Gender Relations in Global Perspective

Gender Relations in Global Perspective

Essential Readings

Edited by Nancy Cook

Canadian Scholars' Press Inc.

Toronto

Gender Relations in Global Perspective: Essential Readings
edited by Nancy Cook

First published in 2007 by
Canadian Scholars' Press Inc.
180 Bloor Street West, Suite 801
Toronto, Ontario
M5S 2V6

www.cspi.org

Canadian Scholars' Press Inc. gratefully acknowledges financial support for our publishing activities from the Government of Canada through the Book Publishing Industry Development Program (BPIDP) and the Government of Ontario through the Ontario Book Publishing Tax Credit Program.

Library and Archives Canada Cataloguing in Publication

Gender relations in global perspective : essential readings / edited by Nancy Cook.

Includes bibliographical references.
ISBN 978-1-55130-328-4

      1. Sex role. 2. Sex differences--Social aspects. 3. Gender identity.
4. Sex discrimination. I. Cook, Nancy, 1961-

HQ1075.G465 2007   305.3   C2007-901378-3

Cover design: Susan MacGregor/Digital Zone
Cover art: Leo Cinezi. "501576_Barbie," from StockXchng.
Interior design and layout: Aldo Fierro

Printed and bound in Canada

Canadä

To Nina, as she negotiates gender regimes now, then, here, and there

TABLE OF CONTENTS

Part XI
Gender, Imperialism, and Globalization

PREFACE

This book is a product of several abridged undergraduate reading lists I've developed for courses in both my home discipline of Sociology and the multidisciplinary contexts of Women's Studies and Global Studies. My goal for the collection is to give students a broad sense of the scope of feminist scholarship that integrates gender analyses with those of intersecting social processes that shape gender relations in various institutional sites, drawing from the work of feminists across disciplines and around the world. Introductory sections on feminist theory and its historical development lay the groundwork for specific studies of the institutions through which gender relations are constituted. Global and historical analyses allow students to examine gender relations in comparative and cross-cultural perspective, which highlights global inequalities, as well as the diversity of gender relations.

A NOTE FROM THE PUBLISHER

Thank you for selecting *Gender Relations in Global Perspective*, edited by Nancy Cook. The editor and publisher have devoted considerable time and careful development (including meticulous peer reviews) to this book. We appreciate your recognition of this effort and accomplishment.

TEACHING FEATURES

This volume distinguishes itself on the market in many ways. One key feature is the book's well-written and comprehensive part openers, which help to make the readings all the more accessible to undergraduate students. The part openers add cohesion to the section and to the whole book. The themes of the book are very clearly presented in these section openers.

The general editor, Nancy Cook, has also greatly enhanced the book by adding pedagogy to close and complete each section. Each part ends with detailed, chapter-specific discussion questions; annotated further readings; relevant films (also annotated), and annotated relevant Web sites.

INTRODUCTION

WHAT ARE GENDER RELATIONS?

Gender relations refer to complex, culturally and historically specific social systems that organize and regulate interactions between women and men, as well as their relative social value. They simultaneously encompass ideas, practices, representations, and identities that pertain to gender. For example, dominant ideas about gender throughout much of the world value those things associated with men and masculinity rather than with women and femininity, which produces gender hierarchies, a ranking of men's and women's social worth. Feminist research shows that these gendered ideas, practices, and identities are not determined biologically as a direct result of anatomical characteristics such as hormones, chromosomes, and sex organs. Rather, masculinity and femininity, the central components of gender relations, are social constructions, products of everyday social interactions that are linked in complex ways to the material reality of our (trans)gendered bodies. Because gender is often misunderstood as being the study of women and femininity only, I want to emphasize that gender relations focus on the relationships between masculinity and femininity, the valuation of women and men, and their relative access to and control of resources.

As a social system, gender relations are a central organizing principle of society that govern, in part, processes of production and reproduction, consumption, and the distribution of resources. Gender relations do not operate in isolation, but are influenced and shaped by other systems that organize social interactions between groups of people, including the economy, sexuality, "race," and ability. Feminists examine the ways in which a gendered society is created by studying how key social institutions—divisions of labour, health, education, family, work, popular culture, and the media—have been structured by gender relations. Consequently, we need to keep in mind that gender is a property of all social institutions and of society more generally, as much as it is a feature of an individual's identity, embodiment, and daily behaviour.

When we examine gender relations over time in one place or across space in the same temporal moment, we see that many different forms of gender relations have been conceived and implemented. This collection of readings will give you some nascent idea of what these different forms are, how they relate to one another, and what clear trends, if any, there have been in the development of gender relations around the world. By employing numerous feminist theoretical frameworks to examine the complex world of gender relations globally, the book demonstrates that there are many forms of masculinity and femininity and different relationships between the two across time and space.

THE IMPORTANCE OF INTERSECTIONALITY

As you read these analyses of men's position in the family, women's relationship to work and the global economy, and the gendered problems of imperialism and reproduction, you will quickly find that to investigate gender dynamics adequately, feminist scholars simultaneously pay attention to processes of racialization, class, state formation, colonialism, and sexuality that interweave with gender to produce complex forms of oppression and privilege. This framework for analyzing the ways in which various systems work together to affect social life is called intersectionality. Many feminists claim that we cannot fully understand the gendered social world without considering how multiple social processes mutually construct one another.

Intersectionality is a feminist tool of analysis, as well as a conceptual orientation. As an analytic tool, intersectionality enables us more fully to grasp the complexity and specificity of a particular group's experiences of oppression and privilege than if we attended to gender relations alone. Feminist analyses of this sort offer more complete pictures of the economic, social, political, and cultural situations that contextualize our lives, which in turn allows us to design institutions, policies, and laws that can more completely and precisely target avenues of progressive social change in a current global environment characterized by fundamentalist forces, neo-liberal economic policies, militarization, and entrenched imperialism that threaten an equitable social future. These textured analyses examine the full context and quality of the experience of various forms of oppression and discrimination.

Intersectionality as a feminist conceptual orientation starts from two main premises. First, women and men do not constitute dichotomous and homogeneous gender groups. Rather, these groups are internally fractured by different experiences of class, "race," sexuality, and ability, as well as by different forms of embodiment. In other words, individuals are members of more than one group or community at the same time, even across gender groupings, and therefore can simultaneously experience oppression and privilege. For instance, a White woman may be a respected and affluent professor, but suffer abuse at home and sexual harassment at work. In this way, intersectional analyses challenge dominant thinking about power that presumes we are either privileged or oppressed and one person's privilege comes at the expense of another's.

Second, in terms of an individual's identity, intersectionality posits that people live multiple, layered identities derived from the numerous social relations, histories, and structures of power mentioned above. Intersectional analyses aim to reveal these multiple identities, exploring the different types of oppression and disadvantages that occur as a consequence of their combination by taking account of the full context of an individual's life and recognizing the particular experiences that result from the intersection of different categories of identity. But this orientation also stresses that we should not understand the combining of identities as additively increasing an individual's burden, but rather as producing substantively distinct and sometimes contradictory experiences. The aim is not to demonstrate that one group is more victimized or privileged than another, but to reveal meaningful distinctions and similarities in order to struggle against oppressive social conditions. In summary, a feminist intersectional analysis emphasizes that we have multiple identities and therefore face multiple, intersecting oppressions that prevents us from being slotted into rigid, essential social categories and groups.

A MULTIDISCIPLINARITY APPROACH

Multidisciplinarity characterizes a form of knowledge that mobilizes multiple or multi-layered approaches to examine the formation and perpetuation of gender relations. It arises from a conviction that the theory and analytical tools of one discipline alone are unable fully to address complex gender relations in their entirety. Feminists, like many other scholars, have come to realize over time that our most pressing social problems can only be analyzed by exploring them from a full range of perspectives and vantage points. This is to say that the study of gender relations requires a holistic approach, one that provides a coherent understanding of the problem and its potential solutions through the combination of numerous types of analysis. We pay an intellectual and social price for narrow disciplinary compartmentalization, especially the risk that facile generalizations will be made that create harmful inaccuracies.

In keeping with this approach, I draw together the work of feminist researchers from a range of disciplines—Sociology, Geography, Anthropology, History, English, French, Biology, Law, and Education—who focus on exploring gender relations around the world using a variety of theoretical and topical perspectives. They examine gender relations from different angles, creating a feminist dialogue that constructs a detailed, integrated whole where "symptoms" are not treated in isolation and short-term political solutions are eschewed.

WHY GENDER RELATIONS IN GLOBAL PERSPECTIVE?

Gender relations configure the multiple social relationships among different groups of women and men across "race," class, and sexual lines in the global North. The same is true throughout the rest of the world, although the concepts and structures that define gender relations often differ significantly. Many of the readings in this collection examine global constructions of gender by focusing on the significance of national and transnational economic, cultural, and historical processes that shape women's and men's experiences, identities, and practices.

These readings comprise an interesting range of comparative and cross-cultural gender analyses from various world regions, including the Middle East, South Asia, South East Asia, Europe, the Americas, and Africa. As they are dialogically situated in this text, readers will be able to analyze gender similarities and differences around the globe and to learn about the diversity of gender experiences across cultures and regions.

More generally, this range of analyses demonstrates how a global perspective enriches feminist analyses. Not only are local and global inequalities more explicitly highlighted, but a familiarity with the gender dynamics in other cultures, as well as their gendered interactions with our own, enables us to view those dynamics and interactions in our own more clearly.

OVERVIEW OF THE READER

The text opens with a section that provides insight into the historical development of feminist analyses of gender relations. This section is followed by four readings that outline some of the main strands of contemporary feminist theory, including symbolic interactionism, Marxism, and post-structuralism. The remaining parts engage the main social institutions through which gender relations are created and organized: the family, work, education, the media, the state, imperialism, and globalization. Interspersed with these readings are those that examine gender as an embodied experience that incorporates regimes of beauty, ability, violence, and racism.

⊕ ⊕ ⊕

PART I

HISTORICAL PERSPECTIVES

The opening section of this book includes some of the key readings in the historical development of feminist thinking in the North American context. Three decades of pioneering work
by feminist scholars across disciplines has made us aware of the centrality of gender in shaping every aspect of social life. Gender, therefore, can be understood as one of the central organizing
principles around which social life revolves. These multidisciplinary articles introduce many of the
central themes related to gender that are raised in this reader, namely work, the relationship between
family and work, sexuality, the nature versus nurture debate, and cross-cultural differences in the
social organization of gender relations.

Louise Lamphere, a famous American feminist anthropologist, opens the collection by reviewing anthropological literature in the study of women beginning in the early 1970s. In particular,
she engages the claim made by her peer Michelle Rosaldo in 1974 that, despite some cross-cultural
variation in gender roles, there is universal asymmetry between the genders in which the masculine
identities, roles, and activities enacted in the public sphere are always valued over those performed
by women in the feminine domestic domain. She then moves on to discuss the shifts that have
taken place in feminist thinking about this issue since that time, especially in light of the mounting
empirical evidence that questions the previous hypothesis of the universal subordination of women
and the dichotomous relationship between women's social location in the domestic sphere and men's
in the public.

Canadian sociologist Meg Luxton, in her well-known book *More Than a Labour of Love: Three
Generations of Women's Work in the Home*, provides an early feminist exploration of the life circumstances and unpaid labour of Canadian housewives. In the introduction to the book she argues that
this work, rather than simply being a "labour of love" on the part of nurturing wives and mothers,
serves as a patriarchal foundation for capitalist work relations. The book as a whole is a key socialist
feminist text that analyzes the relationship between paid (seen and valued) and unpaid (invisible
and undervalued) work that is performed by men and women in the public and private spheres
respectively.

Taking up a more contemporary issue in the history of feminist thinking, biologist Anne Fausto-Sterling argues for a feminist reconceptualization of the relationship between sex and gender as intertwined, rather than dichotomous as feminists previously theorized. In thinking through this complex relationship, she provides a rich discussion of the ways in which science constructs "truths" about sexuality, biological sex differences, and sexual identity, including an assessment of past and current research on intersexed individuals, sex-based brain differences, and sex hormones that, as she demonstrates, are all organized by mainstream gender politics.

The final chapter in Part I is written by Leslie Feinberg, a prominent feminist theorist of transgendered bodies. Feinberg's piece is a personal narrative that explores the invisibility of "trans" people throughout White American history, the acts of persecution directed against them, and the places we can "find" references to them hidden away in our museums, historical writings, and traditional First Nations practices.

CHAPTER 1

THE DOMESTIC SPHERE OF WOMEN AND THE PUBLIC WORLD OF MEN
The Strengths and Limitations of an Anthropological Dichotomy

Louise Lamphere

Since 1974, there has been a burgeoning interest within anthropology in the study of women, sex roles, and gender. Anthropology has long been a discipline that contained important women (Elsie Clews Parsons, Ruth Benedict, and Margaret Mead among the most famous) and a field in which women have been studied as well (e.g., Kaberry 1939, 1952; Landes 1938, 1947; Leith-Ross 1939; Underhill 1936; and Paulme 1963). However, with the publication of *Woman, Culture, and Society* (Rosaldo and Lamphere 1974) and *Toward an Anthropology of Women* (Reiter 1975a) women scholars, many of whom were identified as feminists, began to critique the androcentric bias in anthropology, to explore women's status in a wide variety of societies, and to provide explanatory models to understand women's position cross-culturally.

One of the most powerful and influential models was proposed by Michelle Rosaldo in her introductory essay to *Woman, Culture, and Society* (1974). Her argument began by asserting that although there is a great deal of cross-cultural variability in men's and women's roles, there is a pervasive, universal asymmetry between the sexes. "But what is perhaps most striking and surprising," Rosaldo writes, "is the fact that male, as opposed to female, activities are always recognized as predominantly important, and

cultural systems give authority and value to the roles and activities of men" (Rosaldo 1974:19).

One of the quotes we chose to appear at the beginning of the book, a passage from Margaret Mead's *Male and Female*, sums up what we saw in 1974 in all the ethnographies and studies we examined. "In every known society, the male's need for achievement can be recognized. Men may cook, or weave, or dress dolls or hunt hummingbirds, but if such activities are appropriate occupations of men, then the whole society, men and women alike, votes them as important. When the same occupations are performed by women, they are regarded as less important" (Mead 1949:125). Not only were there differential evaluations of women's activities, but, Rosaldo argues, "everywhere men have some authority over women, that [is] they have culturally legitimated right to her subordination and compliance" (1974:21).

Having argued for a pervasive sexual asymmetry across cultures, not just in terms of cultural values, but also in terms of power and authority, Rosaldo accounted for this difference between men and women in terms of a dichotomy.[1] She argued that women are associated with a "domestic orientation," while men are primarily associated with extradomestic, political, and military spheres of activity. By "domestic"

Rosaldo meant "those minimal institutions and modes of activity that are organized immediately around one or more mothers and their children." In contrast, the "public" referred to "activities, institutions, and forms of association that link, rank, organize, or subsume particular mother-child groups. Put quite simply, men have no single commitment as enduring, time-consuming, and emotionally compelling—as close to seeming necessary and natural—as the relation of a woman to her infant child; and so men are free to form those broader associations that we call 'society,' universalistic systems of order, meaning, and commitment that link particular mother-child groups."

Rosaldo, along with Sherry Ortner and Nancy Chodorow who also wrote essays in *Woman, Culture, and Society*, insisted that the connection between women's role in reproduction (the fact that women everywhere lactate and give birth to children) and their domestic orientation is not a necessary one. In other words, biology is not destiny. Women's domestic orientation was structurally and culturally constructed and "insofar as woman is universally defined in terms of a largely maternal and domestic role, we can account for her universal subordination" (Rosaldo 1974:7).

"Although," Rosaldo writes, "I would be the last to call this a necessary arrangement or to deny that it is far too simple as an account of any particular empirical case, I suggest that the opposition between domestic and public orientations (an opposition that must, in part, derive from the nurturant capacities of women) provides the necessary framework for an examination of male and female roles in any society" (Rosaldo 1974:24).

For Rosaldo, then, women were involved in the "messiness" of daily life; they were always available for interruption by children. Men could be more distanced and may actually have separate quarters (such as men's houses) away from women's activities. Men could thus "achieve" authority and create rank, hierarchy, and a political world away from women. The confinement of women to the domestic sphere and men's ability to create and dominate the political sphere thus accounted for men's ability

to hold the greater share of power and authority in all known cultures and societies.

At the time Rosaldo wrote her overview and in the introduction we both wrote, we were faced with building a framework where none existed. Despite the number of monographs on women, Margaret Mead's work and that of Simone de Beauvoir (1953) were the most provocative, and perhaps the only, theoretical works we knew.[2] The argument for universal sexual asymmetry followed in a long tradition in anthropology where scholars have sought to look for what is broadly "human" in all cultures. In addition to language, anthropologists have discussed the universality of the incest taboo, marriage, and the family. The notion that women might be universally subordinate to men thus made sense as a first attempt at theory building in this newly revived "subfield" within anthropology.

Although Rosaldo argued for universal subordination, she was careful to make clear that women are not powerless. They exercise informal influence and power, often mitigating male authority or even rendering it trivial (Rosaldo 1974:21). In addition, there are important variations in women's roles in different cultures, and variation was discussed in most of the rest of the articles in the collection. For example, Sanday and Sacks compared women's status in a number of different societies, while Leis examined the structural reasons why women's associations are strong in one Ijaw village in Nigeria, yet absent in another. Finally, in my own article I examined the differences in women's strategies within domestic groups in a number of societies, which related to the relative integration or separation of domestic and political spheres.

Since 1974, the hypothesis of universal subordination of women and the dichotomous relationship between women in the domestic sphere and men in the public sphere have been challenged and critiqued by a number of feminist anthropologists. As appealing as this dichotomy seemed in the abstract, it turned out to be difficult to apply when actually looking at examples of women's activities in different cultures. For example, in an important article written about the same time as Rosaldo's introduction, Rayna Reiter (now Rayna Rapp) described women's and men's distinct lives in a small French village in the south of France. They inhabited different domains, one public, one private. While men fraternized with whomever they found to talk to in public places, women were much more enmeshed in their families and their kinship networks" (Reiter 1975b:253). However, two categories of public space fell into women's domain: the church and three shops, including the local bakery. Men tended to avoid women's places, entering the bakery, for example, only when several men were together and joking, "Let's attack now" (Reiter 1975b:257).

Reiter argues that men and women use public space in different ways and at different times. "The men go early to the fields, and congregate on the square or in the cafes for a social hour after work. Sometimes they also fraternize in the evenings. These are the times when women are home cooking and invisible to public view. But when the men have abandoned the village for the fields, the women come out to do their marketing in a leisurely fashion. The village is then in female hands. In the afternoon, when the men return to work, the women form gossip groups on stoops and benches or inside houses depending on the weather" (Reiter 1975b:258). Despite the powerful imagery—women associated with the private or domestic domain and men with public space—the description also shows that the dichotomy is not neat. After all women are in public a great deal; they have taken over, in some sense, the church and the shops and even the public square in the middle of the day.

In Margery Wolf's description of women in a Taiwanese village based on data she collected in the late 1950s, she emphasizes that because researchers have focused on the dominance of patrilineal descent in the family, they have failed to see women's presence. "We have missed not only some of the system's subtleties but also its near-fatal weaknesses" (Wolf 1972:37). Women have different interests than men and build uterine families—strong ties to their daughters, but primarily to their sons who give their mothers loyalty and a place in the patrilineal extended family. Outside the family in the community

women formed neighborhood groups—around a store, at a platform where women washed their clothes in the canal, or under a huge old tree. In a village strung out between a river and a canal, there was no central plaza dominated by men as in the South of France.

In Peihotien, Wolf did not describe a cultural geography where women were in a private sphere and men in the public one; rather there was more of a functional separation—men and women had different activities and interests. They were often located in the same places but had a different relationship to the patrilineal extended family and the male-dominated community. Women's lack of power led them to different strategies, different tactics that often undermined male control of the household and even the community. As Sylvia Yanagisako (1987:111) has pointed out, the notion of domestic-public entails both a spatial metaphor (of geographically separated or even nested spaces) and a functional metaphor (of functionally different activities or social roles) in the same conceptual dichotomy. Analysts often "mix" these different metaphors in any particular analysis—sometimes using domestic-public spatially and at other times functionally.

Even in the Middle East, the association of women with a private domain (and a lack of power) and men with a public domain (and the center of politics) was too simple, as Cynthia Nelson pointed out in her article, "Public and Private Politics: Women in the Middle Eastern World" (1974). Because they are born into one patrilineal group and marry into another, women are important structural links between social groups and often act as mediators. Because there are segregated social worlds, all-female institutions are important for enforcing social norms: Women fill powerful ritual roles as sorceresses, healers, and mediums; women are important sources of information for their male kin; and women act as "information brokers," mediating social relations within both the family and the larger society.

From Rosaldo's point of view, these aspects of women's power are primarily "informal" and very different from the public, legitimate roles of men. Nevertheless, even though Nelson affirms the separation of male and female worlds (both spatially and functionally), what is "domestic" has public ramifications (the arrangement of a marriage, the transmission of highly charged political information) and the shadow of the family and kin group (the "domestic") is present in even the most "public" of situations. What at first seemed like a simple straightforward dichotomy, in light of actual case material seems very "slippery" and complex.

Furthermore, in many cultures, particularly those with an indigenous band or tribal structure, a separation of "domestic" and "public" spheres makes no sense because household production was simultaneously public, economic, and political. Leacock pointed out the following after reviewing the literature on the Iroquois during the seventeenth and eighteenth century:

> Iroquois matrons preserved, stored, and dispensed the corn, meat, fish, berries, squashes, and fats that were buried in special pits or kept in the long house. Brown (1970:162) hates that women's control over the dispensation of the foods they produced, and meat as well, gave them de facto power to veto declarations of war and to intervene to bring about peace.... Women also guarded the "tribal public treasure" kept in the long house, the wampum quill and feather work, and furs.... The point to be stressed is that this was "household management" of an altogether different order from management of the nuclear or extended family in patriarchal societies. In the latter, "women may cajole, manipulate, or browbeat men, but always behind the public facade; in the former case, "household management" was itself the management of the "public economy."
> (Leacock 1978:253)

Sudarkasa has made much the same point about women in West African societies such as the Yoruba. She argues that many of the political and economic activities anthropologists discuss as public are actually embedded in households (Sudarkasa 1976, as quoted in Rapp 1979:509). Furthermore, "in West Africa,

the 'public domain' was not conceptualized as 'the world of men.' Rather, the public domain was one in which both sexes were recognized as having important roles to play" (Sudarkasa 1986:99).

A more appropriate conception would be to recognize two domains, "one occupied by men and another by women, both of which were internally ordered in a hierarchical fashion and both of which provided 'personnel' for domestic and extradomestic (or public) activities" (Sudarkasa 1986:94).

Furthermore, a careful examination of "domestic domain" indicates that the categories of "woman" and "mother" overlap in Western society, but the meaning of motherhood may be vastly different in another society. Women may not be exclusively defined as mothers and childrearers in terms of their status and cultural value (see Moore 1988:20–29 for a discussion of this point).

In addition to the issue of whether the domestic-public dichotomy can provide an adequate description of men's and women's spatial and functional relationships in our own and other societies, the model has problems as an explanation of women's status. One of these problems is the inherent circularity of the model. A central point is to account for the nature of these domains, yet they are already assumed to exist widely and are treated as categories in terms of which women's activities (such as food preparing, cooking, childcare, washing) can be classified (as opposed to male hunting, warfare, political councils). Comaroff says that the model "can only affirm what has already been assumed—that is, that the distinction between the domestic and politico-jural is an intrinsic, if variable, fact of social existence" (Comaroff 1987:59). When the model is used to explain women's positions in different societies in relation to these two orientations, the reasoning is equally circular. To put it in the words of Yanagisako and Collier, "The claim that women become absorbed in domestic activities because of their role as mothers is tautological given the definition of 'domestic' as 'those minimal institutions and modes of activity that are organized immediately around one or more mothers and their children'" (Yanagisako and Collier 1987:19).

Finally, we have come to realize that the concepts of domestic and public were bound up in our own history and our own categories grounded particularly in a Victorian heritage. Rosaldo, in a thoughtful revaluation of her model, came to argue this position herself.

> The turn-of-the-century social theorists whose writings are the basis of most modern social thinking tended without exception to assume that women's place was in the home. In fact, the Victorian doctrine of separate male and female spheres was, I would suggest, quite central to their sociology. Some of these thinkers recognized that modern women suffered from their association with domestic life, but none questioned the pervasiveness (or necessity) of a split between the family and society. (Rosaldo 1980:401–402)

Rosaldo traced the historical roots of domestic-public from the nineteenth-century evolutionists through twentieth-century structural functionalists to her own work. Instead of two opposed spheres (different and apart), Rosaldo suggested an analysis of gender relationships, an examination of inequality and hierarchy as they are created particularly through marriage (Rosaldo 1980:412–413).

The dichotomy has been usefully employed in several ways since 1974. First, several authors have shown us how it works in Western societies (e.g., France and the United States, where it arose historically and still has an important ideological function) (Reiter 1975b; Collier, Rosaldo, and Yanagisako 1982). In a related way, analysts have explored the meanings surrounding domestic activities of women, putting together a much more complex picture of women's relation to men in this sphere (Chai 1987; and Murcott 1983). Second, anthropological analysis has helped us to understand the historical development of domestic-public spheres in societies under colonialism. John Comaroff's analysis of the Tshidi chiefdom in South Africa during the early twentieth century is an excel-

lent example of this approach (1987:53–85). Finally, some analysts have used the cultural concepts of other societies to critique our own model of domestic-public orientations. Sylvia Yanagisako's essay on the clear separation of "inside-outside" domains (a spatial metaphor) and "work-family" activities (a functional dichotomy) in Japanese American culture demonstrates how the anthropological model of domestic-public mixes these metaphors, which has made analysis confusing and difficult (Yanagisako 1987).

Despite these useful attempts at examining women's lives through the lens of a domestic-public opposition, many of us would agree with Rayna Rapp's 1979 summary of the problems with this dichotomy.

> We cannot write an accurate history of the West in relation to the Rest until we stop assuming that our experiences subsume everyone else's. Our public/private conflicts are not necessarily the same as those of other times and places. The specific oppression of women cannot be documented if our categories are so broad as to decontextualize what "womanness" means as we struggle to change that definition. A Tanzanian female farmer, a Mapuche woman leader, and an American working-class housewife do not live in the same domestic domain, nor will the social upheavals necessary to give them power over their lives be the same. We must simultaneously understand the differences and the similarities, but not by reducing them to one simple pattern. (Rapp 1979:511)

Thus, many of us have tired of the domestic-public dichotomy. We feel it is constraining, a "trap," while new approaches try to get away from dichotomous thinking. These approaches do one of several things. Often they take history seriously, examining women's situation as it has evolved, often in a colonial context. Furthermore, they treat women as active agents and following Collier (1974), as people who have interests, often divergent from men, and who act on them. Third, they often focus on gender relationships, rather than only on women. Finally, they do not treat all women as part of a single universal category of "woman." Rather women are usually analyzed in terms of their social location. Age, class, race, ethnicity, and kinship are all likely to divide women, so newer analyses examine women's strategies and identities as they are differently shaped. Several examples will illustrate some of the different approaches taken in recent years.

Collier's examination of Comanche, Cheyenne, and Kiowa gender relationships (1988) illustrates the recent focus on gender and on the multiple positions that men and women hold in societies in which the domestic-public dichotomy seems inappropriate. This is because these "spheres" are integrated, and there is no firm line between domestic and public space (see Lamphere 1974 and Leacock 1978).

The Comanche are an example of a bride service society in which, like many hunter-gatherer societies, men and women were relatively autonomous, the concept of femininity was not elaborated, and the greatest status differences were between unmarried and married men. Marriage established men as having something " to achieve (e.g., a wife), leaving women without such a cultural goal. Young men, through providing meat for their in-laws (bride service), become equal adults, and older men, through egalitarian relations and generosity, become the repositories of wisdom and knowledge. Politics focused on the issue of sexuality and on male-male relationships, which often erupted in conflict and violence. Women celebrated their health and sexuality, and hence the roles of "woman the gatherer" or even "woman the mother" did not emerge as cultural themes.

Among the Cheyenne, an equal bridewealth society, and among the Kiowa, an unequal bridewealth society, marriage relationships were structured in a much different way in the nineteenth century, so gender relationships had a much different content, politics were more hierarchical, and ideology played a different role. Collier's interest is not in the subordination of women in these three societies, because in all three there are several kinds of inequality: between men and women, between older women and girls, between unmarried men and married men, and between kin and affines. An interest in "spheres" and "domains" has been replaced by an emphasis on relationships and an analysis that focuses on the ways in which inequality gets reproduced through marriage transactions, claims on the labor of others, and giving and receiving of gifts. Dominance and subordination become a much more layered, contextualized phenomenon—more interesting than the simple assertion that women are universally subordinated. The processes through which women's inequality (and that of young men) is constructed are laid bare, rather than flatly asserted.

Mary Moran's study of civilized women (1990) explores the historical beginnings and present-day construction of the category "civilized," which does confine educated women among the Glebo of southeastern Liberia to a "domestic sphere." The dichotomy between "civilized" and "native" (or even tribal or country) is a result of missionization and has created a status hierarchy differentially applied to men and to women. Men, once educated and with a history of paid wage work, never lose their status as "civilized," while women, even though married to a "civilized man," may lose their status if they do not dress correctly, keep house in specific ways, and refrain from farming and marketing. Native women, who market or have farms, are more economically independent but occupy positions of lower prestige. Here we see not only the importance of historical data in examining how cultural categories evolve, but also the ways in which both civilized and native women actively manage their status positions. Civilized women, through the practice of fosterage, recruit younger women to their households to carry out the more elaborate household routines in which they must engage and to train these fostered daughters to become civilized themselves.

The civilized-native dichotomy represents the juxtaposition of two systems. One is a parallel-sex system in which native men and women are represented by their own leaders in two linked but relatively autonomous prestige hierarchies (as suggested by Sudarkasa 1986). The other is a single-sex system (based on a Western model) in which men in political positions represent both sexes, and women have little access to prestige except through their husbands. Thus, this is a much more complex system than one based on a domestic-public dichotomy. There are dichotomous categories—civilized-native, male-female—but they do not fit neatly together. Moran speaks of categories as "gender sensitive" and suggests that "The Glebo have inserted gender into the civilized/native dichotomy to the point that women's status is not only more tenuous and vulnerable than men's but also very difficult to maintain without male support." In some respects civilized women trade off dependency for prestige, but Moran provides a sympathetic picture of how both civilized and native women manage their lives.

Lila Abu-Lughod's study (1986) of Bedouin women's ritual poetry gives us further insights into the complexity of women who in 1974 we would have simply thought of as "confined to a domestic sphere." Among the Bedouin, women's marriages are arranged; wives wear black veils and red belts (symbolizing their fertility); and women must behave within a code of behavior that emphasizes family honor and female modesty and shame. When confronted with loss, poor treatment, or neglect, the public discourse is one of hostility, bitterness, and anger. In the case of lost love the discourse is of militant indifference and denial of concern. In contrast, Bedouin poetry, a highly prized and formally structured art, expresses sentiments of devastating sadness, self-pity, attachment, and deep feeling (Abu-Lughod 1986:187). Although both men and women recite poetry for women, it may express conflicting feelings concerning an arranged marriage, a sense of loss over a divorce, or sentiments of betrayal when a husband marries a new wife. The poems are used to elicit sympathy and get help, but they also constitute a dissident and subversive discourse. Abu-Lughod sees ritual poetry as a corrective to "an obsession with morality and an overzealous adherence to the ideology of honor.... Poetry reminds people of another way of being and encourages, as it reflects, another side of experience.... And maybe the vision [offered through poetry] is cherished because people see that the costs of this system,

in the limits it places on human experiences, are just too high" (Abu-Lughod 1986:259). Bedouin women in this portrait are not simply victims of patriarchy confined to a domestic sphere; they are active individuals who use a highly valued cultural form to express their deepest sentiments, acknowledge an alternative set of values, and leave open the possibility of subverting the system in which they are embedded.

A large number of studies have been conducted in the United States that loosely focus on what used to be termed the domestic sphere and the public world of work. As in the Native American, African, and Middle Eastern cases cited previously, when one begins to examine a topic in detail, global notions like domestic-public seem too simple to deal with the complexities of women's lives. Clearly work and home are distinctly separated spheres in the United States. Women who have been employed in the paid labor force have experienced the disjunction of spending eight or more hours of the day in a place of employment where they are "female workers" and the rest of their time in the home where they are daughters, wives, and/or mothers. With this comes responsibilities for cooking, cleaning, and providing nurturance, care, and intimacy for other family members. Several recent studies have examined the contradictions women face when combining work and family, the impact of paid employment on family roles, and vice versa. I will refer to only three examples of this growing literature.

Patricia Zavella's research on Chicana cannery workers examines women's networks that link the workplace and the family (Zavella 1987). Calling these "work-related networks," Zavella describes groups of friends who saw each other outside work and who were members of a kin network employed in the same cannery. Women used work-related networks as sources of exchange for information, baby sitters, and emotional support. Networks operated in more political ways as workers organized a women's caucus and filed a complaint with the Fair Employment Practices Commission. Women's cannery work was seasonal and had relatively little impact on power relations in the family or the household division of labor. On the other hand, work-related networks of friends or kin were an important "bridging mechanism" helping women to deal with the contradictions and demands that came from two different spheres.

Karen Sacks's study of hospital workers at the Duke Medical center examines the ways in which black and white women brought family notions of work, adulthood, and responsibility to work with them and used these values to organize a walk out and subsequent union drive (1988). Sacks focuses on the activities of "center women"—leaders in the union drive. Unlike the men who were often the public speakers at rallies and events, the center women organized support on an interpersonal, one-to-one basis. Rather than emphasizing the bridging aspect of women's networks, Sacks shows how the family is "brought to work" or in the old terminology how the "domestic" influences the "public."

In my own research I have traced the changes in the relationship between women, work, and family historically through the study of immigrant women in a small industrial community, Central Falls, Rhode Island (Lamphere 1987). Using the twin notions of productive and reproductive labor, I examined the rise of the textile industry in Rhode Island and the recruitment of working daughters and later of working mothers to the textile industry and to the other light industries that have replaced it since World War II. Rather than seeing production and reproduction as a rigid dichotomy (like public and domestic), I have used these categories to study relationships and to examine the kinds of strategies that immigrant women and their families forged in confronting an industrial system where wage work was a necessity and where working-class families had no control over the means of production. Such an approach revealed a great deal of variability both between and within ethnic groups— the Irish, English, French-Canadian, and Polish families who came to Central Falls between 1915 and 1984 and the more recent Colombian and Portuguese immigrants. Examination of strikes and walkouts in the 1920s and 1930s and my own experience as a sewer in an apparel plant in 1977 led me to emphasize the strategies of resistance the women workers used on the job, as well as the impact of women's paid labor on the family itself. When daughters were recruited as workers in textile mills, the internal division of labor within the household did not materially change because wives and mothers continued to do much of the reproductive labor necessary to maintain the household. Fathers, teenage sons, and daughters worked for wages. In the current period, in contrast, as more wives have become full-time workers, immigrant men have begun to do some reproductive labor, particularly child care. Immigrant couples often work different shifts and prefer to care for children themselves rather than trust baby sitters from their own ethnic group. In my study I argue that "the productive system as constituted in the workplaces has shaped the family more than issues of reproduction have shaped the workplace" (Lamphere 1987:43).

More recently, Patricia Zavella, Felipe Gonzalez, and I have found that young working mothers in sunbelt industries have moved much further than Cannery women or New England industrial immigrant women in changing the nature of the household division of labor (Lamphere, Zavella, Gonzalez, and Evans 1993). These new committed female workers have been employed since high school and do not drop out of the labor force for long periods of time to have children. Thus, they and their husbands construct a family life around a two-job household. Although some couples have a "traditional" division of housework (women do the cooking and the majority of the cleaning and husbands take out the garbage, do minor repairs, and fix the car), many husbands participate in "female chores" and do substantial amounts of childcare (often caring for children while the wife is at work). Here we see the impact of what we used to call the "public sphere" on the domestic one, but in our analysis, we have focused more on the varied ways that Anglos and Hispanics (including single mothers) have negotiated household and child-care arrangements, viewing husbands and wives as mediating contradictions. Subtle similarities and differences among and between working-class Anglo and Hispanic women have emerged from this analysis, making it clear that the impact of work in the public world is not a monolithic but a variegated process.

In summary, the dichotomy between the public world of men and domestic world of women was, in 1974, an important and useful starting point for thinking about women's roles in a cross-cultural perspective. As anthropologists have written more detailed and finegrained studies of women's lives in a wide variety of other cultures and in our own society, we have gone beyond the use of dichotomies to produce analyses of the complex and layered structure of women's lives. We now treat women more historically, viewing them as social actors and examining the variability among women's situations within one culture and in their relationship to men.

NOTES

1. Rosaldo says that "the opposition does not determine cultural stereotypes or asymmetries in the evaluations of the sexism, but rather underlies them, to support a very general ... identification of women with domestic life and of men with public life" (Rosaldo 1974:21–22). Thus, I would argue, Rosaldo did not attempt to explain women's subordination through the dichotomy, but saw it as an underlying structural framework in any society that supported subordination and that would have to be reorganized to change women's position.
2. It is interesting that we did not know of Elsie Clews Parsons's extensive feminist writing during 1910 to 1916, much of which is reminiscent of the kind of position we took in *Woman, Culture, and Society*. In another article, I have noted the similarities between Shelly's prose and that of Parsons (see Lamphere 1989 and Parsons 1913, 1914, 1915).

REFERENCES

Abu-Lughod, Lila. 1986. *Veiled Sentiments: Honor and Poetry in a Bedouin Society*. Berkeley and Los Angeles: University of California Press.

Brown, Judith. 1970. Economic organization and the position of women among the Iroquois, *Ethnohistory* 17(3/4):131–167.

Chai, Alice Yun. 1987. Freed from the elders but locked into labor: Korean immigrant women in Hawaii. *Women's Studies* 13:223–234.

Collier, Jane. 1974. Women in politics. In Michelle Z. Rosaldo and Louise Lamphere (eds.), *Woman, Culture, and Society*. Stanford: Stanford University Press.

———. 1988. *Marriage and Inequality in Classless Societies*. Stanford: Stanford University Press.

Collier, Jane, Michelle Rosaldo, and Sylvia Yanagisako. 1982. Is there a family? New anthropological views. In Barrie Thorne and Marilyn Yalom (eds.), *Rethinking the Family: Some Feminist Questions*. New York and London: Longman.

Comaroff, John L. 1987. Sui generis: Feminism, kinship theory, and structural "domains." In Jane Fishburne Collier and Sylvia Junko Yanagisako (eds.), *Gender and Kinship: Essays Toward a Unified Analysis*. Stanford: Stanford University Press.

de Beauvoir, Simone. 1953. *The Second Sex*. New York: Alfred A. Knopf. Originally published in French in 1949.

Kaberry, Phyllis M. 1939. *Aboriginal Women, Sacred and Profane*. London: G. Routledge.

———. 1952. *Women of the Grassfields*. London: H.M. Stationery Office.

Lamphere, Louise. 1974. Strategies, cooperation, and conflict among women in domestic groups. In Michelle Z. Rosaldo and Louise Lamphere (eds.), *Woman, Culture, and Society*. Stanford: Stanford University Press.

———. 1987. *From Working Daughters to Working Mothers: Immigrant Women in a New England Industrial Community*. Ithaca, NY: Cornell University Press.

———. 1989. Feminist anthropology: The legacy of Elsie Clews Parsons. *American Ethnologist* 16(3):518–533.

Lamphere, Louise, Patricia Zavella, Felipe Gonzales, and Peter Evans 1993. *Sunbelt Working Mothers: Reconciling Family and Factory*. Ithaca, NY: Cornell University Press.

Landes, Ruth. 1938. *The Ojibiua Woman, Part 1: Youth*. New York: Columbia University. *Contributions to Anthropology*, Vol. 31.

———. 1947. *The City of Women: Negro Women Cult Leaders of Bahia, Brazil*. New York: Macmillan.

Leacock, Eleanor. 1978. Women's status in egalitarian society: Implications for social evolution. *Current Anthropology* 19(2):247–275.

Leith-Ross, Sylvia. 1939. *African Women: Study of the Ibo of Nigeria*. London: Faber and Faber.

Mead, Margaret. 1949. *Male and Female*. New York: William Morrow and Co.

Moran, Mary H. 1990. *Civilized Women: Gender and Prestige in Southeastern Liberia*. Ithaca, NY: Cornell University Press.

Moore, Henrietta L, 1988. *Feminism and Anthropology*. Minneapolis: University of Minnesota Press.

Murcott, Anne. 1983. "It's a pleasure to cook for him": Food, mealtimes and gender in some South Wales households. In Eva Gamarnikow, D.H.J. Morgan, June Purvis, and Daphne Taylorson (eds.), *The Public and the Private*. London: Heinemann Educational Books.

Nelson, Cynthia. 1974. Public and private politics: Women in the Middle East. *American Ethnologist* 1:551–563.

Parsons, Eisie Clews. 1913. *The Old Fashioned Woman*. New York: G.P. Putnam's Sons.

———. 1914. *Fear and Conventionality*. New York: G.P. Putnam's Sons.

———. 1915. *Social Freedom: A Study of the Conflicts between Social Classifications and Personality*. New York: G.P. Putnam's Sons.

Paulme, Denise (ed.). 1963. *Women of Tropical Africa*. Berkeley: University of California Press.

Rapp, Rayna. 1979. Anthropology. *Signs* 4(3): 497–513.

Reiter, Rayna (ed.). 1975a. *Toward an Anthropology of Women*. New York: Monthly Review Press.

———. 1975b. Men and women in the South of France: Public and private domains. In Rayna Reiter (ed.), *Toward an Anthropology of Women*. New York: Monthly Review Press.

Rosaldo, Michelle. 1974. Woman, culture and society: A theoretical overview. In Michelle Z. Rosaldo and Louise Lamphere (eds.), *Woman, Culture, and Society*. Stanford: Stanford University Press.

———. 1980. The uses and abuses of anthropology. *Signs* 5(3):389–417.

Rosaldo, Michelle Z. and Louise Lamphere (eds.). 1974. *Woman, Culture, and Society*. Stanford: Stanford University Press.

Sacks, Karen. 1988. *Caring by the Hour: Women, Work, and Organizing at the Duke Medical Center*. Urbana and Chicago: University of Illinois Press.

Sudarkasa, Niara. 1976. Female employment and family organization in West Africa. In Dorothy McGuigan (ed.), *New Research on Women and Sex Roles*. Ann Arbor: Center for Continuing Education of Women.

———. 1986. The status of women in indigenous African Societies. *Feminist Studies* 12:91–104.

Underhill, Ruth. 1936. *Autobiography of a Papago Woman. Supplement to American Anthropologist* 38(3), Part II. Millwood, NY: American Anthropological Association.

Wolf, Margery. 1972. *Women and the Family in Rural Taiwan*. Stanford: Stanford University Press.

Yanagisako, Sylviajunko. 1987. Mixed metaphors: Native and anthropological models of gender and kinship domains. In Jane Fishburne Collier and Sylviajunko Yanagisako (eds.), *Gender and Kinship: Essays Toward a Unified Analysis*. Stanford: Stanford University Press.

Yanagisako, Sylvia Junko and Jane Fishburne Collier. 1987. Toward a unified analysis of gender and kinship. In Jane Fishburne Collier and Sylvia Junko Yanagisako (eds.), *Gender and Kinship: Essays Toward a Unified Analysis*. Stanford: Stanford University Press.

Zavella, Patricia. 1987. *Women's Work and Chicane Families: Cannery Workers of the Santa Clara Valley*. Ithaca, NY: Cornell University Press.

CHAPTER 2

"INTRODUCTION" TO MORE THAN A LABOUR OF LOVE:

Three Generations of Women's Work in the Home

Meg Luxton

A man works from sun to sun;
A woman's work is never done.

—Proverb

Housewives make up one of the largest occupational groups in Canada. In 1980 more than half of the married women in Canada were working as full-time housewives. At the same time, in spite of the fact that the percentage of married women in the wage labour force has steadily increased since 1945, married women who work for pay have not relinquished their domestic responsibilities. Instead they have taken on a double day of work, labouring as both wage workers and domestic workers. Thus the vast majority of Canadian women perform domestic labour on a regular daily basis.[1]

For most wage workers there is a distinct separation between their workplace and home, between their coworkers and family, between their work and leisure. They leave their homes each workday to go off to their jobs and return at the end of the workday to rest and relax. For housewives, whose work is based on marriage and parenting, such distinctions do not exist. Housewives are not employed—they work for their husbands and children. Their work is unpaid and performed in their family home. It is therefore both private and unseen. Because their work is rooted in the intense and important relationships

of the family, it seems to be a "labour of love." It appears that there are two distinct and unrelated spheres: the public world of work, based on economic relations, and the private world of the family household, based on love relations.[2]

Domestic labour seems to be invisible. It is neither understood nor recognized as work. For example, women are asked: "Do you work, or are you a housewife?" Women who do both wage labour and domestic labour are described as "working wives" or "working mothers," as if to deny that what they do in the home is also work. When women themselves are asked to describe what they do, they often have no name for it:

> I never really thought about it before. It's just what I do every day. It's a bit startling to try and think about it as something more than just me living my life. But it is important to ask why I do things the way I do and especially how what I do is like what other women do. (Generation III, b. 1951)[3]

As a "labour of love," this work is not respected in the same way as wage work, partly because it is not directly supervised and because its standards and schedules seem to be determined by the women who do it. As a job it is full of contradictions. On the one hand, it is important, necessary and potentially satisfying. On the other hand, it has a low status and is often isolating and frustrating:

> It's looking after your family and what could be more important? You don't have anyone standing over you so you get to do what you want, sort of. But you don't get paid, so you're dependent on your husband, and you have to be there all the time, and there's always something needs doing. I feel so confused because it could be so good and it never is. (Generation II, b. 1930)

This book analyses the work that women do in the home. It is based on a case study of three generations of working-class housewives in Flin Flon, a mining town in northern Manitoba. Because the experiences of these housewives are typical for working-class women in general, their stories illustrate what it is to be a working-class wife and mother and what it means to run a home. The study describes the actual work that women do, shows how their work has changed over three generations and isolates the various forces that shape and change domestic labour. This analysis distinguishes between the way particular women organize their daily work and the patterns that are essential to the occupation of housewife.

Some Flin Flon women themselves recognized both the universal characteristics and the social importance of their work:

> When I think about what I do every day—I cook meals for my family, I make cereal for breakfast and sandwiches for lunch and meat and potatoes for supper. Nothing unusual about that. But when I think about all those thousands of other women all doing the same thing, then I realize I'm not just making porridge. I'm part of a whole army of women who are feeding the country. (Generation II, b. 1937)

By placing the specific, personal experiences of individual women in a larger social and economic framework, the book argues that women's work in the home is one of the most important and necessary labour processes of industrial capitalist society.

THE WORKING-CLASS HOUSEHOLD

In *The Origin of the Family, Private Property and the State*, a classic Marxist analysis of the family, Frederick Engels recognized as false the apparent separation of the family from other labour processes. He suggested a way to develop an integrated analysis:

> According to the materialist conception of history, the determining factor in history is, in the final instance, the production and reproduction of immediate life. This, again, is of a twofold character: on the one side, the production of the means of existence, of food, clothing, and shelter and the tools necessary for that production; on the other side, the production of human beings themselves, the production of the species. The social organization under which the people of a particular historical epoch and a particular country live is determined by both kinds of production: by the stage of development of labour on the one hand and of the family on the other.[4]

Unfortunately, the promise of Engels' statement—to deliver a balanced and comprehensive view of the total labour process—has been largely unfulfilled. From Marx onward, Marxists have tended to focus on the "production of the means of existence" and have left out of their analysis "the production of human beings themselves." This is particularly the case in studies of industrial capitalist society. Most Marxists have concentrated on the activities of wage workers engaged in industrial production, assuming that the eight-hour-shift experience is sufficient to explain capitalist labour processes.[5]

As feminists have pointed out, this concentration on industrial production ignores the fact that workers live a twenty-four-hour day. With such a limited view, it is virtually impossible either to analyze the sexual division of labour under capitalism or to explain what domestic labour actually is. If the perspective is expanded from a preoccupation with the eight or ten hours a day that wage workers spend in wage labour to a consideration of the complete twenty-four-hour cycle of daily life of the working class as a whole, then it becomes clear that domestic labour is one of the central labour processes of industrial capitalism. It is this particular and indispensable labour that converts the wages of the paid worker into the means of subsistence for the entire household and that replenishes the labour power of household members again and again so that it can be resold the next day, the next year and in the next generation.[6]

Domestic labour takes the form it does because one of the distinctive characteristics of capitalist society is that the production of commodities—items produced for sale in the market—becomes generalized to the extent that even labour becomes a commodity.[7] Under capitalism, individual workers—proletarians—do not own the means of production, either land to grow their own food or machinery to produce goods to sell. Because they are divorced from these means of production, the first thing that workers must do in the daily cycle for survival is to go to the labour market and make a deal with an employer to sell the only commodity they possess, which is their capacity to work—their labour power—in exchange for wages. They do so freely, compelled only by their own needs. With their wages they can purchase housing, food and other consumer goods and services.

Once workers enter the employ of a boss, they become unfree in the sense that the employer determines what they do on the job. The employer's main objective is to extract as much work as possible from the workers. At the end of the work shift, they are worn out; their capacity to labour is exhausted. Because labour power is expended in the industrial production process, it has been used up or consumed. If it is to be sold again, it must be regenerated or reproduced. When wage workers are hired, they sell the use of their labour capacity for a limited time period, which means that workers retain ownership of their labour power.

Unlike slave or feudal societies where the owners of the means of production are at least partly responsible for the subsistence of their workers, the capitalist mode of production ruptures the relationship between the production of commodity goods and the production of human beings themselves. The production of commodities is taken over while workers remain free and thus responsible for their own survival. Because workers retain possession of their labour power, they, rather than their employers, are responsible for reproducing it.

Once workers leave their bosses' premises at the end of each shift, they are on their own. How they choose to live their lives is left almost entirely up to them. They are able to live because they are richer by one day's pay. Thus the nature of the wage worker/employer relationship is one that makes it possible for the working class to create a place—the private household—outside of capitalist production where they can live their daily lives. At the same time, it constantly reasserts the necessity of the private household where workers live and reproduce themselves.

While the wages they earn make it possible for workers to maintain themselves in their own households, money itself will not shelter or feed them. Instead, further work must be expended to transform money into housing, food and other consumer goods and services. And so workers go to the consumer goods market to obtain the necessary means of subsistence. Once these have been purchased and the wages spent, the working-class household still cannot consume most commodities directly but must perform additional work, based on their residence, to put the means of subsistence in a directly consumable form. For example, the groceries have to be put away and the food cooked for supper. With these goods, household members meet their daily needs.

Simultaneously, wage earners in the household rest and restore their energies—reproduce their labour power—so that the next day they are able to leave home once again to go to work. This completes the twenty-four-hour cycle of working-class subsistence and shows that the working class is formed, as a class, at two locations—on the job and at home—and its members are necessarily involved in two distinct labour processes in the course of a single day. This double day of work—wage labour and domestic labour—is necessary for the survival of all members of the working class.[8]

THE FAMILY HOUSEHOLD AND THE SEXUAL DIVISION OF LABOUR

There are many different types of working-class households. Some people live alone, or with a friend of the same sex, or with a group of unrelated friends. But the most typical household form is based on the nuclear family, that is, a woman, a man and their children.[9] This nuclear family household is itself based on a division of labour. The man leaves the household regularly to earn money elsewhere. The women may or may not leave the household to work for money.

Whether or not the woman has a paid job, she is primarily responsible for domestic labour.[10] This involves producing goods and services for the family's use, such as cooked meals, clean clothes and a pleasant environment in the home. At the same time, the work includes the preparation of labour power for sale. Thus women's work in the home has two dimensions: meeting household needs and producing labour power. Because household subsistence depends on wages, the production of labour power for exchange must always take precedence over production for family use. So, for example, the daily rhythms of family life—what time the family eats, gets up and goes to bed—are usually set by the schedules of the wage worker's job rather than by family preferences.

Domestic labour is also a production process that is conducted between two arenas of economic exchange—the labour or job market and the consumer goods market. The patterns of domestic labour are determined by the conditions of these two markets. For example, if the price of meat goes way up, women may learn to cook other foods, or if massive lay-offs occur in local industries, families may have to move in search of paid work. However, the working class is not passive in the cycle of capitalist production. While the working-class household is formed and limited by the system of capitalist development, it is also shaped by the working class as an expression of its needs and wants.[11] Women's labour in the home is one of the ways in which the working class adapts and modifies the effects that external market forces have on its households.

Through their work, women are instrumental in creating the face that the household presents to the world.[12] By managing their homes skillfully and helping household members maintain comfortable relations with each other, women try to achieve the highest standard of living and the greatest degree of emotional and physical well-being possible. During periods of economic crisis, for example, women intensify different aspects of their labour in an effort to stretch the budget. They may shop more frugally, do more mending, or take on a paid job. In addition, they are expected to provide emotional support for members of the household who are unemployed, ill, retired, or under some other form of stress. This never-ending work is vitally important in making life tolerable for household members.

Although domestic labour, as a labour of subsistence for the working-class household, does not fall under the direct auspices of capitalist production, it is profoundly determined by capitalist production and functions at the heart of the social relations integral to the capitalist mode of production. One woman described her work this way:

> I send my husband off to work each day and my kids off to school. It's women like me keep the whole system running. Weren't for us, the men wouldn't work and there wouldn't be no kids to grow up, would there? (Generation II, b. 1927)

As the necessary complement of the wage labour/capital relationship, domestic labour is a central labour process of industrial capitalism.

WOMEN'S DOMESTIC LABOUR

Women experience domestic labour as a continuous series of activities, all geared to running their households and looking after their families. These daily activities consist of many intricately woven threads that together form the fabric of their work. In order to study domestic labour and to understand its effects on women's lives, this fabric must be unravelled and each thread examined in turn, while at the same time showing how they are woven together into the whole that is domestic labour. Domestic labour actually consists of four related but distinct work processes, each composed of a variety of tasks and each having its own history, its own internal rhythms and pressures and its own particular pattern of change. The first two are directly involved with people, while the last two maintain the physical infrastructure of the household.

The woman's most immediate task involves looking after herself, her husband and other adult members of the household. Because the household depends for its existence on wages, the dominant requirement is that the labour power of the wage earner be reproduced on a daily basis. However, the household also depends on domestic labour, which makes the reproduction of this labour power on a daily basis similarly important.

The second component of domestic labour is childbearing and childrearing. For most working-class people, their expectation that they will have children is a major reason for marrying and setting up family-based households. Although people have children for a variety of personal reasons, the social effect is the production of labour power for the next generation.

The third component of domestic labour is housework. It includes all those activities, such as cooking, cleaning and washing clothes, that are necessary for maintaining the house and servicing household members.

The final component of domestic labour involves the transformation of wages into goods and services for the household's use. This process of "making ends meet" involves money management and shopping. Sometimes it also requires that women take on additional work to bring more money into the household.

Domestic labour is, however, not simply four distinct work processes going on simultaneously. Each component is affected by, and in turn affects, each of the others. Changes in one reverberate throughout the whole labour process, reorganizing its internal composition. The analysis of domestic labour must examine how these processes are interwoven to form the total fabric of women's work. It is important therefore to look at domestic labour in an historical context.

Throughout the twentieth century, the development and expansion of industrial capitalism has reduced the range of production activities that go on in the household. Some activities, such as making clothes or preserving food, have been removed from the household and socialized in factories. Certain services, such as education and some health care, have also been taken out of the household. The modern household has been left with only one main productive function, the most fundamental and essential one—the production of labour power.

The labour that has remained in the household has also been profoundly affected by the technological revolution, and this has created another contradiction for the modern housewife.[13] Although new technological innovations (such as indoor plumbing, electricity, washing machines and other appliances) seem to be labour saving, modern women working in the home with up-to-date technology spend almost as much time at their work as their grandmothers did without using modern conveniences.[14]

Popular myth has it that modern housewives tend to make work for themselves. According to this myth, in the old days housewives really had to work hard doing everything at home by hand, while modern women can buy most of the things they need ready made as well as the conveniences to make their work easier. It seems then that running a home is no longer a full-time job and those women who do it full time are either inefficient, lazy or self-indulgent. This myth is a source of anxiety for some women:

> I know that I work hard all day. I don't think I'm inefficient either. But I keep thinking about how much easier things are for me than they were for my mother. Everybody keeps telling me how with all the modern things I have, I shouldn't have to work very hard. Is there something wrong with me? (Generation III, b. 1949)

But as another housewife pointed out, this myth is based on an inadequate understanding of what women's work actually involves:

> Sure things are easier today. Modern houses are much easier to keep up. No one's denying that. But the same is true of mining. Mining today with power drills and trains and all that is much easier than mining was in my grandfather's day. But no one ever says that modern mining isn't work anymore. So the people who say housework isn't full-time, demanding, hard work are full of it. All that proves is they don't know what housework is really all about. (Generation III, b. 1950)

What women do in the home is not just housework. It is domestic labour—the production of both family subsistence and labour power. As domestic labour has changed, certain tasks have either been eliminated or have become less onerous. But no matter what specific tasks they do, or do not do, women are always responsible for maintaining the household. To understand why such work is never ending, it is important to distinguish between two measures that are relevant to domestic labour: production time and labour time.[15] Production time measures the duration of a task from start to finish; labour time measures the specific period during which a worker is actually expending labour. For example, the production time involved in roasting meat may be as much as ten hours from the time the woman takes the meat out of the freezer until she puts it on the table ready to eat. The actual labour time may be as little as half an hour, and it includes the time involved in actually putting the meat in the oven, basting it and later removing it to a serving dish. Similarly, a woman may spend an hour putting her child to bed. Once the child is asleep, she is apparently free to do other things, including going to sleep herself. But she remains on duty, responsible for the care of her child all through the night. Although labour time expended is only an hour, the production time is the duration of the night.

Both the production time and the labour time of specific aspects of domestic labour have been reduced considerably. Household technology has definitely eased the housewife's labour time in some specific tasks, such as washing and cleaning. However the central task—the production of life itself—is an on going, endlessly recurring process. Its production time can never be reduced. Whereas wage workers sell their labour power for a specific, limited period of time, "from sun to sun" domestic labour is "never done."

NOTES

1. Monique Proulx, *Five Million Women: A Study of the Canadian Housewife* (Ottawa: Advisory Council on the Status of Women, 1978). For a discussion of the increased participation of married women in the paid labour force, see Patricia Connelly, *Last Hired, First Fired* (Toronto: The Women's Press, 1978). For a discussion of the numbers of women who are full-time housewives and what happens when they take on paid work as well, see *The Report of the Royal Commission on the Status of Women in Canada* (Ottawa: Information Canada, 1970), p. 33; or Pat Armstrong and Hugh Armstrong, *The Double Ghetto* (Toronto: McClelland & Stewart, 1978).

2. For a discussion of the historical development of these two spheres, see Eli Zaretsky, "Capitalism, the Family and Personal Life," *Socialist Revolution* 13 and 14 (January–April 1973); and 15 (May–June 1973).

3. Quotations such as this one are drawn from my interviews with Flin Flon housewives, which were conducted specifically for this study. To identify the speaker, I have indicated in which of three generations she set up her household in Flin Flon and the date of her birth.

4. Frederick Engels, *The Origin of the Family, Private Property and the State* (New York: New World Paperbacks, 1972), pp. 71–72.

5. For three examples, see Harry Braverman, *Labor and Monopoly Capital: The Degradation of Work in the Twentieth Century* (New York: Monthly Review Press, 1974); Michael Burawoy, *Manufacturing Consent: Changes in the Labour Process under Monopoly Capitalism* (Chicago: University of Chicago Press, 1979);

Andrew Friedman, *Industry and Labour: Class Struggle at Work and Monopoly Capitalism* (London: Macmillan, 1978).

6. As far as I can determine, the term "domestic labour" was first applied to women's work in the home in an article by Wally Seccombe, "The Housewife and Her Labour under Capitalism," *New Left Review* 83 (January–February 1974). Subsequently, the term was taken up by numerous authors in what became known as "the domestic labour debate." The most recent publication on this topic is a collection of essays, which includes an extensive annotated bibliography, edited by Bonnie Fox, *Hidden in the Household: Women's Domestic Labour under Capitalism* (Toronto: The Women's Press, 1980). For a more detailed theoretical argument about the importance of a twenty-four-hour perspective, see Margaret Luxton and Wally Seccombe, "The Making of the Working Class: Two Labours, Not One" (paper presented at the annual meeting of the Canadian Sociology and Anthropology Association, June 1980, Montreal, Quebec).

7. Once in the employ of capital, the worker's labour power actually becomes a part of capital—the elastic or variable part. Karl Marx, *Capital, Vol. 1: A Critique of Political Economy* (London: Penguin Books, 1976).

8. For a full elaboration of the Marxist theory of the proletarian condition and the necessity of a private household sphere, see Wally Seccombe, "Domestic Labour and the Working-Class Household"; and "The Expanded Reproduction Cycle of Labour Power in Twentieth-Century Capitalism," in Fox, *Hidden in the Household*, pp. 25–99; pp. 219–268.

9. A household may refer to any number of possibilities ranging from that of one person living alone in a rented room to that of several adults and children living together in a privately owned house. In fact, people live in many different types of households. The capitalist mode of production allows for such a variety in household living arrangements, but the nuclear family form remains typical. It is the particular form that is reinforced by the state and ideologically encouraged in a thousand ways. It is possible to live as a proletarian outside of nuclear family households, but it is not easy. In one way or another, those who make a habit of rejecting nuclear family living arrangements are considered abnormal.

10. Domestic labour is women's work par excellence. However, this does not mean that only women do domestic labour. All men help out occasionally and some men do their own domestic labour regularly. In some households, domestic labour is organized collectively so that all the members of the household divide the work equally. See Margaret Luxton, "Urban Communes and Co-ops in Toronto" (M. Phil, dissertation, University of Toronto, 1973). Those people who can afford to can either pay others (cleaning ladies, nannies) to do their domestic labour for them in their homes or purchase these services elsewhere (restaurants, cleaners, hotels, prostitutes). Despite these alternatives, domestic labour is still primarily women's work. See Ann Oakley, *Women's Work: The Housewife Past and Present* (New York: Vintage Books, 1976).

11. While it has its roots in pre-existing household and family forms, the working-class household, as a part of working-class social relations, emerged as a new social form with the rise of capitalism. Too often investigators assume that the household is determined by capital, forgetting that it is formed and shaped by class struggle. For a discussion of the historical development of the working-class household, see E.P. Thompson, *The Making of the English Working Class* (Harmondsworth, England: Pelican Books, 1968); Eli Zaretsky, "Capitalism, the Family and Personal Life"; Peter Sterns, *Lives of Labour: Work in a Maturing Industrial Society* (London: Croom Helm Publishing, 1975); Jane Humphries, "The Working-Class Family, Women's Liberation and Class Struggle: The Case of Nineteenth-Century British History," *The Review of Radical Political Economics: Women, Class and the Family* 9, no. 3 (fall 1977).

12. John Littlejohn, *Westrigg: The Sociology of a Cheviot Parish* (London: Routledge and Kegan Paul, 1963), pp. 122–123.

13. Schwartz Cowan has noted, "The industrialization of the home was a process very different

from the industrialization of other means of production, and the impact of that process was neither what we have been led to believe it was nor what students of the industrial revolution would have been led to predict." Ruth Schwartz Cowan, "The 'Industrial Revolution' in the Home: Household Technology and Social Change in the Twentieth Century," *Technology and Culture* 17, no. 1 (January 1976), p. 1.

14. Joann Vanek, "Keeping Busy: Time Spent in Housework, United States, 1920–1970" (Ph.D. dissertation, University of Michigan, 1974).

15. Karl Marx, *Capital, Vol. 2* (London: Progress Books, 1969), p. 127.

BIBLIOGRAPHY

Armstrong, Pat and Armstrong, Hugh. *The Double Ghetto: Canadian Women and their Segregated Work.* Toronto: McClelland & Stewart, 1978.

Braverman, Harry. *Labour and Monopoly Capitalism: The Degradation of Work in the Twentieth Century.* New York: Monthly Review Press, 1974.

Burawoy, Michael. *Manufacturing Consent: Changes in the Labor Process under Monopoly Capitalism.* Chicago: University of Chicago Press, 1979.

Connelly, Patricia. *Last Hired, First Fired: Women and the Canadian Work Force.* Toronto: The Women's Press, 1978.

Cowan, Ruth Schwartz. "The 'Industrial Revolution' in the Home: Household Technology and Social Change in the Twentieth Century." *Technology and Culture* 17, no. 1 (1976).

Engels, Frederick. *The Origins of the Family, Private Property and the State.* 1884. Reprint. New York: New World Paperbacks, 1972.

Fox, Bonnie, ed. *Hidden in the Household: Women and Their Domestic Labour under Capitalism.* Toronto: The Women's Press, 1980.

Friedman, Andrew. *Industry and Labour: Class Struggle at Work and Monopoly Capitalism.* London: Macmillan, 1978.

Humphries, Jane. "The Working-Class Family, Women's Liberation, and Class Struggle: The Case of Nineteenth-Century British History." *The Review of Radical Political Economics* 9, no. 3 (fall 1977), pp. 25–42.

Littlejohn, John. *Westrigg: The Sociology of a Cheviot Parish.* London: Routledge and Kegan Paul, 1963

Luxton, Margaret. "Urban Communes and Co-ops in Toronto." M. Phil, dissertation, University of Toronto, 1973.

Luxton, Margaret, and Seccombe, Wally. "The Making of a Working Class: Two Labours, Not One." Paper presented at the annual meeting of the Canadian Sociology and Anthropology Association, June 1980, Montreal, Quebec.

Marx, Karl. *Capital, Volume I: A Critique of Political Economy.* 1867. Reprint. London: Penguin Books, 1976.

_____. *Capital, Volume 2.* 1893. Reprint. London: Progress Press, 1969.

Oakley, Ann. *Woman's Work: The Housewife Past and Present.* New York: Vintage Books, 1976.

Proulx, Monique. *Five Million Women: A Study of the Canadian Housewife.* Ottawa Advisory Council on the Status of Women, 1978.

Seccombe, Wally. "The Expanded Reproduction Cycle of Labour Power in Twentieth-Century Capitalism." In *Hidden in the Household*, edited by Bonnie Fox. Toronto: The Women's Press, 1980.

_____. "The Housewife and Her Labour under Capitalism." *New Left Review* 83 (January-February 1974), pp. 3–24.

Sterns, Peter. *Lives of Labour: Working in a Maturing Industrial Society.* London: Croon Helm Publishing, 1975.

Thompson, E.P. *The Making of the English Working Class.* Harmondsworth, England: Pelican Books, 1968.

Vanek, Joann. "Keeping Busy: Time Spent in Housework, United States, 1920–1970." Ph.D. dissertation. University of Michigan.

Zaretsky, Eli. "Capitalism, the Family and Personal Life." *Socialist Revolution* 13 and 14 (January–April 1973); and 15 (May–June 1973)

CHAPTER 3

DUELING DUALISMS

Anne Fausto-Sterling

MALE OR FEMALE?

In the rush and excitement of leaving for the 1988 Olympics, Maria Patiño, Spain's top woman hurdler, forgot the requisite doctor's certificate stating, for the benefit of Olympic officials, what seemed patently obvious to anyone who looked at her: she was female. But the International Olympic Committee (IOC) had anticipated the possibility that some competitors would forget their certificates of femininity. Patiño had only to report to the "femininity control head office,"[1] scrape some cells off the side of her cheek, and all would be in order—or so she thought.

A few hours after the cheek scraping she got a call. Something was wrong. She went for a second examination, but the doctors were mum. Then, as she rode to the Olympic stadium to start her first race, track officials broke the news: she had failed the sex test. She may have looked like a woman, had a woman's strength, and never had reason to suspect that she wasn't a woman, but the examinations revealed that Patiño's cells sported a Y chromosome, and that her labia hid testes within. Furthermore, she had neither ovaries nor a uterus. According to the IOC's definition, Patiño was not a woman. She was barred from competing on Spain's Olympic team.

Spanish athletic officials told Patiño to fake an injury and withdraw without publicizing the embarrassing facts. When she refused, the European press heard about it and the secret was out. Within months after returning to Spain, Patiño's life fell apart. Spanish officials stripped her of past titles and barred her from further competition. Her boyfriend deserted her. She was evicted from the national athletic residence, her scholarship was revoked, and suddenly she had to struggle to make a living. The national press had a field day at her expense. As she later said, "I was erased from the map, as if I had never existed. I gave twelve years to sports."[2]

Down but not out, Patiño spent thousands of dollars consulting doctors about her situation. They explained that she had been born with a condition called androgen insensitivity. This meant that, although she had a Y chromosome and her testes made plenty of testosterone, her cells couldn't detect this masculinizing hormone. As a result, her body had never developed male characteristics. But at puberty her testes produced estrogen (as do the testes of all men), which, because of her body's inability to respond to its testosterone, caused her breasts to grow, her waist to narrow, and her hips to widen. Despite a Y chromosome and testes, she had grown up as a female and developed a female form.

Patiño resolved to fight the IOC ruling. [...] After two and a half years the International Amateur Athletic Federation (IAAF) reinstated her, and by 1992 Patiño had rejoined the Spanish Olympic squad, going down in history as the first woman ever to challenge sex testing for female athletes. Despite the IAAF's flexibility, however, the IOC has remained adamant: even if looking for a Y chromosome wasn't the most scientific approach to sex testing, testing *must* be done.

*****

Although the IOC didn't require modern chromosome screening in the interest of international politics until 1968, it had long policed the sex of Olympic competitors in an effort to mollify those who feared that women's participation in sports threatened to turn them into manly creatures. [...] Olympic officials rushed to certify the femininity of the women they let through the door, because the very act of competing seemed to imply that they could not be true women. In the context of gender politics, employing sex police made a great deal of sense.

SEX OR GENDER?

Until 1968, female Olympic competitors were often asked to parade naked in front of a board of examiners. Breasts and a vagina were all one needed to certify one's femininity. But many women complained that this procedure was degrading. Partly because such complaints mounted, the IOC decided to make use of the modern "scientific" chromosome test. The problem, though, is that this test, and the more sophisticated polymerase chain reaction to detect small regions of DNA associated with testes development that the IOC uses today, cannot do the work the IOC wants it to do. A body's sex is simply too complex. There is no either/or. Rather, there are shades of difference. [...] One of the major claims I make [...] is that labeling someone a man or a woman is a social decision. We may use scientific knowledge to help us make the decision, but only our beliefs about gender—not science—can define our sex. Furthermore, our beliefs about gender affect what kinds of knowledge scientists produce about sex in the first place.

Over the last few decades, the relation between social expression of masculinity and femininity and their physical underpinnings has been hotly debated in scientific and social arenas. In 1972, the sexologists John Money and Anke Ehrhardt popularized the idea that sex and gender are separate categories. Sex, they argued, refers to physical attributes and is anatomically and physiologically determined. Gender they saw as a psychological transformation of the self—the internal conviction that one is either male or female (gender identity) and the behavioral expressions of that conviction.

Meanwhile, the second-wave feminists of the 1970s also argued that sex is distinct from gender—that social institutions, themselves designed to perpetuate gender inequality, produce most of the differences between men and women. Feminists argued that although men's and women's bodies serve different reproductive functions, few other sex differences come with the territory, unchangeable by life's vicissitudes. If girls couldn't learn math as easily as boys, the problem wasn't built into their brains. The difficulty resulted from gender norms—different expectations and opportunities for boys and girls. Having a penis rather than a vagina is a sex difference. Boys performing better than girls on math exams is a gender difference. Presumably, the latter could be changed even if the former could not.

Money, Ehrhardt, and feminists set the terms so that sex represented the body's anatomy and physiological workings and gender represented social forces that molded behavior. Feminists did not question the realm of physical sex; it was the psychological and cultural meanings of these differences—gender—that was at issue. But feminist definitions of sex and gender left open the possibility that male/female differences in cognitive function and behavior could *result* from sex differences, and thus, in some circles, the matter of sex versus gender became a debate about how "hardwired" intelligence and a variety of behaviors are in the brain, while in others there seemed no choice but to ignore many of the findings of contemporary neurobiology.

In ceding the territory of physical sex, feminists left themselves open to renewed attack on the grounds of biological difference. Indeed, feminism has encountered massive resistance from the domains of biology, medicine, and significant components of social science. Despite many positive social changes, the 1970s optimism that women would achieve full economic and social equality once gender inequity was addressed in the social sphere has faded in the face of a seemingly recalcitrant inequality. All of which has prompted feminist scholars, on the one hand, to question the notion of sex itself, while on the other to deepen their inquiry into what we might mean by words such as *gender, culture, and experience.*

*****

Our bodies are too complex to provide clear-cut answers about sexual difference. The more we look for a simple physical basis for "sex," the more it becomes clear that "sex" is not a pure physical category. What bodily signals and functions we define as male or female come already entangled in our ideas about gender.

*****

The IOC may use chromosome or DNA tests or inspection of the breasts and genitals to ascertain the sex of a competitor, but doctors faced with uncertainty about a child's sex use different criteria. They focus primarily on reproductive abilities (in the case of a potential girl) or penis size (in the case of a prospective boy). If a child is born with two X chromosomes, oviducts, ovaries, and a uterus on the inside, but a penis and scrotum on the outside, for instance, is the child a boy or a girl? Most doctors declare the child a girl, despite the penis, because of her potential to give birth, and intervene using surgery and hormones to carry out the decision. Choosing which criteria to use in determining sex, and choosing to make the determination at all, are social decisions for which scientists can offer no absolute guidelines.

REAL OR CONSTRUCTED?

[F]eminist theorists view the body not as essence, but as a bare scaffolding on which discourse and performance build a completely acculturated being. Feminist theorists write persuasively and often imaginatively about the processes by which culture molds and effectively creates the body. Furthermore, they have an eye on politics (writ large). [...] Most feminist scholars concern themselves with real-world power relationships. They have often come to their theoretical work because they want to understand (and change) social, political, and economic inequality. [...] [F]eminist theorists reject what Donna Haraway, a leading feminist theoretician, calls "the God-trick"—producing knowledge from above, from a place that denies the individual scholar's location in a real and troubled world. Instead, they understand that all scholarship adds threads to a web that positions racialized bodies, sexes, genders, and preferences in relationship to one another. New or differently spun threads change our relationships, change how we are in the world.

*****

[A]s a biologist, I believe in the material world. As a scientist, I believe in building specific knowledge by conducting experiments. But as a feminist Witness (in the Quaker sense of the word) and in recent years as a historian, I also believe that what we call "facts" about the living world are not universal truths. Rather, as Haraway writes, they "are rooted in specific histories, practices, languages and peoples."[3] Ever since the field of biology emerged in the United States and Europe at the start of the nineteenth century, it has been bound up in debates over sexual, racial, and national politics. And as our social viewpoints have shifted, so has the science of the body.

Many historians mark the seventeenth and eighteenth centuries as periods of great change in our concepts of sex and sexuality. During this period, a notion of legal equality replaced the feudal exercise of arbitrary and violent power given by divine right. As the historian Michel Foucault saw it, society still required some form of discipline. A growing capitalism needed new methods to control the "insertion of bodies into the machinery of production and the adjustment of the phenomena of population to economic processes."[4] Foucault divided this power over living bodies (bio-power) into two forms. The first centered on the individual body. The role of many science professionals (including the so-called human sciences—psychology, sociology, and economics) became to optimize and standardize the body's function. In Europe and North America, Foucault's standardized body has, traditionally, been male and Caucasian. [...] Understanding how race and gender work—together and independently—helps us learn more about how the social becomes embodied.

Foucault's second form of bio-power—"*a biopolitics of the population*"[5]— emerged during the early nineteenth century as pioneer social scientists began to develop the survey and statistical methods needed to supervise and manage "births and mortality, the level of health, life expectancy and longevity."[6] For Foucault, "discipline" had a double meaning. On the one hand, it implied a form of control or punishment; on the other, it referred to an academic body of knowledge—the discipline of history or biology. The disciplinary knowledge developed in the fields of embryology, endocrinology, surgery, psychology, and biochemistry have encouraged physicians to attempt to control the very gender of the body—including "its capacities, gestures, movements, location and behaviors."[7]

By helping the normal take precedence over the natural, physicians have also contributed to populational biopolitics. We have become, Foucault writes, "a society of normalization."[8] One important mid-twentieth-century sexologist went so far as to name the male and female models in his anatomy text Norma and Normman (*sic*).[9] Today we see the notion of pathology applied in many settings—from the sick, diseased, or different body to the single-parent family in the urban ghetto. But imposing a gender norm is socially, not scientifically, driven. The lack of research into the normal distributions of genital anatomy, as well as many surgeons' lack of interest in using such data when they do exist

[...] clearly illustrate this claim. From the viewpoint of medical practitioners, progress in the handling of intersexuality involves maintaining the normal. Accordingly, there *ought* to be only two boxes: male and female. The knowledge developed by the medical disciplines empowers doctors to maintain a mythology of the normal by changing the intersexual body to fit, as nearly as possible, into one or the other cubbyhole.

One person's medical progress, however, can be another's discipline and control. Intersexuals such as Maria Patiño have unruly—even heretical—bodies. They do not fall naturally into a binary classification; only a surgical shoehorn can put them there. But why should we care if a "woman" (defined as having breasts, a vagina, uterus, ovaries, and menstruation) has a "clitoris" large enough to penetrate the vagina of another woman? Why should we care if there are individuals whose "natural biological equipment" enables them to have sex "naturally" with both men and women? Why must we amputate or surgically hide that "offending shaft" found on an especially large clitoris? The answer: to maintain gender divisions, we must control those bodies that are so unruly as to blur the borders. Since intersexuals quite literally embody both sexes, they weaken claims about sexual difference.

[...] I am deeply committed to the ideas of the modern movements of gay and women's liberation, which argue that the way we traditionally conceptualize gender and sexual identity narrows life's possibilities while perpetuating gender inequality. In order to shift the politics of the body, one must change the politics of science itself. Feminists (and others) who study how scientists create empirical knowledge have begun to reconceptualize the very nature of the scientific process. As with other social arenas, such scholars understand practical, empirical knowledge to be imbued with the social and political issues of its time. I stand at the intersection of these several traditions. On the one hand, scientific and popular debates about intersexuals and homosexuals—bodies that defy the norms of our two-sex system—are deeply intertwined. On the other, beneath the debates about what these bodies mean and how to treat them lie struggles over the meaning of objectivity and the timeless nature of scientific knowledge.

*****

Many scholars mark the start of modern scientific studies of human homosexuality with the work of Alfred C. Kinsey and colleagues, first published in 1948. Their surveys of sexual behavior in men and women provided modern sex researchers with a set of categories useful for measuring and analyzing sexual behaviors.[10] For both men and women, they used a rating scale of 0 to 6, with 0 being 100 percent heterosexual, 6 being 100 percent homosexual. (An eighth category—"X"—was for individuals who experienced no erotic attractions or activities.) Although they designed a scale with discrete categories, Kinsey and co-workers stressed that "the reality includes individuals of every intermediate type, lying in a continuum between the two extremes and between each and every category on the scale."[11]

The Kinsey studies offered new categories defined in terms of sexual arousal—especially orgasm—rather than allowing terms such as *affection*, *marriage*, or *relationship* to contribute to definitions of human sexuality. Sexuality remained an individual characteristic, not something produced within relationships in particular social settings. Exemplifying my claim that with the very act of measuring, scientists can change the social reality they set out to quantify, I note that today Kinsey's categories have taken on a life of their own. Not only do sophisticated gays and lesbians occasionally refer to themselves by a Kinsey number (such as in a personal ad that might begin "tall, muscular Kinsey 6 seeks ... "), but many scientific studies use the Kinsey scale to define their study population.

******

[A] recent explosion of scholarship on the social history of human sexuality showed that the social organization and expression of human sexuality are neither timeless nor universal. Historians are just beginning to pry loose information from the historical record, and any new overviews written are sure to differ. [...]

*****

The social scientist Mary McIntosh's 1968 article, "The Homosexual Role," provided the touchstone that pushed scholars to consider sexuality as a historical phenomenon.[12] Most Westerners, she pointed out, assumed that people's sexuality could be classified two or three ways: homosexual, heterosexual, and bisexual. McIntosh argued that this perspective wasn't very informative. A static view of homosexuality as a timeless, physical trait, for instance, didn't tell us much about why different cultures defined homosexuality differently, or why homosexuality seemed more acceptable in certain times and places than others. An important corollary to McIntosh's insistence on a history of homosexuality is that heterosexuality, and indeed all forms of human sexuality, have a history.

*****

Many historians believe that our modern concepts of sex and desire first made their appearance in the nineteenth century. Some point symbolically to the year 1869, when a German legal reformer seeking to change antisodomy laws first publicly used the word *homosexuality*.[13] Merely coining a new term did not magically create twentieth-century categories of sexuality, but the moment does seem to mark the beginning of their gradual emergence. It was during those years that physicians began to publish case reports of homosexuality—the first in 1869 in a German publication specializing in psychiatric and nervous illness.[14] As the scientific literature grew, specialists emerged to collect and systematize the narratives. The now-classic works of Krafft-Ebing and Havelock Ellis completed the transfer of homosexual behaviors from publicly accessible activities to ones managed at least in part by medicine.

The emerging definitions of homo- and heterosexuality were built on a two-sex model of masculinity and femininity. The Victorians, for example, contrasted the sexually aggressive male with the sexually indifferent female. But this created a mystery. If only men felt active desire, how could two women develop a mutual sexual interest? The answer: one of the women had to be an *invert*, someone with markedly masculine attributes. This same logic applied to male homosexuals, who were seen as more effeminate than heterosexual men. [...] [T]hese concepts linger in late-twentieth-century studies of homosexual behaviors in rodents. A lesbian rat is she who mounts; a gay male rat is he who responds to being mounted.

[...] [B]y the early part of the twentieth century, someone engaging in homosexual acts *was* [...] a homosexual, a person constitutionally disposed to homosexuality. Historians attribute the emergence of this new homosexual body to widespread social, demographic, and economic changes occurring in the nineteenth century. In America, many men and eventually some women who had in previous generations remained on the family farm found urban spaces in which to gather. Away from the family's eyes, they were freer to pursue their sexual interests. Men seeking same-sex interactions gathered in bars or in particular outdoor spots; as their presence became more obvious, so too did attempts to control their behavior. In response to police and moral reformers, self-consciousness about their sexual behaviors emerged—a budding sense of identity.

*****

Homosexuality may have been born in 1869, but the modern heterosexual required another decade of gestation. In Germany in 1880, the word *heterosexual* made its public debut in a work defending homosexuality. In 1892, heterosexuality crossed the ocean to America, where, after some period of debate, a consensus developed among medical men that "heterosexual referred to a normal 'other-sex' Eros. [The doctors] proclaimed a new heterosexual separatism—an erotic apartheid that forcefully segregated the sex normals from the sex perverts."[15]

Through the 1930s the concept of heterosexuality fought its way into the public consciousness, and by World War II, heterosexuality seemed a permanent feature of the sexual landscape. Now, the concept has come

under heavy fire. Feminists daily challenge the two-sex model, while a strongly self-identified gay and lesbian community demands the right to be thoroughly normal. Transsexuals, transgendered people, and [...] a blossoming organization of intersexuals all have formed social movements to include diverse sexual beings under the umbrella of normality.

The historians whose work I've just recounted emphasize discontinuity. They believe that looking "for general laws about sexuality and its historical evolution will be defeated by the sheer variety of past thought and behavior."[16] But some disagree. The historian John Boswell [...] regards sexuality as "real" rather than "socially constructed." While Halperin sees desire as a product of cultural norms, Boswell implies we are quite possibly born with particular sexual inclinations wired into our bodies. Growth, development, and the acquisition of culture show us how to express our inborn desires, he argues, but do not wholly create them.

*****

There is no way to decide whose interpretation is right. Despite surface similarities, we cannot know whether yesterday's *tribade* is today's butch or whether the middle-aged Greek male lover is today's pedophile.

NATURE OR NURTURE?

While historians have looked to the past for evidence of whether human sexuality is inborn or socially constructed, anthropologists have pursued the same questions in their studies of sexual behaviors, roles, and expressions found in contemporary cultures around the globe. [...]

*****

Anthropologists study vastly differing peoples and cultures with two goals in mind. First, they want to understand human variation—the diverse ways in which human beings organize society in order to eat and reproduce.

Second, many anthropologists look for human universals. Like historians, anthropologists are divided about what information drawn from any one culture can tell them about another, or whether underlying differences in the expression of sexuality matter more or less than apparent commonalities. In the midst of such disagreements, anthropological data are, nevertheless, often deployed in arguments about the nature of human sexual behaviour.

The anthropologist Carol Vance writes that the field of anthropology today reflects two contradictory strains of thought. The first she refers to as the "cultural influences model of sexuality," which, even as it emphasizes the importance of culture and learning in the molding of sexual behavior, nevertheless assumes "the bedrock of sexuality ... to be universal and biologically determined; in the literature it appears as the 'sex drive' or 'impulse.'"[17] The second approach, Vance says, is to interpret sexuality entirely in terms of social construction. A moderate social constructionist might argue that the same physical act can carry different social meanings in different cultures, while a more radical constructionist might argue that "sexual desire is itself constructed by culture and history from the energies and capacities of the body."[18]

*****

When they turn their attention more generally to the relationships between gender and systems of social power, anthropologists face the same sorts of intellectual difficulties when studying "third" genders in other cultures. During the 1970s European and North American feminist activists hoped that anthropologists could provide empirical data to support their political arguments for gender equality. If, somewhere in the world, egalitarian societies existed, wouldn't that imply that our own social structures were not inevitable? Alternatively, what if women in every culture known to humankind had a subordinate status? Didn't such cross-cultural similarity mean [...] that women's secondary standing must be biologically ordained?

When feminist anthropologists traveled around the world in search of cultures sporting the banner of equity, they did not return with happy tidings. Most thought, as the feminist anthropologist Sherry Ortner writes, "that men were in some way or other 'the first sex.'"[19] But critiques of these early cross-cultural analyses mounted, and in the 1990s some prominent feminist anthropologists reassessed the issue. The same problem encountered with collecting information by survey emerges in cross-cultural comparisons of social structures. Simply put, anthropologists must invent categories into which they can sort collected information. Inevitably, some of the invented categories involve the anthropologists' own unquestioned axioms of life, what some scholars call "incorrigible propositions." The idea that there are only two sexes is an incorrigible proposition, and so too is the idea that anthropologists would know sexual equality when they saw it.

*****

But feminists, too, have incorrigible propositions, and a central one has been that all cultures, as the Nigerian anthropologist Oyeronke Oyewumi writes, "organize their social world through a perception of human bodies" as male or female.[20] In taking European and North American feminists to task over this proposition, Oyewumi shows how the imposition of a system of gender—in this case, through colonialism followed by scholarly imperialism—can alter our understandings of ethnic and racial difference. In her own detailed analysis of Yoruba culture, Oyewumi finds that relative age is a far more significant social organizer. Yoruba pronouns, for example, do not indicate sex, but rather who is older or younger than the speaker. What they think about how the world works shapes the knowledge that scholars produce about the world. That knowledge, in turn, affects the world at work.

If Yoruba intellectuals had constructed the original scholarship on Yoruba-land, Oyewumi thinks that "seniority would have been privileged over gender."[21] Seeing Yoruba society through the lens of seniority rather than that of gender would have two important effects. First, if Euro-American scholars learned about Nigeria from Yoruba anthropologists, our own belief systems about the universality of gender might change. Eventually, such knowledge might alter our own gender constructs. Second, the articulation of a seniority-based vision of social organization among the Yoruba would, presumably, reinforce such social structures. Oyewumi finds, however, that African scholarship often imports European gender categories. And "by writing about any society through a gendered perspective, scholars necessarily write gender into that society.... Thus scholarship is implicated in the process of gender-formation."[22]

Thus historians and anthropologists disagree about how to interpret human sexuality across cultures and history. Philosophers even dispute the validity of the words *homosexual* and *heterosexual*—the very terms of the argument. But wherever they fall along the social constructionist spectrum, most argue from the assumption that there is a fundamental split between nature and culture, between "real bodies" and their cultural interpretations. I take seriously the ideas of Foucault, Haraway, Scott, and others that our bodily experiences are brought into being by our development in particular cultures and historical periods. But especially as a biologist, I want to make the argument more specific. As we grow and develop, we literally, not just "discursively" (that is, through language and cultural practices), construct our bodies, incorporating experience into our very flesh. To understand this claim, we must erode the distinctions between the physical and the social body.

DUALISMS DENIED

"A devil, a born devil, on whose nature nurture can never stick." So Shakespeare's Prospero denounces Caliban in *The Tempest*. Clearly, questions of nature and nurture have troubled European culture for some time. Euro-American ways of understanding how the world works depend heavily on the use of dualisms—pairs of opposing concepts, objects, or belief systems. This book focuses especially on three of these:

sex/gender, nature/nurture, and real/constructed. We usually employ dualisms in some form of hierarchical argument. Prospero complains that nature controls Caliban's behavior and that his, Prospero's, "pains humanely taken" (to civilize Caliban) are to no avail. Human nurture cannot conquer the devil's nature. [...] But in virtually all cases, I argue that intellectual questions cannot be resolved nor social progress made by reverting to Prospero's complaint. Instead, as I consider discrete moments in the creation of biological knowledge about human sexuality, I look to cut through the Gordian knot of dualistic thought. I propose to modify Halperin's bon mot that "sexuality is not a somatic fact, it is a cultural effect,"[23] arguing instead that sexuality is a somatic fact *created by* a cultural effect. [...]

Why worry about using dualisms to parse the world? I agree with the philosopher Val Plumwood, who argues that their use makes invisible the inter-dependencies of each pair. This relationship enables sets of pairs to map onto each other. Consider an extract of Plumwood's list:

Reason	Nature
Male	Female
Mind	Body
Master	Slave
Freedom	Necessity (nature)
Human	Nature (nonhuman)
Civilized	Primitive
Production	Reproduction
Self	Other

In everyday use, the sets of associations on each side of the list often run together. "Culture," Plumwood writes, accumulates these dualisms as a store of weapons "which can be mined, refined and redeployed. Old oppressions stored as dualisms facilitate and break the path for new ones."[24] For this reason, even though my focus is on gender, I do not hesitate to point out occasions in which the constructs and ideology of race intersect with those of gender.

Ultimately, the sex/gender dualism limits feminist analysis. The term *gender*, placed in a dichotomy, necessarily excludes biology. As the feminist theorist Elizabeth Wilson writes: "Feminist critiques of the stomach or hormonal structure ... have been rendered unthinkable."[25] [...] Such critiques remain unthinkable because of the real/constructed divide (sometimes formulated as a division between nature and culture), in which many map the knowledge of the real onto the domain of science (equating the constructed with the cultural). Dichotomous formulations from feminists and nonfeminists alike conspire to make a sociocultural analysis of the body seem impossible.

Some feminist theorists, especially during the last decade, have tried—with varying degrees of success—to create a nondualistic account of the body. Judith Butler, for example, tries to reclaim the material body for feminist thought. Why, she wonders, has the idea of materiality come to signify that which is irreducible, that which can support construction but cannot itself be constructed. We have, Butler says (and I agree), to talk about the material body. There are hormones, genes, prostates, uteri, and other body parts and physiologies that we use to differentiate male from female, that become part of the ground from which varieties of sexual experience and desire emerge. Furthermore, variations in each of these aspects of physiology profoundly affect an individual's experience of gender and sexuality. But every time we try to return to the body as something that exists prior to socialization, prior to discourse about male and female, Butler writes, "we discover that matter is fully sedimented with discourses on sex and sexuality that prefigure and constrain the uses to which that term can be put."[26]

*****

Since matter already contains notions of gender and sexuality, it cannot be a neutral recourse on which to build "scientific" or "objective" theories of sexual development and differentiation. At the same time, we have to acknowledge and use aspects of materiality "that pertain to the body." "The domains of biology, anatomy, physiology, hormonal and chemical composition, illness, age, weight, metabolism, life and death" cannot "be denied."[27] The critical theorist Bernice Hausman concretizes this point in her discussion of surgical technologies

available for creating male-to-female versus female-to-male transsexual bodies. "The differences," she writes, "between vagina and penis are not merely ideological. Any attempt to engage and decode the semiotics of sex ... must acknowledge that these physiological signifiers have functions in the real that will escape ... their function in the symbolic system."[28]

To talk about human sexuality requires a notion of the material. Yet the idea of the material comes to us already tainted, containing within it preexisting ideas about sexual difference. Butler suggests that we look at the body as a system that simultaneously produces and is produced by social meanings, just as any biological organism always results from the combined and simultaneous actions of nature and nurture.

*****

BEYOND DUALISMS

[...] Humans are biological and thus in some sense natural beings *and* social and in some sense artificial—or, if you will, constructed entities. Can we devise a way of seeing ourselves, as we develop from fertilization to old age, as simultaneously natural and unnatural? During the past decade an exciting vision has emerged that I have loosely grouped under the rubric of developmental systems theory, or DST. What do we gain by choosing DST as an analytic framework?

Developmental systems theorists deny that there are fundamentally two kinds of processes: one guided by genes, hormones, and brain cells (that is, nature), the other by the environment, experience, learning, or inchoate social forces (that is, nurture). The pioneer systems theorist, philosopher Susan Oyama promises that DST: "gives more clarity, more coherence, more consistency and a different way to interpret data; in addition it offers the means for synthesizing the concepts and methods ... of groups that have been working at cross-purposes, or at least talking past each other for decades." Nevertheless, developmental systems theory is no magic bullet. Many will resist its insights because, as

Oyama explains," it gives less ... guidance on fundamental truth" and "fewer conclusions about what is inherently desirable, healthy, natural or inevitable."[29]

How, specifically, can DST help us break away from dualistic thought processes? Consider an example described by systems theorist Peter Taylor, a goat born with no front legs. During its lifetime it managed to hop around on its hind limbs. An anatomist who studied the goat after it died found that it had an S-shaped spine (as do humans), "thickened bones, modified muscle insertions, and other correlates of moving on two legs."[30] This (and every goat's) skeletal system developed as part of its manner of walking. Neither its genes nor its environment determined its anatomy. Only the ensemble had such power. Many developmental physiologists recognize this principle. As one biologist writes, "enstructuring occurs during the enactment of individual life histories."[31]

A few years ago, when the neuroscientist Simon LeVay reported that the brain structures of gay and heterosexual men differed (and that this mirrored a more general sex difference between straight men and women), he became the center of a firestorm. Although an instant hero among many gay males, he was at odds with a rather mixed group. On the one hand, feminists such as myself disliked his unquestioning use of gender dichotomies, which have in the past never worked to further equality for women. On the other, members of the Christian right hated his work because they believe that homosexuality is a sin that individuals can choose to reject. LeVay's, and later geneticist Dean Harner's, work suggested to them that homosexuality was inborn or innate. The language of the public debate soon became polarized. Each side contrasted words such as *genetic, biological, inborn, innate,* and *unchanging* with *environmental, acquired, constructed,* and *choice.*

The ease with which such debates evoke the nature/nurture divide is a consequence of the poverty of a nonsystems approach. Politically, the nature/nurture framework holds enormous dangers. Although some hope that a belief in the nature side of things will lead to greater tolerance, past history suggests that the opposite is also possible. Even the scientific architects of the nature argument recognize the dangers. In an extraordinary passage in the pages of *Science*, Dean Hamer and his collaborators indicated their concern: "It would be fundamentally unethical to use such information to try to assess or alter a person's current or future sexual orientation. Rather, scientists, educators, policy-makers and the public should work together to ensure that such research is used to benefit all members of society."[32]

The feminist psychologist and critical theorist Elisabeth Wilson uses the hubbub over LeVay's work to make some important points about systems theory. Many feminist, queer, and critical theorists work by deliberately displacing biology, hence opening the body to social and cultural shaping. This, however, is the wrong move to make. Wilson writes: "What may be politically and critically contentious in LeVay's hypothesis is not the conjunction neurology-sexuality per se, but the particular manner in which such a conjunction is enacted."[33] An effective political response, she continues, doesn't have to separate the study of sexuality from the neurosciences. Instead, Wilson, who wants us to develop a theory of mind and body—an account of psyche that joins libido to body—suggests that feminists incorporate into their worldview an account of how the brain works that is, broadly speaking, called connectionism.

The old-fashioned approach to understanding the brain was anatomical. Function could be located in particular parts of the brain. Ultimately function and anatomy were one. This idea underlies the corpus callosum debate [...], for example, as well as the uproar over LeVay's work. Many scientists believe that a structural difference represents the brain location for measured behavioral differences. In contrast, connectionist models argue that function emerges from the complexity and strength of many neural connections acting at once. The system has some important characteristics: the responses are often nonlinear, the networks can be "trained" to respond in particular ways, the nature of the response is not easily predictable, and information is not located anywhere— rather, it is the net result of the many different connections and their differing strengths.

The tenets of some connectionist theory provide interesting starting points for understanding human sexual development. Because connectionist networks, for example, are usually nonlinear, small changes can produce large effects. One implication for studying sexuality: we could easily be looking in the wrong places and on the wrong scale for aspects of the environment that shape human development. Furthermore, a single behavior may have many underlying causes, events that happen at different times in development. I suspect that our labels of homosexual, heterosexual, bisexual, and transgender are really not good categories at all, and are best understood only in terms of unique developmental events affecting particular individuals. Thus, I agree with those connectionists who argue that "the developmental process itself lies at the heart of knowledge acquisition. Development is a process of emergence."[34]

*****

NOTES

1. Hanley 1983
2. Quoted in Carlson 1991 p. 27.
3. Haraway 1997, p. 217.
4. Foucault 1978, p. 141.
5. Foucault 1978, p.139; emphasis in the original.
6. Ibid.
7. Sawicki 1991, p. 67.
8. Foucault 1980, p. 107.
9. Quoted in Moore and Clarke 1995, p. 271.
10. Kinsey et al., 1948; Kinsey et al., 1953.
11. When they looked at accumulated homosexual encounters, from adolescence through age forty, they reported that homosexual responses had reached 28 percent for women and almost 50 percent for men. When they asked about interactions that led to orgasm, the numbers were still high: 13 percent for women and 37 percent for men (ibid., p. 471). Kinsey did not endorse the notion of homosexuality as a natural category. His system, emphatically, did not carve nature at the joints.
12. McIntosh 1968.

13. Katz 1990 and 1995
14. Hansen 1989 and 1992.
15. Katz 1990, p. 16.
16. Nye 1998, p. 4.
17. Vance 1991, p. 878.
18. Vance 1991, p. 878.
19. Ortner 1996.
20. Oyewumi 1998, p. 1053.
21. Oyewumi 1998, p. 1061.
22. Oyewumi 1997, p. xv.
23. Halperin 1993, p. 416.
24. Plumwood 1993, p. 43.
25. Wilson 1998, p. 55.
26. Butler 1993, p. 66.
27. Ibid., p. 29.
28. Hausmann 1995, p. 69.
29. Oyama 1985, p. 9.
30. Taylor 1998, p. 24.
31. Ho 1989, p. 34.
32. Hamer et al., 1993, p. 326.
33. Wilson 1998, p. 203.
34. Elman et al. 1996, p. 359.

BIBLIOGRAPHY

Butler, J. 1993. *Bodies That Matter: On the Discursive Limits of Sex.* New York: Routledge.

Carlson, A. 1991. When Is a Woman Not a Woman? *Women's Sport and Fitness* 13:24–29.

Elman, J.L., E.A. Bates, et al. 1996. *Rethinking Innateness: A Connectionist Perspective on Development.* Cambridge: MIT Press.

Foucault M. 1978. *The History of Sexuality.* New York: Pantheon.

———. 1980. Two Lectures. In *Power/Knowledge: Selected Interviews and Other Writings 1972–1977 by Michel Foucault,* ed. C. Gordon. New York: Pantheon, pp. 78–108.

Halperin, D.A. 1993. Is There a History of Sexuality? In *The Lesbian and Gay Reader,* ed. H. Abelove, M.A. Barale, and D.A. Halperin. New York: Routledge, 416–31.

Hamer, D., S. Hu, et al. 1993. Linkage between DNA Markers on the X Chromosome and Male Sexual Orientation. *Science* 261: 321–25.

Hanley, D.F. 1983. Drug and Sex Testing: Regulations for International Competitions. *Clinics in Sports Medicine* 2: 13–17.

Hansen, B. 1989. American Physicians' Earliest Writings about Homosexuals, 1880–1900. *Milbank Quarterly* 67 (suppl. 1): 92–108.

_____. 1992. American Physicians' Discovery of Homosexuals, 1880–1900: A New Diagnosis in a Changing Society. In *Framing Disease*, ed. C. Rosenberg and J. Golden. New Brunswick, NJ: Rutgers University Press, 104–33.

Haraway, D. 1997. *Modest_witness@second_millenium.femaleman_meets_oncomouse*™. New York: Routledge.

Hausman, B.L. 1995. *Changing Sex: Transsexualism, Technology and the Idea of Gender in the 20th Century*. Durham, NC: Duke University Press.

Ho, M.-W. 1989. A Structuralism of Process: Towards a post-Darwinian Rational Morphology. In *Dynamic Structures in Biology*, ed. B. Goodwin, A. Sibatani, and G. Webster. Edinburgh: Edinburgh University Press, 31–48.

Katz, J. 1990. The Invention of Heterosexuality. *Socialist Review* 20: 7–34.

_____. 1995. *The Invention of Heterosexuality*. New York: Dutton.

Kinsey, A.C., W.B. Pomeroy, et al. 1948. *Sexual Behaviour in the Human Male*. Philadelphia: Saunders.

_____. 1953. *Sexual Behaviour in the Human Female*. Philadelphia: Saunders.

McIntosh, M. 1968. The Homosexual Role. *Social Problems* 16: 182–92.

Moore, L.J., and A.E. Clarke. 1995. Clitoral Conventions and Transgressions: Graphic Representations in Anatomy Texts, c1900–1991. *Feminist Studies* 21 (2): 255–301.

Nye, R.A. 1998. Introduction. In *Oxford Readers: Sexuality*, ed. R.A. Nye. Oxford, UK: Oxford University Press, 3–15.

Ortner, S.B. 1996. *Making Gender: The Politics and Erotics of Culture*. Boston: Beacon Press.

Oyama, S. 1985. *The Ontogeny of Information*. Cambridge, UK: Cambridge University Press.

Oyewumi, O. 1997. *The Invention of Women: Making an African Sense of Western Gender*. Minneapolis: University of Minnesota Press.

_____. 1998. De-confounding Gender: Feminist Theorizing and Western Culture, a Comment on Hawkesworth's "Confounding Gender." *Signs* 23(4): 1049–62.

Plumwood, V. 1993. *Feminism and the Mastery of Nature*. New York: Routledge.

Sawicki, J. 1991. *Disciplining Foucault*. New York: Routledge.

Taylor, P.J. 1998. Natural Selection: A Heavy Hand In Biological and Social Thought. *Science as Culture* 7(1): 5–32.

Vance, C.S. 1991. Anthropology Rediscovers Sexuality: A Theoretical Comment. *Social Science and Medicine* 33(8): 875–84.

Wilson, E. 1998. Communicating in Science. In E. Bearne (Ed.), *The Use of Language at Key Stage 3*. New York: Routledge.

CHAPTER 4

THE GIVE AWAY

Leslie Feinberg

I found my first clue that trans people have not always been hated in 1974. I had played hooky from work and spent the day at the Museum of the American Indian in New York City.

The exhibits were devoted to Native history in the Americas. I was drawn to a display of beautiful thumb-sized clay figures. The ones to my right had breasts and cradled bowls. Those on the left were flat chested, holding hunting tools. But when I looked closer, I did a double-take. I saw that several of the figures holding bowls were flat chested; several of the hunters had breasts. You can bet there was no legend next to the display to explain. I left the museum curious.

What I'd seen gnawed at me until I called a member of the curator's staff. He asked, "Why do you want to know?" I panicked. Was the information so classified that it could only be given out on a "need to know" basis? I lied and said I was a graduate student at Columbia University.

Sounding relieved, he immediately let me know that he understood exactly what I'd described. He said he came across references to these berdache[1] practically every day in his reading. I asked him what the word meant. He said he thought it meant transvestite or trans-sexual in modern English. He remarked that Native peoples didn't seem to abhor them the way "we" did. In fact, he added, it appeared that such individuals were held in high esteem by Native nations.

Then his voice dropped low. "It's really quite disturbing, isn't it?" he whispered. I hung up the phone and raced to the library. I had found the first key to a vault containing information I'd looked for all my life.

"Strange country this," a white man wrote in 1850 about the Crow nation of North America, "where males assume the dress and perform the duties of females, turn men and mate with their own sex!"[2]

I found hundreds and hundreds of similar references, such as those in Jonathan Ned Katz's ground-breaking *Gay American History: Lesbians and Gay Men in the U.S.A.*, published in 1976, which provided me with additional valuable research. The quotes were anything but objective. Some were statements by murderously hostile colonial generals, others by the anthropologists and missionaries who followed in their bloody wake.

Some only referred to what today might be called male-to-female expression. "In nearly every part of the continent," Westermarck concluded in 1917, "there seem to have been, since ancient times, men dressing themselves in the clothes and performing the functions of women...."[3]

But I also found many references to female-to-male expression. Writing about his expedition into northeastern Brazil in 1576, Pedro de Magalhães noted females among the Tupinamba who lived as men and were accepted by other men, and who hunted and went to war. His team of explorers, recalling the Greek Amazons, renamed the river that flowed through that area the *River of the Amazons*.[4]

Female-to-male expression was also found in numerous North American nations. As late as 1930, ethnographer Leslie Spier observed of a nation in the Pacific Northwest: Transvestites or berdaches ... are found among the Klamath, as in all probability among all other North American tribes. These are men and women who for reasons that remain obscure take on the dress and habits of the opposite sex."[5]

I found it painful to read these quotes because they were steeped in hatred. "I saw a devilish thing," Spanish colonialist Alvar Nuñez Cabeza de Vaca wrote in the sixteenth century.[6] "Sinful, heinous, perverted, nefarious, abominable, unnatural, disgusting, lewd"—the language used by the colonizers to describe the acceptance of sex/gender diversity, and of same-sex love, most accurately described the viewer, not the viewed. And these sensational reports about Two-Spirit people were used to further "justify" genocide, the theft of Native land and resources, and destruction of their cultures and religions.

But occasionally these colonial quotes opened, even if inadvertently, a momentary window into the humanity of the peoples being observed. Describing his first trip down the Mississippi in the seventeenth century, Jesuit Jacques Marquette chronicled the attitudes of the Illinois and Nadouessi to the Two-Spirits. "They are summoned to the Councils, and nothing can be decided without their advice. Finally, through their profession of leading an Extraordinary life, they pass for Manitous,—That is to say, for Spirits,—or persons of Consequence."[7]

Although French missionary Joseph François Lafitau condemned Two-Spirit people he found among the nations of the western Great Lakes, Louisiana, and Florida, he revealed that those Native peoples did not share his prejudice. "They believe they are honored ..." he wrote in 1724, "they participate in all religious ceremonies, and this profession of an extraordinary life causes them to be regarded as people of a higher order...."[8]

But the colonizers' reactions toward Two-Spirit people can be summed up by the words of Antonio de la Calancha, a Spanish official in Lima. Calancha wrote that during Vasco Nuñez de Balboa's expedition across Panama, Balboa "saw men dressed like women; Balboa learnt that they were sodomites and threw the king and forty others to be eaten by his dogs, a fine action of an honorable and Catholic Spaniard."[9]

This was not an isolated attack. When the Spaniards invaded the Antilles and Louisiana, "they found men dressed as women who were respected by their societies. Thinking they were hermaphrodites, or homosexuals, they slew them."[10]

Finding these quotes shook me. I recalled the "cowboys and Indians" movies of my childhood. These racist films didn't succeed in teaching me hate; I had grown up around strong, proud Native adults and children. But I now realized more consciously how every portrayal of Native nations in these movies was aimed at diverting attention from the real-life colonial genocide. The same bloody history was ignored or glossed over in my schools. I only learned the truth about Native cultures later, by re-educating myself—a process I'm continuing.

Discovering the Two-Spirit tradition had deep meaning for me. It wasn't that I thought the range of human expression among Native nations was identical to trans identities today. I knew that a Crow *badé*, Cocopa *warhameh*, Chumash *joya*, and Maricopa *kwiraxame'* would describe themselves in very different ways from an African-American *drag queen* fighting cops at Stonewall or a white *female-to-male transsexual* in the 1990s explaining his life to a college class on gender theory.

What stunned me was that such ancient and diverse cultures allowed people to choose more sex/gender paths, and this diversity of human expression was honored as sacred. I had to chart the complex geography of sex and gender with a compass needle that only pointed to north or south.

You'd think I'd have been elated to find this new information. But I raged that these facts had been kept from me, from all of us. And so many of the Native peoples who were arrogantly scrutinized by military men, missionaries, and anthropologists had been massacred. Had their oral history too been forever lost?

In my anger, I vowed to act more forcefully in defense of the treaty, sovereignty, and self-determination rights of Native nations. As I became more active in these struggles, I began to hear more clearly the voices of Native peoples who not only reclaimed their traditional heritage, but carried the resistance into the present: the takeover of Alcatraz, the occupation of Wounded Knee, the Longest Walk, the Day of Mourning at Plymouth Rock, and the fight to free political prisoners like Leonard Peltier and Norma Jean Croy.

Two historic developments helped me to hear the voices of modern Native warriors who lived the sacred Two-Spirit tradition: the founding of Gay American Indians in 1975 by Randy Burns (Northern Paiute) and Barbara Cameron (Lakota Sioux), and the publication in 1988 of *Living the Spirit: A Gay American Indian Anthology*. Randy Burns noted that the History Project of Gay American Indians "has documented these alternative gender roles in over 135 North American tribes."[11]

Will Roscoe, who edited *Living the Spirit*, explained that this more complex sex/gender system was found "in every region of the continent, among every type of native culture, from the small bands of hunters in Alaska to the populous, hierarchical city-states in Florida."[12]

Another important milestone was the 1986 publication of *The Spirit and the Flesh*[13] by Walter Williams, because this book included the voices of modern Two-Spirit people.

I knew that Native struggles against colonialization and genocide—both physical and cultural—were tenacious. But I learned that the colonizers' efforts to outlaw, punish, and slaughter the Two-Spirits within those nations had also met with fierce resistance. Conquistador Nuño de Guzman recorded in 1530 that the last person taken prisoner after a battle, who had "fought most courageously, was a man in the habit of a woman...."[14]

Just trying to maintain a traditional way of life was itself an act of resistance. Williams wrote,

"Since in many tribes berdaches were often shamans, the government's attack on traditional healing practices disrupted their lives. Among the Klamaths, the government agent's prohibition of curing ceremonials in the 1870s and 1880s required shamans to operate underground. The berdache shaman White Cindy continued to do traditional healing, curing people for decades despite the danger of arrest."[15]

Native nations resisted the racist demands of U.S. government agents who tried to change Two-Spirit people. This defiance was especially courageous in light of the power these agents exercised over the economic survival of the Native people they tried to control. One such struggle focused on a Crow *badé* (*boté*) named *Osh-Tisch* (Finds Them and Kills Them). An oral history by Joe Medicine Crow in 1982 recalled the events: "One agent in the late 1890s ... tried to interfere with Osh-Tisch, who was the most respected *badé*. The agent incarcerated the *badé*s, cut off their hair, made them wear men's clothing. He forced them to do manual labor, planting these trees that you see here on the BIA grounds. The people were so upset with this that Chief Pretty Eagle came into Crow Agency, and told [the agent] to leave the reservation. It was a tragedy, trying to change them."[16]

How the *badé*s were viewed within their own nation comes across in this report by S.C. Simms in 1903 in *American Anthropologist*: "During a visit last year to the Crow reservation, in the interest of the Field Columbian Museum, I was informed that there were three hermaphrodites in the Crow tribe, one living at Pryor, one in the Big Horn district, and one in Black Lodge district. These persons are usually spoken of as 'she,' and as having the largest and best appointed tipis; they are also generally considered to be experts with the needle and the most efficient cooks in the tribe, and they are highly regarded for their many charitable acts....

"A few years ago an Indian agent endeavored to compel these people, under threat of punishment, to wear men's clothing, but his efforts were unsuccessful."[17]

White-run boarding schools played a similar role in trying to force generations of kidnapped children to abandon their traditional ways. But many Two-Spirit children escaped rather than conform.

Lakota medicine man Lame Deer told an interviewer about the sacred place of the *winkte* ("male-to-female") in his nation's traditions, and how the *winkte* bestowed a special name on an individual. "The secret name a *winkte* gave to a child was believed to be especially powerful and effective," Lame Deer said. "Sitting Bull, Black Elk, even Crazy Horse had secret *winkte* names." Lakota chief Crazy Horse reportedly had one or two *winkte* wives.[18]

Williams quotes a Lakota medicine man who spoke of the pressures on the *winktes* in the 1920s and 1930s. The missionaries and the government agents said *winktes* were no good, and tried to get them to change their ways. Some did, and put on men's clothing. But others, rather than change, went out and hanged themselves."[19]

Up until 1989, the Two-Spirit voices I heard lived only in the pages of books. But that year I was honored to be invited to Minneapolis for the first gathering of Two-Spirit Native people, their loved ones, and supporters. The bonds of friendship I enjoyed at the first event were strengthened at the third gathering in Manitoba in 1991. There, I found myself sitting around a campfire at the base of tall pines under the rolling colors of the northern lights, drinking strong tea out of a metal cup. I laughed easily, relaxed with old friends and new ones. Some were feminine men or masculine women; all shared same-sex desire. Yet not all of these people were transgendered, not all of the Two-Spirits I'd read about desired people of the same sex. Then what defined this group?

I turned to Native people for these answers. Even today, in 1995, I read research papers and articles about sex/gender systems in Native nations in which every source cited is a white social scientist. When I began to write this book, I asked Two-Spirit people to talk about their own cultures, in their own words.

Chrystos, a brilliant Two-Spirit poet and writer from the Menominee nation, offered me this understanding: "Life among First Nation people, before first contact, is hard to reconstruct. There's been so much abuse of traditional life by the Christian Church. But certain things

have filtered down to us. Most of the nations that I know of traditionally had more than two genders. It varies from tribe to tribe. The concept of Two-Spiritedness is a rather rough translation into English of that idea. I think the English language is rigid, and the thought patterns that form it are rigid, so that gender also becomes rigid.

"The whole concept of gender is more fluid in traditional life. Those paths are not necessarily aligned with your sex, although they may be. People might choose their gender according to their dreams, for example. So even the idea that your gender is something you dream about is not even a concept in Western culture—which posits you are born a certain biological sex and therefore there's a role you must step into and follow pretty rigidly for the rest of your life. That's how we got the concept of queer. Anyone who doesn't follow their assigned gender role is queer; all kinds of people are lumped together under that word."[20]

Does being Two-Spirit determine your sexuality? I asked Chrystos. "In traditional life a Two-Spirit person can be heterosexual or what we would call homosexual," she replied. "You could also be a person who doesn't have sex with anyone and lives with the spirits. The gender fluidity is part of a larger concept, which I guess the most accurate English word for is 'tolerance.' It's a whole different way of conceiving how to be in the world with other people. We think about the world in terms of relationship, so each person is always in a matrix, rather than being seen only as an individual—which is a very different way of looking at things."[21]

Chrystos told me about her Navajo friend Wesley Thomas, who describes himself as *nadleeh*-like. A male *nadleeh*, she said, "would manifest in the world as a female and take a husband and participate in tribal life as a female person." I e-mailed Wesley, who lives in Seattle, for more information about the *nadleeh* tradition. He wrote back that "*nadleeh* was a category for women who were/are masculine and also feminine males."[22]

The concept of *nadleeh*, he explained, is incorporated into Navajo origin or creation stories. "So, it is a cultural construction," he wrote, "and was part of the normal Navajo culture, from the Navajo point of view, through the nineteenth century. It began changing during the first half of the twentieth century due to the introduction of western education and most of all, Christianity. *Nadleeh* since then has moved underground."[23]

Wesley, who spent the first thirty years of life on the Eastern Navajo reservation, wrote that in his initial fieldwork research he identified four categories of sex: female/woman, male/man, female/man, and male/woman. "Where I began to identify gender on a continuum—meaning placing female at one end and male on the other end—I placed forty-nine different gender identifications in between. This was derived at one sitting, not from carrying out a full and comprehensive fieldwork research. This number derived from my own understanding of gender within the Navajo cosmology."[24]

I have faced so much persecution because of my gender expression that I also wanted to hear about the experiences of someone who grew up as a "masculine girl" in traditional Native life. I thought of Spotted Eagle, whom I had met in Manitoba, and who lives in Georgia. Walking down an urban street, Spotted Eagle's gender expression, as well as her nationality, could make her the target of harassment and violence. But she is White Mountain Apache, and I knew she had grown up with her own traditions on the reservation. How was she treated?

"I was born in 1945," Spotted Eagle told me. "I grew up totally accepted. I knew from birth, and everyone around me knew I was Two-Spirited. I was honored. I was a special creation; I was given certain gifts because of that, teachings to share with my people and healings. But that changed—not in my generation, but in generations to follow."

There were no distinct pronouns in her ancient language, she said. There were three variations: the way the women spoke, the way the men spoke, and the ceremonial language." Which way of speaking did she use? "I spoke all three. So did the two older Two-Spirit people on my reservation."[25]

Spotted Eagle explained that the White Mountain Apache nation was small and isolated, and so had been less affected early on by colonial culture. As a result, the U.S. government didn't set up the mission school system on the White Mountain reservation until the late 1930s or early 1940s. Spotted Eagle said she experienced her first taste of bigotry as a Two-Spirit in those schools. "I was taken out of the mission school with the help of my people and sent away to live with an aunt off reservation, so I didn't get totally abused by Christianity. I have some very horrible memories of the short time I was there."[26]

"But as far as my own people," Spotted Eagle continued, "we were a matriarchy, and have been through our history. Women are in a different position in a matriarchy than they are out here. It's not that we have more power or more privilege than anyone else, it's just a more balanced way to be. Being a woman was a plus and being Two-Spirit was even better. I didn't really have any negative thoughts about being Two-Spirit until I left the reservation."[27]

Spotted Eagle told me that as a young adult she married. "My husband was also Two-Spirit and we had children. We lived in a rather peculiar way according to standards out here. Of course it was very normal for us. We faced a lot of violence, but we learned to cope with it and go on."[28]

Spotted Eagle's husband died many years ago. Today her partner is a woman. Her three children are grown. "Two of them are Two-Spirit," she said proudly. "We're all very close."[29]

I asked her where she found her strength and pride. "It was given to me by the people around me to maintain," she explained. "If your whole life is connected spiritually, then you learn that self-pride—the image of self—is connected with everything else. That becomes part of who you are and you carry that wherever you are."[30]

What was responsible for the imposition of the present-day rigid sex/gender system in North America? It is not correct to simply blame patriarchy, Chrystos stressed to me. "The real word is 'colonization' and what it has done to the world. Patriarchy is a tool of colonization and exploitation of people and their lands for wealthy white people."[31]

"The Two-Spirit tradition was suppressed," she explained. "Like all Native spirituality, it underwent a tremendous time of suppression. So there's gaps. But we've continued on with our spiritual traditions. We are still attached to this land and the place of our ancestors and managed to protect our spiritual traditions and our languages. We have always been at war. Despite everything—incredible onslaughts that even continue now—we have continued and we have survived.[32]

Like a gift presented at a traditional give away, Native people have patiently given me a greater understanding of the diverse cultures that existed in the Western hemisphere before colonization.

But why did many Native cultures honor sex/gender diversity, while European colonialists were hell-bent on wiping it out? And how did the Europeans immediately recognize Two-Spiritedness? Were there similar expressions in European societies?

Thinking back to my sketchy high-school education, I could only remember one person in Europe whose gender expression had made history [Joan of Arc].

NOTES

1. "Berdache" was a derogatory term European colonizers used to label any Native person who did not fit their narrow notions of woman and man. The blanket use of the word disregarded distinctions of self-expression, social interaction, and complex economic and political realities. Native nations had many respectful words in their own languages to describe such people; Gay American Indians (GAI) has gathered a valuable list of these words. However, cultural genocide has destroyed and altered Native languages and traditions. So Native people ask that the term "Two-Spirit" be used to replace the offensive colonial word—a request I respect.

    In a further attempt to avoid analyzing oppressed peoples' cultures, I do not make a distinction between sex and gender expression in this chapter. Instead, I use sex/gender.

2. Edwin Thompson Denig, *Five Indian Tribes of the Upper Missouri*, ed. John C. Ewers (Norman: University of Oklahoma Press, 1961) 199.

3. Edward Westermarck, "Homosexual Love," *The Origin and Development of Moral Ideas*, 2nd ed., 2 vols. (London: Macmillan, 1917) 2:456.

4. Pedro de Magalhães, *The Histories of Brazil*, trans. John B. Stetson, Jr. (New York: The Cortes Society, 1922) 89–90.

5. Leslie Spier, "Klamath Ethnography," *University of California Publications in American Archaeology and Ethnology* 30 (1930): 51–53.

6. Alyar Nunez Cabeza de Vaca, "Naufragios," *Historiadores primitivos delndias*, ed. Enrique de Vedia (Madrid: M. Rivadeneyra, 1852) 538, Vol. 1 of *Biblioteca de autores espanoles*, quoted in Jonathan Katz, *Gay American History: Lesbians and Gay Men in the U.S.A.* (New York: Harper & Row, 1976) 285.

7. Jacques Marquette, *Of the First Voyage Made by Father Marquette toward New Mexico, and How the Idea Thereof Was Conceived*, ed. Reuben Gold Thwaites (Cleveland: Burrows, 1895–1901) 129, Vol. 59 of *The Jesuit and Allied Documents*, quoted in Katz, 287.

8. Joseph Francois Lafitau, *Moeurs des sauvages ameriquains, comparées aux moeurs des premiers tempts*, 2 vols. (Paris: Saugrain, 1724) 1:52, 603–10, quoted in Katz, 288–89.

9. Francisco Guerra, *The Pre-Columbian Mind* (London: Seminar Press, 1971) 190, cited in Walter Williams, *The Spirit and the Flesh: Sexual Diversity in American Indian Culture* (Boston: Beacon Press, 1986) 137.

10. Cora Dubois, cited in Richard Green, "Historical and Cross-Cultural Survey," *Sexual Identity Conflict in Children and Adults* (New York: Basic Books, 1974) 11.

11. Randy Burns, "Preface," and the Gay American Indian History Project, "North American Tribes with Berdache and Alternative Gender Roles," *Living the Spirit: A Gay American Indian Anthology*, compiled by Gay American Indians, coordinating ed. Will Roscoe (New York: St. Martin's Press, 1988) 1, see language list on 217–22.

12. Will Roscoe, *The Zuni Man-Woman* (Albuquerque: University of New Mexico Press, 1988) 5.

13. Walter Williams, *The Spirit and the Flesh: Sexual Diversity in American Indian Culture* (Boston: Beacon Press, 1986).

14. Ibid., 137.

15. Ibid., 178.

16. Ibid., 179.

17. S.C. Simms, "Crow Indian Hermaphrodites," *American Anthropologist* no. 5 (1903): 580–81.

18. C. Daryll Forde, "Ethnography of the Vuma Indians," *University of California Publications in American Archaeology and Ethnology* 28.4 (1931): 157, quoted in Williams, *Spirit and Flesh*, 38; Lakota informant as cited in Williams, 112.

19. Williams, *Spirit and Flesh*, 182.

20. Chrystos, telephone interview, 14 March 1995.

21. Ibid.

22. Wesley Thomas, e-mail communication, 5 April 1995.

23. Ibid.

24. Ibid.

25. Spotted Eagle, telephone interview, 16 March 1995.

26. Ibid.

27. Ibid.

28. Ibid.

29. Ibid.

30. Ibid.

31. Chrystos, telephone interview, 14 March 1995.

32. Ibid.

DISCUSSION QUESTIONS: LAMPHERE

1. Explain the conclusions early feminist anthropologists reached about gender roles cross-culturally in the 1970s. What precipitated a shift in their thinking?
2. Discuss major pieces of feminist anthropological research that contributed to a retheorization of women's universal subordination as a result of their association with the domestic sphere.
3. Summarize what has become a more subtle and widely accepted feminist anthropological understanding of cross-cultural gender relations.

DISCUSSION QUESTIONS: LUXTON

1. Explain why non-feminist theorists of labour largely ignore the issue of domestic labour. Why do feminists argue that this issue is of crucial importance to understanding the workings of capitalism?
2. Discuss in detail what Luxton means when she argues that domestic labour is a process of production, as well as reproduction.
3. How does Luxton differentiate "housework" from "domestic labour"?

DISCUSSION QUESTIONS: FAUSTO-STERLING

1. Explain the recent shifts in feminist thinking about the relationship between sex and gender, and between the social expressions of gender and their physical underpinnings.
2. Discuss why intersexuals are understood to have "unruly" or "heretical" bodies in the context of dominant gender relations.
3. Fausto-Sterling argues that sexuality has a history. Explain.

DISCUSSION QUESTIONS: FEINBERG

1. Feinberg ends the piece by asking, "Why did many Native cultures honour sex/gender diversity, while European colonialists were hell-bent on wiping it out?" Provide some of your own answers to this question, considering dominant European gender relations at the time, as well as Fausto-Sterling's ideas about gender dualism.

2. Explain indigenous American traditions that created social space for "alternative" sex/gender arrangements.

3. How does the invisibility of a range of sex/gender arrangements serve particular political and social purposes?

FURTHER READINGS

1. de Beauvoir, Simone. 1953 [1949]. *The Second Sex*. Translated by H.M. Parshley. New York: Knopf.

    This is a classic and extraordinarily rich text written by a famous feminist philosopher. Beauvoir was one of the first thinkers to examine in a sustained manner the ways in which women are socially constructed as "other," and what social implications follow from that construction. While men are understood as agents in the world, making history, they look at women as "different," as other than themselves, as a passive part of nature. She deconstructs these androcentric representations that "describe the world from [men's] point of view, which they confuse with absolute truth" (1953:133).

2. Chodorow, Nancy. 1978. *The Reproduction of Mothering: Psychoanalysis and the Sociology of Gender*. Berkeley: University of California Press.

    One of the first feminists to employ psychoanalytic theory in analyzing the family, Chodorow develops an original thesis detailing how the traditional family structure, in which women have the primary responsibility for child care and nurturing, shapes women's and men's psychic development and results in the reproduction of gender roles from generation to generation.

3. Gilligan, Carol. 1982. *In a Different Voice: Psychological Theory and Women's Development*. Cambridge: Harvard University Press.

    In this famous study, Gilligan reveals the male bias in Lawrence Kohlberg's widely accepted theory of moral development. While Kohlberg's scale of moral development was constructed to represent progress to moral reasoning based on research results with 84 boys, Gilligan studied women to determine why they seemed to become stalled at the middle of the scale, which implied that women are deficient in the development of moral judgment. She found that many women follow a different path to moral development than most men. Women seem to have a morally "different voice" from the one Kohlberg identified as definitive of moral judgment, one that expresses an "ethics of care," rather than an "ethics of justice."

4. Rich, Adrienne. 1980. Compulsory Heterosexuality and Lesbian Existence. *Signs: Journal of Women in Society and Culture*, 5, 631–660.

    In this article, a lesbian poet tries to understand the hostility and homophobia lesbians face in their daily lives, constructing what has become the classic analysis of the "heterosexual prescription." Her analysis of anthropological literature about women across time and cultures details how men have enforced heterosexuality on women as a form of gender power through arranged marriages, harems, pornography, rape, enforced motherhood and sexual harassment.

5. Wollstonecraft, Mary. 1975 [1792]. *A Vindication of the Rights of Women*. Edited by Miriam Krammick. Harmondsworth: Penguin Books.

    Wollstonecraft (1759–1797) was one of the first feminist philosophers to make a place for herself in history. A British journalist and author who tried to support herself economically, she found she was unable to do so due to the social barriers against women's economic independence. In addition to this preoccupation, she argued against dominant notions that women are inferior in reasoning. She claimed that women are socialized to be creatures of emotion rather than reason, and to remedy this situation, she called for women to receive educations comparable to men.

RELEVANT FILMS

1. *20th Century Gals*, 2001, 46 minutes, Magic Lantern Communications
   Cathy Jones from "This Hour Has 22 Minutes" (masquerading as Babe) reviews women's progress through the 20th century. This fast-paced and hilarious film includes archival and documentary footage, historical re-enactments, and live interviews to determine how women have come to fare in the social fields of politics, sexuality, family, and work through the last 100 years.

2. *Multiple Genders: Mind and Body in Conflict*, 1997/1998, 40 minutes, Films for the Humanities and Sciences
   This film engages the topics of transsexuality and intersexuality, thereby raising the question of whether or not there are only two sexes. A doctor and theologian address the numbers and moral implications of an increasingly visible multisexual and polygendered orientation as they grapple with the relationship between sex and gender and intersexuality as a common phenomenon in nature.

3. *Juchitan Queer Paradise*, 2002, 64 minutes, McNabb and Connolly
   In Juchitan, a small Mexican city near the Guatemalan border, homosexuality is an accepted part of citizens' sexual lives. Gays and lesbians are understood simply as a "third gender," and many families recognize their "third gender" children as blessings. This film profiles three Juchitan residents who demonstrate the sexual fluidity and tolerance that characterizes this community.

4. *Transamazon: A Gender Queer Journey*, 2003, 41 minutes, UNH Video Services
   In this documentary film Joelle Ruby Ryan, a transactivist, questions the dominant gender binary by exploring transgendered identities. In the course of this exploration, Ryan investigates the meanings of "trans," "gender queer," and "passing," as well as the violence and hate crimes transgendered people experience.

5. *Women Organize!* 2000, 32 minutes, Women Make Movies
   Women from across the United States are portrayed in this documentary as they organize various activities as part of the global struggle for racial, gender, and economic justice.

RELEVANT WEB SITES

1. www.library.csi.cuny.edu/dept/history/lavender/182links.html
   This Web site provides information on and further links to women's history and strands of feminist theory. Topics discussed include a timeline of women's history, a history of feminism and women's movements and organizations, influential women, and changing feminist perspectives through time.

2. www.history.unimelb.edu.au/lilith/
   Lilith is an online journal of feminist history. It provides links to published, peer reviewed feminist research on women's history.

3. www.cddc.vt.edu/feminism/hist.html
   This is another Web site that provides a solid general history and broad overview of feminist history and feminist theory. Included are numerous links to further foundational readings in the field.

4. www.feministsforlife.org/history/foremoth.htm
   Feminist history is the focus of this site, including a list of important feminist foremothers, their publications, and their noteworthy contributions.

5. www.mith2.umd.edu/WomensStudies/Bibliographies/feminist-historiography
   The bibliography found at this site covers literature on American women's history published between 1968 and 1991. All articles are written from a feminist perspective.

⊕ ⊕ ⊕

PART II

THEORY AND THE SOCIAL CONSTRUCTION OF GENDER

There are a number of strands of feminist theory. Each one engages a particular central issue or set of concerns that shed light on how gender relations are shaped and perpetuated in everyday life. None of these theories is exhaustive or without its faults, but successive cohorts of feminist scholars have engaged each other's work, critiquing and expanding their peers' ideas in an attempt to develop subtler and more comprehensive explanations of gender arrangements. The following readings illustrate the spirit and challenge of these feminist debates, which productively advance feminist theory as a rigorous body of scholarship.

What different strands of feminist theory have in common is the principle that gender relations are socially constructed. Rather than supposing that we are simply biologically programmed for social behaviour, feminists argue that we actively shape our gendered lives in the particular historical and social contexts in which we live. We respond to the world we encounter, shaping, modifying, and creating our own identities and actions through our interactions with other people within various social institutions. The basis for a social constructivist position within feminist theory entails four empirical findings that cast doubt on the notion of a universal, stable, biologically based gender regime: definitions of masculinity and femininity vary from culture to culture; they vary in any one culture over time; they also vary over the course of an individual's life; and they vary within any one culture at any one time by class, race, age, sexuality, educational achievement, ability, region, etc.

For much of the life of feminist theory, scholars have been preoccupied with studying femininity and the lives of women, primarily because those lives and their position within a gendered society were largely invisible in mainstream academic literature. But in the past two decades, feminists have paid increasing attention to the social construction of masculinity. They are particularly attentive to making masculinity visible, to making men visible as gendered beings. But even that project has now been diversified as scholars argue that these two terms are inaccurate; they imply that there is only one definition of masculinity and femininity. More recent social constructivist approaches to gender explore the differences among men and among women, as these differences are now understood as

47

often more decisive than those between men and women. These differences among men and among women have led feminists such as Michael Kimmel to claim that several meanings of masculinity and femininity coexist in any one time and place based on men's and women's position with hierarchies of class, race, age, and sexuality, although one particular definition tends to become dominant or "hegemonic" in any particular social context. Consequently, we now speak of masculinities and femininities, acknowledging that gender identities and practices mean different things to different people at different times.

This selection of readings offers an introduction to a range of contemporary feminist theories. Roberta Hamilton provides an excellent overview of some (but not all) of the dominant strands of feminist theory, including liberal, Marxist, socialist, radical, anti-racist, and post-structuralist variants. Following that broad synopsis, Candice West and Don Zimmerman, in their famous article "Doing Gender," narrow our attention to an ethnomethodologically informed (the authors will explain) theory of gender. They argue that gender is less a component of a fixed identity that precedes social interactions than it is a *product* of those interactions. They contend that "a person's gender is not simply that aspect of what one is, but, more fundamentally, it is something that one *does*, and does recurrently, in interaction with others." We are thus constantly "doing" gender, performing the activities and exhibiting the traits that society prescribes.

Next, Michael Kimmel, whom I mentioned earlier, takes up the issue of the social construction of masculinity using a Freudian model of psychoanalysis. In outlining his theory of multiple masculinities, as well as the hegemonic form masculinity takes in contemporary American society, he explains how men simultaneously benefit and suffer from dominant gender relations. Homophobia seems to be the animating condition of the dominant definition of masculinity, which harms and socially excludes other men who perform "alternative" masculinities.

Finally, in an admittedly more difficult read, Judith Butler offers readers an introduction to post-structural feminist thinking. Butler is currently one of the most influential feminist theorists in North America. Her concern in the book *Undoing Gender*, which is reflected in the introduction, is to explore what it means to have a "livable life" in terms of societal rules for gender behaviour and identity. As she demonstrates, these norms "undo" the lives of the gender marginalized. Her writing compels us to contemplate how they can be actively resisted or made "undone" in order to make more lives more livable in a more open gender regime.

CHAPTER 5

FEMINIST THEORIES

Roberta Hamilton

Theory is a word that sends most mortals rushing from the room, convinced that what is coming is too rarefied, too pretentious, too difficult, or completely irrelevant. But I want to argue three things: first, that theory is very much intertwined with how we make sense of the world in an ordinary, day-to-day way; second, that we can gain something from being more systematic and probing about this activity of making sense; and third, that feminists have made very good use, indeed, of this more systematic process.

*****

Trying to understand the nature of social life, and how to transform inequitable social relationships has [...] taken many forms. Feminists have produced an enormous, diverse, and eclectic range of interpretations in their attempts to explain how sexual hierarchies are created and sustained as well as to provide strategies for confronting these hierarchies. Taken together, these interpretations constitute an unprecedented historical challenge to the organization of social life and the categories through which that life previously has been apprehended. This challenge involves examining the ways in which sexual oppression informs and is informed by

the many social practices through which people are privileged and disadvantaged, included and excluded, wield and submit to power. Feminist literature in its diversity, complexity, internal debates, and many languages defies summary. Yet all of it is provoked by unease with current social arrangements. My concern is that we not lose sight of its origins within feminist movements that seek to transform our relationships to each other on the intimate, local, and global levels. This chapter delineates the contours of contemporary feminist theories and their relationship to each other, and emphasizes their collective indebtedness to past and present feminist movements.

*****

Sociologist Philip Abrams (1982, xiii) chose the expression "the paradox of human agency" to convey the idea that what people choose to do is never straightforward. We live in particular times and places and face varying sorts of constraint and possibility; even what we can imagine we would like to do is shaped by these circumstances. This may not seem like a contestable proposition. But this way of understanding the individual and society actually stands against the ideology of the rational, autonomous individual "man" that has dominated Western thought in the past two or three centuries. These dominant ideas had their origins in the Enlightenment and have had powerful adherents throughout this age of capitalism, never more so, perhaps, than in its present neo-liberal incarnation that seeks to privatize the public sector, reduce the scale and scope of government spending, and throw each of us on our own resources (Leys 1996, 18). Marx's challenge to this ideology is encapsulated in his famous passage, "Men make their own history, but they do not make it just as they please; they do not make it under circumstances chosen by themselves, but under circumstances directly encountered, given and transmitted from the past" (Marx 1969 [1869], 398). As Marx indicates, we are born into particular, if always shifting, sets of relationships, within families and households, communities, and states. Such relationships confer obligation and responsibility and shape access or lack of access to everything from economic power and privilege to care and intimacy.

Feminists have had different ways of conveying the important idea that we are born into particular arrangements that shape all aspects of our lives. Indeed, the question of who and what constrains, oppresses, and subordinates women, and how, not only unites feminists but also divides them.

FEMINISTS AND THE DEBATE ABOUT HUMAN AGENCY

There are many proliferating and overlapping feminist perspectives (Shanley and Narayan 1997, xxi). My intention is not to contribute to the drawing of firm boundaries between them, boundaries that may only imitate conventional disciplinary boundaries and make it more difficult to ask questions about the origins and perpetuation of hierarchical relations between the sexes. Yet for students of feminist scholarship, it is necessary to know something about the history of these differences. The labels have been used a good deal and, even when labels are increasingly abandoned, it is important to know what is being abandoned and why.

Let us return to Marx's statement and see how feminists of differing persuasions—liberal feminists, socialist feminists, radical feminists, lesbian feminists, lesbian separatists, black feminists, and feminists of colour—would elaborate, modify, or overturn it. We also have to consider the ways in which feminists (who might also be in one or more of the above categories) have drawn on the insights of [...] poststructuralism and discourse analysis in considering this question of (wo)men making their own history but not under conditions chosen by themselves.

Liberal Feminism

Feminism's history is intertwined with the individualistic ideology of liberalism. When Mary Wollstonecraft (1759–97) wrote *A Vindication of the Rights of Woman* in 1792, she was in broad agreement with the liberal democratic slogan—Liberty, Equality, Fraternity—of the French Revolution. She argued that women, like men, are rational beings with the potential to be fully responsible for their own lives. Although she wrote in scathing terms about men's treatment of women, and provided them with reasoned arguments to treat women as their equals, she also lambasted aristocratic and middle-class women for exchanging "health, liberty, and virtue" for food and clothing (147), that is for a life of dependence on fathers and husbands.

She urged women not to be taken in by chivalry. Women "constantly demand homage as women though experience should teach them that the men who pride themselves upon paying this arbitrary insolent respect to the sex, with the most scrupulous exactness, are most inclined to tyrannize over, and despise the very weakness they cherish" (146).

For her, and for the liberal feminists who came after her, including those of our own time, the circumstances that shaped women's lives were the laws and prejudices (shared by men and women) that excluded them from the public sphere and from the right to earn their own living on an equal footing with men.

*****

During the next 200 years, with much ebb and flow, women struggled for the right to higher education, entrance into the professions, the right to own property and hold public office, and for suffrage, the right that came to symbolize full citizenship. For liberal feminists, the laws that decreed that women were lesser beings than men were a product of ignorance. The expectation was that as men and women educated themselves on this subject, these laws and the prejudices that underwrote them would gradually be replaced by extending equality of opportunity to women. As will become evident in this chapter, liberal feminism has been subjected to many criticisms. But several feminist theorists, notably Martha Nussbaum (2001), have recently reworked liberalism in their attempt to show that feminist goals can be accommodated within the paradigm.

Marxism and the Woman Question

The issue of economic independence figures prominently in Marx and his collaborator Friedrich Engels' theory on the subordination of women. Like other socialists, they conceptualized this as the "woman question." The problem was important, but clearly secondary to the central issue of social class.

Engels argued that our early ancestors lived in a state of primitive communism: everyone had to labour to survive and all that was available was shared. With the invention of cultivation and animal husbandry, people created the possibility of accumulating surplus. This development was of monumental importance in human history. It opened up the possibility of longer, more secure lives. But the underside was that this surplus could be controlled by some and used in the interests of the few against the many. The surplus would be claimed by the few as their private property. Some would labour so that others might prosper. Those men with a surplus wanted their own children to inherit the wealth they had amassed. But how would men know who were their own children? Only

women have this assurance. The solution was to turn women themselves into private property. If a man owned a woman, she would labour for him, and she would be permitted to have sexual relations only with him. Thus the idea of legitimacy was born. Legitimacy means that a man's legal children are the biological children of his wife. They are assumed to be his biological children because he owns their mother.

In this interpretation, class society and male dominance enter onto the world stage together. For Engels these developments constituted the "world historic defeat of the female sex" (1948 [1884], 57). It followed, then, that with the abolition of private property (under communism), women would be emancipated. Under capitalism, Engels detected a first step towards women's emancipation, as economic desperation forced working-class women to become wage labourers, and hence propelled them into de facto equality with their husbands. Economically dependent bourgeois women, on the other hand, remained the property of their husbands. For Marxists, then, the circumstances that shape women's lives are the relations of private property and, in our era, capitalist relations. They are the same relations that shape the lives of men, albeit in different ways.

Historically, liberal feminism and the Marxist perspective on the woman question not only had different explanations for, and solutions to, the subordination of women but also occupied different, and sometimes hostile, political territory. Marxists accused feminists of being "bourgeois," interested only in ensuring that women would share in the privilege (or destitution) of their class. Feminism was potentially dangerous to working-class struggles because sex-specific ideas about oppression would pit working men and women against each other and might create (false) grounds for class collaboration between upper- and working-class women. Feminists, for their part, often accused left-wing men and their political parties of being as uninterested, if not as hostile, as their class enemies to the rights of women.

Not until the late 1960s did another feminism develop that put liberal feminism and the

Marxist perspective on the woman question into dialogue with each other and made fully visible the hitherto unexplored fragments in Wollstonecraft's writings. For this feminism launched a critique not only of the public world but also of the private world—the world of family, love, sexuality, pregnancy, and childcare. Furthermore, these feminists argued that the interconnections between public and private worlds were pivotal for understanding the sexual hierarchy. Women's liberation, therefore, depended upon the transformation of both worlds.

But this feminism soon divided along political and theoretical lines into those calling themselves socialist feminists and those calling themselves radical feminists. For the purpose of this discussion, the difference between them centred upon the question of explanation: who and what oppressed women and why.

Socialist Feminism

Socialist feminists argued, with Marxists, that the relations of capital, and therefore class relations, are pivotal for understanding women's oppression. But they differed from Marxists in insisting that the oppressive relations between the sexes are not simply derivative of class. They argued that the interconnections between sex oppression and class exploitation had to be addressed. In other words, for socialist feminists, it was no longer enough to talk only about the woman question, and they did not assume that the basis for women's oppression would disappear automatically with the overthrow of capitalism. These feminists focused upon the ways in which the labour done by women in the household—which they called domestic labour—helps to sustain the capitalist system. On both a daily and generational level, women contribute to the reproduction of labour power by having and rearing children and by looking after husbands between their wearying days (or nights) in mines and factories (Armstrong and Armstrong 1994; 2002; Hamilton 1978; Luxton 1980; Luxton and Corman 2001; Vosko 2002). As a result, both capitalists and individual men

benefit from the unpaid and personal service of women in the home.

Socialist feminists analyzed the interconnections between the public sphere of capitalist and state relations and the private sphere of the family/household. Not only did the complex range of tasks done in the home prop up the capitalist edifice and allow the system to function at a fraction of its real cost, but in many ways the appearance of the distinction between private and public created and sustained the unequal relations between men and women throughout society. Challenging the dominant interpretation that men in the work force "bring home the bacon" and that nurturing women at home provide sustenance, socialist feminists uncovered the historically specific development of this relationship during the rise of industrial capitalism. Men of capital, together with middle-class philanthropists and social reformers and the better-paid male skilled workers, engaged in diverse, but mutually reinforcing, strategies to push women out of the labour force with promises of a family wage for male workers. For women, the results of this long historical manoeuvre were doubly exploitative and oppressive. First, denied access to higher education and the professions, women were also pushed out of the better-paying jobs; only the worst-paid and least-protected jobs remained open to them. Second, most men never earned a family wage but were nonetheless expected to support a wife and children. Women compensated for inadequate wages by increasing household labour, taking in boarders, laundry, and other people's children, and putting the needs of others before their own. Third, men earned the (main) wage, and this relative privilege reinforced their power over their wives and children. Men were exploited in the work force, and many responded by flexing their muscles, literally and figuratively, at home.

Socialist feminists pointed to the final irony that when men deserted their families, women, encouraged from birth to believe that men would care for them and their children, had to earn a living in the capitalist marketplace with "one hand tied behind their back" (Liddington and Norris 1978). Most women had no marketable skills, they were denied access to education and better-paying jobs, and they had no social supports for childcare. The family wage, portrayed as a form of security for working-class people, was unmasked as a fraud. Primarily, the idea of a family wage functioned as a rationale for excluding women from better-paying jobs and secure incomes, for paying them less, hiring them last, and firing them first (Connelly 1978). It served as a justification for women's sole responsibility for childcare and housework coupled with a lifetime of personal service to a particular man. No wonder that sociologists and socialist feminists Pat and Hugh Armstrong wanted to call *The Double Ghetto* (their pathbreaking book on women's work in Canada) *Everyone Needs a Wife*.

During the 1970s, socialist feminism developed through heated debates and open dialogue with radical feminism, quickly taking up many of its insights while eschewing many of its explanations.

Radical Feminism

Radical feminists did not dispute the exploitative nature of capitalist relations, but they argued that, buried deeper in human society, both historically and psychically, are the relations of domination and subordination between the sexes. Writing at the dawn of the contemporary women's movement, Shulamith Firestone (1970) located these differences between men and women in nature's unequal allotment of reproductive tasks. Women bore, suckled, and raised children, while men had the time and opportunity to develop social institutions—including the family—through which they were able to appropriate power and control over women and children. The bottom line was that men oppress women. Overthrowing that oppression constituted the primary struggle in which feminists should engage.

Radical feminism was neither static nor monolithic. As its critique developed, many radical feminists began to locate men's power over women in their ability to control women

sexually and to develop the institutions that ensure continuing control (Eisenstein 1984). Adrienne Rich (1980) coined the famous phrase *compulsory heterosexuality* to encapsulate the social and cultural imperatives that close off all sexual options for women except monogamous heterosexual permanent coupling, usually called marriage. In a world of unequal power relations between men and women, compulsory heterosexuality ensures not only women's sexual dependence upon men but also their economic, social, and psychological dependence. From this perspective—sometimes called *lesbian feminism*, though it was by no means confined to lesbians—women's lives in patriarchal society are shaped by the myriad legal institutions and cultural messages that enjoin women (from the time they are young girls) to look to men for sexual satisfaction, personal validation, and life-long companionship, and to accept their subordination to men in general and their husbands in particular as part of the bargain (Martindale 1995; see also *Resources for Feminist Research* 1990). From this critical position, some lesbian feminists took the short but dramatic step to a lesbian separatist position that women should no longer try to change the whole society but rather find ways to live apart from men and build a society alone (Rudy 2001).

More generally, early radical feminism was eclipsed by what has been called cultural feminism—overlapping with, but not confined by, a separatist perspective (Echots 1989). Women should build their own institutions from health clinics and women's shelters to small businesses, art galleries, publishing houses, and magazines. The rationale for these developments varies widely: for some it is a way of building a permanent women's world; for others it is a refuge from the pain of day-to-day struggle with men; for still others such autonomous organizing is intended to build a power base from which the whole society could be transformed (Rudy 2001).

What is key for the discussion on human agency is that radical, lesbian, and cultural feminists argue that women are born into arrangements that force them to live their lives in subservience to men. These feminists might alter Marx's statement to something like "Men make their own history; women have no history of their own." Socialist feminists agree that most men of all social classes have the opportunity in both their intimate and work lives to dominate and oppress women. Yet they also argue that men's and women's lives are shaped by the relations of capital, which privilege a few at the expense of the many.

Anti-racist Feminisms

For over a century, feminists argued that for women sex (and class, for socialist feminists) constituted the most important and sustaining form of oppression and exploitation. Within dominant feminist discourses, this became self-evident, and much effort went into charting the long and varied history of patriarchal relationships.

From the 1980s, women of colour and Aboriginal women began publicly challenging the universalism inherent in liberal, radical, and socialist feminism, all of which ignored—or at best sidelined—the histories of colonialism and imperialism, the legacies of slavery and genocide, and the systemic racism that produced lives of brutality and exclusion for some, and lives of unearned and unrecognized privilege for others (Brand 1984; Dua 1999; Carty 1999; Tynes 1987; 1990). By claiming to speak for all women, white feminists denied their social and economic advantages, perpetuated racism in their own theories, failed to make their movements relevant to women of colour, and excluded the struggles against racism from the histories of feminism.

These challenges led in different directions. Some feminists began to intertwine an analysis of racism with the Marxist focus on class and the radical feminist focus on the sexual hierarchy. Such a perspective is prominently announced in the titles of books and courses—"Race, Class and Gender" (Brand 1984; Vorst et al. 1989; Creese and Stasiulis 1996), and this formulation has motivated a good deal of important scholarship and political campaigns. The race-class-gender list, however, presupposes the possibility of coherent theoretical perspectives that can grapple

with the interconnections between these three dimensions of inequality, and this is no easy matter. Michele Barrett has argued that "existing theories of social structure, already taxed by attempting to think about the inter-relations of class and gender, have been quite unable to integrate a third axis of systemic inequality into their conceptual maps" (1988, xii).

Going further, Vijay Agnew has declared "that the mantra of 'race, class and gender' [had been] repeated so routinely that all its force as a critique of mainstream feminism had been lost" (1996, 3). The point is that mainstream feminism can hardly be left intact once interrogated for racialist assumptions. For the assumption of universalism—that a sexual hierarchy constitutes the most basic and important form of inequality for all women—is revealed as a racist assumption for writing so many women and their experiences out of feminist scripts while remaining silent on the privileges of whiteness.

Feminists from across the spectrum have responded to anti-racist feminisms and redrawn their theoretical perspectives and political agendas. For example, by looking at the lives of men and women in particular historical and social contexts, many feminists have abandoned the question of whether class, race, or sex is the more salient relation for analysis in favour of understanding the historical specificity of complex relations of power (Adamson, Briskin, and McPhail 1988; Dua 1999). The "circumstances directly encountered, given and transmitted from the past" must include those relations that are the living legacy of colonialism, imperialism, and slavery. Furthermore, they have argued—in opposition to the radical feminist perspective on sexual hierarchy—that, while these relations of racism shape the lives of men and women differently, they do not necessarily privilege men over women (Feminist Review 1985–86; hooks 1988; Lorde 1984; Silvera 1986; Williams 1991). Disavowing universalistic assumptions in favour of historically specific interpretations opens space for women in different social locations to address the most pertinent forms of oppression in their lives. Many African Canadian and Aboriginal women insist that racism has been the force that most constrains and brutalizes their lives. Not surprisingly then, historically they struggled against racist practices while struggles for gender equality went "glaringly missing" (Dua 1999, 12). Feminist thought did not speak to their lives and its program for equality was (silently) predicated on the perpetuation of racialized privilege for white women.

Women in Canada are now studying the lives of their forebears from the African diaspora and Asia "to provide some answers to questions of how they experienced oppression and exploitation [and] what priority they gave to different struggles at different periods of time" (Agnew 1996, 27). The emergence of anti-racist feminists push us, in Enakshi Dua's words, "to rethink Canadian society from the standpoint of women who have been racial-ized as dangerous, as alien, as hyphenated Canadians" (1999, 28).

Many feminists now agree that the "circumstances directly encountered, given and transmitted from the past" include those racialized relations that are the living legacy of colonialism, imperialism, and slavery (hooks 1988; Lorde 1984; Silvera 1986; Williams 1991; Agnew 1996; Carty 1999; Dua 1999). This challenge initially seemed to create irreconcilable differences among feminists. Michèle Barrett, for example, argued that the proposition that racism must have equal billing with class and sex dislodged the claim of socialist feminists to have a coherent theory of inequality. "Existing theories of social structure, already taxed by attempting to think about the inter-relations of class and gender, have been quite unable to integrate a third axis of systemic inequality into their conceptual maps" (1988, xii).

Feminism and [Poststructuralism]

*****

Although [these] theories insist correctly that gender is made not born, they tend, nonetheless, to "invoke a language of binaries [...]" (Hird 2002, 39). That is, once gender is established, and these theories portray this as a necessary and normal accomplishment, masculinity and

femininity become givens, and patriarchal power appears virtually unchallengeable.

But these binaries—men and women (as well as others like gay and straight)—that have been seen as so basic are not standing up well. They have been challenged within social movements, and within the daily lives of many people who have developed new words and concepts to describe themselves: transgender, transsexual—sometimes just "trans" (Hausman 2001, 448; Devor 1997; MacDonald 1998, 5). Some of these challenges appear to re-inscribe sex categories as a kind of ontological truth (what I "really" am). Yet the traffic between male and female not only shakes up the categories but also some of these challenges provoke the question, in Eleanor MacDonald's words, "of how those categories are established [and] maintained [and how] the boundaries of what is normal is 'policed'" (1998, 9). In subsequent chapters, we turn to these dramatic challenges to binary assumptions, but here we focus on the central theoretical challenges poststructuralist theories pose to binary thinking.

Poststructuralism is indebted, in part, to theories about discourse and about how language works. We tend to think that what we say conveys something that is already there, in our mind, awaiting verbalization. When teachers tell their students, "Don't worry about how you say something, just get your ideas down on paper," they contribute to this belief. Our common sense notions tend to hold that language is simply a tool for expressing an underlying reality or fully developed thought. But, as Susan Heald puts it, "[P]oststructuralism begins from the perspective that it is language which makes meaning possible, that words do not name pre-existing differences but inform us about what differences are visible and matter in any given situation" (1997, 32).

We need to notice, however, that words do not simply describe or identify. Words make distinctions and create oppositions. They tell us what is encompassed in a symbol and, by implication, what is not. Think of the words *hot* and *cold*. These words structure how we describe everything from soup to sex. Yet, as we know, temperature comes on a continuum, and hot and cold are always relative. Hot and cold, when applied to sexual activity, still carry with them the connotations of lust and evil that have so informed Western civilization and the presumed identities of men and women. Medieval Catholic writers depicted women as full of lust, waiting to tempt unsuspecting men into a life of sin. Later, Protestant writers developed a language about women that described them as asexual; it was men who had to control their own lust (Hamilton 1978). Opposing concepts like hot and cold, rational and irrational (emotional), or aggressive and passive serve to distinguish men from women by depicting each sex as either one way or the other, and ignoring all the points on the continuum that are in between. In this way "we can only know what 'man' is through its opposition, 'woman.' The female is everything that is absent from the male and vice versa" (Hird 2002, 23).

Language, together with gestures and all the other symbols that convey meaning, make up fields of thought that are called discourses. Any discourse makes some thought possible and others less possible or impossible. Contemporary feminists have drawn heavily on the work of Michel Foucault, who showed through several historically engaged studies how discourses "bring the true into existence" (Barrett 1991; Butler 1993; Westlund 1999). Their analyses reveal that discourses are not only thoroughly informed by prevailing power relations—of class, race, sex, age, and sexuality, among others—but also by a common-sense rationale for accepting those power relations as given, as the only way things could be (Belsey 1980).

Prevailing discourses also provide the possibilities and constraints for constructing our own identities, identities that are not fixed—as in the expression "the real me"—but rather are fragmented, changing, and contradictory. Freud argued that our psyches are a kind of lifelong battleground among the id, ego, and superego—or, put differently, among desire, possibility, and conscience. More recent theories of discourse accept Freud's idea of the fragmented self. But they shift the ground for explanation away from the body as such to the way that the body—including need and

desire—is constituted by the discourse, again as a lifelong, fragmented, contradictory, illusory process. Why illusory? Because discourse can never capture "reality." This is an impossible task for two related reasons. First, the terms of a discourse are always time-bound, space-bound, culture-bound, bound by the multiplicities of power relations that inform daily life. Second, there is no "pure" reality outside of what is represented in discourse. There is no "something" outside of that which is already interpreted, except that which is to be interpreted in some future moment. As one of my students wrote in her honours thesis on "femininity" and "feminism," beauty magazines suggest that "femininity is natural but in constant need of improvement and intervention" (Wakelin 2003, 38). In this sense, discourse does not represent reality; it shapes and creates that-which-is-believed-to-be-reality.

Using this kind of analysis, feminists have argued that identities are not fixed, but rather are continually constructed in particular times and places. They are not unified, but rather are fragmented: in some circumstances, we feel ourselves to be strong and powerful, in others weak and fragile, in others perhaps creative, stupid, lackadaisical, determined—the list is yours to make and remake. If this is so, the argument goes, how can we then talk about women and men as if these categories mean something that we can all agree upon? Our language helps create the sense that our identities are not only fixed, but gender-determined. When feminists hold this language up for scrutiny, they open the space for consideration of identities that are not bound by biological sex, race, age, sexuality, ethnicity, or any other category that we use to fix and freeze identities.

If we say that men are aggressive, we are comparing them directly and indirectly to those—women—who are not. In like manner, if men are rational, women are irrational; if men independent, women are dependent. The point is not that men and women "really" are this way, although in particular times and places they may behave so or they may be believed to be so. Let us reiterate that the discourse does not convey "reality"; rather it constitutes what appears to be reality. Furthermore, women who are not perceived to be passive and emotional may be defined as "not real women," and men who are not perceived to be aggressive may be called effeminate. In such ways, the discourse permits acknowledgment that men and women do not always conform to these oppositions. But the point is that this acknowledgment is made only in the terms of the discourse itself: the categories are retained, but the individual people are labelled as deviants. In this sense, we can speak of discourses as "closed systems"; they make thought that is not consonant with the prevailing discourses difficult.

In her pathbreaking book *The Gender of Breadwinners*, Joy Parr explained why feminists need poststructuralist analysis. The task, she wrote, is to

> unmake the chain of binary oppositions—masculine/feminine, market/non-market, public/private, waged/non-waged—and rethink the categoricalism that cantonizes gender, class, race, ethnicity and nationality, so as to see past the conceptual signage, which has illuminated the previously invisible but now threatens to obstruct our view of the living space beyond. (1990, 8)

Her argument here is two-pronged. She acknowledges that it was necessary for feminists to use the category of woman in order to "illuminate the previously invisible." Women had been invisible, present only in what was left unexamined, unexplored, unstated. But her main point is that this process of making visible must "see past the conceptual signage." We must not simply recapitulate the pattern of androcentric perspectives and continue to use the categories men and women as though they really described the world.

For by doing this, we fall into three errors. First, we perpetuate the categories of the discourse that once left women invisible. We refer to women and men as if we knew what they were, and we perpetuate the oppositional character of those identities. Women still are defined by what men are not, even though we may now place more value on what-men-are-

not. Second, we assume that when we use the word woman we are referring to all women; we collapse the differences among women that accrue from class, racism, heterosexism, imperialism, even the idiosyncrasies of taste and talent. In this way, the theoretical challenges to feminism from women of colour, disabled women, lesbians, bisexuals, and older women converged with those of poststructuralism. The command is "do not tell me what I am."

Third, the male/female binary makes the assumption that biologically there really are only two sexes despite the evidence that intersexuals may account for as many as 4 percent of all births (Anderson 1996, 334; Fausto-Sterling 1993). Medical practitioners in North America treat children born with ambiguous genitalia "in such a way that they conform as soon as possible to the two-sex model of sexual dimorphism in order to relieve the psychological trauma and suffering" (Anderson 1996, 345) that is believed to accompany this condition. But this response also stems from the strong cultural belief that "all bodies should conform to the binary classification of male/female" (346). If you read carefully you can see that this is a circular argument: the belief in social difference drives the impetus to ensure that all of us are male or female. Yet if you ask—why is there a social difference between men and women?—the answer will be: biology. Poststructuralism helps analyze how the categories of male and female are kept afloat in the face of medical and historical evidence that reveals a much more complicated state of affairs (MacDonald 1998). [...]

Let us return then to the question of how feminist poststructuralists might respond to the issue of human agency, and in particular to Marx's statement that we make our history "under circumstances directly encountered, given and transmitted from the past." The difference from Marx could be located in the definition poststructuralists might give to "circumstances": they want to look at the process through which the categories of male/female, black/white, work/home, public/private are constituted in time and place, and how those categories, as they are defined at any particular time, contribute to the range of possibility and constraint. Furthermore, unlike Marx and most feminists before them, they argue that the ways in which male and female are defined are also implicated in all other categorization, whether of class, race, or sexual preference. How, for example, has "working class" as a category in the language informed shifting definitions of masculinity and, through inclusion and exclusion, shifting definitions of femininity? At the same time, how do notions of class infuse gender definitions?

Language appears innocent, in that it appears simply as an instrument through which our ideas can be expressed. Let us take a familiar example to see how language does not express our pre-existing thought, but actually shapes that thought. The term *working mother* has come into the language in the last 20 years with the great influx into the formal waged economy of women who have children. Embedded in the phrase, implicitly, are a whole host of shifting, value-laden, gendered, and classed characters. Counterposed to working mother are *women who don't work* (and who "just" keep house and look after children) and the victims of working mothers, *neglected children* (those whose mothers do not "just" look after them). Implicit in the phrase *working mothers* is a cast of male characters. Whoever heard of a *working father*, or children who were neglected because their father worked? Working mother can also designate those women who take jobs away from men, therefore contributing to the category *unemployed men*—fathers who don't work and therefore are, by definition, *bad fathers*. Furthermore, working mother is more likely to be used with reference to women who do certain kinds of *class-related* occupations that have relatively low monetary rewards and little status. Women who work in other sorts of class-related occupations may be defined as *professionals* rather than working mothers. Here we see the operation of a kind of implicit override clause: sometimes gender terms take precedence, other times class terms, or racist terms, or terms referring to women's sexual lives [...].

Consider also the ways in which social movement activists and cultural radicals take words that have been used to humiliate, ridicule, or authorize discrimination, and fashion them for their own use—as displays of irony, resistance, even badges of honour. So successfully did gays and lesbians redefine the word "queer" that "queer theory" now stands for sophisticated approaches to sexuality and identity and lends its name to conferences, academic journals, and courses. [...]

In the late 1980s, I discovered that high school girls used the word *slut* as a derogatory word to describe girls outside their own circle (and one could easily fall out) who were believed to have any sexual experience (Currie 1999, 234–36). In my introductory course in sociology, I asked if there was a "boy" version of slut—or whether the double standard still prevailed. A male student brought the house down with the words "male whore" as an equivalent. Everyone got it: he needed to invoke a pejorative label for a woman to come up with a phrase suitable for a male. Equally interesting as a form of resistance is how "seemingly outrageous ... unruly and ironic play with and on, female sexuality via various verbal ... twists on words like 'slut,' 'bitch,' 'chick,' and 'whore' have now become staples of third wave feminists" (Diner 2001, 76). They circulate their ideas in small noncommercial magazines called zines, on Web pages, in feminist anthologies and among themselves (Ferris 2001; Bell 2001). Even the word "girls" changed spelling and took on new meaning in the movement "Riot Grrrls" comprising "Young female punks who were fed up with the overwhelming maleness of punk rock [and] with sexism in general" (Jacques 2001, 64; Brasile 2001). Words, as you can see, do not just say what they appear to say; they carry and create shifting identities, possibilities, and constraints.

*****

REFERENCES

Abrams, Philip. 1982. *Historical Sociology*. Somerset, England: Open Books Publishing.

Adamson, Nancy, Linda Briskin, and Margaret McPhail. 1988. *Feminist Organizing for Change*. Toronto: Oxford University Press.

Agnew, Vijay. 1996. *Resisting Discrimination: Women from Asia, Africa and the Caribbean and the Women's Movement in Canada.* Toronto: University of Toronto Press.

Anderson, Karen. 1996. *Sociology.* Scarborough: Nelson.

Armstrong, Pat and Hugh Armstrong. 1994. *The Double Ghetto: Canadian Women and Their Segregated Work.* 3rd ed. Toronto: McClelland & Stewart.

_____. 2002. "Thinking It Through: Women and Work in the New Millennium." *Canadian Woman Studies/les cahiers de la femme* 21/22 (4/1): 44–50.

Barrett, Michèle. 1988. *Women's Oppression Today.* 2nd ed. London: Verso.

_____. 1991. *The Politics of Truth.* Stanford: Stanford University Press.

Bell, Brandi Leigh-Ann. 2001. "Women-Produced Zines Moving into the Mainstream." *Canadian Woman Studies/les cahiers de la femme* 20/21 (4/1): 56–60.

Belsey, Catherine. 1980. *Critical Practice.* London: Methuen.

Brand, Dionne. 1984. "A Working Paper on Black Women in Toronto: Gender, Race and Class." *Fireweed* 19: 26–43.

Brasile, Monica. 2001. "From Riot Grrrl to Mamagirl in Omaha Nebraska." *Canadian Woman Studies/les cahiers de la femme* 20/21 (4/1): 63–8.

Butler, Judith. 1993. *Bodies That Matter: On the Discursive Limits of "Sex."* New York: Routledge.

Carty, Linda. 1999. "The Discourse of Empire and the Social Construction of Gender." In *Scratching the Surface: Canadian Anti-racist Feminist Thought.* Ed. Enakshi Dua and Angela Robertson. Toronto: Women's Press.

Connelly, Patricia. 1978. *Last Hired: First Fired.* Toronto: Women's Press.

Creese, Gillian, and Daiva Stasiulis. 1996. "Intersections of Gender, Race, Class and Sexuality." *Studies in Political Economy* 51: 5–14.

Currie, Dawn. 1999. *Girl Talk: Adolescent Magazines and Their Readers.* Toronto: University of Toronto Press.

Devor, Holly. 1997. *FTM: Female-to-Male Transsexuals in Society.* Bloomington: Indiana University Press.

Diner, Robyn. 2001. "Things to Do with the 'F' Word: The Ironic and Unruly Adventures of Liz Phair and Courtney Love." *Canadian Woman Studies/les cahiers de la femme* 20/21 (4/1): 76–81.

Dua, Enakshi. 1999. "Introduction." In *Scratching the Surface: Canadian Anti-racist Feminist Thought.* Ed. Enakshi Dua and Angela Robertson. Toronto: Women's Press.

Echols, Alice. 1989. *"Daring to Be Bad": Radical Feminism in America, 1967–1975.* Minneapolis: University of Minnesota Press.

Eisenstein, Hester. 1984. *Contemporary Feminist Thought.* London: Allen & Unwin.

Engels, F. 1948 [1884]. *The Origin of the Family, Private Property and the State.* Moscow: Progress Publishers.

Fausto-Sterling, Anne. 1993. "The Five Sexes." *The Sciences* (March/April): 20–21.

Feminist Review. 1985–86. Vols. 20, 22, 23.

Ferris, Melanie A. 2001, "Resisting Mainstream Media: Girls and the Act of Making Zines." *Canadian Woman Studies/les cahiers de la femme* 20/21 (4/1): 51–55.

Firestone, Shulamith. 1970. *The Dialectic of Sex.* New York: William Morrow & Co.

Hamilton, Roberta. 1978. *The Liberation of Women: A Study of Patriarchy and Capitalism.* London: Allen and Unwin.

Hausman, Bernice. 2001. "Recent Transgender Theory." *Feminist Studies* 27 (2): 465–490.

Heald, Susan. 1997. "Telling Feminist Truths: Research and Writing about Feminist Organizing." *Atlantis* 22 (I): 31–42.

Hird, Myra. 2002. *Engendering Violence: Heterosexual Interpersonal Violence from Childhood to Adulthood.* Hampshire, England: Ashgate.

hooks, bell. 1988. *Thinking Feminist, Thinking Black.* Toronto: Garamond Press.

Jacques, Alison. 2001. "You Can Run But You Can't Hide: The Incorporation of Riot Grrrl into Mainstream Culture." *Canadian Woman Studies/les cahiers de la femme* 20/21 (4/1) 46–50.

Leys, Colin. 1996. *The Rise and Fall of Development Theory.* London: James Currey.

Liddington, Jill, and Jill Norris. 1978. *One Hand Tied behind Us: The Rise of the Women's Suffrage Movement.* London: Virago.

Lorde, Audre. 1984. *Sister Outsider.* Trumansburg, New York: Crossing Press Feminist Series.

Luxton, Meg. 1980. *More Than a Labour of Love.* Toronto: Women's Press.

———, and June Corman. 2001. *Getting by in Hard Times*. Toronto: University of Toronto Press.

MacDonald, Eleanor. 1998. "Critical Identities: Rethinking Feminism through Transgendered Politics." *Atlantis* 23 (1): 3–12.

Martindale, Kathleen. 1995. "What Makes Lesbianism Thinkable: Theorizing Lesbianism from Adrienne Rich to Queer Theory." In *Feminist Issues: Race, Class and Sexuality*. Ed. Nancy Mandell. Scarborough, ON: Prentice-Hall.

Marx, Karl. 1969 [1869]. "The 18th Brumaire of Louis Bonaparte." In Karl Marx and Friedrich Engels, *Selected Works*. Vol. 1: 394–87, Moscow: Progress Publishers.

Nussbaum, Martha C. 2001. "Comment on Quillen's 'Feminist Theory, Justice, and the Lure of the Human.'" *Signs* 27(1): 123-35.

Parr, Joy. 1990. *The Gender of Breadwinners*. Toronto: University of Toronto Press.

Resources for Feminist Research. 1990. Special issue: Confronting Hetero-sexuality 19, 3/4 (Sept.–Dec.).

Rich, Adrienne. 1980. "Compulsory Heterosexuality and Lesbian Existence." *Signs* 5 (Summer): 631–60.

Rudy, Kathy. 2001. "Radical Feminism, Lesbian Separatism, and Queer Theory." *Feminist Studies* 27 (1): 191–222.

Shanley, Mary Lyndon, and Uma Narayan. 1997. "Introduction: Contentious Concepts." In *Reconstructing Political Theory: Feminist Perspectives*. Ed. Mary Lyndon Shanley and Uma Narayan, xi–xxi. University Park, Pennsylvania: Pennsylvania University Press.

Silvera, Makeda, ed. 1986. *Fireworks: The Best of Fireweed*. Toronto: Women's Press.

Tynes, Maxine. 1987. *Borrowed Beauty*. Porters Lake, NS: Pottersfield Press.

———. 1990. *Woman Talking Woman*. Lawrencetown Beach, NS: Pottersfield Press.

Vorst, Jessie et al., eds. 1989. *Race, Class, Gender: Bonds and Barriers*. Toronto: Between the Lines.

Vosko, Leah F. 2002. "The Pasts and Futures of Feminist Political Economy in Canada: Reviving the Debate." *Studies in Political Economy* 68: 55–83.

Wakelin, Amy. 2003. "An Elusive Dichotomy: Exploring the Inconsistencies and Contradictions between 'Femininity' and 'Feminism' in Western Culture." Unpublished undergraduate thesis, Department of Sociology, Queen's University.

Westlund, Andrea. 1999. "Pre-modern and Modern Power: Foucault and the Case of Domestic Violence." *Signs* 24 (4): 1045–1066.

Williams, Patricia. 1991. *The Alchemy of Race and Rights*. Cambridge: Harvard University Press.

Wollstonecraft, Mary. 1992 [1792]. *A Vindication of the Rights of Woman*. London: Penguin.

CHAPTER 6

DOING GENDER

Candace West and Don H. Zimmerman

*****

Our purpose in this article is to propose an ethnomethodologically informed, and therefore distinctively sociological, understanding of gender as a routine, methodical, and recurring accomplishment. We contend that the "doing" of gender is undertaken by women and men whose competence as members of society is hostage to its production. Doing gender involves a complex of socially guided perceptual, interactional, and micropolitical activities that cast particular pursuits as expressions of masculine and feminine "natures."

When we view gender as an accomplishment, an achieved property of situated conduct, our attention shifts from matters internal to the individual and focuses on interactional and, ultimately, institutional arenas. In one sense, of course, it is individuals who "do" gender. But it is a situated doing, carried out in the virtual or real presence of others who are presumed to be oriented to its production. Rather than as a property of individuals, we conceive of gender as an emergent feature of social situations: both as an outcome of and a rationale for various social arrangements and as a means of legitimating one of the most fundamental divisions of society.

*****

To elaborate our proposal, we suggest at the outset that important but often overlooked distinctions be observed among *sex*, *sex category*, and *gender*. Sex is a determination made through the application of socially agreed upon biological criteria for classifying persons as females or males. The criteria for classification can be genitalia at birth or chromosomal typing before birth, and they do not necessarily agree with one another. Placement in a sex category is achieved through application of the sex criteria, but in everyday life, categorization is established and sustained by the socially required identificatory displays that proclaim one's membership in one or the other category. In this sense, one's sex category presumes one's sex and stands as proxy for it in many situations, but sex and sex category can vary independently; that is, it is possible to claim membership in a sex category even when the sex criteria are lacking. *Gender*, in contrast, is the activity of managing situated conduct in light of normative conceptions of attitudes and activities appropriate for one's sex category. Gender activities emerge from and bolster claims to membership in a sex category.

*****

PERSPECTIVES ON SEX AND GENDER

In Western societies, the accepted cultural perspective on gender views women and men as naturally and unequivocally defined categories of being [...] with distinctive psychological and behavioral propensities that can be predicted from their reproductive functions. Competent adult members of these societies see differences between the two as fundamental and enduring—differences seemingly supported by the division of labor into women's and men's work and an often elaborate differentiation of feminine and masculine attitudes and behaviors that are prominent features of social organization. Things are the way they are by virtue of the fact that men are men and women are women—a division perceived to be natural and rooted in biology, producing in turn profound psychological, behavioral, and social consequences. The structural arrangements of a society are presumed to be responsive to these differences.

Analyses of sex and gender in the social sciences, though less likely to accept uncritically the naive biological determinism of the view just presented, often retain a conception of sex-linked behaviors and traits as essential properties of individuals [...]. The "sex differences approach" [...] is more commonly attributed to psychologists than to sociologists, but the survey researcher who determines the "gender" of respondents on the basis of the sound of their voices over the telephone is also making trait-oriented assumptions. Reducing gender to a fixed set of psychological traits or to a unitary "variable" precludes serious consideration of the ways it is used to structure distinct domains of social experience [...].

Taking a different tack, role theory has attended to the social construction of gender categories, called "sex roles" or, more recently, "gender roles" and has analyzed how these are learned and enacted. Beginning with Linton (1936) and continuing through the works of Parsons (Parsons 1951; Parsons and Bales 1955) and Komarovsky (1946, 1950), role theory has emphasized the social and dynamic aspect of role construction and enactment [...]. But at the level of face-to-face interaction, the application

of role theory to gender poses problems of its own [...]. Roles are *situated* identities—assumed and relinquished as the situation demands—rather than *master identities* [...], such as sex category, that cut across situations. Unlike most roles, such as "nurse," "doctor," and "patient" or "professor" and "student," gender has no specific site or organizational context.

Moreover, many roles are already gender marked, so that special qualifiers—such as "female doctor" or "male nurse"—must be added to exceptions to the rule. Thorne (1980) observes that conceptualizing gender as a role makes it difficult to assess its influence on other roles and reduces its explanatory usefulness in discussions of power and inequality. Drawing on Rubin (1975), Thorne calls for a reconceptualization of women and men as distinct social groups, constituted in "concrete, historically changing—and generally unequal—social relationships" (Thorne 1980, p. 11).

We argue that gender is not a set of traits, nor a variable, nor a role, but the product of social doings of some sort. What then is the social doing of gender? It is more than the continuous creation of the meaning of gender through human actions [...]. We claim that gender itself is constituted through interaction. To develop the implications of our claim, we turn to Goffman's (1976) account of "gender display." Our object here is to explore how gender might be exhibited or portrayed through interaction, and thus be seen as "natural," while it is being produced as a socially organized achievement.

GENDER DISPLAY

Goffman contends that when human beings interact with others in their environment, they assume that each possesses an "essential nature"—a nature that can be discerned through the "natural signs given off or expressed by them" (1976, p. 75). Femininity and masculinity are regarded as "prototypes of essential expression—something that can be conveyed fleetingly in any social situation and yet something that strikes at the most basic characterization of the individual" (1976, p. 75). The means through which we provide such expressions are "perfunctory, conventionalized acts" (1976, p. 69), which convey to others our regard for them, indicate our alignment in an encounter, and tentatively establish the terms of contact for that social situation. But they are also regarded as expressive behavior, testimony to our "essential natures."

Goffman (1976, pp. 69–70) sees *displays* as highly conventionalized behaviors structured as two-part exchanges of the statement-reply type, in which the presence or absence of symmetry can establish deference or dominance. These rituals are viewed as distinct from but articulated with more consequential activities, such as performing tasks or engaging in discourse. Hence, we have what he terms the "scheduling" of displays at junctures in activities, such as the beginning or end, to avoid interfering with the activities themselves. Goffman (1976, p. 69) formulates *gender display* as follows:

> If gender be defined as the culturally established correlates of sex (whether in consequence of biology or learning), then gender display refers to conventionalized portrayals of these correlates.

These gendered expressions might reveal clues to the underlying, fundamental dimensions of the female and male, but they are, in Goffman's view, optional performances. Masculine courtesies may or may not be offered and, if offered, may or may not be declined (1976, p. 71). Moreover, human beings "themselves employ the term 'expression', and conduct themselves to fit their own notions of expressivity" (1976, p. 75). Gender depictions are less a consequence of our "essential sexual natures" than interactional portrayals of what we would like to convey about sexual natures, using conventionalized gestures. Our *human* nature gives us the ability to learn to produce and recognize masculine and feminine gender displays—"a capacity [we] have by virtue of being persons, not males and females" (1976, p. 76).

*****

There are fundamental equivocations in this perspective. By segregating gender display from the serious business of interaction, Goffman obscures the effects of gender on a wide range of human activities. Gender is not merely something that happens in the nooks and crannies of interaction, fitted in here and there and not interfering with the serious business of life. While it is plausible to contend that gender displays—construed as conventionalized expressions—are optional, it does not seem plausible to say that we have the option of being seen by others as female or male.

It is necessary to move beyond the notion of gender display to consider what is involved in doing gender as an ongoing activity embedded in everyday interaction. Toward this end, we return to the distinctions among sex, sex category, and gender introduced earlier.

SEX, SEX CATEGORY, AND GENDER

Garfinkel's (1967, pp. 118–40) case study of Agnes, a transsexual raised as a boy who adopted a female identity at age 17 and underwent a sex reassignment operation several years later, demonstrates how gender is created through interaction and at the same time structures interaction. Agnes, whom Garfinkel characterized as a "practical methodologist," developed a number of procedures for passing as a "normal, natural female" both prior to and after her surgery. She had the practical task of managing the fact that she possessed male genitalia and that she lacked the social resources a girl's biography would presumably provide in everyday interaction. In short, she needed to display herself as a woman, simultaneously learning what it was to be a woman. Of necessity, this full-time pursuit took place at a time when most people's gender would be well accredited and routinized. Agnes had to consciously contrive what the vast majority of women do without thinking. She was not "faking" what "real" women do naturally. She was obliged to analyze and figure out how to act within socially structured circumstances and conceptions of femininity that women born with appropriate biological credentials come to take for granted early on. As in the case of others who must "pass," [...] Agnes's case makes visible what culture has made invisible—the accomplishment of gender.

*****

Sex

Agnes did not possess the socially agreed upon biological criteria for classification as a member of the female sex. Still, Agnes regarded herself as a female, albeit a female with a penis, which a woman ought not to possess. The penis, she insisted, was a "mistake" in need of remedy (Garfinkel 1967, pp. 126–27, 131–32). Like other competent members of our culture, Agnes honored the notion that there are "essential" biological criteria that unequivocally distinguish females from males. However, if we move away from the commonsense viewpoint, we discover that the reliability of these criteria is not beyond question [...]. Moreover, other cultures have acknowledged the existence of "cross-genders" [...] and the possibility of more than two sexes [...].

More central to our argument is Kessler and McKenna's (1978, pp. 1–6) point that genitalia are conventionally hidden from public inspection in everyday life; yet we continue through our social rounds to "observe" a world of two naturally, normally sexed persons. It is the *presumption* that essential criteria exist and would or should be there if looked for that provides the basis for sex categorization. Drawing on Garfinkel, Kessler and McKenna argue that "female" and "male" are cultural events—products of what they term the "gender attribution process"—rather than some collection of traits, behaviors, or even physical attributes. Illustratively they cite the child who, viewing a picture of someone clad in a suit and a tie, contends, "It's a man, because he has a pee-pee" (Kessler and McKenna 1978, p. 154). Translation: "He must have a pee-pee [an essential characteristic] because I see the insignia of a suit and tie." Neither initial sex assignment (pronouncement at birth as a female or male) nor the actual ex-

istence of essential criteria for that assignment (possession of a clitoris and vagina or penis and testicles) has much—if anything—to do with the identification of sex category in everyday life. There, Kessler and McKenna note, we operate with a moral certainty of a world of two sexes. We do not think, "Most persons with penises are men, but some may not be" or "Most persons who dress as men have penises." Rather, we take it for granted that sex and sex category are congruent—that knowing the latter, we can deduce the rest.

Sex Categorization

*****

The categorization of members of society into indigenous categories such as "girl" or "boy," or "woman" or "man," operates in a distinctively social way. The act of categorization does not involve a positive test, in the sense of a well-defined set of criteria that must be explicitly satisfied prior to making an identification. Rather, the application of membership categories relies on an "if-can" test in everyday interaction [...]. This test stipulates that if people *can be seen* as members of relevant categories, *then categorize them that way*. That is, use the category that seems appropriate, except in the presence of discrepant information or obvious features that would rule out its use. This procedure is quite in keeping with the attitude of everyday life, which has us take appearances at face value unless we have special reason to doubt [...]. It should be added that it is precisely when we have special reason to doubt that the issue of applying rigorous criteria arises, but it is rare, outside legal or bureaucratic contexts, to encounter insistence on positive tests [...].

Agnes's initial resource was the predisposition of those she encountered to take her appearance (her figure, clothing, hair style, and so on), as the undoubted appearance of a normal female. Her further resource was our cultural perspective on the properties of "natural, normally sexed persons." Garfinkel (1967, pp. 122–28) notes that in everyday life, we live in a world of two—and only two—sexes. This arrangement has a moral status, in that we include ourselves and others in it as "essentially, originally, in the first place, always have been, always will be, once and for all, in the final analysis, either 'male' or 'female'" (Garfinkel 1967, p. 122).

*****

[...] Not only do we want to know the sex category of those around us (to see it at a glance, perhaps), but we presume that others are displaying it for us, in as decisive a fashion as they can.

Gender

[...] Sex categorization and the accomplishment of gender are not the same. Agnes's categorization could be secure or suspect, but did not depend on whether or not she lived up to some ideal conception of femininity. Women can be seen as unfeminine, but that does not make them "unfemale." Agnes faced an ongoing task of being a woman—something beyond style of dress (an identificatory display) or allowing men to light her cigarette (a gender display). Her problem was to produce configurations of behavior that would be seen by others as normative gender behavior.

*****

Popular culture abounds with books and magazines that compile idealized depictions of relations between women and men. Those focused on the etiquette of dating or prevailing standards of feminine comportment are meant to be of practical help in these matters. However, the use of any such source *as a manual of procedure* requires the assumption that doing gender merely involves making use of discrete, well-defined bundles of behavior that can simply be plugged into interactional situations to produce recognizable enactments of masculinity and femininity. The man "does" being masculine by, for example, taking the woman's arm to guide her across a street, and she "does"

being feminine by consenting to be guided and not initiating such behavior with a man.

Agnes could perhaps have used such sources as manuals, but, we contend, doing gender is not so easily regimented [...]. Such sources may list and describe the sorts of behaviors that mark or display gender, but they are necessarily incomplete [...]. And to be successful, marking or displaying gender must be finely fitted to situations and modified or transformed as the occasion demands. Doing gender consists of managing such occasions so that, whatever the particulars, the outcome is seen and seeable in context as gender-appropriate or, as the case may be, gender-*in*appropriate, that is, *accountable*.

GENDER AND ACCOUNTABILITY

As Heritage (1984, pp. 136–37) notes, members of society regularly engage in "descriptive accountings of states of affairs to one another," and such accounts are both serious and consequential. These descriptions name, characterize, formulate, explain, excuse, excoriate, or merely take notice of some circumstance or activity and thus place it within some social framework (locating it relative to other activities, like and unlike).

Such descriptions are themselves accountable, and societal members orient to the fact that their activities are subject to comment. Actions are often designed with an eye to their accountability, that is, how they might look and how they might be characterized. The notion of accountability also encompasses those actions undertaken so that they are specifically unremarkable and thus not worthy of more than a passing remark, because they are seen to be in accord with culturally approved standards.

*****

If sex category is omnirelevant (or even approaches being so), then a person engaged in virtually any activity may be held accountable for performance of that activity as a woman or a man, and their incumbency in one or the other sex category can be used to legitimate or discredit their other activities [...]. Accordingly, virtually any activity can be assessed as to its womanly or manly nature. And note, to "do" gender is not always to live up to normative conceptions of femininity or masculinity; it is to engage in behavior *at the risk of gender assessment.* While it is individuals who do gender, the enterprise is fundamentally interactional and institutional in character, for accountability is a feature of social relationships and its idiom is drawn from the institutional arena in which those relationships are enacted. If this be the case, can we ever *not* do gender? Insofar as a society is partitioned by "essential" differences between women and men and placement in a sex category is both relevant and enforced, doing gender is unavoidable.

RESOURCES FOR DOING GENDER

Doing gender means creating differences between girls and boys and women and men, differences that are not natural, essential, or biological. Once the differences have been constructed, they are used to reinforce the "essentialness"of gender. In a delightful account of the "arrangement between the sexes," Goffman (1977) observes the creation of a variety of institutionalized frameworks through which our "natural, normal sexedness" can be enacted. The physical features of social setting provide one obvious resource for the expression of our "essential" differences. For example, the sex segregation of North American public bathrooms distinguishes "ladies" from "gentlemen" in matters held to be fundamentally biological, even though both "are somewhat similar in the question of waste products and their elimination" (Goffman 1977, p. 315). These settings are furnished with dimorphic equipment (such as urinals for men or elaborate grooming facilities for women), even though both sexes may achieve the same ends through the same means (and apparently do so in the privacy of their own homes). [...]

*****

Standardized social occasions also provide stages for evocations of the "essential female and male natures." Goffman cites organized sports as one such institutionalized framework for the expression of manliness. There, those qualities that ought "properly" to be associated with masculinity, such as endurance, strength, and competitive spirit, are celebrated by all parties concerned—participants, who may be seen to demonstrate such traits, and spectators, who applaud their demonstrations from the safety of the sidelines (1977, p. 322).

*****

Gender may be routinely fashioned in a variety of situations that seem conventionally expressive to begin with, such as those that present "helpless" women next to heavy objects or flat tires. But, as Goffman notes, heavy, messy, and precarious concerns can be constructed from any social situation, "even though by standards set in other settings, this may involve something that is light, clean, and safe" (Goffman 1977, p. 324). Given these resources, it is clear that *any* interactional situation sets the stage for depictions of "essential" sexual natures. In sum, these situations "do not so much allow for the expression of natural differences as for the production of that difference itself" (Goffman 1977, p. 324).

Many situations are not clearly sex categorized to begin with, nor is what transpires within them obviously gender relevant. Yet any social encounter can be pressed into service in the interests of doing gender. Thus, Fishman's (1978) research on casual conversations found an asymmetrical "division of labor" in talk between heterosexual intimates. Women had to ask more questions, fill more silences, and use more attention-getting beginnings in order to be heard. Her conclusions are particularly pertinent here:

> Since interactional work is related to what constitutes being a woman, with what a woman is, the idea that it is work is obscured. The work is not seen as what women do, but as part of what they are. (Fishman 1978, p. 405)

We would argue that it is precisely such labor that helps to constitute the essential nature of women as women in interactional contexts [...].

Individuals have many social identities that may be donned or shed, muted or made more salient, depending on the situation. One may be a friend, spouse, professional, citizen, and many other things to many different people—or, to the same person at different times. But we are always women or men—unless we shift into another sex category. What this means is that our identificatory displays will provide an ever-available resource for doing gender under an infinitely diverse set of circumstances.

*****

[T]he heart of the matter is that [...] gender is still something one is accountable for. Thus a woman physician (notice the special quali-fier in her case) may be accorded respect for her skill and even addressed by an appropriate title. Nonetheless, she is subject to evaluation in terms of normative conceptions of appropri-ate attitudes and activities for her sex category and under pressure to prove that she is an "es-sentially" feminine being, despite appearances to the contrary [...]. Her sex category is used to discredit her participation in important clinical activities [...], while her involvement in medicine is used to discredit her commitment to her responsibilities as a wife and mother [...]. Simultaneously, her exclusion from the physi-cian colleague community is maintained and her accountability as a woman is ensured.

In this context, "role conflict" can be viewed as a dynamic aspect of our current "arrangement between the sexes" (Goffman 1977), an arrangement that provides for oc-casions on which persons of a particular sex category can "see" quite clearly that they are out of place and that if they were not there, their current troubles would not exist. What is at stake is, from the standpoint of interaction, the management of our "essential" natures, and from the standpoint of the individual, the continuing accomplishment of gender. If, as we have argued, sex category is omnirelevant,

then any occasion, conflicted or not, offers the resources for doing gender.

*****

What are the consequences of this theoretical formulation? If, for example, individuals strive to achieve gender in encounters with others, how does a culture instill the need to achieve it? What is the relationship between the pro-duction of gender at the level of interaction and such institutional arrangements as the division of labor in society? And, perhaps most impor-tant, how does doing gender contribute to the subordination of women by men?

RESEARCH AGENDAS

To bring the social production of gender under empirical scrutiny, we might begin at the be-ginning, with a reconsideration of the process through which societal members acquire the requisite categorical apparatus and other skills to become gendered human beings.

Recruitment to Gender Identities

The conventional approach to the process of becoming girls and boys has been sex-role so-cialization. In recent years, recurring problems arising from this approach have been linked to inadequacies inherent in role theory per se—its emphasis on "consensus, stability and continu-ity" (Stacey and Thorne 1985, p. 307), its ahis-torical and depoliticizing focus (Thorne 1980, p. 9; Stacey and Thorne 1985, p. 307), and the fact that its "social" dimension relies on "a general assumption that people choose to maintain ex-isting customs" (Connell 1985, p. 263).

In contrast, Cahill (1982, 1986a, 1986b) analyzes the experiences of preschool children using a social model of recruitment into nor-mally gendered identities. Cahill argues that categorization practices are fundamental to learning and displaying feminine and mascu-line behavior. Initially, he observes, children are primarily concerned with distinguishing between themselves and others on the basis of social competence. Categorically, their concern resolves itself into the opposition of "girl/boy" classification versus "baby" classification (the latter designating children whose social behavior is problematic and who must be closely supervised). It is children's concern with being seen as socially competent that evokes their initial claims to gender identities.

*****

Subsequently, little boys appropriate the gender ideal of "efficaciousness," that is, being able to affect the physical and social environment through the exercise of physical strength or appropriate skills. In contrast, little girls learn to value "appearance," that is, managing themselves as ornamental objects. Both classes of children learn that the recognition and use of sex categorization in interaction are not optional, but mandatory [...].

Being a "girl" or a "boy" then, is not only being more competent than a "baby," but also being competently female or male, that is, learning to produce behavioral displays of one's "essential" female or male identity. In this respect, the task of four- to five-year-old children is very similar to Agnes's:

> For example, the following interaction occurred on a preschool playground. A 55-month-old boy (D) was attempting to unfasten the clasp of a necklace when a preschool aide walked over to him.
>
> A: Do you want to put that on?
> D: No. It's for girls.
> A: You don't have to be a girl to wear things around your neck. Kings wear things around their necks. You could pretend you're a king.
> D: I'm not a king. I'm a boy. (Cahill 1986a, p. 176)

As Cahill notes of this example, although D may have been unclear as to the sex status of a king's identity, he was obviously aware that necklaces are used to announce the identity "girl." Having claimed the identity "boy" and having developed a behavioral commitment to it, he was leery of any display that might furnish grounds for questioning his claim.

In this way, new members of society come to be involved in a *self-regulating process* as they begin to monitor their own and others' conduct with regard to its gender implications. The "recruitment" process involves not only the appropriation of gender ideals (by the valuation of those ideals as proper ways of being and behaving) but also *gender identities* that are important to individuals and that they strive to maintain. Thus gender differences, or the sociocultural shaping of "essential female and male natures," achieve the status of objective facts. They are rendered normal, natural features of persons and provide the tacit rationale for differing fates of women and men within the social order.

*****

Gender and the Division of Labor

Whenever people face issues of *allocation*—who is to do what, get what, plan or execute action, direct or be directed, incumbency in significant social categories such as "female" and "male" seems to become pointedly relevant. How such issues are resolved conditions the exhibition, dramatization, or celebration of one's "essential nature" as a woman or man.

Berk (1985) offers elegant demonstration of this point in her investigation of the allocation of household labor and the attitudes of married couples toward the division of household tasks. Berk found little variation in either the actual distribution of tasks or perceptions of equity in regard to that distribution. Wives, even when employed outside the home, do the vast majority of household and child-care tasks. Moreover, both wives and husbands tend to perceive this as a "fair" arrangement. Noting the failure of conventional sociological and economic theories to explain this seeming contradiction, Berk contends that something more complex is involved than rational arrangements for the production of household goods and services:

Hardly a question simply of who has more time, or whose time is worth more, who has more skill or more power, it is clear that a complicated relationship between the structure of work imperatives and the structure of normative expectations attached to work as gendered determines the ultimate allocation of members' time to work and home. (Berk 1985, pp. 195–96)

She notes, for example, that the most important factor influencing wives' contribution of labor is the total amount of work demanded or expected by the household; such demands had no bearing on husbands' contributions. Wives reported various rationales (their own and their husbands') that justified their level of contribution and, as a general matter, underscored the presumption that wives are essentially responsible for household production.

Berk (1985, p. 201) contends that it is difficult to see how people "could rationally establish the arrangements that they do solely for the production of household goods and services"—much less, how people could consider them "fair." She argues that our current arrangements for the domestic division of labor support *two* production processes: household goods and services (meals, clean children, and so on) and, at the same time, gender. As she puts it:

Simultaneously, members "do" gender, as they "do" housework and child care, and what [has] been called the division of labor provides for the joint production of household labor and gender; it is the mechanism by which both the material and symbolic products of the household are realized. (1985, p. 201)

It is not simply that household labor is designated as "women's work," but that for a woman to engage in it and a man not to engage in it is to draw on and exhibit the "essential nature" of each. What is produced and reproduced is not merely the activity and artifact of domestic life, but the material embodiment of wifely and husbandly roles, and derivatively, of womanly and manly conduct [...]. What are also frequently produced and reproduced are the dominant and subordinate statuses of the sex categories.

How does gender get done in work settings outside the home, where dominance and subordination are themes of overarching importance? Hochschild's (1983) analysis of the work of flight attendants offers some promising insights. She found that the occupation of flight attendant consisted of something altogether different for women than for men:

As the company's main shock absorbers against "mishandled" passengers, their own feelings are more frequently subjected to rough treatment. In addition, a day's exposure to people who resist authority in a woman is a different experience than it is for a man.... In this respect, it is a disadvantage to be a woman. And in this case, they are not simply women in the biological sense. They are also a highly visible distillation of middle-class American notions of femininity. They symbolize Woman. Insofar as the category "female" is mentally associated with having less status and authority, female flight attendants are more readily classified as "really" females than other females are. (Hochschild 1983, p. 175)

In performing what Hochschild terms the "emotional labor" necessary to maintain airline profits, women flight attendants simultaneously produce enactments of their "essential" femininity.

Sex and Sexuality

What is the relationship between doing gender and a culture's prescription of "obligatory heterosexuality" [...]? As Frye (1983, p. 22) observes, the monitoring of sexual feelings in relation to other appropriately sexed persons requires the ready recognition of such persons "before one can allow one's heart to beat or one's blood to flow in erotic enjoyment of that person." The appearance of heterosexuality is produced through emphatic and unambiguous indicators of one's sex, layered on in ever more conclusive fashion (Frye 1983, p. 24). Thus, lesbians and gay men concerned with passing as heterosexuals can rely on these indicators for camouflage; in contrast, those who would avoid the assumption of heterosexuality may foster ambiguous indicators of their categorical status through their dress, behaviors, and style. But "ambiguous" sex indicators are sex indicators nonetheless. If one wishes to be recognized as a lesbian (or heterosexual woman), one must first establish a categorical status as female. Even as popular images portray lesbians as "females who are not feminine" (Frye 1983, p. 129), the accountability of persons for their "normal, natural sexedness" is preserved.

*****

GENDER, POWER, AND SOCIAL CHANGE

Let us return to the question: Can we avoid doing gender? Earlier, we proposed that insofar as sex category is used as a fundamental criterion for differentiation, doing gender is unavoidable. It is unavoidable because of the social consequences of sex-category membership: the allocation of power and resources not only in the domestic, economic, and political domains but also in the broad arena of interpersonal relations. In virtually any situation, one's sex category can be relevant, and one's performance as an incumbent of that category (i.e., gender) can be subjected to evaluation. Maintaining such pervasive and faithful assignment of lifetime status requires legitimation.

But doing gender also renders the social arrangements based on sex category accountable as normal and natural, that is, legitimate ways of organizing social life. Differences between women and men that are created by this process can then be portrayed as fundamental and enduring dispositions. In this light, the institutional arrangements of a society can be seen as responsive to the differences—the social order being merely an accommodation to the natural order. Thus if, in doing gender, men are also doing dominance and women are

doing deference [...], the resultant social order, which supposedly reflects "natural differences," is a powerful reinforcer and legitimator of hierarchical arrangements. [...]

*****

If we do gender appropriately, we simultaneously sustain, reproduce, and render legitimate the institutional arrangements that are based on sex category. If we fail to do gender appropriately, we as individuals—not the institutional arrangements—may be called to account (for our character, motives, and predispositions).

Social movements such as feminism can provide the ideology and impetus to question existing arrangements, and the social support for individuals to explore alternatives to them. Legislative changes, such as that proposed by the Equal Rights Amendment, can also weaken the accountability of conduct to sex category, thereby affording the possibility of more widespread loosening of accountability in general. [...] What such proposed changes can do is provide the warrant for asking why, if we wish to treat women and men as equals, there needs to be two sex categories at all [...].

The sex category/gender relationship links the institutional and interactional level [...]. Doing gender furnishes the interactional scaffolding of social structure [...]. In appreciating the institutional forces that maintain distinctions between women and men, we must not lose sight of the interactional validation of those distinctions that confers upon them their sense of "naturalness" and "rightness."

Social change, then, must be pursued both at the institutional and cultural level of sex category and at the interactional level of gender. [...] Reconceptualizing gender not as a simple property of individuals but as an integral dynamic of social orders implies a new perspective on the entire network of gender relations:

> [T]he social subordination of women, and the cultural practices which help sustain it; the politics of sexual object-choice, and particularly the oppression of homosexual people; the sexual division of labor, the

formation of character and motive, so far as they are organized as femininity and masculinity; the role of the body in social relations, especially the politics of childbirth; and the nature of strategies of sexual liberation movements. (Connell 1985, p, 261)

Gender is a powerful ideological device, which produces, reproduces, and legitimates the choices and limits that are predicated on sex category. An understanding of how gender is produced in social situations will afford clarification of the interactional scaffolding of social structure and the social control processes that sustain it.

REFERENCES

Berk, Sarah F. 1985. *The Gender Factory: The Apportionment of Work in American Households*. New York: Plenum.

Cahill, Spencer E. 1982. "Becoming Boys and Girls." Ph.D. dissertation, Department of Sociology, University of California, Santa Barbara.

_____. 1986a. "Childhood Socialization as Recruitment Process: Some Lessons from the Study of Gender Development." Pp. 163–86 in *Sociological Studies of Child Development*, edited by P. Adler and P. Adler. Greenwich, CT: JAI Press.

_____. 1986b. "Language Practices and Self-Definition: The Case of Gender Identity Acquisition." *The Sociological Quarterly* 27:295–311.

Connell, R.W. 1985. "Theorizing Gender." *Sociology* 19:260–72.

Fishman, Pamela. 1978. "Interaction: The Work Women Do." *Social Problems* 25:397–406.

Frye, Marilyn. 1983. *The Politics of Reality: Essays in Feminist Theory*. Trumansburg, NY: The Crossing Press.

Garfinkel, Harold. 1967. *Studies in Ethnomethodology*. Englewood Cliffs, NJ: Prentice-Hall.

Goffman, Erving. 1976. "Gender Display." *Studies in the Anthropology of Visual Communication* 3:69–77.

_____. 1977. "The Arrangement between the Sexes." *Theory and Society* 4:301–31.

Heritage, John. 1984. *Garfinkel and Ethnomethodology*. Cambridge, England: Polity Press.

Hochschild, Arlie R. 1983. *The Managed Heart: Commercialization of Human Feeling*. Berkeley: University of California Press.

Kessler, Suzanne J., and Wendy McKenna. 1978. *Gender: An Ethnomethodological Approach*. New York: Wiley.

Komarovsky, Mirra. 1946. "Cultural Contradictions and Sex Roles." *American Journal of Sociology* 52:184–89.

_____. 1950. "Functional Analysis of Sex Roles." *American Sociological Review* 15:508–16.

Linton, Ralph. 1936. *The Study of Man*. New York: Appleton-Century.

Parsons, Talcott. 1951. *The Social System*. New York: Free Press.

_____, and Robert F. Bales. 1955. *Family, Socialization and Interaction Process*. New York: Free Press.

Rubin, Gayle. 1975. "The Traffic in Women: Notes on the 'Political Economy' of Sex." Pp. 157–210 in *Toward an Anthropology of Women*, edited by R. Reiler. New York: Monthly Review Press.

Stacey, Judith, and Barrie Thorne. 1985. "The Missing Feminist Revolution in Sociology." *Social Problems* 32:301–16.

Thorne, Barrie. 1980. "Gender ... How Is It Best Conceptualized?" Unpublished manuscript.

CHAPTER 7

MASCULINITY AS HOMOPHOBIA
Fear, Shame, and Silence in the Construction of Gender Identity

Michael S. Kimmel

We think of manhood as eternal, a timeless essence that resides deep in the heart of every man. We think of manhood as a thing, a quality that one either has or doesn't have. We think of manhood as innate, residing in the particular biological composition of the human male, the result of androgens or the possession of a penis. We think of manhood as a transcendent tangible property that each man must manifest in the world, the reward presented with great ceremony to a young novice by his elders for having successfully completed an arduous initiation ritual. [...]

In this chapter, I view masculinity as a constantly changing collection of meanings that we construct through our relationships with ourselves, with each other, and with our world. Manhood is neither static nor timeless; it is historical. Manhood is not the manifestation of an inner essence; it is socially constructed. Manhood does not bubble up to consciousness from our biological makeup; it is created in culture. Manhood means different things at different times to different people. We come to know what it means to be a man in our culture by setting our definitions in opposition to a set of "others"—racial minorities, sexual minorities, and, above all, women.

Our definitions of manhood are constantly changing, being played out on the political and social terrain on which the relationships between women and men are played out. In fact, the search for a transcendent, timeless definition of manhood is itself a sociological phenomenon—we tend to search for the timeless and eternal during moments of crisis, those points of transition when old definitions no longer work and new definitions are yet to be firmly established.

This idea that manhood is socially constructed and historically shifting should not be understood as a loss, that something is being taken away from men. In fact, it gives us something extraordinarily valuable—agency, the capacity to act. It gives us a sense of historical possibilities to replace the despondent resignation that invariably attends timeless, ahistorical essentialisms. Our behaviors are not simply "just human nature," because "boys will be boys." From the materials we find around us in our culture—other people, ideas, objects—we actively create our worlds, our identities. Men, both individually and collectively, can change.

In this chapter, I explore this social and historical construction of both hegemonic masculinity and alternate masculinities, with an eye toward offering a new theoretical model of American manhood.[1] To accomplish this I first uncover some of the hidden gender meanings in classical statements of social and political philosophy, so that I can anchor the emergence of contemporary manhood in specific historical and social contexts. I then spell out the ways in which this version of masculinity emerged in the United States, by tracing both psychoanalytic developmental sequences and a historical trajectory in the development of marketplace relationships.

CLASSICAL SOCIAL THEORY AS A HIDDEN MEDITATION OF MANHOOD

I begin this inquiry by looking at [...] passages from that set of texts commonly called classical social and political theory. You will, no doubt, recognize them, but I invite you to recall the way they were discussed in your undergraduate or graduate courses in theory:

> The bourgeoisie cannot exist without constantly revolutionizing the instruments of production, and thereby the relations of production, and with them the whole relations of society. Conservation of the old modes of production in unaltered form, was, on the contrary, the first condition of existence for all earlier industrial classes. Constant revolutionizing of production, uninterrupted disturbance of all social conditions, everlasting uncertainty and agitation distinguish the bourgeois epoch from all earlier ones. All fixed, fast-frozen relations, with their train of ancient and venerable prejudices and opinions are swept away, all new-formed ones become antiquated before they can ossify. All that is solid melts into air, all that is holy is profaned, and man is at last compelled to face with sober senses, his real conditions of life, and his relation with his kind. (Marx & Engels, 1848/1964)

An American will build a house in which to pass his old age and sell it before the roof is on; he will plant a garden and rent it just as the trees are coming into bearing; he will clear a field and leave others to reap the harvest; he will take up a profession and leave it, settle in one place and soon go off elsewhere with his changing desires.... At first sight there is something astonishing in this spectacle of so many lucky men restless in the midst of abundance. But it is a spectacle as old as the world; all that is new is to see a whole people performing in it. (Tocqueville, 1835/1967)

*****

Did anyone ever mention that in all [...] cases the theorists were describing men? Not just "man" as in generic mankind, but a particular type of masculinity, a definition of manhood that derives its identity from participation in the marketplace, from interaction with other men in that marketplace—in short, a model of masculinity for whom identity is based on homosocial competition? Three years before Tocqueville found Americans "restless in the midst of abundance," Senator Henry Clay had called the United States "a nation of self-made men."

What does it mean to be "self-made"? What are the consequences of self-making for the individual man, for other men, for women? It is this notion of manhood—rooted in the sphere of production, the public arena, a masculinity grounded not in landownership or in artisanal republican virtue but in successful participation in marketplace competition—this has been the defining notion of American manhood. Masculinity must be proved, and no sooner is it proved that it is again questioned and must be proved again—constant, relentless, unachievable, and ultimately the quest for proof becomes so meaningless than it takes on the characteristics [...] of a sport. He who has the most toys when he dies wins.

Where does this version of masculinity come from? How does it work? What are the consequences of this version of masculinity for women, for other men, and for individual men themselves? These are the questions I address in this chapter.

MASCULINITY AS HISTORY AND THE HISTORY OF MASCULINITY

The idea of masculinity expressed in the previous extracts is the product of historical shifts in the grounds on which men rooted their sense of themselves as men. To argue that cultural definitions of gender identity are historically specific goes only so far; we have to specify exactly what those models were. In my historical inquiry into the development of these models of manhood, I chart the fate of two models for manhood at the turn of the 19th century and the emergence of a third in the first few decades of that century.

In the late 18th and early 19th centuries, two models of manhood prevailed. The *Genteel Patriarch* derived his identity from landownership. Supervising his estate, he was refined, elegant, and given to casual sensuousness. He was a doting and devoted father, who spent much of his time supervising the estate and with his family. Think of George Washington or Thomas Jefferson as examples. By contrast, the *Heroic Artisan* embodied the physical strength and republican virtue that Jefferson observed in the yeoman farmer, independent urban craftsman, or shopkeeper. Also a devoted father, the Heroic Artisan taught his son his craft, bringing him through ritual apprenticeship to status as master craftsman. Economically autonomous, the Heroic Artisan also cherished his democratic community, delighting in the participatory democracy of the town meeting. Think of Paul Revere at his pewter shop, shirtsleeves rolled up, a leather apron—a man who took pride in his work.

Heroic Artisans and Genteel Patriarchs lived in casual accord, in part because their gender ideals were complementary (both supported participatory democracy and individual autonomy, although patriarchs tended to support more powerful state machineries and also supported slavery) and because they rarely saw one another: Artisans were decidedly urban and the Genteel Patriarchs ruled their rural estates. By the 1830s, though, this casual symbiosis was shattered by the emergence of a new vision of masculinity, *Marketplace Manhood*.

Marketplace Man derived his identity entirely from his success in the capitalist marketplace, as he accumulated wealth, power, status. He was the urban entrepreneur, the businessman. Restless, agitated, and anxious, Marketplace Man was an absentee landlord at home and an absent father with his children, devoting himself to his work in an increasingly homosocial environment—a male-only world in which he pits himself against other men. His efforts at self-making transform the political and economic spheres, casting aside the Genteel Patriarch as an anachronistic feminized dandy—sweet, but ineffective and outmoded, and transforming the Heroic Artisan into a dispossessed proletarian, a wage slave.

As Tocqueville would have seen it, the coexistence of the Genteel Patriarch and the Heroic Artisan embodied the fusion of liberty and equality. Genteel Patriarchy was the manhood of the traditional aristocracy, the class that embodied the virtue of liberty. The Heroic Artisan embodied democratic community, the solidarity of the urban shopkeeper or craftsman. Liberty and democracy, the patriarch and the artisan, could, and did, coexist. But Marketplace Man is capitalist man, and he makes both freedom and equality problematic, eliminating the freedom of the aristocracy and proletarianizing the equality of the artisan. In one sense, American history has been an effort to restore, retrieve, or reconstitute the virtues of Genteel Patriarchy and Heroic Artisanate as they were being transformed in the capitalist marketplace.

Marketplace Manhood was a manhood that required proof, and that required the acquisition of tangible goods as evidence of success. It reconstituted itself by the exclusion of "others"—women, nonwhite men, nonnative-born men, homosexual men—and by terrified flight into a pristine mythic homosocial Eden where men could, at last, be real men among other men. The story of the ways in which Marketplace Man becomes American Everyman is a tragic tale, a tale of striving to live up to impossible ideals of success leading to chronic terrors of emasculation, emotional emptiness, and a gendered rage that leave a wide swath of destruction in its wake.

MASCULINITIES AS POWER RELATIONS

Marketplace Masculinity describes the normative definition of American masculinity. It describes his characteristics—aggression, competition, anxiety—and the arena in which those characteristics are deployed—the public sphere, the marketplace. If the marketplace is the arena in which manhood is tested and proved, it is a gendered arena, in which tensions between women and men and tensions among different groups of men are weighted with meaning. These tensions suggest that cultural definitions of gender are played out in a contested terrain and are themselves power relations.

All masculinities are not created equal; or rather, we are all *created* equal, but any hypothetical equality evaporates quickly because our definitions of masculinity are not equally valued in our society. One definition of manhood continues to remain the standard against which other forms of manhood are measured and evaluated. Within the dominant culture, the masculinity that defines white, middle-class, early middle-aged, heterosexual men is the masculinity that sets the standards for other men, against which other men are measured and, more often than not, found wanting. Sociologist Erving Goffman (1963) wrote that in America, there is only "one complete, unblushing male":

> a young, married, white, urban, northern heterosexual, Protestant father of college education, fully employed, of good complexion, weight and height, and a recent record in sports. Every American male tends to look out upon the world from this perspective.... Any male who fails to qualify in any one of these ways is likely to view himself ... as unworthy, incomplete, and inferior. (p. 128)

This is the definition that we will call "hegemonic" masculinity, the image of masculinity of those men who hold power, which has become the standard in psychological evaluations, sociological research, and self-help and advice literature for teaching young men to become "real men" (Connell, 1987). The hegemonic definition of manhood is a man *in* power, a man *with* power, and a man *of* power. We equate manhood with being strong, successful, capable, reliable, in control. The very definitions of manhood we have developed in our culture maintain the power that some men have over other men and that men have over women.

*****

This definition of manhood has been summarized cleverly by psychologist Robert Brannon (1976) into four succinct phrases:

1. "No Sissy Stuff!" One may never do anything that even remotely suggests femininity. Masculinity is the relentless repudiation of the feminine.
2. "Be a Big Wheel." Masculinity is measured by power, success, wealth, and status. As the current saying goes, "He who has the most toys when he dies wins."
3. "Be a Sturdy Oak." Masculinity depends on remaining calm and reliable in a crisis, holding emotions in check. In fact, proving you're a man depends on never showing your emotions at all. Boys don't cry.
4. "Give 'em Hell." Exude an aura of manly daring and aggression. Go for it. Take risks.

These rules contain the elements of the definition against which virtually all American men are measured. Failure to embody these rules, to affirm the power of the rules and one's achievement of them is a source of men's confusion and pain. Such a model is, of course, unrealizable for any man. But we keep trying, valiantly, and vainly, to measure up. American masculinity is a relentless test. The chief test is contained in the first rule. Whatever the variations by race, class, age, ethnicity, or sexual orientation, being a man means "not being like women." This notion of anti-femininity lies at the heart of contemporary and historical conceptions of manhood, so that masculinity is defined more by what one is not rather than who one is.

MASCULINITY AS THE FLIGHT FROM THE FEMININE

Historically and developmentally, masculinity has been defined as the flight from women, the repudiation of femininity. Since Freud, we have come to understand that developmentally the central task that every little boy must confront is to develop a secure identity for himself as a man. As Freud had it, the oedipal project is a process of the boy's renouncing his identification with and deep emotional attachment to his mother and then replacing her with the father as the object of identification. Notice that he reidentifies but never reattaches. This entire process, Freud argued, is set in motion by the boy's sexual desire for his mother. But the father stands in the son's path and will not yield his sexual property to his puny son. The boy's first emotional experience, then, the one that inevitably follows his experience of desire, is fear—fear of the bigger, stronger, more sexually powerful father. It is this fear, experienced symbolically as the fear of castration, Freud argues, that forces the young boy to renounce his identification with mother and seek to identify with the being who is the actual source of his fear, his father. In so doing, the boy is now symbolically capable of sexual union with a motherlike substitute, that is, a woman. The boy becomes gendered (masculine) and heterosexual at the same time.

Masculinity, in this model, is irrevocably tied to sexuality. The boy's sexuality will now come to resemble the sexuality of his father (or at least the way he imagines his father)—menacing, predatory, possessive, and possibly punitive. The boy has come to identify with his oppressor; now he can become the oppressor himself. But a terror remains, the terror that the young man will be unmasked as a fraud, as a man who has not completely and irrevocably separated from mother. It will be other men who will do the unmasking. Failure will de-sex the man, make him appear as not fully a man. He will be seen as a wimp, a Mama's boy, a sissy.

After pulling away from his mother, the boy comes to see her not as a source of nurturance and love, but as an insatiably infantalizing creature, capable of humiliating him in front of his peers. She makes him dress up in uncomfortable and itchy clothing, her kisses smear his cheeks with lipstick, staining his boyish innocence with the mark of feminine dependency. No wonder so many boys cringe from their mothers' embraces with groans of "Aw, Mom! Quit it!" Mothers represent the humiliation of infancy, helplessness, dependency. "Men act as though they were being guided by (or rebelling against) rules and prohibitions enunciated by a moral mother," writes psychohistorian Geoffrey Gorer (1964). As a result, "all the niceties of masculine behavior—modesty, politeness, neatness, cleanliness—come to be regarded as concessions to feminine demands, and not good in themselves as part of the behavior of a proper man" (pp. 56, 57).

The flight from femininity is angry and frightened, because mother can so easily emasculate the young boy by her power to render him dependent, or at least to remind him of dependency. It is relentless; manhood becomes a lifelong quest to demonstrate its achievement, as if to prove the unprovable to others, because we feel so unsure of it ourselves. Women don't often feel compelled to "prove their womanhood"—the phrase itself sounds ridiculous. Women have different kinds of gender identity crises; their anger and frustration, and their own symptoms of depression, come more from being excluded than from questioning whether they are feminine enough.

The drive to repudiate the mother as the indication of the acquisition of masculine gender identity has three consequences for the young boy. First, he pushes away his real mother, and with her the traits of nurturance, compassion, and tenderness she may have embodied. Second, he suppresses those traits in himself, because they will reveal his incomplete separation from mother. His life becomes a lifelong project to demonstrate that he possesses none of his mother's traits. Masculine identity is born in the renunciation of the feminine, not in the direct affirmation of the masculine, which leaves masculine gender identity tenuous and fragile.

Third, as if to demonstrate the accomplishment of these first two tasks, the boy also learns to devalue all women in his society, as the living embodiments of those traits in himself he has learned to despise. Whether or not he was aware of it, Freud also described the origins of sexism—the systematic devaluation of women—in the desperate efforts of the boy to separate from mother. We may *want* "a girl just like the girl that married dear old Dad," as the popular song had it, but we certainly don't want to *be like* her.

This chronic uncertainty about gender identity helps us understand several obsessive behaviors. Take, for example, the continuing problem of the school-yard bully. Parents remind us that the bully is the *least* secure about his manhood, and so he is constantly trying to prove it. But he "proves" it by choosing opponents he is absolutely certain he can defeat; thus the standard taunt to a bully is to "pick on someone your own size." He can't, though, and after defeating a smaller and weaker opponent, which he was sure would prove his manhood, he is left with the empty gnawing feeling that he has not proved it after all, and he must find another opponent, again one smaller and weaker, that he can again defeat to prove it to himself.[2]

*****

When does it end? Never. To admit weakness, to admit frailty or fragility, is to be seen as a wimp, a sissy, not a real man. But seen by whom?

MASCULINITY AS A HOMOSOCIAL ENACTMENT

Other men: We are under the constant careful scrutiny of other men. Other men watch us, rank us, grant our acceptance into the realm of manhood. Manhood is demonstrated for other men's approval. It is other men who evaluate the performance. Literary critic David Leverenz (1991) argues that "ideologies of manhood have functioned primarily in relation to the gaze of male peers and male authority" (p. 769). Think of how men boast to one another of their accomplishments—from their latest sexual conquest to the size of the fish they caught—and how we

constantly parade the markers of manhood—wealth, power, status, sexy women—in front of other men, desperate for their approval.

That men prove their manhood in the eyes of other men is both a consequence of sexism and one of its chief props. "Women have, in men's minds, such a low place on the social ladder of this country that it's useless to define yourself in terms of a woman," noted playwright David Mamet. "What men need is men's approval." Women become a kind of currency that men use to improve their ranking on the masculine social scale. (Even those moments of heroic conquest of women carry, I believe, a current of homosocial evaluation.) Masculinity is a *homosocial* enactment. We test ourselves, perform heroic feats, take enormous risks, all because we want other men to grant us our manhood.

*****

MASCULINITY AS HOMOPHOBIA

If masculinity is a homosocial enactment, its overriding emotion is fear. In the Freudian model, the fear of the father's power terrifies the young boy to renounce his desire for his mother and identify with his father. This model links gender identity with sexual orientation: The little boy's identification with father (becoming masculine) allows him to now engage in sexual relations with women (he becomes heterosexual). This is the origin of how we can "read" one's sexual orientation through the successful performance of gender identity. Second, the fear that the little boy feels does not send him scurrying into the arms of his mother to protect him from his father. Rather, he believes he will overcome his fear by identifying with its source. We become masculine by identifying with our oppressor.

But there is a piece of the puzzle missing, a piece that Freud, himself, implied but did not follow up. If the pre-oedipal boy identifies with mother, he *sees the world through mother's eyes.* Thus, when he confronts father during his great oedipal crisis, he experiences a split vision: He sees his father as his mother sees his father, with a combination of awe, wonder, terror, *and desire.*

He simultaneously sees the father as he, the boy, would like to see him—as the object not of desire but of emulation. Repudiating mother and identifying with father only partially answers his dilemma. What is he to do with that homoerotic desire, the desire he felt because he saw father the way that his mother saw father?

He must suppress it. Homoerotic desire is cast as feminine desire, desire for other men. Homophobia is the effort to suppress that desire, to purify all relationships with other men, with women, with children of its taint, and to ensure that no one could possibly ever mistake one for a homosexual. Homophobic flight from intimacy with other men is the repudiation of the homosexual within—never completely successful and hence constantly reenacted in every homosocial relationship. [...]

Even if we do not subscribe to Freudian psychoanalytic ideas, we can still observe how, in less sexualized terms, the father is the first man who evaluates the boy's masculine performance, the first pair of male eyes before whom he tries to prove himself. Those eyes will follow him for the rest of his life. Other men's eyes will join them—the eyes of role models such as teachers, coaches, bosses, or media heroes; the eyes of his peers, his friends, his workmates; and the eyes of millions of other men, living and dead, from whose constant scrutiny of his performance he will never be free. [...]

That nightmare from which we never seem to awaken is that those other men will see that sense of inadequacy, they will see that in our own eyes we are not who we are pretending to be. What we call masculinity is often a hedge against being revealed as a fraud, an exaggerated set of activities that keep others from seeing through us, and a frenzied effort to keep at bay those fears within ourselves. Our real fear "is not fear of women but of being ashamed or humiliated in front of other men, or being dominated by stronger men" (Leverenz, 1986, p. 451).

This, then, is the great secret of American manhood: *We are afraid of other men.* Homophobia is a central organizing principle of our cultural definition of manhood. Homophobia is more than the irrational fear of gay men, more than the fear that we might be perceived as gay. "The word 'faggot' has nothing to do with homosexual experience or even with fears of homosexuals," writes David Leverenz (1986). "It comes out of the depths of manhood: a label of ultimate contempt for anyone who seems sissy, untough, uncool" (p. 455). Homophobia is the fear that other men will unmask us, emasculate us, reveal to us and the world that we do not measure up, that we are not real men. We are afraid to let other men see that fear. Fear makes us ashamed, because the recognition of fear in ourselves is proof to ourselves that we are not as manly as we pretend, that we are, like the young man in a poem by Yeats, "one that ruffles in a manly pose for all his timid heart." Our fear is the fear of humiliation. We are ashamed to be afraid.

Shame leads to silence—the silences that keep other people believing that we actually approve of the things that are done to women, to minorities, to gays and lesbians in our culture. The frightened silence as we scurry past a woman being hassled by men on the street. That furtive silence when men make sexist or racist jokes in a bar. That clammy-handed silence when guys in the office make gay-bashing jokes. Our fears are the sources of our silences, and men's silence is what keeps the system running. This might help to explain why women often complain that their male friends or partners are often so understanding when they are alone and yet laugh at sexist jokes or even make those jokes themselves when they are out with a group.

*****

As adolescents, we learn that our peers are a kind of gender police, constantly threatening to unmask us as feminine, as sissies. One of the favorite tricks when I was an adolescent was to ask a boy to look at his fingernails. If he held his palm toward his face and curled his fingers back to see them, he passed the test. He'd looked at his nails "like a man." But if he held the back of his hand away from his face, and looked at his fingernails with arm outstretched, he was immediately ridiculed as a sissy.

As young men we are constantly riding those gender boundaries, checking the fences we have constructed on the perimeter, making sure that nothing even remotely feminine might show through. The possibilities of being unmasked are everywhere. Even the most seemingly insignificant thing can pose a threat or activate that haunting terror. On the day the students in my course "Sociology of Men and Masculinities" were scheduled to discuss homophobia and male-male friendships, one student provided a touching illustration. Noting that it was a beautiful day, the first day of spring after a brutal northeast winter, he decided to wear shorts to class. "I had this really nice pair of new Madras shorts," he commented. "But then I thought to myself, these shorts have lavender and pink in them. Today's class topic is homophobia. Maybe today is not the best day to wear these shorts."

Our efforts to maintain a manly front cover everything we do. What we wear. How we talk. How we walk. What we eat. Every mannerism, every movement contains a coded gender language. Think, for example, of how you would answer the question: How do you "know" if a man is homosexual? When I ask this question in classes or workshops, respondents invariably provide a pretty standard list of stereotypically effeminate behaviors. He walks a certain way, talks a certain way, acts a certain way. He's very emotional; he shows his feelings. One woman commented that she "knows" a man is gay if he really cares about her; another said she knows he's gay if he shows no interest in her, if he leaves her alone.

Now alter the question and imagine what heterosexual men do to make sure no one could possibly get the "wrong idea" about them. Responses typically refer to the original stereotypes, this time as a set of negative rules about behavior. Never dress that way. Never talk or walk that way. Never show your feelings or get emotional. Always be prepared to demonstrate sexual interest in women that you meet, so it is impossible for any woman to get the wrong idea about you. In this sense, homophobia, the fear of being perceived as gay, as not a real man, keeps men exaggerating all the traditional rules of masculinity, including sexual predation with women. Homophobia and sexism go hand in hand.

The stakes of perceived sissydom are enormous—sometimes matters of life and death.

We take enormous risks to prove our manhood, exposing ourselves disproportionately to health risks, workplace hazards, and stress-related illnesses. Men commit suicide three times as often as women. Psychiatrist Willard Gaylin (1992) explains that it is "invariably because of perceived social humiliation," most often tied to failure in business.

*****

In one survey, women and men were asked what they were most afraid of. Women responded that they were most afraid of being raped and murdered. Men responded that they were most afraid of being laughed at (Noble, 1992, pp. 105–106).

*****

POWER AND POWERLESSNESS IN THE LIVES OF MEN

I have argued that homophobia, men's fear of other men, is the animating condition of the dominant definition of masculinity in America, that the reigning definition of masculinity is a defensive effort to prevent being emasculated. In our efforts to suppress or overcome those fears, the dominant culture exacts a tremendous price from those deemed less than fully manly: women, gay men, nonnative-born men, men of color. This perspective may help clarify a paradox in men's lives, a paradox in which men have virtually all the power and yet do not feel powerful (see Kaufman, 1993).

*****

This feminist definition of masculinity as the drive for power is theorized from women's point of view. It is how women experience masculinity. But it assumes a symmetry between the public and the private that does not conform to men's experiences. Feminists observe that women, as a group, do not hold power in our society. They also observe that individually, they, as women, do not feel powerful. They feel afraid, vulnerable. Their observation of the social reality and their individual experiences are therefore symmetrical. Feminism also observes that men, as a group, are in power. Thus, with the same symmetry, feminism has tended to assume that individually men must feel powerful.

*****

Men's feelings are not the feelings of the powerful, but of those who see themselves as powerless. These are the feelings that come inevitably from the discontinuity between the social and the psychological, between the aggregate analysis that reveals how men are in power as a group and the pyschological fact that they do not feel powerful as individuals. They are the feelings of men who were raised to believe themselves entitled to feel that power, but do not feel it. No wonder many men are frustrated and angry.

*****

Often the purveyors of the mythopoetic men's movement, that broad umbrella that encompasses all the groups helping men to retrieve this mythic deep manhood, use the image of the chauffeur to describe modern man's position. The chauffeur appears to have the power—he's wearing the uniform, he's in the driver's seat, and he knows where he's going. So, to the observer, the chauffeur looks as though he is in command. But to the chauffeur himself, they note, he is merely taking orders. He is not at all in charge.[3]

Despite the reality that everyone knows chauffeurs do not have the power, this image remains appealing to the men who hear it at these weekend workshops. But there is a missing piece to the image, a piece concealed by the framing of the image in terms of the individual man's experience. That missing piece is that the person who is giving the orders is also a man. Now we have a relationship between men—between men giving orders and other men taking those orders. The man who identifies with the chauffeur is entitled to be the man giving the orders, but he is not. ("They," it turns out, are other men.)

The dimension of power is now reinserted into men's experience not only as the product of individual experience but also as the product of relations with other men. In this sense, men's experience of powerlessness is *real*—the men actually feel it and certainly act on it—but it is not *true*, that is, it does not accurately describe their condition. In contrast to women's lives, men's lives are structured around relationships of power and men's differential access to power, as well as the differential access to that power of men as a group. Our imperfect analysis of our own situation leads us to believe that we men need *more* power, rather than leading us to support feminists' efforts to rearrange power relationships along more equitable lines.

*****

Why, then, do American men feel so powerless? Part of the answer is because we've constructed the rules of manhood so that only the tiniest fraction of men come to believe that they are the biggest of wheels, the sturdiest of oaks, the most virulent repudiators of femininity, the most daring and aggressive. We've managed to disempower the overwhelming majority of American men by other means—such as discriminating on the basis of race, class, ethnicity, age, or sexual preference.

Masculinist retreats to retrieve deep, wounded, masculinity are but one of the ways in which American men currently struggle with their fears and their shame. Unfortunately, at the very moment that they work to break down the isolation that governs men's lives, as they enable men to express those fears and that shame, they ignore the social power that men continue to exert over women and the privileges from which they (as the middle-aged, middle-class white men who largely make up these retreats) continue to benefit—regardless of their experiences as wounded victims of oppressive male socialization.

Others still rehearse the politics of exclusion, as if by clearing away the playing field of secure gender identity of any that we deem less than manly—women, gay men, nonnative-born men, men of color—middle-class, straight, white men can reground their sense of themselves without those haunting fears and that deep shame that they are unmanly and will be exposed by other men. This is the manhood of racism, of sexism, of homophobia. It is the manhood that is so chronically insecure that it trembles at the idea of lifting the ban on gays in the military, that is so threatened by women in the workplace that women become the targets of sexual harassment, that is so deeply frightened of equality that it must ensure that the playing field of male competition remains stacked against all newcomers to the game.

Exclusion and escape have been the dominant methods American men have used to keep their fears of humiliation at bay. The fear of emasculation by other men, of being humiliated, of being seen as a sissy, is the leitmotif in my reading of the history of American manhood. Masculinity has become a relentless test by which we prove to other men, to women, and ultimately to ourselves, that we have successfully mastered the part. The restlessness that men feel today is nothing new in American history; we have been anxious and restless for almost two centuries. Neither exclusion nor escape has ever brought us the relief we've sought, and there is no reason to think that either will solve our problems now. Peace of mind, relief from gender struggle, will come only from a politics of inclusion, not exclusion, from standing up for equality and justice, and not by running away.

NOTES

1. Of course, the phrase "American manhood" contains several simultaneous fictions. There is no single manhood that defines all American men; "America" is meant to refer to the United States proper, and there are significant ways in which this "American manhood" is the outcome of forces that transcend both gender and nation, that is, the global economic development of industrial capitalism. I use it, therefore, to describe the specific hegemonic version of masculinity in the United States, that normative constellation of attitudes, traits, and behaviors that became the standard against which all other masculinities are measured and against which individual men measure the success of their gender accomplishments.

2. Such observations also led journalist Heywood Broun to argue that most of the attacks against feminism came from men who were shorter than 5 ft. 7 in. "The man who, whatever his physical size, feels secure in his own masculinity and in his own relation to life is rarely resentful of the opposite sex" (cited in Symes, 1930, p. 139).

3. The image is from Warren Farrell, who spoke at a workshop I attended at the First International Men's Conference, Austin, Texas, October 1991.

REFERENCES

Brannon, R. (1976). The male sex role—and what it's done for us lately. In R. Brannon & D. David (Eds.), *The forty-nine percent majority* (pp. 1–40). Reading, MA: Addison-Wesley.

Connell, R.W. (1987). *Gender and power.* Stanford, CA: Stanford University Press.

Gaylin, W. (1992). *The male ego.* New York: Viking.

Goffman, E. (1963). *Stigma.* Englewood Cliffs, NJ: Prentice Hall.

Gorer, G. (1964). *The American people: A study in national character.* New York: Norton.

Kaufman, M. (1993). *Cracking the armour: Power and pain in the lives of men.* Toronto: Viking Canada.

Leverenz, D. (1986). Manhood, humiliation and public life: Some stories. *Southwest Review, 71,* Fall.

Leverenz, D. (1991). The last real man in America: From Natty Bumppo to Batman. *American Literary Review, 3/4,* pp. 753-81.

Marx, K., & F. Engels. (1848/1964). The communist manifesto. In R. Tucker (Ed.), *The Marx-Engels reader.* New York: Norton.

Noble, V. (1992). A helping hand from the guys. In K.L. Hagan (Ed.), *Women respond to the men's movement.* San Francisco: HarperCollins.

Symes, L. (1930). The new masculinism. *Harper's Monthly, 161,* January.

Tocqueville, A. de. (1835/1967). *Democracy in America.* New York: Anchor.

What men need is men's approval. (1993, January 3). *The New York Times,* p. C-11.

CHAPTER 8

INTRODUCTION
Acting in Concert

Judith Butler

The essays included here represent some of my most recent work on gender and sexuality focusing on the question of what it might mean to undo restrictively normative conceptions of sexual and gendered life. Equally, however, the essays are about the experience of *becoming undone* in both good and bad ways. Sometimes a normative conception of gender can undo one's personhood, undermining the capacity to persevere in a livable life. Other times, the experience of a normative restriction becoming undone can undo a prior conception of who one is only to inaugurate a relatively newer one that has greater livability as its aim.

If gender is a kind of a doing, an incessant activity performed, in part, without one's knowing and without one's willing, it is not for that reason automatic or mechanical. On the contrary, it is a practice of improvization within a scene of constraint. Moreover, one does not "do" one's gender alone. One is always "doing" with or for another, even if the other is only imaginary. What I call my "own" gender appears perhaps at times as something that I author or, indeed, own. But the terms that make up one's own gender are, from the start, outside oneself, beyond oneself in a sociality that has no single author (and that radically contests the notion of authorship itself).

Although being a certain gender does not imply that one will desire a certain way, there is nevertheless a desire that is constitutive of gender itself and, as a result, no quick or easy way to separate the life of gender from the life of desire. What does gender want? To speak in this way may seem strange, but it becomes less so when we realize that the social norms that constitute our existence carry desires that do not originate with our individual personhood. This matter is made more complex by the fact that the viability of our individual personhood is fundamentally dependent on these social norms.

The Hegelian tradition links desire with recognition, claiming that desire is always a desire for recognition and that it is only through the experience of recognition that any of us becomes constituted as socially viable beings. That view has its allure and its truth, but it also misses a couple of important points. The terms by which we are recognized as human are socially articulated and changeable. And sometimes the very terms that confer "humanness" on some individuals are those that deprive certain other individuals of the possibility of achieving that status, producing a differential between the human and the less-than-human. These norms have far-reaching consequences for how we understand the model of the human entitled to rights or included in the participatory sphere of political deliberation. The human is understood differentially depending on its race, the legibility of that race, its morphology, the recognizability of that morphology, its sex, the perceptual verifiability of that sex, its ethnicity, the categorical understanding of that ethnicity. Certain humans are recognized as less than human, and that form of qualified recognition does not lead to a viable life. Certain humans are not recognized as human at all, and that leads to yet another order of unlivable life. If part of what desire wants is to gain recognition, then gender, insofar as it is animated by desire, will want recognition as well. But if the schemes of recognition that are available to us are those that "undo" the person by conferring recognition, or "undo" the person by withholding recognition, then recognition becomes a site of power by which the human is differentially produced. This means that to the extent that desire is implicated in social norms, it is bound up with the question of power and with the problem of who qualifies as the recognizably human and who does not.

If I am a certain gender, will I still be regarded as part of the human? Will the "human" expand to include me in its reach? If I desire in certain ways, will I be able to live? Will there be a place for my life, and will it be recognizable to the others upon whom I depend for social existence?

There are advantages to remaining less than intelligible, if intelligibility is understood as that which is produced as a consequence of recognition according to prevailing social norms. Indeed, if my options are loathsome, if I have no desire to be recognized within a certain set of norms, then it follows that my sense of survival depends upon escaping the clutch of those norms by which recognition is conferred. It may well be that my sense of social belonging is impaired by the distance I take, but surely that estrangement is preferable to gaining a sense of intelligibility by virtue of norms that will only do me in from another direction. Indeed, the capacity to develop a critical relation to these norms presupposes a distance from them, an ability to suspend or defer the need for them,

even as there is a desire for norms that might let one live. The critical relation depends as well on a capacity, invariably collective, to articulate an alternative, minority version of sustaining norms or ideals that enable me to act. If I am someone who cannot *be* without *doing*, then the conditions of my doing are, in part, the conditions of my existence. If my doing is dependent on what is done to me or, rather, the ways in which I am done by norms, then the possibility of my persistence as an "I" depends upon my being able to do something with what is done with me. This does not mean that I can remake the world so that I become its maker. That fantasy of godlike power only refuses the ways we are constituted, invariably and from the start, by what is before us and outside of us. My agency does not consist in denying this condition of my constitution. If I have any agency, it is opened up by the fact that I am constituted by a social world I never chose. That my agency is riven with paradox does not mean it is impossible. It means only that paradox is the condition of its possibility.

As a result, the "I" that I am finds itself at once constituted by norms and dependent on them but also endeavors to live in ways that maintain a critical and transformative relation to them. This is not easy, because the "I" becomes, to a certain extent unknowable, threatened with unviability, with becoming undone altogether, when it no longer incorporates the norm in such a way that makes this "I" fully recognizable. There is a certain departure from the human that takes place in order to start the process of remaking the human. I may feel that without some recognizability I cannot live. But I may also feel that the terms by which I am recognized make life unlivable. This is the juncture from which critique emerges, where critique is understood as an interrogation of the terms by which life is constrained in order to open up the possibility of different modes of living; in other words, not to celebrate difference as such but to establish more inclusive conditions for sheltering and maintaining life that resists models of assimilation.

The essays in this text are efforts to relate the problematics of gender and sexuality to the tasks of persistence and survival. My own thinking has been influenced by the "New Gender Politics" that has emerged in recent years, a combination of movements concerned with transgender, transsexuality, intersex, and their complex relations to feminist and queer theory.[1] I believe, however, that it would be a mistake to subscribe to a progressive notion of history in which various frameworks are understood to succeed and supplant one another. There is no story to be told about how one moves from feminist to queer to trans. The reason there is no story to be told is that none of these stories are the past; these stories are continuing to happen in simultaneous and overlapping ways as we tell them. They happen, in part, through the complex ways they are taken up by each of these movements and theoretical practices.

Consider the intersex opposition to the widespread practice of performing coercive surgery on infants and children with sexually indeterminate or hermaphroditic anatomy in the name of normalizing these bodies. This movement offers a critical perspective on the version of the "human" that requires ideal morphologies and the constraining of bodily norms. The intersex community's resistance to coercive surgery moreover calls for an understanding that infants with intersexed conditions are part of the continuum of human morphology and ought to be treated with the presumption that their lives are and will be not only livable, but also occasions for flourishing. The norms that govern idealized human anatomy thus work to produce a differential sense of who is human and who is not, which lives are livable, and which are not. This differential works for a wide range of disabilities as well (although another norm is at work for invisible disabilities).

A concurrent operation of gender norms can be seen in the *DSM IV*'s Gender Identity Disorder diagnosis. This diagnosis that has, for the most part, taken over the role of monitoring signs of incipient homosexuality in children assumes that "gender dysphoria" is a psychological disorder simply because someone of a given gender manifests attributes of another gender or a desire to live as another gender. This imposes a model of coherent gendered life that demeans the complex ways in which gendered lives are crafted and lived. The diagnosis, however, is crucial for many individuals who seek insurance support for sex reassignment surgery or treatment, or who seek a legal change in status. As a result, the diagnostic means by which transsexuality is attributed implies a pathologization, but undergoing that pathologizing process constitutes one of the important ways in which the desire to change one's sex might be satisfied. The critical question thus becomes, how might the world be reorganized so that this conflict can be ameliorated?

The recent efforts to promote lesbian and gay marriage also promote a norm that threatens to render illegitimate and abject those sexual arrangements that do not comply with the marriage norm in either its existing or its revisable form. At the same time, the homophobic objections to lesbian and gay marriage expand out through the culture to affect all queer lives. One critical question thus becomes, how does one oppose the homophobia without embracing the marriage norm as the exclusive or most highly valued social arrangement for queer sexual lives? Similarly, efforts to establish bonds of kinship that are not based on a marriage tie become nearly illegible and unviable when marriage sets the terms for kinship, and kinship itself is collapsed into "family." The enduring social ties that constitute viable kinship in communities of sexual minorities are threatened with becoming unrecognizable and unviable as long as the marriage bond is the exclusive way in which both sexuality and kinship are organized. A critical relation to this norm involves disarticulating those rights and obligations currently attendant upon marriage so that marriage might remain a symbolic exercise for those who choose to engage in it, but the rights and obligations of kinship may take any number of other forms. What reorganization of sexual norms would be necessary for those who live sexually and affectively outside the marriage bond or in kin relations to the side of marriage either to be legally and culturally recognized for the endurance and importance of their intimate ties or, equally important, to be free of the need for recognition of this kind?

If a decade or two ago, gender discrimination applied tacitly to women, that no longer serves as the exclusive framework for understanding its contemporary usage. Discrimination against women continues—especially poor women and women of color, if we consider the differential levels of poverty and literacy not only in the United States, but globally—so this dimension of gender discrimination remains crucial to acknowledge. But gender now also means gender identity, a particularly salient issue in the politics and theory of transgenderism and transsexuality. Transgender refers to those persons who cross-identify or who live as another gender, but who may or may not have undergone hormonal treatments or sex reassignment operations. Among transsexuals and transgendered persons, there are those who identify as men (if female to male) or women (if male to female), and yet others who, with or without surgery, with or without hormones, identify as *trans*, as transmen or transwomen; each of these social practices carries distinct social burdens and promises.

Colloquially, "transgender" can apply to the entire range of these positions as well. Transgendered and transsexual people are subjected to pathologization and violence that is, once again, heightened in the case of trans persons from communities of color. The harassment suffered by those who are "read" as trans or discovered to be trans cannot be underestimated. They are part of a continuum of the gender violence that took the lives of Brandon Teena, Mathew Shephard, and Gwen Araujo.[2] And these acts of murder must be understood in connection with the coercive acts of "correction" undergone by intersexed infants and children that often leave those bodies maimed for life, traumatized, and physically limited in their sexual functions and pleasures.

Although intersex and transsex sometimes seem to be movements at odds with one another, the first opposing unwanted surgery, the second sometimes calling for elective surgery, it is most important to see that both challenge the principle that a natural dimorphism should be established or maintained at all costs. Intersex activists work to rectify the erroneous assumption that every body has an inborn "truth" of sex that medical professionals can discern and bring to light on their own. To the extent that the intersex movement maintains that gender ought to be established through assignment or choice, but noncoercively, it shares a premise with transgendered and transsexual activism. The latter opposes forms of unwanted coercive gender assignment, and in this sense calls for greater claims of autonomy, a situation that parallels intersex claims as well. What precisely autonomy means, however, is complicated for both movements, since it turns out that choosing one's own body invariably means navigating among norms that are laid out in advance and prior to one's choice or are being articulated in concert by other minority agencies. Indeed, individuals rely on institutions of social support in order to exercise self-determination with respect to what body and what gender to have and maintain, so that self-determination becomes a plausible concept only in the context of a social world that supports and enables that exercise of agency. Conversely (and as a consequence), it turns out that changing the institutions by which humanly viable choice is established and maintained is a prerequisite for the exercise of self-determination. In this sense, individual agency is bound up with social critique and social transformation. One only determines "one's own" sense of gender to the extent that social norms exist that support and enable that act of claiming gender for oneself. One is dependent on this "outside" to lay claim to what is one's own. The self must, in this way, be dispossessed in sociality in order to take possession of itself.

One tension that arises between queer theory and both intersex and transsexual activism centers on the question of sex assignment and the desirability of identity categories. If queer theory is understood, by definition, to oppose all identity claims, including stable sex assignment, then the tension seems strong indeed. But I would suggest that more important than any presupposition about the plasticity of identity or indeed its retrograde status is queer theory's claim to be opposed to the unwanted legislation of identity. After all, queer theory and activism acquired political salience by insisting that antihomophobic activism can be engaged in by anyone, regardless of sexual orientation, and that identity markers are not prerequisites for political participation. In the same way that queer theory opposes those who would regulate identities or establish epistemological claims of priority for those who make claims to certain kinds of identities, it seeks not only to expand the community base of antihomophobic activism, but, rather, to insist that sexuality is not easily summarized or unified through categorization. It does not follow, therefore, that queer theory would oppose all gender assignment or cast doubt on the desires of those who wish to secure such assignments for intersex children, for instance, who may well need them to function socially even if they end up changing the assignment later in life, knowing the risks. The perfectly reasonable assumption here is that children do not need to take on the burden of being heroes for a movement without first assenting to such a role. In this sense, categorization has its place and cannot be reduced to forms of anatomical essentialism.

Similarly, the transsexual desire to become a man or a woman is not to be dismissed as a simple desire to conform to established identity categories. As Kate Bornstein points out, it can be a desire for transformation itself, a pursuit of identity as a transformative exercise, an example of desire itself as a transformative activity.[3] But even if there are, in each of these cases, desires for stable identity at work, it seems crucial to realize that a livable life does require various degrees of stability. In the same way that a life for which no categories of recognition exist is not a livable life, so a life for which those categories constitute unlivable constraint is not an acceptable option.

The task of all of these movements seems to me to be about distinguishing among the norms and conventions that permit people to breathe, to desire, to love, and to live, and those norms and conventions that restrict or eviscerate the conditions of life itself. Sometimes norms function both ways at once, and sometimes they function one way for a given group, and another way for another group. What is most important is to cease legislating for all lives what is livable only for some, and similarly, to refrain from proscribing for all lives what is unlivable for some. The differences in position and desire set the limits to universalizability as an ethical reflex. The critique of gender norms must be situated within the context of lives as they are lived and must be guided by the question of what maximizes the possibilities for a livable life, what minimizes the possibility of unbearable life or, indeed, social or literal death.

None of these movements is, in my view, postfeminist. They have all found important conceptual and political resources in feminism, and feminism continues to pose challenges to these movements and to function as an important ally. And just as it no longer works to consider "gender discrimination" as a code for discrimination against women, it would be equally unacceptable to propound a view of gender discrimination that did not take into account the differential ways in which women suffer from poverty and illiteracy, from employment discrimination, from a gendered division of labor within a global frame, and from violence, sexual and otherwise. The feminist framework that takes the structural domination of women as the starting point from which all other analyses of gender must proceed imperils its own viability by refusing to countenance the various ways that gender emerges as a political issue, bearing a specific set of social and physical risks. It is crucial to understand the workings of gender in global contexts, in transnational formations, not only to see what problems are posed for the term "gender" but to combat false forms of universalism that service a tacit or explicit cultural imperialism. That feminism has always countered violence against women, sexual and nonsexual, ought to serve as a basis for alliance with these other movements, since phobic violence against bodies is part of what joins antihomophobic, antiracist, feminist, trans, and intersex activism.

Although some feminists have worried in public that the trans movement constitutes an effort to displace or appropriate sexual difference, I think that this is only one version of feminism, one that is contested by views that take gender as an historical category, that the framework for understanding how it works is multiple and shifts through time and place. The view that transsexuals seek to escape the social condition of femininity because that condition is considered debased or lacks privileges accorded to men assumes that female-to-male (FTM) transsexuality can be definitively explained through recourse to that one framework for understanding femininity and masculinity. It tends to forget that the risks of discrimination, loss of employment, public harassment, and violence are heightened for those who live openly as transgendered persons. The view that the desire to become a man or a transman or to live transgendered is motivated by a repudiation of femininity presumes that every person born with female anatomy is therefore in possession of a proper femininity (whether innate, symbolically assumed, or socially assigned), one that can either be owned or disowned, appropriated or expropriated. Indeed, the critique of male-to-female (MTF) transsexuality has centered on the "appropriation" of femininity, as if it belongs properly to a given sex, as if sex is discretely given, as if gender identity could and should be derived unequivocally from presumed anatomy. To understand gender as a historical category, however, is to accept that gender, understood as one way of culturally configuring a body, is open to a continual remaking, and that "anatomy" and "sex" are not without cultural framing (as the intersex movement has clearly shown). The very attribution of femininity to female bodies as if it were a natural or necessary property takes place within a normative framework in which the assignment of femininity to femaleness is one mechanism for the production of gender itself. Terms such as "masculine" and "feminine" are notoriously changeable; there are social histories for each term; their meanings change radically depending upon geopolitical boundaries and cultural constraints on who is imagining whom, and for what purpose. That the terms recur is interesting enough, but the recurrence does not index a sameness, but rather the way in which the social articulation of the term depends upon its repetition, which constitutes one dimension of the performative structure of gender. Terms of gender designation are thus never settled once and for all but are constantly in the process of being remade.

*****

Feminist work on reproductive technology has generated a host of ethical and political perspectives that have not only galvanized feminist studies but have made clear the implications for thinking about gender in relation to biotechnology, global politics, and the status of the human and life itself. Feminists who criticize technologies for effectively replacing the maternal body with a patriarchal apparatus must nevertheless contend with the enhanced autonomy that those technologies have provided for women. Feminists who embrace such technologies for the options they have produced nevertheless must come to terms with the uses to which those technologies can be put, ones that may well involve calculating the perfectibility of the human, sex selection, and racial selection. Those feminists who oppose technological innovations because they threaten to efface the primacy of sexual difference risk naturalizing heterosexual reproduction. The doctrine of sexual difference in this case comes to be in tension with antihomophobic struggles as well as with the intersex movement and the transgender movement's interest in securing rights to technologies that facilitate sex reassignment.

In each of these struggles, we see that technology is a site of power in which the human is produced and reproduced—not just the humanness of the child but also the humanness of those who bear and those who raise children, parents and nonparents alike. Gender likewise figures as a precondition for the production and maintenance of legible humanity. If there is important coalitional thinking to be done across these various movements, all of which comprise the New Gender Politics, it will doubtless have to do with presumptions about bodily dimorphism, the uses and abuses of technology, and the contested status of the human, and of life itself. If sexual difference is that which ought to be protected from effacement from a technology understood as phallocentric in its aims, then how do we distinguish between sexual difference and normative forms of dimorphism against which intersex and transgendered activists struggle on a daily basis? If technology is a resource to which some people want access, it is also an imposition from which others seek to be freed. Whether technology is imposed or elected is salient for intersex activists. If some trans people argue that their very sense of personhood depends upon having access to technology to secure certain bodily changes, some feminists argue that technology threatens to take over the business of making persons, running the risk that the human will become nothing other than a technological effect.

Similarly, the call for a greater recognition of bodily difference made by both disability movements and intersex activism invariably calls for a renewal of the value of life. Of course, "life" has been taken up by right-wing movements to limit reproductive freedoms for women, so the demand to establish more inclusive conditions for valuing life and producing the conditions for viable life can resonate with unwanted conservative demands to limit the autonomy of women to exercise the right to an abortion. But here it seems important not to cede the term "life" to a right-wing agenda, since it will turn out that there are within these debates questions about when human life begins and what constitutes "life" in its viability. The point is emphatically not to extend the "right to life" to any and all people who want to make this claim on behalf of mute embryos, but rather to understand how the "viability" of a woman's life depends upon an exercise of bodily autonomy and on social conditions that enable that autonomy. Moreover, as in the case with those seeking to overcome the patholo-gizing effects of a gender identity disorder diagnosis, we are referring to forms of autonomy that require social (and legal) support and protection, and that exercise a transformation on the norms that govern how agency itself is differentially allocated among genders; thus, a women's right to choose remains, in some contexts, a misnomer.

Critiques of anthropocentrism have made clear that when we speak about human life we are indexing a being who is at once human and living, and that the range of living beings exceeds the human. In a way, the term "human life" designates an unwieldy combination, since "human" does not simply qualify "life," but "life" relates human to what is nonhuman and living, establishing the human in the midst of this relationality. For the human to be human, it must relate to what is nonhuman, to what is outside itself but continuous with itself by virtue of an interimplication in life. This relation to what is not itself constitutes the human being in its livingness, so that the human exceeds its boundary in the very effort to establish them. To make the claim, "I am an animal," avows in a distinctively human language that the human is not distinct. This paradox makes it imperative to separate the question of a livable life from the status of a human life, since livability pertains to living beings that exceed the human. In addition, we would be foolish to think that life is fully possible without a dependence on technology, which suggests that the human, in its animality, is dependent on technology, to live. In this sense, we are thinking within the frame of the cyborg as we call into question the status of the human and that of the livable life.

The rethinking of the human in these terms does not entail a return to humanism. When Frantz Fanon claimed that "the black is not a man," he conducted a critique of humanism that showed that the human in its contemporary articulation is so fully racialized that no black man could qualify as human.[4] In his usage, the formulation was also a critique of masculinity, implying that the black man is effeminized. And the implication of that formulation would be that no one who is not a "man" in the masculine sense is a human, suggesting that both masculinity and racial privilege shore up the notion of the human. His formulation has been extended by contemporary scholars, including the literary critic Sylvia Wynter, to pertain to women of color as well and to call into question the racist frameworks within which the category of the human has been articulated.[5] These formulations show the power differentials embedded in the construction of the category of the "human" and, at the same time, insist upon the historicity of the term, the fact that the "human" has been crafted and consolidated over time.

The category of the "human" retains within itself the workings of the power differential of race as part of its own historicity. But the history of the category is not over, and the "human" is not captured once and for all. That the category is crafted in time, and that it works through excluding a wide range of minorities means that its rearticulation will begin precisely at the point where the excluded speak to and from such a category. If Fanon writes that "a black is not a man," who writes when Fanon writes? That we can ask the "who" means that the human has exceeded its categorical definition, and that he is in and through the utterance opening up the category to a different future. If there are norms of recognition by which the "human" is constituted, and these norms encode operations of power, then it follows that the contest over the future of the "human" will be a contest over the power that works in and through such norms. That power emerges in language in a restrictive way or, indeed, in other modes of articulation as that which tries to stop the articulation as it nevertheless moves forward. That double movement is found in the utterance, the image, the action that articulates the struggle with the norm. Those deemed illegible, unrecognizable, or impossible nevertheless speak in the terms of the "human," opening the term to a history not fully constrained by the existing differentials of power.

*****

Psychoanalysis has sometimes been used to shore up the notion of a primary sexual difference that forms the core of an individual's psychic life. But there it would seem that sexual difference gains its salience only through assuming that sperm and egg imply heterosexual parental coitus, and then a number of other psychic realities, such as the primal scene and oedipal scenario. But if the egg or sperm comes from elsewhere, and is not attached to a person called "parent," or if the parents who are making love are not heterosexual or not reproductive, then it would seem that a new psychic topography is required. Of course, it is possible to presume, as many French psychoanalysts have done, that reproduction follows universally from heterosexual parental coitus, and that this fact provides a psychic condition for the human subject. This view proceeds to condemn forms of nonheterosexual unions, reproductive technology, and parenting outside of nuclear heterosexual marriage as damaging for the child, threatening to culture, destructive of the human. But this recruitment of psychoanalytic vocabularies for the purpose of preserving the paternal line, the transmission of national cultures, and heterosexual marriage is only one use of psychoanalysis, and not a particularly productive or necessary one.

It is important to remember that psychoanalysis can also serve as a critique of cultural adaptation as well as a theory for understanding the ways in which sexuality fails to conform to the social norms by which it is regulated. Moreover, there is no better theory for grasping the workings of fantasy construed not as a set of projections on an internal screen but as part of human relationality itself. It is on the basis of this insight that we can come to understand how fantasy is essential to an experience of one's own body, or that of another, as gendered. Finally, psychoanalysis can work in the service of a conception of humans as bearing an irreversible humility in their relations to others and to themselves. There is always a dimension of ourselves and our relation to others that we cannot know, and this not-knowing persists with us as a condition of existence and, indeed, of survivability. We are, to an extent, driven by what we do not know, and cannot know, and this "drive" (Trieb) is precisely what is neither exclusively biological nor cultural, but always the site of their dense convergence.[6] If I am always constituted by norms that are not of my making, then I have to understand the ways that constitution takes place. The staging and structuring of affect and desire is clearly one way in which norms work their way into what feels most properly to belong to me. The fact that I am other to myself precisely at the place where I expect to be myself follows from the fact that the sociality of norms exceeds my inception and my demise, sustaining a temporal and spatial field of operation that exceeds my self-understanding. Norms do not exercise a final or fatalistic control, at least, not always. The fact that desire is not fully determined corresponds with the psychoanalytic understanding that sexuality is never fully captured by any regulation. Rather, it is characterized by displacement, it can exceed regulation, take on new forms in response to regulation, even turn around and make it sexy. In this sense, sexuality is never fully reducible to the "effect" of this or that operation of regulatory power. This is not the same as saying that sexuality is, by nature, free and wild. On the contrary, it emerges precisely as an improvisational possibility within a field of constraints. Sexuality, though, is not found to be "in" those constraints as something might be "in" a container: it is extinguished by constraints, but also mobilized and incited by constraints, even sometimes requiring them to be produced again and again.

It would follow, then, that to a certain extent sexuality establishes us as outside of ourselves; we are motivated by an elsewhere whose full meaning and purpose we cannot definitively establish.[7] This is only because sexuality is one way cultural meanings are carried, through both the operation of norms and the peripheral modes of their undoing.

Sexuality does not follow from gender in the sense that what gender you "are" determines what kind of sexuality you will "have." We try to speak in ordinary ways about these matters, stating our gender, disclosing our sexuality, but we are, quite inadvertently, caught up in ontological thickets and epistemological quandaries. Am I a gender after all? And do I "have" a sexuality?

Or does it turn out that the "I" who ought to be bearing its gender is undone by being a gender, that gender is always coming from a source that is elsewhere and directed toward something that is beyond me, constituted in a sociality I do not fully author? If that is so, then gender undoes the "I" who is supposed to be or bear its gender, and that undoing is part of the very meaning and comprehensibility of that "I." If I claim to "have" a sexuality, then it would seem that a sexuality is there for me to call my own, to possess as an attribute. But what if sexuality is the means by which I am dispossessed? What if it is invested and animated from elsewhere even as it is precisely mine? Does it not follow, then, that the "I" who would "have" its sexuality is undone by the sexuality it claims to have, and that its very "claim" can no longer be made exclusively in its own name? If I am claimed by others when I make my claim, if gender is for and from another before it becomes my own, if sexuality entails a certain dispossession of the "I," this does not spell the end to my political claims. It only means that when one makes those claims, one makes them for much more than oneself.

NOTES

1. The Human Rights Campaign, situated in Washington, D.C., is the main lobbying organization for lesbian and gay rights in the United States. It has maintained that gay marriage is the number one priority of lesbian and gay politics in the U.S. See www.hrc.org. See also the The Intersex Society of North America at www.isna.org.

2. Brandon Teena was killed on December 30, 1993, in Falls City, Nebraska after being raped and assaulted a week earlier for being transgendered. Mathew Shephard was killed (beaten and tied to a post) in Laramie, Wyoming, on October 12, 1998, for being a "feminine" gay man. Gwen Araujo, a transgendered woman, was found dead in the foothills of the Sierra mountains after being assaulted at a party in Newark, California, on October 2, 2002.

3. See Kate Bornstein, *Gender Outlaw.*

4. Frantz Fanon, *Black Skin, White Masks,* 8.

5. Sylvia Wynter, "Disenchanting Discourse: 'Minority' Literary Criticism and Beyond," in Abdul JanMohammed and David Lloyd, *The Nature and Context of Minority Discourse.*

6. See Sigmund Freud, "Instincts and their Vicissitudes."

7. See Maurice Merleau-Ponty, "The Body in its Sexual Being," in *The Phenomenology of Perception,* 154–73.

WORKS CITED

Bornstein, Kate. *Gender Outlaw*. New York: Routledge, 1994.

Fanon, Frantz. *Black Skin, White Masks*. New York: Grove, 1967.

Freud, Sigmund. "Instincts and Their Vicissitudes." *The Standard Edition of the Complete Works of Sigmund Freud*. Vol. 14, edited by James Strachey et al. London: The Hogarth Pres and the Institute of Psychoanalysis, 1953–1974.

Merleau-Ponty, Maurice. " The Body in Its Sexual Being." In *The Phenomenology of Perception*. Translated by Colin Smith. New York: Routledge, 1967.

Wynter, Sylvia. "Disenchanting Discourse: 'Minority' Literary Criticism and Beyond." In The Nature and Context of Minority Discourse, edited by Abdul JanMohammed and David Lloyd. Oxford: Oxford University Press, 1997.

DISCUSSION QUESTIONS: HAMILTON

1. Compare and contrast these dominant strands of feminist theory, paying particular attention to how each one theorizes human agency.
2. Over the last century, liberal feminists in Canada have lobbied the state for laws that challenge women's exclusion from the public sphere and enable them to be economically independent from men. What liberal feminist organizations, as well as particular women, have played this role in Canada during this time period? What laws has the Canadian state implemented to address the concerns of these feminists?
3. Imagine that Friedrich Engels and Adrienne Rich were scheduled to give the keynote address opening the annual Canadian Women's Studies Association conference, in which they would summarize their new theoretical collaboration. Describe what the conference participants might hear during that lecture.

DISCUSSION QUESTIONS: WEST AND ZIMMERMAN

1. Explain in detail what West and Zimmerman mean when they argue that gender is "situated doing," as opposed to a set of traits or roles, that has implications for social structure and social control.
2. Discuss how theoretical conversations with the work of sociologists Erving Goffman and Harold Garfinkel have been instrumental to this feminist perspective on gender relations.
3. Imagine some critiques that might be levelled at this variant of feminist theory by other strands outlined by Roberta Hamilton.

DISCUSSION QUESTIONS: KIMMEL

1. Outline the three main models of manhood Kimmel discusses in this history of masculinity, explaining how competing definitions of masculinity are subordinated to one particular hegemonic standard.
2. Describe the characteristics of "hegemonic masculinity" according to Kimmel.
3. Like other readings in this collection, Kimmel's article theorizes the interrelationship of power relations, such as the relationship between masculinity and femininity, and masculinity and sexuality. Explain these interrelationships, providing examples from the reading.

DISCUSSION QUESTIONS: BUTLER

1. Like West and Zimmerman, Butler understands gender as something that we "do." However, her post-structural notion of gender "performance" is very unlike the ethnomethodological perspective on "doing gender" employed by West and Zimmerman. Tease out the differences between these feminist theories, drawing on Hamilton's, as well as Butler's own explanations as a guide.
2. Butler argues that "intelligibility" is vital to "livability." Explain this interrelationship.
3. Within the framework of the "New Gender Politics," which social groups concern Butler most in terms of the "livability" of their lives within contemporary social relations? Why? What, in her opinion, needs to change in order to make more lives more livable?

FURTHER READINGS

1. Alexander, M. Jacqui, and Chandra Talpade Mohanty (eds.). 1997. *Feminist Genealogies, Colonial Legacies, and Democratic Futures.* London: Routledge.

    In this book, the editors compel us to consider feminist theories and practices in a new light within an intersectional and transnational framework. Feminist activists engaged in research and political projects in Asia, Africa, Europe, and North America write about the intersection of sexual, gender, and racial relations of domination in the context of advanced global capitalism, with the hopes of producing analyses that will lead to a more socially democratic future.

2. Alvi, Sajida Sultana, Homa Hoodfar, and Sheila McDonough (eds). 2003. *The Muslim Veil in North America: Issues and Debates.* Toronto: Women's Press.

    These three Canadian feminist scholars have collected together eight essays that investigate contemporary veiling practices in Muslim communities in North America, which has become a salient site of feminist analysis and social struggle since September 11, 2001. Each author explores the multiple and contested meanings of head coverings for Muslim women in this context, including a way to strengthen identity and take advantage of educational and political participation opportunities.

3. Dua, Enaski, and Angela Robertson (eds.) 2003. *Scratching the Surface: Canadian Anti-racist Feminist Thought.* Toronto: Women's Press.

    This is another noteworthy Canadian anthology that draws together the work of 13 authors who examine the issues of citizenship and the nation using a critical anti-racist feminist framework. Contributors cover a wide range of historical periods—from the colonial era to the late 20th century—and draw much-needed attention to the activism of racialized women in relation to these issues.

4. Thornham, Sue. 2000. *Feminist Theory and Cultural Studies: Stories of Unsettled Relations.* London: Arnold.

    An important contribution to feminist cultural studies, this book outlines the key theoretical approaches and debates within the field, drawing on psychoanalytic theories, ethnographic studies, and the literature in the area of cultural consumption and the body to summarize the major contributions feminist theory has made to the larger field of cultural studies.

5. Walby, Sylvia. 1990. *Theorizing Patriarchy.* London: Blackwell.

    Although this monograph is over a decade old, it continues to provide a thorough yet succinct overview of feminist theoretical debates over the "origins," facets, and consequences of gender inequality. Walby discusses Marxist, radical, liberal, post-structural, and dual-systems strands of feminist theory, showing how each can be applied to a range of gendered phenomenon from paid work, housework, and the state to culture, sexuality, and violence.

RELEVANT FILMS

1. *The Gender Tango*, 1997, 47 minutes, Films for the Humanities and Sciences

   This film examines how women define themselves and are defined by others in several national contexts around the world. It includes excerpts of a beauty contest in the United States, Latin American women selling cosmetics door to door in the Amazon jungle, women passing as men to gain acceptance in the world of jazz music, and competing Aboriginal constructions of femininity.

2. *Sexism in Language: Thief of Honour, Shaper of Lies*, 1995, 29 minutes, University of California Extension Centre for Media and Independent Learning

   Sexism in Language analyzes the gender biases that permeate everyday language in the United States.

3. *Tough Guise: Media Images and the Crisis of Masculinity*, 1999, 40 minutes, Wellesley Centre of Women

   In this analytic documentary, filmmakers systematically examine the relationship between dominant images in popular culture and the social construction of masculine identities in late 20th-century America.

4. *Cross-cultural Comparisons: Gender Roles* (Volume 1), 1995, Western Illinois University

   By outlining Hindu, Chinese, and Islamic gender roles, this film compares and contrasts gendered cultural practices across the globe that give men authority over women.

5. *Wrestling with Manhood*, 2003, 60 minutes, Kinetic

   This informative, yet disturbing, documentary analyzes WWE professional wrestling, addressing its relationship to the construction of masculinity among young men in the United States. Sut Jhally and Jackson Katz discuss wrestling's inculcation in violence again women, bullying in schools, homophobia, sexual assault, workplace harassment, and relationship violence. Consequently, they argue that wrestling is a cultural site vital to the construction of hegemonic masculinity and the process of boys becoming "men" in American society.

RELEVANT WEB SITES

1. www.cddc.vt.edu/feminism/enin.html

   This feminist theory Web site provides research materials and information for students, activists, and scholars interesting in understanding the circumstances of women's lives and their daily struggles around the globe. Searchable fields include topics in feminist theory, different national feminisms, and individual feminist theories.

2. http://pers-www.wlv.ac.uk/~le1810/theory.htm

   Links provided here give information on feminist theories, women's movements, women and work, and women's sexuality and health. Included are Internet resources, articles, archives, and lists of women's organizations and feminist journals.

3. http://newmedia.colorado.edu/~socwomen/resources/genderscfilms.html

   The bibliography found at this address lists numerous films that demonstrate the social construction of gender.

4. http://employees.oneonta.edu/farberas/arth/arth200/gender.html

   This Web site, entitled *The Social Construction of Gender*, is an image-based essay that explains how the category "Woman" is produced through a masculine gaze and how they are seen and represented by men in paintings, films, ads, and television shows; an informative and innovative site.

5. http://bailiwick.lib.uiowa.edu/wstudies/theory.html

   Four main sections are listed pertaining to feminist theory: French feminisms, a review of feminist theory books, a photo gallery of feminist theorists, and links to feminist articles and journals.

⊕ ⊕ ⊕

PART III

THE GENDERED FAMILY

The family is conventionally understood as a place of nurturing and care central to women's and men's lives. Anthropologists claim it is a significant organizing unit for all known societies, a site of child rearing, marriage, and aging. But feminists argue that the family, especially in its nuclear form (man, woman, and their biological children), is a gendered institution, one that is crucial to determining gender, sexual, and racial inequalities in society at large.

Nuclear family members are often unwitting accomplices in the process of creating, maintaining, and perpetuating gender inequality by implicitly assuming that women are solely responsible for unpaid and undervalued domestic duties while men, although tied to family, should be properly dedicated to more important concerns in the public sphere such as paid work and political activities. Parents also raise children as gendered actors as they serve as examples for "appropriate" gender performances in heterosexual nuclear family units.

In the last few decades, we have seen a historic transformation in family life as the number of same-sex and single-parent families (usually headed by women) grows and (once)-married women enter the workforce in ever greater numbers. With this mass movement of women out of the domestic sphere, women have encountered a new problem: the double day. Housework and child care must be completed in order for families to function, but women are still largely saddled with this reproductive work, which needs to be undertaken after the paid workday is over. Feminists ask why this movement of women from home to work has not been accompanied by a comparable movement of men back into the home. Andrea Doucet's reading addresses just this question.

The readings collected in this section investigate the gendered, sexual, and racial dynamics at work in the family in order to make visible how social inequalities are produced within family units, especially through their interrelationship with other social institutions. Authors also suggest forward-looking changes to existing family structures that are considered socially appropriate. As the structure of the family changes, so do its gendered nature, meanings, and effects. To begin, Andrea Doucet, in her article "It's Almost Like I Have a Job, But I Don't Get Paid: Fathers at Home Reconfiguring Work, Care and Masculinity," analyzes the qualitative interviews she conducted with 70 stay-at-home fathers in Canada. In particular, she explores how these fathers combine family care responsibilities and self-provisioning and community work in order to remain connected to sources of traditional masculine identity. These fathers discuss the daily pressures of hegemonic masculinity as it relates to their lives as primary caregivers, which they deal with by distancing themselves from and devaluing femininity at the same time as they actively reconfigure masculine care to include femininity. These interviews, therefore, give us some insight into men's more general reluctance to take primary responsibility for reproductive labour in a domestic setting, even though many find child rearing a rewarding experience.

Enaski Dua rounds out this collection of readings by investigating the role played by the discourse of race in the development of the nuclear family as a sexist institution in Canada. Her piece includes a review of White feminist critiques of this family form, which contend that patriarchy and capitalism have shaped the nuclear family. In contrast, her "integrative" feminist approach that explicitly considers race relations shows that the nuclear family has operated differently in Canadian communities of colour. She also explores the social construction of race and gender in metropolitan and White settler communities to demonstrate that the familial, gender, and sexual relationships characteristic of the nuclear family emerged out of racialized projects of 19th-century nation-building. These insights lead her to argue that, in addition to organizing gender relations, the institution of the nuclear family also organizes race relations in Canadian society, and it is these politics of race and nation that explain why White women and women of colour have different experiences within the nuclear family form.

CHAPTER 9

"IT'S ALMOST LIKE I HAVE A JOB, BUT I DON'T GET PAID"

Fathers at Home Reconfiguring Work, Care, and Masculinity

Andrea Doucet

It's funny. There were lots of pros and cons about being home.... One of the things I missed was that you lose a sense of stature, a sense of common ground between myself and other men, a sense of being able to say— "Hey, I'm a man too." I think a lot of that revolved around not having employment. Not working and being at home. For me, not working was the bigger issue than being at home.... I liked the domestic stuff, cooking and all that. I like that stuff a lot. But I missed work.... As a man you have no status at all if you don't work. (Adam)

*****

Adam, a 42-year-old man living in rural Ontario, was a stay-at-home father of three children for a decade. He is one of 70 fathers in the study, as well as part of a larger study of Canadian fathers who self-define as primary caregivers of their children. [...]

*****

It was clear that while fathers were at home, they were [...] carving out complex sets of relations between home, paid and unpaid work, community work, and their own sense of masculinity. In seeking to explore the ways that work and family interact for stay-at-home fathers, this paper argues that they reconstruct the meanings of both, while also demonstrating complex intersections between work, home, community, and masculinity.

The paper makes three key arguments, all of which pull together these intricate connections. First, fathers retain very close links to paid work even when they have temporarily or permanently left a career to care for children. While there are three dominant patterns that characterize fathers' home-work balances, all of the fathers fall under the weight of community scrutiny for being primary caregivers and not primary breadwinners, thus confirming research that has argued that mothers' and fathers' "moral" responsibilities as carers and earners remain differently framed and experienced (Berk, 1985; Finch & Mason, 1993; McMahon, 1995). Second, where fathers have given up a formal investment in the full-time labor force, many replace employment with "self-provisioning" work [...] that allows them to contribute economically to the household economy as well as to display masculine practices, both to themselves and their wider community. That is, although stay-at-home fathers "trade cash for care" (Hobson & Morgan, 2002, p. 1), they also remain connected to traditionally masculine sources of identity such as paid work as well as self-provisioning at home and in the community as public displays of masculinity. Their narratives speak volumes about the ways in which the long shadow of hegemonic masculinity hangs over them. Third and finally, this paper argues that stay-at-home fathers' narratives of emergent and generative practices of caring represent a slow process of critical resistance as they begin to critique concepts of "male time" (Daly, 1996 [...]) and market capitalism approaches to work and care (Crittenden, 2001; [...] Williams, 2000).

The paper concludes by suggesting that fathers neither reproduce nor challenge hegemonic masculinity, as has been argued recently by some authors (Brandth & Kvande, 1998 [...]). Rather, stay-at-home fathers create new forms of masculinity that, while enacted against a weighty backdrop of hegemonic masculinity, nevertheless incorporate varied aspects of femininities. This paper hints at the need for discussions on men and masculinities to move into new theoretical ground that can assist us in making sense of fathers living and working in traditional female dominated or symbolically feminine domains. These arguments and findings are based on a qualitative research project with and on Canadian fathers, which will be described below, following a brief outline of the theoretical perspectives informing this work.

THEORETICAL FRAMEWORKS

*****

Symbolic Interactionism and Family Life

The study that informs this paper is rooted in principles of symbolic interactionism and by a rich tradition of family research that employs such principles (Barker, 1994; Daly, 1996, 2002; Finch & Mason, 1993; McMahon, 1995). Particular emphasis is placed on attempts to gain people's accounts of their own understandings and actions as well as how they, in turn, interpret these understandings and actions in light of the observations and judgments of other people. A central concept within my work has been that of moral dimensions of fathering and mothering, as well detailed in Janet Finch and Jennifer Mason's work (1993) [...]. Drawing on symbolic interactionist ideas, they argue that it is "through human interaction that people develop a common understanding of what a particular course of action will *mean*" [...] (Finch & Mason, 1993, p. 61). These ideas are applicable to our understandings of mothering and fathering and are intricately connected to "people's identities as moral beings" [...] (Finch & Mason, 1993, p. 170). To add a moral dimension is to incorporate an understanding of the critical role of social networks, how fathers and mothers feel they should act, and how they think others within their community networks will view these actions [...].

Studies on Fatherhood and Gender Divisions of Domestic Labour

My study is also rooted in a burgeoning [...] body of scholarship on fatherhood and gender divisions of domestic labor. This literature has drawn attention to the continued salience of key obstacles to greater fatherhood involvement including, for example, the role of work in fathers' lives ([...] Dowd, 2000 [...]), parental modeling after one's own father (Coltrane, 1996; [...]; Daly, 1993 [...]), maternal gatekeeping from wives or female partners (Allen & Hawkins, 1999; Parke, 1996 [...]), co-constructed processes of "doing gender" by both mothers and fathers (Berk, 1985; Coltrane, 1989, 1996 [....]) gender identities and ideologies [...], and discourses of fatherhood (Dienhart, 1998; Lupton & Barclay, 1997; Mandell, 2002). My work recognizes the validity of all of these facilitating and constraining factors in fathers' involvement but also gives greater emphasis to the role of social networks and the community as well as to the moral assumptions about what it means to be a "good mother" or a "good father," which are held and reinforced within particular communities.

Men and Masculinities

In addition to symbolic interactionist studies on families and research on gender divisions of labour, my work on fathering is also heavily influenced by theoretical literature on men and masculinities. Five points, gleaned from the literature on masculinities, underpin this paper. First, while there has been much debate on the usefulness of the concept "masculinities" (Clatterbaugh, 1998; Hearn, 1996), I hold with Connell that "we need some way of talking about men and women's involvement in the domain of gender" and that masculinities and femininities remain theoretically useful concepts to assist us with making sense of understanding gender relations as well as "gender ambiguity" (Connell, 2000, pp. 16–17). Second, there are a plurality of masculinities (Brittan, 1989; Hearn & Morgan, 1990); the meanings of masculinities differ across and within settings, and there are, at the level of practice, varied kinds of relations between different kinds of masculinities (Connell, 2000). Third, masculinities are not essences but occur in social relations where issues of power and difference are at play and where masculinities exist at both the level of agency and structure. As detailed by Connell, "The patterns of conduct our society defines as masculine may be seen in the lives of individuals, but they also have an existence beyond the individual. Masculinities are defined in culture and sustained in institutions" (Connell, 2000, p. 11). A fourth point is that there is a distinction between men and masculinities in that "sometimes masculine conduct or masculine identity goes together with a female body" and, similarly, it is also "very common for a (biological) man to have elements of feminine identity, desire and patterns of conduct" (Connell, 2000, p. 16). These observations are particularly astute when studying men who are engaging in female-dominated or feminine-identified work such as caregiving.

A fifth critical point about masculinity relates to the much-discussed concept of "hegemonic masculinity" (Coltrane, 1994; Connell, 1987, 1995, 2000; Kimmel, 1994; Messner, 1997). Traditionally it has been defined as "the most honored or desired" form of masculinity (Connell 2000, p. 10), one that usually aligns itself with traditional masculine qualities of "being strong, successful, capable, reliable, in control. That is (t)he hegemonic definition of manhood is a man *in* power, a man *with* power, and a man *of* power" (Kimmel, 1994, p. 125). Further, as Connell points out, hegemonic masculinity is perhaps most strongly identified "as the opposite of femininity" (Connell, 2000, p. 31). Other forms of masculinity, then, have come to be viewed as *subordinated* (especially gay masculinities), *marginalized* (exploited or oppressed groups such as ethnic minorities), and *complicit* masculinities (those organized around the complicit acceptance of what has come to be termed a "patriarchal dividend" (Connell, 1995, 2000).

*****

A key question, then, in empirical studies of fathers' lives is how their everyday caring practices confirm or challenge current theoretical understandings of masculinities. Given the continuing salience of the concept of hegemonic masculinity, it is thus worth asking whether or not fathers as carers exhibit subordinated, complicit or hegemonic masculinity. Furthermore, given that hegemonic masculinity is largely associated with the devaluation of the feminine while caring is often equated with feminine practice, what is the relationship between hegemonic masculinity and care? Does fathers' caregiving disrupt the smooth surfaces of hegemonic masculinity? In examining stay-at-home fathers' home-work balances, this question will be explored in this paper.

*****

Paid Work and Home

For the 70 stay-at-home fathers, three sets of patterns, with varying degrees of overlap, characterized their home-work balances. First, there were 12 fathers who had achieved financial and professional success and wanted to take a break from working and/or were seeking to move into another line of work once their children were in school. The overarching commonality with this group of fathers was that they seemed to have achieved their career goals and were looking for other forms of fulfillment, one of which was caring for their children as well as alternative work or leisure interests (e.g., travel, sports, writing). Second, 28 fathers were taking a break from working (as was the case with the two fathers on extended parental leave), were in a clear transition between jobs, were planning to go back to college or university for further education or training, or were currently taking evening courses along this path. Third, 30 fathers were working part-time, flexibly from a home office, or as an employee in their wife/partner's business; of these 30 fathers, 10 (one-third) were both working part-time and in transition between jobs. For all of these stay-at-home fathers, the decision to relinquish full-time employment was a result of a complex mix of factors that included variations of the following themes: their wife/partner having the higher income with employment benefits and a stronger career interest (at this stage of their lives); strong views on the importance of home care; the view that there was a paucity of good childcare facilities in Canada; the cost of childcare; and, in some cases, a child with particular developmental, physical or health needs. Each of the three patterns of home-work balances will be illustrated through a briefcase study.

Fathers with Work Success: "It's Not Like I'm Saying 'This Kid Is Holding Me Back'"

The first pathway to staying at home is well represented in the case study of Rory, a 53-year-old stay-at-home father living in Calgary, Alberta, who gave up his consulting business as quality-control expert on gas pipelines to stay at home with Tristan, who is now seven years old. His wife is a high-level civil servant with the provincial government. At home for four years, he has been president of the school's parent council, takes language courses to assist

with French immersion schooling, and cooks a daily special diet for his son, who has debilitating food allergies. He also renovates the home and takes on community work that relates to his son's interests. In his words, "The way I see it, if my son is really interested in something, I am really interested in it. If not, I don't have the time." Rory describes the reasoning behind his decision to leave work:

> He had been having problems with a stutter and he had been in a home daycare. We were both working. The kids in the daycare all had colds, so I kept him home. Things were pretty slow at work that week. So we decided I would stay home with him that week. His stutter started to get better. The next week he stayed home because he had the cold. Then his stutter got even better. And so I said to my wife, "If this is what it is going to take to get him better, then this is what I will do."

Unlike many of the stay-at-home fathers, Rory seems to have a particular sense of ease about his time at home. At the end of the interview, he adds that they have no debt, the house has been paid off, his wife is younger than he is, it was her turn for her career to take off, and his age is definitely a factor in his sense of ease.

*****

Richard, a French Canadian stay-at-home father of three who was a car mechanic for many years, is quite blunt about his aspirations for a career: "I've done it. I did it before. I made money. I went to work. I used to have expectations and dreams. And I don't want to work anymore."

Fathers like Rory [...] and Richard who identified themselves as having met their own standards of employment success were a small part of the study. It was more likely that most of the fathers, as described in the next two sections, were in transition between jobs and/or working part-time.

FATHERS IN TRANSITION: "THIS IS NOT THE KIND OF THING I WANT TO DO FOR THE REST OF MY LIFE"

Approximately 37% of the stay-at-home fathers (28 fathers) were in transition between jobs or careers. Craig, a 40-year-old stay-at-home father to triplets, four-year-old Michael and Zachary, and Jonathon who had recently died, typifies the "in transition" father. [...] When I ask him how he came to be at home with his sons, he responds:

> When my wife became pregnant—my wife is a psychiatric nurse, she has a career.... I am a musician from a long time ago, and that's what I like to do primarily. My job was just that, it was not a career, so it was a very easy choice. We looked at it, and I was working in auto parts, mostly car dealerships, and before that I was in forklifts and things like that, parts for these machines. But we looked at it, and when we found out that it was going to be triplets and without even thinking that there would be anything other than three happy normal bouncing kids running around, my salary would have been eaten up by daycare, and I figured well, what the heck, we're going to be in the same boat financially, so I'll stay home until they go to school. That's how we came to the decision; it took us like not even a minute to come to that decision.

*****

Within this group of in-transition fathers, some had lost their jobs, others went through a serious illness that forced them to re-think their career paths at the same time as they were juggling expensive childcare arrangements, and still others found that their jobs were "dead-end" ones that did not justify two stressful jobs and the high cost of childcare. While some men took a break altogether in order to concentrate on the demands of childcare while simultaneously preparing for a new career, others, as described in the next section, took on part-time

work or moved their jobs into a more home-based setting.

Fathers Juggling Paid Work and Caring: "My Shop Is in the Garage"

Of the 70 stay-at-home fathers in the study, 30 fathers were employed in part-time jobs or were working flexible hours from a home-based workplace. Within this group, one-third of the fathers were also in transition between careers but were working part-time to supplement the family income. Shahin, a 43-year-old Iranian Canadian, provides a good example of the home-working father. Shahin began staying at home with his son, now six years old, when his wife, a French-Canadian lawyer, went back to work after a four-month maternity leave. A self-employed cabinetmaker, he has a workshop in his garage. [...]

*****

In his long descriptions about his routine when his son was an infant, he frequently invoked the way in which he juggled work at home and childcare:

> My shop is in my garage. It's rather practical. So I had the monitor in the shop.... He had this rocking chair ... you know, you put the baby in there, and it goes back and forth. He loved to sleep in it and it was 45 minutes, I think, the cycle. So I used to run every half an hour and crank it up.

Shahin and 29 other fathers kept their hand in paid work through part-time or home-based working. The range of occupations and creative flexibility within this group was astounding. Of the 30 stay-at-home fathers who work part-time, several diverse examples can be highlighted. Sam is a driving instructor two evenings a week and Saturdays. Jamal, a Somali immigrant father, takes care of his two sons during the day while his wife studies English, and he works nights conducting surveys by phone. Brandon, a sole-custody father, has balanced the raising of his three sons with running his organic farm. Jerome, at home for the past 11 years, works about eight hours a week as office manager in his wife's pediatrician practice in a small Nova Scotia town. [...]

The patterns described above could be viewed as somewhat similar to those taken by mothers as they seek to find creative ways of combining working and caring. [...] One large difference, however, is that the majority of fathers in my study felt compelled to talk about paid work in relation to caring, whereas mothers, as described by Garey (1999), were more likely to focus on how their caring responsibilities were not hindered by working. There is thus a slight shift in the balance of emphasis with fathers feeling the weight and pull of moral responsibilities as earners whereas mothers feel pulled by a moral responsibility to care. This is explored more fully in the section that follows.

The Weight of Social Scrutiny and Gendered Moral Responsibilities: "I Felt I Wasn't Being a Good Man"

Each and every father interviewed referred in some way to the weight of community scrutiny and how he felt social pressure to be earning. Some fathers claimed that they were unaffected by this pressure, but nevertheless they all felt this societal gaze upon them. Peter, a stay-at-home father of two young sons for the past five years, describes this quite well. His former job in desktop publishing was gradually phased out, but he was able to maintain his connection with his former employer and take on contract work for about 12 hours a week from a home office. His wife is a high school teacher. He very much identifies with the "stay-at-home father" label and has done some media appearances on this. Nevertheless, he says:

> Despite that fact, I've always—in social occasions, dinner parties, talking with other people, or whatever—other men, I guess, especially—just being able to talk about something I do in the "real world" was kind of important socially—that

didn't make me sound limited, or stuck ... to show that I am able to work, although I have chosen to do this.

*****

[A] final example of the expression of this negative social gaze on fathers who relinquish a primary identity as breadwinner is given by Jesse, a freelance artist and stay-at-home father, for two years, of a now three-year-old daughter. He pulls together the ways in which these perceptions are "so engrained" through men's upbringing, how it "can weigh on you" and the particularly gendered quality of this ("*It's a guy thing*"):

> These things are so ingrained in us.... It can weigh on you, those kinds of things. Sometimes I do wonder if people have that sort of perception of me as a stay-at-home father. I am still not sure if there is a widespread acceptance of it. I think some people still wonder, "Why is the father at home? Like he can't earn as much as his partner or something?" I struggle with that, because it is also my own internalized kind of condition, too, that I have this struggle. You know, my background, working class, a strong work ethic. And it's a guy thing.

In referring to "a guy thing," these fathers are implicitly referring to the connections between dominant or hegemonic masculinity and paid work and the associated sense of vertigo that men feel when they relinquish earning as a primary part of their identity [...]. Fathers remained connected with paid work partly to maintain a link with masculine conceptions of identity and to respond to deeply felt moral precepts that, as one father put it, "There's a certain male imperative to be bringing in money, to feel like you are actually caring for your family, a sense of providing." One of the ways that men deal with these losses is to take on unpaid work that has masculine qualities.

UNPAID WORK AND HOME

Whatever the status of their relationship with paid work, the overwhelming majority of fathers made it a point to let me know that they were taking on self-provisioning work, mainly "working on the house," and/or doing community work. These two strands of unpaid work will be examined here.

Self-Provisioning: "We Get Together and Talk Tools"

Most of the stay-at-home fathers spoke about work they were doing on the house, landscaping, carpentry, woodworking or repairing cars. Richard, for example, a 39-year-old French Canadian father, draws attention to this issue without even being asked about it. He left his work as an electronic technician two years ago to be at home with his children, now aged seven and two, plus a two-month-old infant. In his joint interview with his wife, Richard takes out a photo album and shows me before-and-after pictures of his household renovation, saying, "Now you can see how much I've done." He enjoys the domestic routine and has excelled at making award-winning birthday cakes for the kids (and proudly shows photos of his creations); he also makes homemade baby food and does a batch of jams and jellies every fall. When I ask him about the long-term plans, he says, "I am not going back to work," but rather, as he says:

> I'll be doing work on the house. Renovations. Cooking, cleaning. They're only gone for six hours. I'll probably be more involved in the school. I'll do these things I've been wanting to do for years. Simple things like organizing my recipes. Organizing my tapes and music.... I have a lot of projects that I want to do in woodworking, but I don't have the time.

Like Richard, many of the stay-at-home fathers in this study reconstruct the meanings of work and home to include unpaid self-provisioning work (Pahl, 1984; Wallace & Pahl, 1985),

specifically "male self-provisioning activities" (Mingione, 1988, p. 560) that include "building, renovation ... carpentry, electrical repairs and plumbing, furniture making, decorating, constructing doors and window frames, agricultural cultivation for own use, repairing vehicles" (see Mingione, 1988, pp. 560–561). While some of these can be viewed as masculine hobbies, which these men would have likely picked up from their fathers or male peers, these are also activities that display or justify men's masculinity and seem to alleviate some of the discomfort men feel with giving up breadwinning.

*****

For many men in my study, the impulse to take on self-provisioning was partly financial, but it was also part of an effort to justify their being at home through emphasizing more masculine work and hobbies that involve traditional male qualities, such as building, construction, and physical strength. This very much carried over into the community work that men took on, where the emphasis was often on sports and occasionally on traditional masculine roles of physical labor and leadership/management.

Community Work: "They Call Me 'Bob the Builder'"

In addition to unpaid self-provisioning work, men also take on unpaid community work, particularly involvement in school and extracurricular activities. This is well illustrated by Bob, a former sign-maker who lives in rural Quebec. He [...] has a particular involvement at his son's school:

> I'm head of maintenance at my son's kindergarten.... They call me "Bob the Builder"—"fix this, fix that." Every time I go in, they are always asking me to do things.... [...]

The unpaid community work done by fathers often has gender-neutral tones such as volunteering in the classroom or on school trips, but fathers also emphasize work that has masculine qualities. Building on traditional male interests such as sports [...] and physical labor, men translated these skills into assets in their caregiving and became involved in recreational sports as organizers and coaches and took on tasks involving physical labor in the classroom. Some fathers also took on leadership positions in school councils and community organizations. Archie, for example, highlights how his position as president of the parent-teacher council became "a full-time job."

It is also important to emphasize that this community work constitutes a part of domestic labor in that it builds bridges between parents, between households, and between households and other social institutions (schools, health settings, community centers). [...] This recognition of community work as part of domestic labour is a further insight that this research adds to work on fathering and divisions of domestic labour (see also Doucet, 2000, 2001 [...]).

It is important to point out that the majority of unpaid work in communities remains in the hands of women. An extensive body of research evidence suggests that women typically do a varied range of work that links the household to the school and to the wider community ([...] Crittenden, 2001; [...] Doucet, 2000, 2001; Stueve & Pleck, 2003). While Anita Garey has pointed out that "homework, volunteer work and extracurricular activities are ways in which mothers link their children to the public world—and are symbolic arenas in their strategies of being mothers" (Garey, 1999, p. 40), fathers also play a role in children's extracurricular activities such as sporting as well as in community work which emphasizes leadership, sports, construction, and building. [...] Many stay-at-home fathers view coaching and assisting in children's sports at school and in the community as a venue that makes their fathering more enjoyable for themselves while also easing community scrutiny of their decision to give up work. Moreover, fathers' involvement in children's lives in a manner that builds on traditional male interests also provides for the possibility of building their own community networks on the basis of traditional areas of

male connection such as sports. As argued below, this involvement reflects the way in which fathers seek to distinguish their caring from mothering and to reconstruct particular kinds of "masculine care" (Brandth & Kvande, 1998).

RECONSTRUCTING CARING, FATHERING, AND MASCULINITIES

While taking on masculine self-provisioning and/or community work that sometimes involved masculine qualities, what seemed very clear in most fathers' narratives was that they were quite adamant, from within their practices and identities of caring, to distinguish themselves as men, as heterosexual (with the exception of gay fathers), as masculine, and as fathers, not as mothers. In my first focus group with fathers, Sam, stay-at-home father of two for five years, interjected several times, half jokingly: "Well, we're still men, aren't we?" Another father, Mitchell, stay-at-home father of three for seven years, made several pointed references in his interview to how he often worked out at a gym and enjoyed "seeing the women in lycra." These men's words add further support to what theorists of work have underlined about men working in nontraditional or female-dominated occupations (such as nursing or elementary school teaching) and how they must actively work to expel the idea that they might be gay, unmasculine, or not men ([...] Sargent, 2000; Williams, 1992). This leads to men finding ways of reinforcing their masculinity—such as engaging in sports or physical labor so as to maintain masculine affiliations and to exhibit public displays of masculinity (see Bird, 1996). Additionally, the men in my study are attempting to carve out their own paternal and masculine identities within spaces traditionally considered maternal and feminine. These processes of masculine identification and distancing from the feminine occurred in at least three ways.

First, the overwhelming majority of fathers spoke about their efforts to impart a more "masculine quality" to their family care through promoting their children's physical and outdoor activities, independence, risk taking, and the fun and playful aspects of care (see Brandth & Kvande, 1998; Doucet, 2004). Second, given that domestic space, the home, is metaphorically configured as a maternal space with feminine connotations of comfort and care ([...] Walker, 2002) many fathers, as described above, more readily identified with the house as something to build and rebuild. Finally, many men also made it a point of saying how they had to "hang out with the guys"—playing traditionally male sports such as hockey or baseball or working with men on activities involving physical labor—so as to balance out the time that they were home caring. Owen, a stay-at-home father of two children for seven years, says: "At the same time *I was still needing the men thing*. I needed a break from the kids.... I would build sets for the theater. I would hang out with the guys."

A set of theoretical assumptions that can initially assist us in making sense of these processes are feminist theoretical discussions on how men distance themselves from and devalue the feminine (Bird, 1996; [...] Connell, 1987, 1995, 2000; Johnson, 1988 [...]) as well as the concept of hegemonic masculinity. While there have been varied discussions of the meanings and relevance of hegemonic masculinity, most recently the author who penned it, Connell, has boiled it down to being defined partly "as the opposite of femininity" (Connell, 2000, p. 31). These fathers' narratives, as touched upon in this paper, are filled with visible and inchoate contradictions that tell about how fathers are both determined to distance themselves from the feminine, but are also, in practice, radically revisioning masculine care to include some aspects of femininities. In effect, their narratives move us beyond the issue of whether they reproduce or challenge hegemonic masculinity [...] and, rather, speak to the ways in which they are creating new kinds of masculinities that join together varied configurations of masculinities and femininities.

Audible effects of this revisioning of masculinity can be picked up in these fathers' narratives because they are spoken partly from the borders of the most traditional arena of men's dominance within the "gender order," that of paid work. When men—like the stay-at-home fathers described in this paper—relinquish their

identities and practices as full-time workers and primary breadwinners, it is inevitable that processes of personal and social readjustment will occur. Perhaps most notable is that fathers' relation to paid work begins to shift, their meanings of work are dramatically altered, and men begin, at least partially, to take on perspectives that are more aligned with women's social positioning [...] and ultimately feminine [...] or feminist [...] vantage points. There are many instances demonstrating the ways in which these movements occur, three of which will be briefly mentioned here.

First, fathers noted ensuing personal and "generative" [...] changes as they make the shift from worker to carer. Aaron, for example, who used to be a lawyer in a "cutthroat" environment "where you have to be strong," says that "my hard edges have softened" and how he had a steep learning curve "about sharing, feelings, and spending time with them, sort of mellowing out a little." In a similar way, many fathers also find that their time at home gives them the opportunity to reflect on what it is they actually want to do once they return to the work force. [...]

Second, most fathers mentioned how parenting is the "hardest" or "most difficult" job they have ever done. In the words of Archie, at home for seven years, "it's the hardest work I ever done in my whole life," and "it's like I have a full-time job, but I don't get paid." From this place where they see that it is "hard"—and yet some of them admit they have "softened"—men also come to appreciate how vitally important caring work is and yet also socially devalued. They thus add their voices to a large chorus of generations of women who have argued for the valuing of unpaid work (Crittenden, 2001; Luxton, 1997; Luxton & Vosko, 1998; [...]).

A third way that stay-at-home fathers' relation to paid work changes is that they are adamant that they will remain very involved with their children if and when they go back to full-time employment. While issues of home-work balance have been configured largely as women's issues for decades, with women being the ones who make adjustments in work schedules to accommodate children (Brannen & Moss, 1991; Hochschild, 1989), fathers at home come to join their female partners in recognizing the need for what researchers have recently termed greater "work-life integration" (Johnson, Lero, & Rooney, 2001). In two-parent families, many men commented on how their ideal home-work arrangement was that both parents worked part-time or that one parent worked from home. [...]

*****

CONCLUSIONS

Just as Adam, mentioned at the beginning of this paper, let me know how he repaired cars while his children toddled around him, most of the 70 stay-at-home fathers within my larger study on Canadian fathers as primary caregivers viewed staying at home as a way of combining part-time paid work, "working on the house," caring, and housework. Sometimes these skills extended into the community as fathers often volunteered to coach sports, a venue that allowed them to be involved in their children's lives while also building on a traditional area of male interests. Most of the fathers maintained a connection with paid work, through working part-time, studying part-time for a new career, or taking a break from work in order to carve out a new line of work. The narratives of these fathers and their activities represent the complex intersections between the sites and theoretical concepts of home, work, community and masculinity. Moreover, at a practical level, it could be reasonably argued that the term "stay-at-home" father may be a slight misnomer since most fathers bring together varied configurations of home, paid and unpaid work, and community work. Just as Anita Garey (1999) uses the metaphor of "weaving" to discuss the ways in which mothers weave together complex patterns of employment and motherhood, stay-at-home fathers are in the process of "building" new models of varied employment patterns and fatherhood that represent not only changes in the institution of fatherhood but also suggest potential shifts in social relations between women and men in the social institution of work.

*****

A final concluding point refers to the political implications that can be drawn from this work and to the potential role that men could play in the social recognition and valuing of unpaid work (Armstrong & Armstrong, 1993; Doucet, 2004; Luxton, 1980, 1997; Luxton & Vosko, 1998). Freed somewhat from the breadwinner imperative that is the norm for most men in most societies, the stay-at-home fathers in this study can be viewed as representing some of what Karin Davies refers to in her Swedish study of women, work and time. Davies argues that decisions to work part-time or to take time off from work constitute "breaking the pattern" (p. 217) out of "wage labor as the over-riding structure and an unconditional adherence to male time" (Davies, 1990, p. 208). She maintains that "by limiting the time spent in wage labor, a soil is provided whereby visions of what is important to fight and strive for can find space" (p. 208). While writing about women two decades ago, the views of Davies as applied to men have a particularly powerful effect because the "the overriding structure" and "male time" she refers to have strong connections with masculinity, especially hegemonic masculinity. It is men's overall privileged access to the rewards of paid employment and their concurrent lesser role in the care of dependent others that partly account for the overall dominance and associated "patriarchal dividend" (Connell, 1995) from which men benefit. The slow process of critical resistance documented here by fathers as they critique concepts of "male time" constitutes some unraveling of their relation to the structural effects of hegemonic masculinity.

Nevertheless, these stories are marginal ones; they sit quietly on the borders of most men's lives in most contemporary societies. Connell poignantly cautions that "the gender order does not blow away at a breath" and "the historical process around masculinity is a process of struggle in which, ultimately, large resources are at stake" (2000, p. 14). We are reminded of the need to move beyond these vignettes of everyday caring and the generative changes that ensue to focus on wider social relations and the need for greater structural changes and policy measures to assist both women and men in achieving work-life integration. [...] While Davies' work highlights how "it is up to women to exert influence" in this vein since they are more likely to have "experience of rejecting male time" and thus "concrete knowledge and understanding of how we can produce and re-produce new forms of daily life ... which are not so oppressive" (1990, p. 247), this study suggests that stay-at-home fathers are also lodged in this distinctive position as well. Indeed, adding father's voices to these issues can also "exert in-fluence" very loudly indeed, both theoretically and politically.

REFERENCES

Allen, S.M., & Hawkins, A.J. (1999). Maternal gate-keeping: Mothers' beliefs and behaviors that inhibit greater father involvement in family work. *Journal of Marriage and the Family, 61,* 199–212.

Armstrong, P., & Armstrong, H. (1993). *The double ghetto* (3rd ed.). Toronto: McClelland & Stewart.

Barker, R.W. (1994). *Lone fathers and masculinities.* Avebury, UK: Aldershot.

Berk, S.F. (1985). *The gender factory: The apportion-ment of work in American households.* New York: Plenum.

Bird, S.R. (1996). Welcome to the men's club: Homo-sociality and the maintenance of hegemonic masculinity. *Gender & Society, 19*(2), 120–132.

Brandth, B., & Kvande, E. (1998). Masculinity and child care: The reconstruction of fathering. *The Sociological Review, 46*(2), 293–313.

Brannen, J., & Moss, P. (1991). *Managing mothers: Dual earner households after maternity leave.* London: Unwin Hyman.

Brittan, A. (1989). *Masculinity and power.* Oxford: Basil Blackwell.

Clatterbaugh, K. (1998). What is problematic about masculinities? *Men and Masculinities, 7*(1), 24–45.

Coltrane, S. (1989). Household labor and the routine production of gender. *Social Problems, 36*(5), 473–490.

Coltrane, S. (1994). Theorizing masculinities in contemporary social science. In H. Brod & M. Kaufman (Eds.), *Theorizing masculinities* (pp. 39–60). Thousand Oaks: Sage Publications.

Coltrane, S. (1996). *Family man: Fatherhood, housework, and gender equity.* Oxford: Oxford University Press.

Connell, R.W. (1987). *Gender and power.* Cambridge, UK: Polity Press.

Connell, R.W. (1995). *Masculinities.* London: Polity Press.

Connell, R.W. (2000). *The men and the boys.* Berkeley: University of California Press.

Crittenden, A. (2001). *The price of motherhood: Why the most important job in the world is still the least valued.* New York: Henry Holt and Company.

Daly, K. (1993). Reshaping fatherhood: Finding the models. *Journal of Family Issues, 74,* 510–530.

Daly, K. (1996). *Families and time: Keeping pace in a hurried culture.* Thousand Oaks, CA: Sage Publications.

Daly, K. (2002). Time, gender, and the negotiation of family schedules. *Symbolic Interaction, 25*(3), 323–342.

Davies, K. (1990). *Women, time and weaving the strands of everyday life.* Avebury, UK: Gower Publishing Company.

Dienhart, A. (1998). *Reshaping fatherhood: The social construction of shared parenting.* London: Sage Publications.

Doucet, A. (2000). "There's a huge difference be-tween me as a male carer and women": Gender, domestic responsibility, and the community as an institutional arena. *Community Work and Family, 3*(2), 163–184.

Doucet, A. (2001). "You see the need perhaps more clearly than I have": Exploring gendered pro-cesses of domestic responsibility. *Journal of Family Issues, 22,* 328–357.

Doucet, A. (2004). Fathers and the responsibility for children: A puzzle and a tension. *Atlantis: A Women's Studies Journal, 28*(2), 103–114.

Dowd, N.E. (2000). *Redefining fatherhood.* New York: New York University Press.

Finch, J., & Mason, J. (1993). *Negotiating family re-sponsibilities.* London: Routledge.

Garey, A.I. (1999). *Weaving work and motherhood.* Philadelphia: Temple University Press.

Hearn, J. (1996). Is masculinity dead? A critique of the concept of masculinity/masculinities. In M. Mac an Ghaill (Ed.), *Understanding masculinities* (pp. 202–217). Buckingham, UK: Open University Press.

Hearn, J., & Morgan, D.H.J. (1990). Men, masculinities and social theory. In D.H.J. Morgan (Ed.), *Men, masculinities and social theory* (pp. 1–17). London: Unwin Hyman.

Hobson, B., & Morgan, D.H.J. (2002). Introduction: Making men into fathers. In B. Hobson (Ed.), *Men, masculinities and the social politics of fatherhood* (pp. 1–21). Cambridge, UK: Cambridge University Press.

Hochschild, A.R. (1989). *The second shift.* New York: Avon Books.

Johnson, K.L., Lero, D.S., & Rooney, J.A. (2001). *Work-life compendium 2001: 150 Canadian statistics on work, family and well-being.* Guelph, Ontario: Centre for Families, Work and Well-Being, University of Guelph.

Johnson, M.M. (1988). *Strong mothers, weak wives: The search for gender equality.* Berkeley: University of California Press.

Kimmel, M.S. (1994). Masculinity as homophobia: Fear, shame and silence in the construction of gender identity. In H. Brod & M. Kaufman (Eds.), *Theorizing masculinities* (pp. 119–141). Thousand Oaks, CA: Sage Publications.

Lupton, D., & Barclay, L. (1997). *Constructing fatherhood: Discourses and experiences.* London: Sage Publications.

Luxton, M. (1980). *More than a labor of love: Three generations of women's work in the home.* Toronto: Women's Press.

Luxton, M. (Ed.). (1997). *Feminism and families: Critical policies and changing practices.* Halifax: Fernwood Publishing.

Luxton, M., & Vosko, L. (1998). The Census and women's work. *Studies in Political Economy, 56,* 49–82.

Mandell, D. (2002). *Deadbeat dads: Subjectivity and social construction.* Toronto: University of Toronto Press.

McMahon, M. (1995). *Engendering motherhood: Identity and self-transformation in women's lives.* New York: The Guilford Press.

Messner, M.A. (1997). *Politics of masculinities: Men in movements.* Thousand Oaks, CA: Sage Publications.

Mingione, E. (1988). Work and informal activities in urban southern Italy. In R.E. Pahl (Ed.), *On work: Historical, comparative and theoretical approaches* (pp. 548–578). Oxford: Basil Blackwell.

Pahl, R.E. (1984). *Divisions of labour.* Oxford: Basil Blackwell.

Parke, R.D. (1996). *Fatherhood.* Cambridge, Massachusetts: Harvard University Press.

Sargent, P. (2000). Real men or real teachers? Contradictions in the lives of men elementary teachers. *Men and Masculinities, 2*(4), 410–433.

Stueve, J.L., & Pleck, J.H. (2003). Fathers' narratives of arranging and planning: Implications for understanding parental responsibility. *Fathering, 1*(1), 51–70.

Walker, L. (2002). Home making: An architectural perspective. *Signs: Journal of Women in Culture and Society, 27*(3), 823–836.

Wallace, C.D., & Pahl, R.E. (1985). Household work strategies in an economic recession. In N. Redclift & E. Mingione (Eds.), *Beyond employment* (pp. 189–227). Oxford: Basil Blackwell.

Williams, C.L. (1992). The glass escalator: Hidden advantage for men in the "female" professions. *Social Problems, 39*(3), 253–267.

Williams, J. (2000). *Unbending gender: Why family and work conflict and what to do about it.* Oxford: Oxford University Press.

CHAPTER 10

BEYOND DIVERSITY
Exploring the Ways in Which the Discourse of Race Has Shaped the Institution of the Nuclear Family

Enakshi Dua

For more than a decade, feminists have been debating the relative importance of the nuclear family in shaping the ways in which women of colour experience gender oppression. For many mainstream feminists, the nuclear family has been the starting point for exploring the roots of gender oppression in society. Mainstream feminists have argued that the institution of the nuclear family is the primary site in which gender oppression is produced and experienced by women. They point out that it is through the nuclear family that gender socialization, the appropriation of women's unpaid labour, and the unequal power relationships between men and women are organized in society (Barrett and McIntosh 1982). However, in *Ain't I a Woman* (1981), bell hooks shattered the hegemony of mainstream feminist analyses, when she argued that these theories failed to address the ways in which racism shape the social construction of gender. hooks and others went on to argue that due to the racism in western societies, women of colour's experiences with the family deviate considerably from the model put forward in mainstream feminist analyses (see, for example, Amos and Parmar 1984).

Based on this critique, many feminist scholars have called for theorizing that is inclusive of how women of colour experience the family and

that take into account the diversity of women's experiences with the family. For example, Mandell argues that "previous historical accounts ... have uncritically superimposed a European framework onto a Canadian past" and calls for research "that stress[es] the diversity and multiplicity of family histories" (1995, 17). The starting point for such research has been the task of integrating the historical dimensions of racism into investigations of gender and class.

Not all feminists agree that integrating racism into analyses of gender would alter feminist theorizing on the family. Recently, Okin dismissed the significance of such diversity in experiences with the family, cautioning scholars "not to overreact to differences by losing sight of their broadly relevant insights about families, their gendered division of labour, and its effect on sex inequality in all spheres of life" (1997, 19). Okin calls for a re-evaluation of feminist theories of the family, arguing that

> there are obvious benefits to such reevaluations of earlier second-wave feminist theories about families that a decade or more of scholarship had been inclined to jettison as racist, classist, ethnocentric or heterosexist. Indeed when such theories are given a fair second chance rather

than rejected as essentialist, they can sometimes be found to apply or to have considerable relevance to those persons they had thought to neglect and thereby discriminate against. (1997, 20)

Despite such disagreements over the relevance of mainstream feminist theories on the nuclear family for women of colour, feminist analyses of the family have failed to investigate the ways in which racism has shaped the institution of the nuclear family. While mainstream feminist analyses have been preoccupied with investigating the forces that led to the historical emergence of the nuclear family, they have assumed that the discourse of race has had little to do with the nuclear family. As a result, this body of work has concentrated on discerning the ways in which male power interacted with the historical development of capitalism to produce the nuclear family as a sexist institution. For writers such as Okin, racism as a discourse and as a form of systemic discrimination[1] seems to have little to do with the way in which gender has come to be socially organized or with the historical development of the family.

In contrast, writers who attempt to integrate race and gender have challenged the universalizing tendencies in mainstream feminist analyses, pointing out that the family is experienced differently according to a woman's social class, race, and sexual orientation. Surprisingly, though, these writers do not tell us why such diversity exists. In particular, they do not explain why racism alters a woman of colour's experience with the family, nor how the dynamics of racism have shaped the way in which the institution of the nuclear family has historically come to be organized. As a result, racism is seen as only relevant in explaining how women of colour experience the family, not in how white women experience the family, nor in explaining the social organization of sexism.

This chapter explores the role of the discourse of race in the emergence of the nuclear family as a sexist institution. First, through a review of mainstream feminist approaches to the family, I examine the ways in which the historical development of patriarchy and capitalism led to the emergence of the nuclear family in Canada. Next, through a review of integrative feminist approaches, I show that the nuclear family operated very differently in Canadian communities of colour. The last section outlines the ways in which the discourse of racism led to the emergence of the nuclear family. Drawing on an emerging body of literature which explores the social construction of race and gender in both metropolitan and white settler societies, I will demonstrate that the familial, gender, and sexual relationships characteristic of the nuclear family emerge out of the imperatives of racialized projects of nineteenth-century nation-building. In addition to organizing gender relations, the institution of the nuclear family also organizes race relations in society. It is these politics of race and nation that explain why white women and women of colour[2] have different experiences with the nuclear family.

MAINSTREAM FEMINIST APPROACHES TO THE NUCLEAR FAMILY: PATRIARCHY OR CAPITALISM?

The question of how the nuclear family emerged as a sexist institution has been a central concern in mainstream feminist theory. In the 1960s and 1970s, feminists began challenging the hegemonic idea that the institution of the family was a complementary unit which provides for the needs of all of its members. Starting with Betty Friedan's *The Feminine Mystique* (1963), mainstream feminists have argued that the gender division of labour within the family, which delegated to women unpaid motherwork and domestic work, created power differences as unpaid domestic work made women dependent on a male wage. These writers linked the division of labour within the family to the subordination of women in society. As the private sphere (domestic and mother work) was associated with women, the public sphere (paid work) became associated with men; the private sphere also became devalued.

*****

Marxist feminists argued that the origins of the nuclear family were located in the social relations of capitalism. These writers began their analysis by extending conventional Marxist categories of production and class exploitation, illustrating that domestic work was indeed a form of labour and that social reproduction was a form of production. Benston (1969), Dalla Costa (1972) argued that the nuclear family served the interests of capitalism, which required the reproduction of cheap labour. Subsequently, others argued that not only did the nuclear family serve the needs of capitalism but its origins are located in the transition from feudal to capitalist society (Fox 1980; Seccombe 1980). In contrast, radical feminists argued that the origins of the sex-gender system predated capitalism, and were located in earlier cleavages between men and women. Firestone (1970) argued that these cleavages arose out of a male imperative to control women's reproduction—where such control was socially organized through the institutions of marriage and the family.

Rather than asserting the primacy of one over the other, one resolution of this debate was to integrate the two approaches. The attention of theorists shifted to how the historical development of capitalist relations of production combined with the historical development of social relations of reproduction to create gender oppression (see, for example, Coontz and Henderson 1986; Fox 1988; Eisenstein 1979; Armstrong and Armstrong 1984; Ursel 1992). As a result, feminist scholars began to undertake detailed historical studies of the nuclear family. However, given the intellectual context of theorizing on the nuclear family, the role of racism continued to be treated as irrelevant to the historical development of capitalism, the organization of social reproduction in a capitalist society and the institution of the nuclear family.

*****

In Canada, the nuclear family, as an institution, begins to emerge for the bourgeoisie during the late eighteenth century, typified by a strong sense of separation of parents and children from the extended family, marked by a norm of complementarity between husband and wife, and the special role of the mother in shaping the character of her children (Bradbury 1982). Several writers have demonstrated that the institutionalization of the nuclear family among working-class and settler households, in part, was a response to the changes brought about by industrialization, particularly to the extension of wage labour to a larger proportion of the population. After 1850, what constitutes the character of household life begins to change for working-class and settler households, as relations of production give way to relations of sexuality, intimacy, and consumption.

As Armstrong and Armstrong (1984) and Ursel (1992) have shown, the shift to industrialization meant that men, women, and children became dependent on the wages earned by family members for survival. In the initial period of industrialization, all members of a household worked in the wage labour force, and wages were pooled. As Ursel (1992) has shown, the entry of all members of the household into the paid labour force was accompanied by a breakdown in the power of the patriarch. In addition, declining birth rates in this period led to a societal concern for social reproduction. The crisis in social reproduction gave legitimacy to the notion of the family wage, which in turn allowed the nuclear family to be institutionalized and women's labour to once again be tied to the household (1992, 61–122). The family was transformed into a set of relations that specialized in procreation, child rearing, consumption, and affection. Notably, the nuclear family widened the division between many men's and women's tasks: husbands became responsible for breadwinning and wives became responsible for homemaking and child rearing.

Several agents participated in the process of institutionalizing the nuclear family. The most noted role is that of state managers. The Canadian state, through a variety of social welfare and family protection legislation, preserved the concept of the household as a distinct unit. As Ursel (1992) and Pupo (1988) show, child labour legislation, protective labour legislation for women, the creation of Mother's Pensions, reform of property and divorce legislation, and the notion of the family wage were measures designed to preserve both familial and patriarchal relations. Such interventions allowed women's labour to once again become tied to the household. By transforming men into breadwinners, male authority was both maintained and transformed.

However, the state was not the only agent working to preserve patriarchal authority. In Canada, as well as elsewhere, the entrenchment of the nuclear family was located in a politics of bourgeois morality. As noted earlier, the nuclear family first became entrenched in middle-class homes, leading the middle class to glorify motherhood and the ideology of domesticity, and to work towards institutionalizing these gender and familial relations in society. As several researchers have shown, in the late nineteenth and early twentieth century, the nuclear family was the focus of social reform movements in most western societies (Pupo 1988; Ursel 1992). Social reformers worked to entrench the bourgeois ideal of the nuclear family among the working class, as well as immigrants and First Nations people (see also Dubinsky 1992; Marks 1992). Private charities spearheaded attempts to make poor and immigrant European families conform to the new ideal of domesticity. These organizations advocated legislation that would keep families intact, where husbands were engaged in paid work, wives laboured in domestic work and childcare, children went to school, and no one other than parents and children lived within the home.[3] Notably, middle-class women dominated the social reform movement, playing a major role in shaping state policies as activists, lobbyists, and clients.

This literature suggests the importance of a more contingent, historically sensitive approach that locates the development of the nuclear family in several forces—such as patriarchy, capitalism, wage labour, the social organization of reproduction, state authority, and bourgeois morality. However, these studies treat the development of the nuclear family as isolated from the social organization of racism. This work is missing an analysis of how these forces operate in the lives of women of colour.

While there is a recognition of the complexities of class and gender, these writers assume that these forces have organized familial relations in the same way for women of colour. Moreover, how racism has shaped the social organization of white male power, "Black" male power, wage labour, reproduction, and bourgeois morality are unexplored.

INTEGRATIVE PERSPECTIVES ON THE FAMILY

It was not until women of colour began to challenge mainstream feminist thought that the issue of racism was raised. Perhaps reflecting the importance of the family not only in feminist theorizing but also in all women's lives, women of colour began deconstructing mainstream feminist theories by pointing to the absence of an analysis of how racism alters women's experiences with the family.

In a series of articles, Amos and Parmar (1984), Bhavani and Coulson (1986), and hooks (1981) argue that in the context of a racist society, the family becomes not only a site of gender oppression but, as importantly, a refuge against racism. [...]

*****

[...] Collins (1990) and Das Gupta (1995) have pointed out, in the context of the historical inadequacy of the Black male wage and of high rates of Black female labour force participation rates, the ability to do unpaid domestic work becomes a form of resistance against racism.

*****

As a result, many writers rejected the idea that the family is the main institution that structures inequality for women of colour (see also Parmar 1985; Trivedi 1984; Bhavani and Coulson 1986; Ramazanoglu 1986; Kazi 1986; Lees 1986). Others, such as Collins (1990), and Das Gupta (1995), argue that while the family does operate differently in the lives of women of colour, it would be premature to deny that it does not also organize gender and sexual relations for women of colour [...]. One way to resolve this debate is to distinguish between how women of colour experience the family, and how the family is socially organized in communities of colour (see Collins 1990; Dua 1992). Das Gupta (1995) has called for work which identifies the historically specific characteristics of the institution of the family in communities of colour.

While very few studies have specifically focused on this question, there is a large body of historical research from which we can begin to discern how the family has been organized in Canadian communities of colour. This literature suggests that there are several important differences in how the institution of the family is organized in communities of colour. Das Gupta summarizes these differences, arguing that people of colour and immigrants have often been denied the right to live in a family context, or the right to have the "family" form of their choice, a denial that has been historically constructed by the Canadian state (1995, 142–4).

Indeed, the following examination of state policies towards familial relations in First Nations [...] communities supports this argument. [...] In [this] case, Canadian state managers have acted to destroy, prevent, or disrupt the ability of people of colour to participate in family relations. This body of research suggests that women of colour do experience the family in very different ways than women of European descent. Through this research we can begin to see the ways in which racism operates to (dis)organize familial and gender relations.

Both French and British colonizers undertook a series of campaigns to reconstruct familial relations in First Nations communities (Anderson 1991; Bourgeault 1988.) The attack on family forms in First Nations communities began in the seventeenth century when French colonial authorities through the missions identified the familial practices in First Nations communities as problematic. As Anderson (1991) shows, French colonizers were threatened by the social organization of social, gender, and sexual relations in First Nations communities: the economic, social, and political equality men and women possessed; the absence of hierarchal relationships; the personal freedom enjoyed by men and women; the existence of consensual conjugal relations, spousal autonomy, sexual freedom inside and outside marriage; the ease with which spousal relations could be ended; the indulgence of children; and absence of physical punishment [...].

In contrast, the world of the colonizers was hierarchial and patriarchal. Authority was vested in a few senior officers; soldiers and traders were subject to harsh discipline. French ideas of familial relations were bound by relations of authority, discipline, and dependency. As a result, the French colonizers, through the missions, undertook an active campaign to not only destroy gender, sexual, and familial relations in First Nations communities, but moreover to replace them with an alternate set of relationships organized around monogamy, patriarchy, and bounded by discipline and dependency (Andersen 1991). As Andersen (1991) suggests, the transformation of gender and familial relations was part of a larger project to bring First Nations people into the nexus of authoritarian and hierarchial relations of the colonial regime.

British colonizers also focused on familial relationships in First Nations communities. However, the focus shifted from an attempt to transform familial relations, to an attempt to disrupt the ability of First Nations people to participate in either European or First Nations patterns of families. As Ponting (1986) and Jamieson (1986) show, after 1806, customary marriages were outlawed by the North West Company. Several factors account for this change. First, as the fur trade declined in importance, and the Canadian economy shifted to agriculture production for the world market, the importance of the labour of First Nations people to the fur trade declined (Laxer 1973; Naylor 1975). Second, as Jamieson (1986) notes, there was a shift in British colonial policy after the Hudson Bay Company merged with the North West Company. During this period, trading companies were further tied to British imperial interests. These political and economic changes were accompanied by an increasing emphasis on British moral codes, especially class and racial classification codes. These changes meant that company officials, government representatives, and missionaries began to denounce interracial marriages in an effort to promote racial segregation. As Bourgeault suggests, the shift to a politics of racial purity needs to be located in the project of creating a white settler colony with political power in the hands of white settlers (Bourgeault 1988).

With Confederation, the politics of racial purity would not only encourage state officials to regulate intermarriages but also to regulate the ability of First Nations men and women to participate in familial relations. Under the policy of assimilation, government policies set out to destroy languages, familial relations, and community structures in these communities (Ponting 1986). A series of acts, culminating in the Indian Act of 1876, legislated the system of reservations and policies which regulated all aspects of social life in First Nations communities. State regulation focused on family forms. Residential schools and later child welfare policies were mechanisms used to destroy the fabric of social, familial, gender, and sexual relations. Through residential schools and child welfare agencies, children were forcibly separated from biological parents and First Nations communities. Notably, child welfare officers were most likely to remove these children from parents who did not conform to the norms of a patriarchal nuclear family (Locust 1990; Brant 1988). Monture-Angus (1995) has argued that the purpose behind such polices was not simply to alter family practices but to destroy the fabric of First Nations communities (Monture-Angus 1995; [...]). Thus, an examination of the institution of the family in First Nations communities demonstrates that colonial and Canadian state policies have often denied First Nations people the right to live in a family context and the right to have the "family" form of their choice.

*****

In the case of First Nations [...] communities, the state has spent considerable effort to target existing familial practices in these communities as problematic and developed strategies to eliminate such practices. In the case of First Nations communities, this involved replacing egalitarian or matrilineal familial relationships with patriarchal ones. [...] This body of research suggests that women of colour do experience the family in very different ways than women of European descent. This difference can be summed up quite simply: while the Canadian state has acted in ways to ensure the participation of white women in nuclear familial relations, the state has acted to restrict women of colour's ability to participate in familial relations.

While this body of work has been important for suggesting that race matters—that white women and women of colour have significantly different relationships to the institution of the family—it does not explain why race matters. In other words, what remains unexplained is why women of colour experience the family differently than white women. Why have Canadian state managers instituted policies which encourage white women to participate in nuclear family relations, yet been reluctant to ensure that women of colour do so? Ironically, by not asking why race matters, such an examination does not tell us much about how racism has shaped the social organization of familial and gender relations in Canada. Without such an analysis, the restrictions that people of colour have faced appear as deviations from the way in which the nuclear family operates in Canadian society.

TOWARDS A TRINITY—INTEGRATING RACE, PATRIARCHY, AND CAPITALISM: THEORIZING THE IMPACT OF RACISM ON THE FAMILY

In order to understand the ways in which racism has shaped the development of the nuclear family, we need to place it in the context of late nineteenth-century projects of nation-building. An emerging literature in sociology, history, political science, and post-colonial and feminist studies explores the connections between nationalism and the social construction of race and gender in metropolitan and colonial settings. Importantly for our purposes, this literature points to the ways in which nineteenth-century discourses of race influenced the social organization of capitalism, nations, bourgeois morality, and the nuclear family. During this period, as nations became constituted through a discourse of race, the nuclear family emerged as one of the main institutions for constructing a racialized and gendered nation-state. This link between the discourse of race, the nation, and the nuclear family explains why white women and women of colour experience the family differently.

Several important economic and political changes were taking place in the nineteenth century. In Europe, and many settler societies, this period was not only characterized by the consolidation of the capitalist mode of production, but also by the development of the nation-state. The emergence of the nation-state played an important role in ensuring capitalist relations of production. The spatial division of the world and the formation of a centralized political authority claiming sovereignty within each space allowed for the organization of wage labour and the consolidation of markets (see Corrigan and Sayer 1986; Hobsbawm 1990; Miles 1989). As importantly, this spatial division of the world into nations allowed for the consolidation of a bourgeois project (Stoler 1995; Hobsbawm 1990).

However, as nations are far from "natural," the consolidation of nation-states required reconstituting social identities. The emergence of many, though not all, nineteenth-century nations was accompanied by projects of nation-building. As Anderson (1983) points out, these projects focused on creating an "imagined community," where members of a nation-state acquired a sense of fraternity with an extended community based on an emotional sense of shared distinctiveness. As Gellner (1983), Anderson (1983), and Hobsbawm (1990) show, despite the allegory of a historical continuum, national identities are a product of nation-states, rather than vice versa. Balibar (1991) suggests that in order to promote such a sense of distinctiveness, nineteenth-century nationalists promoted a sense of a "fictive ethnicity," the notion that

members of nation-states share a pre-existing unity with others who are part of the nation-state.

Historically, the discourse of race has played a significant role in the construction of a fictive ethnicity or national identity. As several writers have illustrated, in both metropolis and colonial settings, nineteenth-century nationalists often employed notions of race to imagine the nation (Miles 1989; Balibar 1991; Huttenback 1976; McClintock 1995; Stoler 1995). [...]

*****

The discourse of race allowed nationalists to put forward four interconnected representations of the nation. First, that a nation was composed of naturally occurring distinct populations. Second, the discourse of race allowed the distinct character of each nation to be located in biology—an inborn national spirit—so that each nation came to be seen as composed of races, of people who were biologically distinct from those in other nations. Third, as citizens of a nation-state came to be defined as belonging to a common race, nations came to be represented as natural and inevitable. Fourth, the discursive construction of the nation as composed of a common race linked such nationalist projects into a politics of racial purity, as nationalists argued that the biological stock of a nation needed to be protected, otherwise the nation would decline. In the language of the period, nationalists argued that nations need to be guarded against "race deterioration" or "race degeneration" (see Davin 1978; Valverde 1991; McLaren 1990).

*****

Importantly, in both metropolitan and settler settings, this discourse shaped how national identities were constituted, for it tied those who resided within a nation-state together through the metaphors of blood, inborn essences, and biology. It is this racialized process of constituting national identities that underpins the institutionalization of the nuclear family in metropolitan and settler settings. For, a nation that imagines itself on the basis of race, in its imagining redefines the family and gender relations within the family. As Balibar (1991) points out, a nation which is constituted through the imagery of a racial community has a tendency to present itself through the common envelope of family relations, or as one big family. Indeed, in nineteenth-century nationalist discourses, the icon of family became a powerful symbol through which national identities were constructed and where individuals were tied to the nation through a national genealogy.

As importantly, as national identities were constituted through the metaphors of blood, inborn essences, and biology, the nuclear family and its associated set of gender and sexual relations would become the anchoring point for a racialized nation. Balibar (1991) suggests that in a racialized nation, the importance of the family does not derive solely from the role it plays in the reproduction of labour, but from its role in physically reproducing the nation. Nations that are based on the notion of racially distinct groups require that such distinct groups be physically reproduced. By the end of the nineteenth century, in most metropolitan and white settler colonies, the importance of "race instinct for reproduction" (cited in McLaren 1990, 21) was an accepted notion (also see Valverde 1992).

*****

It is in this context that the nuclear family became entrenched. As the racialized and classed (re)production of the nation was not something nationalists could take for granted, nationalists focused considerable attention reorganizing familial relations, particularly in ensuring that the nuclear family and its concomitant racial, gender, sexual relations were adopted by those women deemed important for the reproduction of the nation. Eugenicists such as Lochhead systematically advocated that improving the race called for "more stringent marriage laws" (cited in McLaren 1990, 13). Eugenicists were not alone in advocating the institutionalization of the nuclear family. In the context of the moral panic over racial degeneration, several agents,

ranging from social reformers to state managers, argued that the nuclear family was central to national strength and vitality (see Davin 1978; McLaren 1990; Ursel 1992; Valverde 1992)

The institutionalization of the nuclear family allowed nationalists to organize race, class, gender, and sexuality according to the racialized nationalist project. Foremost, the institutionalization of the family allowed nationalists to entrench the class character of the nation-state. As Ursel (1992), Valverde (1992), and Stoler (1995) show, the fear of race deterioration allowed social reformers and state managers to link the nuclear family and its associated gender relations to bourgeois morality. As the racial stock of working-class women was suspect (see also Davin 1978; McLaren 1990), nationalists, eugenicists and social reformers argued that no matter what the costs, middle-class women needed to focus their energies on reproducing a racialized and classed citizenry.

This bourgeois project was not simply based on the notion of racial purity. It was also based on notions of colonized people. As Stoler has suggested, both the construction of bourgeois civility and the racial inferiority of the working class were juxtaposed against the inferiority of colonized peoples and the threat that they posed to the racial vitality of a nation (Stoler 1995; Huttenback 1976; Miles 1989). The danger posed by colonized people depended on the setting. In the metropolis, as Davin (1978), Ware (1992), and Stoler (1995) have shown, the dangers of racial deterioration were placed in the context of imperialism. As population was linked to power, the ability of white, middle-class women to reproduce a virile race was widely perceived as paramount to the imperial strength and success. Childbearing and improving the racial stock became not just a national but also an imperial duty. As a British nationalist proclaimed in 1909, "the history of nations is determined not on the battlefields but in the nursery, and the battalions which give lasting victory are the battalion of babies. The politics of the future will be domestics" (cited in Davin 1978, 29).

*****

To reproduce the class and racial character of the nation, nationalists needed to transform gender and sexual practices. Most importantly, gender practices within bourgeois households needed to be reorganized so that white, bourgeois women's labour was tied to the (re)production of the nation. Several writers have demonstrated how in this period white bourgeois women came to be seen as exalted breeders of a virile race of nation- and empire-builders, as "mothers of the nation" (see Burton 1994; Yuval-Davis and Anthias 1989). New emerging ideologies of motherhood allowed this to take place. These ideologies of motherhood, domesticity, and childbearing stressed the importance of white bourgeois women's work in preserving the race and nation. According to a writer of a manual on motherhood published in 1911, "If every woman who takes upon herself the sacred relationship of motherhood could be led to realize how she is responsible for the future of the baby-life, and the true greatness of the individual constitutes the true grandeur of nations, we should have healthier babies and happier homes, and the disintegration of family life would be a menace no more" (cited in Davin 1978, 24).

In the emerging rhetoric, white, bourgeois women were not only responsible for physically reproducing the nation but also for socially re-producing a generation of empire-builders. Davin (1978) illustrates that as theories of eugenics were used to bolster ideas of innate superiority of the white race in the late nineteenth century, the ideology of motherhood was redefined so that it was the duty and destiny of women not only to breed but also to raise healthy members of the race. As she states, "a responsible mother would study expert opinion so that the eugeni-cally conceived baby would be reared to its best advantage" (1978, 21). The emerging ideology of femininity tied bourgeois women to raising citizens for the nation. A nineteenth-century child welfare manual warned, "the child of today will be the citizen of the coming years and must take up duties of statesmanship, defence from foes, the conduct of labour, the direction of progress ... and all other necessities for the perpetuation of an imperial race" (cited in Davin 1978, 43).

*****

In British, white settler colonies (Canada, South Africa, Australia, New Zealand, and the United States), nationalist projects had a more complex racial politics. While white, working-class people were suspect, the racial inferiority of people of colour was immutable. Nationalists and eugenicists pointed out that the inclusion of colonized people made race deterioration an immediate threat. In these cases, nationalist projects were based on the creation of a white settler society. Foremost, this involved the marginalization of indigenous peoples from the emerging body politic, which involved legal, residential, and social separation. This included legal regulations of interracial sexuality. They also were characterized by settlement and immigration policies that recruited suitable "white" settlers and excluded people of colour. Eugenicists preached the danger of waves of "defective immigrants" for racial deteriora-tion (in Canada, see McLaren 1990; Valverde 1991). However, while white, working-class immigrants were suspect, people of colour were defined as truly dangerous foreigners. In Canada, as well as other settler colonies, racial purity was premised on the Asian peril—the danger of Anglo-Saxons being overrun by more fertile races (see Roy 1989; Valverde 1991; Dua forthcoming). As a result, a series of immigra-tion and naturalization regulations prevented Asians from entering Canada.

*****

Not only would the discourse of race shape the organization of the nuclear family and its associated gender and sexual relations, more-over, nation-building projects would racialize the institution of the family itself. By the end of the nineteenth century, the family would be-come a symbolic signifier of national difference. McClintock (1995) shows that the institution of the nuclear family was employed to construct notions of modernity and progress. In colonial-ist narratives, the nuclear family was employed to construct a discourse of racial superiority as it was tied to civilization, superiority, and whiteness. In contrast, symbols of alternative familial and gender relationship were employed to represent colonized people as backwards, arrested, natural, and in an unreasonable state of savagery. Projecting the emergence of the nuclear family into a discourse of national and imperial progress enabled colonial administrators to legitimate colonialism as modernizing, progressive, and as the unfolding of natural decree. McClintock points out that after 1850, the image of the natural patriarchal family in alliance with social Darwinism came to constitute the organizing trope for marshalling an array of societies into a single global narrative, ordered and managed by Europeans (1995, 21–51).

*****

In this context, women of colour threatened the racialized project of nation-building in several ways. As the social organization of reproduction in the racialized nation was premised on the politics of racial purity, women of colour's reproductive activities posed a threat to the nation. In contrast to the exalted fertility of white, middle-class women, women of colour were depicted in the iconography of degeneration. In Canada, First Nations and Chinese women were linked to primitive sexuality (Roy 1989; Valverde 1991), while the submissiveness of Hindu women was linked to a decline into premodern conditions (Dua 1998). While white bourgeois women were racially gendered as mothers of the nation, colonized women were racially gendered as dangerous to the nation-state.

In the racialized narrative of the family, women became symbolic boundary markers of nations and empires (Yuval Davis and Anthias 1989; McClintock 1995). As colonial women and colonial patterns of gender relations became associated with power and progress, colonized women and colonized patterns of gender relations became associated with degeneracy and inferiority. Departures from bourgeois patterns of family life by colonized women were used to define these women simultaneously as racially inferior, in need of colonial relationships, and a danger to the nation-state and empire.

CONCLUSION

It is only by integrating the interconnections between the discourse of race and the forces of capitalism, imperialism, nation-building, and bourgeois morality that we can understand the emergence of the nuclear family and its concomitant gender and sexual relations. In important ways, the racialized projects of nation-building and imperialism both underpin the emergence of the nuclear family and shapes its associated gender and sexual relations. [...] The nuclear family was crucial to constituting the nation-state; projects of nationalism have been central in institutionalizing the nuclear family.

Through an exploration of the interconnections between nation-building, the politics of racial purity, and the nuclear family we can explain why white women and women of colour experience the family differently. As projects of nation-building were constituted on a discourse of race, the nuclear family organized gender and sexual relations to ensure a racialized nation. The nuclear family not only regulated gender relations in society, it also regulated race relations. In this process white women and women of colour were racially gendered in starkly different ways. White women were racially gendered as mothers of the nation whose participation in the nuclear family was crucial for the (re)production of the nation. In contrast, women of colour were racially gendered as posing a triple threat to the racialized nation as they could not reproduce a white population, allowed for the possibility of interracial sexuality, and challenged, by their presence within the nation-state, the very racialized moral order that the nuclear family was to protect. Given this, it is not surprising that the Canadian state has both disrupted the ability of women of colour to participate in families and systematically attacked alternative ways of organizing familial relations.

NOTES

1. In this paper, following Miles (1989), I will define the discourse of race as the idea that human beings can be categorized into biologically distinct populations; racism as a representational form which by designating discrete human collectivities, necessarily functions as an ideology of inclusion and exclusion; and systemic discrimination as the exclusionary practices that arise from a racist discourse.

2. Despite their limitations, I will use the terms white women and women of colour. As we shall see, whiteness and colour were two of the crucial signifiers for racializing women. This process of racialization led white women and women of colour to be treated in radically different ways. As we shall see, this is not to deny that both categories hide other forms of racial distinctions.

3. Nicholson (1997) has recently pointed out that it was not until the post-war era that the nuclear family became a mass phenomenon. It would be the boom of the 1950s that was accompanied by an increase in real wages that would allow white, working-class Americans to live in separate households.

REFERENCES

Amos, Valerie, and Pratibha Parmar. "Challenging Imperial Feminism." *Feminist Review*, vol. 17 (1984): 3–19.

Anderson, Benedict. *Imagined Communities: Reflections on the Origins and Spread of Nationalism*. London: Verso, 1983.

Anderson, Karen. *Chain by Her Foot: The Subjection of Native Women in Seventeenth-Century New France*. New York: Routledge, 1991.

Armstrong, Pat, and Hugh Armstrong. *The Double Ghetto: Canadian Women and Their Segregated Work*. Toronto: McClelland & Stewart, 1984.

Balibar, Etienne. "The Nation Form: History and Ideology." In *Race, Nation, Class*, eds. Etienne Balibar and Immanuel Wallerstem. London: Verso, 1991.

Barrett, Michele, and Mary McIntosh. *The Anti-Social Family*. London: Verso, 1982.

Benston, Margaret. "The Political Economy of Women's Liberation." *Monthly Review*, vol. 21 (Sept. 1969): 13–27.

Bhavnani, Kum-Kum, and Margaret Coulson. "Transforming Socialist-Feminism: The Challenge of Racism." *Feminist Review*, vol. 23 (1986): 81–92.

Bourgeault, Ron. "Race and Class under Mercantilism: Indigenous People in Nineteenth-Century Canada." In *Racial Oppression in Canada*, eds. Singh Bolaria and Peter Li. Toronto: Garamond Press, 1988.

Bradbury, Bettina. "The Fragmented Family: Family Strategies in the Face of Death, Illness, and Poverty, Montreal, 1860–1885." In *Childhood and Family in Canadian History*, ed. Joy Parr. Toronto: McClelland & Stewart, 1982.

Brant, Beth. "A Long Story." In *A Gathering of Spirit*, ed. Beth Brant. Toronto: Women's Press, 1988.

Burton, Antoinette. *Burdens of History: British Feminists, Indian Women, and Imperial Culture, 1865–1915*. Chapel Hill: University of North Carolina Press, 1994.

Collins, Patricia. *Black Feminist Thought*. Boston: Unwin Hyman, 1990.

Coontz, Stephanie, and Peta Henderson. *Women's Work: The Origins of Gender and Class*. London: Verso, 1986.

Corrigan, P., and D. Sayer. *The Great Arch: English State Formation as Cultural Revolution*. Oxford: Basil Blackwell, 1986.

Dalla Costa, Mariarosa. *Women and the Subversion of the Community*. Bristol: Falling Wall Press, 1972.

Das Gupta, Tania. "Families of Native Peoples, Immigrants, and People of Colour." In *Canadian Families: Diversity, Conflict and Change*, eds. Nancy Mandell and Ann Duffy. Toronto: Harcourt Brace, 1995.

Davin, Anna. "Motherhood and Imperialism." *History Workshop 5* (1978): 9–57.

Dua, Enakshi. "Racism or Gender: Understanding Gender Oppression of South-Asian Canadian Women." *Canadian Woman Studies*, vol. 13, no. 1 (1992): 6–10.

———. "The Hindu Woman's Question: Canadian Nation-Building and the Social Construction of Gender for South Asian-Canadian Women." In *Canadian Reader on Anti-Racism*, eds. George Dei and Agnes Calliste. Toronto: University of Toronto Press, forthcoming.

Dubinsky, Karen. "'Maidenly Girls' or 'Designing Women'? The Crime of Seduction in Turn-of-the-Century Toronto." In *Gender Conflicts: New Essays in Women's History*, eds. Franca Iacovetta and Mariana Valverde. Toronto: University of Toronto Press, 1992.

Eisenstein, Zillah. *Capitalist Patriarchy and the Case for Socialist Feminism*. New York: Monthly Review Press, 1979.

Firestone, Shulamith. *The Dialectic of Sex: The Case for Feminist Revolution*. New York: William Morrow, 1970.

Friedan, Betty. *The Feminist Mystique*. New York: Penguin, 1963.

Fox, Bonnie. *Hidden in the Household: Women's Domestic Labour under Capitalism*. Toronto: Women's Press, 1980.

———. "Conceptualizing 'Patriarchy.'" *Canadian Review of Sociology and Anthropology*, vol. 25, no. 2 (1988): 273–84.

Gellner, Ernest. *Nations and Nationalism*. Oxford: Basil and Blackwell, 1983.

Hobsbawm, Eric. *Nations and Nationalism Since 1780*. Cambridge: Cambridge University Press, 1990.

hooks, bell. *Ain't I a Woman: Black Women and Feminism*. Boston: South End Press, 1981.

Huttenback, Robert. *Racism and Empire*. Ithaca: Cornell University Press, 1976.

Jamieson, Kathleen. "Sex Discrimination and the Indian Act." In *Arduous Journey: Canadian Indians and Decolonization*, ed. J.R. Ponting. Toronto: McClelland & Stewart, 1986.

Kazi, Hamida. "The Beginning of a Debate Long Due: Some Observations on Ethnocentrism and Socialist Feminist Theory." *Feminist Review*, vol. 17 (1986).

Laxer, Robert. *(Canada) Limited: The Political Economy of Dependency*. Toronto: McClelland & Stewart, 1973.

Lees, Sue. "Sex, Race and Culture: Feminism and the Limits of Cultural Pluralism." *Feminist Review*, vol. 17 (1986): 92–102.

Locust, Carol. "Discrimination against American Indian Families in Child Abuse Cases." *Indian Child Welfare Digest* (1990): 7–9.

Mandell, Nancy, and Ann Duffy. *Canadian Families: Diversity, Conflict and Change*. Toronto: Harcourt Brace, 1995.

Marks, Lynne. "The 'Hallelujah Lasses': Working-Class Women in the Salvation Army in English Canada, 1882–92." In *Gender Conflicts: New Essays in Women's History*, eds. Franca Iacovetta and Mariana Valverde. Toronto: University of Toronto Press, 1992.

McClintock, Anne. *Imperial Leather: Race, Gender and Sexuality in the Colonial Conquest*. London: Routledge, 1995.

McLaren, Angus. *Our Own Master Race: Eugenics in Canada, 1885–1945*. Toronto: McClelland & Stewart, 1990.

Miles, Robert. *Racism*. London: Routledge, 1989.

Monture-Angus, Patricia. *Thunder in My Soul: A Mohawk Woman Speaks*. Halifax, Nova Scotia: Fernwood Publishing, 1995.

Naylor, Tom. *The History of Canadian Business, 1867–1914*. 2nd ed. Toronto: McClelland & Stewart, 1975.

Nicholson, Linda. "The Myth of the Traditional Family." In *Feminism and Families*, ed. Hilde L. Nelson. London: Routledge, 1997.

Okin, Susan. "Families and Feminist Theory: Some Past and Present Issues." In *Feminism and Families*, ed. Hilde L. Nelson. London: Routledge, 1997.

Parmar, Prathiba. "Gender, Race, and Class: Asian Women in Resistance." In *The Empire Strikes Back: Race and Racism in 70s Britain*. The Centre for Contemporary Studies. London: Hutchinson, 1985.

Ponting, Rick. *Arduous Journey: Canadian Indians and Decolonization*. Toronto: McClelland & Stewart, 1986.

Pupo, Norene. "Preserving Patriarchy: Women, the Family and the State." In *Reconstructing the Canadian Family: Feminist Perspectives*, eds. Nancy Mandell and Ann Duffy. Toronto: Butterworths, 1988.

Ramazanoglu, Caroline. "Ethnocentrism and Socialist Feminist Theory: A Response to Barrett and McIntosh." *Feminist Review*, vol. 22 (1986): 83–86.

Roy, Patricia. *White Canada Forever*. Vancouver: University of British Columbia Press, 1989.

Seccomb, Wally. "The Expanded Reproduction Cycle of Labour in 20th-Century Capitalism." In *Hidden in the Household*, ed. Bonnie Fox. Toronto: Women's Press, 1980.

Stoler, Ann Laura. *Race and the Education of Desire.* Durham: Duke University Press, 1995.

Trivedi, Parita. "To Deny Our Fullness: Asian Women in the Making of History. *Feminist Review*, vol. 17 (1984): 37–48.

Ursel, Jane. *Private Lives, Public Policy.* Toronto: Women's Press, 1992.

Valverde, Mariana. *The Age of Light, Soap, and Water: Moral Reform in English Canada, 1885–1925.* Toronto: McClelland & Stewart, 1991.

———. "'When the Mother of the Race is Free': Race, Reproduction, and Sexuality in First-Wave Feminism." In *Gender Conflicts: New Essays in Women's History*, eds. Franca Iacovetta and Mariana Valverde. Toronto: University of Toronto Press, 1992.

Ware, Vron. *Beyond the Pale: White Women, Racism and History.* London: Verso, 1992.

Yuval-Davis, Nira, and Floya Anthias, eds. *Women-Nation-State.* London: MacMillan Press, 1989.

DISCUSSION QUESTIONS: DOUCET

1. Doucet argues that stay-at-home fathers are creating new forms of masculinity that are enacted against the backdrop of hegemonic masculinity. Explain the details of this argument, drawing on empirical details provided in the article.

2. The men in Doucet's study experienced a loss of masculinity with a loss of paid employment. How did they retrieve that sense of masculinity in the context of their unpaid caring work, and what implications do those efforts have on gender relations in their families?

3. What social policy recommendations does Doucet make based on her understandings of stay-at-home fathers and their impact on current dominant gender relations? Why?

DISCUSSION QUESTIONS: DUA

1. Outline the dominant feminist explanations of how the nuclear family emerged as a sexist institution.

2. What challenges did anti-racist feminists pose to those dominant explanations of the historical development of the nuclear family? What difference do these challenges make for theorizing women's position in the family?

3. Explain what role the Canadian state played in the development of the nuclear family as a racist and sexist social institution.

FURTHER READINGS

1. Baker, Christina Looper, and Christina Baker Kline. 1996. *The Conversation Begins: Mothers and Daughters Talk about Living Feminism.* New York: Bantam Books.
   This book explores the parental relationship between 23 pioneering American feminists and their third wave daughters, including the tensions and satisfactions these mothers experienced as they raised children according to feminist principles. Interviews with both daughters and mothers reveal that the experiment was both painful and rewarding, giving them opportunities to assess early feminist mandates for family life as they define new agendas for the future.

2. Bell-Scott, Patricia, Beverly Guy-Sheftall, Jacqueline DeCosta Willis, and Lucie Fultz (eds). 1991. *Double Stitch: Black Women Write about Mothers and Daughters*. Boston: Beacon Press.

   Maya Angelou provides a foreword to this collection of 47 stories, poems, and essays written by African American feminists about their mother-daughter relationships. Well-known authors such as bell hooks, June Jordan, Audre Lorde, Sonia Sanchez, Alice Walker, and Patricia Hill-Collins highlight the dynamics of Black family life, Black lesbian families, and Black women's relationships with familial men.

3. Mernissi, Fatima. 1994. *Dreams of Trespass: Tales of a Harem Girlhood*. New York: Perseus Books.

   In this memoir, Mernissi constructs a rich narrative of her childhood in Fez, Morocco, which was largely lived inside the gates of a domestic harem. She details her life there, as well as those of the other women in her family, who found imaginative ways of informing themselves about the world and enacting agency in it. It is a provocative and informative story of an extended family of Muslim women who use their material and mental resources to forge satisfying gendered lives in a mid-century Islamic context.

4. Nelson, F. 1996. *Lesbian Motherhood: An Exploration of Canadian Lesbian Families*. Toronto: University of Toronto Press.

   Based on interviews with lesbian mothers in Canada, this groundbreaking study explores several topics related to this non-traditional family form, including reproductive decision making, the social context of lesbian mothering, strategies of child rearing and step-parenting, and the sharing of domestic and parenting roles.

5. Ouzgane, Lahoucine (ed.). 2006. *Islamic Masculinities*. London: Zed Books.

   While much scholarly attention is paid to understanding femininity in the Middle East and North Africa, very little has been devoted to studies of Islamic masculinity. This edited collection gathers together previously published material on this topic that analyzes how masculinities are integral to gender relations in Muslim cultures in the modern Middle East, especially within the context of the family. For articles specifically addressing masculinity and the family, see chapters 5, 9, 10, 11, and 12.

RELEVANT FILMS

1. *Gender Wars* (Part 6 of *The Human Sexes*), 1997, 50 minutes, The Learning Channel

   In this documentary, Desmond Morris, the author of the book of the same name, travels the world looking at modern vestiges of ancient male dominance over women in the context of the family, such as wedding rings and the annual wife-carrying contest in Finland. Morris also chronicles the rise of the 20th-century feminist movement, beginning with a drive for women's suffrage and equality within the family.

2. *Full Circle*, 1995, 58 minutes, Filmmakers Library

   The first settlers on Israeli Kibbutzim adhered to the ideal of gender equality. Consequently, women participated fully in the economic and work life of these communities, and were not solely responsible for child rearing. However, in the 1960s the children of these women reinstated a traditional gender division of labour. Without women's participation in the sphere of production, the original egalitarian gender ideals of the community have been compromised, if not lost.

3. *Divorce Iranian Style*, 1998. 80 minutes, Women Make Movies

   This hilarious yet tragic view of an Iranian divorce court gives an intimate perspective on the domestic lives of Iranian women. Women filing for divorce due to abuse, estrangement, and emotional dissatisfaction use all their strength and ingenuity to get custody of their children, as well as their marriage money in the face of patriarchal laws, judges, and family members. The film dispels any sense we might have of Muslim women as passive victims of Islamic social systems.

4. *Fatherhood USA: Juggling Family and Work*, 1998, 60 minutes, The Fatherhood Project

   Men are traditionally understood as breadwinners in the context of the nuclear family, while women take on the reproductive domestic duties. But this film documents the lives of three men in the United

States who chose to stay home and raise their children rather than build a career. They each discuss how this choice has impacted their lives, including their self-conceptions as fathers and the new opportunities this work provides them.

5. *The Double Shift*, 1994, 47 minutes, Films for the Humanities and Sciences

Most women who participate in paid employment work a double shift, one outside the home and another inside the home for which they are not paid. This documentary, by examining that reality in detail, raises questions about the possibility of gender equality in the face of this intersection between family and work life.

RELEVANT WEB SITES

1. www.undp.org/rblac/gender/legislation/

This site is entitled *Gender and Legislation in Latin America and the Caribbean*. Once you're at the site, link to "Gender and Family," where you'll find an overview of the relationship between gender and family, a definition of family, the constitution of family in Latin American and the Caribbean, and a discussion of gender discrimination in marriage, reproductive rights, and existing legislation at the national and international levels related to gender and family. Importantly, the site includes an agenda for advancing the equality of women within the family in this context.

2. www12.statcan.ca/english/censuso1/products/analytic/companion/fam/contents.cfm

The Statistics Canada Web site lists results on "family" from the most recent Canadian census of 2001. It includes information on trends in the constitution of families in Canada, family size, and the division of household responsibilities at the federal, provincial, and sub-provincial levels.

3. http://web.uvic.ca/hrd/cfpl

The Canadian Families Project is a research project based at the University of Victoria in British Columbia. The researchers involved in the project study families in Canada, in particular the historical discourses of family; class, ethnicity, and religion as they relate to the family; the history of single parenthood and "fragmented" families; fertility decline; language, education, and the family; religion and family; families in rural and urban Canadian settings; and family income and standards of living.

4. www.apa.org/pi/parent.html

This Web site on *Lesbian and Gay Parenting*, constructed by Charlotte Patterson from the University of Virginia, reviews research findings on lesbian and gay parenting to ameliorate the negative effects of the prejudices that are often experienced by members of this family form. Dr. Patterson also supplies an excellent annotated bibliography on this body of research.

5. www.brandeis.edu/projects/fse/Pages/linksislam.html

The Feminist Sexual Ethics Project site provides an ISLAM link to various articles and resources relating to women, gender and Islam, including family issues such as veiling, Islamic family law, domestic violence, honour killings, and queer Muslim families.

PART IV

GENDERED BODIES

People tend to speak of their bodies as private possessions they control completely, or, conversely, as biological entities that are utterly outside their sphere of influence. Feminists claim that both of these stances are inaccurate. Instead they argue that bodies are socially constructed with our active participation; we inscribe them with a wide range of already available cultural signs that usually express well-established social norms and practices related to gender, sexuality, race, etc. In this way, our bodies are social texts whose meaning and significance are shaped by particular cultural ideals that affect how we experience our bodies and how they are interpreted or "read" by others in particular cultural contexts. Not only will different social conceptions of the body affect how individuals in different times and places experience their bodies, but the meaning of the body can also vary within a society according to an individual's gender, age, ability, class, sexual orientation, and race.

Historically, as these readings show, women's bodies have been significantly more vulnerable than men's to cultural ideals that include extreme forms of bodily manipulation and control. Strategies of control such as corsets, foot-binding, high heels, and enforced motherhood (through prohibited contraception) discipline and regulate women's bodies to maintain gendered power relations. Therefore, feminists understand the body as a site of political domination and struggle. They protest the cultural constraints placed on women's bodies, including ideals and regimes of feminine beauty, and argue for women's rightful control of their own bodies.

The first reading is taken from Rose Weitz's book *The Politics of Women's Bodies: Sexuality, Appearance and Behaviour*. In this chapter, she outlines a short history of women's bodies, beginning with women's legal status as property in the earliest written legal codes. Moving through the 18th and 19th centuries, when enslaved African American women were freed and suffrage movements won White women the right to vote and go to school, Weitz discusses how each of these social changes related to women's bodies challenged power relations between women and men in American society, which incited new patriarchal counter-reactions, new incursions on women's bodies such as gynecological surgeries. These shifting strategies of bodily control helped foster the women's movement in which feminists of different theoretical stripes challenged accepted ideas about women's bodies, appearance, and social position.

Jacqueline Urla and Alan Swedlund draw our attention to one of the most predominant of these strategies of bodily control for women: embodied norms of feminine beauty. They begin by noting how many women in the United States perceive their bodies as defective, as never feminine enough to meet the criteria for socially acceptable femininity. These idealized notions of femininity have a long and shifting history that has been shaped by images from high art, science, and popular culture. Urla and Swedlund focus on the domain of pop culture to investigate the role the Barbie doll has played in determining what counts as a desirable body for women.

The third reading continues this feminist examination of the cultural ideals and social regulation of embodied femininity, but this time through a comparative cross-cultural analysis. During Fatima Mernissi's Western tour to promote her book *Dreams of Trespass: Tales of a Harem Girlhood*, she was surprised to learn of Western harems. In *Scheherazade Goes West: Different Cultures, Different Harems* she presents her observations about Western harems, drawing on her experience as a Moroccan feminist and professor of Sociology who was raised in a harem in Fez. In this particular chapter she juxtaposes gender relations in Europe with those in the Muslim world in terms of women's clothing, showing how the obligatory size 6 for Western women is as much a gendered bodily constraint as any Muslim harem.

Expanding notions of gendered embodiment beyond cultural ideals of femininity and beauty, feminist lawyer Fiona Sampson focuses on how women with disabilities in Canada are affected by the workings of the capitalist economy in the current era of globalization. These women are disadvantaged in this context as they seek employment in a shrinking job market and work in insecure jobs with low wages. They also must deal with the problems of government downsizing and the association of state and familial dependency with personal culpability in a neo-liberal socio-economic era, all of which compounds the effects of economic restructuring on disabled women. Sampson concludes her analysis by discussing two strategies for advancing the equality rights of women with disabilities in light of the threats posed by economic globalization.

As I mention above, gender relations pertain to masculinity as much as femininity. Well-known American feminist theorist of the body, Susan Bordo, in her piece *Pills and Power Tools*, relates masculinity and embodiment in this short comment on the prominence of Viagara advertising in North America, which implicitly invokes the gendered horror of men's impotence and consequent lack of masculinity and sexual virility. In this advertising, as well as in movies, television shows, and music videos, men's bodies (especially their penises) are portrayed as power tools that guarantee perpetual performance as a feature of masculinity. Viagara promises performance whenever masculine failure threatens. But Bordo argues that, rather than popping pills, men should deconstruct and actively resist the gendered expectation that they should be always already prepared to perform like power tools.

CHAPTER 11

A HISTORY OF WOMEN'S BODIES

Rose Weitz

Throughout history, ideas about women's bodies have played a dramatic role in either challenging or reinforcing power relationships between men and women. We can therefore regard these ideas as political tools in an ongoing political struggle. This article presents a brief history of women's bodies, looking at how ideas about the female body have changed over time in western law and biological theory.

Beginning with the earliest written legal codes, and continuing nearly to the present day, the law typically has defined women's bodies as men's property. In ancient societies, women who were not slaves typically belonged to their fathers before marriage and to their husbands thereafter. For this reason, Babylonian law, for example, treated rape as a form of property damage, requiring a rapist to pay a fine to the husband or father of the raped woman, but nothing to the woman herself. Similarly, marriages in ancient societies typically were contracted between prospective husbands and prospective fathers-in-law, with the potential bride playing little, if any, role.

Women's legal status as property reflected the belief that women's bodies were inherently different from men's in ways that made women both defective and dangerous. This belief comes through clearly in the writings of Aristotle,

whose ideas about women's bodies formed the basis for "scientific" discussion of this topic in the west from the fourth century B.C. through the eighteenth century (Martin 1987; Tuana 1993). Aristotle's biological theories centered around the concept of heat. According to Aristotle, only embryos that had sufficient heat could develop into fully human form. The rest became female. In other words, woman was, in Aristotle's words, a "misbegotten man" and a "monstrosity"—less than fully formed and literally half-baked. Building on this premise, Galen, a highly influential Greek doctor, later declared that women's reproductive organs were virtually identical to men's, but were located internally because female embryos lacked the heat needed for those organs to develop fully and externally. This view remained common among doctors until well into the eighteenth century.

Lack of heat, classical scholars argued, also produced a plethora of other deficiencies in women, including a smaller stature, a frailer constitution, a less developed brain, and emotional and moral weaknesses that could endanger any men who fell under women's spell. These ideas later would resonate with ideas about women embedded in Christian interpretations of Mary and Eve. Christian theologians argued that Eve caused the fall from divine grace and the expulsion from the Garden of Eden by succumbing when the snake tempted her with the forbidden fruit. This "original sin" occurred, these theologians argued, because women's nature made them inherently more susceptible to sexual desire and other passions of the flesh, blinding them to reason and morality and making them a constant danger to men's souls. Mary avoided the pitfalls of passion only by remaining virginal. Such ideas later would play a large role in fueling the witchcraft hysteria in early modern Europe and colonial America. Women formed the vast majority of the tens of thousands of people executed as witches during these centuries because both Protestants and Catholics assumed that women were less intelligent than men, more driven by sexual passions, and hence more susceptible to the Devil's blandishments (Barstow 1994).

By the eighteenth century, women's legal and social position in the western world had changed little. When the famous English legal theorist, Sir William Blackstone, published his encyclopedic codification of English law in 1769, non-slave women's legal status still remained closer to that of property than to that of non-slave men. According to Blackstone, "By marriage, the husband and wife are one person in the law; that is, the very being and legal existence of the woman is suspended during the marriage, or at least is incorporated into that of her husband under whose wing, protection and cover she performs everything" (1904, 432). In other words, upon marriage a woman experienced "civil death," losing any rights as a citizen, including the right to own or bestow property, make contracts or sue for legal redress, hold custody of minor children, or keep any wages she earned. Moreover, as her "protector," a husband had a legal right to beat his wife if he believed it necessary, as well as a right to her sexual services. These principles would form the basis of marital law in the United States from its founding.

Both in colonial America and in the United States for its first 89 years, slave women were property. Moreover, both the law and contemporary scientific writings often described African-American women (and men) as animals,

rather than humans. Consequently, neither slave women nor slave men held any rights of citizenship. By the same token, female African-American slaves were completely subject to their white masters. Rape was common, both as a form of "entertainment" for white men and as a way of breeding more slaves, since the children of slave mothers were automatically slaves, regardless of their fathers' race. Nor did African-American women's special vulnerability to rape end when slavery ended.

Both before and after the Civil War, the rape of African-American women was explained, if not justified, by an ideology that defined African-Americans, including African-American women, as animalistically hypersexual, and thus responsible for their own rapes (Gilman 1985; Giddings 1995). For example, an article published by a white southern woman on March 17, 1904 in a popular periodical, the *Independent*, declared:

> Degeneracy is apt to show most in the weaker individuals of any race; so Negro women evidence more nearly the popular idea of total depravity than the men do. They are so nearly lacking in virtue that the color of a Negro woman's skin is generally taken (and quite correctly) as a guarantee of her immorality.... I sometimes read of a virtuous Negro woman, hear of them, but the idea is absolutely inconceivable to me.

These ideas about sexuality, combined with ideas about the inherent inferiority of African Americans, are vividly reflected in the 1861 Georgia penal code. That code left it up to the court whether to fine or imprison men who raped African-American women, recommended two to 20 years' imprisonment for white men convicted of raping white women, and mandated the death penalty for African-American men convicted of raping white women (Roberts 1990, 60). Moreover, African-American men typically were lynched before being brought to trial if suspected of raping a white woman, while white men were rarely convicted for raping white women and probably never convicted for raping African-American women.

For both free and slave women in the United States, the legal definition of women's bodies as men's property experienced its first serious challenges during the nineteenth century. In 1839, Mississippi passed the first Married Women's Property Act. Designed primarily to protect family farms and property from creditors rather than to expand the rights of women (Speth 1982), the law gave married women the right to retain property they owned before marriage and wages they earned outside the home. By the end of the nineteenth century, similar laws had been passed in all the states.

Also during the 19th century, both white and African-American women won the right to vote in Wyoming, Utah, Colorado, and Idaho, and a national suffrage campaign took root. Beginning with Oberlin College in 1833, a growing number of colleges began accepting women students, including free African-American women, with more than 5,000 women graduating in 1900 alone (Flexner 1974, 232). At the same time, the industrial revolution prompted growing numbers of women to seek paid employment. By 1900, the U.S. census listed more than five million women as gainfully employed outside the home (Flexner 1974, 250). This did not reflect any significant changes in the lives of African-American women—who had worked as much as men when slaves and who often worked full-time post-slavery (Jones 1985)—but was a major change for white women.

Each of these changes challenged the balance of power between men and women in American society. In response to these challenges, a counterreaction quickly developed. This counterreaction combined new "scientific" ideas with older definitions of women's bodies as ill or fragile to argue that white middle-class women were unable to sustain the responsibilities of political power or the burdens of education or employment.

Ideas about middle-class women's frailty drew heavily on the writings of Charles Darwin, who had published his groundbreaking *On the Origin of Species* in 1872 (Tuana 1993). As part of his theory of evolution, Darwin argued that males compete for sexual access to females, with only the fittest succeeding and reproducing. As

a result, males continually evolve toward greater "perfection." Females, on the other hand, need not compete for males, and therefore are not subject to the same process of natural selection. Consequently, in any species, males are more evolved than females. In addition, Darwin argued, females must expend so much energy on reproduction that they retain little energy for either physical or mental development. As a result, women remain subject to their emotions and passions: nurturing, altruistic, and child-like, but with little sense of either justice or morality.

Darwin's theories meshed well with Victorian ideas about middle-class white women's sexuality, which depicted women as the objects of male desire, emphasized romance and downplayed female sexual desire, and reinforced a sexual double standard. Middle-class women were expected to have passionate and even romantic attachments to other women, but these attachments were assumed to be emotional, rather than physical. Most women who had "romantic friendships" with other women were married to men, and only those few who adopted male clothing or behavior were considered lesbians (Faderman 1981). Lesbianism became more broadly identified and stigmatized only in the early twentieth century, when women's entry into higher education and the workforce enabled some women to survive economically without marrying, and lesbianism therefore became a threat to male power.

With women's increasing entry into education and employment, ideas about the physical and emotional frailty of women—with their strong echoes of both Christian and Aristotelian disdain for women and their bodies—were adopted by nineteenth-century doctors as justifications for keeping women uneducated and unemployed. So, for example:

> The president of the Oregon State Medical Society, R.W. Van Dyke, in 1905, claimed that hard study killed sexual desire in women, took away their beauty, and brought on hysteria, neurasthenia [a mental disorder], dyspepsia [indigestion], astigmatism [a visual disorder], and

dysmenorrhea [painful menstruation]. Educated women, he added, could not bear children with ease because study arrested the development of the pelvis at the same time it increased the size of the child's brain, and therefore its head. The result was extensive suffering in childbirth by educated women. (Bullough and Voght 1984, 32)

Belief in the frailty of middle-class women's bodies similarly fostered the epidemic rise during the late nineteenth century in gynecological surgery (Barker-Benfield 1976; Longo 1984). Many doctors routinely performed surgery to remove healthy ovaries, uteruses, or clitorises from women who experienced an extremely wide range of physical and mental symptoms— including symptoms such as rebelliousness or malaise, which reflected women's constrained social circumstances more than their physical health. These operations were not only unnecessary but dangerous, with mortality rates of up to 33 % (Longo 1984).

Paradoxically, at the same time that scientific "experts" emphasized the frailty of middle-class white women, they emphasized the robustness of poorer women, both white and nonwhite. As Jacqueline Jones (1985, 15) explains:

> Slaveholders had little use for sentimental platitudes about the delicacy of the female constitution.... There were enough women like Susan Mabry of Virginia, who could pick 400 or 500 pounds of cotton a day (150 to 200 pounds was considered respectable for an average worker) to remove from a master's mind all doubts about the ability of a strong, healthy woman field worker. As a result, he conveniently discarded his time-honored Anglo-Saxon notions about the type of work best suited for women.

Similar attitudes applied to working-class white women. Thus, Dr. Lucien Warner, a popular medical authority, could in 1874 explain how middle-class women were made frail by their affluence, while "the African negress, who toils beside her husband in the fields of the south, and Bridget [the Irish maid], who washes and scrubs and toils in our homes at the north, enjoy for the most part good health, with comparative immunity from uterine disease" (cited in Ehrenreich and English 1973, 12–13).

At any rate, despite the warnings of medical experts, women continued to enter both higher education and the paid workforce. However, although education clearly benefited women, entering the workforce endangered the lives and health of many women due to hazardous working conditions.

Although male workers could hope to improve their working conditions through union agitation, this tactic was far less useful for women, who more often worked in non-unionized jobs, were denied union membership, or were not interested in joining unions. As a result, some feminists began lobbying for protective labor laws that would set maximum working hours for women, mandate rest periods, and so on (Erickson, 1982). In 1908, the U.S. Supreme Court first upheld such a law in *Muller v. Oregon*. Unfortunately, it soon became clear that protective labor laws hurt women more than they helped, by bolstering the idea that female workers were inherently weaker than male workers.

Twelve years after the *Muller* decision, in 1920, most female U.S. citizens finally won the right to vote in national elections. (Most Asian-born and Native American women, however, were ineligible for citizenship, and most African-American women—like African-American men—were prevented from voting through legal and illegal means.) Unfortunately, suffrage largely marked the close of decades of feminist activism rather than the start of any broader reforms in women's legal, social, or economic positions.

By the 1960s, women's status had hardly changed. For example, although the fourteenth amendment (passed in 1868) guaranteed equal protection under the law for all U.S. citizens, not until 1971, in *Reed v. Reed*, did the Supreme Court rule that differential treatment based on sex was illegal. Similarly, based still on Blackstone's interpretation of women's legal position and the concept of women as men's property, until the 1970s courts routinely refused to prosecute wife batterers unless they killed their wives, and not until 1984 did any court convict a man for raping a woman to whom he was married and with whom he still legally resided.

Recognition of these and other inequities led to the emergence of a new feminist movement beginning in the second half of the 1960s (Evans 1979). In its earliest days, this movement adopted the rhetoric of liberalism and the civil rights movement, arguing that women and men were morally and intellectually equal and that women's bodies were essentially similar to men's bodies. The (unsuccessful) attempts to pass the Equal Rights Amendment, which stated that "equality of rights under the law shall not be denied or abridged by the United States or any state on account of sex," reflected this strain of thinking about gender.

The goal of these liberal feminists was to achieve equality with men within existing social structures—for example, to get men to assume a fair share of child-care responsibilities. Soon, however, some feminists began questioning whether achieving equality within existing social structures would really help women, or whether women would be served better by radically restructuring society to create more humane social arrangements—for example, establishing communal living arrangements in which child care could be more broadly shared rather than trying to allocate child-care responsibilities more equitably within a nuclear family. Along with this questioning of social arrangements came questions about the reality not only of sex differences but also of the categories "male" and "female."

In contrast, a more recent strand of feminist thought, known as "cultural feminism," has re-emphasized the idea of inherent differences between men and women. Unlike those who made this argument in the past, however, cultural feminists argue that women's bodies (as well as their minds and moral values) are superior to men's. From this perspective, women's ability to create human life makes women (especially mothers) innately more pacifistic, loving, moral, creative, and life-affirming than men (e.g., Daly 1978). For the same reason, some feminists, such as Susan Griffin (1978), now argue that women also have an inherently deeper connection than men to nature and to ecological concerns. (Ironically, many in the antiabortion movement and on the far right use rhetoric similar to that of cultural feminists to argue that women belong at home.)

Despite the differences among feminists in ideology and tactics, all share the goal of challenging accepted ideas about women's bodies and social position. Not surprisingly, as the modern feminist movement has grown, a backlash has developed that has attempted to reinforce more traditional ideas (Faludi 1991). This backlash has taken many forms, including (1) increasing pressure on women to control the shape of their bodies, (2) attempts to define premenstrual and postmenopausal women as ill, and (3) the rise of the anti-abortion and "fetal rights" movements.

Throughout history, women have experienced social pressures to maintain acceptable appearances. However, as Susan Faludi (1991), Naomi Wolf (1991), and many others have demonstrated, the backlash against modern feminism seems to have increased these pressures substantially. For example, the average weight of both Miss America winners and Playboy centerfolds has decreased steadily since 1978, even though the average height has increased (Wiseman et al. 1992). Current appearance norms call for women to be not only painfully thin, but muscular and buxom—qualities that can occur together only if women spend vast amounts of time on exercise, money on cosmetic surgery, and emotional energy on diet (Seid 1989).

The backlash against feminism also has affected women's lives by stimulating calls for the medical control of premenstrual women. Although first defined in the 1930s, the idea of a "premenstrual syndrome" (PMS) did not garner much attention either inside or outside medical circles until the 1970s. Since then, innumerable popular and medical articles have argued that to function at work or school, women with PMS need medical treatment to control their anger and discipline their behaviors. Similarly, many doctors now believe that menopausal women need drugs to maintain their sexual attractiveness and to control their behavior and emotions.

Finally, the backlash against feminism has restricted women's lives by encouraging the rise of the antiabortion and "fetal rights" movements. Prior to the twentieth century, abortion was generally considered both legally and socially acceptable, although dangerous. By the mid-twentieth century, abortion had become a safe medical procedure, but was legal only when deemed medically necessary. Doctors were deeply divided, however, regarding when it was necessary, with some performing abortions only to preserve women's lives and others doing so to preserve women's social, psychological, or economic well-being (Luker 1984). To protect themselves legally, beginning in the 1960s, those doctors who favored more lenient indications for abortion, along with women who considered abortion a right, lobbied heavily for broader legal access to abortion. This lobbying culminated in 1973 when the U.S. Supreme Court ruled, in *Roe v. Wade*, that abortion was legal in most circumstances. However, subsequent legislative actions and Court decisions (including the 1976 Hyde Amendment and the Supreme Court's 1989 decision in *Webster v. Reproductive Health Services*) have reduced legal access to abortion substantially, especially for poor and young women.

Embedded in the legal battles over abortion is a set of beliefs about the nature of women and of the fetus (Luker 1984). On one side stand those who argue that unless women have an absolute right to control their own bodies, including the right to abortion, they will never attain fully equal status in society. On the other side stand those who argue that the fetus is fully human and that women's rights to control their bodies must be subjugated to the fetus's right to life.

This latter belief also underlies the broader social and legal pressure for "fetal rights." For example, pregnant women around the country—almost all of them nonwhite and poor—have been arrested for abusing alcohol or illegal drugs while pregnant, on the grounds that they had no right to expose their fetuses to harmful substances. Others—again, mostly poor and nonwhite—have been forced to have cesarean sections against their will. In these cases, the courts have ruled that fetuses' interests are more important than women's right to

determine what will happen to their bodies—in this case, the right to refuse invasive, hazardous surgery—and that doctors know better than mothers what is in a fetus's best interests. Still other women have been denied jobs by employers who have argued that hazardous work conditions might endanger a pregnant worker's fetus; these employers have ignored evidence that the same conditions would also damage men's sperm and thus any resulting fetuses.

In sum, throughout history, ideas about women's bodies have centrally affected the strictures within which women live. Only by looking at the embodied experiences of women, as well as at how those experiences are socially constructed, can we fully understand women's lives, women's position in society, and the possibilities for resistance against that position.

REFERENCES

Barker-Benfield, G.J. 1976. *The Horrors of the Half-Known Life: Male Attitudes towards Women and Sexuality in Nineteenth-Century America*. New York: Harper.

Barstow, Anne Llewellyn. 1994. *Witchcraze: A New History of the European Witch Hunts*. San Francisco: Pandora.

Blackstone, Sir William. 1904. *Commentaries on the Laws of England in Four Books*. Vol. 1 edited by George Sharswood. Philadelphia: Lippincott.

Bullough, Vern, and Martha Voght. 1984. Women, menstruation, and nineteenth-century medicine. In *Women and Health in America: Historical Readings*, edited by Judith Walzer Leavitt. Madison: University of Wisconsin Press.

Daly, Mary. 1978. *Gyn/Ecology: The Metaethics of Radical Feminism*. Boston: Beacon.

Darwin, Charles. 1872. *On the Origin of Species*. Akron, OH: Werner.

Ehrenreich, Barbara, and Deirdre English. 1973. *Complaints and Disorders: The Sexual Politics of Sickness*. Old Westbury, NY: Feminist Press.

Erickson, Nancy S. 1982. Historical background of "protective" labor legislation: *Muller v. Oregon*. In *Women and the Law: A Social Historical Perspective*. Vol. 2, edited by D. Kelly Weisberg. Cambridge, MA: Schenkman.

Evans, Sara M. 1979. *Personal Politics: The Roots of Women's Liberation in the Civil Rights Movement and the New Left.* New York: Vintage.

Faderman, Lillian. 1981. *Surpassing the Love of Men: Romantic Friendship and Love between Women from the Renaissance to the Present.* New York: William Morrow.

Faludi, Susan. 1991. *Backlash: The Undeclared War against American Women.* New York: Crown.

Flexner, Eleanor. 1974. *Century of Struggle: The Women's Rights Movement in the United States.* New York: Atheneum.

Giddings, Paula. 1995. The last taboo. In *Words of Fire: An Anthology of African-American Feminist Thought*, edited by Beverly Guy-Sheftall. New York: New Press.

Gilman, Sander. 1985. Black bodies, white bodies: Toward an iconography of female sexuality in late nineteenth-century art, medicine, and literature. In *"Race," Writing, and Difference*, edited by Henry Louis Gates. Chicago: University of Chicago Press.

Griffin, Susan. 1978. *Woman and Nature: The Roaring inside Her.* New York: Harper.

Jones, Jacqueline. 1985. *Labor of Love, Labor of Sorrow: Black Women, Work, and the Family from Slavery to the Present.* New York: Basic.

Longo, Lawrence D. 1984. The rise and fall of Battey's operation: A fashion in surgery. In *Woman and Health in America*, edited by Judith Walzer Leavitt. Madison: University of Wisconsin Press.

Luker, Kristin. 1984. *Abortion and the Politics of Motherhood.* Berkeley: University of California Press.

Martin, Emily. 1987. *The Woman in the Body: A Cultural Analysis of Reproduction.* Boston: Beacon.

Roberts, Dorothy E. 1990. The future of reproductive choice for poor women and women of color. *Women's Rights Law Reporter* 12(2):59–67.

Seid, Roberta Pollack. 1989. *Never Too Thin: Why Women Are at War with Their Bodies.* Englewood Cliffs, NJ: Prentice Hall.

Speth, Linda E. 1982. The Married Women's Property Acts, 1839–1865: Reform, reaction, or revolution? In *Women and the Law: A Social Historical Perspective.* Vol. 2, edited by D. Kelly Weisberg. Cambridge, MA: Schenkman.

Tuana, Nancy. 1993. *The Less Noble Sex: Scientific, Religious, and Philosophical Conceptions of Woman's Nature.* Bloomington: Indiana University Press.

Wiseman, Claire V., James J. Gray, James E. Mosimann, and Anthony H. Ehrens. 1992. Cultural expectations of thinness in women: An update. *International Journal of Eating Disorders* 11:85–89.

Wolf, Naomi. 1991. *The Beauty Myth: How Images of Beauty Are Used against Women.* New York: William Morrow.

CHAPTER 12

MEASURING UP TO BARBIE
Ideals of the Feminine Body in Popular Culture

Jacqueline Urla and Alan C. Swedlund

It is no secret that thousands of healthy women in the United States perceive their bodies as defective. The signs are everywhere: from potentially lethal cosmetic surgery and drugs to the more familiar routines of dieting, curling, crimping, and aerobicizing, women seek to take control over their unruly physical selves. Every year at least 150,000 women undergo breast implant surgery (Williams 1992), while Asian women have their noses rebuilt and their eyes widened to make themselves look "less dull" (Kaw 1993). Studies show the obsession with body size and sense of inadequacy starts frighteningly early; as many as 80% of 9-year-old suburban girls are concerned about dieting and their weight (Bordo 1991:125). Reports like these, together with the dramatic rise in eating disorders among young women, are just some of the more noticeable fall-out from what Naomi Wolf calls "the beauty myth." Fueled by the hugely profitable cosmetic, weight loss, and fashion industries, the beauty myth's glamorized notions of the ideal body reverberate back upon women as "a dark vein of self hatred, physical obsessions, terror of aging, and dread of lost control" (Wolf 1991:10).

It is this paradox—that female bodies are never feminine enough, that they require deliberate and oftentimes painful refashioning

to be what "nature" intended—that motivates our inquiry into the feminine ideal. Neither universal nor changeless, idealized notions of both masculine and feminine bodies have a long history that shifts considerably across time, racial or ethnic group, class, and culture. Body ideals in twenty-first-century North America are influenced and shaped by images from classical or "high art," the discourses of science and medicine, as well as a multitude of commercial interests, ranging from mundane life insurance standards, to the more high-profile fashion, fitness, and entertainment industries. Each has played contributing and sometimes conflicting roles in determining what counts as a desirable body for us today. In this essay, we focus our attention on the domain of popular culture and the ideal feminine body as it is conveyed by one of pop culture's longest lasting and most illustrious icons: the Barbie doll.

Making her debut in 1959 as Mattel's new teenage fashion doll, Barbie rose quickly to become the top-selling toy in the United States. Several decades and a women's movement later, Barbie dolls remain one of Mattel's biggest-selling items netting over one billion dollars in revenues worldwide (Adelson 1992), or roughly one Barbie sold every two seconds (Stevenson 1991). By the nineties, Mattel was estimating that in the U.S. over 95% of girls between the ages of 3 and 11 own at least one Barbie and that the average number of dolls per owner is seven (Shapiro 1992). Barbie is clearly a force to contend with, eliciting, over the years, a combination of critique, parody, and adoration. A legacy of the post-war era, she remains an incredibly resilient visual and tactile model of femininity for pre-pubescent girls.

It is not our intention to settle the debate over whether Barbie is a good or bad role model for little girls. Though that issue surrounds Barbie like a dark cloud, we are more concerned with how Barbie has been able to survive and remain popular in a period marked by the growth of consumer society, intense debate over gender and racial relations, and changing notions of the body. Our aim, then, is not to offer another rant against Barbie, but to explore how this doll crystallizes some of the predicaments of femininity and feminine bodies in late twentieth-century North America.

A DOLL IS BORN

*****

Legend has it that Barbie was the brainchild of Mattel owner Ruth Handler, who first thought of creating a three-dimensional fashion doll after seeing her daughter play with paper dolls. As an origin story, this one is touching and no doubt true. But Barbie was not the first doll of her kind nor was she just a mother's invention. Making sense of Barbie requires that we look to the larger socio-political and cultural milieu that made her genesis both possible and meaningful. Based on a German prototype, the "Lili" doll, Barbie was from "birth" implicated in the ideologies of the cold war and the research and technology exchanges of the military-industrial complex. Her finely crafted durable plastic mold was, in fact, designed by Jack Ryan, well known for his work in designing the Hawk and Sparrow missiles for the Raytheon Company. Conceived at the hands of a military weapons designer-turned-toy inventor, Barbie dolls came onto the market the same year as the infamous Nixon-

Khrushchev "kitchen debate" at the American National Exhibition in Moscow. There, in front of the cameras of the world, the leaders of the capitalist and socialist worlds faced off, not over missile counts, but over "the relative merits of American and Soviet washing machines, televisions, and electric ranges" (May 1988:16). As Elaine Tyler May has noted in her study of the Cold War, this much-celebrated media event signaled the transformation of American-made commodities and the model suburban home into key symbols and safeguards of democracy and freedom. It was thus with fears of nuclear annihilation and sexually charged fantasies of the perfect bombshelter running rampant in the American imaginary that Barbie and her torpedo-like breasts emerged into popular culture as an emblem of the aspirations of prosperity, domestic containment, and rigid gender roles that were to characterize the burgeoning post-war consumer economy and its image of the American Dream.

Marketed as the first "teenage" fashion doll, Barbie's rise in popularity also coincided with and no doubt contributed to the postwar creation of a distinctive teenage lifestyle.[1] Teens, their tastes and behaviors, were becoming the object of both sociologists and criminologists, as well as market survey researchers intent on capturing their discretionary dollars. While J. Edgar Hoover was pronouncing "the juvenile jungle" a menace to American society, we have retailers, the music industry, and movie-makers declaring the 13- to 19-year-old age bracket "the seven golden years" (Doherty 1988:51–52).

Barbie dolls seemed to cleverly reconcile both of these concerns by personifying the good girl who was sexy, but didn't have sex, and was willing to spend, spend and spend. Amidst the palpable moral panic over juvenile delinquency and teenagers' newfound sexual freedom, Barbie was a reassuring symbol of solidly middle-class values. Popular teen magazines, advertising, television and movies of the period painted a highly dichotomized world divided into good (i.e., middle class) and bad (i.e., working class) kids: the clean-cut college-bound junior achiever versus the street corner boy; the wholesome American Bandstander versus the uncontrollable bad seed (cf. Doherty 1988; and Frith 1981 for England). It was no mystery where Barbie stood in this thinly disguised class discourse. [...] In lieu of back-seat sex and teenage angst, Barbie had pajama parties, barbecues, and her favorite pastime, shopping.

*****

Perhaps what makes Barbie such a perfect icon of late capitalist constructions of femininity is the way in which her persona pairs endless consumption with the achievement of femininity and the appearance of an appropriately gendered body. By buying for Barbie, girls practice how to be discriminating consumers knowledgeable about the cultural capital of different name brands, how to read packaging, and the overall importance of fashion and taste for social status (Motz 1983:131–132). Being a teenage girl in the world of Barbie dolls becomes quite literally a performance of commodity display requiring numerous and complex rehearsals. [...] [T]o the extent that little girls *do* participate in the prepackaged world of Barbie, they come into contact with a number of beliefs central to femininity under consumer capitalism. Little girls learn, among other things, about the crucial importance of their appearance to their personal happiness and ability to gain favor with their friends. [...] Through [...] play scenarios, little girls learn [...] about the importance of hygiene, occasion-specific clothing, knowledgeable buying, and artful display as key elements to popularity and a successful career in femininity.

Barbie exemplifies the way in which gender has become a commodity itself, "something we can buy into ... the same way we buy into a style" (Willis 1991:23). In her insightful analysis of the logic of consumer capitalism, cultural critic Susan Willis pays particular attention to the way in which children's toys like Barbie and the popular muscle-bound "He-Man" for boys link highly conservative and narrowed images of masculinity and femininity with commodity consumption (1991:27). Being or becoming a teenager, having a "grown-up" body, observes Willis, is presented as inextricably bound up with the acquisition of certain commodities, signaled by styles of clothing, cars, music, etc. In play groups and fan clubs (collectors are a whole world unto themselves), children exchange knowledge about the latest accessories and outfits, their relative merit, and how to find them. They become members of a community of Barbie owners whose shared identity is defined by the commodities they have or desire to have. The articulation of social ties through commodities is, as Willis argues, at the heart of how sociality is experienced in consumer capitalism. In this way, we might say that playing with Barbie serves not only as a training ground for the production of the appropriately gendered woman, but also as an introduction to the kinds of knowledge and social relations one can expect to encounter in late capitalist society.

BARBIE IS A SURVIVOR

For anyone tracking Barbie's history, it is abundantly clear that Mattel's marketing strategies have been sensitive to a changing social climate. When the women's movement gained momentum in the seventies, Barbie dolls became a target of criticism (Billyboy 1987; Lord 1994). Mattel responded by giving Barbie new outfits to "reflect the activities and professions that modern women are involved in" (quoted in *Harpers*, August 2, 1990, p. 20). Just as Barbie graduated from Candy striper and ballerina to astronaut and doctor, Mattel also tried to diversify her lily-white image beginning in 1967 with Barbie's first Black friend, "Colored Francie." With the expansion of sales worldwide, Barbie has acquired multi-national guises (Spanish Barbie, Jamaican Barbie, Malaysian Barbie, etc.).[2] In addition, her cohort of "friends" has become increasingly ethnically diversified, as has Barbie advertising, which now regularly feature Asian, Hispanic and Afro-American little girls playing with Barbie. Today, Barbie pals include a smattering of brown and yellow plastic friends, like Teresa, Kira, and Miko who appear on her adventures and, very importantly, can share her clothes.

Perhaps Mattel's most glamorous concession to multiculturalism was Shani who premiered at the 1991 Toy Fair with great fanfare and media attention. Unlike her predecessors who were essentially "brown plastic poured into blond Barbie's mold," Shani, together with her two friends, Asha and Nichelle (each a slightly different shade of brown), and boyfriend Jamal created in 1992, were decidedly Afro-centric, with outfits in "ethnic" fabrics rather than the traditional Barbie pink (Jones 1991). The packaging also announced that these dolls' bodies and facial features were meant to be more realistic of African-American women, although as we will see, the differences, while meaningful, don't preclude interchanging clothes with Barbie. Now, Mattel announced, "ethnic Barbie lovers will be able to dream in their own image" (*Newsweek* 1990:48). Multiculturalism cracked open the door to Barbie-dom and diversity could walk in as long as she was big busted, slim hipped, had long flowing hair, tiny feet, and was very very thin.[3]

In looking over the course of Barbie's career, it is clear that part of her resilience, continuing appeal, and profitability stems from the fact that her identity is constructed primarily through fantasy and is consequently open to change and reinterpretation. As a fashion model, Barbie continually creates her identity anew with every costume change. In that sense, we might want to call Barbie emblematic of the restless desire for change that permeates post-modern capitalist society (Wilson 1985:63). Not only can her image be renewed with a change of clothes, Barbie is also seemingly able to clone herself effortlessly into new identities—"Malibu Barbie"; "Totally Hair Barbie"; "Teen Talk Barbie"; even Afro-centric Shani—without somehow suggesting a serious personality disorder. Furthermore, as a perpetual teenager, Barbie's owners are at liberty to fantasize any number of life choices for her; she might be a high-powered fashion executive or she just might marry Ken and "settle down" in her luxury condo. Her history is a barometer of changing fashions, changing gender and race relations, and a keen index of corporate America's anxious attempts to find new and more palatable ways of selling the

beauty myth and commodity fetishism to new generations of parents and their daughters.

What is striking, then, is that while Barbie's identity may be mutable—one day she might be an astronaut, another a cheerleader—her hyper-slender, big-chested body has remained fundamentally unchanged over the years—a remarkable fact in a society that fetishizes the new and improved. Barbie, of course, did acquire flexible arms and legs as we know, her face has changed significantly, and her hair has grown by leaps and bounds (Melosh and Simmons 1986). But her body measurements, pointed toes, and proportions have not altered significantly. It is to that body and to the results of our class experiment in the anthropometry of Barbie that we now turn. But before taking out our calipers on Barbie and her friends to see how their bodies measure up, we want to offer a very brief historical overview of anthropometry to help us understand how the notion of the "average" American female body was debated in post-war United States.

THE MEASURED BODY: NORMS AND IDEALS

*****

Anthropometry, the science of measuring human bodies, belongs to a long line of techniques of the 18th and 19th centuries—craniometry, phrenology, comparative anatomy—concerned with measuring, comparing, and interpreting variability in the physical dimensions of the human body. [...] Head shape (especially cranial capacity) was a constant source of special fascination, but by the early part of this century, physical anthropologists, together with anatomists and medical doctors, were developing a precise and routine set of measurements for the entire body that they hoped would permit systematic comparison of the human body across race, nationality, and gender.[4]

Anthropometry developed in the United States under the aegis of Ernest Hooton, Ales Hrdlicka, and Franz Boas, located respectively at Harvard, the Smithsonian, and Columbia University. Their main areas of interest were (1) identifying the physical features of racial and or national types, (2) the measurement of adaptation and "degeneracy," and (3) a comparison of the sexes. As is well documented by now, women and non-Europeans did not fare well in these emerging sciences of the body, which held white males as the pinnacle of evolution (see the work of Blakey 1987; Gould 1981, Schiebinger 1989; Fee 1979; Russett 1989). Hooton, in his classic book, *Up from the Ape* (1931), regularly likened women and especially non-Europeans of both sexes to non-human primates. [...]

When it came to defining racial or national types, men, not women were the most commonly studied.[5] Although Hrdlicka and others considered it necessary to measure both males and females, early physical anthropology textbooks reveal that more often than not it was the biologically male body that was selected to visually represent a particular race or humanity as a whole. [...] Women's bodies were frequently described as deviations from the generic or ideal type [...]. Scientists seem to agree that what most dictated a woman's physical shape was her reproductive function. All other features were subordinated to and could be explained by this capacity to bear children. Not surprisingly, given this assumption, it was women's, particularly African or non-European women's, reproductive organs, genitalia, and secondary sexual characteristics that were the most carefully scrutinized and measured (see Fausto-Sterling 1995).

In the United States, we begin to find an attempt to scientifically define a normative "American" female body in the late 19th and early 20th centuries. By the 1860s, Harvard as well as other universities had begun to regularly collect anthropometric data on their male student populations, and in the 1890s comparable data began to be collected from the East Coast women's colleges as well. It was thus upper-class, largely WASP, young people who were the basis of some of the early attempts to define the measurements of the "normal" American male and female. By basing themselves in elite colleges, "other" Americans [...] were effectively

excluded from defining the norm. Rather, their bodies were more often the subject of racist evolutionary-oriented studies concerned with "race crossing," degeneracy, and the effects of the "civilizing" process (see Blakey 1987).

[...] By the early part of the twentieth century industry began to make widespread commercial use of practical anthropometry: the demand for standardized measures of the "average" body manifested in everything from designs for labor-efficient workstations and kitchens to standardized sizes in the ready-to-wear clothing industry (cf. Schwartz 1986). [...] Between 1900 and 1920, the first medicoactuarial standards of weight and height began to appear. The most significant of these, the Dublin Standard Table of Heights and Weights, [...] became the authoritative reference in every doctor's office (cf. Bennett and Gurin 1982:130–138). However, what began as a table of statistical averages soon became a means of setting ideal "norms." Within a few years of its creation, the Dublin table shifted from providing a record of statistically "average" weights to becoming a guide to "desirable" weights, which, interestingly enough, began to fall notably below the average weight for most adult women. [...]

By the 1940s, the search to describe the normal American male and female body in anthropometric terms was being conducted on many fronts fueled by a deepening concern about the physical fitness of the American people. Did Americans constitute a distinctive physical type? Were they physically stronger or weaker than their European ancestors? Could they defend themselves in time of war? [...] Questions such as these fed into an already long-standing preoccupation with defining a specifically American national character and, in 1945, led to the creation of some of the most celebrated and widely publicized life-size anthropometric statues of the century: Norm and Norma, the average American male and female. These statues, sculpted by Malvina Hoffman, were based on the composite measurements of thousands of white 18- to 25-year-old subjects. Both figures were put on display, but it was Norma who received the greatest media attention when the Cleveland Health Museum, which had purchased the pair, decided to sponsor a contest to find the woman in Ohio whose body most closely matched the dimensions of Norma. Under the catchy headline, "Are you Norma, Typical Woman?" the publicity surrounding this contest instructed women how to take their measurements for the contest. Within ten days, 3863 women had sent in their measurements to compete for the $100 prize in U.S. War Bonds that would go to the woman who most resembled the average American girl.

Besides bolstering the circulation of the *Cleveland Plain Dealer*, the idea behind the contest was to promote interest in physical fitness. Norma was described in the press as everything the young American woman should be in a time of war: fit, strong-bodied and at the peak of her reproductive potential. Newspaper articles emphasized that women had a national responsibility to be fit if America was to continue to excel after the war. Few contestants apparently measured up to the challenge (Shapiro 1945). Only one percent came close to Norma's proportions. Commenting on the search for Norma, Dr. Gebhard, director of the Cleveland Health Museum, was quoted in one of the many newspaper articles as saying that "if a national inventory of the female population of this country were taken there would be as many "4Fs" among the women as were revealed among the men in the draft" (Robertson 1945:4). The contest provided the occasion for many health reformers to voice their concern about the weakening of the "American stock" and to call for eugenic marital selection and breeding.

Norma and Norman were thus always more than statistical composites, they were prescriptive ideals that, like the college studies that preceded them, erased Americans' racial and ethnic differences. The "average American" of the post-war period was still imagined as a youthful white body. However, there were competing ideals. Health reformers, educators, and doctors who approved and promoted Norma as an ideal for American women were well aware that her sensible, strong, thick-waisted body differed significantly from the tall, slim-hipped bodies of fashion models in vogue at the time.[6] As the post-war period advanced, Norma would be overshadowed by the array of images of fashion models and pin-up girls put out by advertisers, the entertainment industry, and a burgeoning consumer culture. These fashion images were becoming increasingly thin in the sixties and seventies while the "average" woman's body was in fact getting heavier.

THE ANTHROPOMETRY OF BARBIE: TURNING THE TABLES

Anthropometry, like the very notion of a "normal" body it has been used to construct, is part of an unsavory history. Nevertheless, in the contemporary cultural context where an impossibly thin image of women's bodies has become the most popular children's toy ever sold, it strikes us it might just be the power tool we need for destabilizing a fantasy spun out of control. It was with this in mind that we asked students in one of our social biology classes to measure Barbie to see how her body compared to the average measurements of young American women of the same period. Besides estimating what Barbie's dimensions would be if she were life-size, we see the experiment as an occasion to turn the anthropometric tables from disciplining the bodies of living women, to measuring the ideals by which we have come to judge ourselves and others. We also see it as an opportunity for students who have grown up under the regimes of normalizing science, students who no doubt have been measured, weighed, and compared to standards since birth, to use those very tools to unsettle a highly popular cultural ideal.

Our initial experiment involved measuring many Barbies and Kens from different decades as well as some of their friends. Here we will only report on the results for Barbie and Ken from the Glitter Beach collection, as well as Jamal and Shani, Barbie's more recent African-American friends. Mattel had marketed these latter dolls as having a more authentic African-American appearance and a "rounder more athletic" body, and we wanted to test that out.

After practicing with the calipers, discussing potential observational errors, and performing repeated trial runs, we began to record. In scaling Barbie to be life-sized, the students decided to translate her measurements using two standards: (a) If Barbie were a fashion model (5'10") and (b) if she were of average height for women in the United States (5'4"). We also decided to measure Ken, in the same way, using an average male stature, which we designated as 5'8", and the more "idealized" stature for men, 6'. We report here only the highlights of the measurements taken on the newer Barbie and newer Ken, Jamal, and Shani, scaled at the fashion-model height. For purposes of comparison, we include data on average body measurements from the standardized published tables of the 1988 Anthropometric Survey of the Army Personnel. We have dubbed these composites for the female and male recruits "Army Norma" and "Army Norm," respectively.

Both Barbie and Shani's measurements at 5'10" reveal the extreme thinness expected of the runway model. Both dolls have considerably smaller measurements than Army Norma at all points, even though they are six inches taller than her. When we scaled the dolls to 5'4"—the same as Army Norma—we can see just how skewed the dimensions are: Barbie's chest, waist, and hip measurements come out as 32"–17"–28," clinically anorexic to say the least. We also wanted to see if Mattel had physically changed the Barbie mold in making Shani. Most of the differences we could find appeared to be in the face. Shani's nose is broader and her lips are slightly larger. The only significant difference we found in the bodies was that Shani's back is arched in such a way that it tilts her buttocks up, producing the visual illusion of a higher, rounder butt. Perhaps this is what Mattel was referring to in claiming that Shani has a realistic or ethnically correct body (Jones 1991).

When it came to the male dolls, we did not find the same kind of dramatic difference between them and Army Norm as we did in the female dolls. [...] Ken and Jamal were largely identical to each other, and they were only somewhat slimmer than the average soldier. Visually Ken and Jamal appear very tight and muscular and "bulked out," while the U.S. Army males tend to carry slightly more fat,

judging from the photographs and data presented in the 1988 study.

OUR BARBIES, OUR SELVES

*****

Our venture into anthropometry revealed that Barbie has a much more "abnormal" body than does Ken. But her hyper-thin body was by no means exceptional. Studies tracking the body measurements of Playboy magazine centerfolds and Miss America contestants show that between 1959 and 1978 the average weight and hip size for women in both of these groups has decreased steadily while the average weight of women was increasing (Wiseman, Gray, Mosimann and Ahrens 1992). A follow-up study for the years 1979–1988 found this trend continuing into the eighties: approximately 69% of Playboy centerfolds and 60% of Miss America contestants were weighing in at 15% or more below their expected age and height category. In short, the majority of women presented to us in the media as having desirable feminine bodies, were, like Barbie, well on their way to qualify for anorexia nervosa.

On the surface, at least, it might seem that Barbie's signature thin body would seem at odds with the doll's seemingly endless desire for consumption and self-transformation. Being thin for most women requires repression of desire and self-discipline, neither of which are traits we associate with the consummate shopper. And yet, as Susan Bordo (1990) has argued in regard to anorexia, these two phenomena—hyper-thin bodies and hyper consumption—are very much linked in advanced capitalist economies which depend upon commodity excess. Bodies, says Bordo, are where the regulation of desire is played out most keenly. The imperative to manage the body and to "be all that you can be"—in fact the idea that you can choose the body that you want to have—is a pervasive feature of consumer culture. Keeping control of one's body, not getting too fat or flabby, in other words, conforming to gendered norms of fitness and weight, have become signs of an individual's social and moral worth. But as Bordo, Sandra Bartky (1990), and other feminist scholars have been quick to point out, not all bodies are subject to the same degree of scrutiny or the same repercussions if they fail. It is women's bodies and desires in particular where the structural contradictions—the simultaneous incitement to consume and social condemnation for overindulgence—appear to be most acutely manifested in bodily regimes of intense self-monitoring and discipline. Just as it is women's appearance which is subject to greater social scrutiny, so it is that women's desires, hunger, and appetites which are seen as most threatening and in need of control in a patriarchal society.

This cultural context is relevant to making sense of Barbie and the meaning her body holds in late consumer capitalism. In dressing and undressing Barbie, combing her hair, bathing her, turning and twisting her limbs in imaginary scenarios, children acquire a very tactile and intimate sense of Barbie's body. Barbie is presented in packaging and advertising as a role model, a best friend or older sister to little girls. Television jingles use the refrain, "I want to be just like you," while look-alike clothes and look-alike contests make it possible for girls to live out the fantasy of being Barbie. In short, there is every reason to believe that girls (or adult women) link Barbie's body shape with her popularity and glamour.

This is exactly what worries many people. As our measurements show, Barbie's body differs wildly from anything approximating "average" female body weight and proportions. Over the years her wasp-waisted body has evoked a steady stream of critique for having a negative impact on little girls' sense of self-esteem. [...]

*****

There is no doubt that Barbie's body contributes to what Kim Chernin (1981) has called "the tyranny of slenderness." But is repression all her hyper-thin body conveys? In her work on how anorexic women see themselves, Susan Bordo writes that, "for anorexics, [the slender ideal] may have a very different meaning; it may

symbolize, not so much the containment of female desire, as its liberation from a domestic, reproductive destiny" (Bordo 1990:103).

Similar observations have been made about cosmetic surgery: women often explain their experience as one of empowerment, of taking charge of their bodies and lives (Balsamo 1993; Davis 1991). What does this mean for making sense of Barbie and her long-lasting appeal? We would suggest that a sub-text of agency and independence, even transgression, accompanies this pencil-thin icon of femininity. On the one hand, one can argue that Barbie's body displays conformity to dominant cultural imperatives for a disciplined body and contained feminine desires. On the other hand, however, her excessive slenderness can also signify a rebellious manifestation of willpower, a refusal of the maternal ideal, symbolized by pendulous breasts, rounded stomach and hips. Hers is a body of hard edges, distinct borders, and self-control. It is literally impenetrable. While the anorectic woman becomes increasingly androgynous the more she starves herself, Barbie, in the realm of plastic fantasy, is able to remain powerfully sexualized with her large gravity-defying breasts, even while she is distinctly non-reproductive. Like the "hard bodies" in fitness advertising, Barbie's body may signify for women the pleasure of control and mastery both of which are highly valued traits in American society and both of which are predominantly associated with masculinity (Bordo 1990:105). Putting these elements together with her apparent independent wealth can make for a very different reading of Barbie than that of bimbo. To paraphrase one Barbie doll owner: she owns a Ferrari and doesn't have a husband; she must be doing something right![7]

By invoking these testimonies of anorectic women, we are not trying to suggest that playing with Barbie, or trying to become like Barbie, are paths to empowerment for little girls. Rather we want to signal the complex and contradictory meanings that her body has in contemporary American society. And we also want to underscore that our bodies, whatever the reigning ideal might be, continue to function as a vitally important stage on which gender—as well as race and class—conformity and transgression are played out.[8] It is clear that a next step we would want to take in the cultural interpretation of Barbie is an ethnographic study of Barbie doll owners. It is sensible to assume that the children who play with Barbie are themselves creative users who respond variously to the messages about femininity encoded in her fashions and appearance. In the hands of their adult and child owners, Barbies have become Amazon cave warriors, drag queens, dutiful mommies, and evil axe murderers.[9] As we consider Barbie's many meanings, we should also note that the doll has become a world traveler. A product of the global assembly-line, Barbie dolls owe their existence to the internationalization of the labor market and global flows of capital and commodities that today characterize the toy industry as well as other industries in the post-war era. Designed in Los Angeles, manufactured in Taiwan or Malaysia, distributed worldwide, Barbie™ is American-made in name only. Speeding her way into an expanding global market, Barbie brings with her some of the North American cultural subtext we have outlined in this analysis. How this teenage survivor has inserted herself into the cultural landscapes of Mayan villages, Bombay high rises, and Malagasy towns is a rich topic that begs to be explored.

NOTES

1. While the concept of adolescence as a distinct developmental stage between puberty and adulthood was not new to the fifties, Thomas Doherty (1988) notes that it wasn't until the end of World War II that the term "teenager" became standard usage in the American language.

2. More work needs to be done on how Barbie dolls are adapted to appeal to various national markets. For example, Barbie dolls manufactured in Japan for Japanese consumption are reputed to have noticeably larger, rounder eyes than those marketed in the United States (see Billyboy 1987). For some suggestive thoughts on the cultural implications of the transnational flow of toys like Barbie dolls, TransFormers, and

He-Man, see Carol Breckenridge's (1990) brief but intriguing editor's comment to *Public Culture*.

3. On Black Barbies see DuCille (1995).

4. Though measurements of skulls, noses, facial angles for scientific comparison had been going on throughout the 19th century, it wasn't until the 1890s that any serious attempts were made to standardize anthropometric measurements of the living body. This culminated in the Monaco agreement of 1906, one of the first international meetings to standardize anthropometric measurement. For a brief review of the attempts to use and systematize photography in anthropometry, see Spencer (1992).

5. In her study of 18th-century physical sciences, Schiebinger (1989) remarks that male bodies (skulls in particular) were routinely assumed to embody the prototype of their race in the various typologies devised by comparative anatomists of the period. "When anthropologists did compare women across cultures, their interest centered on sexual traits—feminine beauty, redness of lips, length and style of hair, size and shape of breasts or clitorises, degree of sexual desire, fertility, and above all the size, shape, and position of the pelvis" (1989:156). In this way, the male body "remained the touchstone of human anatomy," while females were regarded as a sexual subset of the species (1989:159–60).

6. Historians have noted a long-standing conflict between the physical culture movement, eugenicists and health reformers on the one hand, and the fashion industry on the other that gave rise to competing ideals in American society of the fit and the fashionably fragile woman (e.g., Banner 1983; Cogan 1989).

7. "Dolls in Playland." 1992. Colleen Toomey, producer. BBC.

8. For an illuminating case study of race, class, and gender codings of the female body, see Krause (1998).

9. Barbie has become a somewhat celebrated figure among avant-garde and pop artists, giving rise to a whole genre of Barbie satire known as "Barbie Noire" (Kahn 1991; Ebersole and Peabody 1993). On queer appropriations of Barbie and Ken, see Rand (1995).

REFERENCES

Adelson, Andrea. 1992. And Now, Barbie Looks Like a Billion. *New York Times*. Nov. 26. pg. D3.

Balsamo, Anne. 1993. On the Cutting Edge: Cosmetic Surgery and the Technological Production of the Gendered Body. *Camera Obscura* 28:207–238.

Banner, Lois W. 1983. *American Beauty*. New York: Knopf.

Bartky, Sandra Lee. 1990. "Foucault, Femininity, and the Modernization of Patriarchal Power." In *Femininity and Domination: Studies in the Phenomenology of Oppression*, pp. 63–82, New York: Routledge.

Bennett, William and Joel Gurin. 1982. *The Dieter's Dilemma: Eating Less and Weighing More*. New York: Basic Books.

Billyboy. 1987. *Barbie, Her Life and Times, and the New Theater of Fashion*. New York: Crown Publishers.

Blakey, Michael L.1987. Skull Doctors: Instrinsic Social and Political Bias in the History of American Physical Anthropology. *Critique of Anthropology* 7(2):7–35.

Bordo, Susan R. 1990. "Reading the Slender Body." In *Body/Politics: Women and the Discourses of Science*. M. Jacobus, E. Fox Keller, and S. Shuttleworth, eds. pp. 83–112. New York: Routledge.

Bordo, Susan R. 1991. "'Material Girl': The Effacements of Postmodern Culture." In *The Female Body: Figures, Styles, Speculations*. L. Goldstein, ed. pp. 106–130. Ann Arbor, MI: The University of Michigan Press.

Breckenridge, Carol A. 1990. Editor's Comment: On Toying with Terror. *Public Culture* 2(2):i–iii.

Chernin, Kim. 1981. *The Obsession: Reflections on the Tyranny of Slenderness*. New York: Harper.

Cogan, Frances B. 1989. *All-American Girl: The Ideal of Real Woman-hood in Mid-Nineteenth Century America*. Athens and London: University of Georgia Press.

Davis, Kathy. 1991. Remaking the She-Devil: A Critical Look at Feminist Approaches to Beauty. *Hypatia* 6(2):21–43.

Doherty, Thomas. 1988. *Teenagers and Teenpics. The Juvenilization of American Movies in the 1950s*. Boston: Unwin Hyman.

DuCille, Ann. 1995. "Toy Theory: Blackface Barbie and the Deep Play of Difference." In *The Skin Trade: Essays on Race, Gender and Merchandising of Difference*. Cambridge: Harvard University Press.

Ebersole, Lucinda and Richard Peabody, eds.1993. *Mondo Barbie*. New York: St. Martin's Press.

Fausto-Sterling, Anne. 1995. "Gender, Race and Nation: The Comparative Anatomy of 'Hottentot' Women in Europe, 1815–1817." In *Deviant Bodies: Critical Perspectives on Difference in Science and Popular Culture*. J. Terry and J. Urla, eds. Bloomington: Indiana University Press.

Fee, Elizabeth. 1979. Nineteenth-Century Craniology: The Study of the Female Skull. *Bulletin of the History of Medicine* 53:415–433.

Frith, Simon. 1981. *Sound Effects: Youth, Leisures, and the Politics of Rock'n'Roll*. New York: Pantheon.

Gould, Steven Jay. 1981. *The Mismeasure of Man*. New York: Norton.

Hooton, E.A. 1931 *Up from the Ape*. New York: The MacMillan Company.

Jones, Lisa. 1991. Skin Trade: A Doll Is Born. *Village Voice*. March 26, p. 36.

Kahn, Alice. 1991. A Onetime Bimbo Becomes a Muse. *New York Times*. September 29.

Kaw, Eugenia. 1993. Medicalization of Racial Features: Asian American Women and Cosmetic Surgery. *Medical Anthropology Quarterly* 7(1):74–89.

Krause, Elizabeth. 1998. A Bead of Raw Sweat in a Field of Dainty Perspirers: Nationalism, Whiteness and the Olympic Ordeal of Tonya Harding. *Transforming Anthropology* 7(1).

Lord, M.G. 1994. *Forever Barbie: The Unauthorized Biography of a Real Doll*. New York: William Morrow.

May, Elaine Tyler. 1988. *Homeward Bound: American Families in the Cold War Era*. New York: Basic Books.

Melosh, Barbara and Christina Simmons. 1986. "Exhibiting Women's History." In *Presenting the Past: Essays on History and the Public*. Susan Porter Benson, Stephen Brier, and Roy Rosenzweig, eds. Philadelphia: Temple University Press.

Motz, Marilyn Ferris. 1983. "'I Want to Be a Barbie Doll When I Grow Up': The Cultural Significance of the Barbie Doll." In *The Popular Culture Reader,* 3rd ed. Christopher D. Geist and Jack Nachbar, eds. pp. 122–136. Bowling Green: Bowling Green University Popular Press.

Newsweek. 1990 Finally, Barbie Dolls Go Ethnic. *Newsweek* (August 13), p. 48.

Rand, Erica. 1995. *Barbie's Queer Accessories*. Durham and London: Duke University Press.

Robertson, Josephine. 1945. Theatre Cashier, 23, Wins Tide of "Norma." *Cleveland Plain Dealer*. September 21, pp. 1, 4.

Russett, Cynthia Eagle. 1989. *Sexual Science: The Victorian Construction of Womanhood*. Cambridge, MA: Harvard University Press.

Schiebinger, Londa. 1989. *The Mind Has No Sex: Women in the Origins of Modern Science*. Cambridge: Harvard University Press.

Schwartz, Hillel. 1986. *Never Satisfied: A Cultural History of Diets, Fantasies and Fat*. New York: The Free Press.

Shapiro, Eben. 1992. "Total Hot, Totally Cool." Long-Haired Barbie Is a Hit. *New York Times*. June 22. p. D-9.

Shapiro, Harry L. 1945. *Americans: Yesterday, Today, Tomorrow*. Man and Nature Publications (Science Guide No. 126). New York: The American Museum of Natural History.

Spencer, Frank. 1992. "Some Notes on the Attempt to Apply Photography to Anthropometry during the Second Half of the Nineteenth Century. In *Anthropology and Photography: 1860–1920*. Elizabeth Edwards, ed. pp. 99–107. New Haven, CT: Yale University Press.

Stevenson, Richard. 1991. Mattel Thrives as Barbie Grows. *New York Times*. December 2.

Williams, Lena. 1992. Woman's Image in a Mirror: Who Defines What She Sees? *New York Times*. February 6. A1; B7.

Willis, Susan. 1991. *A Primer for Daily Life*. London and New York: Routledge.

Wilson, Elizabeth. 1985. *Adorned in Dreams: Fashion and Modernity*. London: Virago.

Wiseman, C., Gray, J., Mosimann, J. and Ahrens, A. 1992. Cultural Expectations of Thinness in Women: An Update. *International Journal of Eating Disorders* II (l):85–89.

Wolf, Naomi. 1991. *The Beauty Myth: How Images of Beauty are Used against Women*. New York: William Morrow.

CHAPTER 13

SIZE 6
The Western Women's Harem

Fatima Mernissi

It was during my unsuccessful attempt to buy a cotton skirt in an American department store that I was told my hips were too large to fit into a size 6. That distressing experience made me realize how the image of beauty in the West can hurt and humiliate a woman as much as the veil does when enforced by the state police in extremist nations such as Iran, Afghanistan, or Saudi Arabia. Yes, that day I stumbled onto one of the keys to the enigma of passive beauty in Western harem fantasies. The elegant saleslady in the American store looked at me without moving from her desk and said that she had no skirt my size. "In this whole big store, there is no skirt for me?" I said. "You are joking." I felt very suspicious and thought that she just might be too tired to help me. I could understand that. But then the saleswoman added a condescending judgment, which sounded to me like an Imam's *fatwa*. It left no room for discussion:

"You are too big!" she said.

"I am too big compared to what?" I asked, looking at her intently, because I realized that I was facing a critical cultural gap here.

"Compared to a size 6," came the saleslady's reply.

Her voice had a clear-cut edge to it that is typical of those who enforce religious laws.

"Size 4 and 6 are the norm," she went on, encouraged by my bewildered look. "Deviant sizes such as the one you need can be bought in special stores."

That was the first time that I had ever heard such nonsense about my size. In the Moroccan streets, men's flattering comments regarding my particularly generous hips have for decades led me to believe that the entire planet shared their convictions. It is true that with advancing age, I have been hearing fewer and fewer flattering comments when walking in the medina, and sometimes the silence around me in the bazaars is deafening. But since my face has never met with the local beauty standards, and I have often had to defend myself against remarks such as *zirafa* (giraffe), because of my long neck, I learned long ago not to rely too much on the outside world for my sense of self-worth. In fact, paradoxically, as I discovered when I went to Rabat as a student, it was the self-reliance that I had developed to protect myself against "beauty blackmail" that made me attractive to others. My male fellow students could not believe that I did not give a damn about what they thought about my body. "You know, my dear," I would say in response to one of them, "all I need to survive is bread, olives, and sardines. That you think my neck is too long is your problem, not mine."

147

In any case, when it comes to beauty and compliments, nothing is too serious or definite in the medina, where everything can be negotiated. But things seemed to be different in that American department store. In fact, I have to confess that I lost my usual self-confidence in that New York environment. Not that I am always sure of myself, but I don't walk around the Moroccan streets or down the university corridors wondering what people are thinking about me. Of course, when I hear a compliment, my ego expands like a cheese souffle, but on the whole, I don't expect to hear much from others. Some mornings, I feel ugly because I am sick or tired; others, I feel wonderful because it is sunny out or I have written a good paragraph. But suddenly, in that peaceful American store that I had entered so triumphantly, as a sovereign consumer ready to spend money, I felt savagely attacked. My hips, until then the sign of a relaxed and uninhibited maturity, were suddenly being condemned as a deformity.

"And who decides the norm?" I asked the saleslady, in an attempt to regain some self-confidence by challenging the established rules. I never let others evaluate me, if only because I remember my childhood too well. In ancient Fez, which valued round-faced plump adolescents, I was repeatedly told that I was too tall, too skinny, my cheekbones were too high, my eyes were too slanted. My mother often complained that I would never find a husband and urged me to study and learn all that I could, from storytelling to embroidery, in order to survive. But I often retorted that since "Allah had created me the way I am, how could he be so wrong, Mother?" That would silence the poor woman for a while, because if she contradicted me, she would be attacking God himself. And this tactic of glorifying my strange looks as a divine gift not only helped me to survive in my stuffy city, but also caused me to start believing the story myself. I became almost self-confident. I say almost, because I realized early on that self-confidence is not a tangible and stable thing like a silver bracelet that never changes over the years. Self-confidence is like a tiny fragile light, which goes off and on. You have to replenish it constantly.

"And who says that everyone must be a size 6?" I joked to the saleslady that day, deliberately neglecting to mention size 4, which is the size of my skinny twelve-year-old niece.

At that point, the saleslady suddenly gave me an anxious look. "The norm is everywhere, my dear," she said. "It's all over, in the magazines, on television, in the ads. You can't escape it. There is Calvin Klein, Ralph Lauren, Gianni Versace, Giorgio Armani, Mario Valentino, Salvatore Ferragamo, Christian Dior, Yves Saint-Laurent, Christian Lacroix, and Jean-Paul Gaultier. Big department stores go by the norm." She paused and then concluded, "If they sold size 14 or 16, which is probably what you need, they would go bankrupt."

She stopped for a minute and then stared at me, intrigued. "Where on earth do you come from? I am sorry I can't help you. Really, I am." And she looked it too. She seemed, all of a sudden, interested, and brushed off another woman who was seeking her attention with a cutting, "Get someone else to help you, I'm busy." Only then did I notice that she was probably my age, in her late fifties. But unlike me, she had the thin body of an adolescent girl. Her knee-length, navy blue, Chanel dress had a white silk collar reminiscent of the subdued elegance of aristocratic French Catholic schoolgirls at the turn of the century. A pearl-studded belt emphasized the slimness of her waist. With her meticulously styled short hair and sophisticated makeup, she looked half my age at first glance.

"I come from a country where there is no size for women's clothes," I told her. "I buy my own material and the neighborhood seamstress or craftsman makes me the silk or leather skirt I want. They just take my measurements each time I see them. Neither the seamstress nor I know exactly what size my new skirt is. We discover it together in the making. No one cares about my size in Morocco as long as I pay taxes on time. Actually, I don't know what my size is, to tell you the truth."

The saleswoman laughed merrily and said that I should advertise my country as a paradise for stressed working women. "You mean you don't watch your weight?" she inquired, with a tinge of disbelief in her voice. And then, after a brief moment of silence, she added in a lower register, as if talking to herself: "Many women working in highly paid fashion-related jobs could lose their positions if they didn't keep to a strict diet."

Her words sounded so simple, but the threat they implied was so cruel that I realized for the first time that maybe "size 6" is a more violent restriction imposed on women than is the Muslim veil. Quickly I said good-bye so as not to make any more demands on the saleslady's time or involve her in any more unwelcome, confidential exchanges about age-discriminating salary cuts. A surveillance camera was probably watching us both.

Yes, I thought as I wandered off, I have finally found the answer to my harem enigma. Unlike the Muslim man, who uses space to establish male domination by excluding women from the public arena, the Western man manipulates time and light. He declares that in order to be beautiful, a woman must look fourteen years old. If she dares to look fifty, or worse, sixty, she is beyond the pale. By putting the spotlight on the female child and framing her as the ideal of beauty, he condemns the mature woman to invisibility. In fact, the modern Western man enforces Immanuel Kant's nineteenth-century theories: To be beautiful, women have to appear childish and brainless. When a woman looks mature and self-assertive, or allows her hips to expand, she is condemned as ugly. Thus, the walls of the European harem separate youthful beauty from ugly maturity.

These Western attitudes, I thought, are even more dangerous and cunning than the Muslim ones because the weapon used against women is time. Time is less visible, more fluid than space. The Western man uses images and spotlights to freeze female beauty within an idealized childhood, and forces women to perceive aging—that normal unfolding of the years—as a shameful devaluation. "Here I am, transformed into a dinosaur," I caught myself saying aloud as I went up and down the rows of skirts in the store, hoping to prove the saleslady wrong—to no avail. This Western time-defined veil is even crazier than the space-defined one enforced by the Ayatollahs.

The violence embodied in the Western harem is less visible than in the Eastern harem because aging is not attacked directly, but rather masked as an aesthetic choice. Yes, I suddenly felt not only very ugly but also quite useless in that store, where, if you had big hips, you were simply out of the picture. You drifted into the fringes of nothingness. By putting the spotlight on the prepubescent female, the Western man veils the older, more mature woman, wrapping her in shrouds of ugliness. This idea gives me the chills because it tattoos the invisible harem directly onto a woman's skin. Chinese foot-binding worked the same way: Men declared beautiful only those women who had small, childlike feet. Chinese men did not force women to bandage their feet to keep them from developing normally—all they did was to define the beauty ideal. In feudal China, a beautiful woman was the one who voluntarily sacrificed her right to unhindered physical movement by mutilating her own feet, and thereby proving that her main goal in life was to please men. Similarly, in the Western world, I was expected to shrink my hips into a size 6 if I wanted to find a decent skirt tailored for a beautiful woman. We Muslim women have only one month of fasting, Ramadan, but the poor Western woman who diets has to fast twelve months out of the year. "*Quelle horreur*," I kept repeating to myself, while looking around at the American women shopping. All those my age looked like youthful teenagers.

According to the writer Naomi Wolf, the ideal size for American models decreased sharply in the 1990s. "A generation ago, the average model weighed 8 percent less than the average American woman, whereas today she weighs 23 percent less.... The weight of Miss America plummeted, and the average weight of Playboy Playmates dropped from 11 percent below the national average in 1970 to 17 percent below it in eight years."[1] The shrinking of the ideal size, according to Wolf, is one of the primary reasons for anorexia and other health-related problems: "Eating disorders rose exponentially, and a mass of neurosis was promoted that used food and weight to strip women of ... a sense of control."[2]

Now, at last, the mystery of my Western

harem made sense. Framing youth as beauty and condemning maturity is the weapon used against women in the West just as limiting access to public space is the weapon used in the East. The objective remains identical in both cultures: to make women feel unwelcome, inadequate, and ugly.

The power of the Western man resides in dictating what women should wear and how they should look. He controls the whole fashion industry, from cosmetics to underwear. The West, I realized, was the only part of the world where women's fashion is a man's business. In places like Morocco, where you design your own clothes and discuss them with craftsmen and -women, fashion is your own business. Not so in the West. As Naomi Wolf explains in *The Beauty Myth*, men have engineered a prodigious amount of fetish-like, fashion-related paraphernalia: "Powerful industries—the $33-billion-a-year diet industry, the $20-billion cosmetic industry, the $300-million cosmetic surgery industry, and the $7-billion pornography industry—have arisen from the capital made out of unconscious anxieties, and are in turn able, through their influence on mass culture, to use, stimulate, and reinforce the hallucination in a rising economic spiral."[3]

But how does the system function? I wondered. Why do women accept it?

Of all the possible explanations, I like that of the French sociologist, Pierre Bourdieu, the best. In his latest book, *La Domination Masculine*, he proposes something he calls "*la violence symbolique*": "Symbolic violence is a form of power which is hammered directly on the body, and as if by magic, without any apparent physical constraint. But this magic operates only because it activates the codes pounded in the deepest layers of the body."[4] Reading Bourdieu, I had the impression that I finally understood Western man's psyche better. The cosmetic and fashion industries are only the tip of the iceberg, he states, which is why women are so ready to adhere to their dictates. Something else is going on on a far deeper level. Otherwise, why would women belittle themselves spontaneously? Why, argues Bourdieu, would women make their lives more difficult, for example, by preferring men who are taller or older than they are? "The majority of French women wish to have a husband who is older and also, which seems consistent, bigger as far as size is concerned," writes Bourdieu.[5] Caught in the enchanted submission characteristic of the symbolic violence inscribed in the mysterious layers of the flesh, women relinquish what he calls "*les signes ordinaires de la hiérarchie sexuelle*," the ordinary signs of sexual hierarchy, such as old age and a larger body. By so doing, explains Bourdieu, women spontaneously accept the subservient position. It is this spontaneity Bourdieu describes as magic enchantment.[6]

Once I understood how this magic submission worked, I became very happy that the conservative Ayatollahs do not know about it yet. If they did, they would readily switch to its sophisticated methods, because they are so much more effective. To deprive me of food is definitely the best way to paralyze my thinking capabilities.

Both Naomi Wolf and Pierre Bourdieu come to the conclusion that insidious "body codes" paralyze Western women's abilities to compete for power, even though access to education and professional opportunities seem wide open, because the rules of the game are so different according to gender. Women enter the power game with so much of their energy deflected to their physical appearance that one hesitates to say the playing field is level. "A cultural fixation on female thinness is not an obsession about female beauty," explains Wolf. It is "an obsession about female obedience. Dieting is the most potent political sedative in women's history; a quietly mad population is a tractable one."[7] Research, she contends, "confirmed what most women know too well—that concern with weight leads to a 'virtual collapse of self-esteem and sense of effectiveness' and that ... 'prolonged and periodic caloric restriction' resulted in a distinctive personality whose traits are passivity, anxiety, and emotionality."[8] Similarly, Bourdieu, who focuses more on how this myth hammers its inscriptions onto the flesh itself, recognizes that constantly reminding women of their physical appearance destabilizes them emotionally because it reduces them to exhibited objects. "By confining women to the status of symbolical objects to be seen and perceived by the other, masculine domination ... puts women in a state of constant physical insecurity.... They have to strive ceaselessly to be engaging, attractive, and available."[9] Being frozen into the passive position of an object whose very existence depends on the eye of its beholder turns the educated modern Western woman into a harem slave.

"I thank you, Allah, for sparing me the tyranny of the 'size 6 harem,'" I repeatedly said to myself while seated on the Paris-Casablanca flight, on my way back home at last. "I am so happy that the conservative male elite does not know about it. Imagine the fundamentalists switching from the veil to forcing women to fit size 6."

How can you stage a credible political demonstration and shout in the streets that your human rights have been violated when you cannot find the right skirt?

NOTES

1. Naomi Wolf, *The Beauty Myth: How Images of Beauty Are Used against Women* (New York; Anchor Books, Doubleday, 1992), p. 185.

2. Ibid., p. 11.

3. Ibid., p. 17.

4. Pierre Bourdieu: "La force symbolique est une forme de pouvoir qui s'exerce sur les corps, directement, et comme par magie, en dehors de toute contraine physique, mais cette magie n'opére qu'en s'appuyant sur des dispositions déposées, tel des ressorts, au plus profond des corps." In *La Domination Masculine* (Paris: Editions du Seuil, 1998), op. cit. p. 44.

5. *La Domination Masculine*, op. cit., p. 41.

6. Bourdieu, op. cit., p. 42.

7. Wolf, op. cit., p. 187.

8. Wolf, quoting research carried out by S.C. Woolly and O.W. Woolly, op. cit., pp. 187–188.

9. Bourdieu, *La Domination Masculine*, p. 73.

CHAPTER 14

GLOBALIZATION AND THE INEQUALITY OF WOMEN WITH DISABILITIES

Fiona Sampson

I. INTRODUCTION

Many interrelated processes characterize the phenomenon of globalization, including trade liberalization, changing patterns of financial flows, a growth in the size and power of corporations, political choices made by governments to cede power to regulate capital, and advances in information and communication technology. These processes interact to affect, to varying degrees, the enjoyment of human rights.[1]

This article focuses on one disadvantaged group—women with disabilities—whose members are affected in multiple ways by the operation of the market economy in the current era of globalization. To give just one example, women with disabilities in Canada are vulnerable to the experience of gendered disability discrimination when seeking employment. This form of discrimination is compounded by the insecurities associated with globalization, such as the lowering of wages, the shrinking job market for low-income earners, and government downsizing.[2] Moreover, it is well established that non-disabled women are disadvantaged by the restructuring of the private sector through changes in household incomes and the pressure to assume more of the burden of unpaid domestic labour.[3] However, many women with disabilities do not have the luxury of a spouse or a domestic environment to act as a potential buffer; therefore, for them, the effects of restructuring are compounded. Finally, because they are largely excluded from our consumer-oriented culture, women with disabilities are vulnerable to the increased dominance of corporate rule in the political economy. They are deprived of the influence that comes with the ability to make consumer choices.

In the face of such rising inequities, this article seeks to galvanize support for the protection and advancement of the rights of women with disabilities to equality. In considering the relative merits of future legal claims seeking recognition and redistribution of equality rights for women with disabilities,[4] it is important to identify critical issues for women with disabilities relating to globalization so that priorities for future political and legal reform can be established. Accordingly, this article's central concern is the invisibility of women with disabilities in the context of globalization, and the increased discrimination against women with disabilities resulting from globalization. The goal here is to highlight an underdeveloped area of research and activism in the hopes of spurring interest in and support for the protection and advancement of the equality rights of women with disabilities.

This article addresses four areas of concern relating to globalization and the equality rights of women with disabilities: the replacement of citizenship with consumerism; the introduction of non-standardized employment arrangements; the association of dependency with culpability in neo-liberal thinking; and, finally, the threat globalization poses to the independence of women with disabilities. The article will conclude with a discussion of two strategies for the advancement of the equality rights of women with disabilities in light of the threats posed by globalization.

II. WOMEN WITH DISABILITIES AND ECONOMIC INEQUALITY

Women with disabilities are especially vulnerable to the experience of unemployment and poverty, and particularly disadvantaged by its effects.[5] Poverty is more than just a shortage of money—poverty affects the enjoyment of all other human rights. Due in part to their relative poverty, women with disabilities do not have equal access to the justice system and find it harder to participate in political life. Poverty affects the health of women with disabilities, and it affects their ability to improve their status and life conditions. Poverty also leaves women with disabilities—as it does women generally[6]—vulnerable to violence, sexual exploitation, and coercion.

Equal treatment and equal opportunity in employment represent ways of overcoming poverty for women with disabilities. Employment can provide a sense of identity. It can also offer opportunities to learn and develop, to belong to a social group, and to make a contribution to society. For women with disabilities, so often segregated from mainstream society, employment means the ability to lead more conventional lives, become economically self-sufficient, and escape the stigma often associated with disability. The provision of health benefits is another attraction of permanent employment for women with disabilities. Unfortunately, employment is especially difficult to secure for women with disabilities as a result of the gendered disability discrimination that confronts them. The unemployment rate of women with disabilities in Canada was placed at 74 per cent in 1997.[7] Even on more conservative estimates, the employment rate for women with disabilities in Canada is about one-third less than the rate for non-disabled women[8] and about 15 per cent less than the rate for men with disabilities.[9]

The reality of the disadvantage experienced by women with disabilities is also reflected in income statistics relating to their status in Canadian society. Adults with disabilities in Canada are more likely to live in poverty. Forty-three per cent of adults with disabilities have an annual income of less than $10,000, and 26 per cent have an income of less than $5,000. These figures do not represent the full economic hardship experienced by persons with disabilities, as they do not take into account the high costs often associated with having a disability.[10] In 1990, of all women with disabilities, excluding those living in an institution, those aged 35 to 54 had the highest annual incomes: an average of $17,000, still only 55 per cent of the average annual income of men with disabilities in the same age range.[11] The 1996 census results show that in 1995 the rate of poverty for women with disabilities aged 15 to 64 was twice that of non-disabled women in the same age bracket: 36 per cent compared to 18 per cent.[12] The more severe a woman's disability, the lower her income tended to be.[13] These trends have not abated. Indeed, recently the United Nations committee that reviews Canada's compliance with the Convention on the Elimination of All Forms of Discrimination against Women[14] expressed its concern over the high percentage of women with disabilities living in poverty in Canada. The number of disabled women who are poor, the committee found, has grown because of governmental budgetary adjustments and related cuts in social services since 1995.[15]

Those women with disabilities who manage to secure employment may face discrimination related to their disability once in the workforce. An employer may make inaccurate assumptions about a woman's capabilities and her needs based on the application of a traditional construction of disability. The attitude may be that the problem is located in the individual woman with the disability, rather than in society. Traditional assumptions of weakness associated both with women and with disability can combine to expose women with disabilities to a compounded form of discrimination. It is interesting to note that women with disabilities are less likely to initiate human rights complaints alleging disability discrimination in the employment context.[16] The under-representation of women with disabilities in the human rights complaint process may be a result of their under-representation within the work force generally. It may also stem from the disempowerment of women with disabilities in the workplace, making it difficult for them to challenge discrimination. Whatever the reason for the disparity, the relative power imbalance relating to gendered disability must operate to the disadvantage of women with disabilities in employment.

Beyond a particular employer or position, women with disabilities may also be disadvantaged by society-wide, able-bodied norms that define the employment experience. Norms such as efficiency, productivity, and competition have become central features of contemporary, post-industrial society. Janice Stein argues in *The Cult of Efficiency* that efficiency has become a value in its own right and one of the overriding goals associated with the delivery of public goods.[17] Efficiency has been used to justify a political agenda obsessed with the reduction of costs and insensitive to the needs of the desperately poor and insecure,[18] such as persons with disabilities. Thus, the time and attention needed to train or accommodate a woman with a disability may often be understood as incompatible with a commitment to non-neutral norms like efficiency. This perceived incompatibility might make women with disabilities appear unsuitable as potential employees.

Male-biased norms, such as the definition of the "ideal worker," may also contribute to the disadvantage experienced by women with disabilities in the employment context. Non-disabled women often experience gender bias as a result of male norms and expectations that define the employment experience.

These include the ability to work long hours, including unpaid overtime, and the ability to relocate easily. Women with disabilities are further disadvantaged by these expectations. It may be physically impossible for women with disabilities to work long hours, and requests for reduced hours may not be considered cost efficient by an employer. Employers may deny requests for accommodation advanced by women with disabilities by relying on a defence of undue hardship.[19] It may also be more difficult for women with disabilities to relocate because of difficulties in duplicating an established support system—that is, a home designed to accommodate their disability, or familiarity with and access to local support services.

The operation of traditional social constructions of gender and disability may also make equality of treatment in employment elusive for women with disabilities. Sexual harassment is a good example of how the social constructions of gender and disability can interact to disadvantage women with disabilities once they have entered the workforce. The commonplace experience of sexual harassment is an affront to the equality rights of all women,[20] including women with disabilities. The social construction of women as subordinate to men leaves women vulnerable to objectification and sexual harassment. Similarly, the social construction of persons with disabilities as inferior to non-disabled persons contributes to the vulnerability of women with disabilities to exploitation through exercises of power and control, such as sexual harassment. All victims of sexual harassment feel its harmful effects, including debilitating stress reactions that affect women's physical and psychological health.[21] It can have an especially oppressive effect on women with disabilities, whose physical or psychological health may already be precarious.

Women in Canada are forced to deal with an allegedly gender-neutral standard of socially acceptable behaviour, which makes the male workplace culture the standard against which equality is measured. This leaves all women vulnerable to harassment in the workplace.[22] For women with disabilities the risk of sexual harassment may be even greater. It is well established that women with disabilities are exceptionally vulnerable to sexual assault.[23] Similarly, they may be at greater risk of sexual harassment in the workplace, compared to non-disabled women, because of the same socially constructed myths and stereotypes that make them vulnerable to sexual assault—myths to the effect that women with disabilities are desperate for sex, or that they are sexually promiscuous. The sexual harassment of women with disabilities can contribute to the creation of a hostile work environment in which continued employment may prove untenable, thereby contributing to the economic insecurity experienced by these women.[24]

III. THE REPLACEMENT OF CITIZENSHIP WITH CONSUMERISM

Government downsizing and the downloading of state responsibilities to private sector corporations have had an obvious negative economic effect on women with disabilities who depend on the state for assistance. But government downsizing also means women with disabilities lose the ability to influence the policies of a service provider that is accountable to the public (or at least theoretically accountable to the public). As corporate rule overtakes government rule, women with disabilities find themselves even further alienated from the centres of political power in Canada.

It is more difficult for women with disabilities to exercise power and influence in the market as consumers than it is for more economically advantaged members of society. Women with disabilities cannot afford to access the new political arena of consumerism. While the anti-corporate and anti-globalization movement criticizes the lack of consumer choice that now exists, women with disabilities experience such a high degree of poverty that they often cannot afford to participate in the economy as consumers. For them, the question of which products to buy, which corporations to support or boycott, is a non-issue.

The exclusion of women with disabilities from consumerism in the new global economy is evidenced by their absence from the marketing campaigns of global companies such as Nike, The Gap, and McDonald's, to name just three better-known examples.[25] Non-disabled feminists and anti-racism leaders have expressed outrage, and legitimately so, at the commercial co-optation of their identity politics and the exploitation of feminist and anti-racist messages to sell shoes, jeans, and hamburgers.[26] However, the equality rights of women with disabilities are not considered a sufficiently visible social justice issue to merit repackaging. Women with disabilities are excluded from marketing hype. This invisibility reflects their exclusion from consumer culture overall, and their inability to influence the policies of multinational corporations. Naomi Klein, author of *No Logo: Taking Aim at Brand Bullies*, has concluded that cultural diversity has become the mantra of global capital.[27] If so, it is a form of diversity that excludes women with disabilities.

IV. NON-STANDARDIZED EMPLOYMENT ARRANGEMENTS

With the rise of non-standard employment arrangements such as part-time, contract, and temporary work,[28] it is difficult for many persons to find traditional, standard jobs with conventional hours, health benefits, and a predictable routine.[29] For women with disabilities, this has aggravated the difficulty in breaking through the occupational hierarchy that operates against them. Good jobs are no longer readily available to even the most attractive employees—white, non-disabled men—so there is more competition for the inferior jobs for which women with disabilities might formerly have been viable candidates. Women with disabilities who are employed are heavily over-represented in the lowest wage sectors.[30] They comprise a marginal labour force that is especially vulnerable to work reductions and layoffs. Therefore, as the competition for inferior, non-standardized work increases, women with disabilities will find it increasingly difficult to secure employment and achieve economic equality.

An example of the disadvantage experienced by women with disabilities resulting from the rise of non-standardized employment relationships and the application of gendered disability discrimination is found in the federal government's 1996 reforms to the *Employment Insurance Act*.[31] The main changes to the Act relevant to the equality concerns of women with disabilities are in sections 6(1) and 7(2). To be eligible for regular benefits, claimants (other than new entrants and certain re-entrants to the job market) require between 420 and 700 hours of insurable employment, depending on the rate of unemployment in their region, in the preceding fifty-two-week qualifying period. Under the old *Unemployment Insurance Act*, a claimant had to show he or she had worked 20 or more weeks, with a week defined as 15 hours or 20 per cent of his or her maximum weekly earnings.[32] The change in the criteria needed to qualify for benefits means that it is significantly more difficult for part-timers to qualify for benefits under the new Act. When they do qualify, benefits are often available for a shorter period of time than they had been under the *Unemployment Insurance Act*.[33]

Women with disabilities are the least likely persons in society to have full-time, year-round employment.[34] As such, they find it more difficult to accumulate the number of hours needed to qualify for regular, sickness, maternity, or parental insurance benefits under the new Act. The denial of benefits under the Act to women with disabilities who are also part-time workers amounts to discrimination within the meaning of section 15(1) of the *Canadian Charter of Rights and Freedoms*.[35] The adverse impact of the amendments to the Act on women with disabilities is made worse by the trend toward non-standardized employment arrangements associated with globalization. This is a trend to which women with disabilities are particularly susceptible, leaving them at increased risk of disadvantage because of the higher eligibility thresholds under the Act.

V. THE LINK BETWEEN DEPENDENCY AND CULPABILITY

The entrenchment of globalization and the erosion of the welfare state also affect the way other members of Canadian society treat women with disabilities. Within the market economy, the individual is viewed as responsible for her own condition, so that poverty is assumed to be the individual's fault. This neo-liberal thinking is bad news for women with disabilities. The disadvantage experienced by persons with disabilities within the economy will be viewed as a problem located in the individual, not a problem with society or the economy's response to a person's condition.[36] This, in turn, is used to justify the majority-rule, able-bodied response to disability. The trend toward blaming individuals who live in a state of economic dependency rather than understanding the condition as a result of systemic dysfunctions also reinforces the tendency for mainstream society to adopt essentialist assumptions about normalcy. These kinds of assumptions lead to the isolation, and often the abandonment, of individuals outside the norm, such as women with disabilities.

The problem of victim blaming is compounded by the negative connotations attached to the condition of dependency. In the new market economy, all adults who depend on the state for support are considered suspect.[37] With greater competition for fewer jobs, more women with disabilities will require state assistance (which may well not be available) and therefore will be subject to the harsh judgments directed at persons who rely on state assistance. The increased tendency to link dependency and culpability may provide mainstream society with a pretext to further restrict access to employment insurance and other government-subsidized support programs.

VI. THE THREAT TO THE INDEPENDENCE OF WOMEN WITH DISABILITIES

Globalization jeopardizes the independence of many non-disabled women. This is the result of the reduction or elimination by governments of spending on social assistance and support programs, and of the decreased availability of jobs within the private sector in Canada.[38] To survive financially, women may be forced to retreat into the private family sphere. However, all women are vulnerable to violence in the context of the family, where they are unequal to male partners and may be subject to abuse.[39]

While concerns about non-disabled women retreating to the private sphere of the family are certainly legitimate, women with disabilities may not even have a family to which they can retreat. Women with disabilities are predominantly single. Those women who acquire a disability after marriage have a higher rate of separation and divorce.[40] Many women with disabilities do not have the option of the family as refuge. This means women with disabilities will fall between the cracks of the public and private spheres, and they will be made even more vulnerable to the experiences of homelessness, violence, sexual exploitation, and coercion.

VII. CONCLUSION: PRIORITIES FOR THE FUTURE

Women with disabilities find themselves in a precarious position because of the increased risks of economic inequality and poverty associated with globalization. Yet, while the issue of gender and globalization has received significant attention from academics and activists, the issue of gendered disability and globalization continues to be overlooked. In this conclusion, I make two recommendations. First, anti-globalization activists must take meaningful steps to include women with disabilities in their movement. Second, legal and political advocacy by and on behalf of women with disabilities should focus on achieving economic redistribution rather than recognition.

Transnational corporations, government actors, and activist groups all play a role in the globalization experience, yet all three ignore the impact of globalization on women with disabilities. Transnational corporations seek to dominate and control global economies without resistance from those people whose human rights, including those of women with disabilities, might be violated in the process. The invisibility of women with disabilities, along with the invisibility of other disenfranchised groups, facilitates the domination process.

Governments disregard women with disabilities for a similar reason—their invisibility facilitates social spending cutbacks. Finally, within the anti-globalization movement the experience of women with disabilities is also lost, but for a different reason. In this context, human rights issues are too often oversimplified, such that the experience of gendered disability discrimination disappears.

The concerns of women with disabilities relating to globalization need to be acknowledged and addressed. Women with disabilities could achieve this goal, in part, by increasing their visibility within the anti-globalization movement. This would enable them to have their concerns receive the attention they need and deserve. If women with disabilities can participate effectively in the anti-globalization movement, they will be better placed to oppose corporate and government policies and practices.

In order for women with disabilities to achieve visibility within the anti-globalization movement, participants in the movement, including academics and lawyers, need to develop a more comprehensive understanding of the effects of globalization and more representative equality rights advocacy strategies. Pro forma processes of inclusion, such as consultations amounting to no more than tokenistic objectifications of women with disabilities, are not helpful. This kind of inclusion can be as disempowering as outright exclusion.[41] Inclusion needs to mean more than grafting a gendered disability perspective onto an established theory or strategy for reform. Meaningful inclusion would mean that women with disabilities are incorporated into the movement as equals. Decision making about reform strategies needs to involve women with disabilities to ensure their perspective is represented. Sherene Razack has written about the need to adopt a "politics of accountability" in the context of feminism:[42]

> What would a politics of accountability look like? Clearly it begins with anti-essentialism and the recognition that there is no one stable core we can call women's experience. Equally important, it is a politics

guided by a search for the ways in which we are complicitous in the subordination of others.[43]

Razack's goal is seemingly to develop a politics by which human rights advocates can achieve honesty and responsibility in their work, which will contribute to a more valuable equality rights product. A politics of accountability could increase the accessibility of the anti-globalization movement for all disadvantaged persons. This could be achieved by exposing relations of privilege and domination among those involved in globalization and ensuring the examination of these relations. Central to a politics of accountability in the globalization context would be a recognition that there is no single experience that can be identified as the universal experience of oppression resulting from globalization, and that those affected by globalization may be complicit in the subordination of others. Through the incorporation of a politics of accountability, inclusion and representation may become more than mere empty gestures. If women with disabilities assume leadership positions within the movement, they will then be better positioned to educate others about their experience and to advocate for change on their own behalf.

Another priority for the future is the need for women with disabilities to focus their energies on redistributive remedies. While the demands for recognition and accommodation of difference that have been the focus of past advocacy efforts remain important, many of the harms associated with recognition inequality are intensified as a result of economic inequalities. A concentration of advocacy efforts on redistribution remedies is needed to prevent the further marginalization of women with disabilities. Possible legal challenges for redistribution could include equality rights challenges to retroactive government policies and legislation that diminish the economic security of women with disabilities.[44] If domestic courts fail to recognize the equality rights infractions inherent in government policies and legislation that threaten the economic security of women with disabilities,

an appeal to an international human rights forum, such as the United Nations Human Rights Commission, might be possible. Such an appeal would be based on international human rights mechanisms that recognize the rights of women with disabilities, such as the *Convention on the Elimination of All Forms of Discrimination against Women*,[45] although of course there are no guarantees for success in an international forum either.

Legal actions for economic redistribution could lead to incremental reform. However, more radical changes are needed to address the large-scale harms associated with globalization. Challenges to the underlying structures of political and economic oppression are necessary. Reforms could be achieved through advocacy efforts that challenge established sexist and ableist perspectives. Women with disabilities need to make dominant groups (both the dominant groups within the anti-globalization movement and beyond) self-conscious about their status as dominant groups; discomfort can be an effective stimulus for change.[46] In this way, prevailing norms can be exposed, challenged, and, hopefully, displaced.

Women with disabilities, through a combination of political and legal advocacy, need to address issues of economic redistribution. They need the opportunity to assert their rights, both in a political and legal context.

There is work to be done by the anti-globalization movement to ensure that such an opportunity is made available in a meaningful way. Women with disabilities also need to work to expose the socio-political and legal implications of gendered disability discrimination associated with globalization. Through increased information sharing, education, and understanding of the experience of gendered disability discrimination as it is intensified by globalization, the beginnings of an effective resistance and reform strategy designed to challenge globalization can take shape, and the economic security of women with disabilities may be advanced.

NOTES

1. Robert McCorquodale & Richard Fairbrother, "Globalization and Human Rights" (1999) 21:3 Hum. Rts. Q. 735; Alison Brysk, "Introduction" in Alison Brysk, ed., *Globalization and Human Rights* (Berkeley: University of California Press, 2002) 1.

2. Brenda Cossman & Judy Fudge, "Conclusion: Privatization, Polarization, and Policy" in Brenda Cossman & Judy Fudge, eds., *Privatization, Law, and the Challenge of Feminism* (Toronto: University of Toronto Press, 2002) 403 at 409–10; Cossman & Fudge, "Introduction: Privatization, Law, and the Challenge to Feminism" in Cossman & Fudge, ibid. 3 at 14–16; Brysk, *supra* note 1; Kenneth K. Lee, "Urban Poverty in Canada: A Statistical Profile" (Ottawa: Canadian Council on Social Development, 2000) at 55, online: Canadian Council on Social Development <http://www.ccsd.ca/pubs/2000/up/chapter3.pdf>.

3. See Isabella Bakker, "Engendering Macro-economic Policy Reform in the Era of Global Restructuring and Adjustment" in Isabella Bakker, ed., *The Strategic Silence: Gender and Economic Policy* (Ottawa: The North-South Institute, 1994) at 1; Janine Brodie, "Shifting the Boundaries: Gender and the Politics of Restructuring" in Bakker, ed., *The Strategic Silence*, ibid. 46 at 51, 56; Janine Brodie, "Restructuring and the New Citizenship" in Isabella Bakker, ed., *Rethinking Restructuring; Gender and Change in Canada* (Toronto: University of Toronto Press, 1996) 126 at 126–27; Cossman & Fudge, "Conclusion," *supra* note 2; Valentine M. Moghadam, "Gender and Globalization: Female Labor and Women's Mobilization" (1999) 5:2 *Journal of World Systems Research* 367–88; Canadian Feminist Alliance for International Action, "The Other Side of the Story: A Feminist Critique of Canada's National Response to the U.N. Questionnaire on the Implementation of the Beijing Platform for Action" (December 1999), online: European and North American Women Action <http://www.enawaorg/NGO/canadal.html>.

4. See Nancy Fraser, *Justice Interruptus: Critical Reflections on the "Postsocialist" Condition* (New York: Routledge, 1997) at 11–41, esp. 13–16. Fraser makes an analytical distinction between redistribution remedies directed at economic injustice and recognition remedies, directed at cultural injustice. She argues, however, that recognition and redistribution claims should be pursued together.

5. Shelagh Day & Gwen Brodsky, *Women and the Equality Deficit: The Impact of Restructuring Canada's Social Programs* (Ottawa: Status of Women Canada, 1998) at 5–8; Monica Townson, *Report Card on Poverty* (Ottawa: Canadian Centre for Policy Alternatives, 2000) at 3–8; Clarence Lochhead & Katherine Scott, *The Dynamics of Women's Poverty in Canada* (Ottawa: Status of Women Canada, 2000) at 15–18.

6. Day & Brodsky, *Women and the Equality Deficit*, ibid., at 94–95; Marika Morris, *Women and Poverty* (Ottawa: Canadian Research Institute for the Advancement of Women, 2002), online: Canadian Research Institute for the Advancement of Women <http://www.criaw-icref.ca/Poverty_fact_sheet.htm>. See also *Gosselin v. Quebec* (Attorney General), 2002 SCC 84 (Factum of intervenes National Association of Women and the Law) at paras, 39–41, online: PovNet <http://www.povnet.org/gosselin/gosselin_part2-3.htm>.

7. Freda L. Paltiel, "The Disabled Women's Network in Canada" (1997) 15:1 *Sexuality and Disability* 47.

8. Statistics Canada, *A Portrait of Persons with Disabilities* (Ottawa: Minister of Industry, Science, and Technology, 1995) at 46–49.

9. Human Resources Development Canada, *Improving Social Security in Canada. Persons with Disabilities: A Supplementary Paper* (Hull, Que.: Government of Canada, 1994) at 50–51.

10. Human Resources Development Canada, *Lessons Learned from Evaluation of Disability Policy and Programs* (Hull, Que.: Human Resources Development Canada, 1999), online: Human Resources Development Canada <http://www-ll.hrdc-drhc.gc.ca/pls/edd/DPPTR.lhtml>.

11. Statistics Canada, *Women in Canada: A Statistical Report*, 3d ed. (Ottawa: Minister of Industry, Science, and Technology, 1995) at 166 [*Women in Canada*].

12. Gail Fawcett, *Bringing Down the Barriers: The Labour Market and Women with Disabilities in Ontario* (Ottawa: Canadian Council on Social Development, 2000), online: Canadian Council on Social Development <http://www.ccsd.ca/pubs/2000/wd/sectionl.htm>.

13. See generally *Women in Canada, supra* note 11.

14. 18 December 1979, 1983 A.T.S. No. 9; 19 I.L.M. 33, online: U.N. Office of the High Commissioner for Human Rights <http://www.unhchr.ch/html/menu3/b/ elcedaw.htm> [CEDAW]. The Convention was adopted by the United Nations General Assembly in 1979, and Canada signed it in 1980.

15. Committee on the Elimination of Discrimination against Women, *Draft Report/Consideration of Reports of State Parties/Canada/Fifth Periodic Report*, UN CEDAWOR, 28th Sess., UN Doc. C/2OO3/I/CRP.3/Add.5/Rev.l (2003) 1 at 6, online: U.N. Division for the Advancement of Women <http://www.un.org/womenwatch/daw/cedaw/cedaw28/ConComCanada. PDF>. The committee also expressed concern about other marginalized groups of women, including elderly women, Aboriginal women, women of colour, single mothers, and immigrant women.

16 Judith Mosoff, "Is the Human Rights Paradigm 'Able' to Include Disability: Who's in? Who Wins? What? Why?" (2000) 26 *Queen's L.J.* 225 at paras. 27–29 (QL).

17. Janice Gross Stein, *The Cult of Efficiency* (Toronto: House of Anansi Press, 2001).

18. Ibid., at 9.

19. Where a complainant establishes a prima facie case of discrimination because of disability, the respondent can argue in defence that he or she cannot accommodate the needs of the complainant without undue hardship. The issues relevant to an undue hardship analysis include cost, health, and safety concerns. A successful defence of undue hardship depends on the facts of the specific case. See, e.g., *British Columbia (Public Service Employee Relations Commission) v. B.C.G.S.E.U.*, [1999] 3 S.C.R. 3 (QL).

20. Arjun P. Aggarwal & Madhu M. Gupta, "Same-Sex Sexual Harassment: Is It Sex Discrimination? A Review of Canadian and American Law" (2000)

27 *Man. L.J.* 333 at para. 1 (QL); Sandy Welsh, Myrna Dawson & Elizabeth Griffiths, "Sexual Harassment Complaints to the Canadian Human Rights Commission" in Donna Greschner et al. *Women and the Canadian Human Rights Act: A Collection of Policy Research Reports* (Ottawa: Status of Women Canada, 1999) at 187, 214; James E. Gruber, "The Impact of Male Work Environments and Organizational Policies on Women's Experiences of Sexual Harassment" (1998) 12(3) *Gender & Society* 301 at 302–05; Laura L. O'Toole & Jessica R. Schiffman, "Sexual Harassment" in Laura L. O'Toole &. Jessica R. Schiffman, eds., *Gender Violence: Interdisciplinary Perspectives* (New York: New York University Press, 1997) 131 at 132–33.

21. Barbara A. Gutek &. Mary P. Koss, "Changed Women and Changed Organizations: Consequences of and Coping with Sexual Harassment" in O'Toole &. Schiffman, ibid. 151 at 154–55.

22. Judy Fudge, "Rungs on the Labour Law Ladder: Using Gender to Challenge Hierarchy" (1996) *Sask. L. Rev.* 237 (QL).

23. Dick Sobsey, "Patterns of Sexual Abuse and Assault" (1991) 9 *Sexuality and Disability* 243 at 248–49; Helen Meekosha, "Body Battles: Bodies, Gender, and Disability" in Tom Shakespeare, ed., *The Disability Reader* (New York: Cassell, 1998) at 177; Marika Morris, *Violence against Women and Girls: A Fact Sheet* (Ottawa: Canadian Research Institute for the Advancement of Women, 2002), online: Canadian Research Institute for the Advancement of Women <http://www.criaw-icref.ca/Violence_fact_sheet_a.htm>.

24 Constance Backhouse & Leah Cohen, *Sexual Harassment on the Job* (Englewood Cliffs, N.J.: Prentice Hall, 1981); Arjun P. Aggarwal, *Sexual Harassment in the Workplace* (Toronto: Butterworths Canada, 1992). See also Ontario Women's Directorate, "The Nature of Sexual Harassment" in *Employer's Guide: A Time for Action on Sexual Harassment in the Workplace* (Toronto: Ontario Women's Directorate, 1993), online: Education Wife Assault <http://www. womanabuseprevention.com/html/employers.html>; O'Toole & Schiffman, "Sexual Harassment," *supra* note 20 at 136.

25. The corporate phenomenon of mining popular culture for sources of meaning and identity to attach to commercial products and the phenomenon of "brandmasters" or "change agents" targeting the same cultural groups as part of aggressive marketing campaigns are discussed in Naomi Klein, *No Logo: Taking Aim at Brand Bullies* (Toronto: Random House, 2000) at 365–79.

26. Ibid., at 360.

27. Ibid., at 115.

28. Leah F. Vosko, *Temporary Work: The Gendered Rise of a Precarious Employment Relationship* (Toronto: University of Toronto Press, 2000) at 3–13, 27–44.

29. Ibid.

30. Edward B. Harvey & Lorne Tepperman, *Selected Socio-Economic Consequences of Disability for Women* (Ottawa: Statistics Canada, 1990) at A-13.

31. *Employment Insurance Act*, S.C. 1996, c. 23.

32. *Unemployment Insurance Act*, R.S.C. 1985, c. U-l. Reforms to the legislation introduced in 1996 via the *Employment Insurance Act*, ibid., changed the eligibility criteria. Under section 6(1) of the Act, a major attachment claimant is now defined as "a claimant who qualifies to receive benefits and has 700 or more hours of insurable employment in their qualifying period." Section 7(2) of the Act goes on to establish a threshold for employment insurance benefit eligibility based only on hours of insurable employment—between 420 and 700, depending on the regional rate of unemployment. The total hours specified must be worked within the qualifying period, which is generally fifty-two weeks. Sections 22 and 23 of the Act provide that only major attachment claimants are eligible to receive maternity and parental benefits.

33. *Lesiuk v. Canada (Employment insurance Commission)*, CUB 51142, R.E. Salhany, Umpire, March 22, 2001 at para. 32, rev'd 2003 KC.A. 3, leave to appeal to S.C.C. requested.

34. Fawcett, *supra* note 12.

35. Part I of the *Constitution Act*, 1982, being Schedule B to the *Canada Act* 1982 (U.K.), 1982, c. 11. While a specific challenge to sections 6 and 7 of the *Employment Insurance Act* on the basis of gendered disability discrimination has not

been advanced, the provisions have been challenged as unconstitutional based on allegations of sex and family status discrimination. The umpire in *Lesiuk*, *supra* note 33, found that the disadvantage experienced under the Act by able-bodied women who are mothers as well as part-time workers constitutes discrimination in violation of section 15(1) of the Charter. The umpire's decision in *Lesiuk* was recently overruled by the Federal Court of Appeal, and application for leave to appeal the Court of Appeal's decision has been filed with the Supreme Court.

36. There have been some advances made in terms of the legal perception of disability discrimination incorporating an awareness of the social construction of disability (thereby de-emphasizing the focus on the individual). For example, see Ontario Human Rights Commission, "Policy and Guidelines on Disability and the Duty to Accommodate" (November 2000) at 8–11, online: Ontario Human Rights Commission <http://www.ohrc.on.ca/english/publications/disability-policy.shtml>.

37. Brodie, "Restructuring and the New Citizenship," *supra* note 3 at 134–35, 136–37.

38. Day & Brodsky, *supra* note 5; Christa Freiler & Judy Cerny, *Benefiting Canada's Children: Perspectives on Gender and Social Responsibility* (Ottawa: Status of Women Canada, 1998). Executive Summary available online: Status of Women Canada <http://www.swc-cfc.gc.ca/pubs/0662634691/199803_0662634691_e.html>.

39. Over a quarter (29 per cent) of Canadian women have been assaulted by a spouse. There are approximately sixty-seven intimate femicides per year in Canada in which women are the victims and men are the murderers. See Morris, *supra* note 23.

40. Jennifer Lee & Shirley White, "Economic Sufficiency of Women with Disability" (1998) 1:3 *Asia & Pacific Journal on Disability* at para. 10, online: Disability Information Resources <http://www.dinf.ne.jp/doc/english/asia/resource/zOOap/003/zOOap00305.htm>; Adrienne Asch & Michelle Fine, "Nurturance, Sexuality, and Women with Disabilities" in Lennard J. Davis, ed., *The Disability Studies Reader* (New York: Routledge, 1997) 241 at 241–43.

41. See Kimberly Crenshaw, "Mapping the Margins: Intersectionality, Identity, Politics, and Violence against Women of Color" (1991) 43 *Stan. L. Rev.* 1241 at 1249.

42. Sherene Razack, *Looking White People in the Eye* (Toronto: University of Toronto Press, 1998) at 157–70.

43. Ibid., at 159.

44. Two cases currently before the courts in Canada have potential to generate affirmative redistributive remedies that could benefit women with disabilities: *Lesiuk, supra* note 33, and *Falkiner v. Ontario (Ministry of Community and Social Services, Income Maintenance Branch)* (2002), 59 O.R. (3d) 481 (Ont. C.A.), leave to appeal to S.C.C. granted, [2002] S.C.C.A. No. 297. At issue in *Falkiner* is whether amendments to Ontario's social assistance regulations changing the definition of "spouse" for the purposes of receiving social assistance violate sections 7 and 15 of the Charter. The new regulations provide that if a social assistance recipient lives with a person of the opposite sex, the two are presumed to be spouses, and the social assistance recipient is presumed to have access to the income of the other person. Such presumptions of financial dependency may be relevant to women with disabilities who live with caregivers. The Supreme Court's recent decision in *Gosselin v. Quebec (Attorney General)*, 2002 SCC 84,12002] S.C.J. No. 85 (QL), should be relevant to the appeals of *Lesiuk* and *Falkiner*. In *Gosselin*, at para. 82, the Court left open the question of whether governments have positive obligations under the Charter to ensure adequate financial assistance to persons in Canada.

45. The application of the universal principle of non-discrimination entrenched in CEDAW, *supra* note 14, could he applied by women with disabilities to the disability context. In support of the legitimacy of this strategy, General Recommendation No. 18 of the Committee on the Elimination of Discrimination against Women discussed the specific government reporting duties regarding the rights of women with disabilities under CEDAW. The committee also mentioned women with disabilities in its General Recommendation No. 24, which refers to women and health. See UN GAOR, 54th Sess., Supp. No. 38, UN Doc. A/54/38 (Part I) at 5.

46. Nitya Iyer has written about the need for those outside of the dominant norm to generate, among members of the dominant group, a consciousness of their dominance. This exposes the norms against which human rights claimants are measured. See Nitya Iyer, "Categorical Denials: Equality Rights and the Shaping of Social Identity" (1993) 19 *Queen's L.J.* 179.

CHAPTER 15

PILLS AND POWER TOOLS

Susan Bordo

Viagra. "The Potency Pill," as *Time* magazine's cover describes it. Since it went on sale, it has had "the fastest takeoff of a new drug" that the RiteAid drugstore chain has ever seen. It is all over the media. Users are jubilant, claiming effects that last through the night, youth restored, better "quality" erections. "This little pill is like a package of dynamite," says one.

Some even see Viagra as a potential cure for social ills. Bob Guccione, publisher of *Penthouse*, hails the drug as "freeing the American male libido" from the emasculating clutches of feminism. This diagnosis does not sit very comfortably with current medical wisdom, which has declared impotence to be a physiological problem. I, like Guccione, am skeptical of that declaration—but would suggest a deeper meditation on what has put the squeeze on male libido.

Think, to begin with, of the term *impotence*. It rings with disgrace, humiliation—and it was not the feminists who invented it. Writer Philip Lopate, in an essay on his body, says that merely to say the word out loud makes him nervous. Yet remarkably, *impotence*—rather than the more forgiving, if medicalized, *erectile dysfunction*—is still a common nomenclature among medical researchers. *Frigidity*, with its suggestion that the woman is cold, like some barren tundra, went by the board a while ago.

But *impotence*, no less loaded with ugly gender implications, remains. Lenore Tiefer, who researches medical terminology, suggests that we cannot let go of *impotence* because to do so would force us to also let go of *potency* and the cultural mythology that equates male sexuality with power. But to hold on to that mythology, men must pay a steep price.

Impotence. Unlike other disorders, impotence implicates the whole man, not merely the body part. He is impotent. Would we ever say about a man with a headache "He is a headache?" Yet this is just what we do with impotence, as Warren Farrell notes in *Why Men Are the Way They Are*. "We make no attempt to separate impotence from the total personality." Then, we expect the personality to perform like a machine.

That expectation of men is embedded throughout our culture. Think of our slang terms, so many of which encase the penis, like a cyborg, in various sorts of metal or steel armor. Big rig. Blow torch. Bolt. Cockpit. Crank. Crowbar. Destroyer. Dipstick. Drill. Engine. Hammer. Hand tool. Hardware. Hose. Power tool. Rod. Torpedo. Rocket. Spear. Such slang—common among teenage boys—is violent in what it suggests the machine penis can do to another, "softer" body. But the terms are also metaphorical protection against the failure of potency. A human organ of flesh and blood is subject to anxiety, ambivalence, uncertainty. A torpedo or rocket, on the other hand, would never let one down.

Contemporary urologists have taken the metaphor of man the machine even further. Erectile functioning is "all hydraulics," says Irwin Goldstein of the Boston University Medical Center, scorning a previous generation of researchers who stressed psychological issues. But if it is all a matter of fluid dynamics, why keep the term *impotent*, whose definitions (according to *Webster's Unabridged*) are "want of power," "weakness," "lack of effectiveness, helplessness" and (appearing last) "lack of ability to engage in sexual intercourse." In keeping the term *impotence*, the drug companies, it seems, get to have it both ways: reduce a complex human condition to a matter of chemistry while keeping the old shame machine working, helping to assure the flow of men to their doors.

We live in a culture that encourages men to think of their sexuality as residing in their penises and that gives men little encouragement to explore the rest of their bodies. The beauty of the male body has finally been brought out of the cultural closet by Calvin Klein, Versace, and other designers. But notice how many of those new underwear ads aggressively direct our attention to the (often extraordinary) endowments of the models. Many of the models stare coldly, challengingly at the viewer, defying the viewer's gaze to define them in any way other than how they have chosen to present themselves: powerful, armored, emotionally impenetrable. "I am a rock," their bodies seem to proclaim. Commercial advertisements depict women stroking their necks, their faces, their legs, lost in sensual reverie, taking pleasure in touching themselves—all over. Similar poses with men are very rare. Touching oneself languidly, lost in the sensual pleasure of the body, is too feminine, too "soft," for a real man. Crotch-grabbing, thrusting, putting it "in your face"—that is another matter.

There is a fascinating irony in the fact that although it is women whose bodies are most sexually objectified by this culture, women's bodies are permitted much greater sexual expression in our cultural representations than men's. In sex scenes, the moaning and writhing of the female partner have become the conventional cinematic code for heterosexual ecstasy and climax. The male's participation largely gets represented via caressing hands, humping buttocks, and—on rare occasions—a facial expression of intense concentration. She is transported to another world; he is the pilot of the ship that takes her there. When men are shown being transported themselves, it is usually being played for comedy (as in Al Pacino's shrieks in *Frankie and Johnny*, Eddie Murphy's moaning in *Boomerang*, Kevin Kline's contortions in *A Fish Called Wanda*), or it is coded to suggest that something is not quite normal with the man—he is sexually enslaved, for example (as with Jeremy Irons in *Damage*). Men's bodies in the movies are action-hero toys, power tools—wind them up and watch them perform.

Thankfully, the equation between penis and power tool is now being questioned in other movies. Earlier this year, *The Full Monty* brought us a likable group of unemployed workers in Sheffield, England, who hatch the moneymaking scheme of displaying all in a male strip show and learn what it is like to be what feminist theorists call "the object of the gaze." Paul Thomas Anderson's *Boogie Nights* told the story of the rise and fall (so to speak) of a mythically endowed young porn star, Dirk Diggler, who does fine so long as he is the most celebrated stallion in the stable but loses his grip in the face of competition. On the surface, the film is about a world far removed from the lives of most men, a commercial underground where men pray for "wood" and lose their jobs unless they can achieve erection on command. On a deeper level, however, the world of the porn actor is simply the most literalized embodiment—and a perfect metaphor—for a masculinity that demands constant performance from men.

Even before he takes up a career that depends on it, Diggler's sense of self is constellated around his penis; he pumps up his ego by looking in the mirror and—like a coach mesmerizing the team before a game—intoning mantras about his superior gifts. That works well, so long as he believes it. But unlike a real power tool, the motor of male self-worth cannot simply be switched on and off. In the very final shot of the movie, we see Diggler's fabled organ itself. It is a prosthesis, actually (a fact that annoyed several men I know until I pointed out that it was no more a cheat than implanted breasts passing for the real thing). But prosthesis or not and despite its dimensions, it is no masterful tool. It points downward, weighted with expectation, with shame, looking tired and used.

Beginning with the French film *Ridicule* (in which an aristocrat, using his penis as an instrument of vengeance, urinates on the lap of another man), we have seen more unclothed penises in films this year than ever before. But what is groundbreaking about *Boogie Nights* is not that it displays a nude penis, but that it so unflinchingly exposes the job that the mythology of unwavering potency does on the male body. As long as the fortress holds, the sense of power may be intoxicating; but when it cracks—as it is bound to do at some point—the whole structure falls to pieces. Those of whom such constancy is expected (or who require it of themselves) are set up for defeat and humiliation.

Unless, of course, he pops his little pill whenever "failure" threatens. I have no desire to withhold Viagra from the many men who have been deprived of the ability to get an erection by accidents, diabetes, cancer, and other misfortunes to which the flesh—or psyche—is heir. I would just like CNN and *Time* to spend a fraction of the time they devote to describing "how Viagra cures" to looking at how our culture continues to administer the poison for whose effects we now claim a cure. Let us note, too, that the official medical definition of erectile dysfunction (like the definitions of depression and attention deficit disorder) has broadened coincident with the development of new drugs. Dysfunction is no longer defined as "inability

to get an erection" but inability to get an erection that is adequate for "satisfactory sexual performance." Performance. Not pleasure. Not feeling. Performance.

Some of what we now call impotence may indeed be physiological in origin; some may be grounded in deep psychic fears and insecurities. But sometimes, too, a man's penis may simply be instructing him that his feelings are not in synch with the job he is supposed to do—or with the very fact that it's a "job." So, I like Philip Lopate's epistemological metaphor for the penis much better than the machine images. Over the years, he has come to appreciate, he writes, that his penis has its "own specialized form of intelligence." The penis knows that it is not a torpedo, no matter what a culture expects of it or what drugs are relayed to its blood vessels. If we accept that, the notion that a man requires understanding and tolerance when he does not "perform" would go by the wayside ("It's OK. It happens" still assumes that there is something to be excused.) So, too, would the idea that there ought to be one model for understanding nonarousal. Sometimes, the penis's "specialized intelligence" should be listened to rather than cured.

Viagra, unfortunately, seems to be marketed—and used—with the opposite message in mind. Now men can perform all night! Do their job no matter how they feel! (The drug does require some degree of arousal, but minimal.) The hype surrounding the drug encourages rather than deconstructs the expectation that men perform like power tools with only one switch—on or off. Until this expectation is replaced by a conception of manhood that permits men and their penises a full range of human feeling, we will not yet have the kind of "cure" we really need.

DISCUSSION QUESTIONS: WEITZ

1. Using examples from Weitz's piece, discuss how ideas about women's bodies through history have been used as political tools to shape and challenge dominant gender relations.
2. What patriarchal reasoning was used to justify women's legal status as property? What has been the historical legacy of this reasoning for White and African-American women according to Weitz?

3. As women make social gains through protest and struggle that challenge patriarchal power structures, usually "counterreactions" develop to contain their progress. Describe some of these "counterreactions" from the 19th and 20th centuries that have impacted women's bodies.

DISCUSSION QUESTIONS: URLA AND SWEDLUND

1. Explain the socio-political and cultural contexts that made the "birth" of Barbie possible and meaningful.
2. Discuss the relationship between anthropometry and the development of the Barbie doll.
3. Describe the differences Urla and Swedlund found among the measurements of Barbie's body dimensions and those of Shani, Ken, Jamal, Army Norma, and Army Norm. What conclusions and implications do the authors draw from these differences?

DISCUSSION QUESTIONS: MERNISSI

1. How can the clothing norm of size 6 for Western women be understood as a gendered bodily constraint more restrictive than the Muslim veil or harem?
2. What differences does Mernissi describe between Western and Islamic patriarchal control over women and their bodies?

DISCUSSION QUESTIONS: SAMPSON

1. Explain the many ways in which women with disabilities are particularly vulnerable to economic restructuring processes that are part of global capitalism.
2. Discuss in detail the four main ways in which globalization processes are frustrating the equality rights of women with disabilities in Canada.
3. What two strategies does Sampson propose for advancing equality rights of women with disabilities in light of the current threat of globalization? Why?

DISCUSSION QUESTIONS: BORDO

1. How is Viagara implicated in the problematic notion that men should be always already able to perform like a machine?
2. In what other areas of our culture do we see this association of man and machine?
3. Where can you find cultural challenges to this particular embodied construction of masculinity?

FURTHER READINGS

1. Bordo, Susan. 1993. *Unbearable Weight: Feminism, Western Culture, and the Body*. Berkeley: University of California Press.
   In this classic monograph Bordo provides a cultural analysis of the contemporary female body, including an in-depth discussion of the myths, ideologies, and practices that socially construct, regulate, and discipline it. She focuses most particularly on the commodification of women's bodies, arguing that

consumption "normalizes" these bodies and leads some women and girls to physically discipline themselves to such an extent that they endanger their lives.

2. Conboy, Katie, Nadia Median, and Sarah Stanbury (eds.). 1997. *Writing on the Body: Female Embodiment and Feminist Theory*. New York: Columbia University Press.

   This collection of essays by leading feminist theorists is organized by the metaphor of "writing the body" to explore how women's bodies are "read," constituted, performed, and experienced.

3. Fausto-Sterling, Anne. 2000. *Sexing the Body: Gender Politics and the Construction of Sexuality*. New York: Basic Books.

   This feminist biologist provides a rich examination of the role of science in constructing "truths" about sexuality, biological sex differences, and sexual identity. She accesses past and current research on intersexed individuals, sex-based brain differences, and sex hormones, showing how gender politics organize each of these spheres of scientific research.

4. Mohanran, Radhika. 1999. *Black Body: Women, Colonialism, and Space*. Minneapolis: University of Minnesota Press.

   A colonial lens has rendered the female Black body, no matter where it is situated around the globe, as dangerous, unknown, and alien. With her sights on the Antipodes, Mohanran explores the associations of the Black body with nature and landscape, as the White body is associated with knowledge. She draws on post-colonial feminist theory to interrogate the relationship between female Black bodies and White male bodies, as well as Northern and Southern theories of the body, which she argues parallels the unequal political relationship between the two hemispheres.

5. Thomas, Rosmarie Garland (ed.). 1996. *Freakery: Cultural Spectacles of the Extraordinary Body*. New York: New York University Press.

   This multidisciplinary collection of essays focuses on how racialized and disabled bodies have historically been commodified and turned into spectacles for Western viewing, whether in circuses, museums, and fairs, or, more recently, on television.

RELEVANT FILMS

1. *The Pill*, 2003, 56 minutes, PBS Home Video

   This PBS documentary presents one-on-one interviews with the first generation of women to have access to the birth control pill in the United States. The women interviewed discuss how this hormone-controlling medication affected their lives, unleashing both a personal and larger social revolution.

2. *La Operacion*, 1982, 40 minutes, Cinema Guild

   Despite the date of this film, it effectively examines the persistent and controversial practice of female sterilization as a means of population control in Puerto Rico, which has the highest incidence of this practice in the world.

3. *Whose Bodies, Whose Rights*, 1996, 56 minutes, University of California Extension Centre for Media and Independent Learning

   Male circumcision is an increasingly contentious practice in North America. This documentary demonstrates that it is performed based mainly on medical and cultural myths, as opposed to a firm medical rationale.

4. *Killing Us Softly III*, 1999, 30 minutes, Cambridge Documentary Films

   This documentary outlines the psychological, sexual, and gender constructs that organize advertising in North America. It is an updated version of Kilbourne's now classic documentary, which examines how the images of women in advertising have evolved over the last two decades.

5. *Fire Eyes: Female Circumcision*, 1994, 60 minutes, Filmmakers Library

   The culturally explosive issue of female circumcision in Africa is the topic of this film. Doctors explain the various forms this practice can take, as well as the medical problems that result. Women who have undergone the procedure discuss their contrasting experiences, as well as their views on its practice in the future. In addition, we hear from men, who also have conflicting insights about its cultural relevance.

RELEVANT WEB SITES

1. http://newmedia.colorado.edu/~socwomen/resources/body.html
    This Web site, constructed by *Sociologists for Women in Society*, provides an excellent and thorough list of resources pertaining to feminism, gender, and the body.
2. www.femtap.com/id13.html
    Disarming Venus: Disability and the Revision of Art History includes a discussion of feminist performance art that is part of the larger feminist art movement. These performances expose how visual culture has depended on sexual exploitation and violence against women's bodies, with the effect of erasing the female subject. Feminist performers use their bodies as art to challenge these constructions. The site pays particular attention to a 1995 live performance at a Disability Arts Conference by Mary Duffy.
3. www.grhf.harvard.edu/frame1/researchlib.html
    Harvard's GRHF Research library on gender and reproduction includes references and resources regarding gender and abortion, contraception, biological technology, HIV/AIDS, maternal health, family planning, women's reproductive rights, and STDs and RTIs. Many of the same topics are suitably framed for teenaged reading.
4. www.genderads.com
    Gender Ads analyzes the dominant gender tropes that organize advertising using women's bodies. It provides samples of ads, as well as cartoons from *Hustler* and *Playboy*, and explains how to read them from a feminist perspective. In doing so it supplies pictorial evidence of the bodily misogyny and violence inherent in much media and advertising. This site is interesting and novel.
5. www.mwlusa.org/pulications/positionpapers/fgm.html
    The *Muslim Women's League* is a non-profit American Muslim organization that aims to achieve the equal status of women in society. Their Web site includes important and instructive essays about and links to further information about Islam, as well as body issues including female genital mutilation, Muslim women's dress and veiling practices, violence against Muslim women, and rape.

⊕ ⊕ ⊕

PART V

GENDERED VIOLENCE

Gender violence is a problem of significant proportions that affects many societies around the world. Since the early 1970s, thanks to the feminist movement, there has been an enormous growth in the amount of public and professional attention given to gendered violence in Western capitalist societies, and this attention has now spread globally. However, many people remain unaware of the magnitude, causes, and consequences of gender violence as it plays out in marital, dating, and cohabiting relationships. Even less awareness exists about the violence enacted on women by employers and state actors.

Men's violence against women is often understood as the actions of a few "sick" men perpetrated upon a few unruly women. Consequently, it is widely conceived of as individually motivated behaviours that have few serious social consequences, which means that men's violence against women is seldom identified as a social site of patterned relations between women and men. Feminists, however, argue that men's violence against women has all the characteristics of a social structure, and that it cannot be understood outside an analysis of unequal gender relations in a patriarchal social context. Indeed, scholars in this field of feminist research have found that in gender-equitable cultures, violence against women is largely unknown.

These readings present some of the issues associated with two particular types of gender violence, but also propose ways to prevent and eradicate them. First, Russell Dobash and his colleagues, in their article "The Myth of Sexual Symmetry in Marital Violence," relate the body of feminist research that documents wife abuse as a widespread and severe social problem that is used as a tool to dominate and control women, even as it continues to be ignored and treated ineffectually by American justice, medical, and social service institutions. What worries them is the number of recent researchers who claim that assaults on men by their wives constitutes a social problem comparable in nature and magnitude to that of wife-beating. To address their concern, the authors examine these data, research methodologies, and arguments in depth, demonstrating that the claim of sexual symmetry in marital violence is exaggerated, and that wives' and husbands' uses of violence differ greatly, both quantitatively and qualitatively. They claim that, if violence is gendered, then we need to demonstrate gender's relevance to violence, instead of conceiving violence as a widespread pattern in intimate human relationships.

Next, Helene Moussa analyzes the types of violence that are perpetrated against refugee women in their home countries and refugee camps, as well as by the Canadian state and society more generally when they settle in Canada as refugees. Not even their new family lives in Canada are violence-free. Moussa discusses the effects of gender, sexual, and racial violence on refugee women's mobility, security, self-esteem, and ability to integrate into Canadian society. She argues that we need to understand how gender relations inform the realities of violence in countries of origin and asylum by analyzing the social systems and structures that contribute to the oppression of refugee women, such as immigrant and refugee social policy in Canada.

CHAPTER 16

THE MYTH OF SEXUAL SYMMETRY IN MARITAL VIOLENCE

Russell P. Dobash, R. Emerson Dobash, Margo Wilson, and Martin Daly

Long denied, legitimized, and made light of, wife-beating is at last the object of widespread public concern and condemnation. Extensive survey research and intensive interpretive investigations tell a common story. Violence against wives (by which term we encompass *de facto* as well as registered unions) is often persistent and severe, occurs in the context of continuous intimidation and coercion, and is inextricably linked to attempts to dominate and control women [...]. Historical and contemporary investigations further reveal that this violence has been explicitly decriminalized, ignored, or treated in an ineffectual manner by criminal justice systems, by medical and social service institutions, and by communities [...]. Increased attention to these failures has inspired increased efforts to redress them, and in many places legislative amendments have mandated arrest and made assault a crime whether the offender is married to the victim or not.

A number of researchers and commentators have suggested that assaults upon men by their wives constitute a social problem comparable in nature and magnitude to that of wife-beating [...]. Two main bodies of evidence have been offered in support of these authors' claims that husbands and wives are similarly victimized: (1) self-reports of violent acts perpetrated and suffered by survey respondents, especially those in two U.S. national probability samples [...]; and (2) U.S. homicide data. Unlike the case of violence against wives, however, the victimization of husbands allegedly continues to be denied and trivialized. "Violence by wives has not been an object of public concern," note Straus and Gelles (1986:472). "There has been no publicity, and no funds have been invested in ameliorating this problem because it has not been defined as a problem."

We shall argue that claims of sexual symmetry in marital violence are exaggerated, and that wives' and husbands' uses of violence differ greatly, both quantitatively and qualitatively. We shall further argue that there is no reason to expect the sexes to be alike in this domain, and that efforts to avoid sexism by lumping male and female data and by the use of gender-neutral terms such as "spouse-beating" are misguided. If violence is gendered, as it assuredly is, explicit characterization of gender's relevance to violence is essential. The alleged similarity of women and men in their use of violence in intimate relationships stands in marked contrast to men's virtual monopoly on the use of violence in other social contexts, and we challenge the proponents of the sexual symmetry thesis to

173

develop coherent theoretical models that would account for a sexual monomorphism of violence in one social context and not others.

*****

THE CLAIM OF SEXUALLY SYMMETRICAL MARITAL VIOLENCE

Authoritative claims about the prevalence and sexual symmetry of spousal violence in America began with a 1975 U.S. national survey in which 2,143 married or cohabiting persons were interviewed in person about their actions in the preceding year. Straus (1977/78) announced that the survey results showed that the "marriage license is a hitting licence," and moreover that the rates of perpetrating spousal violence, including severe violence, were higher for wives than for husbands. [...] In 1985, the survey was repeated by telephone with a new national probability sample including 3,520 husband-wife households, and with similar results. In each survey, the researchers interviewed either the wife or the husband (but not both) in each contacted household about how the couple settled their differences when they had a disagreement. The individual who was interviewed was presented with a list of 18 "acts" ranging from "discussed an issue calmly" and "cried" to "threw something at him/her/you" and "beat him/ her/you up," with the addition of "choked him/her/you" in 1985 (Straus 1990a:33). These acts constituted the Conflict Tactics Scales (CTS) and were intended to measure three constructs: "Reasoning," "Verbal Aggression," and "Physical Aggression" or "Violence," which was further subdivided into "Minor Violence" and "Severe Violence" according to a presumed potential for injury (Straus and Gelles 1990). Respondents were asked how frequently they had perpetrated each act in the course of "conflicts or disagreements" with their spouses (and with one randomly selected child) within the past year, and how frequently they had been on the receiving end. Each respondent's self-reports of victimization and perpetration contributed to estimates of rates of violence by both husbands and wives.

According to both surveys, rates of violence by husbands and wives were strikingly similar [...]. The authors estimated that in the year prior to the 1975 survey 11.6 percent of U.S. husbands were victims of physical violence perpetrated by their wives, while 12.1 percent of wives were victims of their husbands' violence. In 1985, these percentages had scarcely changed, but husbands seemed more vulnerable: 12.1 percent of husbands and 11.3 percent of wives were victims. In both surveys, husbands were more likely to be victims of acts of "severe violence": in 1975, 4.6 percent of husbands were such victims versus 3.8 percent of wives, and in 1985, 4.4 percent of husbands versus 3.0 percent of wives were victims. In reporting their results, the surveys' authors stressed the surprising assaultiveness of wives.

*****

[...] One of Straus and Gelles's collaborators in the 1975 survey, Steinmetz (1977/78), used the same survey evidence to proclaim the existence of "battered husbands" and a "battered husband syndrome." She has remained one of the leading defenders of the claim that violence between men and women in the family is symmetrical [...]. Steinmetz and her collaborators maintain that the problem is not wife-beating perpetrated by violent men, but "violent couples" and "violent people" (see also Shupe et al. 1987). Men may be stronger on average, argues Steinmetz, but weaponry equalizes matters, as is allegedly shown by the nearly equivalent numbers of U.S. husbands and wives who are killed by their partners. The reason why battered husbands are inconspicuous and seemingly rare is supposedly that shame prevents them from seeking help.

Straus and his collaborators have sometimes qualified their claims that their surveys demonstrate sexual symmetry in marital violence, noting, for example, that men are usually larger and stronger than women and thus able to inflict more damage and that women are more likely to use violence in self-defense or retaliation [...]. However, the survey results indicate a symmetry not just in the perpetration of violence but in its initiation as well, and from this further symmetry, Stets and Straus (1990:154–155) conclude

174

that the equal assaultiveness of husbands and wives cannot be attributed to the wives acting in self-defense, after all.

*****

Some authors maintain not only that wives initiate violence at rates comparable to husbands, but that they rival them in the damage they inflict as well. [...] The most dramatic evidence invoked in this context is again the fact that wives kill: spousal homicides—for which detection should be minimally or not at all biased because homicides are nearly always discovered and recorded—produce much more nearly equivalent numbers of male and female victims in the United States than do sublethal assault data, which are subject to sampling biases when obtained from police, shelters and hospitals. [...]

A corollary of the notion that the sexes are alike in their use of violence is that satisfactory causal accounts of violence will be gender-blind. Discussion thus focuses, for example, on the role of one's prior experiences with violence as a child, social stresses, frustration, inability to control anger, impoverished social skills, and so forth, without reference to gender [...]. This presumption that the sexes are alike not merely in action but in the reasons for that action is occasionally explicit, such as when Shupe et al. (1987:56) write: "Everything we have found points to parallel processes that lead women and men to become violent.... Women may be more likely than men to use kitchen utensils or sewing scissors when they commit assault, but their frustrations, motives and lack of control over these feelings predictably resemble men's."

In sum, the existence of an invisible legion of assaulted husbands is an inference which strikes many family violence researchers as reasonable. Two lines of evidence—homicide data and the CTS survey results—suggest to those supporting the sexual-symmetry-of-violence thesis that large numbers of men are trapped in violent relationships. These men are allegedly being denied medical, social welfare, and criminal justice services because of an unwillingness to accept the evidence from homicide statistics and the CTS surveys [...].

VIOLENCE AGAINST WIVES

Any argument that marital violence is sexually symmetrical must either dismiss or ignore a large body of contradictory evidence indicating that wives greatly outnumber husbands as victims. While CTS researchers were discovering and publicizing the mutual violence of wives and husbands, other researchers—using evidence from courts, police, and women's shelters—were finding that wives were much more likely than husbands to be victims [...]. After an extensive review of extant research, Lystad (1975) expressed the consensus: "The occurrence of adult violence in the home usually involves males as aggressors towards females." This conclusion was subsequently supported by numerous further studies of divorce records, emergency room patients treated for non-accidential injuries, police assault records, and spouses seeking assistance and refuge [...]. Analyses of police and court records in North America and Europe have persistently indicated that women constitute 90 to 95% of the victims of those assaults in the home reported to the criminal justice system [...].

Defenders of the sexual-symmetry-of-violence thesis do not deny these results, but they question their representativeness: these studies could be biased because samples of victims were self-selected. However, criminal victimization surveys using national probability samples similarly indicate that wives are much more often victimized than husbands. Such surveys in the United States, Canada and Great Britain have been replicated in various years, with essentially the same results. [...] The 1981 Canadian Urban Victimization Survey [...] and the 1987 General Social Survey [...] produced analagous findings, from which Johnson (1989) concluded that "women account for 80–90 percent of victims in assaults or sexual assaults between spouses or former spouses. In fact, the number of domestic assaults involving males was too low in both surveys to provide reliable estimates" (1–2). The 1982 and 1984 British Crime Surveys found that women accounted for all the victims of marital assaults [...].

The national crime surveys also indicate that women are much more likely than men to suffer injury as a result of assaults in the home [...]. After analyzing the results of the U.S. National Crime Surveys, Schwartz (1987:67) concludes, "there are still more than 13 times as many women seeking medical care from a private physician for injuries received in a spousal assault." This result again replicates the typical findings of studies of police or hospital records. For example, women constituted 94 percent of the injury victims in an analysis of the spousal assault cases among 262 domestic disturbance calls to police in Santa Barbara County, California [...]; moreover, the women's injuries were more serious than the men's.

In response, defenders of the sexual-symmetry-of-violence thesis contend that data from police, courts, hospitals, and social service agencies are suspect because men are reluctant to report physical violence by their wives. [...] Shupe et al. (1987) maintain that men are unwilling to report their wives because "it would be unmanly or unchivalrous to go to the police for protection from a woman" (52). However, the limited available evidence does not support these authors' presumption that men are less likely to report assaults by their spouses than are women. Schwartz's (1987) analysis of the 1973–1982 U.S. National Crime Survey data found that 67.2 percent of men and 56.8 percent of women called the police after being assaulted by their spouses. One may protest that these high percentages imply that only a tiny proportion of the most severe spousal assaults were acknowledged as assaults by respondents to these crime surveys, but the results are nonetheless contrary to the notion that assaulted men are especially reticent. Moreover, Rouse et al. (1988), using "act" definitions of assaults which inspired much higher proportions to acknowledge victimization, similarly report that men were likelier than women to call the police after assaults by intimate partners, both among married couples and among those dating. In addition, a sample of 337 cases of domestic violence drawn from family court cases in Ontario showed that men were more likely than women to press charges against their spouses [...]. What those who ar-

gue that men are reluctant or ashamed to report their wives' assaults overlook is that women have their own reasons to be reticent, fearing both the loss of a jailed or alienated husband's economic support and his vengeance. Whereas the claim that husbands underreport because of shame or chivalry is largely speculative, there is considerable evidence that women report very little of the violence perpetrated by their male partners [...].

The CTS survey data indicating equivalent violence by wives and husbands thus stand in contradiction to injury data, to police incident reports, to help-seeking statistics, and even to other, larger, national probability sample surveys of self-reported victimization. The CTS researchers insist that their results alone are accurate because husbands' victimizations are unlikely to be detected or reported by any other method. It is therefore important to consider in detail the CTS and the data it generates.

DO CTS DATA REFLECT THE REALITY OF MARITAL VIOLENCE?

The CTS instrument has been much used and much criticized. Critics have complained that its exclusive focus on "acts" ignores the actors' interpretations, motivations, and intentions; that physical violence is arbitrarily delimited, excluding, for example, sexual assault and rape; that retrospective reports of the past year's events are unlikely to be accurate; that researchers' attributions of "violence" (with resultant claims about its statistical prevalence) are based on respondents' admitting to acts described in such an impoverished manner as to conflate severe assaults with trivial gestures; that the formulaic distinction between "minor" and "severe violence" (whereby, for example, "tried to hit with something" is definitionally "severe" and "slapped" is definitionally "minor") constitutes a poor operationalization of severity; that the responses of aggressors and victims have been given identical evidentiary status in deriving incidence estimates, while their inconsistencies have been ignored; that the CTS omits the contexts of violence, the events precipitating it, and the sequences of events by which it progresses; and that it fails to connect outcomes, especially injury, with the acts producing them.

Straus (1990b) has defended the CTS against its critics, maintaining that the CTS addresses context with its "verbal aggression" scale (although the assessment of "verbal aggression" is not incident-linked with the assessment of "violence"); that the minor-severe categorization "is roughly parallel to the legal distinction between 'simple assault' and 'aggravated assault'" (58); that other measurement instruments have problems, too; and that you cannot measure everything. Above all, the defense rests on the widespread use of the instrument, on its reliability, and on its validity. That the CTS is widely used cannot be gainsaid, but whether it is reliable or valid is questionable.

Problems with the Reliability and Validity of CTS Responses

*****

The crucial matter of interobserver reliability is [...] problematic. The degree of concordance in couples' responses is an assay of "interspousal reliability" (Jouriles and O'Leary 1985), and such reliability must be high if CTS scores are to be taken at face value. For example, incidence estimates of husband-to-wife and wife-to-husband violence have been generated from national surveys in which the CTS was administered to only one adult per family, with claims of victimization and perpetration by male and female respondents all granted equal evidentiary status and summated [...]. The validity of these widely cited incidence estimates is predicated upon interspousal reliability.

Straus (1990b:66) considers the assessment of spousal concordance to constitute an assay of "concurrent validity" rather than "interspousal reliability," in effect treating each partner's report as the violence criterion that validates the other. But spousal concordance is analogous to interobserver reliability: it is a necessary but by no means sufficient condition for concluding that the self-reports accurately reflect reality. If

couples generally produce consistent reports—Mr. and Mrs. Jones both indicate that he struck her, while Mr. and Mrs. Smith both indicate that neither has struck the other—then it is possible though by no means certain that their CTS self-reports constitute valid (veridical) information about the blows actually struck. However, if couples routinely provide discrepant CTS responses, data derived from the CTS simply cannot be valid.

In this light, studies of husband/wife concordance in CTS responses should be devastating to those who imagine that the CTS provides a valid account of the respondents' acts. In what Straus correctly calls "the most detailed and thorough analysis of agreement between spouses in response to the CTS," Szinovacz (1983) found that 103 couples' accounts of the violence in their interactions matched to a degree little greater than chance. On several CTS items, mainly the most severe ones, agreement was actually below chance. On the item "beat up," concordance was nil: although there were respondents of both sexes who claimed to have administered beatings and respondents of both sexes who claimed to have been on the receiving end, there was not a single couple in which one party claimed to have administered and the other to have received such a beating.

Straus (1990b) acknowledges that these and the other studies he reviews "found large discrepancies between the reports of violence given by husbands and by wives" (69). He concludes, however, that "validity measures of agreement between family members are within the range of validity coefficients typically reported" (71), and that "the weakest aspect of the CTS are [sic] the scales that have received the least criticism: Reasoning and Verbal aggression" (71), by which he implies that the assessment of violence is relatively strong.

Ultimately, Straus's defense of the CTS is that the proof of the pudding is in the eating: "The strongest evidence concerns the construct validity of the CTS. It has been used in a large number of studies producing findings that tend to be consistent with previous research (when available), consistent regardless of gender of respondent, and theoretically meaningful" [...].

And indeed, with respect to marital violence, the CTS is capable of making certain gross discriminations. Various studies have found CTS responses to vary as a function of age, race, poverty, duration of relationship, and registered versus de facto marital unions [...] and these effects have generally been directionally similar to those found with less problematic measures of violence such as homicides [...]. However, the CTS has also failed to detect certain massive differences, and we do not refer only to sex differences.

Consider the case of child abuse by stepparents versus birth parents. In various countries, including the United States, a stepparent is more likely to fatally assault a small child than is a birth parent, by a factor on the order of 100-fold [...]; sublethal violence also exhibits huge differences in the same direction [...]. Using the CTS, however, Gelles and Harrop (1991) were unable to detect any difference in self-reports of violence by step- versus birth parents. Users of the CTS have sometimes conceded that the results of their self-report surveys cannot provide an accurate picture of the prevalence of violence, but they have made this concession only to infer that the estimates must be gross underestimates of the true prevalence. However, the CTS's failure to differentiate the behavior of step- versus birth parents indicates that CTS-based estimates are not just underestimates but may misrepresent between-group differences in systematically biased ways. One must be concerned, then, whether this sort of bias also arises in CTS-based comparisons between husbands and wives.

Problems with the Interpretation of CTS Responses

With the specific intention of circumventing imprecision and subjectivity in asking about such abstractions as "violence," the CTS is confined to questions about "acts": Respondents are asked whether they have "pushed" their partners, have "slapped" them, and so forth, rather than whether they have "assaulted" them or behaved "violently." This focus on "acts" is intended to reduce problems of self-serving and biased definitional criteria on the part of the respondents. However, any gain in objectivity has been undermined by the way that CTS survey data have then been analyzed and interpreted. Any respondent who acknowledges a single instance of having "pushed," "grabbed," "shoved," "slapped" *or* "hit or tried to hit" another person is deemed a perpetrator of "violence" by the researchers, regardless of the act's context, consequences, or meaning to the parties involved. Similarly, a single instance of having "kicked," "bit," "hit or tried to hit with an object," "beat up," "choked," "threatened with a knife or gun," or "used a knife or fired a gun" makes one a perpetrator of "severe violence."

Affirmation of any one of the "violence" items provides the basis for estimates such as Straus and Gelles's (1990b:97) claim that 6.8 million U.S. husbands and 6.25 million U.S. wives were spousal assault victims in 1985. Similarly, estimates of large numbers of "beaten" or "battered" wives and husbands have been based on affirmation of any one of the "severe violence" items. For example, Steinmetz (1986:734) and Straus and Gelles (1987:638) claim on this basis that 1.8 million U.S. women are "beaten" by their husbands annually. But note that any man who once threw an "object" at his wife, regardless of its nature and regardless of whether the throw missed, qualifies as having "beaten" her; some unknown proportion of the women and men who are alleged to have been "beaten," on the basis of their survey responses, never claimed to have been struck at all. Thus, the "objective" scoring of the CTS not only fails to explore the meanings and intentions associated with the acts but has in practice entailed interpretive transformations that guarantee exaggeration, misinterpretation, and ultimately trivialization of the genuine problems of violence.

Consider a "slap." The word encompasses anything from a slap on the hand chastising a dinner companion for reaching for a bite of one's dessert to a tooth-loosening assault intended to punish, humiliate, and terrorize. These are not trivial distinctions; indeed, they constitute the essence of definitional issues concerning violence. Almost all definitions of violence and violent acts refer to intentions. Malevolent intent is crucial, for example, to legal definitions of "assault" (to which supporters of the CTS have often mistakenly claimed that their "acts" correspond; e.g., Straus 1990b:58). However, no one has systematically investigated how respondents vary in their subjective definitions of the "acts" listed on the CTS. If, for example, some respondents interpret phrases such as "tried to hit with an object" literally, then a good deal of relatively harmless behavior surely taints the estimates of "severe violence." Although this problem has not been investigated systematically, one author has shown that it is potentially serious. In a study of 103 couples, Margolin (1987) found that wives surpassed husbands in their use of "severe violence" according to the CTS, but unlike others who have obtained this result, Margolin troubled to check its meaningfulness with more intensive interviews. She concluded:

> While CTS items appear behaviorally specific, their meanings still are open to interpretation. In one couple who endorsed the item "kicking," for example, we discovered that the kicking took place in bed in a more kidding, than serious, fashion. Although this behavior meets the criterion for severe abuse on the CTS, neither spouse viewed it as aggressive, let alone violent. In another couple, the wife scored on severe physical aggression while the husband scored on low-level aggression only. The inquiry revealed that, after years of passively accepting the husband's repeated abuse, this wife finally decided, on one occasion, to retaliate by hitting him over the head with a wine decanter (1987:82).

By the criteria of Steinmetz (1977/78:501), this incident would qualify as a "battered husband" case. But however dangerous this retaliatory blow may have been and however reprehensible or justified one may consider it, it is not "battering," whose most basic definitional criterion is its repetitiveness. A failure to consider intentions, interpretations, and the history of the individuals' relationship is a significant shortcoming of CTS research. Only through

a consideration of behaviors, intentions, and intersubjective understandings associated with specific violent events will we come to a fuller understanding of violence between men and women [...]. Studies employing more intensive interviews and detailed case reports addressing the contexts and motivations of marital violence help unravel the assertions of those who claim the widespread existence of beaten and battered husbands. Research focusing on specific violent events shows that women almost always employ violence in defense of self and children in response to cues of imminent assault in the past and in retaliation for previous physical abuse [...]. Proponents of the sexual-symmetry-of-violence thesis have made much of the fact that CTS surveys indicate that women "initiate" the violence about as often as men, but a case in which a woman struck the first blow is unlikely to be the mirror image of one in which her husband "initiated." A noteworthy feature of the literature proclaiming the existence of battered husbands and battering wives [...] is how little the meager case descriptions resemble those of battered wives and battering husbands [...]. Especially lacking in the alleged male victim cases is any indication of the sort of chronic intimidation characteristic of prototypical woman battering cases.

Any self-report method must constitute an imperfect reflection of behavior, and the CTS is no exception. That in itself is hardly a fatal flaw. But for such an instrument to retain utility for the investigation of a particular domain such as family violence, an essential point is that its inaccuracies and misrepresentations must not be systematically related to the distinctions under investigation. The CTS's inability to detect the immense differences in violence between stepparents and birth parents, as noted above, provides strong reason to suspect that the test's shortcomings produce not just noise but systematic bias. In the case of marital violence, the other sorts of evidence reviewed in this paper indicate that there are massive differences in the use of confrontational violence against spouses by husbands versus wives, and yet the CTS has consistently failed to detect them. CTS users have taken this failure as evidence for the null hypothesis, apparently assuming that their questionnaire data have a validity that battered women's injuries and deaths lack.

HOMICIDES

The second line of evidence that has been invoked in support of the claim that marital violence is more or less sexually symmetrical is the number of lethal outcomes:

> Data on homicide between spouses suggest that an almost equal number of wives kill their husbands as husbands kill their wives (Wolfgang 1958). Thus it appears that men and women might have equal potential for violent marital interaction; initiate similar acts of violence; and when differences of physical strength are equalized by weapons, commit similar amounts of spousal homicide (Steinmetz and Lucca 1988:241).

McNeely and Robinson-Simpson (1987:485) elevated the latter hypothesis about the relevance of weapons to the status of a fact: "Steinmetz observed that when weapons neutralize differences in physical strength, about as many men as women are victims of homicide."

*****

Husbands are indeed almost as often slain as are wives in the United States, then. However, there remain several problems with Steinmetz and Lucca's (as well as McNeely and Robinson-Simpson's) interpretation of this fact. Studies of actual cases [...] lend no support to the facile claim that homicidal husbands and wives "initiate similar acts of violence." Men often kill wives after lengthy periods of prolonged physical violence accompanied by other forms of abuse and coercion; the roles in such cases are seldom if ever reversed. Men perpetrate familicidal massacres, killing spouse and children together; women do not. Men commonly hunt down and kill wives who have left them; women hardly ever behave similarly. Men kill wives as

part of planned murder-suicides; analogous acts by women are almost unheard of. Men kill in response to revelations of wifely infidelity; women almost never respond similarly, though their mates are more often adulterous. The evidence is overwhelming that a large proportion of the spouse-killings perpetrated by wives, but almost none of those perpetrated by husbands, are acts of self-defense. Unlike men, women kill male partners after years of suffering physical violence, after they have exhausted all available sources of assistance, when they feel trapped, and because they fear for their own lives [...].

A further problem with the invocation of spousal homicide data as evidence against sex differences in marital violence is that this numerical equivalence is peculiar to the United States. Whereas the ratio of wives to husbands as homicide victims in the United States was 1.3:1 [...], corresponding ratios from other countries are much higher: 3.3:1 for a 10-year period in Canada, for example, 4.3:1 for Great Britain, and 6:1 for Denmark (Wilson and Daly forthcoming). The reason why this is problematic is that U.S. homicide data and CTS data from several countries have been invoked as complementary pieces of evidence for women's and men's equivalent uses of violence [...]. One cannot have it both ways. If the lack of sex differences in CTS results is considered proof of sexually symmetrical violence, then homicide data must somehow be dismissed as irrelevant, since homicides generally fail to exhibit this supposedly more basic symmetry. [...]

A possible way out of this dilemma is hinted at in Steinmetz and Lucca's (1988) allusion to the effect of weapons: perhaps it is the availability of guns that has neutralized men's advantage in lethal marital conflict in the United States. Gun use is indeed relatively prevalent in the U.S., accounting for 51 percent of a sample of 1706 spousal homicides in Chicago, for example, as compared to 40 percent of 1060 Canadian cases, 42 percent of 395 Australian cases, and just 8 percent of 1204 cases in England and Wales (Wilson and Daly forthcoming). Nevertheless, the plausible hypothesis that gun use can account for the different sex ratios among victims fails. When shootings and other spousal homicides are analyzed separately, national differences in the sex ratios of spousal homicide remain dramatic. For example, the ratio of wives to husbands as gunshot homicide victims in Chicago was 1.2:1, compared to 4:1 in Canada and 3.5:1 in Britain; the ratio of wives to husbands as victims of non-gun homicides was 0.8:1 in Chicago, compared to 2.9:1 in Canada and 4.5:1 in Britain (Wilson and Daly forthcoming). Moreover, the near equivalence of husband and wife victims in the U.S. antedates the contemporary prevalence of gun killings. In Wolfgang's (1958) classic study, only 34 of the 100 spousal homicide victims were shot (15 husbands and 19 wives), while 30 husbands were stabbed and 31 wives were beaten or stabbed. Whatever may explain the exceptionally similar death rates of U.S. husbands and wives, it is not simply that guns "equalize."

Nor is the unusual U.S. pattern to be explained in terms of a peculiar convergence in the United States of the sexes in their violent inclinations or capabilities across all domains and relationships. Although U.S. data depart radically from other industrialized countries in the sex ratio of spousal homicide victimization, they do not depart similarly in the sex ratios of other sorts of homicides (Wilson and Daly forthcoming). For example, in the United States as elsewhere men kill unrelated men about 40 times as often as women kill unrelated women [...].

Even among lethal acts, it is essential to discriminate among different victim-killer relationships, because motives, risk factors, and conflict typologies are relationship-specific (Daly and Wilson 1988). Steinmetz (1977/78, Steinmetz and Lucca 1988) has invoked the occurrence of maternally perpetrated infanticides as evidence of women's violence, imagining that the fact that some women commit infanticide somehow bolsters the claim that they batter their husbands, too. But maternal infanticides are more often motivated by desperation than by hostile aggression and are often effected by acts of neglect or abandonment rather than by assault [...]. To conflate such acts with aggressive attacks is to misunderstand their utterly distinct motives, forms, and perpetrator profiles, and the distinct social and material circumstances in which they occur.

HOW TO GAIN A VALID ACCOUNT OF MARITAL VIOLENCE?

How ought researchers to conceive of "violence"? People differ in their views about whether a particular act was a violent one and about who was responsible. [...]

Unfortunately, the presumed gain in objectivity achieved by asking research subjects to report only "acts," while refraining from elaborating upon their meanings and consequences, is illusory. As noted above, couples exhibit little agreement in reporting the occurrence of acts in which both were allegedly involved, and self-reported acts sometimes fail to differentiate the behavior of groups known to exhibit huge differences in the perpetration of violence. The implication must be that concerns about the validity of self-report data cannot be allayed merely by confining self-reports to a checklist of named acts. [...]

If these "acts" were scored by trained observers examining the entire event, there might be grounds for such behavioristic austerity in measurement [...]. However, when researchers have access only to self-reports, the cognitions of the actors are neither more nor less accessible to research than their actions. Failures of candor and memory threaten the validity of both sorts of self-report data, and researchers' chances of detecting such failures can only be improved by the collection of richer detail about the violent event. The behavioristic rigor of observational research cannot be simulated by leaving data collection to the subjects, nor by active inattention to "subjective" matters like people's perceptions of their own and others' intentions, attributions of loss of control, perceived provocations and justifications, intimidatory consequences, and so forth. Moreover, even a purely behavioristic account could be enriched by attending to sequences of events and subsequent behavior rather than merely counting acts.

Enormous differences in meaning and consequence exist between a woman pummelling her laughing husband in an attempt to convey strong feelings and a man pummelling his weeping wife in an attempt to punish her for coming home late. It is not enough to acknowledge such contrasts (as CTS researchers have sometimes done), if such acknowledgments neither inform further research nor alter such conclusions as "within the family or in dating and cohabiting relationships, women are about as violent as men" (Straus and Gelles 1990b:104). What is needed are forms of analysis that will lead to a comprehensive description of the violence itself as well as an explanation of it. In order to do this, it is, at the very least, necessary to analyze the violent event in a holistic manner, with attention to the entire sequences of distinct acts as well as associated motives, intentions, and consequences, all of which must in turn be situated within the wider context of the relationship.

THE NEED FOR THEORY

If the arguments and evidence that we have presented are correct, then currently fashionable claims about the symmetry of marital violence are unfounded. How is it that so many experts have been persuaded of a notion that is at once counterintuitive and counterfactual? Part of the answer, we believe, is that researchers too often operate without sound (or indeed any) theoretical visions of marital relationships, of interpersonal conflicts, or of violence.

[...] [Many such analyses obscure] all that is distinctive about violence against wives, which occurs in a particular context of perceived entitlement and institutionalized power asymmetry. Moreover, marital violence occurs around recurring themes, especially male sexual jealousy and proprietariness, expectations of obedience and domestic service, and women's attempts to leave the marital relationship [...]. In the self-consciously gender-blind literature on "violent couples," these themes are invisible.

Those who claim that wives and husbands are equally violent have offered no conceptual framework for understanding why women and men should think and act alike. Indeed, the claim that violence is gender-neutral cannot easily be reconciled with other coincident claims. For example, many family violence researchers who propose sexual symmetry in violence attribute the inculcation and legitimation

of violence to socializing processes and cultural institutions [...], but then overlook the fact that these processes and institutions define and treat females and males differently. If sexually differentiated socialization and entitlements play a causal role in violence, how can we understand the alleged equivalence of women's and men's violent inclinations and actions?

Another theoretical problem confronting anyone who claims that violent inclinations are sexually monomorphic concerns the oft-noted fact that men are larger than women and likelier to inflict damage by similar acts. Human passions have their own "rationality" [...] and it would be curious if women and men were identically motivated to initiate assaults in contexts where the expectable results were far more damaging for women. Insofar as both parties to a potentially violent transaction are aware of such differences, it is inappropriate to treat a slap (or other "act") by one party as equivalent to a slap by the other, not only because there is an asymmetry in the damage the two slaps might inflict, but because the parties differ in the responses available to them and hence in their control over the denouement. Women's motives may be expected to differ systematically from those of men wherever the predictable consequences of their actions differ systematically. Those who contend that women and men are equally inclined to violence need to articulate why this should be so, given the sex differences in physical traits, such as size and muscularity, affecting the probable consequences of violence.

*****

We cannot hope to understand violence in marital, cohabiting, and dating relationships without explicit attention to the qualities that make them different from other relationships. It is a cross-culturally and historically ubiquitous aspect of human affairs that women and men form individualized unions, recognized by themselves and by others as conferring certain obligations and entitlements, such that the partners' productive and reproductive careers become intertwined. Family violence research might usefully begin by examining the consonant and discordant desires, expectations, grievances, perceived entitlements, and preoccupations of husbands and wives, and by investigating theoretically derived hypotheses about circumstantial, ecological, contextual, and demographic correlates of such conflict. Having described the conflicts of interest that characterize marital relationships with explicit reference to the distinct agendas of women and men, violence researchers must proceed to an analysis that acknowledges and accounts for those gender differences. It is crucial to establish differences in the patterns of male and female violence, to thoroughly describe and explain the overall process of violent events within their immediate and wider contexts, and to analyze the reasons why conflict results in differentially violent action by women and men.

REFERENCES

Daly, Martin, and Margo Wilson. 1988. *Homicide.* Hawthorne, N.Y.: Aldine de Gruyter.

Gelles, Richard J., and John W. Harrop. 1991. "The risk of abusive violence among children with nongenetic caretakers." *Family Relations* 40:78–83.

Johnson, Holly. 1989. "Wife assault in Canada." Paper presented at the Annual Meeting of the American Society of Criminology, November, Reno, Nevada.

Jouriles, Ernest N., and K. Daniel O'Leary. 1985. "Interspousal reliability of reports of marital violence." *Journal of Consulting and Clinical Psychology* 53:419–421.

Lystad, Mary H. 1975 "Violence at home: A review of literature." *American Journal of Orthopsychiatry* 45:328–345.

Margolin, Gayla. 1987. "The multiple forms of aggressiveness between marital partners: How do we identify them?" *Journal of Marital and Family Therapy* 13:77–84.

McNeely, R.L., and Gloria Robinson-Simpson. 1987. "The truth about domestic violence: A falsely framed issue." *Social Work* 32:485–490.

Rouse, Linda P., Richard Breen, and Marilyn Howell. 1988. "Abuse in intimate relationships: A comparison of married and dating college students." *Journal of Interpersonal Violence* 3:414–429.

Schwartz, Martin D. 1987. "Gender and injury in spousal assault." *Sociological Focus* 20:61–75.

Shupe, Anson, William A. Stacey, and Lonnie R. Hazelwood. 1987. *Violent Men, Violent Couples: The Dynamics of Domestic Violence.* Lexington Mass.: Lexington Books.

Steinmetz, Suzanne K. 1977/78. "The battered husband syndrome." *Victimology* 2:499–509.

———. 1986. "Family violence. Past, present, and future." In *Handbook of Marriage and the Family*, ed. Marvin B. Sussman and Suzanne K. Steinmetz, 725–765. New York: Plenum.

Steinmetz, Suzanne K., and Joseph S. Lucca. 1988. "Husband battering." In *Handbook of Family Violence*, ed. Vincent B. Van Hasselt, R.L. Morrison, A.S. Bellack, and M. Hersen, 233–246. New York: Plenum Press.

Stets, Jan E., and Murray A. Straus. 1990. "Gender differences in reporting marital violence and its medical and psychological consequences." In *Physical Violence in American Families*, ed. Murray A. Straus and Richard J. Gelles, 151–165. New Brunswick, N.J.: Transaction Publishers.

Straus, Murray A. 1977/78. "Wife-beating: How common, and why?" *Victimology* 2:443–458.

———. 1990a. "Measuring intrafamily conflict and violence: The Conflict Tactics (CT) Scales." In *Physical Violence in American Families*, ed. Murray A. Straus and Richard J. Gelles, 29–47. New Brunswick, N.J.: Transaction Publishers.

———. 1990b. "The Conflict Tactics Scales and its critics: An evaluation and new data on validity and reliability." In *Physical Violence in American Families*, ed. Murray A. Straus and Richard J. Gelles, 49–73. New Brunswick, N.J.: Transaction Publishers.

Straus, Murray A., and Richard J. Gelles, eds. 1990. *Physical Violence in American Families.* New Brunswick, N.J.: Transaction Publishers.

———. 1990b. "How violent are American families? Estimates from the National Family Violence Resurvey and other studies." In *Physical Violence in American Families*, ed. Murray A. Straus and Richard J. Gelles, 95–112. New Brunswick, N.J.: Transaction Publishers.

Straus, Murray A., and Richard J. Gelles. 1986. "Societal change and change in family violence from 1975 to 1985 as revealed by two national surveys." *Journal of Marriage and the Family* 48:463–480.

———. 1987. "The costs of family violence." *Public Health Reports* 102:638–641.

Szinovacz, Maximiliane E. 1983 "Using couple data as a methodological tool: The case of marital violence." *Journal of Marriage and the Family* 45:633–644.

Wilson, Margo, and Martin Daly. Forthcoming. "Who kills whom in spouse-killings? On the exceptional sex ratio of spousal homicides in the United States." *Criminology.*

Wolfgang, Marvin E. 1958. *Patterns in Criminal Homicide.* Philadelphia: University of Pennsylvania Press.

CHAPTER 17

VIOLENCE AGAINST REFUGEE WOMEN
Gender Oppression, Canadian Policy, and the International Struggle for Human Rights

Helene Moussa

INTRODUCTION

Since the 1985 United Nations Women's Decade Conference in Nairobi, international women's groups, particularly those from the South, have been organizing women at the grassroots and national levels to raise public consciousness on the issue of gender oppression, and lobbying governments to recognize violence against women as both a form of gender oppression and a human rights issue. In 1990, when the United Nations announced that its World Conference on Human Rights would be held in Vienna in June 1993, women's organizations were quick to note that women's issues were not even named on the agenda. By the time of the conference, women's organizations had a petition with half a million names from 124 countries demanding that gender violence be recognized as a violation of human rights. Even though the 150 governments represented at the conference had been lobbied at home, it was not until the conference took place that the international women's organizations succeeded in winning their demand that the government delegates address women's rights at every level of their debates. In addition, women, including refugee women, testified at the Global Tribunal on Violations of Human Rights, held in conjunction with the conference. Based on their testimonies, the following types of violence and violations of human rights that women around the world suffer were identified: persecution for political participation; violation of social and economic rights; sexual violence committed against women in war-torn countries; violence against women in the family; and violation of women's bodily integrity (Reilly, 1994, pp. 2–3).

Another accomplishment of the conference, which was a direct result of the intensive feminist networking and lobbying between 1985 and 1993, was the adoption of principles and actions to eradicate gender oppression. Paragraph 18 of the final Vienna Declaration and Programme of Action affirmed that,

> The human rights of women and the girl-child are an inalienable, integral and indivisible part of human rights.... Gender-based violence and all forms of sexual harassment and exploitation, including those resulting from cultural prejudice and international trafficking, are incompatible with the dignity and worth of the human person, and must be eliminated. (Bauer, 1993, p. 73)

While it is not within the United Nations' mandate to enforce international conventions, it is within its purview to promote and encourage the application of these decisions. International instruments also play the important role of setting standards. One of the strengths of the Vienna Declaration is that it can be "translated" to the reality of refugee women and children who, in effect, do not have rights as citizens but in the context of the Declaration do have rights as "human persons."

*****

International NGO networks and their allies in the UN system also succeeded in having the following demands included in the Beijing Declaration and Platform of Action: that governments address the root causes of forced displacement; the redress of economic marginalization of refugee women; inclusion of refugee women in decision-making that affects them; greater access to education and training for refugee women, including training and education about their human rights; the application of a gender perspective to legal instruments and practices that affect refugee women; the prevention and elimination of violence against women and the recognition of refugee women's human rights; and adequate gender-sensitive training for the judiciary, police, border guards and refugee camp personnel.

Women's lobbying efforts to have gender oppression recognized have made some governments respond. Three months before the Vienna Conference, the Canadian Immigration and Refugee Board issued "Guidelines on Women Refugee Claimants Fearing Gender-Related Persecution" (March 1993). This recognition that women can experience persecution primarily because they are women is without doubt a landmark decision in Canadian and international legal jurisprudence. In May 1995, the United States Naturalization and Immigration Service issued guidelines entitled "Consideration for Officers Adjudicating Asylum Claims for Women." And in 1996, the Australian government indicated that they were studying comparative practices domestically and internationally with the objective of establishing gender guidelines for decision-makers in the asylum process.

These policies are important because they signal that governments are beginning to acknowledge the role violence and gender oppression play in the lives of refugee women. These acts of violence can take different forms: economic exploitation, including the feminization of poverty and the commoditization of women in the media; sexual violence, including sexual assault, wife assault and psychological abuse, genital mutilation and sexual slavery/trafficking; dowry death; and the abortion of female fetuses after sex-determination tests. To understand how this violence is perpetrated against refugee women and how it restricts their freedom and mobility, security, and well-being, one must understand how gender relations inform the social, economic, cultural, and political realities in the countries of origin and in the countries where they seek asylum.

In this article, I attempt to develop this understanding by looking at the systems that contribute to the gender-related violence and oppression perpetrated against refugee women. I provide an overview of the context in which refugee women experience sexual violence and oppression in their countries of origin—experiences which may cause them to flee. Their vulnerability during flight and in asylum countries is briefly touched on, while an extensive discussion of international and Canadian refugee policy reveals how such policies can both hinder and protect refugee women's interests in their struggle to find safety in a receiving-country. Finally, using Canada as the example country, I provide an overview of the options available to refugee women who face violence in the home and how racism and gender barriers hinder their attempts to find refuge inside their receiving country.

Refugee women are, of course, a diverse group of women. They come from different racial, ethnic, and class backgrounds, represent a wide range of ages, have varying levels of education and come from different political orientations. [...] While recognizing that the experience of refugee women is not homogeneous, in this article I will nonetheless focus on the similarities and patterns in their experience to underscore how violence and gender oppression affect all refugee women regardless of their background. Patriarchal culture not only legitimates and perpetuates the domination of women but also tolerates violence against women as a justification of their "place" in gender relations. As Roxanna Carrillo states, "Women experience violence as a form of control that limits their ability to pursue options in almost every area of life from the home to the schools, workplaces, and most public spaces. Violence is used to control women's labour in both productive and reproductive capacities" (1991, p. 27).

*****

THE GLOBAL REFUGEE SITUATION

Today, about 80 to 90 percent of the world's refugees are women and their dependants and 50 percent of these are children (Forbes Martin, 1991, p. 1). The numbers of refugees since the Second World War have increased dramatically. For example, immediately following the Second World War the number of refugees in the world was estimated at 2 million, and they were predominantly located in Europe. By 1995, the estimated number of refugees under the protection of the United Nations High Commission for Refugees (UNHCR) was estimated at 27.5 million (United Nations High Commissioner for Refugees, 1995, p. 19). These figures do not include the 2.4 million Palestinians refugees who are under the care of the United Nations Relief Works Agency for Palestinian Refugees (Bannenbring, 1991, p. 6). [...] If the total refugee number approximates 29.5 million people, then there are about 22 million to 25 million refugee women and their dependants in the world today.

*****

What has generated this enormous movement of displaced women, children and men? One cause is the prevalence of armed conflict around the world. Ruth Sivard's 1987 study on world militarism documented that, since the Second World War, 119 of the 120 wars have been waged in the third world (Sivard, 1987, p. 11). Many of these wars occurred in the process of decolonization and the establishment of neo-colonial policies. Between 1960 and 1986, there were 144 successful coups d'état and 50% of all third world countries were controlled by the military (ibid., p. 26). In 1990, 64 third world governments were under military control, and 28 of the 37 armed conflicts under way were in third world countries (Sivard, 1991, p. 11). Amnesty International's 1993 Annual Report revealed that 161 countries (out of 181 member nations of the United Nations) exercised "gruesome" methods to control dissent and to humiliate and force people to sign false confessions (Amnesty International, 1993, p, 2). The lack of democracy and the flagrant violation of human rights by many third world governments are major causes for the flow of refugees. In 1994 alone, 4 million people fled their countries because of armed conflict and human rights violations.

By 1995, the total number of wars had reached 130 (Kane, 1995, p. 18) and with the collapse of the Soviet Union, these wars were no longer restricted to the third world. The most dramatic exclusion and expulsion of people in the mid-1990s took place in the Caucuses region, the former Yugoslavia, and Rwanda. Violence and persecution motivated by ethnic, racial, and religious differences is destructive of the social fabric and economic structures of entire nation states. The destruction of community and resulting human rights violations of human dignity remain the most dramatic causes for forced displacement.

While the human rights record of refugee-producing countries is inextricably related to global militarization, the developed countries are complicit in this escalating trend of violence. For example, Sivard documents that in 1990 developed countries provided $56 billion (US) in economic aid to developing countries and exported $35 billion (US) in arms. Furthermore, developed countries spend as much on military power in one year as the poorest 2 billion people earn in total income (Sivard, 1993, p. 5). Between 1984 and 1990, 56 percent of arms sent to the third world went to countries with highly repressive governments (Sivard, 1991, p. 19). Regehr's study, *Arms Canada*, documents that 60 percent of the countries purchasing Canada's military commodities have been reported by Amnesty International and the United Nations Commission on Human Rights as regular violators of human rights (Regehr, 1987, p. 157). While Canadian arms sales to the US and Europe declined in 1992, third world sales "leaped ahead" irrespective of human rights abuses in those countries receiving arms (Regehr, 1993, p. 8).

Economic inequalities between the North and the South is another causal factor for forced displacement of people. These inequalities have not only placed constraints on the development of third world countries but have also aggravated the "tensions that are inherent in major economic and political transformations" (Zolberg, et al., 1986:158). Structural adjustment policies introduced by the World Bank and the International Monetary Fund (IMF) since the 1970s have further aggravated the processes of democratization and the gap between the rich and poor within third world countries and on a global scale. Today, many third world governments face a situation whereby half of their export earnings must go to pay the servicing of debt (the interest and fees) while the principal, the original amount borrowed, remains untouched. Thus governments borrow more money to pay debt while trying to implement the conditions imposed by lenders. Typically the IMF requires the imposition of structural adjustment policies that include devaluation of national currency (thus making imports more expensive), reduction of public sector spending, stimulus to exports, and easing restriction on foreign investment. These policies may lead to displacement of people for political reasons. As governments are forced to implement unpopular policies to meet conditions imposed by the World Bank and the IMF, they often implement more repressive measures against their dissenting population. Spending on the police and military forces is justified as a way of maintaining public order in the face of popular opposition to government policies.

The end of the Cold War brought the announcement of the triumph of a "universalized"

global market economy. Perhaps the most disturbing aspect of this global system is that the formidable power and mobility of global corporations is (directly or indirectly) undercutting the effectiveness of national governments to carry out essential policies on behalf of the people. Leaders of nation states are losing substantial control of their own territory. They conform to the demands of the corporations who in the new world economy have unrestricted ability to cross national boundaries.

According to the International Labour Office (ILO) the poor and most vulnerable groups (usually women, children and the elderly) bear the heaviest debt burden (Fromont, 1995, p. 29). Widespread unemployment and marginalization have been a significant cause of social and civil strife in many countries. The risk of war is most likely to occur in countries experiencing difficult financial circumstances: for example, 24 out of 27 countries involved in war in the past 10 years are heavily indebted. The total indebtedness of third world countries rose from $250 billion (US) in 1970 to $1,900 billion (US) in 1995 (George, 1995, pp. 23–24).

The refugee situation today is no longer ad hoc or temporary. It is a continuous phenomenon, and for many refugees a permanent life situation. In the post-Cold War era, the growing number of refugees and internally displaced peoples is no longer caused by ideological conflict between the Capitalist West and Communist East. Rather, it is caused primarily by armed conflict and militarization of governments, as well as economic and political instability often created by Western intervention. [...] Refugee women and men with whom I have had personal conversations, interviewed or heard speak at meetings always underscore that they never considered living anywhere else before the circumstances that led them to make the decision to flee their countries of origin.

SEXUAL VIOLENCE IN THE COUNTRIES OF ORIGIN

In situations of war and repression, men, women and children are equally vulnerable to human rights abuses, including sexual violence and torture. Women and girls, however, are particularly vulnerable to sexual violence under repressive regimes and especially during civil strife and wars. Not all refugee women and girls are tortured or sexually violated in their countries of origin; many, however, will flee their countries of origin to escape such violence.

As I have noted, repressive regimes exist in 161 out of 181 countries today (Amnesty International, 1993). In most of these countries, women are arrested and sexually tortured because of their political actions, the political actions of other family members, or for belonging to certain social, ethnic, religious, or political groups. Once in prison, women are at great risk of being raped by prison guards and in the torture chamber. Women are raped with such objects as sticks and bottles. In some countries dogs have been trained to sexually violate women. They can be raped in front of their husbands, partners, parents, or children; they can be made to witness the rape and torture of their sisters, mothers and grandmothers, and the torture of male members of their family or political group. Women, too, are often victims of sexual torture at the hands of the police and military (Amnesty International, 1990; Amnesty International, 1995, pp. 1–8).

Sexual torture of women is designed to destroy their identity as women. It can be inflicted upon women as a "punishment" for not conforming to cultural norms and it is used as a form of intimidation that forces women to reveal information about political activities of family members, individuals and groups allegedly involved in political activities against the state. Sexual torture relates political activity with sexual activity (Agger, 1989). In the case of women, it is usually men who torture women. The reverse is not the case for men.

Under repressive conditions and because of the stigma associated with women's sexuality, women have very little recourse. Obviously, they cannot seek the protection of the police, let alone the law. Indeed, the police and the military may themselves be the perpetrators of sexual violence "on behalf" of the state. In many cases women cannot count on the support of their

family and community since a woman's loss of virginity is perceived as a shame to the family in some cultures. Survivors of sexual violence will often choose to remain silent about such experiences. In addition to the trauma of being raped, these women will often become pregnant and not be able to abort the fetus of their rapist because abortion is either not available to them or it is illegal (Amnesty International, 1990; Allodi and Stiasny, 1990; Agger, 1989,1987; *Manavi Newsletter* 1991; Mollica and Son, 1989). Having to carry the child of their rapist is the epitome of patriarchal control over women's reproductive power.

In times of war, women are even more vulnerable to rape. Women's bodies become the site of combat when they are raped as a vengeance to the "enemy" (Enloe, 1988, pp. 18–46; Korac, 1995, pp. 12–15; Moussa, 1993; *Women's World* no. 24, 1990/91). Often, they are "captured" by fighting armies on either side and forced to serve as maids and housekeepers, as well as forced to render sexual services.

The sexual violation of women and girls intensifies during "ethnic" conflicts. The 1990s have witnessed the beginning of an era of widespread "ethnic" conflicts, which have resulted in civil wars, "ethnic cleansing," and brutal expulsion of peoples. These in turn have become major causes of forced human displacement. Political leaders in countries where "ethnic" battles rage—for example, the former Yugoslavia—use religion and ethnicity to uphold narrow nationalistic control of populations to maintain their grip on power. A central strategy of "ethnic cleansing" is to rape women and girls.

*****

Victims of "ethnic cleansing" in Rwanda and the former Yugoslavia have sought refuge in countries bordering their own or in camps within their own borders. Even in these temporary asylums, women and girls are not safe, but are the victims of rape by the men who are military and camp officials. Similarly, women who flee their homes and country of origin to escape repression or war are most often at risk whether they travel alone or in groups, by land or by sea. While crossing the border to the country of asylum, women may once again experience intimidation, sexual harassment, and rape—this time in "exchange" for "safe passage." Once in the asylum country, they are equally vulnerable to sexual violence in the refugee camps and settlements, in urban areas, and when they seek to register their status with the police, other state organs or the staff of the United Nations High Commission on Refugees (UNCHR). State officials whose role it is to protect refugees and members of society are often perpetrators of violence against refugee women. Male (refugee) members of their families are also powerless and unable to protect women. Refugee women may also be raped by members of their own refugee male population (Agger, 1993; Forbes Martin, 1991; Mollica and Son, 1989; Moussa, 1993; Tu Khuong, 1988). The double bind for refugee women is that the word "refugee," in effect, signifies powerlessness and subjection while ostensibly conveying protection. But, refugees have no rights. It is the prerogative of states to grant them asylum, refugee status and immigrant status, or to deport them. To become a refugee is a lived experience, marked by sharp, if not violent discontinuities of identities, social and economic status, culture, family, and community relationships.

*****

CANADIAN POLICY AND REFUGEE WOMEN

There are two ways refugees can apply for re-settlement in Canada. The first is to apply at a visa office abroad. This is called the "overseas determination process." The second is to arrive at the Canadian border by land, air or sea and claim refugee status. This is called the "refugee claimant process."

In the overseas determination process, women and men who are applying outside Canada have to meet two criteria: they have to be eligible according to the United Nations'

Convention and Protocol as stated in Canada's Immigration Act, and they have to meet Canadian immigration admissibility criteria designated to ensure that they can successfully (that is, economically) establish themselves in Canadian society. Since such criteria are based on skills and the employability of refugees/immigrants, refugee women will often be at a disadvantage. Women are seen as dependants. Their skills and strengths are not seen as "assets" in the family or the public sphere. [...] For these reasons, it is not surprising that male refugees are by far the largest number of "principal applicants" landed between 1986 and 1993. [...]

*****

The irony of the "employability" criteria is that highly qualified refugee women (and men) will, as do immigrants, have to start at the bottom of the job market. As compared with Canadian-born women, immigrant and refugee women are heavily concentrated in factory occupations (Boyd, 1984, 1986; Ng and Das Gupta, 1981). Refugee women are also at a disadvantage because the Canadian job market is gendered both in the kind of jobs that are available for women and because women do not receive equal pay for equal work. In addition, media stories and images of refugees do not portray them as contributing to the economy, culture (beyond "exotic" food and music) and history of Canada. Rather, they are portrayed as abusers of the Canadian refugee and welfare systems, as well as criminals and drug-dealers. In contrast, many studies in Canada, Europe, and the US have shown that refugees and migrants make significant economic and cultural contributions to their host countries (for example: Beiser et al., 1995; Richmond, 1994, pp. 123–129; Spencer, 1994, p. xxi; Stalker, 1994, p. 51–56). While the categories of "principal applicant" and "spouse" are gender neutral, in reality the landing statistics [...] not only reflect the stereotype that women are dependent but also reinforce the role of women in the home, that is, as non-productive labourers. The home-care skills and efforts of refugee women to hold their families together in the adjustment process are not only invisible but also are not recognized in economic terms. Furthermore the refugee determination process totally ignores the critical role refugee women play in the survival of family members in asylum countries and in Canada.

*****

IMMIGRATION AND REFUGEE BOARD

On March 8, 1993, Nurjehan Mawani, the Chairperson of the IRB, officially issued the IRB Guidelines on "Women Refugee Claimants Fearing Gender-Related Persecution."

*****

The Guidelines do not add gender persecution to the enumerated grounds of admissible forms of persecution. Instead, the Guidelines aim to assist IRB members in establishing the link between gender persecution and one or more of the grounds as accepted by the UN Convention—race, religion, nationality, membership in a particular social group and political opinion. [...] Since the Guidelines were issued, claims relating to sexual assault, wife abuse, enforced sterilization, female genital mutilation among other oppressive actions solely directed towards women have been linked to the persecution of refugee women.

While on the one hand policies such as the gender Guidelines are established to offer refugee women fearing gender-based persecution an opportunity to find safe haven in Canada, on the other hand policies are established that make it particularly difficult for refugee women to remain in Canada. The "Right to Landing Fee" (commonly referred to as the "Head Tax") established in February 1995 by the Minister of Immigration is a specific example. Before permanent status in Canada can be granted, a fee of $975 is now imposed on all immigrants and refugees (each individual member of a family are charged this fee). The fee has been justified by the Minister of Immigration as a measure to reduce the national deficit. Not only will this fee reduce the chances for refugee women to come

to Canada but those who are in Canada will undoubtedly find it very difficult to pay the fee in order to remain in this country.

VIOLENCE AS A BARRIER IN THE RECONSTRUCTION OF REFUGEE WOMEN'S LIVES

Once in Canada, refugee women encounter a new set of barriers in their attempts to reconstruct their lives, for example, in seeking services (language, legal, etc.) and paid employment. These barriers are rooted in the pervasiveness of racism, sexism and classism in Canadian society. The pressures on arrival in Canada are generally extensive for all refugees. Refugee claimants under the "refugee claimant process," for example, are in limbo until they are granted refugee and landed immigrant status. The stress of "waiting" further intensifies the fear of deportation, which is a prevalent feeling among all refugees.

Keeping the family together has particular significance for refugee women. Members of a family can arrive separately; children may have been separated from parents in flight or even in the country of origin. Whether it is the male or female spouse who arrived first, the family will never be the same as it was in their country of origin. Renegotiating relationships and identities is critical for the well-being of all family members. Separation from the extended family, [...] in addition to concern about their family's safety in the war-torn countries of origin or in countries under repressive regimes, add to the accumulation of stress. The pressures to find housing, work, schooling, and so on, let alone not knowing how institutions function and dealing with pervasive racism, leave very little space to process the grief of the personal and material losses since fleeing their homes and country. Refugee women will often defer and suppress their own emotional needs to hold the family together.

The alienation which is part of North American life affects refugees in a much more drastic way because they experience multiple losses of the structures that under normal circumstances sustain their identities. For example, they lose their home and country, their network of family, friends, and acquaintances, the familiarity of their neighbourhood and religious institutions, the security of work, their cultural food and language, their health and education benefits, and their citizenship. Racism and hostility towards refugees create additional layers of alienation for refugees during and after the initial settlement process.

An abused refugee woman claimant may be in a particularly precarious position if her status is dependent on her partner's refugee claim. In some cases, if the woman arrives before her spouse, she may have developed a sense of her own autonomy and familiarity with Canadian society and institutions. While she may look forward to the arrival of her spouse, once he rejoins his wife and children, the process of adaptation as a family in a new country is stressful on relationships.

*****

The support and advice of elders in their countries of origin are often named by refugee women as a possible source of restraint on men's abuse of their female partners. While the intervention of elders does not preclude the possibility of sexist decisions, women can sometimes find a family member to give them support and refuge. Lacking the extended family and not knowing where to seek support in Canadian society, newly arrived refugee women are more likely to suffer in silence. Furthermore, racism and hostility towards refugees makes it even harder to break the silence. A community worker in an "ethnic" agency, for instance, informed me that battered refugee women will choose solidarity with their community rather than seek personal safety. These refugee women believe that revealing male violence will only exacerbate the "violent," "terrorist" image that the media portrays and that many Canadians believe about their people.

Family members and friends (in Canada and at home) may also collude to prevent reporting male violence and may even blame the woman. Some refugee male abusers have also been known to threaten relatives and even friends as a means of silencing them and withdrawing their support from the wife. Whatever the "reason," community denial rather than sanctions against male violence inevitably reinforces the isolation of the woman, if not the continuation of violence perpetrated against her in her own home. [...]

Fear of further reprisals from their abusive partner is another reason why refugee women may remain silent. Since the majority of refugee women enter Canada as a sponsored "spouse," [...] abused refugee women fear that they will lose their sponsorship and be deported and separated from their children, or that the abuser (or in-laws who may have sponsored the couple or the woman) will use the sponsorship support as a threat to silence them. Nor will an abused refugee woman consider the option of divorce. Not only do they fear that divorce will result in their loss of sponsorship and subsequent deportation, religious beliefs, such as those of Catholics and Muslims, as well as gendered cultural traditions, make it difficult for refugee women to perceive that they have a "right" to seek divorce. [...]

*****

Sexual assault counselling and assistance to abused refugee women also requires different approaches. Sometimes sexual assault in the family becomes entangled with the way women have dealt or not dealt with their past. Sexual abuse can very likely become the catalyst to remembering premigration and migration experiences of torture (sexual or otherwise); witnessing torture; sexual assault in flight; or sexual assault in the asylum countries. The support and counselling needs of refugee women who are abused by their spouse but who escaped the above violations will still necessitate recognition of their refugee experience.

*****

Research and reports on violence against immigrant and refugee women in Canada do underscore the fact that analysis and solutions from the experience of the mainstream women's movement cannot be transplanted (Moussa, 1995). The battered women's shelter movement is an example of an institution which was developed to meet mainstream women's needs. For many abused refugee women a shelter is not necessarily a viable option. Moving out of their homes is once again an uprooting experience and a reexperiencing of refugee "homelessness" and "poverty." Conditions of confinement and sharing limited space can be a reminder of a prison, or a refugee camp (Moussa, 1995).

It is essential to encourage and support refugee and immigrant women who are actively exploring and testing models of intervention that work to protect and assist refugee women living with violent men (Moussa, 1995). Ethnospecific communities also have to deconstruct ideologies and practices which condone male power and superiority over women.

CONCLUSION

While Canada is the first country to have established a set of guidelines that specifically addresses gender-related persecution, the application of these guidelines may not consistently benefit all refugee women. Ongoing assessment of the Guidelines needs to be undertaken to determine their effectiveness and the implications of their interpretation.

There are two key processes that particularly need to be assessed. The first of these are the decisions made about refugees by the senior immigration officers at Canadian border stations. These crucial first decisions determine whether a refugee is eligible to pursue a claim for refugee status or is turned back and not allowed to enter Canada. The second is the consistency or lack of consistency in the reasons which determine which refugee claims are accepted or rejected.

In addition, there are several improvements that should be made to strengthen the application of the Guidelines. The application of the Guidelines should be mandatory and not be left to the choice of individual IRB members. Canadian policy should be consistent in its application. The Guidelines should also be applied

in the overseas selection process and not limited to the refugee claimant process, IRB members should be interviewed and screened prior to their appointment to determine their position on sexism, racism, classism, and other forms of discrimination. Anti-racist and anti-sexist education of all IRB members and cultural interpreters should be mandatory. These educational activities should be monitored to ensure that anti-racist and anti-sexist behaviours and actions are integrated into the IRB. Women refugee claimants should be informed that they can choose legal counsel to assist them and should be assisted in finding counsel. They must be informed that they can apply independently of their spouse in case of death or if the relationship breaks down before the heating. Refugee women need to be well prepared by their lawyers, and the lawyers should understand the political context of the refugee woman's experience. It may be easier for a refugee woman to share her experience with a female lawyer; however, in many cultures, it is taboo for women to discuss sex and the private parts of their bodies with anyone else. Lawyers must respect these cultural norms and listen carefully to refugee women when discussing their experiences.

Despite these applications and efforts to improve the Guidelines, however, we will still look at refugee women and their cultures through the lens of our own history, culture and ideology unless we undertake a deeper analysis of our perceptions. The difficult question is, How can we cross this bridge to be able to listen to what refugee women are saying? The highly legal discourse of the Guidelines assumes that "fairness" and "objectivity" are in place in the process of determining a refugee claim. The implications of ideological perspective(s) towards women from other cultures, social classes, and races are assumed to be dealt with when IRB members attend educational workshops to improve their "gender/cultural sensitivity." But is it enough to be "culturally sensitive" or "gender sensitive"? These concepts are often used in Canada as a way of relating in a positive manner to the cultural background of refugee women. "Sensitivity" is a psychological response and as such is only a partial strategy. Moreover, this approach can inadvertently pathologize other cultures. To truly hear refugee women's stories, the listener has to deconstruct her or his own sexist and racist assumptions.

*****

Refugee women themselves may find it difficult to recognize the political nature of their experience. It is therefore important for those working with refugee women who have been sexually violated or tortured to understand the inter-relationship of the historical and political realities in the countries of origin of these women. In their counselling of refugee women, Mollica and Son clearly describe the interactive cultural, political, and historical dimensions of sexual trauma (1989, pp. 363–379). While their focus is geared to psychoanalytic "treatment" of sexually tortured or raped refugee women, the concepts and approaches could very well be adapted in the refugee determination process and by refugee women's legal counsel in preparation for hearings. The psychoanalytic treatment used by Inger Agger and Soren Buus Jensen (1990, 1996) also enables women to analyze the political context of the violence exerted on them (for example, rape in time of war, sexual torture in prison). Similar to Mollica and Son (1989), this analysis enables women to understand their disclosures of violence as being a testimony about or a "witnessing" of a political context of violence which leads to becoming a refugee rather as opposed to a "confession" from a victim. In this approach, sexual violence is perceived as political rather than a private experience.

Violence against refugee women is gender oppression and a crime against human rights. We must address the root causes to put a halt to the economic and social forces that create refugees. At the same time, Canada must continue to ensure that services provided to refugee women respect their human rights and that they have access to education and employment that will enable them to fulfil their potentials. We must continue to lobby for changes in refugee policy and practice that are responsible and just. Finally, we must ensure that refugee determina-

tion personnel and officers of the courts receive appropriate education and the tools to analyze gender-based refugee claims, as they are, in the end, the final gatekeepers of refugee women's safety and wellbeing.

*****

REFERENCES

Agger, Inger. *The Blue Room: Trauma and Testimony among Refugee Women a Psychosocial Experience.* London: Zed Press, 1993.

Agger, Inger. "Sexual Torture of Political Prisoners: An Overview." *Journal of Traumatic Stress* vol. 2, no. 3 (1989), pp. 305–317.

Agger, Inger. "The Female Political Prisoner. A Victim of Sexual Torture." Paper presented at the Eighth World Congress of Sexology, Heidelberg, June 14–20, 1987, pp. 1–40.

Agger, Inger and Soren Buus Jensen. *Trauma and Healing under State Terrorism.* London: Zed Press, 1996.

Agger, Inger and Soren Buus Jensen. "Testimony as Ritual and Evidence in Psychotherapy for Political Refugees." *Journal of Traumatic Stress* vol. 3, no. 1 (1990), pp. 115–130.

Allodi, F. and S. Stiasny. "Women as Torture Victims." *Canadian Journal of Psychiatry* no. 35 (1990), pp. 144–148.

Amnesty International 1995 Report. New York: Amnesty International, 1995.

Amnesty International 1993 Report. New York: Amnesty International, 1993.

Amnesty International. *Women in the Front Line: Human Rights Violations against Women.* New York: Amnesty International, 1990.

Bannenbring, Fredo. "Refugees: A New Challenge to Foreign and Development Policy." *Development and Cooperation* no. 1 (1991), p. 6.

Bauer, Jan. "Report on UN Conference on Human Rights. June 14–25, 1993." Prepared by Article 19 (UK) and Canadian Network on International Human Rights, Ottawa, 31, October, 1993.

Beiser, Morton et al. "The Mental Health of South East Asian Refugees Resettling in Canada." Final Report to Canada Health and Welfare NHRDL, 1995.

Boyd, Monica. "Immigrant Women in Canada," in *International Migration: The Female Experience*. Rita J. Simon and Caroline Bretell, eds. Totowa, New Jersey: Rowman and Allhanheld, 1986, pp. 45–61.

Boyd, Monica. "At a Disadvantage: The Occupational Attainments of Foreign-Born Women in Canada." *International Migration Review* vol. 18, no. 4 (1984), pp. 109–119.

Canada, An Act to Amend the Immigration Act, 1976 and to Amend other Acts in consequence thereof, 21 July, 1988. Ottawa.

Carrillo, Roxana. "Violence against Women: An Obstacle for Development." In Charlotte Bunch and Roxana Carrillo, *Gender Violence: A Development and Human Rights Issues*. New Jersey: Center for Women's Global Leadership, 1991.

Enloe, Cynthia. *Does Khaki Become You? The Militarisation of Women's Lives*. London: Pandora Press, 1988.

Forbes Martin, Susan. *Women Refugees*. London: Zed Press, 1991.

Fromont, Michel. "Poverty and Exclusion: The Infernal Duo." *The World of Work*. Geneva: International Labour Organization, 1995.

George, Susan. "Le danger d'un chaos financier généralisé." *Le Monde Diplomatique* July 1995, pp. 23–24.

Immigration and Refugee Board. "Guidelines issued by the Chairperson. Pursuant to Section 65(3) of the Immigration Act: Guidelines on Women Refugee Claimants Fearing Gender-Related Persecution." Ottawa, March 9, 1993.

Kane, Hal. *The Hour of Departure: Forces That Create Refugees and Migrants*. Washington, DC: World Watch Institute, 1995.

Korac, Maya. "Women's Groups in the Former Yugoslavia: Working with Refugees." *Refuge* vol. 14, no. 8 (1995), pp. 12–15.

Manavi Newsletter vol. 3, no. 2 (1991). Special issue on violence against women.

Mollica, Richard F. and Linda Son. "Cultural Dimensions in the Evaluation of Treatment of Sexual Trauma." *Psychiatric Clinics of North America* vol. 12, no. 2 (1989), pp. 378–363.

Moussa, Helene. *Women Claiming Power Together: A Handbook to Set Up and Assess Support Groups for/with Immigrant and Refugee Women*. Toronto: Education Wife Assault, 1995.

Moussa, Helene. *Storm and Sanctuary: The Journey of Ethiopian and Eritrean Women Refugees*. Dundas, Ontario: Artemis Enterprises, 1993.

Ng, Roxana and Tania Das Gupta. "Nation Builders: The Captive Labour Force of Non-English Speaking Immigrant Women." *Canadian Woman Studies* vol. 3, no. 1 (1981), pp. 83–89.

Regehr, Ernie. "Key Canadian Components Missing: UN Reports First Arms Trade Register." *The Ploughshares Monitor* vol. 14, no. 4 (1993), pp. 10 and 19.

Regehr, Ernie. *Arms Canada*. Toronto: Lorimer Publishers, 1987.

Reilly, Niamh. *Testimonies of the Global Tribunal on Violations of Women's Rights, Vienna 1993*. New Jersey: Centre for Women's Global Leadership, 1994.

Richmond, Anthony. *Global Apartheid: Refugees, Racism and the New World Order*. Oxford: Oxford University Press, 1994.

Sivard, Ruth Leger. *The World Military and Social Expenses*. Washington, DC: World Priorities, 1993.

Sivard, Ruth Leger. *World Military and Social Expenditure, 1991*. Washington, DC: World Priorities, 1991.

Sivard, Ruth Leger. *World Military Expenditure*. Washington, DC: World Priorities, 1987.

Spencer, Sarah, ed. *Immigration as an Economic Assistance: The German Experience*. London: Tretham Books, 1994.

Stalker, Peter. *The World of Strangers: A Survey of Immigrant Labour Migration*. Geneva: International Labour Organization, 1994.

Tu Khuong, Dao. "Victims of Violence: South China Sea." In *Refugees: The Trauma of Exile*. Diana Miserez, ed. Boston: Martinus Nijhof Publishers, 1988, pp. 13–17.

United Nations High Commission for Refugees. *The State of the World's Refugees: In Search of Solutions*. Oxford: Oxford University Press, 1995.

United Nations High Commission for Refugees. *Sexual Violence against Refugees: Guidelines on Prevention and Response*. Geneva: UNHCR, 1995.

United States Naturalization and Immigration Service. "Consideration for Officers Adjudicating Asylum Claims for Women." Washington, DC, May 26, 1995.

Memorandum to all INS Asylum Officers and HQASM Coordinators. From: Phyllis Coven, Office of International Affairs, pp. 1–19.

Women's World no. 24 (1990/91). Special issue of ISIS-WICCE on Poverty and Prostitution.

Zolberg, Aristides et al. "International Factors in the Formation of Refugee Movements," *International Migration Review* vol. 20, no. 2 (1986), pp. 151–169.

DISCUSSION QUESTIONS: DOBASH ET AL.

1. Outline the argument used by researchers to claim a sexual symmetry in marital violence using national surveys of spousal violence, as well as homicide rates in the United States.

2. Now describe the larger body of evidence that indicates that wives greatly outnumber husbands as victims of martial violence.

3. Describe in detail the authors' critique of the methodology used to make the claim for symmetrical marital violence, including an analysis of the CTS instrument's reliability and validity and the interpretation of CTS data. What conclusions and theoretical and policy implications stem from this critique?

DISCUSSION QUESTIONS: MOUSSA

1. Outline Moussa's characterization of violence and its uses in relation to women's lives.

2. Describe in detail the three levels of violence refugee women experience in their global movement from home to asylum country. Include examples from the chapter in that description.

3. What policy and process recommendations does Moussa make pertaining to the Canadian state? What does she hope will be achieved with their implementation?

FURTHER READINGS

1. Bowker, L. (ed.). 1998. *Masculinities and Violence.* Newburg Park: Sage Publications.

   This book is part of a series entitled Research on Men and Masculinities. These particular essays examine the causes and settings of men's violence, including how men learn violence, repeat it, and use it to victimize women, children, and other men both in the family and at work. Each author shows that empirical analyses of the intersection of masculinity and violence are important to finding ways to mitigate the problem.

2. DeKeseredy, Walter, and Ronald Hinch. 1991. *Woman Abuse: Sociological Perspectives.* Toronto: Thompson Educational Publishing.

   Although the book is fairly old, it remains a concise and indispensable treatment of the central issues related to violence against women, including basic definitions, statistics, and theories related to physical and sexual violence against women in dating, marital, and cohabiting relationships. The authors also provide an excellent discussion of men's violence against and harassment of women in the workplace.

3. Kaufman, Michael. 1997. The Construction of Masculinity and the Triad of Men's Violence. In Michael Kimmel and Michael Messner (eds.), *Men's Lives* (4th ed.). Boston: Allyn and Bacon, p. 4–17.

   In this article Kaufman contends that acts of violence perpetrated by individual men occur within a triad, rather than being solely directed at women. Men's violence against women is linked to men's violence against other men and themselves in a patriarchal context where violence is an accepted mechanism for establishing social hierarchies. He offers ideas about how this situation can be changed to reduce men's violence and improve individual men's lives.

4.   Tetreault, Mary Ann. 1997. Justice for All: Wartime Rape and Women's Human Rights. *Global Governance*, 3, 197–212.

Tetreault's claim in this article is that an individual's control over his or her body should be considered a fundamental human right. With this claim in mind, she supports retribution for acts of wartime rape. Using examples from the Iraqi offensive into Kuwait and the Bosnia-Herzegovina war, she demonstrates that cultural norms in individual societies and criminal courts obstruct the prosecution of wartime rapists and frustrate justice for women rape victims.

5.   Zaman, Habiba. 1999. Violence against Women in Bangladesh: Issues and Responses. *Women's Studies International Forum*, 22(1), 37–48.

In this article Zaman demonstrates that women are everyday targets of exploitation and violence in Bangladesh. She outlines the various forms of violence women suffer, and roots them in the socio-political and ideological relations between women and men in this context. Moreover, she explores the role played by women's organizations and non-governmental organizations in resisting these acts of violence in women's lives.

RELEVANT FILMS

1.   *Against My Will*, 2002, 50 minutes, Humanist Broadcasting Foundation

This film documents violence against women in Pakistan, which is partly a product of cultural concepts such as family honour and women's status as men's private property. The practice of honour killing is discussed, the murder of women by husbands and other family members for "inappropriate" gender and sexual behaviour. We hear personal testimonies from women at the Dastak women's shelter in Lahore about the gendered violence they experience.

2.   *Rape: A Crime of War*, 1996, 60 minutes, National Film Board of Canada

Filmed from the perspective of women who were raped during the conflict in the former Yugoslavia, this Canadian documentary examines rape as a systematic weapon of war used by states around the world. We learn of women's experiences of rape during wartime and the effects of those experiences on their relationships with partners and children, and we meet the perpetrators of rape at the international tribunal at The Hague, which is investigating these state-sanctioned crimes.

3.   *Why Don't You Just Leave?* 1996, 28 minutes, Moving Images

Addressing the question posed in the title, which is often asked of women who are abused by their partners, this film innovatively explores the dilemma of wife abuse using symbolic imagery. Abusive men who are part of the Family Violence Project in Victoria, British Columbia, speak about their behaviours, exposing the implications of domestic violence against women in a society that seems disinclined to confront the issue seriously.

4.   *Insh'Allah Dimanche*, 2002, 98 minutes

This French film (with English subtitles) begins by exploring post-World War II France as it replenishes its workforce by recruiting men from North Africa. In 1974, with the passing of the family reunification law, these men's families joined them. The film details the story of one women émigré who struggles with the alienating experiences of immigration, dislocation, and family reunification in a foreign land.

5.   *After the Montreal Massacre*, 1991, 27 minutes, National Film Board of Canada

Filmmakers retrospectively examine the murders of 14 women at L'Ecole Polytechnique one year after what has come to be known as the Montreal Massacre. The story is told from the perspectives of a survivor and the journalists who covered the story in December 1989. All of these people associate these particular murders with the larger social problem of men's violence against women.

RELEVANT WEB SITES

1. www.undp.org/rblac/gender/legislation/

   Once again, the Gender and Legislation in Latin America and the Caribbean Web site contains a link to a Gender and Violence subtopic, which defines and analyzes gender violence in this context. It includes empirical data to illustrate the parameters of the problem, discusses legislation that is itself violent to women, and defines the necessity of implementing new laws that will help eradicate, prevent, and prosecute gender violence.

2. www.who.int/gender/violence/en/

   The World Health Organization provides an interesting outline of gender-based violence, reporting on a Multi-country Study of Women's Health and Domestic Violence against Women. The study incorporates data on the topic from 10 countries including Brazil, Ethiopia, Japan, and Thailand. It outlines sexual violence as a global problem, and suggests ways to strengthen the global health care response to this violence. The report also explains a new Sexual Violence Research Initiative it is implementing, which links violence against women and HIV infection rates.

3. www.irinnews.org/webspecials/GBV/fearap.asp

   This Web site, hosted by the United Nations Office for the Coordination of Humanitarian Affairs, discusses gender-based violence in conflict zones, including an argument about how rape is used as a systematic weapon of war. The site documents these crimes and suggests preventative action, as well as avenues of support for affected women.

4. www.apiahf.org/apidvinstitue/GenderViolence/analyse.htm

   The Asian and Pacific Islander Institute on Domestic Violence uses this site to analyze violence against women in Asia and the Pacific Islands. It outlines the dynamics and continuum of violence women experience throughout their lives. Information is available in English, Chinese, Farsi, Korean, Tagalog, Vietnamese, and Punjabi.

5. http://policyresearch.gc.ca/page.asp?pagenm=v5n2_art_06

   The researchers involved with the Policy Research Initiatives, which is funded by the government of Canada, explain here the relationship among women, gender, and immigration. They outline the need for more research on gender and integration to develop better public social policy about this issue. Noteworthy Canadian feminist geographers, including Valerie Preston and Isabel Dyck, provide links to their research about Canadian immigration law and recent immigrants in the Canadian labour market.

PART VI

THE GENDERED CLASSROOM

In addition to teaching a program of official knowledge, schools and educators, through what is called the "informal" curriculum, help socialize girls and boys to be appropriately feminine and masculine—obedient, respectful, and quiet, or competitive, independent, and resourceful—thereby (re)producing dominant gender relations and gendered individuals. Feminist educational theorists are interested in these, as well as other structures of power that constitute and mediate the division of labour within schools, teacher-student relations, student-student relations, forms of evaluation, and the curriculum. Practices of gender, racial, class, and sexual domination and exclusion operate in all these spheres, from the classroom to the schoolyard, to discipline students to acquire particular ideas, identities, certificates, and degrees, and to participate in specific activities.

Both of the following articles are based on research conducted in Britain that shows how these inequalities are (re)produced in school cultures. Jon Swain's ethnography of boys' culture in a British junior school focuses on the role clothing plays in the construction of gender identity, especially hegemonic masculinity, which is policed by homophobia. For example, when boys' clothing (e.g., running shoes) or behaviour (e.g., not playing sports) does not conform to hegemonic masculine ideals, they are called "boffs" or "fags" to discipline gendered and sexual identities and practices.

Diane Reay, in her article "'Spice Girls', 'Nice Girls', and 'Tomboys': Gender Discourses, Girls' Culture, and Femininities in the Primary Classroom," starts her examination of the gendered nature of educational institutions by engaging the recent societal premise that boys as a group are underachieving in primary schools due to their masculinity. She argues that the notion that girls are doing better in school is more complicated than the popular discourse suggests when we consider gendered power relations in that context. Her study demonstrates that girls perform various femininities in ways that bolster boys' social and educational positions at the expense of their own, as they widely believe it is "better" to be a boy. Consequently, there is little gender equality at work in these schools, and boys do not come out at the bottom of school hierarchies. Even when boys behave badly and do poorly in school, everyone, including teachers, understands them as better, causing girls to attempt to be more masculine in order to succeed.

CHAPTER 18

THE RIGHT STUFF
Fashioning an Identity through Clothing in a Junior School

Jon Swain

INTRODUCTION

There has been very little empirical research into pupils' clothing as an expression of identity, particularly in the junior school. Although clothing may be one of the surface facets of schooling, in certain circumstances it becomes intrinsically linked to the pupils' own self-appraisals of identity, showing how they wish to present themselves to the world. It is therefore, as an issue, neither trivial nor inconsequential. Epstein and Johnson (1998) point out that the compulsory wearing of school uniform is almost unknown in the state sector in countries outside the UK and some of its ex-colonies. However, since the mid-1980s, there appears to have been an increase in both the implementation, and enforcement, of school uniform in both the secondary and the primary school sectors (Heron, 1990; Lepkowska, 1997), which needs to be explained in the context of devolution and the marketization of schools (Meadmore & Symes, 1997). The 1986 Education Act (see also, *School Governor's Manual*, 1999) advises that responsibility for uniforms should rest with school governors rather than with local authorities, and many headteachers, governors and parents seem to view a smart uniform as a ritualized symbol of order and discipline,

community, tradition, and higher academic standards (Meadmore & Symes, 1996). Moreover, as schools have begun to operate in a competitive market, uniform has come to be used as a tactic of impression management in the projection of school identity (Davis & Ellison, 1991).

BACKGROUND AND METHODOLOGY

The study is located at Westmoor Abbey Junior School [...] where I spent three separate periods of a month each, beginning in October 1998 and ending in June 1999. The research was part of a wider comparative project (my PhD thesis) [...] investigating the construction of masculinity amongst 10–11 year-olds in three schools selected on the basis of social class. Westmoor Abbey was my designated working-class school and was situated on the outskirts of a small town in southern England. It is an average sized junior school, with 11 classes, and less than one percent of the pupils came from homes where English was not the first language. Although 23% of pupils were stipulated as having special educational needs, only 14% were eligible for free school meals, the standard measurement of social deprivation used by government and local education authorities.

The main focus of this study is one class, 6M. This is where I spent the majority of my time, studying the peer group culture and pupil networks. The class consisted of 12 boys (one other had been permanently excluded) and 13 girls (a total of 25 pupils), a small number by state school standards. Most of the early research period was spent observing and getting to know the children in the playground, around the school, but mainly in the classroom, where I often helped and joined in with their work. Over the whole research period, I conducted a series of 27 loosely structured interviews with 6M, talking to the whole class in friendship groups of two to three pupils. All of these discussions took place during class time. Many pupils were interviewed a number of times, and I also observed and carried out 10 further interviews with a number of pupils from the other two Year 6 classes (I also interviewed the class teacher of 6M and the headteacher.) During the interviews, my role was chiefly one of facilitator, with the children being encouraged to express their views freely, and share their experiences, on a wide range of topics. However, I also used direct questioning to test out emerging theories, clarify issues, and as a means to cross-check data from other interviewees.

*****

UNIFORM POLICY: REGULATION AND CONTROL

There was no school uniform when Mr Lane arrived at the school in 1990, but by 1995, a proposition from the school governors that pupils should wear specified school colours had been accepted by a parental ballot and included in the school prospectus. In fact, there appears to have been a good deal of apathy towards this issue and the voting turnout was actually very low. According to the school handbook, the pupils had a choice of two colours of sweatshirt (royal blue or yellow), three colours of polo shirt (royal blue, yellow or white), and two colours of trousers or skirts (grey or black). A distinction must be made between school

"uniform" and school "colours," for it became apparent that, in practice, Mr Lane and his staff did not pay as much attention to trousers, skirts or footwear, but concentrated on the colours of the pupils' tops. Any top that was plain blue, yellow, white, black or grey was deemed acceptable. In fact, my personal (although not formally researched) observations indicate that many primary schools have chosen the option of school colours (usually *one*, in the form of polo/T-shirts and sweatshirts) rather than uniform. Where Westmoor Abbey differed was that even tops displaying motifs and designer labels were permitted, so long as they were in one of the five specified colours. Only football shirts were prohibited, but even here, two or three boys in 6M still sometimes wore them.

I am not suggesting that schools should enforce school uniform or colours, but merely making the observation that many of them do so. Both the other two schools in my study had a rigid policy of enforcement, and I was curious to find out the reasons for the more relaxed approach taken at Westmoor Abbey. When I asked Mr Lane why he was not stricter on the application of uniform, he told me directly that "the main reason is because we can't ... and the parents know their rights." It is important to note that the school had no legal entitlement to impose a school uniform [...], and so it was not so much a question whether Mr Lane *should* enforce school uniform, but whether he *could* enforce it considering the lack of parental support, or, in some cases, their outright opposition. Schools need parental consensus, and if some parents were not prepared to back him, he was going to find rigid implementation an uphill struggle. So, it was largely for pragmatic reasons that he had decided to concentrate on "colours" rather than on "uniform." [...]

In fact, even the "colours" rule had turned out to be "an ongoing battle," and it appeared to me that although Mr Lane could (in theory) have spent a large part of his day "picking up" pupils on their uniform transgressions, he had deliberately chosen to focus his energies on priorities elsewhere, especially in other areas of school discipline. [...] Within class 6M, only one boy, Chris, wore full school uniform (including grey trousers and black shoes). Although, given such a wide choice of colours, it was almost harder not to find an approved colour, only about 14–15 out the 25 pupils in 6M wore correct colours on a regular basis. The rest (about 10—five boys and five girls) wore various tops in various colours emblazoned with designer labels and motifs. Within the context of clothing, there was an inextricable link to sport. Nearly all the pupils in 6M wore tracksuit bottoms (in varying colours), and only three girls usually wore skirts. One of the most controversial parts of school uniform often concerns the type of footwear. There was no mention of everyday footwear in the school prospectus (apart from plimsolls for indoor physical education), and whereas in some schools all forms of training shoes are strictly prohibited, "trainers" at Westmoor Abbey were the norm.

All schools contain relations of (teacher) control and (pupil) resistance (Epstein & Johnson, 1998), and the wearing of non-school uniform (or parts of non-school uniform) is a major resource for pupils in the outward/public display of resistance to school regulation (Meadmore & Symes, 1996). By the lack of rigid control and surveillance of school uniform at Westmoor Abbey, a space, or trajectory (which is often denied to the pupils at schools where uniform is strictly enforced), was opened up for the pupils to express themselves. Some pupils seemed to have decided on an almost contemptuous dismissal of school dress codes, with much clothing being highly individualized, and representing a direct challenge to school regulations. What made this situation so difficult for the school to confront was that the pupils' style of clothing was worn in collusion with their parents. Indeed, the class teacher of 6M, Miss Morris, told me during interview that many of the parents she dealt with wore the same style of clothes as their children. Of course, the vast majority of the pupils' clothes were bought by the parents. These children were generally too young to earn money to pay for these expensive items, and there was no evidence that they procured them by illegal means.

*****

MASCULINITIES AND PUPIL CULTURES

An integral part of the ongoing formation of young boys' identity is the negotiation and renegotiation of their masculinity. Many of the most convincing arguments concerning the theoretical conceptualization of masculinity emanate from the work of Connell (1987, 1995, 1996, 2000), who views masculinity as an interrelational social construction, whereby various masculinities are constructed in relation to each other, as well as in relation to femininities. Incorporating Gramsci's concept of hegemony into the area of gender relations, Connell has placed power at the centre of his analysis. Power is differentiated with a number of hierarchical, competing, and frequently contradictory versions of masculinity on view in each particular site (which in this case is the school). However, one hegemonic strand of masculinity often tends to dominate an institution at any one time, exerting the greatest influence and authority, and claiming the highest status. Connell defines hegemonic as "culturally exalted" or "idealised" (Connell, 1990, p. 83), while Kenway and Fitzclarence (1997, pp. 119–120) refer to hegemonic masculinity as the "standard-bearer" of what it means to be a "real boy," with other males drawing inspiration from it, and at least attempting to emulate its form. Most significantly, this hegemonic form is able to regulate thought and action by defining the norm which gains the consent of other masculine forms. There was a group of dominant boys in 6M (who also had friendship links with boys in the other two Year 6 classes). To be included, you had to be what Thornton (1997) calls "in the know"; that is, you not only had to adhere to the right look, you also had to be able to talk about the right subjects, use the right speech, use the right body language, play the right playground games and so on. It was the hegemonic group that defined what "right" actually was.

The school itself is a thoroughly gendered institution and plays an important role in the formation of masculine identity [...]. Connell (1996, p. 213) maintains that each school has its own gender regime and Gilbert and Gilbert

(1998) site three key areas of "masculinizing practices": management and policy organizational practices, teacher and pupil relation, and the curriculum. Moreover, it should not be forgotten that there are at least two cultures in every school: a formal/official school culture (academic, social, policy/organizational structures) and an informal/unofficial pupil peer culture (Connell et al., 1982; Pollard, 1985; Pollard & Filer, 1999), each having its own particular hierarchy, rules, and evaluation criteria. The production of the dominant form of pupil masculinity at Westmoor Abbey was centred on a counter-school culture, which was achieved in and through resistance to the authority of the formal school culture. Those boys who were not able to be included in the dominant group were necessarily marginalized (pushed to the edges) or stigmatized/subordinated (actively pursued). That said, the majority of boys at Westmoor Abbey were content to follow a kind of complicit masculinity by imitating and adopting some of the hegemonic features of the informal culture, which was partly due to the need to gain social recognition and abrogate the risk of abuse and ridicule (Connell, 1995; Parker, 1996a).

Butler (1990) refers to masculinity as part of a gender performance. The main features of the hegemonic masculinity at Westmoor Abbey were bound up with a highly visible kind of presentation, and were expressed as a style. You needed to look and be tough and be a successful fighter, to look and be sporty/athletic, to show that you were not working in class (even if you actually were), to publicly undermine the authority of teachers (for example, by calling out in class and/or being cheeky), and show you were "cool" by the wearing of fashionable items of non-school clothing. There was a need to be seen to be doing these things, and it was a kind of perpetual performance.

*****

Although the majority of the boys consented to, and colluded with, the hegemonic regime, they either chose not to, or were unable to, perform many of its features. In fact James, Eric, Jimmy, Robert, Chris, Dave and Tom had tended to become rather marginalized by the core dominant group. They were sporty/athletic, played rough games, were often cheeky to the teachers, wore the fashionable clothes, but were not really tough enough to be able to impose themselves physically. Exclusion was part of the hegemonic masculine form at Westmoor Abbey, and two boys (Simon and Sam) had become subordinated, or victimized, by the other boys in 6M, mainly because of what they were unable (and to a certain extent) unwilling, to be or do. [...]

*****

Although, at this age, boys' appearance in general is fundamentally presented and performed for the benefit of their own male peer culture, both boys and girls in 6M took keen note of what each other was wearing. Girls also ran the risk of taunts and insults for conforming too closely to school dress codes and regulations (from both boys and girls). In fact, the majority wore the same unofficial "uniform" as the boys, that is, tracksuit bottoms and training shoes, although they did not appear to have the same compulsive need to wear designer makes/brands, and more of them wore the Westmoor Abbey sweatshirt. Clothing was, however, used to promote heterosexual attraction in settings outside school, such as at a series of locally organized discos which many of the boys and girls attended, and where they would consciously and conspicuously "dress up" for the occasion.

It is important to stress, firstly, that models of hegemonic masculinity do not necessarily need to be the most common form on show, and that, secondly, they are contextually bound and will assume different meanings in different places. For instance, the undermining of a teacher's authority or the ability to be a good fighter may be qualities that are generally despised rather than valorized at other schools. Moreover, the wearing of fashionable clothing at many schools is not even an option open for consideration. There are different alternatives, or possibilities, of *doing boy* within each school setting using the meanings and practices available, and these will often be interconnected to the formal/

official school culture. For instance, some schools may consciously promote and sanction school games/sport while others do not. One of the main ways of gaining status at one of the other schools in my study was by working hard, and gaining academic qualifications, but this trajectory was not open to those at Westmoor Abbey, or at least it was a much more difficult one to attempt to both perform and succeed in without being derided as a "boff." In fact, although many of the boys had relatively low levels of academic attainment (as against national norms as measured by Standard Assessment Task results and Office for Standards in Education reports) [...], they did not appear to interpret their schooling experience in terms of failure, for they were evaluating their school life in a different way, the way which was open to them at their school. In essence, they were negotiating a different "set of storylines" and "repertoires of action" (Gilbert & Gilbert, 1998, p. 51).

PUPIL CULTURES AND PUPIL NETWORKS

"Pupil cultures refer to a "way of life," or "shared guidelines" (Dubbs & Whitney, 1980, p. 27), providing boys with a series of shared meanings of what it is to be a boy. Mac an Ghaill (1994) points out that peer group cultural networks are used as a kind of "institutional infrastructure," in which both individual and collective identities are constructed, negotiated, and performed. Within every class there are a number of overlapping pupil cultures to which boys are going to be variably affiliated (Woods, 1983, 1990). As the period of research progressed, it became apparent that there were three main groups of boys within 6M, saturated and structured by power relations, and governed by a number of clear rules defining attitudes, expectations, and expressions of tastes and behaviour.

Of course, these groups were not as discrete as this. Real life is far more complex, and there was quite lot of inter-group mixing, particularly, in the playground games. Nevertheless, these typologies do point to the range of masculinities on show within one class. The groupings came

from my own observations, and from the boys themselves during interview sessions. Each interview group had slightly different perceptions of how the boys' peer groupings were constituted in 6M. The boy's classifications of their peers also revealed much about themselves, for as Bourdieu states, "nothing classifies somebody more the way he or she classifies" (Bourdieu, 1990, p. 132). For Bourdieu, the social world functions in unison as a system of power relations, and as a symbolic system in which distinctions of taste are used as a basis for social judgement. He also views taste and fashion as an important form of cultural capital which can be used as currencies to gain advancement in the social hierarchy. In his empirical study of taste in French society, Bourdieu (1984) demonstrates that fashion (including clothing styles) has an important function in classifications, and taste in clothing was one way that the pupils used as a means of uniting, including and differentiating themselves from others. For Bourdieu, taste distinguishes a person in an essential way, "since taste is the basis of all that one has ... and all that one is for others, whereby one classifies oneself and is classified by others" (Bourdieu, 1984, p. 56).

LOOKING RIGHT, AND WEARING THE RIGHT STUFF

For the pupils at Westmoor Abbey, appearance was a central part of how they defined themselves, and clothing seemed to signify self-worth. Moreover, styles of dress formed a part of how the pupils wished to be publicly represented, and the designer labels and names so prominently displayed were a vital visible component in that promotion. In contemporary mass cultures, children, like adults, consume signs. During the third week of my fieldwork, I remember Dan and Alan proudly showing me their jackets in the cloakroom, outside their classroom, and Alan saying, "This one's worth £100," and also the disappointment on Dan's face when I failed to recognize the make of Kappa, which was emblazoned on the side of his jacket. The importance of displaying the labels, getting oneself noticed, and making sure one was part of the "in" crowd is illustrated in the following conversation:

> JS: Have you heard of Tommy Sports? I saw Leah wearing Tommy, that's meant to be quite good isn't it?
>
> Eric: Yeah that's quite good, the watch is [interrupted]
>
> Robert: It's very quiet, though.
>
> JS: What do you mean, "very quiet"?
>
> Robert: It don't stand out.
>
> Eric: Not many people wear it.
>
> JS: So have you got to have something that stands out?
>
> Robert: Yeah.
>
> JS: Yeah, I mean the more it stands out the more you get noticed?
>
> Robert: I've got a luminous yellow T-shirt, this is a good make, Diadora.
>
> JS: Is it important to wear something that stands out and everyone goes, "Oh look, you've got that on"?
>
> Robert: No, they don't go, "You've got that on," but they won't take the mick out of you. If I wear this, it's all right.

Robert's last comment draws our attention to the risks involved for anyone not conforming to the group norms, for the wearing of certain clothes was very much a cultural imperative. It was as if masculine competence was on trial or on show, and looking good and having the right stuff to wear needed commitment and dedication, knowledge, and importantly, peer group recognition, validation, and legitimation. Although the boys' appearance was equated with their performance, and in many ways "to look was to be" (Skeggs, 1997, p. 116), there was also the need "to look" in order to be safe.

Within peer group relations, certain items acquired a specific, localized, symbolic value, such as particular brand names, and these were ascribed a higher cultural value than others. There was a hierarchy of brand names in play, and some of the most popular included "Tommy Sports," "Kappa," "Reebok" and "Adidas." It was the training shoes that had the greatest currency in terms of status, with their signifiers

of wealth, choice, freedom, equality, sportiness, casualness, anti-school, and of collective belonging. [...]

*****

[...] As with the tracksuit tops (and also T-shirts, jackets, etc.), there was a hierarchy of brand names. Two of the lowest ranking were "Ascot" and "Gola." During an interview with two pupils from another class, aesthetic style was highlighted again, but so was the associated high price, and having the ability to afford it. *Real* training shoes were bought in real sports shops with their higher associated symbolic value. [...]

*****

SUBORDINATED FORMS OF MASCULINITY: GAYS AND BOFFS

Those who did not conform to the right "look" at Westmoor Abbey were categorized as "other." It was the whole look, the whole package, that was required, and this was policed by the boys from both the hegemonic and marginalized groups. If a 6M boy wore anything associated with the regulation school uniform, apart from the sweatshirt, they would often be called either "gay" or a "boff." The following extract comes from an interview with Chris, Jimmy and Tom. Chris was a particularly unusual and, therefore, interesting case, being the only boy in the class who wore a recognizable school uniform of white shirt, black school trousers and black, "ordinary," shoes. This was due to his mother's insistence, rather than any choice of his own, and he was often ridiculed for it. However, as he displayed many of the other characteristics of hegemonic masculinity, and was often "one of the lads," he did not pay such a heavy price as, perhaps, other boys might have done. Chris was quick to point out that Dan, the main leader of the dominant group, sometimes wore the official school top, and his rather defiant assertion at the end of the conversation that he did not care about wearing school uniform seemed to lack conviction and probably had more to do with the way he was presenting himself to me, the adult researcher. Moreover, Chris wanted to make the point that his identity at home, and around the estate, was unaffected by what he looked like at school:

JS: What about the way you dress?

Chris: Some people say, like, you have to dress cool, but it don't matter 'cos they reckon, they call you "boffins" if you just dress in school uniform like I do, but it don't matter 'cos when you go home you can open your wardrobe and show 'em and you've got all these sports clothes like [...] that's what my mum tells me, I've got loads of jogging bottoms, Giorgio tops.

JS: So some people, if they came to the school, would be called boff with a school uniform? I mean you've got a school uniform. [indicating Chris]

Chris: [...] Yeah, but Joe don't normally say it anymore 'cos he wears a school jumper, and a school shirt.

JS: [...] I can see a lot of you wear trainers, but you haven't got trainers on today have you? [indicating Chris]

Chris: No, I leave my trainers for football day, PE, and when I get home I change into something else ... he knows [indicating Dave] that I don't wear all these fake things [...] because I come out in jogging bottoms and things like that ...

J.S.: So you feel it's all right to wear the school uniform?

Chris: Yeah, I don't care what I wear.

Getting Called "Gay"

Gilbert and Gilbert maintain that "heterosexuality has been found to be a powerful marker of masculine identity in most studies of boys' school cultures" (Gilbert & Gilbert, 1998, p. 129) and at Westmoor Abbey, the valorized, dominant masculinity was partly shaped by homophobia. A number of researchers have recognised homosexuality as being a key

form of subordinated masculinity (see, for example, Connell, 1987, 1995, 2000; Mac an Ghaill, 1994; Nayak & Kehily, 1996; Epstein, 1997; Redman & Mac an Ghaill, 1997; Martino, 1999; Skelton, 2001), and it was no different here. Parker (1996a) argues that insults such as "gay" and/or "poofter" need to be implicitly conceptualized in terms of *gender* as opposed to *sexuality* and, therefore, connote to being "non-masculine" and effeminate rather than being homosexual. Certainly, at Westmoor Abbey, these terms were essentially used to control the general behaviour of boys, rather than their sexual preference. "Gay" was used as a means of positioning particular boys at the bottom of the masculine hierarchy and was used ubiquitously as a term of abuse which could be applied to a whole range of actions in different situations. Basically, "gay" meant "naff" or "terrible." A boy could ask a gay question in class; he could do gay work (rather incongruously, by either producing a poor piece of work, or by actually working too well); he could even make a "gay pass" in football and so on. Even the clothes that he wore could be called "gay," and this included his choice of shoe. I had already been alerted to the fact that shoes could be deemed "gay" in an interview with Jimmy and Tom:

Jimmy: Some people say that Tom has got gay trainers because they're old.

Tom: These are old, but I'm getting new ones.

This next extract comes from an interview with two other boys as I am attempting to find out some of the reasons why some boys are labelled "gay":

JS: I've heard of people just doing their work and they get called gay, why is that?

Eric: Because of, like, being too good [...] and if someone is doing, like, rubbish work they go, "Oh that's gay, something like that."

JS: So you've just got to be doing rubbish work then, to be called. [interrupted]

Eric: It's not necessarily, just like being horrid to someone about your work.

JS: What else?

Eric: Some of the clothes you wear, like the shoes.

JS: So you get called gay if you wear different shoes and things?

Eric: Yeah.

Simon: Like Jimmy.

Eric: He goes, "They're gay shoes."

JS: Gay shoes!? What sort are gay shoes then?

Eric: They're like Ascots [*the type of cheap training shoe, mentioned earlier*], they're worn by people like [*inaudible*]

Sam: No, now he's got shoes like mine, and mine are [*interrupted*]

JS: As far as I can see the only person in the class who actually has proper shoes is Chris Dowland, he actually has black shoes doesn't he?

Eric: Yeah ones like that. [*points to my shoes*]

JS: How are they called?

Eric: They're sometimes called gay but he won't let [...], no one will be able to call him gay when we go to Broadmead Manor [*the local secondary school*] because you have to wear them when you go to Broadmead Manor.

JS: Everyone's got to wear them.

Eric: Yeah, ones like that. [*points to my shoes*]

It is highly significant to note that the space that was open at Westmoor Abbey for gaining status through the type of footwear and clothing worn was about to be severely restricted when the boys changed school at the end of the year. Although, like primary schools, secondary schools also have no legal entitlement to enforce school uniform, they have a longer tradition in wearing uniform, and parents appear more willing to accept secondary schools' uniform policy and abide by the rules. As far as the pupils at Westmoor Abbey and their parents were concerned, the wearing of school uniform at secondary school was compulsory, and it was, therefore, going to be more difficult to use clothing as a major strategy and resource in the construction of peer group hierarchies. This

is not to say that the school would be unable to close the strategy completely; it just meant that the distinctions of differentiation would become finer. The pupils knew from their older siblings and other Broadmead pupils that it was still possible to customize their uniforms by, for example, the way they wore their ties. At that moment, however, pupil clothing remained highly individualized. Indeed, boys also risked being called gay if two or more of them came to school wearing the same item, and this could even mean that the boys had to plan ahead.

*****

Being Called a "Boff"

The other main term of abuse was "boff." This was often used alongside gay, or on an interchangeable basis with it, but was usually applied to anyone who worked hard and did not reject the official school culture of conformity and academic achievement. That said, the use of the term was not confined simply towards work; it also represented a general indication towards the suitability and appropriateness of "the look." A boy could have a boff shirt, boff trousers, boff shoes, which basically meant anything that was "smart," a term which the pupils equated with conforming to the school regulations:

JS: What sort of person do you think a boff is?

Robert: It's like they do all their work, never get told off, get it all first, get it done neatly ...

JS: What else?

Robert: Don't moan, listen, do as they're told, don't take things as races [*interrupted*]

JS: Don't take?

Robert: Like if it's a race, they take it as a race; if it's a practice, they take it as a practice ... they don't get into fights.

Eric: Like when you're playing runouts, if you get your hand in, normally people go, "You never got me," but the boffs will just go [*puts on a stereotypical upper-class*

accent] "OK, you got me, I'll just go back
to the wall," you know.
JS: And tell me about how they dress?
Eric: Smart trousers. [*interrupted*]
Robert: Smart trousers, smart shoes, school
uniform [*interrupted*]
Eric: Jumper [*interrupted*]
Robert: Smart shirt, not a tie ... Julian John-
son always wears a tie, but he can't help it.

Eric's imitation of an upper-class accent may
suggest an issue of class division, associating
"boffs" with people who speak in an upper
middle-class register, and who are outside local
cultural norms. Robert's last comment also,
possibly, alludes to the fact that some pupils
(like Chris) face greater parental control and
restrictions than others and were made to wear
certain official school clothes. [...]

*****

[...] [T]his [...] demonstrates quite neatly that
meanings are often negotiated and performed,
and are often highly localized. Each school
classroom has its own unique cultural milieu
where, for instance, historic pupil groupings
and individual teacher's policy/organizations
and personalities/ styles can and do make a real
difference to the way children experience and
live out their lives at school. Although, I maintain, that wearing designer clothes was a powerful symbolic marker of identity throughout the
whole informal pupil culture, it did appear to
have a different expression and significance
within each class.

CONCLUSIONS

For the pupils at Westmoor Abbey, their style of
dress was intrinsically linked to their own identity, for as Finkelstein maintains, "fashioning
the body becomes a practice through which the
individual can fashion a self" (Finkelstein, 1996,
p. 50). Clothes acted as a powerful signifier of the
pupils' worth as people, and were an essential
ingredient of social acceptability (or rejection)
within their specific peer group culture.

Clothes/training shoes were part of pupil
performance, a symbol of how they wished to be
interpreted, of how they wished to be known and
perceived. Particular articles of clothing acted as
signifiers of fashion, as well as of the money that
was needed to make the purchase, which meant
that designer labels needed to [be] conspicuously
displayed. "The look" was all-important, and
many clothes were also connected to sport, with
its associations of athleticism, strength and power
(Parker, 1996b). Perhaps the preoccupation with
clothing was so highly valued because the boys
and girls had fewer alternatives of demonstrating
material status compared to pupils from a different social class, or having their value (as people)
legitimized by other means, such as working
hard and achieving academically.

Although pupils had a certain amount of
agency and choice, they were, nevertheless, living their lives in circumstances which were not
of their own choosing, and the symbolic value
attached to dress style was part of the localized
cultural knowledge and attitudes within the
surrounding community. The children brought
their home values into Westmoor Abbey. In
many ways, their lives inside school were an
extension of their lives on the estate, but were
just being performed in a different site.

The school (the head and the teachers) practised a loose form of bodily surveillance, which
was largely due to the fact that a school uniform
was virtually impossible to enforce. But even
Westmoor Abbey's adoption of school colours was
only loosely applied, and a space was created for
the pupils to individualize their clothes and challenge the school's formal authority and control.

There was a range of masculinities and
femininities on view within the class peer group
culture, and the public display of designer labels
on non-school uniform was one key feature of
the dominant, stylized form of masculinity. It
is important to reiterate that this hegemonic
norm was specific to the school (and perhaps
even to 6M) and lost its currency outside the
localized area. In this sense, it formed virtually
no part of the dominant/hegemonic features in
the other two schools where I was carrying out
my research. Here, school uniform was much
more rigidly enforced, and so the opportunities

for using clothes for individual and collective expression were acutely curtailed.

The risks of non-conformity to peer group norms at Westmoor Abbey were severe and would generally result in abuse (often of a homophobic nature), or/and outright rejection and peer group ostracism. The main policing of clothing was conducted by the pupils themselves, and the two prevalent terms of abuse were "gay," which basically connoted "naff" (awful), and "boff," which connoted a conformity to the school's values and authority. Put simply, there was a cultural need to conform and perform to the masculine boundaries in play.

REFERENCES

Bourdieu, P. (1984) *Distinction: A Social Critique of the Judgement of Taste* (London, Routledge).

Bourdieu, P. (1990) *"In Other Words": Essays towards a Reflexive Sociology* (Cambridge, Polity Press).

Butler, J. (1990) *Gender Trouble: Feminism and the Subversion of Identity* (London: Routledge).

Connell, R.W. (1987) *Gender and Power: Society, the Person and Sexual Politics* (Cambridge, Polity Press).

Connell, R.W. (1990) An iron man: The body and some contradictions of hegemonic masculinity, in: M.A. Messner & D.F. Sabo (Eds) *Sport, Men and the Gender Order: Critical Feminist Perspectives* (Champaign, IL, Human Kinetics).

Connell, R.W. (1995) *Masculinities* (Cambridge, Polity Press).

Connell, R.W. (1996) Teaching the boys: New research on masculinity and gender strategies for schools, *Teachers College Record*, 98, pp. 206–235.

Connell, R.W. (2000) *The Men and the Boys* (Cambridge, Polity Press).

Connell, R.W. Ashenden, D.J., Kessler, S. & Dowsett, D.W. (1982) *Making the Difference: Schools, families and social division* (Sydney, George Allen & Unwin).

Davis B. & Ellison, L. (1991) *Marketing the Secondary School* (Harlow, Longman).

Dubbs, P.J. & Whitney, D.D. (1980) *Cultural Contexts: Making Anthropology Personal* (Boston, MA, Allyn and Bacon).

Epstein, D. (1997) Boyz' own stories: Masculinities and sexualities in schools, *Gender and Education*, 9, pp. 105–115.

Epstein, D. & Johnson, R. (1998) *Schooling Sexualities* (Buckingham, Open University Press).

Finkelstein, J. (1996) *Fashion: An Introduction* (New York, New York University Press).

Gilbert, R. & Gilbert, P. (1998) *Masculinity Goes to School* (London, Routledge).

Heron, E. (1990) Slipping into something a little less comfortable, *Times Educational Supplement*, 20 April, p. 10.

Kenway, J. & Fitzclarence, L. (1997) Masculinity, violence and schooling: "Challenging poisonous pedagogies," *Gender and Education*, 9, pp. 117–133.

Lepkowska, D. (1997) From the worst to … better, *Times Educational Supplement*, 24 October, p. 4.

Mac an Ghaill, M. (1994) *The Making of Men: Masculinities, sexualities and schooling* (Buckingham, Open University Press).

Martino, W. (1999). "Cool boys," "party animals," "squids" and "poofters": Interrogating the dynamics and politics of adolescent masculinities in school, *British Journal of Sociology of Education*, 29, pp. 239–263.

Meadmore, D. & Symes, C. (1997) Keeping up appearances: Uniform policy for school diversity? *British Journal of Educational Studies*, 45, pp. 174–186.

Meadmore, D. & Symes, C. (1996) Of uniform appearance: A symbol of school discipline and governmentality, *Discourse*, 17, pp. 209–225.

Nayak, A. & Kehily, M. (1996) Masculinities and schooling: Why are young men so homophobic? In D.L. Steinberg, D. Epstein & R. Johnson (Eds) *Border Patrols: Policing the Boundaries of Heterosexuality* (London, Cassell).

Parker, A. (1996a) The construction of masculinity within boys' physical education, *Gender and Education*, 8, pp. 141–157.

Parker, A. (1996b) Sporting masculinities: Gender relations and the body, in M. Mac an Ghaill (Ed.) *Understanding Masculinities* (Buckingham, Open University Press).

Pollard, A. (1985) *The Social World of the Primary School* (London, Cassell).

Pollard, A. & Filer, A. (1999) *The Social World of Pupil Career: Strategic Biographies through Primary School* (London, Cassell).

Redman, P. & Mac an Ghaill, M. (1997) Educating Peter: The making of a history man, in: D.L. Steinberg, D. Epstein & R. Johnson (Eds) *Border Patrols: Policing the Boundaries of Heterosexuality*. London: Cassell.

School Governor's Manual (1999) (Kingston-upon-Thames, Croner Publications).

Skeggs, B. (1997) *Formation of Class and Gender* (London, Sage).

Skelton, C. (2001) *Schooling the Boys: Masculinities and Primary Education* (Buckingham, Open University Press).

Thornton, S. (1997) The social logic of subcultural capital, in: K. Gelder & S. Thornton (Eds) *The Subcultures Reader* (London, Routledge).

Woods, P. (1983) *Sociology and the School: An Interactionist Viewpoint* (London, Routledge and Kegan Paul).

Woods, P. (1990) *The Happiest Days?* (London, Falmer Press).

CHAPTER 19

"SPICE GIRLS," "NICE GIRLS," "GIRLIES," AND "TOMBOYS"

Gender Discourses, Girls' Cultures and Femininities in the Primary Classroom

Diane Reay

INTRODUCTION

This article attempts to demonstrate that contemporary gendered power relations are more complicated and contradictory than any simplistic binary discourse of "the girls versus the boys" suggests (Heath, 1999). Although prevailing dominant discourses identify girls as "the success story of the 1990s" (Wilkinson, 1994), this small-scale study of a group of seven-year-old girls attending an inner London primary school suggests that, particularly when the focus is on the construction of heterosexual femininities, it is perhaps premature always to assume that "girls are doing better than boys." While girls may be doing better than boys in examinations, this article indicates that their learning in the classroom is much broader than the National Curriculum and includes aspects that are less favourable in relation to gender equity. Although masculinities are touched on in this article, this is only in as far as they relate to girls. This deliberate bias is an attempt to re-focus on femininities at a time when masculinities appear to be an ever-growing preoccupation within education.

However, although the subjects of this research are 14 girls, the position the article takes is that femininities can only be understood relationally. There is a co-dependence between femininities and masculinities, which means that neither can be fully understood in isolation from the other. The article therefore explores how a particular group of primary-aged girls is positioned, primarily in relation to dominant discourses of femininity but also in relation to those of masculinity. There is also an attempt to map out their relationships to transgressive but less prevalent discourses of femininity, which in a variety of ways construct girls as powerful. The findings from such a small-scale study are necessarily tentative and no generalized assertions are made about girls as a group. Rather, the aim is to use the girls' narratives and their experiences in school and, to a lesser extent, those of the boys, to indicate some ways in which the new orthodoxy, namely that girls are doing better than boys, does not tell us the whole story about gender relations in primary classrooms.

The last decade has seen a growing popular and academic obsession with boys' underachievement both in the UK and abroad (Katz, 1999; Smithers, 1999). However, as Lyn Yates points out, much of the "underachieving boys" discourse fails either to deal adequately with power or to see femininity and masculinity as relational phenomena (Yates, 1997).

For instance, within the explosion of concern with masculinities in academia, there has been little focus on the consequences for girls of "boys behaving badly." [...]

*****

Jill Blackmore describes attempts by some male academics in Australia to develop programmes for boys which seek to depict boys as powerless in the face of the progress and success of feminism and girls, and, indeed, as victims of their own male psychology (Blackmore, 1999). Jane Kenway writes more broadly of "the lads' movement" in Australia; a general resurgence of concern that boys and men are getting an unfair deal (Kenway, 1995). In Britain, there has been a growing alarm about "boys doing badly" that preoccupies both mainstream and feminist academics alike (Epstein et al., 1998). What gets missed out in these current concerns is the specificity of the "failing boy" and the ways in which other groups of males continue to maintain their social advantage and hold on to their social power (Arnot et al., 1999; Lucey & Walkerdine, 1999). It is within this context of contemporary preoccupation with boys that this article attempts to problematize issues surrounding gender equity and, in particular, to challenge the view that in millennial Britain it is boys rather than girls who are relatively disadvantaged.

*****

GENDER DISCOURSES

*****

Multiple discourses contribute not only to how researchers appreciate the conditions of childhood but also to how children come to view themselves. Post-structuralist feminists have explored extensively the ways in which different discourses can position girls (Davies, 1993; Hey, 1997; Walkerdine, 1997). It is important to recognize that there are many competing gender discourses, some of which have more power

and potency than others for particular groups of girls (Francis, 1998). Such processes of discursive recognition, of feeling a better fit within one discourse than another (Francis, 1999), are influenced by social class. Similarly, gender discourses are taken up differentially by different ethnic groupings. It is also important to stress that girls can position themselves differently in relation to gender discourses according to the peer group context they find themselves in. For example, it soon became evident in my research that girls assume different positions depending on whether they are in single- or mixed-sex contexts. [...]

*****

I found [...] "complex relations of complicity, tension and opposition" in relation to the nexus of gender discourses that these girls draw on. Yet, any local discursive nexus is framed by a wider social context within which, as Valerie Hey (1997) points out, there is a lack of powerful public discourses for girls, leaving them caught between schooling, which denies difference, and compulsory heterosexuality, which is fundamentally invested in producing it. If this gives the impression of a fluid situation in relation to how contemporary girls position themselves as female, there is also substantial evidence of continuities in which, at least for the girls in this research, conformist discourses continue to exert more power than transgressive or transformative ones.

MASCULINITIES IN THE CLASSROOM: SETTING THE CONTEXT

Although the main focus of this article is how gender discourses position girls at school, in order to understand femininities in this primary classroom, the ways in which masculinities are being played out cannot be ignored. [...] Josh and David, two white, middle-class, 7-year-old boys [...] were the only middle-class boys in a Year 3 class of predominantly working-class children. Existing research has found that the culturally exalted form of masculinity varies from school to school and is informed by the local community (Skelton, 1997; Connolly, 1998). These two boys were adjusting to a predominantly working-class, inner-city peer group in which dominant local forms of masculinity were sometimes difficult for both to negotiate, but in particular, for David (for one thing, he did not like football). They both also found the low priority given to academic work among the other boys problematic. Even so, they were clear that it was still better being a boy.

Both boys, despite their social class positioning, were popular among the peer group. In particular, Josh commanded a position of power and status in the peer group which was virtually unchallenged (see also Reay, 1990). Sociogram data collected from all the children in the class positioned him as the most popular child, not only with the working-class boys in the class but also with the girls. David's positioning is more difficult to understand. His particular variant of middle-class masculinity was far less acceptable to his working-class peers than Josh's. He was studious and hated games. In the exercise where children drew and described their favourite playground activity, David sketched a single figure with a bubble coming out of his head with "thoughts" inside. He annotated it with "I usually like walking about by myself and I'm thinking." However, within the confines of the classroom, for much of the time, he retained both status and power, paradoxically through a combination of being male and clever. When the girls were asked to nominate two boys and two girls they would most like to work with, David was the second most popular male choice after Josh. However, he was the most popular choice with the other boys. The complex issues as to why these two boys were popular when their masculinities did not fit the dominant one within the male peer group are beyond the brief of this article. Rather, what is salient is the relevance of their positioning within the peer group for the group of girls who are the article's main protagonists.

Although the focus has been on "the others" within masculinity, black and white working-class boys (Willis, 1977; Sewell, 1997), it is the association of normativity with white, middle-class masculinity that seems most difficult for girls to challenge effectively. Disruptive, failing boys' behaviour has given girls an unexpected window of opportunity through which some variants of femininities can be valorized over specific pathologized masculinities, particularly within the arena of educational attainment. Both girls and boys were aware of discourses which position girls as more mature and educationally focused than boys and regularly drew on them to make sense of gender differences in the classroom (see also Pattman & Phoenix, 1999). What seems not to have changed is the almost unspoken acceptance of white, middle-class masculinity as the ideal that all those "others"—girls as well as black and white working-class boys—are expected to measure themselves against. Popular discourses position both masculinity and the middle classes as under siege, suggesting an erosion of both male and class power bases (Bennett, 1996; Coward, 1999). While there have been significant improvements in the direction of increasing equity, particularly in the area of gender, the popularity of Josh and David, combined with the uniform recognition among the rest of the peer group that they were the cleverest children in the class, suggests that popular discourses may mask the extent to which white, middle-class male advantages in both the sphere of education and beyond continue to be sustained.

However, 10 of the 12 boys in 3R were working class. The "failing boys" compensatory culture of aggressive "laddism" (Jackson, 1998) had already started to be played out at the micro-level of this primary classroom. The working-class, white and mixed race boys were more preoccupied with football than the academic curriculum (see also Skelton, 1999). When they were not playing football in the playground, they would often be surreptitiously exchanging football cards in the classroom. Alongside regular jockeying for position within the male peer group, which occasionally escalated into full-blown fights, there was routine, casual labelling of specific girls as stupid and dumb. The three Bengali boys at the bottom of this particular male peer group hierarchy compensated by demonizing, in particular, the three middle-class girls. Their strategy echoes that of the subordinated youth in Wight's (1996) study, where in order to gain the approval and acceptance of their dominant male peers, they endeavoured to become active subjects in a sexist discourse which objectified girls.

SUGAR AND SPICE AND ALL THINGS NICE?

3R had four identifiable groups of girls—the "nice girls," the "girlies," the "spice girls" and the "tomboys." The latter two groups had decided on both their own naming as well as those of the "girlies" and the "nice girls," descriptions which were generally seen as derogatory by both girls and boys. "Girlies" and "nice girls" encapsulate "the limited and limiting discourse of conventional femininity" (Brown, 1998), and in this Year 3 class, although there was no simple class divide, the "nice girls" were composed of Donna, Emma and Amrit, the only three middle-class girls in 3R, plus a fluctuating group of one to two working-class girls. The "nice girls," seen by everyone, including themselves, as hard-working and well behaved, exemplify the constraints of a gendered and classed discourse which afforded them the benefits of culture, taste, and cleverness but little freedom. Prevalent discourses, which work with binaries of mature girls and immature boys and achieving girls and underachieving boys, appear on the surface to be liberating for girls. However, the constraints were evident in the "nice girls'" self-surveillant, hypercritical attitudes to both their behaviour and their schoolwork; attitudes which were less apparent amongst other girls in the class. It would appear that this group of seven-year-old, predominantly middle-class girls had already begun to develop the intense preoccupation with academic success that other researchers describe in relation to middle-class, female, secondary school pupils (Walkerdine et al., 2000).

Contemporary work on how masculinities and femininities are enacted in educational contexts stresses the interactions of gender with class, race and sexuality (Mac an Ghaill, 1988;

Hey, 1997; Connolly, 1998). Sexual harassment in 3R (a whole gamut of behaviour which included uninvited touching of girls and sexualized name-calling) was primarily directed at the "girlies" and was invariably perpetuated by boys who were subordinated within the prevailing masculine hegemony either because of their race or social class. However, while sexual harassment was an infrequent occurrence, identifying the "nice girls" as a contaminating presence was not. In the playground, the three working-class Bengali boys were positioned as subordinate to the white and Afro-Caribbean boys; for example, they were often excluded from the football games on the basis that they were not skilful enough. These three boys constructed the "nice girls" as a polluting, contagious "other." They would regularly hold up crossed fingers whenever one of these girls came near them. As a direct result, the "nice girls" began to use the classroom space differently, taking circuitous routes in order to keep as far away from these boys as possible. Barrie Thorne (1993) found similar gender practices in which girls were seen as "the ultimate source of contamination." Like the girls in Thorne's research, the "nice girls" did not challenge the boys but rather developed avoidance strategies which further circumscribed their practices.

*****

This is not to construct the "nice girls" as passive in relation to other groups in the class. They often collaborated with Josh and David on classwork and were vocal about the merits of their approach to schoolwork over those of other girls in the class.

*****

However, the dominant peer group culture in the classroom was working class and, while this had little impact on the popularity of Josh and David, it did have repercussions for the status and social standing of the "nice girls" within the peer group.

"The limited and limiting discourse of conventional femininity" also had a powerful impact on the "girlies," a group of three working-class girls (two white and one Bengali). Kenway et al. (1999) write about "the sorts of femininities which unwittingly underwrite hegemonic masculinity" (p. 120). Certainly, the "girlies," with their "emphasized femininity" (Connell, 1987, p. 187), were heavily involved in gender work which even at the age of 7 inscribed traditional heterosexual relations. Paul Connolly (1998) describes the ways in which sexual orientation and relations defined through boyfriends and girlfriends seems to provide an important source of identity for young children. This was certainly the case for the "girlies." These girls were intensely active in the work of maintaining conventional heterosexual relationships through the writing of love letters, flirting and engaging in regular discussions of who was going out with whom. They were far more active in such maintenance work than the boys.

Both the "girlies" and the "nice girls" were subject to "discourses of denigration" circulating among the wider peer group (Blackmore, 1999, p. 136). In individual interviews, many of the boys and a number of the other girls accounted for the "nice girls'" unpopularity by describing them as "boring" and "not fun to be with," while the "girlies" were variously described by boys as "stupid" and "dumb." While the boys were drawing on a male peer group discourse which positioned the "girlies" as less intelligent than they were, the "girlies" were far from "stupid" or "dumb." Although not as scholarly as the "nice girls," they were educationally productive and generally achieved more highly that their working-class male counterparts. Rather, the working-class discourse of conventional femininity within which they were enmeshed operated to elide their academic achievement within the peer group.

Discourses of conventional femininity also seemed to have consequences for the two Asian girls in the class. Amrit, who was Indian, was from a middle-class background while Shamina was Bengali and working class. Yet, both girls, despite their class differences, shared a high degree of circumscription in relation to the range of femininities available to them in the school context. As Shamina explained, "the spice girls

and the tomboys are naughty. I am a good girl." In contrast to the other girls in the girls' focus group discussion, who all claimed to enjoy playing football, both Shamina and Amrit asserted that "football was a boys' game," and Amrit said, "It's not worth bothering with football. It's too boring. Me and my friends just sit on the benches and talk."

Heidi Mirza (1992) argues that the cultural construction of femininity among African-Caribbean girls fundamentally differs from the forms of femininity found among their white peers. In the case of Amrit and Shamina, there were substantial areas of overlap rather than fundamental differences. However, neither managed to carve out spaces in which to escape gender subordination from the boys in the ways that the "spice girls" and the "tomboys," both all-white groups, did. Racism and its impact on subjectivities may well be an issue here. Although it is impossible to make generalizations on the basis of two children, ethnicity, as well as class, appears to be an important consideration in the possibilities and performance of different femininities.

Membership of the "spice girls" revolved around two white, working-class girls, Carly and Debbie. Jenny, Rachel, Alice and Lisa were less consistently members of the group. Lisa and Alice would sometimes claim to be "tomboys" while Jenny and Rachel, when playing and spending time with the "girlies," and especially when Carly and Debbie were in trouble with adults in the school, would realign themselves as "girlies." Very occasionally, when she had quarrelled both with Carly and Debbie, and with Jodie, the one consistent tomboy among the girls, Alice too would reinvent herself as a "girlie."

Although there were many overlaps between both the practices and the membership of the "girlies" and the "spice girls," aspects of the "spice girls'" interaction with the boys appeared to transgress prevailing gender regimes, while the "girlies'" behaviour followed a far more conformist pattern. Yet, the "spice girls" were, for much of the time, also active in constructing and maintaining traditional variants of heterosexuality. Their espousal of "girl power" did not exclude enthusiastic partaking of the boyfriend/girlfriend games. There was much flirting, letter writing, falling in and out of love and talk of broken hearts. However, they also operated beyond the boundaries of the "girlies'" more conformist behaviour when it came to interaction with the boys. Debbie and Carly, the most stalwart members of the "spice girls," both described the same activity—rating the boys—as their favourite playground game. As Carly explained, "you follow the boys around and give them a mark out of ten for how attractive they are."

The "spice girls'" adherence to so-called girl power also allowed them to make bids for social power never contemplated by the "girlies" or the "nice girls." During a science lesson which involved experiments with different foodstuffs, including a bowl of treacle, Carly and Debbie jointly forced David's hand into the bowl because, as Carly asserted, "he is always showing off, making out he knows all the answers." This incident, which reduced David to tears and shocked the other children, served to confirm the class teacher in her view that the two girls "were a bad lot." The "girls with attitude" stance that Carly and Debbie so valued and their philosophy of "giving as good as they got" were reinterpreted by adults in the school as both inappropriate and counterproductive to learning. Paul Connolly (1998) points out that girls' assertive or disruptive behaviour tends to be interpreted more negatively than similar behaviour in boys, while Robin Lakoff (1975) has described how, when little girls "talk rough" like the boys do, they will normally be ostracized, scolded or made fun of. For the "spice girls," "doing it for themselves" in ways which ran counter to traditional forms of femininity resulted in them being labelled at various times by teachers in the staffroom as "real bitches," "a bad influence," and "little cows." The tendency Clarricoates found in 1978 for girls' misbehaviour to be "looked upon as a character defect, whilst boys' misbehaviour is viewed as a desire to assert themselves" was just as evident in teachers' discourses more than 20 years later.

Debbie and Carly were doubly invidiously positioned in relation to the "girls as mature discourse." They were perceived to be "too mature," as "far too knowing sexually" within adult discourses circulating in the school but they were also seen, unlike the boys and the majority of the girls in 3R, as "spiteful" and "scheming little madams" for indulging in behaviour typical of many of the boys. There were several incidents in the playground of sexual harassment of girls by a small group of boys. Most of the adults dismissed these as "boys mucking about." However, Carly and Debbie's attempts to invert regular processes of gender objectification, in which girls are routinely the objects of a male gaze, were interpreted by teachers as signs of "an unhealthy preoccupation with sex." Their predicament exemplifies the dilemma for girls of "seeking out empowering places within regimes alternatively committed to denying subordination or celebrating it" (Hey, 1997, p. 132). In this classroom, girls like Carly and Debbie seemed to tread a fine line between acceptable and unacceptable "girl power" behaviour. Overt heterosexuality was just about on the acceptable side of the line but retaliatory behaviour towards the boys was not.

Valerie Walkerdine (1997) describes how playful and assertive girls come to be understood as overmature and too precocious. Girls like Debbie and Carly, no less than the girls in Walkerdine's advertisements, occupy a space where girls have moved beyond being "nice" or "girlie." Rather, as sexual little women, they occupy a space where they can be bad. As Walkerdine points out, while it is certainly a space in which they can be exploited, it provides a space of power for little girls, although one which is also subject to discourses of denigration. The forms that denigration take are very different to those experienced by the "nice girls" or the "girlies" but become apparent in teachers' judgements of the two girls' behaviour.

"IT'S BETTER BEING A BOY"—THE TOMBOYS

The most intriguing case in my research was that of the "tomboys." [...]

*****

Jodie was the only girl in the class who was unwavering in her certainty that she was not a girl but a "tomboy," although a couple of the other girls in the class for periods of time decided that they were also "tomboys." One the one hand, Jodie could be viewed as a budding "masculinized new woman at ease with male attributes" (Wilkinson, 1999, p. 37). Yet, her rejection of all things feminine could also be seen to suggest a degree of shame and fear of femininity. Jodie even managed to persuade Wayne and Darren, two of the boys in the class, to confirm her male status. Both, at different times, sought me out to tell me Jodie was "really a boy." It is difficult to know how to theorize such disruptions of normative gender positionings. Jodie's stance combines elements of resistance with recognition. She clearly recognized and responded to prevailing gender hierarchies which situate being male with having more power and status. Jodie appears to operate at the boundaries where femininity meets masculinity. She is what Barrie Thorne calls "active at the edges."

However, while Thorne (1993) reports that it was rarely used among her fourth and fifth graders, the term "tomboy" is frequently used in 3M as a marker of respect by both boys and girls. Being a "tomboy" seems to guarantee male friendship and male respect. Several of the working-class girls in the class, like Alice, appeared to move easily from taking up a position as a "tomboy" through to assuming a "girls with attitude" stance alongside Debbie and Carly to becoming a "girlie" and back again. One week Alice would come to school in army fatigues with her hair scraped back, the next, in lycra with elaborately painted nails and carefully coiffured hair. However, Alice was unusual among the girls in ranging across a number of subject positions. For most of the girls, although they had choices, those choices seemed heavily circumscribed and provided little space for manoeuvre.

The regulatory aspects of the "girlies" and the "nice girls'" self-production as feminine were very apparent, yet the conformity of the "tomboys" to prevailing gender regimes was far more hidden. While it is important to recognize

the transgressive qualities of identifying and rejecting traditional notions of femininity in Jodie's behaviour, the empowering aspects of being a "tomboy" also masked deeply reactionary features embedded in assuming such a gender position. Implicit in the concept of "tomboy" is a devaluing of traditional notions of femininity, a railing against the perceived limitations of being female.

*****

[...] The girls in their study would call each others boys as a compliment: "Girls can be good, bad or—best of all—they can be boys" (p. 200) and this was definitely a viewpoint Jodie adhered to. Jodie's individualized resistance can be set alongside Carly and Debbie's joint efforts to disrupt prevailing gender orders among the peer group. Yet, paradoxically, Jodie, no less than the "girlies," seemed engaged in a process of accommodating the boys. The means of accommodation may differ but the compliance with existing gender regimes remains. Madeline Arnot (1982) writes of the ways in which boys maintain the hierarchy of social superiority of masculinity by devaluing the female world. In 3R, Jodie was also involved in this maintenance work. Although her practices are not rooted in subordination to the boys, she is still acquiescent in prevailing gender hierarchies. Her practices, no less than those of the "girlies" and the "nice girls," are confirmatory of male superiority.

Connell writes that "it is perfectly logical to talk about masculine women or masculinity in women's lives, as well as men's" (Connell, 1995, p. 163). However, so-called "masculine" girls do not seem to disrupt but rather appear to endorse existing gender hierarchies. All the girls at various times were acting in ways which bolstered the boys' power at the expense of their own. Even Jodie's performance of a surrogate masculinity works to cement rather than transform the gender divide. As a consequence, the radical aspects of transgressive femininities like those of Jodie's are undermined by their implicit compliance with gender hierarchies. Being one of the boys seems to result in greater social power but it conscripts Jodie into processes

Sharon Thompson (1994) identifies as "raging misogyny." In my field notes, there are 16 examples of Jodie asserting that "boys are better than girls." Jodie's case is an extreme example of the ways in which girls' ventriloquising of the dominant culture's denigration of femininity and female relations can serve to disconnect them from other girls (Brown, 1998).

CONCLUSION

Performing gender is not straightforward; rather, it is confusing. The seduction of binaries such as male:female, boy:girl often prevents us from seeing the full range of diversity and differentiation existing within one gender as well as between categories of male and female. Both the girls and boys in 3R were actively involved in the production of gendered identities, constructing gender through a variety and range of social processes (Kerfoot & Knight, 1994). Yet, within this "gender work," social and cultural differences generate the particular toolkit of cultural resources individual children have available to them. There is a multiplicity of femininities and masculinities available in this primary classroom. But this is not to suggest that these children have myriad choices of which variant of femininity and masculinity to assume. They do not. Class, ethnicity and emergent sexualities all play their part, and constrain as well as create options.

*****

Yet, despite the multiple masculinities and femininities manifested in 3R, there is evidence of hegemonic masculinity in this classroom no less than outside in the wider social world. Within such a context, it makes sense for girls to seek to resist traditional discourses of subordinate femininity. Yet, attempting to take up powerful positions through articulation with, and investment in, dominant masculinities serves to reinforce rather than transform the gender divide. As a consequence, the prevailing gender order is only occasionally disrupted, in particular by the spice girls through their sex

play and objectification of a number of the boys and also, paradoxically, through their working-class status. Unlike the "nice girls" whose activities are circumscribed through being positioned by the boys as a contagious, polluting other, the "spice girls'" positioning as "rough" in relation to sensitive middle-class boys allows them to take up a "polluting" assignment (Douglas, 1966) and use it as a weapon to intimidate the boys.

The girls' struggle to make meaning of themselves as female constitutes a struggle in which gendered peer group hierarchies such as those in 3R position boys as "better" despite a mass of evidence to show they are neither as academically successful nor as well behaved as girls in the classroom. Peer group discourses constructed girls as harder working, more mature and more socially skilled. Yet, all the boys and a significant number of the girls, if not subscribing to the view that boys are better, adhered to the view that it is better being a boy. There are clearly confusions within the gender work in this classroom. To talk of dominant femininity is to generate a contradiction in terms because it is dominant versions of femininity which subordinate the girls to the boys. Rather, transgressive discourses and the deviant femininities they generate like Jodie's "tomboy" and Debbie and Carly's espousal of "girl power" accrue power in both the male and female peer group, and provide spaces for girls to escape gender subordination by the boys.

*****

Children may both create and challenge gender structures and meanings. However, for much of the time for a majority of the girls and boys in 3R, gender either operates as opposition or hierarchy or most commonly both at the same time. As Janet Holland and her colleagues found in relation to the adolescents in their study, the girls just as much as the boys in this class were "drawn into making masculinity powerful" (Holland et al., 1998, p. 30). The contemporary orthodoxy that girls are doing better than boys masks the complex messiness of gender relations in which, despite girls' better educational attainment, within this peer group, the prevalent view is still that it's better being a boy.

Despite the all-pervading focus on narrow, easily measured, learning outcomes in British state schooling, learning in classrooms is much wider than test results suggest. While test results indicate that girls are more successful educationally than boys, it appears that in this primary classroom girls and boys still learn many of the old lessons of gender relations which work against gender equity. Sue Heath (1999, p. 293) argues that there is a need for school-based work that sensitively addresses issues of gender identity and masculinities within a pro-feminist framework. There is also an urgent need for work that addresses the construction and performance of femininities.

REFERENCES

Arnot, M. (1982) Male Hegemony, Social Class and Women's Education. *Journal of Education*, 16, pp. 64–89.

Arnot, M., David, M. and Weinger, G. (1999) *Closing the Gender Gap: Postwar Education and Social Change* (Cambridge, Polity Press).

Bennett, C. (1996) The Boys with the Wrong Stuff, *Guardian*, 6 November.

Blackmore, J. (1999) *Troubling Women: Feminism, Leadership and Educational Change* (Buckingham, Open University Press).

Brown, L.M. (1998) *Raising Their Voices: The Politics of Girls' Anger* (Cambridge, MA, Harvard University Press).

Clarricoates, K. (1978) Dinosaurs in the Classroom—a Re-examination of Some Aspects of the "Hidden" Curriculum in Primary Schools, *Women's Studies International Forum*, 1, pp. 353–364.

Connell, R.W. (1987) *Gender and Power* (Sydney, Allen & Unwin).

Connell, R.W. (1995) *Masculinities* (Cambridge, Polity Press).

Connolly, P. (1998) *Racism, Gender Identities and Young Children* (London, Routledge).

Coward, R. (1999) The Feminist Who Fights for the Boys, *Sunday Times*, 20 June.

Davies, B. (1993) *Shards of Glass* (Sydney, Allen & Unwin).

Douglas, M. (1966) *Purity and Danger: An Analysis of Concepts of Pollution and Taboo* (London, Routledge & Kegan Paul).

Epstein, D., Elwood, J., Hey, V., and Maw, J. (1998) *Failing Boys? Issues in Gender and Achievement* (Buckingham, Open University Press).

Francis, B. (1998) *Power Plays: Primary School Children's Construction of Gender, Power and Adult Work* (Stoke-on-Trent, Trentham Books).

Francis, B. (1999) Modernist Reductionism or Post-Structuralist Relativism: Can We Move On? An Evaluation of the Arguments in Relation to Feminist Educational Research, *Gender and Education*, 11, pp. 381–394.

Heath, S. (1999) Watching the Backlash: The Problematization of Young Women's Academic Success in 1990s Britain, *Discourse*, 20, pp. 249–266.

Hey, V. (1997) *The Company She Keeps: An Ethnography of Girls' Friendship* (Buckingham, Open University Press).

Holland, J., Ramazanoglu, C., Sharpe, S., & Thomson, R. (1998) *The Male in the Head: Young People, Heterosexuality and Power* (London, Tufnell Publishing).

Jackson, D. (1998) Breaking out of the Binary Trap: Boys' Underachievement, Schooling and Gender Relations, in: D. Epstein, J. Elwood, V. Hey, & J. Maw (Eds) *Failing Boys? Issues in Gender and Achievement* (Buckingham, Open University Press).

Katz, A. (1999) Crisis of the "Low Can Do" Boys, *Sunday Times*, 21 March.

Kenway, J. (1995) Masculinities in Schools: Under Seige, on the Defensive, and under Reconstruction, *Discourse*, 16, pp. 59–79.

Kenway, J. & Willis, S. with Blackmore, J. & Rennie, L. (1999) *Answering Back: Girls, Boys and Feminism in Schools* (London, Routledge).

Kerfoot, D. & Knight, D. (1994) Into the Realms of the Fearful: Identity and the Gender Problematic, in: H.L. Radtke & H.J. Stam (Eds) *Power/Gender: Social Relations in Theory and Practice* (London, Sage).

Lakoff, R.T. (1975) *Language and Woman's Place* (New York, Harper & Row).

Lucey, H. & Walkerdine, V. (1999) Boys' Underachievement: Social Class and Changing

Masculinities, in: T. Cox (Ed) *Combating Educational Disadvantage* (London, Flamer Press).

Mac an Ghaill, M. (1988) *Young, Gifted and Black: Student-Teacher Relations in the Schooling of Black Youth* (Buckingham, Open University Press).

Mirza, S.H. (1992) *Young, Female and Black* (London, Routledge).

Pattman, R. & Phoenix, A. (1999) Constructing Self by Constructing the "Other": 11–14-year-old Boys' Narratives of Girls and Women, Paper presented at the Gender and Education Conference, University of Warwick, 29–31 March.

Reay, D. (1990) Working with Boys, *Gender and Education*, 2, pp. 269–282.

Sewell, T. (1997) *Black Masculinities and Schooling: How Black Boys Survive Modern Schooling* (Stoke-on-Trent, Trentham Books).

Skelton, C. (1997) Primary Boys and Hegemonic Masculinities, *British Journal of Sociology*, 18, pp. 349–369.

Skelton, C. (1999). "A Passion for Football": Dominant Masculinities and Primary Schooling, paper presented to the British Educational Research Association Conference, University of Sussex, 2–5 September.

Smithers, R. (1999) Self-Esteem the Key for Macho Boys Who Scorn "Uncool" School, *Guardian*, 16 March.

Thompson, S. (1994) What Friends Are for: On Girls' Misogyny and Romantic Fusion, in: J. Irvine (Ed.) *Sexual Cultures and the Construction of Adolescent Identities* (Philadelphia, PA, Temple University Press).

Thorne, B. (1993) *Gender Play: Girls and Boys in School* (Buckingham, Open University Press).

Walkerdine, V. (1997) *Daddy's Girl: Young Girls and Popular Culture* (London, Macmillan).

Walkerdine, V., Lucey, H. & Melody, J. (2000) Class, Attainment and Sexuality in Late Twentieth-Century Britain, in: C. Zmroczek & P. Mahoney (Eds) *Women and Social Class: International Feminist Perspectives* (London: UCL Press).

Wight, D. (1996) Beyond the Predatory Male: The Diversity of Young Glasgowegian Men's Discourses to Describe Heterosexual Relationships, in: L. Adkins & V. Merchant (Eds) *Sexualizing the Social: Power and the Organization of Sexuality* (London, Macmillan).

Wilkinson, H. (1994) *No Turning Back: Generations and the Genderquake* (London, Demos).

Wilkinson, H. (1999) The Thatcher Legacy: Power, Feminism, and the Birth of Girl Power, in: N. Walters (Ed.) *On the Move: Feminism for a New Generation* (London, Virago).

Willis, P. (1977) *Learning to Labour: How Working-Class Kids Get Working-Class Jobs* (Farnborough, Saxon House).

Yates, L. (1997) Gender Equity and the Boys Debate: What Sort of Challenge Is It?, *British Journal of Sociology in Education*, 18, pp. 337–348.

DISCUSSION QUESTIONS: SWAIN

1. Explain Swain's argument that low academic achievement for boys is part of the social construction of "hegemonic masculinity." What implications does this relationship have for the recent societal concern about boys' poor performance at school?

2. What does Swain mean when he argues that masculinity is an "interrelational" social construction? Provide examples from the article, as well as from Reay's study about girls' culture in primary classrooms.

3. What evidence does Swain provide for his claim that hegemonic masculinity in this school setting is constructed and expressed through "style," including clothing, personal behaviour, and group activities? Explain the exclusionary effects produced by this particular masculine style.

DISCUSSION QUESTIONS: REAY

1. Enumerate and explain the four dominant femininities performed by the girls in Reay's study, and discuss their relationship to masculinity.
2. Examine the following statistics at your university: the number of men and women students enrolled; the most popular majors for men and women students; the disciplines in which you find the most men and women faculty. Draw on Reay's notion of the social construction of heterosexual femininities in educational settings to explain your findings.
3. Considering Reay's empirical findings and theoretical conclusions, discuss the possible advantages and disadvantages of gender-segregated educational institutions. What are your conclusions about racially segregated schools, such as those recently instituted in Toronto?

FURTHER READINGS

1. Conway, Jill Kerr, and Susan Bourque (eds.). 1993. *The Politics of Women's Education: Perspectives from Asia, Africa, and Latin America.* Ann Arbor: University of Michigan Press.
   This book is a rigorously researched collection of multidisciplinary articles that explore the under-education of women in Asia, Africa, Latin America and the Middle East. Contributors focus in particular on the determinants, nature, and outcomes of women's education in each of these geographical areas.
2. Hannah, Elena, Linda Paul, and Swani Vetnamany-Globus (eds.). 2002. *Women in the Canadian Academic Tundra: Challenging the Chill.* Montreal: McGill-Queen's University Press.
   A collection of personal narratives written by Canadian women academics, this book describes the frustrations they experience working in the often inhospitable environment of the academy. As this androcentric workplace is implicitly constituted on the notion that an academic has a housewife in the shadows providing all "his" material needs so "he" can write, network, and move at will, women academics struggle to meet work expectations as they raise children and fulfill domestic responsibilities. This conflict is usually constructed by other academics as personal failure, rather than the result of gender inequality at work and home.
3. Khayatt, Madiha Didi. 1992. *Lesbian Teachers: An Invisible Presence.* Albany: State University of New York Press.
   Khayatt employs Dorothy Smith's methodology of institutional ethnography to research the lives of 19 lesbian teachers in Ontario, Canada. Her interviews with these women provide rich empirical data on the ways in which these teachers negotiate dominant constructs of sexuality in the school settings that marginalize them.
4. Priegert Coulter, Rebecca. 2003. Boys Doing Good: Young Men and Gender Equity. *Educational Review*, 55(2), 135–146.
   In this article Priegert writes about 10 young male students in three high schools in London, ON, Canada who voluntarily participated in gender equity work. She investigates what experiences, especially within school, encouraged these men to engage critically with gender issues and what actions they took to support their commitment to equality. Her interest in how young men struggle for and against what it means to be masculine, living against the grain to achieve a more socially just world, is novel and compelling.
5. Reimer, Marilee (ed.) 2004. *Inside Corporate U: Women in the Academy Speak Out.* Toronto: Sumach Press.
   Another collection devoted to understanding the position of women in the setting of the Canadian academy, this 14-chapter book highlights the corporate practices that are marginalizing their voices and work at a time when their numbers are on the rise in Canadian universities. Authors examine what is meant

by the "corporatization" of higher education and how it is affecting professors who value the production and teaching of a diverse set of knowledges as the university is recast as a service industry.

RELEVANT FILMS

1. *Science and Gender with Evelyn Fox Keller*, 1990, 30 minutes, Films for the Humanities and Science
   Evelyn Fox Keller decided to become a scientist in the 1950s. As she trained in theoretical physics and mathematical biology, she puzzled about why most of her colleagues were men and why the language of science used only masculine metaphors and incorporated masculine values. Over the years she has grappled with these questions about the gendered nature of science and scientific education.

2. *Hammering It Out: Women in the Construction Zone*, 2000, 54 minutes, Women Make Movies
   This documentary explores the Century Freeway Women's Education Program in California, which trains women for jobs in construction, a traditional preserve of masculine labour.

3. *Fair Play: Achieving Gender Equity in the Digital Age*, 1999, 57 minutes, Films for the Humanities and Sciences
   Set in the context of a middle school in Texas, this film explores the gender inequity that continues to exist in classroom use of computer technology as a learning tool. Filmmakers document classroom practices that discourage girls from using computers, as well as the barriers around technology these girls experience outside of school.

4. *Girls in Action: Speaking Out*, 1997, 15 minutes, Canadian Association for Health, Physical Education, Recreation and Dance
   In Canada, many young girls choose to forego elective physical education classes, despite the health benefits these courses bring. Girls explain this choice as a consequence of the competitive and unwelcoming nature of the classes, as well as the use of inequitable evaluation methods. Filmmakers take up this issue with the hope of both sensitizing adults to the gender inequality that infuses physical education courses and initiating progressive change in how these classes are taught and experienced.

5. *A Better Tomorrow: Transforming the Classroom through Feminist Pedagogy*, 1994, 30 minutes, University of Saskatchewan
   This documentary is prepared by feminist professors at the University of Saskatchewan to introduce teachers to the philosophy and practice of feminist pedagogy. Ten Canadian feminist educators teaching a range of subjects from Mathematics to English Studies demonstrate the practice.

RELEVANT WEB SITES

1. http://rpp.english.ucsb.edu/index.php?s=gender
   The Race and Pedagogy Project at the University of California, Santa Barbara, has constructed a detailed Web site with links to various topics related to race and education. The subsection on gender, for example, lists extensive resources, for both teachers and students, on the topics of race, gender, and sexuality in education, including classroom politics, feminist critical race theory and pedagogies, practical applications of these theories, race and higher education, feminist whiteness studies, and teaching immigration issues in the classroom.

2. http://pages.towson.edu/itow/rgc.htm
   This site provides a bibliography of books and articles that discuss ways of integrating race, gender, and class issues into classroom syllabi. Follow the "Education" link for more references and resources, especially on multicultural education.

3. www.sofweb.vic.edu.au/gender/index.htm

   This government of Australia Web site, entitled "Gender and Education," gives a good overview of the projects, teaching and learning curriculum, resources, and issues pertaining to gender and education that it is currently engaging and developing. The site contains resources for teachers, in particular links to other relevant Web sites and learning technologies. The issues that seem most pressing for the Australian government from browsing the site are Aboriginal student learning, girls' body images, bullying, disabilities, domestic violence, women in higher education, and classroom technology.

4. http://cse.stanford.edu/classes/cs201/Projects/gender-gap-in-education/index.htm

   Gender Relations in Educational Applications of Technology presents readings and resources on the effect of computers on the gender gap in education. It also provides a good introduction to the broader issue of gender inequality in education.

5. www.dfid.gov.uk/pubs/files/edresgenderedpaper19.pdf

   This annotated bibliography on gender, education, and development is compiled by UK scholars for the Department for International Development (DFID). It extensively references work on gender and gender and education in Sub-Saharan Africa, North Africa, the Middle East, Asia, South Asia, South East Asia, Central and East Asia, Latin America, and Tropical Islands.

                              ⊕   ⊕   ⊕

PART VII

THE GENDERED WORKPLACE

According to anthropologists, virtually every society has a division of labour, a way of dividing up the tasks that must be done in order for the society as a whole to survive. Feminists add that gender relations play a major role in that allocation of particular tasks to particular individuals. Because gender is a prominent system of social classification and identity, as well as a structure of power, we should not find the existence of a gendered division of labour surprising, nor the differing social and economic valuation of the work done by men and women.

The gendered division of labour we call "traditional" separates labour into two distinct spheres: the valued paid work done by men in the public sphere—the domain of business, politics, and culture—and the undervalued, largely invisible and "free" reproductive labour undertaken by women in the private sphere of home. (As many societies judge the value of work in terms of economic rewards, the labour provided by housewives is commonly considered "free" and therefore not "work.") This division of labour by gender is often justified based on ostensible differences in the "natural" reproductive roles assigned to women and men.

Gender relations also play out in the public world of work. In the workplace we see the enduring practice of occupational segregation by gender, occupations in which one gender accounts for at least 80 percent of the workforce. Considering how widespread this practice is, women who decide to enter occupations dominated by men find everyday work relations and advancement through the ranks very difficult, which means that most of these women typically remain in the lowest rungs of the work hierarchy. Men, on the other hand, move more quickly through women-dominated oc-cupations to reach higher-level administration or supervisory positions.

Gender affects who is assigned which tasks and what the social worth of that task is in any one culture. But relations of class and race further intervene so that women of colour and poor women are usually found in the most undervalued, underpaid, and unsatisfying types of work. Rhacel Salazar Parreñas' article, which is part of a larger collection that examines how the work lives of women immigrants have been organized by the global economy, studies Filipino women migrant workers who take on child care work for privileged families abroad because they have little chance of good, stable employment in the Philippines. But as they travel abroad to work, they leave behind their children, disrupting local dominant gender ideologies that place women and their labour in the home, at home. Government officials and media denounce these migrating mothers, claiming that they have caused the Filipino family to disintegrate, children to be abandoned, and a crisis of care to unfold. They call for women to return home from work abroad, which ignores the fact that the government, as well as individual families, are increasingly reliant on their remittances. Salazar conducts interviews with young adults who grew up in transnational households in the Philippines, who are not yet reunited with their working mothers, to explore how they experience their mothers' working migration.

CHAPTER 20

THE CARE CRISIS IN THE PHILIPPINES
Children and Transnational Families in the New Global Economy

Rhacel Salazar Parreñas

A growing crisis of care troubles the world's most developed nations. Even as demand for care has increased, its supply has dwindled. The result is a care deficit,[1] to which women from the Philippines have responded in force. Roughly two-thirds[2] of Filipino migrant workers are women, and their exodus, usually to fill domestic jobs,[3] has generated tremendous social change in the Philippines. When female migrants are mothers, they leave behind their own children, usually in the care of other women.[4] Many Filipino children now grow up in divided households, where geographic separation places children under serious emotional strain. And yet it is impossible to overlook the significance of migrant labor to the Philippine economy. Some 34 to 54 percent of the Filipino population is sustained by remittances from migrant workers.[5]

Women in the Philippines, just like their counterparts in postindustrial nations, suffer from a "stalled revolution." Local gender ideology remains a few steps behind the economic reality, which has produced numerous female-headed, transnational households.[6] Consequently, a far greater degree of anxiety attends the quality of family life for the dependants of migrant mothers than for those of migrant fathers. The dominant gender ideology, after

all, holds that a woman's rightful place is in the home, and the households of migrant mothers present a challenge to this view. In response, government officials and journalists denounce migrating mothers, claiming that they have caused the Filipino family to deteriorate, children to be abandoned, and a crisis of care to take root in the Philippines. To end this crisis, critics admonish, these mothers must return. Indeed, in May 1995, Philippine president Fidel Ramos called for initiatives to keep migrant mothers at home. He declared, "We are not against overseas employment of Filipino women. We are against overseas employment at the cost of family solidarity."[7] Migration, Ramos strongly implied, is morally acceptable only when it is undertaken by single, childless women.

The Philippine media reinforce this position by consistently publishing sensationalist reports on the suffering of children in transnational families.[8] These reports tend to vilify migrant mothers, suggesting that their children face more profound problems than do those of migrant fathers; and despite the fact that most of the children in question are left with relatives, journalists tend to refer to them as having been "abandoned." One article reports, "A child's sense of loss appears to be greater when it is the mother who leaves to work abroad."[9] Others link the emigration of mothers to the inadequate child care and unstable family life that eventually lead such children to "drugs, gambling, and drinking."[10] Writes one columnist, "Incest and rapes within blood relatives are alarmingly on the rise not only within Metro Manila but also in the provinces. There are some indications that the absence of mothers who have become OCWs [overseas contract workers] has something to do with the situation."[11] The same columnist elsewhere expresses the popular view that the children of migrants become a burden on the larger society: "Guidance counselors and social welfare agencies can show grim statistics on how many children have turned into liabilities to our society because of absentee parents."[12]

From January to July 2000, I conducted 69 in-depth interviews with young adults who grew up in transnational households in the Philippines. Almost none of these children have yet reunited with their migrant parents. I interviewed 30 children with migrant mothers, 26 with migrant fathers, and 13 with two migrant parents. The children I spoke to certainly had endured emotional hardships; but contrary to the media's dark presentation, they did not all experience their mothers' migration as abandonment. The hardships in their lives were frequently diminished when they received support from extended families and communities, when they enjoyed open communication with their migrant parents, and when they clearly understood the limited financial options that led their parents to migrate in the first place.

To call for the return of migrant mothers is to ignore the fact that the Philippines has grown increasingly dependent on their remittances. To acknowledge this reality could lead the Philippines toward a more egalitarian gender ideology. Casting blame on migrant mothers, however, serves only to divert the society's attention away from these children's needs, finally aggravating their difficulties by stigmatizing their family's choices.

The Philippine media has certainly sensationalized the issue of child welfare in migrating families, but that should not obscure the fact that the Philippines faces a genuine care crisis.

Care is now the country's primary export. Remittances—mostly from migrant domestic workers—constitute the economy's largest source of foreign currency, totaling almost $7 billion in 1999.[13] With limited choices in the Philippines, women migrate to help sustain their families financially, but the price is very high. Both mothers and children suffer from family separation, even under the best of circumstances.

Migrant mothers who work as nannies often face the painful prospect of caring for other people's children while being unable to tend to their own. One such mother in Rome, Rosemarie Samaniego,[14] describes this predicament:

> When the girl that I take care of calls her mother "Mama," my heart jumps all the time because my children also call me "Mama." I feel the gap caused by our physical separation especially in the morning, when I pack [her] lunch, because that's what I used to do for my children.... I used to do that very same thing for them. I begin thinking that at this hour I should be taking care of my very own children and not someone else's, someone who is not related to me in any way, shape, or form.... The work that I do here is done for my family, but the problem is they are not close to me but are far away in the Philippines. Sometimes, you feel the separation and you start to cry. Some days, I just start crying while I am sweeping the floor because I am thinking about my children in the Philippines. Sometimes, when I receive a letter from my children telling me that they are sick, I look up out the window and ask the Lord to look after them and make sure they get better even without me around to care after them. [*Starts crying.*] If I had wings, I would fly home to my children. Just for a moment, to see my children and take care of their needs, help them, then fly back over here to continue my work.

The children of migrant workers also suffer an incalculable loss when a parent disappears overseas. As Ellen Seneriches,[15] a 21-year-old daughter of a domestic worker in New York, says:

> There are times when you want to talk to her, but she is not there. That is really hard, very difficult.... There are times when I want to call her, speak to her, cry to her, and I cannot. It is difficult. The only thing that I can do is write to her. And I cannot cry through the e-mails and sometimes I just want to cry on her shoulder.

Children like Ellen, who was only ten years old when her mother left for New York, often repress their longings to reunite with their mothers. Knowing that their families have few financial options, they are left with no choice but to put their emotional needs aside. Often, they do so knowing that their mothers' care and attention have been diverted to other children. When I asked her how she felt about her mother's wards in New York, Ellen responded:

> Very jealous. I am very, very jealous. There was even a time when she told the children she was caring for that they are very lucky that she was taking care of them, while her children back in the Philippines don't even have a mom to take care of them. It's pathetic, but it's true. We were left alone by ourselves and we had to be responsible at a very young age without a mother. Can you imagine?

Children like Ellen do experience emotional stress when they grow up in transnational households. But it is worth emphasizing that many migrant mothers attempt to sustain ties with their children, and their children often recognize and appreciate these efforts. Although her mother, undocumented in the United States, has not returned once to the Philippines in 12 years, Ellen does not doubt that she has struggled to remain close to her children despite the distance. In fact, although Ellen lives only three hours away from her father, she feels closer to and communicates more frequently with her mother. Says Ellen:

> I realize that my mother loves us very much. Even if she is far away, she would send us her love. She would make us feel like she really loved us. She would do this by always being there. She would just assure us that whenever we have problems to just call her and tell her. [Pauses] And so I know that it has been more difficult for her than other mothers. She has had to do extra work because she is so far away from us.

Like Ellen's mother, who managed to "be there" despite a vast distance, other migrant mothers do not necessarily "abandon" their traditional duty of nurturing their families. Rather, they provide emotional care and guidance from afar.[16] Ellen even credits her mother for her success in school. Now a second-year medical school student, Ellen graduated at the top of her class in both high school and college. She says that the constant, open communication she shares with her mother provided the key to her success. She reflects:

> We communicate as often as we can, like twice or thrice a week through e-mails. Then she would call us every week. And it is very expensive, I know.... My mother and I have a very open relationship. We are like best friends. She would give me advice whenever I had problems.... She understands everything I do. She understands why I would act this or that way. She knows me really well. And she is also transparent to me. She always knows when I have problems, and likewise I know when she does. I am closer to her than to my father.

Ellen is clearly not the abandoned child or social liability the Philippine media describe. She not only benefits from sufficient parental support—from both her geographically distant mother and her nearby father—but also exceeds the bar of excellence in schooling. Her story indicates that children of migrant parents can overcome the emotional strains of transnational family life, and that they can enjoy sufficient family support, even from their geographically distant parent.

Of course, her good fortune is not universal. But it does raise questions about how children withstand such geographical strains; whether and how they maintain solid ties with their distant parents; and what circumstances lead some children to feel that those ties have weakened or given out. The Philippine media tend to equate the absence of a child's biological mother with abandonment, which leads to the assumption that all such children, lacking familial support, will become social liabilities.[17] But I found that positive surrogate parental figures and open communication with the migrant parent, along with acknowledgment of the migrant parent's contribution to the collective mobility of the family, allay many of the emotional insecurities that arise from transnational household arrangements. Children who lack these resources have greater difficulty adjusting.

Extensive research bears out this observation. The Scalabrini Migration Center, a nongovernmental organization for migration research in the Philippines, surveyed 709 elementary-school-age Filipino children in 2000, comparing the experiences of those with a father absent, a mother absent, both parents absent, and both parents present. While the researchers observed that parental absence does prompt feelings of abandonment and loneliness among children, they concluded that "it does not necessarily become an occasion for laziness and unruliness." Rather, if the extended family supports the child and makes him or her aware of the material benefits migration brings, the child may actually be spurred toward greater self-reliance and ambition, despite continued longings for family unity.

Jeek Pereno's life has been defined by those longings. At 25, he is a merchandiser for a large department store in the Philippines. His mother more than adequately provided for her children, managing with her meager wages first as a domestic worker and then as a nurse's aide, to send them $200 a month and even to purchase a house in a fairly exclusive neighborhood in the city center. But Jeek still feels abandoned and insecure in his mother's affection, he believes that growing up without his parents robbed him of the discipline he needed. Like other children of migrant workers, Jeek does not feel that his faraway mother's financial support has been enough. Instead, he wishes she had offered him more guidance, concern, and emotional care.

Jeek was eight years old when his parents relocated to New York and left him, along with his three brothers, in the care of their aunt. Eight years later, Jeek's father passed away, and two of his brothers (the oldest and youngest) joined their mother in New York. Visa complications have prevented Jeek and his other brother from following—but their mother has not once returned to visit them in the Philippines. When I expressed surprise at this, Jeek solemnly replied: "Never. It will cost too much, she said."

Years of separation breed unfamiliarity among family members, and Jeek does not have the emotional security of knowing that his mother has genuinely tried to lessen that estrangement. For Jeek, only a visit could shore up this security after 17 years of separation. His mother's weekly phone calls do not suffice. And because he experiences his mother's absence as indifference, he does not feel comfortable communicating with her openly about his unmet needs. The result is repression, which in turn aggravates the resentment he feels. Jeek told me:

> I talk to my mother once in a while. But what happens, whenever she asks how I am doing, I just say okay. It's not like I am really going to tell her that I have problems here.... It's not like she can do anything about my problems if I told her about them. Financial problems, yes, she can help. But not the other problems, like emotional problems.... She will try to give advice, but I am not very interested to talk to her about things like that.... Of course, you are still young, you don't really know what is going to happen in the future. Before you realize that your parents left you, you can't do anything about it anymore. You are not in a position to tell them not to leave you. They should have not left us. (Sobs)

I asked Jeek if his mother knew he felt this way. "No," he said, "she doesn't know." Asked if he received emotional support from anyone, Jeek replied, "As much as possible, if I can handle it, I try not to get emotional support from anyone. I just keep everything inside me."

Jeek feels that his mother not only abandoned him but failed to leave him with an adequate surrogate. His aunt had a family and children of her own. Jeek recalled, "While I do know that my aunt loves me and she took care of us to the best of her ability, I am not convinced that it was enough.... Because we were not disciplined enough. She let us do whatever we wanted to do." Jeek feels that his education suffered from this lack of discipline, and he greatly regrets not having concentrated on his studies. Having completed only a two-year vocational program in electronics, he doubts his competency to pursue a college degree. At 25, he feels stuck, with only the limited option of turning from one low-paying job to another.

Children who, unlike Jeek, received good surrogate parenting managed to concentrate on their studies and in the end to fare much better. Rudy Montoya, a 19-year-old whose mother has done domestic work in Hong Kong for more than 12 years, credits his mother's brother for helping him succeed in high school:

My uncle is the most influential person in my life. Well, he is in Saudi Arabia now.... He would tell me that my mother loves me and not to resent her, and that whatever happens, I should write her. He would encourage me and he would tell me to trust the Lord. And then, I remember in high school, he would push me to study. I learned a lot from him in high school. Showing his love for me, he would help me with my schoolwork.... The time that I spent with my uncle was short, but he is the person who helped me grow up to be a better person.

Unlike Jeek's aunt, Rudy's uncle did not have a family of his own. He was able to devote more time to Rudy, instilling discipline in his young charge as well as reassuring him that his mother, who is the sole income provider for her family, did not abandon him. Although his mother has returned to visit him only twice—once when he was in the fourth grade and again two years later—Rudy, who is now a college student, sees his mother as a "good provider" who has made tremendous sacrifices for his sake. This knowledge offers him emotional security, as well as a strong feeling of gratitude. When I asked him about the importance of education, he replied, "I haven't given anything back to my mother for the sacrifices that she has made for me. The least I could do for her is graduate, so that I can find a good job, so that eventually I will be able to help her out, too."

Many children resolve the emotional insecurity of being left by their parents the way that Rudy has: by viewing migration as a sacrifice to be repaid by adult children. Children who believe that their migrant mothers are struggling for the sake of the family's collective mobility, rather than leaving to live the "good life," are less likely to feel abandoned and more likely to accept their mothers' efforts to sustain close relationships from a distance. One such child is Theresa Bascara, an 18-year-old college student whose mother has worked as a domestic in Hong Kong since 1984. As she puts it, "[My inspiration is] my mother, because she is the one suffering over there. So the least I can give back to her is doing well in school."

*****

Many of the children I interviewed harbored images of their mothers as martyrs, and they often found comfort in their mothers' grief over not being able to nurture them directly. The expectation among such children that they will continue to receive a significant part of their nurturing from their mothers, despite the distance, points to the conservative gender ideology most of them maintain.[18] But whether or not they see their mothers as martyrs, children of migrant women feel best cared for when their mothers make consistent efforts to show parental concern from a distance. As Jeek's and Ellen's stories indicate, open communication with the migrant parent soothes feelings of abandonment; those who enjoy such open channels fare much better than those who lack them. Not only does communication ease children's emotional difficulties; it also fosters a sense of family unity, and it promotes the view that migration is a survival strategy that requires sacrifices from both children and parents for the good of the family.

For daughters of migrant mothers, such sacrifices commonly take the form of assuming some of their absent mothers' responsibilities, including the care of younger siblings. As Ellen told me:

> It was a strategy, and all of us had to sacrifice for it.... We all had to adjust, every day of our lives.... Imagine waking up without a mother calling you for breakfast. Then there would be no one to prepare the clothes for my brothers. We are all going to school.... I had to wake up earlier. I had to prepare their clothes. I had to wake them up and help them prepare for school. Then I also had to help them with their homework at night. I had to tutor them.

Asked if she resented this extra work, Ellen replied, "No. I saw it as training, a training that helped me become a leader. It makes you more of a leader doing that every day. I guess that is an advantage to me, and to my siblings as well."

Ellen's effort to assist in the household's daily maintenance was another way she reciprocated for her mother's emotional and financial support. Viewing her added work as a positive life lesson, Ellen believes that these responsibilities enabled her to develop leadership skills. Notably, her high school selected her as its first ever female commander for its government-mandated military training corps.

*****

In general, eldest daughters of migrant mothers assume substantial familial responsibilities, often becoming substitute mothers for their siblings. Similarly, eldest sons stand in for migrant fathers. Armando Martinez, a 29-year-old entrepreneur whose father worked in Dubai

for six months while he was in high school, related his experiences:

> I became a father during those six months. It was like, ugghhh, I made the rules.... I was able to see that it was hard if your family is not complete, you feel that there is something missing.... It's because the major decisions, sometimes, I was not old enough for them. I was only a teenager, and I was not that strong in my convictions when it came to making decisions. It was like work that I should not have been responsible for. I still wanted to play. So it was an added burden on my side.

Even when there is a parent left behind, children of migrant workers tend to assume added familial responsibilities, and these responsibilities vary along gender lines. Nonetheless, the weight tends to fall most heavily on children of migrant mothers, who are often left to struggle with the lack of male responsibility for care work in the Philippines. While a great number of children with migrant fathers receive full-time care from stay-at-home mothers, those with migrant mothers do not receive the same amount of care. Their fathers are likely to hold full-time jobs, and they rarely have the time to assume the role of primary caregiver. Of 30 children of migrant mothers I interviewed, only four had stay-at-home fathers. Most fathers passed the caregiving responsibilities on to other relatives, many of whom, like Jeek's aunt, already had families of their own to care for and regarded the children of migrant relatives as an extra burden. Families of migrant fathers are less likely to rely on the care work of extended kin.[19] Among my interviewees, 13 of 26 children with migrant fathers lived with and were cared for primarily by their stay-at-home mothers.

Children of migrant mothers, unlike those of migrant fathers, have the added burden of accepting nontraditional gender roles in their families. The Scalabrini Migration Center reports that these children "tend to be more angry, confused, apathetic, and more afraid than other children."[20] They are caught within an "ideological stall" in the societal acceptance of female-headed transnational households. Because her family does not fit the traditional nuclear household model, Theresa Bascara sees her family as "broken," even though she describes her relationship to her mother as "very close." She says, "A family, I can say, is only whole if your father is the one working and your mother is only staying at home. It's okay if your mother works too, but somewhere close to you."

Some children in transnational families adjust to their household arrangements with greater success than others do. Those who feel that their mothers strive to nurture them as well as to be good providers are more likely to be accepting. The support of extended kin, or perhaps a sense of public accountability for their welfare, also helps children combat feelings of abandonment. Likewise, a more gender-egalitarian value system enables children to appreciate their mothers as good providers, which in turn allows them to see their mothers' migrations as demonstrations of love.

*****

Not surprisingly, when asked if they would leave their own children to take jobs as migrant workers, almost all of my respondents answered, "Never." When I asked why not, most said that they would never want their children to go through what they had gone through, or to be denied what they were denied, in their childhoods. Armando Martinez best summed up what children in transnational families lose when he said:

> You just cannot buy the times when your family is together. Isn't that right? Time together is something that money can neither buy nor replace.... The first time your baby speaks, you are not there. Other people would experience that joy. And when your child graduates with honors, you are also not there.... Is that right? When your child wins a basketball game, no one will be there to ask him how his game went, how many points he made. Is that right? Your family loses, don't you think?

Children of transnational families repeatedly stress that they lack the pleasure and comfort of daily interaction with their parents. Nonetheless, these children do not necessarily become "delinquent," nor are their families necessarily broken, in the manner the Philippine media depicts. Armando mirrored the opinion of most of the children in my study when he defended transnational families: "Even if [parents] are far away, they are still there. I get that from basketball, specifically zone defense." [He laughed.] "If someone is not there, you just have to adjust. It's like a slight hindrance that you just have to adjust to. Then when they come back, you get a chance to recover. It's like that."

Recognizing that the family is an adaptive unit that responds to external forces, many children make do, even if doing so requires tremendous sacrifices. They give up intimacy and familiarity with their parents. Often, they attempt to make up for their migrant parents' hardships by maintaining close bonds across great distances, even though most of them feel that such bonds could never possibly draw their distant parent close enough. But their efforts are frequently sustained by the belief that such emotional sacrifices are not without meaning— that they are ultimately for the greater good of their families and their nature. Jason Halili's mother provided care for elderly persons in Los Angeles for 15 years. Jason, now 21, reasons, "If she did not leave, I would not be here right now. So it was the hardest route to take, but at the same time, the best route to take."

Transnational families were not always equated with "broken homes" in the Philippine public discourse. Nor did labor migration emerge as a perceived threat to family life before the late 1980s, when the number of migrant women significantly increased. This suggests that changes to the gendered division of family labor may have as much as anything else to do with the Philippine care crisis.

The Philippine public simply assumes that the proliferation of female-headed transnational households will wreak havoc on the lives of children. The Scalabrini Migration Center explains that children of migrant mothers suffer more than those of migrant fathers because child rearing is "a role women are more adept at, are better prepared for, and pay more attention to."[21] The center's study, like the Philippine media, recommends that mothers be kept from migrating. The researchers suggest that "economic programs should be targeted particularly toward the absorption of the female labor force, to facilitate the possibility for mothers to remain in the family."[22] Yet the return migration of mothers is neither a plausible nor a desirable solution. Rather, it implicitly accepts gender inequities in the family, even as it ignores the economic pressures generated by globalization.

As national discourse on the care crisis in the Philippines vilifies migrant women, it also downplays the contributions these women make to the country's economy. Such hand-wringing merely offers the public an opportunity to discipline women morally and to resist reconstituting family life in a manner that reflects the country's increasing dependence on women's foreign remittances. This pattern is not exclusive to the Philippines. As Arjun Appadurai observes, globalization has commonly led to "ideas about gender and modernity that create large female work forces at the same time that cross-national ideologies of 'culture,' 'authenticity,' and national honor put increasing pressure on various communities to morally discipline working women."[23]

The moral disciplining of women, however, hurts those who most need protection. It pathologizes the children of migrants, and it downplays the emotional difficulties that mothers like Rosemarie Samaniego face. Moreover, it ignores the struggles of migrant mothers who attempt to nurture their children from a distance. Vilifying migrant women as bad mothers promotes the view that the return to the nuclear family is the only viable solution to the emotional difficulties of children in transnational families. In so doing, it directs attention away from the special needs of children in transnational families—for instance, the need for community projects that would improve communication among far-flung family members, or for special school programs, the like of which did not exist at my field research site.

It's also a strategy that sidelines the agency and adaptability of the children themselves.

To say that children are perfectly capable of adjusting to nontraditional households is not to say that they don't suffer hardships. But the overwhelming public support for keeping migrant mothers at home does have a negative impact on these children's adjustment. Implicit in such views is a rejection of the division of labor in families with migrant mothers, and the message such children receive is that their household arrangements are simply wrong. Moreover, calling for the return migration of women does not necessarily solve the problems plaguing families in the Philippines. Domestic violence and male infidelity, for instance—two social problems the government has never adequately addressed—would still threaten the well-being of children.[24]

Without a doubt, the children of migrant Filipina domestic workers suffer from the extraction of care from the global south to the global north. The plight of these children is a timely and necessary concern for nongovernmental, governmental, and academic groups in the Philippines. Blaming migrant mothers, however, has not helped, and has even hurt, those whose relationships suffer most from the movement of care in the global economy. Advocates for children in transnational families should focus their attention not on calling for a return to the nuclear family but on trying to meet the special needs transnational families possess. One of those needs is for a reconstituted gender ideology in the Philippines; another is for the elimination of legislation that penalizes migrant families in the nations where they work.

If we want to secure quality care for the children of transnational families, gender egalitarian views of child rearing are essential. Such views can be fostered by recognizing the economic contributions women make to their families and by redefining motherhood to include providing for one's family. Gender should be recognized as a fluid social category, and masculinity should be redefined, as the larger society questions the biologically based assumption that only women have an aptitude to provide care. Government officials and the media could then stop vilifying migrant women, redirecting their attention, instead, to men. They could question the lack of male accountability for care work, and they could demand that men, including migrant fathers, take more responsibility for the emotional welfare of their children.

The host societies of migrant Filipina domestic workers should also be held more accountable for their welfare and for that of their families. These women's work allows First World women to enter the paid labor force. As one Dutch employer states, "There are people who would look after children, but other things are more fun. Carers from other countries, if we can use their surplus carers, that's a solution."[25]

Yet, as we've seen, one cannot simply assume that the care leaving disadvantaged nations is surplus care. What is a solution for rich nations creates a problem in poor nations. Mothers like Rosemarie Samaniego and children like Ellen Seneriches and Jeek Pereno bear the brunt of this problem, while the receiving countries and the employing families benefit.

Most receiving countries have yet to recognize the contributions of their migrant care workers. They have consistently ignored these workers' rights and limited their full incorporation into society. The wages of migrant workers are so low that they cannot afford to bring their own families to join them, or to regularly visit their children in the Philippines; relegated to the status of guest workers, they are restricted to the low-wage employment sector, and with very few exceptions, the migration of their spouses and children is also restricted.[26] These arrangements work to the benefit of employers, since migrant care workers can give the best possible care for their employers' families when they are free of care-giving responsibilities to their own families. But there is a dire need to lobby for more inclusive policies, and for employers to develop a sense of accountability for their workers' children. After all, migrant workers significantly help their employers to reduce their families' care deficit.

NOTES

1. Arlie Hochschild, "The Culture of Politics: Traditional, Post-modern, Cold Modern, Warm Modern Ideals of Care," *Social Politics*, vol. 2, no. 3 (1995): pp. 331–46.

2. While women made up only 12 percent of the total worker outflow in 1975, this figure grew to 47 percent twelve years later in 1987 and surpassed the number of men by 1995. IBON Facts and Figures, "Filipinos as Global Slaves," 22, nos. 5–6 (March 15–31,1999), p. 6.

3. Notably, Filipino women have responded to the care crisis in more developed nations in other ways. They also alleviate the care crisis plaguing hospitals and hospices in more developed nations by providing services as professional nurses. At the expense of the quality of professional care in the Philippines, nurses have sought the better wages available outside the country. Between 1992 and 1999, the government deployed more than 35,000 nurses. See Maruja Asis, *Female Labour Migration in South-East Asia: Change and Continuity* (Bangkok, Thailand: Asian Research Centre for Migration, Institution of Asian Studies, Chulalongkorn University, 2001).

4. Using a 1997 national labor force survey, Hector Morada, the director of the Bureau of Labor and Employment Statistics in the Philippines, found that female-headed transnational households have an average of 2.74 children, with .56 aged less than seven years.

5. Gina Mission, "The Breadwinners: Female Migrant Workers," *WIN: Women's International Net Issue* (November 1998): p. 15A.

6. Hochschild and Machung, 1989. By "stalled revolution," Hochschild refers to the fact that the economic contributions of women to the family have not been met with a corresponding increase in male responsibility for household work.

7. Agence France-Presse, "Ramos: Overseas Employment a Threat to Filipino Families," *Philippine Inquirer* (May 26, 1995), p. 11.

8. I base this claim on a survey of articles that appeared in Philippine dailies from 1995 to 1998. I obtained the newspaper articles from the library of the Philippine Overseas Employ-

ment Agency, which catalogs media reports on migrant Filipino workers.

9. Perfecto G. Caparas, "OCWs Children: Bearing the Burden of Separation," *Manila Times* (September 30, n.d.), pp. 1–2.

10. Susan Fernandez, "Pamilya ng OFWs maraming hirap" (Many hardships in the families of OFWs), *Abante* (January 27,1997), p. 5.

11. Lorie Toledo, "Child Sexual Abuse Awareness," *People's Journal* (February 19, 1996), p. 4. Although incest is a social problem in the Philippines, its direct correlation to the emigration of mothers is an unproven speculation. For instance, studies have yet to show that there are higher rates of incest among children of migrant mothers than in other families.

12. Lorie Toledo, "Overseas Job vs. Family Stability," *People's Journal* (December 15, 1993), p. 4.

13. Bureau of Employment and Labor Statistics, "Remittances from Overseas Filipino Workers by Country of Origin Philippines: 1997-Fourth Quarter 1999," *Pinoy Migrants, Shared Government Information System for Migration*, http://emisd.web.dfa.gov.ph/~pinoymigrants/.

14. Rosemarie Samaniego is a pseudonym. This excerpt is drawn from Rhacel Salazar Parreñas, *Servants of Globalization: Women, Migration, and Domestic Work* (Stanford, Calif.: Stanford University Press, 2001).

15. Ellen Seneriches and the names of the other children whom I quote in this article are all pseudonyms.

16. Pierrette Hondagneu-Sotelo and Ernestine Avila, "'I'm Here, but I'm There': The Meanings of Latina Transnational Motherhood," *Gender and Society*, vol. 11, no. 5 (1997), pp. 548–71.

17. A two-part special report by Caparas, "OCWs Children," which appeared on the front page of the *Manila Times*, summarized the media's incredibly negative view on the plight of children in transnational families. It reported that children suffer from a "psychological toll," "extreme loneliness," "unbearable loss," "strained relations," "incest," and consequently delinquency, as indicated, for instance, by rampant "premature pregnancies." See also Caparas's "OCWs and the Changing Lives of Filipino Families," *Manila Times* (August, 29, n.d.), pp. 1, 5.

18. Similarly, I found that children use the corollary image of the struggling "breadwinner" father to negotiate the emotional strains of their transnational household arrangement.

19. Scalabrini Migration Center (SMC), *Impact of Labor Migration on the Children Left Behind* (Quezon City, Philippines: Scalabrini Migration Center, 2000).

20. SMC, 2000, p. 65.

21. SMC, 2000, p. 57.

22. SMC, 2000, p. 65.

23. Arjun Appadurai, "Globalization and the Research Imagination," *International Social Science Journal*, vol. 160 (June 1999), p. 231.

24. National Commission for the Role of Filipino Women, *Philippine Plan for Gender-Responsive Development, 1995–2025* (Manila, Philippines: National Commission for the Role of Filipino Women, 1995).

25. Marije Meerman, "The Care Chain," episode 42 of *The New World* (Netherlands: VPRO-TV); www.dnv.vpro.nl/carechain.

26. Policies in various receiving countries restrict the migration of workers' families. Such restrictions can be found both in countries, such as Singapore and Taiwan, that have illiberal policies and in those, like Canada, with liberal policies. See Abigail Bakan and Daiva Stasiulis, eds., *Not One of the Family: Foreign Domestic Workers in Canada* (Toronto: University of Toronto Press, 1997).

DISCUSSION QUESTIONS: SALAZAR PERREÑAS

1. Explain Salazar's statement that "care" work now has become the Philippines' primary export.
2. What are the local consequences of this global situation?
3. What are the experiences of the children of transnational families as their mothers work abroad caring for other children? How do they cope in the context of global work migration?

FURTHER READINGS

1. Ehrenreich, Barbara, and Arlie Russell Hochschild (eds.). 2002. *Global Woman: Nannies, Maids, and Sex Workers in the New Economy.* New York: Henry Holt.

    The authors gathered in this collection examine the lives of women immigrants from the Dominican Republic, Vietnam, Taiwan, Mexico, Thailand, Sri Lanka, and the Philippines, whose work has been impacted by forces of economic and cultural globalization.

2. Kessler-Harris, Alice. 2003. *Out to Work: A History of Wage-Earning Women in the United States* (20th ed.). Oxford: Oxford University Press.

    This monograph is a history of working women in the United States from the colonial period to the end of the 20th century. The author is particularly interested in the material and ideological relationship between work and family throughout this historical period.

3. Luxton, Meg, and June Corman. 2001. *Getting By in Hard Times: Gendered Labour at Home and on the Job.* Toronto: University of Toronto Press.

    Luxton and Corman integrate analyses of two related studies they undertook in Hamilton, ON, Canada between 1980 and 1996 during a period of intense economic restructuring that resulted in high unemployment, wage cuts, the reorganization of work, and the erosion of the social security system. They interviewed people whose livelihoods depended on employment at Hilton Works, a steel-manufacturing plant owned by Stelco, to see how the home and working lives of White working-class men and women were affected by restructuring processes, and how they renegotiated gender, class, and race relations under these new economic circumstances.

4. McDowell, Linda, and Gill Court. 1994. Performing Work: Bodily Representations in Merchant Banks. *Environment and Planning D: Society and Space,* 12(6), 727–750.

    Feminists have agreed that the workplace is a significant site of the social construction of feminine and masculine identities. But McDowell and Court argue that, with an increase in the number of service sector jobs in the New Economy, gendered bodily performances have become vital to selling products. They draw on the work of Judith Butler to investigate the bodily identities performed by men and women engaged in the interactive service work in a professional capacity in merchant banks in London, England.

5. Williams, Christine. 2004. The Glass Elevator: Hidden Advantages for Men in the "Female" Professions. In Michael Kimmel (ed.), *The Gendered Society Reader.* New York: Oxford University Press, pp. 291–307.

    This paper addresses men's underrepresentation in the women-dominated professions of nursing, elementary school teaching, librarianship, and social work. Williams conducted interviews with 99 women and men in these professions in the United States, which reveal that men do not face discrimination in these occupations, although they do encounter some prejudice from people outside the work environment. Unlike women who enter male-dominated professions, Williams finds that men encounter structural advantages that enhance their careers in occupations dominated by women.

RELEVANT FILMS

1. *Highway Courtesans,* 2005, 71 minutes, Women Make Movies

    This documentary chronicles the life of an Indian woman as she grows from 16 to 23. She is a member of the Bachara community, which commonly sanctions the practice of prostituting eldest daughters as a means of family and community support. The film demonstrates that the Bachara women who sexually service truckers are the core of the local economy, outlining the personal and social costs of this work and questioning the gender relations that place women in this world of paid labour.

2. *Monuments Are for Men, Waffles Are for Women: Gender, Permanence, and Impermanence,* 2000, 37 minutes, University of California Extension Centre for Media and Independent Learning

    Filmmakers eavesdrop on a class at Ohio University to record a discussion about the social construction of gender relations. In particular, students analyze the impermanence of work done by women, compared to the permanence of products of men's work.

3. *The Trickle-Down Theory of Sorrow*, 2002, 15 minutes, Women Make Movies

The film director, Mary Filippo, interviews her mother about her experiences as a labourer in a jewellery factory during the 1940s and 1950s. Mary's mother describes practices of worker exploitation and gender discrimination in the factory, which are compared and contrasted to Mary's own experiences of work, class, and gender relations.

4. *The Life and Times of Rosie the Riveter*, 1980, 65 minutes, Clarity Films

This award-winning documentary examines the lives of five women who worked in American industrial plants during World War II. These women reminisce about their working experiences, as well as the efforts made by the state to force them out of factory work when the war was over to make room for returning veterans. A classic!

5. *A Female Cabby in Sidi Bel-Abbes*, 2000, 52 minutes, First Run Icarus Films

When her husband dies, Soumicha has little choice but to take over her husband's cab as a means of earning a living to support her three children. As the only woman cabby in this Algerian city, she introduces us to the many contradictory aspects of working women's lives as we tour the city from the passenger seat of her car. We meet women from all over the country struggling for more freedom to engage in waged labour, as well as the efforts men have taken to frustrate this struggle.

RELEVANT WEB SITES

1. www.genderwork.ca/index.html

This Canadian Web site constitutes a gender and work database, including six thematic modules (health care, migration, precarious employment, technology, unions, and unpaid labour), library search, and statistical information. The database can be used to obtain information on a topic, or to examine a variety of complex social relations. It takes a feminist political economy approach to gender and work, and is incredibly rich and detailed.

2. www.ilo.org/publis/english/support/publ/textww.htm

The reference list (with links) provided here details numerous books related to gender issues and women's work.

3. www.unpac.ca/economy/llinks.html

The United Nations Platform for Action Committee Manitoba, which grew out of the 1995 UN 4th World Conference on Women in Beijing, has posted this site entitled "Women and the Economy." It provides links to information on women and the economy, women's work, the feminization of poverty, women and globalization, fair trade, no sweatshops, consumerism, and environmentalism. Another rich and detailed set of up-to-date information, resources, and statistics.

4. www.economicsnetwork.ac.uk/books/EconomicsofGender.htm

The Economics Network in the UK lists (and provides links to) books on gender and work/economics. Topics addressed include feminist economics; gender, work and family; race and economics; the feminization of poverty; women in the global economy, and women and welfare states. The information is multidisciplinary and global in perspective.

PART VIII

GENDER AND THE MEDIA

Media are important to gender relations in that they contribute to societal processes of gender identity differentiation. For example, in television ads and programs, girls are often portrayed helping Mommy with domestic chores, while boys help Dad in manly or engaging adventures. As media show stereotyped gender images of the activities of both children and adults, they contribute to expectations of the ways in which both present and future gender relations should be organized and performed. Story lines are also a problem in that they tend to suggest restrictive feminine conduct as appropriate for women, such as when unmarried or divorced working women are portrayed as victims of violence more often than are "respectable" married women. But television story lines, magazine advertising, and music videos are also implicated in creating, maintaining, and perpetuating other social structures of inequality such as class, race, and sexuality using similar strategies of representation.

Candra Gill demonstrates this social process of hierarchy construction as she analyzes the popular television series *Buffy the Vampire Slayer*. This program has been a feminist favourite due to its radical gender edge; images of women in horror settings are recontextualized so that Buffy is characterized as a "transgressive woman warrior" who challenges patriarchal values and institutions rather than acquiescing to them. While Gill agrees with this assessment of the show, she is troubled by how the issue of racism has been neglected both in the series and feminist analyses of it. She undertakes an analysis of the racialized character of the show, reading racism as it plays out in the field of White characters, as well as in the racial stereotypes the show invokes, including representations of any non-White character as evil, marginal, and exotic and story lines that kill them off or at least relegate them to the narrative background.

Joshua Gamson is also preoccupied with the workings of television as a popular form of media that shapes social meaning and significance, but this time of sexuality and class, rather than gender and race. He takes up the interesting question of the visibility of gays and lesbians on American television, where they were once invisible, by asking "Is this progress?" He comes to a conflicted conclusion through his analysis of the ways in which people with non-dominant sexualities are represented on popular television talk shows: increasing visibility does contribute to mainstream society recognizing and confirming these identities and sexual practices, but that visibility simultaneously produces a number of risks for these groups. By examining who gets to speak on popular television talk shows—"rowdy exhibitionists" whose behaviours on screen further marginalize the group, or the more acceptable and respectable middle-class queers who are less "in your face" but reproduce problematic class and racial hierarchies within the group—Gamson provides insights and questions that are relevant to feminist analyses of other forms of media.

CHAPTER 21

'CUZ THE BLACK CHICK ALWAYS GETS IT FIRST

Dynamics of Race in *Buffy the Vampire Slayer*

Candra K. Gill

Since its premiere in 1997, *Buffy the Vampire Slayer* (*BtVS*) has been a feminist favourite. Whip-smart speculative fiction, it crossed horror, fantasy and drama with comedy in a show that both entertained and, often subtly, commented on the difficulties of coming into adulthood in America today. For seven seasons, the show followed Buffy Summers, a young woman living in fictional Sunnydale, California, who, while dealing with the everyday concerns of life, must also fulfill her role as the Chosen One: The Slayer.

There is only one Slayer at a time, and she protects the world from vampires and other supernatural ills. The Slayer is always an adolescent girl, and she is always called to her duty without notice. Others may know if a young woman is a potential Slayer, but the only way to find out for certain who the next Slayer will be is to wait for the previous Slayer to die. When her predecessor dies, the new Slayer's true powers come to light. Since Sunnydale sits on a Hellmouth—a portal to hell—Buffy stays busy.

BtVS featured many regular characters over the years, but at the core were those Joss Whedon, the show's creator, called "the fearsome foursome"[1]—Buffy; Rupert Giles, her Watcher, whose job it was to teach Buffy what she needed to know about being a Slayer and to record her exploits; Willow Rosenberg, Buffy's best friend, who was a bookish nerd in high school but eventually became a powerful witch; and Xander, another high school friend who, unlike Buffy and Willow, had no supernatural abilities, but played an important supportive role.

BtVS purposely recontextualized the image of women in a horror setting. In describing his conception of Buffy, Whedon says:

> I've always been a huge fan of horror movies, and I saw so many horror movies where there was that blonde girl who would always get herself killed. I started feeling bad for her—I thought, you know it's time she had a chance to, you know, "take back the night." And so the idea of Buffy came from just the very simple thought of a beautiful blonde girl walks into an alley, a monster attacks her, and she's not only ready for him, she trounces him.[2]

Several scholars have explored the way *BtVS* recontextualizes women in horror and action settings, particularly through the character of Buffy Summers. A characteristic analysis is that of Frances Early, who argues that Buffy is a "transgressive woman warrior." Early cites Whedon's academic background in film and in women's and gender studies. She quotes him saying he has "...always found strong women interesting because they are not overly represented in cinema" as evidence of his alignment with feminist ideas.[3]

In her study, Early writes, "As a feminist scholar, I appreciate the power of stories that bring women out of the shadows to centre stage and permit protagonists to be disruptive and to challenge patriarchal values and institutions in society."[4] She considers Buffy to be an "open image," a term she attributes to literary critic Sharon MacDonald, in contrast to a "closed image." Closed images are "analogous to symbols and ideals or stereotypes that appear fixed in the public consciousness" whereas open images "are inherently unsettling to the way things are."[5]

Of *BtVS*, Early writes:

> I would like to suggest that the woman warrior theme in Buffy—as presented through the mixed genre of fantasy/horror/adventure—represents an attempt to demystify the closed image of the male warrior-hero not merely by parodying through comedic means this powerful stereotype but also by offering a subversive open image of a just warrior.[6]

Buffy Summers is indeed a subversive warrior, and *BtVS* does recast women in horror settings, but for all its strong feminist imagery and its clever and complex dealings with issues people face through adolescence and early adulthood, the issue of racism has been conspicuously neglected in what fans of the show call the "Buffyverse" (the universe of Buffy). It is important to place this discussion in terms of human-to-human racism, as there are several "races" represented on the show, most notably "demon" races. But when it comes to human characters, *BtVS* is an almost exclusively white show. Few recurring characters have been non-white, and no non-white characters have been featured in the title credits. It took *BtVS*'s spin-off series, *Angel*, to have a character of colour in the opening credits. On *Angel*, the character Charles Gunn appeared late in the first season and eventually became a regular during the second.

What is significant about *BtVS*'s treatment of race is how conventional it is. With few exceptions, the creators of *BtVS* have been content to perpetuate racial stereotypes or to ignore the issue of race altogether. In the African American community, for example, the perception is that in horror movies, if there is a Black character, particularly a Black male character, he or she will die before the film ends.[7] The first six seasons of *BtVS* did nothing to negate this belief: Black characters, or any other characters of colour for that matter, could expect to die by the end of an episode, or by the end of the season if they were lucky.

The people of colour who do appear in Sunnydale fit into two categories. The first: human characters who are actually human. The second, given the supernatural nature of the show, are characters who appear human, but who are not.

In the following sections, I will discuss the way race was handled in the first six seasons. Then, I will contrast this with the way the issue was developed in the seventh and last season.

THE FIRST SIX SEASONS: BUSINESS AS USUAL

For the first six seasons of *BtVS*, people of colour in Sunnydale were portrayed in brief walk-on roles or in the background as non-speaking extras. The few non-white characters with substantial speaking roles could expect to die, be evil, be marginalized/exoticized, or all three.

The show's two-part pilot, called "Welcome to the Hellmouth" and "The Harvest," set the tone. There were very few non-white characters, and though some of them had speaking parts, they were mostly relegated to the background. In the first episode, a Black student at Sunnydale High School finds a dead body in her locker. In the second, a Black bouncer at the Bronze, the all-ages nightclub where Buffy and her friends often hang out, is killed by vampires who take over the club. And that's it. There were no significant non-white characters in the first season.

It was not until the second season's "Inca Mummy Girl" that a non-white character had a large guest role. Ampata was an exchange student from South America who turned out to be an Incan girl who had been sacrificed 500 years before. When the audience first sees Ampata, she is a mummy in a museum that Buffy and her schoolmates visit. Ampata is freed from her imprisonment as a mummy when a seal is broken. To stay alive, Ampata has to suck the life from other people, which she does through kissing.

An Incan man violently defends her and argues that she should return to being a mummy. When he confronts Ampata and tells her that she has already died, he explains: "You are the chosen one. You must die. You have no choice."

Ampata kills him and sucks the life from him, saying: "Yes, I do." Calling Ampata "the chosen one" mirrors Buffy's position as the Slayer, a parallel Buffy notes at the end of the episode when she has defeated Ampata. Buffy kills Ampata to save Xander, with whom Ampata has gone to a school dance. Buffy refers to events in the first season's finale in which she died briefly. But unlike Buffy, of course, Ampata's sacrifice costs her life.

This episode is characteristic of the way indigenous cultures are represented on *BtVS*. They are relegated to museums and art galleries and are presented as lethal curiosities to be fought and overcome. Another example can be found in the third season episode called "Dead Mans Party," in which a Nigerian mask Buffy's mother brings home from her art gallery creates zombies that nearly destroy Buffy's home. The fourth season episode called "Pangs," discussed later in this paper, also fits this pattern.

Kent Ono, who has written about *BtVS* from a post-colonial point of view, has commented on Ampata's role and pointed out her marginalization from Buffy and her friends.[8] At first, she appears to assimilate into their culture. Buffy's mother even notes: "Two days in America and Ampata already seems like she belongs here. She's really fitting in." Ultimately, however, Ampata must be made a mummy once again in order to maintain Sunnydale's safety.

The second season also saw the appearances of Kendra the Vampire Slayer and the vampire Mr. Trick. Kendra first appears in "What's My Line: Part 1." She is a young Black woman who speaks with what sounds like a Caribbean accent. Where Kendra is from is never actually revealed, but the DVD commentary for that episode mentions that the vocal coach who worked with the actor placed the accent as an obscure Jamaican dialect.[9]

When Kendra first appears in Sunnydale, she is presented as a contrast to Buffy. While Buffy works hard to maintain her life outside of being a Slayer, Kendra was given to her Watcher as a child so she could be trained for the possibility she would become The Slayer. Kendra has no life outside of Slaying. She is socially awkward, but extremely professional. By the time she leaves Sunnydale to return to her Watcher, in "What's My Line: Part 2," she has become more like Buffy, which is presented as a positive change. Kendra is able to joke and is even wearing one of Buffy's shirts when she leaves Sunnydale. Later, she returns for the episode "Becoming: Part 1," in which she is ambushed and killed by the vampire Drusilla.

Both Ono and Lynne Edwards, another writer who has explored the politics of race in *BtVS*, have commented on Kendra. Ono sees her as a challenge to Buffy's role as the lone Slayer,[10] while Edwards sees her death as a failed "quest for legitimacy."[11] Both situate her as Other in her relationship with Buffy. Kendra is marginalized, both in her relationship with Buffy and in her role as a Slayer.

The appearance and demise of Mr. Trick, a Black vampire who was once a Black man, provide some of the few instances in the first six seasons where the writers of *BtVS* specifically comment on race. Mr. Trick arrives in Sunnydale in the episode, "Faith, Hope and Trick," working for an ancient vampire named Kakistos. Mr. Trick says about Sunnydale: "The town's got quaint, and the people—he called me 'Sir'—don't you miss that? Admittedly, not a haven for the brothers—strictly for the Caucasian persuasion in the 'Dale. But you gotta stand up and salute that death rate [...] and ain't nobody saying anything about it." With this statement, the writers acknowledge for the first time that Sunnydale is not at all racially diverse.

The death rate to which Mr. Trick refers is the amount of human deaths due to feeding vampires, demons, and other supernatural causes. Ono suggests Mr. Trick is referring specifically to deaths of Black people here, but a close reading of the scene does not support this interpretation. Mr. Trick is simply telling his employer Kakistos about the town and why it is good for them, as vampires, to live there. He is suggesting that the fact that vampires can feed with impunity makes being there worthwhile, but that multiculturally, Sunnydale is lacking. It is worth noting that though Mr. Trick is a vampire, he maintains his Black identity.

The character Faith is also introduced in this episode. She is a white, working-class young woman who was called as a Slayer as a result of Kendra's death. At the end of "Faith, Hope and Trick," Kakistos is killed by Buffy and Faith, who combine efforts, and Mr. Trick goes to work for Sunnydale's evil mayor. Twelve episodes later, in "Consequences," Mr. Trick is killed by Faith. Faith kills him to save Buffy. As Mr. Trick prepares to bite Buffy, he says, "I hear once you've tasted a Slayer, you never want to go back," which is a riff on the saying, "Once you go Black, you never go back." Again, Mr. Trick makes a reference to race. This time, however, he dies.

Looking beyond Mr. Trick's quips, he is portrayed as intelligent and resourceful, but he also, significantly, works exclusively for white vampires and men. Unlike Buffy's other major vampire adversaries, such as The Master in the first season, or Spike and Drusilla in the second, Mr. Trick does not work for himself. And in the end, he does not last a full season (unlike, say, Spike, who becomes a regular character integrated into Buffy's core group).

While the third season briefly acknowledged race as an issue through Mr. Trick, the fourth season showed a return to characters of colour being relegated to minor roles and no acknowledgement of race. In the first episode of the season, "The Freshman," Olivia is introduced. She is a romantic interest for Giles, though little about her is ever revealed. Her character returns toward the middle of the season in "Hush," where we learn that she is visiting from England and that she knows Giles from his life before Sunnydale. The two are shown in bed together, but viewers know little else about their relationship other than that as a result of the events of "Hush," she comes to believe Giles's stories about the supernatural. Olivia is an incidental character who is given little background or significance to the arc of the show.

The fourth season also introduced the character Forrest, an African American man enlisted by The Initiative. The Initiative is a military operation that comes to Sunnydale to fight the supernatural forces there. Forrest is positioned in opposition to Buffy. He sees her as a threat, and repeatedly makes his feelings known. During this season, Buffy dates Riley, a soldier in The Initiative. As their relationship progresses, Riley begins to doubt what The Initiative does. Forrest sees Buffy as the cause of Riley's doubt and eventual desertion. He represents unquestioning military orthodoxy to which Buffy's independence is a threat. Forrest is eventually killed by Adam, a cyborg created by The Initiative as a weapon prototype. The military to which he is so loyal causes his demise. Because of the disproportionately large representation of Black people in the United States' Army, Forrest's death is all the more significant.

That same season, "Pangs" deals with the effects of colonialism through the groundbreaking of a new cultural centre dedicated to the study of the Chumash, a Native American tribe indigenous to southern California. As a result of the digging, the spirit Hus is awakened. Hus kills several people in Sunnydale, including the director of the cultural centre and a priest, as revenge for his people's suffering. Buffy and Willow are conflicted about fighting Hus, as they acknowledge that his people were wronged and he has a right to be angry. The Thanksgiving holiday is used as a framework for a discussion about colonialism, culminating in an attack engineered by Hus on Giles's house as Buffy prepares a meal there.

What at first seems like a progressive handling of this theme actually perpetuates many stereotypes about America's indigenous peoples. In an article addressing "Pangs," Dominic Alessio points out several problems with the episode. First, Hus is portrayed as a violent warrior. Historically, however, the Chumash were a generally peaceful people.[12] Also, they are portrayed as having been wiped out—Hus is seen as the avenging spirit of a dead people. The problem is that the Chumash people still exist.[13] Alessio, while criticizing much of the stereotyping in the episode, gives credit to its writers for even addressing the issue.[14] He concludes that, "(...) the issue of race in [BtVS] remains one demon that Buffy can't deal with, one frontier that Buffy is incapable of crossing."[15] I find it particularly problematic that the discussion of the effects of colonialism is done exclusively by the white characters and there is no real voice given to the people about whom they speak.

Perhaps the most significant episodes in which race was a factor (albeit an unspoken one) were the episodes featuring Buffy's Slayer predecessors. The first such episode was the finale for the fourth season, "Restless," when "the fearsome foursome" are introduced to the First Slayer, who stalks them in their dreams as punishment for invoking her spirit in the preceding episode. The First Slayer is a feral Black woman with a painted face and dreadlocks. She symbolically kills Willow, Xander and Giles in their dreams before encountering Buffy. Interestingly, Olivia appears in this episode—not in the real Sunnydale, but in the Sunnydale of Giles's subconscious during his dream. In this sequence, Giles is positioned as Buffy's father. Olivia is pregnant, pushes a pram and seems to be a part of this ad hoc family. Olivia isn't killed in the dream, but neither does she make any more appearances on the show.

When Buffy meets up with the First Slayer, she is told that what she and her friends have done is wrong. She is told this by the character Tara, Willow's girlfriend, who is serving as an interpreter. For some reason, despite, as Edwards points out, there having been a previous history of telepathic communication on the show, the First Slayer cannot speak directly to Buffy in anything but broken, guttural English.[16] In her confrontation with the First Slayer, Buffy challenges her and eventually saves her friends. Buffy makes her characteristic quips, one of which is about the First Slayer's hair and how unprofessional it is. While this is meant to be seen as an offhand comment, considering the challenges to wearing natural hairstyles Black women have

often faced in the workplace, this statement is more than a joke and can be considered racist when looked at in some contexts. To the writers' credit, in making the First Slayer Black and, as we later learn, African, they are recognizing early human civilizations in Africa.

In the fifth season, we are introduced to two more Slayers in the episode "Fool for Love"—the two Slayers who were killed by the vampire Spike. At this point, Spike is incapable of attacking humans as The Initiative has implanted a behaviour modification chip in his head. Because of this chip, when Spike attacks a human he feels debilitating pain. Through a series of flashbacks, Spike tells Buffy the story of how he became a vampire and about the times he killed two of her predecessors. Both of the Slayers Spike kills are women of colour (one is Chinese, the other African American) and both of their deaths are sexualized.

The first is an unnamed young woman who encounters Spike in what looks like a Buddhist shrine in China during the Boxer Rebellion at the turn of the twentieth century. At one point, she has Spike pinned and is ready to kill him with an ornate, beautifully carved stake. A bomb goes off outside of the temple, knocking her down and giving Spike the chance to pin her. He kills her, drains her of blood and snaps her neck. Before she dies, she asks him in Chinese to tell her mother she is sorry. Spike replies that he does not speak Chinese.

After he kills this Slayer, Spike's sire and then lover, Drusilla, enters the shrine. He says, "You ever hear them say the blood of a Slayer is a powerful aphrodisiac?" Drusilla then places one of Spike's fingers in her mouth, suggestively licking the blood off of it. They have passionate sex. After hearing the story, Buffy is disgusted, saying to Spike, "You got off on it?" Spike replies, "Well, yeah. I suppose you're telling me you don't."

The second story takes place in New York City in 1977, where Spike encounters a Slayer we will later learn is named Nikki Wood. He says of his fight with her, "The first one was all business. But the second—well, she had a touch of your [Buffy's] style. She was cunning, resourceful. Oh, and did I mention, hot?" Spike and Nikki fight in a moving subway car, with each having the upper hand at some point. As he tells Buffy of his fight with Nikki, he and Buffy engage in a parallel sparring match. As the fights end, he is straddling Nikki, but kneeling before Buffy. He tells Buffy how he killed Nikki by snapping her neck.

After his stories, Spike, whose attraction to Buffy was revealed in a previous episode, finally tells her how he feels about her. Buffy rejects him and as a result he decides to kill her, despite the excruciating pain that will ensue. Spike gets a gun and goes to Buffy's house. When he arrives, she is on her porch crying, completely unguarded. Instead of killing her, however, he puts the gun down, sits next to her and asks her what's wrong.

Spike's and Buffy's relationship is like this— problematic and violent, but also considerate and compassionate. The two develop a mutual respect, which plays a part in season seven.

That Spike would be cavalier toward the other Slayers he killed is not out of character. After all, he is a vampire, and the Slayer, whoever she is, is by nature his mortal enemy. What is notable about Spike and the way he treats Buffy in relation to his previous encounters with Slayers is the compassion he shows for her. He falls in love with her. That he kills, and "gets off" on killing, two non-white Slayers and chooses to eventually voluntarily help Buffy in her mission as Slayer, has to be noted. Both Asian women and women of African descent have been historically sexualized and exoticized. That Spike takes the time to love Buffy but brutally kills the other two and eroticizes their deaths, marginalizes and devalues the women of colour who are Slayers.[7]

In fairness, every Slayer before Buffy depicted on the show has been a woman of colour. It shows that the Slayer legacy is not exclusive to white women. It is also significant that in both cases, the Slayer fighting Spike comes close to defeating him—it is only sudden reversals of fortune that lead to their deaths. However, with the exception of Buffy, the only Slayers who die onscreen—and therefore fail in their role as Slayers—are women of colour. And unlike Buffy, these Slayers are not (repeatedly!) resurrected.

SEASON SEVEN: SUNNYDALE GETS SOME COLOUR

The seventh season of *BtVS* showed a marked difference in both the number of people of colour in Sunnydale and the way in which race and racism were approached. While still lacking in many respects, there was a definite improvement, if only in terms of numbers.

The increase in people of colour came after the show moved from the WB network to UPN. Also, in the last year, the shows that aired with *BtVS* in the United States changed. When it first went to UPN, *BtVS* was a lead-in to other speculative shows, including the short-lived *Haunted*. During its last months, *BtVS* ran before a show called *Abby*, which featured a primarily African American cast.

The plot of the seventh season revolved around the return of The First Evil (also called "The First"), a disembodied enemy who had made a brief appearance in the third season. The First decides to destroy the whole line of Slayers, which means killing every girl who is a potential Slayer in the world. In response, Buffy and her friends start to gather all the potential Slayers to Sunnydale, where they can be protected. Ultimately, the final story arc of *BtVS* deals with the battle to defeat The First.

The seventh season featured an unprecedented number of people of colour as characters in Sunnydale. Many of the potential Slayers were women of colour, including Rona, an African American woman; Kennedy, a Latina woman who eventually becomes romantically involved with Willow; and Chao-Ahn, a Chinese woman. Another regular character was introduced in the seventh season—the new principal of Sunnydale High School, an African American man named Robin Wood, who happens to be the son of the second Slayer Spike killed.

In addition to the regular characters, the seventh season featured many single-episode appearances by non-white characters and the return of significant past characters—the First Slayer and Nikki Wood. The *BtVS* writers make several references to race and racism throughout the season. In "Potential," after Rona has been mock-killed in a training exercise, she's asked why she "died." She replies: "'Cuz the Black chick always gets it first." In "The First Date," humorous allusions to cultural stereotypes and expectations are made through Giles's interaction with Chao-Ahn. There is a language barrier, so Giles in particular relies on assumptions that turn out to be erroneous and ethnocentric. It is played in such a way that Giles looks silly for doing this.

Also in "The First Date," Buffy, Xander and Willow each engage in romantic activities with people of colour (Buffy has a date with Robin Wood, Xander has a date with Lissa, played by African American R&B singer Ashanti, and Willow continues to develop her relationship with Kennedy). Factoring in Giles's relationship with Olivia, each of the "fearsome foursome" has interracially dated, though no discussion of this has taken place on the show. In this particular episode, much is made of the fact that Lissa turns out to be a demon who tries to kill Xander, but no one mentions at any point that Buffy, Xander and Willow are each seeing people of colour, nor is it mentioned that, with the exception of Willow and Kennedy, none of the potential relationships work out (this includes Giles and Olivia). This silence on the issue could be seen as a positive normalizing of interracial dating, which would be good. It does, however, seem strange that in a city where people can go days without seeing a non-white person, no one mentions that suddenly everyone's dating them.

The most notable seventh-season episode when it comes to race and racism is "Get It Done." In this episode, the First Slayer appears to Buffy in a dream and talks to her. Apparently the First Slayer can suddenly communicate directly to Buffy in standard English instead of the stereotypical broken English she used previously.

The First Slayer tells Buffy "It's not enough!" The "it" to which she refers is the preparation to fight The First that the "fearsome foursome" and the potential Slayers are all engaged in. Through a mystical shadow box, Buffy is transported through a portal to the place and time of the First Slayer. When she goes through the portal, she encounters three men in non-specific traditional African garb, each carrying a staff. The men speak Kiswahili, but Buffy is able to understand them. They tell her that they have been waiting for her and that they "... can't give her knowledge [...] only power."

When Buffy expresses doubt that the men are real, one of them hits her with his staff and knocks her out. When she awakens, she is chained to a rock. One of the men says, "We are at the Beginning. The Source of your strength. The well of the Slayers' power. This is why we brought you here." When Buffy protests, she is told that "The First Slayer did not talk so much." One of the men then takes a box, opens it, and as a black substance flows into the air, says, "Herein lies your greatest strength. The energy of the demon. Its spirit. Its heart." They reveal that this is the way the First Slayer got her power—by absorbing the demon's heart. Buffy balks, but is told, "It must become one with you" because she needs the strength to fight The First.

Buffy refuses to absorb the power, saying, "By making me less human?" The flowing, black essence of the demon starts to penetrate Buffy, trying to enter her through her nose. She screams, refusing it. It tries to enter her again, this time through her abdomen. Buffy says, "You think I came all this way to get knocked up by some demon dust? I can't fight this. I know that now. But you guys—you're just men—" she breaks her chains "—just the men who did this. To her. Whoever that girl was before she was the First Slayer."

One of the men says, "You do not understand," to which Buffy replies, "No, you don't understand! You violated that girl—made her kill for you because you're weak, you're pathetic, and you obviously have nothing to show me." She then starts to fight the men and knocks two of them down. She breaks one of the staffs of the fallen men and the essence of the demon disappears. She says, "I knew it. It's always the staff." The remaining man says, "We offered you power." Buffy says, "Tell me something I don't know." The man says, "As you wish," and gives Buffy a vision of the army she and the potential Slayers will have to defeat. At that moment, Buffy's friends succeed in their efforts to get

Buffy back through the portal and she returns to Sunnydale.

The scenes that feature the makers of the First Slayer appear to be an exploration and condemnation of patriarchal power. The creation of the First Slayer is presented in terms of a violation, with the demon essence penetrating her. It is also clear that this was done against her will. By refusing the essence and physically overcoming the men who would have given it to her, Buffy challenges the patriarchy in language it can understand—through physical violence.

Another reading of this scene, however, is not as progressive. In having the physically slight, white female confront three Black men and accuse them of violation smacks of early twentieth-century rape narratives in which white women were depicted as the prey of Black men.

The continued problems of race in *BtVS* are encapsulated in the final episode, "Chosen." While people of colour are strongly represented in this episode, the resolution is racially problematic. In "Chosen," Buffy devises a plan to defeat The First once and for all. This plan involves using Willow's abilities as a witch to make each of the girls who is a potential Slayer become an actual Slayer. Buffy questions the tradition of a single Slayer, noting that the only reason there is one Slayer at a time is because the men who made the First Slayer created that rule. "They were powerful men," she says. "But this woman [pointing to Willow] is more powerful." The powerful men to whom she refers are specifically the men who made the First Slayer, the Black men who, in "Get It Done," are coded as rapists.

Willow is able to successfully awaken the Slayer within each of the potentials, both those fighting in Sunnydale and those around the world. In doing so, Willow taps into a great power that turns her hair white and causes her to glow. Willow's normal hair colour is red, but her hair changed colour in previous episodes as well. When she was overcome with evil in the sixth season episode, "Villains," her hair turned completely black. It stayed this way for three episodes, until the evil left her.

When Kennedy sees this final change, she says to Willow, "You're a goddess!" Thus, the climactic moment of empowerment when the potential Slayers all become actual Slayers is brought about by a white goddess standing in opposition to the will of Black male rapists.

Also, near the end of the final episode, the audience is led to believe that Robin Wood has died (to the point where Faith moves to close his eyes) before he stirs. This Black male character has lived, if just barely, through to the end of the show.

CONCLUSION: BETTER ... BUT NOT QUITE THERE YET

In presenting Buffy as a sort of Everygirl (and later, woman), the creators of Buffy failed to acknowledge that not every girl would see herself in Buffy Summers (or Willow Rosenberg, Anya, Cordelia Chase, or any of the other women who have been regulars on *Buffy*). This leaves many fans of colour in a strange place.

Fans are aware of the shortcomings of the show and address them publicly. *Deadbrowalking*, a communal Web log subtitled, "The Principal Wood Death Watch," is a meeting place for fans of the show to approach the show as fans of colour and to discuss issues related to that fandom. The community information page states, "Given that he's an African American and has the Hellmouth in his office, we were convinced that Principal Wood is a man marked for Death (or some other unspeakable evil)." It also makes reference to the increase of people of colour on *BtVS* during the seventh season, facetiously mentioning, "[...] the implementation of court-ordered desegregation in Sunnydale and the resulting influx of people of color in the town [...]."[18]

There is reason to believe that the creators of *BtVS* pay some attention to fans of the show. The sixth season ended controversially with the death of Willow's girlfriend, Tara, and Willow's subsequent grief-driven rampage through Sunnydale, which resulted in her killing the man who killed Tara and attempting to destroy the world. Many fans who were invested in Willow and Tara's relationship felt betrayed by this storyline. Relationships on *BtVS* often ended tragically, so Tara's death was not so much the issue as the circumstances surrounding it. Many felt that killing Tara after she and Willow had sex onscreen perpetuated the stereotype that the punishment for having lesbian sex would be death. Willow's resulting rampage evoked the stereotype of lesbians as dangerous and homicidal.[19]

The seventh season saw the creators of the show addressing these criticisms. When Willow became involved with Kennedy and eventually started sleeping with her, neither of them died, and Willow became more powerful in a decidedly good way. While this does not change the implications of the Tara storyline, it does suggest that the writers are aware of fan response and were willing to address it in the show.

In that brief moment when it seemed as if Robin Wood had died in the finale, it is reasonable to suspect that the writers were giving a nod to the issue of the deaths of people of colour in horror and on their show. It was a welcome acknowledgement, though with the other issues presented in the final episode, it also inspired a mixed reaction.

It is important for feminist fandom to interrogate its favourites and inspect them for other biases and exclusions. Author and cultural critic Samuel R. Delany specifically challenges speculative fiction fandom to deal with its racism. In addressing fandom, Delany says, "How does one combat racism in science fiction, even in such a nascent form as it might be fibrillating, here and there? The best way is to build a certain social vigilance into the system."[20] Part of such vigilance is for us, as fans of shows, to be critical of those shows even as we enjoy them. We must become what Ono calls "resistant readers"[21] who challenge the racism (and other forms of oppression) in our favourites, even if the creators of those favourites often did not intend racism in their creations. We need to approach these works on multiple levels, so we can say, yes, *BtVS* was a great show with transgressive and recontextualized images, but it also ended up perpetuating some racial stereotypes even as it gestured toward critiquing them. Clearly, the Black chick still better watch her back.

NOTES

1. Laura Miller, "The man behind the Slayer," *Salon*, 20 May 2003, <http://www.salon. com/ ent/tv/int/2003/05/20/whedon/priru.html> (23 May 2003).

2. Joss Whedon, "Joss Whedon on 'Welcome to the Hellmouth' and 'The Harvest,'" *Buffy the Vampire Slayer: The Complete First Season on DVD*, Disc 1, Twentieth Century Fox Home Entertainment, Inc., 2001, DVD.

3. Frances H. Early. "Staking Her Claim: Buffy the Vampire Slayer as Transgressive Woman Warrior," *Journal of Popular Culture* 35.3 (2001): (11–27), 12.

4. Early, 12.

5. Early, 12.

6. Early, 18.

7. A popular-culture example of this can be found [...] in *3 Blacks Review Flicks: A Film and Video Guide with Flava!* (New York: Amistad, 2002).

8. Kent Ono, "To Be a Vampire on *Buffy the Vampire Slayer*: Race and ('Other') Socially Marginalizing Positions on Horror TV," *Fantasy Girls: Gender in the New Universe of Science Fiction and Fantasy Television*, ed. Elyce Rae Helford (Lanham, Maryland: Rowan & Littleford Publishers, Inc., 2000: 163–186), 174–177.

9. Marti Noxon, Commentary, "What's My Line Part 2," *Buffy the Vampire Slayer: The Complete Second Season on DVD*, Disc 3, Twentieth Century Fox Home Entertainment, Inc., 2002, DVD.

10. Ono, 174.

11. Lynne Edwards, "Slaying in Black and White: Kendra as Tragic Mulatta in *Buffy*," *Fighting the Forces: What's at Stake in Buffy the Vampire Slayer*, eds. Rhonda V. Wilcox and David Lavery (Lantham, Maryland: Rowan & C. Lirdeford Publishers, Inc., 2002: 85–97), 89.

12. Dominic Alessio, "Things Are Different Now?: A Postcolonial Analysis of: *Buffy the Vampire Slayer*," *The European Legacy* 6 (2001): 731–740, 733, 755.

13. Alessio, 735.

14. Alessio, 738.

15. Alessio, 738.

16. Edwards, 95.

17. These stories are being told by Spike. What he says may or may not be true, but his versions of the stories are all the viewers have.

18. *Deadbrowalking: The Principal Wood Deathwatch*, <http://www.livejournal.com/userinfo. bml?user=deadbrowalking> (20 May 2003).

19. Andy Mangels, "Lesbian sex = death?" *The Advocate*, 20 August 2002, 70–71.

20. Samuel R. Delany, "Racism and Science Fiction," *Dark Matter: A Century of Speculative Fiction from the African Diaspora*, ed. Sheree R. Thomas (New York: Aspect, 2000): 382–397, 396.

21. Ono, 163.

CHAPTER 22

PUBLICITY TRAPS
Television Talk Shows and Lesbian, Gay, Bisexual, and Transgender Visibility

Joshua Gamson

*****

[T]he 1990s have witnessed a storm of "happen to be gay" television, culminating in the much-hyped coming-out of Ellen's central character and star.

By the conventions of much gay and lesbian media studies and advocacy, this is a dream come true. After all, since taking off with Vito Russo's ground-breaking *The Celluloid Closet* (1987), studies of the portrayals of gay men and lesbians in film and television have soundly demonstrated how homosexual lives have been subject to systematic exclusion and stereotyping as victims and villains; how "aspects of gay and lesbian identity, sexuality, and community that are not compatible or that too directly challenge the heterosexual regime are excluded" from mainstream television (Fejes and Petrich 1993: 412; [...]); how television has produced "stereotypical conceptualizations of AIDS that vilify gays and legitimate homophobia" (Netzhammer and Shamp 1994: 104); how even "positive" portrayals of lesbians "serve as mechanisms to perpetuate hetero/sexism" (Hantzis and Lehr 1994: 118; [...]). Now, having made the move from occasional soupy movie-of-the-week issue to soap and sitcom regulars, lesbians and gay men look more or less like everybody else on sitcoms

and soaps: clean, with really good apartments. Their homosexuality is more or less incidental, not much more than a spicy character flip. This would seem to be progress.

The desire to be publicly recognized is especially powerful for marginalized groups, whose cultural visibility is often so minimal, or distant enough from the way people live their lives to render them unrecognizable even to themselves. The positive effects of visibility are quite plain: "Cultural visibility can prepare the ground for gay civil rights protection," as Rosemary Hennessy sums it up, and "affirmative images of lesbians and gays in the mainstream media ... can be empowering for those of us who have lived most of our lives with no validation at all from the dominant culture" (Hennessy 1994–5: 31–2). The desire to be recognized, affirmed, validated, and to lay the cultural groundwork for political change, in fact, are so strong they have tended to inhibit careful analysis of the dynamics of becoming visible. At a time when a major sitcom character and the lesbian playing her have come out amidst a coterie of gay and lesbian supporting characters, when a drag queen has her own talk show on VH-1, when big movie stars no longer see gay roles as career poison, and when one soap opera has had a transsexual storyline and another a gay talk-show-murder storyline, it is no longer enough to think in terms of invisibility and stereotyping. Cultural visibility, especially when it is taking place through commerce, is not a direct route to liberation; in fact, it can easily lead elsewhere.

Talk shows, which have been making nonconforming sex and gender lives public for a good two decades, are a great place to turn for complication. The dramatic new visibility in commercial television fiction, and the slower changes in commercial popular nonfiction media (Alwood 1996) is only the spread of the logic and imagery of TV talk shows, which long ago incorporated lesbians, gay men, transgenders, and bisexuals into their daily dramas. What makes them interesting spots, moreover, is not only the high visibility of gay, lesbian, bisexual, and transgender people, but the (at least partial) *agency* of those people within the genre. Until very recently, lesbians and gay men had little input into our own representation. Almost without exception, the literature on homosexuality and the media has therefore treated the process of representation as a one-sided one.

*****

On talk shows, however, bisexuals, lesbians, transgendered people, and gay men are actively invited to participate, to "play themselves" rather than be portrayed by others, to refute stereotypes rather than simply watch them on the screen. Talk shows mess up our thinking about the difficulties and delights of becoming visible—and, in a more general sense, about the political benefits and dilemmas of cultural representation. And as the dust settles, they can clear our thinking up.

Beginning with a brief introduction to the recent class-cultural history of US daytime television talk, I want to point towards three related political difficulties that talk show visibility brings to the fore and exacerbates. First, drawing from interviews with talk show producers and guests, I suggest that the shows build on and make heavier a class division in gay, lesbian, bisexual, and transgender political organizing—a division tied to the political tension between the pursuit of either a queer difference or an ac-

ceptable sameness. Talk show producers, in part as a response to the organized control activities of activists, have turned to those with little connection to middle-class gay, transgender, bisexual, or lesbian organizing, with little interest or experience in the politics of representation, giving themselves freer reign as producers and infuriating many middle-class activists. The longstanding invisibility (both outside and within gay and lesbian communities) of gay, lesbian, bisexual, and transgender people of color, and of those from lower economic statuses, is cracked open by the talk shows; yet at the same time the shows, with their selection of nasty, rowdy, exhibitionist, not-great-to-look-at poor and working-class guests, encourage those interested in social acceptability to disown the visibility of some of their own. A predicament already present in the politics of sexual social change is brought to a head: as we make ourselves visible, do those among us with less status get to speak just as anyone else (increasing the risk of further stigma as the price for democratic diversity) or do the more acceptable get the upper hand (reproducing class and racial hierarchies as the price for gaining legitimacy)? Any path to visibility must face this question.

Second, drawing from content analysis of talk show transcripts and videos, I argue that the production of rowdy outrageousness draws out and intensifies animosities between the populations (gay men, lesbians, bisexuals, transgendered people) making up the larger movement. Tolerance of visible gayness, put simply, is bought largely through the further stigmatization of bisexuality and gender nonconformity. Talk shows are surely too money-oriented, capricious, and thin to do much deliberate ideological service, but both their loose liberal-therapeutic dogmas and their everyday pursuits—even, and perhaps especially, when they are fixated solely on the "personal"—lead them nonetheless to sharpen political lines of division.

Finally, drawing from focus group interviews with heterosexual talk show viewers, I argue that gay, lesbian, bisexual, and transgender visibility triggers deeper battles over the meaning and ownership of public space. Heterosexual liberal viewers tend to see talk shows as damaging, exploitative contributors to the ongoing victimization of sex and gender deviants. Sympathy for the "exploited," however, is often tempered by a sometimes subtle, sometimes brash animosity towards "trash"—those people who will display themselves outrageously, the bad, low-class queers. Thus, right up next to "leave them alone" is "leave me alone": get out of my face, stop flaunting it. Conservative talk show viewers tend to take this position to the extreme, understanding talk shows as part of a pro-gay publicity apparatus, one of many ways in which queer life is "shoved down their throats."

Talk shows on sex and gender nonconformity are experienced, then, largely as funny pieces in the midst of serious culture wars; primarily through the class divisions to which they are beholden, they encourage viewers to separate "bad" gays from "good" ones, and to link the appearances of sexual nonconformists to inappropriate uses of public space. The various political battles that talk shows elicit, profit from, and amplify, all take a part in a more general war: over the lines between public and private and over who benefits from changing or conserving current public-private divisions. Talk shows open up these cultural battles not so much through the particular discussions they facilitate, not through anything specific that gets said, but through their simple encouragement of publicly visible sex and gender nonconformity. Symbolic political battles over sex and gender norms energize a bigger whirlwind, and are then sucked right into it. Through talk shows, class and sex and publicity and gender provocatively mix, offering more general lessons about the dilemmas of publicity.

CLASS, QUEERNESS, AND PUBLIC VISIBILITY

*****

[T]he talk show genre is fashioned from particular cultural pieces historically associated with different classes: relatively sober, deliberative, "polite" middle-class forms of participating in and presenting public culture

embodied in literary circles and the lyceum, for instance, and irreverent, wild, predominantly lower-class public leisures such as the carnival, the cabaret, the tabloid, and the nineteenth-century theater (see Gamson 1998, ch. 2; Munson 1994; Shattuc 1997).

For their first twenty years, beginning with *Donahue* in the early 1970s, television talk shows were heavily weighted towards the middle-class, people-sitting-around-talking-about-issues model. But with the quick success of *Ricki Lake* in the mid-1990s—which targeted a younger, more mixed-race audience through the programming of rowdy, conflict-filled, interpersonal subjects and a studio audience made up primarily of young audiences—the balance tipped. Ricki and her imitators demonstrated the success of a combination of class voyeurism and class empowerment, inviting guests who were much less likely than *Donahue*'s or *Oprah*'s to be highly educated, organizationally affiliated, and middle class, and audiences who were also more likely to be young, urban, working- or poverty-class people of color. Guests were less commonly recruited, moreover, through organizations, and more commonly through toll-free numbers flashed on the screen: the guests nominated themselves for TV appearances (see Gamson 1998; Grindstaff 1997; Tuchman 1974).

Having discovered the profitable appeal of younger, less educated, more boisterous guests, talk shows have come to feature calm, educated, older guests less and less; they simultaneously appropriate, exaggerate, and give expression to the straightforward, not-afraid-of-conflict emotionalism of some poverty-class and working-class cultures, providing imagery of gays, lesbians, transgenders, and bisexuals from all kinds of racial, cultural, and class backgrounds. At the same time, using the low-risk strategy of class voyeurism, many shows select guests from the bottom of the social barrel. Nearly anyone can feel superior watching people whose speech, dress, bodies, relationships, and accents mark them as "trash."

Especially as the "outrageous" shows took off, and the class (and age) profile of the genre started to shift, middle-class activist guests found themselves and their political agendas edged out. The gay, lesbian, bisexual, and transgendered people who have slowly replaced them—often flamboyant, unaffiliated, untrained in political agendas, and of lower educational, economic, and social status—threaten the mainstreaming agenda of many in the gay movement. They can be loud-mouthed, foul-mouthed, freakish, radical, obnoxious, stereotypical, irrational, emotional: that is, great talk show guests. They emphasize, deliberately and not, a queer difference from the mainstream, and not a terribly appealing one, since on these talk shows it is conflated with "lower class," which is equated with various sorts of ugliness, which do not make the best case for tolerance, acceptance, freedom, and rights.

This dynamic brings to a head class divisions within gay, lesbian, bisexual, and transgender life. Legitimacy, in talk show land as elsewhere, is associated with symbols of social class (educated speech, calm manner, clean dress); uneducated speech, rambunctious manner, and showy dress signify a dismissible lower status. If talk shows are now filled with "trashy" people (many of them people of color), and also with queers, sexual difference is easily conflated with class and racial inferiority; if "classy" white gay people have no monopoly on the conversation, sexual difference can no longer be legitimized by an association with higher educational, racial, and class status. Those seeking mainstream legitimacy therefore avoid the stigma of rowdy, poor, and working-class, mixed-color shows, aligning with the polite, middle-class, predominantly white strand of talk shows. Television talk show visibility thus amplifies the class divisions of the populations on which the shows greedily feed.

Many middle-class activist guests, who had earlier had a virtual monopoly on the non-heterosexual talk show guest list, are trying to move towards the demonstration that gay people (or cross-dressers, or bisexuals, or transsexuals) are regular, civilized, unthreatening, reasonable, conforming folks—for good reason, since media images elsewhere have tipped so heavily in the other direction.

*****

And so two political impulses battle it out through these appearances. We must behave appropriately in public, says one, and work through our ugly stuff in private, in a doctor's office maybe, the way classy people do. Shrink, shmink, says the other, let's go on TV. We are sick of being told what to do and where we can do it, and we're going to take our scary, inappropriate selves as public as we can go.

Ironically, it is in part because of the successes and increased savvy of movement activists in the talk show arena that many middle-class organizers now find themselves on the defensive. For one thing, from the point of view of talk shows, they have pretty much had their time. For another, they have trained themselves in the basics of using-the-talk-show-for-our-own-purposes, and their haggling and negotiating and caution makes them sometimes more trouble than they're worth. It is much easier simply to turn to guests with little agenda other than a few minutes of TV fame and an out-of-town trip. "I wish there was a pool of nice gay folks they called on to do these sorts of things," says [gay writer Eric] Marcus, "but these shows thrive on combativeness, on arguments. They don't want reasonable guests, except as so-called experts."

*****

Opting out, of course, is no guarantee of change. "You get people in our own community who are willing to say anything the producers want them to say in order to create that controversy," says a member of the Manhattan Gender Network, a transgender organization. "The problem is, those of us who don't want to have our brains picked on national television, we leave that to those people who will do whatever is necessary, who look to get on every talk show that they possibly can."

*****

Mainstreaming activists are rightly concerned that talk shows provide a distorted image of gay life—but then again, the image, although more socially acceptable, was no less distorted when it was only white, middle-class, gay movement movers and shakers. Lurking underneath the concern, encouraged by the class dynamics of TV talk, are hints of class, racial, and regional superiority. When gay was just *us*, things were going so well, people seem to want to say. Why did they have to go and give *those* people the microphone?

Talk shows certainly did not *create* the division between moderates with an eye towards assimilation, who want to demonstrate middle-class legitimacy and similarity to heterosexuals, and in-your-face radicals, who use the difference from heterosexuals to create space for themselves. This is a long-standing strategic dispute in sex and gender politics, as it is in most social movements. For a good long time, picking up extra steam in the last decade, civil-rights strategists favoring integration into the "normal" have met with resistance from others favoring a transgressive, confrontational "queer" politics which pushes at the boundaries of normality (D'Emilio 1983; Gamson 1995; Seidman 1996; Vaid 1995; Warner 1993). Of course, it takes a somewhat different form here, since most of the anti-assimilation imagery comes not from organized radical activists, but from unaffiliated individuals seizing the opportunity for televisual confirmation of their social significance. Talk shows, though, take the line between "fringe" and "center"—a divider that, in my own eyes and the eyes of many others, is neither necessary nor productive for political organizing by sex and gender dissidents—and dig away at it, deepening it into an almost unbridgeable chasm. (This comes not just from the strategies of outrageousness-selling shows, but also from those like *Oprah*, which create a "respectable" environment in which people from the wrong side of the tracks are excluded.) The structure of the talk show world intensifies the tension over who rightfully represents "gayness," making it nearly impossible for legitimacy-seeking activists not to close ranks, disrespecting and disowning their own.

This is no deliberate divide-and-conquer on the part of talk show producers. The opening up of the center-fringe, or sameness-difference, fault line is a result of the way producers make

their money, and of the ambivalence built into the talk show genre (high/low class, polite/rude, rational/emotional). An array of "fringe" characters make it to talk TV because of how they play on screen, and because they are easy to recruit and easier to manipulate; they say and do things in public that others are not always willing to say and do. In a genre shot through with class-cultural divisions, in a place where authentic class-cultural expression is indistinguishable from its exaggerated display, where "trash" is a synonym for "lower class," working-class guests (and, through that weird American confusion of race and class, often guests of color as well) are placed directly against the comfortable calm of the middle-class mainstream; bisexual, gay, lesbian, and transgender guests who are not middle class are quite easily placed in the same trash basket. It is not too surprising that many middle-class activists and viewers, informed by a sense that political gains are at stake, are not too excited about joining them there.

NORMALITY AND PUBLIC VISIBILITY

The talk show world rips open existing class divisions within transgender, bisexual, lesbian, and gay politics, but not only these: it also rips away at the tenuous alliance among these nonconforming populations, primarily by rewarding some populations with "acceptability" at the expense of others. Many mainstream gay activist guests and viewers express the worry not only that images of dysfunctional, angry and uneducated parts will be taken to represent the whole, but that disproportionate representation of "abnormal" parts will make it harder for all of us to become "normal." The freaks—especially the gender freaks—are giving us all a bad name.

*****

The talk show world reinforces these divisions not only by using transgendered people as display objects and bisexuals as symbols of promiscuity, but also by offering homosexuals a tempting option: distance yourself from bisexuals and transgendered people, keep your sex and gender practices conservative, and you will be rewarded with acceptance.

Take, for instance, the common "love triangle" structure into which many shows on bisexuality are structured. On a 1992 *Jane Whitney* show on bisexuality, while a white, bearded bisexual guest named Cole is attacking the myth of bisexuality as simultaneous relationships ("I don't have to be in a relationship with both a man and a woman"), a label appears under his image. "Cole," it reads, "Intimate with both men and women." The show, like many others on bisexuality, is structured as a series of triangles: Cole is involved with Hector (who doesn't appear) and with Laura (Latina, bisexual) who is involved with Marcia (African American, lesbian); Jill is involved with both Woody and Rebecca, who has a long-term lover. ("No," says Whitney introducing them, "they're not involved with Laura. They're another bisexual triangle.") Not surprisingly, despite a variety of attempts by panelists to disaggregate bisexuality and non-monogamy, and to distinguish committed, honest non-monogamy from sex-crazed disloyalty, commitment and sexual monogamy become the focus of audience questions and attacks. "How do you decide," asks a young white guy with long, rock-star hair, "flip a coin?" to laughter and applause. "They're changing their preferences every day like they're changing their shirts," says an older white man, and soon a young blond man asks, "Why do you have to have sex with all of them?" to which a tie-wearing, buzz-cut man adds, "As a gay man, I think you're doing a disservice, you should be pursuing the one person and not all this free love." "Don't you believe in commitment?" a series of people ask in a variety of ways. Given the show's Marcia and Laura and Cole and Hector set-up, the answers, all of them well articulated, get lost in the applause for monogamy (Unitel Video 1992).

What is also lost, though, is any concern with the "abnormality" of same-sex relationships, in place of an attack on non-monogamous relationships (equated on the show with bisexual ones). Sexual loyalty, whoever its subjects, is what's really being protected here. In fact, audience members and the host express sympathies and concern for the gay boyfriends and lesbian girlfriends of bisexuals, whose partners "can't

commit" (as when *Jane Whitney*'s Marcia, for example, the sole lesbian on the panel, is encouraged to stop putting up with being a "third wheel"). In these very common "triangle" shows, where bisexuality functions primarily as a stand-in for promiscuity and is therefore denigrated, monogamous sexuality gets the high ground, taking monogamous *homosexuality* along for the ride. In this cultural set-up, from the point of view of gay men or lesbians on the verge of mainstream acceptance and political gains, allying with bisexuals is indeed a risky proposition.

*****

Thus we reach one of the talk show's true political scandals. The scandal isn't so much that talk shows ambush people, or cynically use people's intimate lives to make a buck, or any of that utterly unsurprising and ugly activity. Nor is it even the fact of their drawing of lines that irks; after all, line-drawing is one of the things that culture is always about. The scandal is the *kinds* of lines they emphasize, setting apart potentially powerful sets of political and cultural partners, helping to cut the threads tying working-class lesbian to transsexual to drag queen to gay professional to butch lesbian to bisexual to rural gay kid. That's not of course something they do alone, but they are central to the process, partly because they help it along in such unintentional ways, such entertaining ways, and partly because they mix it, to great effect, with pleas for tolerance, enlightenment, and love. Those alliances are critical because we are engaged in a strange, complicated conflict, which talk shows embody but by no means exhaust: a fight over public space.

SEXUAL NONCONFORMITY AND THE PUBLIC-PRIVATE DIVIDE

*****

"No one's suggesting that you shouldn't be gay," host Jerry Springer tells an 18-year-old gay man in men's pants and sweater, painted nails and high heels, blatantly misrepresenting the sentiments of many in his audience. "If you're gay, you're gay, period. But why is it necessary to just let everybody know all the time?"

*****

His show scripts a backlash against gay visibility (and transgender and bisexual visibility, to a lesser degree) that is quite commonplace, exposing and participating in a culture war that is partly his own creation. "The homosexuals wouldn't have any problem at all if they would just keep it to themselves, and stop trying to act like they're special cause they're gay," says a caller to the *Donahue* show with Reverend Mashore facing off against Sister Sadie, as the camera catches smiling, applauding faces. "Why is there such a need to come out of the closet?" an audience member asks on another *Donahue*, this one on gay cops (Multimedia Entertainment 1994). Indeed, the talk show structural emphasis on separating "appropriate" gay people (middle-class professionals, especially those who pass as heterosexual) from "inappropriate" (lower- and poverty-class people, especially those who do not pass) is powered by an overlapping tension that talk shows manifest: between their push, in alliance with gay people and others, to make "private" matters public, and the various people interested in keeping certain things, such as homosexuality, away from public view. For many in "polite society," it seems, public declarations of lesbian, gay, transgender, or bisexual identity are inherently inappropriate, impolite, and nobody's business.

*****

Daytime talk television, [...] by publicizing the "private," widens yet another fault line in gay and lesbian politics. "Privacy" is already quite a vexed, complex political issue in sexual politics. On the one hand, lesbian and gay political and social life in the past quarter of a century has been built on making sexual identities public, arguing that ours is a political and social status; since everyone is implicated in oppressing us, in part by keeping us invisible and spreading lies

about us, it is everybody's business that we are gay. What we do out of bed, not what we do in bed, is what is most relevant about us. Coming out in public, especially through major public institutions such as schools, the workplace, and communications media, is a way of asserting the public relevance of what others deem private—that is, demonstrating and demonstrating against a second-class, stigmatized social status. (The more recent bisexual and transgender movements have followed this same model.) Talk shows, as we have amply seen, are approached by activists in this light.

At the same time, guided by the logic of constitutional claims-making, gay and lesbian activists have long put forward an argument that retains traditional divisions between private and public, in order to pursue protection under the individual "right to privacy" (Mohr 1988). The only difference between homo and hetero, they have said, is what we do in bed, and what we do in bed is nobody's business, and especially not the business of the government. Thus comments such as this one, from a 30-year-old Latina secretary, in the midst of a discussion of talk shows with a bunch of women: "I feel like it's none of my business. Whatever you do in your bedroom is no concern of mine, just like what I do in my bedroom is none of your business." This is about sex, sex belongs in private, and personal privacy is protected from public intrusion. (The political right, tellingly, has used the basic elements of this argument to great effect, arguing that homosexuality is indeed private, sexual behavior, and that sexual behavior is not the basis for either minority status or rights.) While the legal argument for privacy is certainly not incompatible with public visibility, talk shows seem to run against the rhetorical gist of privacy claims. Many heterosexual talk show participants and viewers seize hold of this conflict: you keep saying how your sexuality is none of my business, yet here you are again on television chatting and yelling and kissing and getting married and making fools of yourselves. If you want privacy, then keep it private.

*****

The divider between inappropriate and appropriate public talk is, moreover, as viewers' conversations capture, a marker of social status; the aversion of middle-class viewers for "sensationalistic," "exploitative" programming expresses an aversion for the declasse. "It's like middle class and lower class," Judi, a 32-year-old homemaker, explains simply, as discussion turns to the comparison of *Oprah*'s audience with *Richard Bey*'s.

*****

It is not just spitting in public that we don't do. We don't *display our sexual selves in public.*

*****

The public display of "private life," especially sexuality, is not something classy people do. It is improper. Watching it, one becomes dirtier, less classy. In the eyes of many middle-class talk show watchers, sexual impropriety is really just the most important and obvious version of un-savory uses of public space. It is not so much the *gayness* that is bothersome, it's the *public-ness.*

So, for many viewers, an ambivalence about homosexuality maps quite effortlessly onto an ambivalence about the making-public of sexual status, which itself maps onto a more general-ized resistance to changes in what they see as their own public territory: a queer presence easily becomes another example of people be-having improperly.

*****

Talk shows make it especially easy for same-sex desire to slide quickly into the category of things that are not the business of polite, civilized, clean, nice people to hear about. They offer occasions for middle-class social anxiet-ies about changes in public space to come into sharper focus, by attaching to the unruly class cultures and unusual sexual beings who seem to populate the public space of talk shows.

*****

Privacy and sexual supremacy, daytime talk and the previously private, talk shows and sex and gender movements—these relationships are undeniably tight. For those with an interest in protecting traditional divisions between public and private, TV talk shows featuring lesbians, gays, bisexuals, and transgenders thus look and feel like a double whammy. The shows want to make public space something entirely different, by giving it to people who have never before made much successful claim on it. Liberal heterosexual viewers worry about exploitation and propriety, beneath which seems to lurk a sense that they are losing control of public space; conservative view-ers bring that anxiety to its extreme, watching those shows, when they can stand to, as though they are holding their fists in front of their faces, ready to fend off the onslaught. While lesbian and gay, bisexual, and transgender activists are waging their struggles for visibility, these viewers are waging their own battle with the television set. They are blocking their throats from the talk shows' fast and furious force-feeding of sex and gender deviance. They are wishing these people would just shut up, not quite understanding why they need to flaunt it in other people's faces, why they have to use television to stick queer noses where they don't belong.

CONCLUSION: VISIBILITY AND COLLECTIVE IDENTITY

All told, talk shows make "good publicity" and "positive images" and "affirmation" hard concepts to hold. They offer a visibility that diversifies even as it amplifies internal class conflicts, that empowers even as it makes public alliances between various sub-populations more difficult, that carves out important new public spaces even as it plays up an association between public queerness and the decay of public decorum. Talk shows suggest that vis-ibility cannot be strategized as either positive or negative, but must be seen as a series of political negotiations.

For instance, a glance at the emphasis on outrageousness that many talk shows have come to promote—the source of much complaining about negative imagery of lesbian, gay, transgender, and bisexual people—makes it hard to hold onto the notion that talk show selection of "the fringes" is necessarily and always a bad thing. This kind of exoticizing imagery certainly makes social acceptability harder to gain by overemphasizing difference, often presented as frightening, pathological, pathetic, or silly; it is annoying and painful for pretty much everybody involved. But at the same time it can push out a space: an emphasis on difference, especially on a scary kind of difference, can keep those watching at a distance. Like the in-your-face radicalism of some recent "queer" organizing, a freaky otherness is useful, for some purposes. When people push away from you, or think of you as harmless and dismissible, they tend to leave you alone, and sometimes being left alone is exactly what is needed for independent political and cultural organizing. As one queer writer put it in the early 1990s, "If I tell them I am queer, they give me room. Politically, I can think of little better. I do not want to be one of them. They only need to give me room" (Chee 1991: 15). The same might be said of the talk shows' money-driven interest in the more provocative edges of lesbian, bisexual, transgender, and gay populations: while they Other us, they also give us *room*. Of course, this is also exactly the problem many people have with them, since at least the appearance of normality seems necessary to winning political *rights*. It's a tension built into talk show visibility, and into the emergence of other marginalized people into commercial media recognition. As Jane Schacter (1997: 728) points out, what's "positive" or "negative" depends "in large part upon what underlying theory of equality has been adopted—one that prizes assimilation or transformation, sameness or difference." The same imagery that is damaging for some kinds of political work (assimilation into the mainstream) is effective for other kinds (the autonomous carving-out of political space). Both kinds of work are necessary. Talk shows, simply through their pursuit of ratings, inadvertently amplify a political dilemma inherent in becoming visible, in which both exaggerating and playing down our collective eccentricity is vital.

*****

Over time, the talk shows have managed to do for their audiences what no one else has: to make televised homosexuality, and even transsexualism and bisexuality, nearly dull. The "fringes," as they show up on TV every week, become run of the mill; they become like a desperate Madonna, whose simulated sex and outside-the-clothing lingerie drew yawns after not too long. Critics of talk shows here have a point: talk shows, through their continual exhibition of the most colorful side-show figures, "define deviance down." From the perspective of those resisting a political and cultural system that labels them deviant, this is a good thing: the edges of normality push ever outward. Tolerance, Crisp informs us, is boredom's offspring. Where exactly is the "positive" in all of this, and where the "negative"?

The difficulty goes much deeper than any talk show will ever go. Talk shows accentuate not only the tension between legitimacy-buying and diversity-promoting visibility but also central dilemmas of collective identity. A sense of collective identification—that this is us, that we are each other—is personally and politically critical: it is an anchor, offering the comforts and resources of family and, at least in this political system, a foundation from which to organize and wage political battles. Identity requires stable, recognizable social categories. It requires difference, knowing where you end and where others begin. It thus makes good sense to do as gay and lesbian movements, modeling themselves on civil rights movements, have done: to build a quasi-ethnicity, with its own political and cultural institutions, festivals, and neighborhoods. Underwriting this strategy, moreover, is typically the notion that gays and lesbians share the same sort of essential self, one with same-sex desires (D'Emilio 1983; Epstein 1987; Seidman 1993). All of this solidifies the social categories of "gay" and "lesbian," clarifying who "we" are and are not, even as it also stabilizes the categories of "heterosexual man" and "heterosexual woman."

At the same time, though, it is exactly through the fixed, dichotomous categorization into apparently distinct species of gay and straight (and male and female) that anti-gay, anti-bisexual, and anti-transgender oppression is perpetuated. Even as the categories that mark us as different are necessary for claiming rights and benefits, making them unworkable provides its own protections; if there is no sure way to distinguish gay from straight, for instance, the basis for anti-gay legislation is arguably weakened. From this angle, *muddying* the categories rather than shoring them up, pointing out their instability and fluidity along with their social roots, is the key to liberation. The political advantages of scrambling the code are always also in competition with those of keeping it clear, not only for people who want to retain their status on a sexual hierarchy, but also for people resisting that hierarchy, who need a coherent sense of collective identity, a cohesive foundation from which to fight, for instance, for rights as gay people.

This tension between a politic that treats the homo-hetero divide as a given and goes about the business of equalizing the sides, and a politic that seeks *to attack the divide itself*, always present in contemporary gay and lesbian politics, has come to the fore most recently with the controversial emergence of "queer" movements in politics and academia. Queer theory and politics, as Michael Warner puts it, protests "not just the normal behavior of the social but the idea of normal behavior" (Warner 1993: xxvii). Especially with the vocal challenge from transgendered and bisexual people—who do not so easily fit into the gay-straight and man-woman binary worldview—the question of the unity, stability, viability, and political utility of sexual identities has been called into question. The queer politics of "carnival, transgression, and parody," with its "anti-assimilationist" and "decentering" politics, has been met with heavy resistance from those rightly seeing it as a threat to civil rights strategies (Stein and Plummer 1996: 134; see also Epstein 1996; Gamson 1995). The problem, of course, is that both the category-strippers and the category-defenders are right: fixed identity categories are both the basis for oppression and the basis for political power.

Talk shows create much of their sex-and-gender fare, especially when transgender and

bisexual people are involved, on exactly this tension. Talk shows, even though they reinstate them, mess up those reassuring dichotomies. On talk shows, the categories stretch and contract, stretch and contract. Much talk show visibility, for one thing, is "queer," in the meaning of the term favored by academics, spotlighting "a proliferation of sexualities (bisexual, transvestite, pre- and post-op transsexual, to name a few) and the compounding of outcast positions along racial, ethnic, and class, as well as sexual lines—none of which is acknowledged by the neat binary division between hetero- and homosexual" (Hennessy 1994–5: 34). The disruptions are fleeting, as audiences work hard to put the categories back together, but they are disturbances nonetheless.

*****

The conditions of visibility, of course, are not of our own making. The tight rope on which bisexuals, transgenders, gays, and lesbians balance as we emerge into visibility gets especially tangled in a time and place where the "public" into which we walk is a space in turmoil. Talk shows, which make their money primarily by publicizing personal issues, only make this anxiety easier to see. Sex and gender nonconformists participate in, and detonate, an anxiety about the shifting boundaries between public and private—much as they have taken a place in other "moral panics," such as the 1950s equation of homosexuality and communism, where pervasive fears and anxieties attach to sexual "deviants" (see D'Emilio 1983; Rubin 1993; Weeks 1981). The very televised presence of gay, lesbian, bisexual, and transgendered people makes public space, to many people, appear to be crawling with indecency. In an environment where public and private have blurred into new forms, gay, lesbian, bisexual, and transgender visibility comes to symbolize a breakdown in the meaning of publicness.

The charge of public indecency is, moreover, a call to get out: this is *my* space, it says, and you do not belong here. Becoming media-visible, especially if your social identity is rooted in a status previously understood to belong to the realm of "private" life, calls the question on who owns public space. The issue of what can and cannot be spoken about and seen in public, which the televised collective coming out of the past twenty years evokes, is really the issue of who is and is not considered a legitimate member of "the public." This ongoing cultural war over public space and public participation is what makes talk shows—even when they are devoid of anything remotely political—socially relevant, and turns them into such zany, vibrant, coarse scenes. In part, they exist to isolate the socially challenging in a discredited space, offering the heady opportunity to be lords and ladies of a vapid kingdom, while the real power-houses command the rest of the empire. In part, they exist to provide a concrete locale at which the question of just what public space can look like, and under just whose jurisdiction it falls, is kept alive for everybody to look at and toss around. Entering media space means joining this fight, and the other ones attached to it, with these questions and predicaments scribbled on your hand.

REFERENCES

Alwood, Edward (1996) *Straight News: Gays, Lesbians, and the News Media*. New York: Columbia University Press.

Chee, Alexander (1991) "A Queer Nationalism," *Out/Look* 11: 15.

D'Emilio, John (1983) *Sexual Politics, Sexual Communities: The Making of a Homosexual Minority in the United States*. Chicago, IL: University of Chicago Press.

Epstein, Steven (1987) "Gay Politics, Ethnic Identity: The Limits of Social Constructionism," *Socialist Review* 17 (3–4): 9–54.

———. (1996) "A Queer Encounter: Sociology and the Study of Sexuality," in Steven Seidman (ed.) *Queer Theory/Sociology*, pp. 145–67. Cambridge, MA: Blackwell Publishers.

Fejes, Fred and Petrich, Kevin (1993) "Invisibility, Homophobia and Heterosexism: Lesbians, Gays and the Media," *Critical Studies in Mass Communication* (December): 396–422.

Gamson, Joshua (1995) "Must Identity Movements Self-Destruct? A Queer Dilemma," *Social Problems* 42 (3): 390–407.

———. (1998) *Freaks Talk Back: Tabloid Talk Shows and Sexual Nonconformity*. Chicago, IL: University of Chicago Press.

Grindstaff, Laura (1997) "Producing Trash, Class, and the Money Shot: A Behind the Scences Account of Daytime TV Talkshows," in James Lull and Stephen Hinerman (eds.) *Media Scandals*. London: Polity Press.

Hantzis, Darlene M. and Leher, Valerie (1994) "Whose Desire? Lesbian (Non) Sexuality and Television's Perpetuation of Hetero/Sexism," in R. Jeffrey Ringer (ed.) *Queer Words, Queer Images: Communication and the Contruction of Homosexuality*, pp. 107–121. New York: New York University Press.

Hennessy, Rosemary (1994–5) "Queer Visibility in Commodity Culture," *Cultural Critique* (winter): 31–75.

Multimedia Entertainment (1994) "Donahue" (*Gay Cops*, June 9).

Munson, Wayne (1994) *All Talk: The Talkshow in Media Culture*. Philadelphia, PA: Temple University Press.

Netzhammer, Emile C. and Shamp, Scott A. (1994) "Guilt by Association: Homosexuality and AIDS on Prime-Time Television," in R. Jeffrey Ringer (ed.) *Queer Words, Queer Images: Communication and the Contruction of Homosexuality*, pp. 98–106. New York: New York University Press.

Rubin, Gayle (1993) [1984] "Thinking Sex" Notes for a radical Theory of the Politics of Sexuality," in Henry Abelove, Michele Aina Barale, and David Halperin (eds.) *The Lesbian and Gay Studies Reader*, pp. 3–44. New York: Routledge.

Schacter, Jane S. (1997) "Skepticism, Culture and the Gay Civil Rights Debate in Post-Civil-Rights Era," *Harvard Law Review* 110 (January): 684–731.

Seidman, Steven (1993) "Identity Politics in a 'Postmodern' Gay Culture: Some Historical and Conceptual Notes," in Michael Warner (ed.) *Fear of a Queer Planet*. Minneapolis: University of Minnesota Press.

——— (ed.) (1996) *Queer Theory/Sociology*. Cambridge, MA: Blackwell Publishers.

Shattuc, Jane (1997) *The Talking Cure: TV Talk Shows and Women.* New York: Routledge.

Stein, Arlene and Plummer, Ken (1996) "'I Can't Even Think Straight': 'Queer' Theory and the Missing Sexual Revolution in Sociology," in Steven Seidman (ed.) *Queer Theory/Sociology,* pp. 129–44. Cambridge, MA: Blackwell Publishers.

Tuchman, Gaye (1974) "Assembling a Network Talk Show," in Gaye Tuchman (ed.) *The TV Establishment: Programming for Power and Profit,* pp. 119–35. Englewood Cliffs, NJ: Prentice-Hall.

Unitel Video (1992) "Jane Whitney" (*Bisexuality,* December 17).

Vaid, Urvashi (1995) *Virtual Equality: The Mainstreaming of Gay and Lesbian Liberation.* New York: Anchor Books.

Warner, Michael, ed. (1993) *Fear of a Queer Planet.* Minneapolis: University of Minnesota Press.

Weeks, Jeffrey (1981) *Sex, Politics, and Society: The Regulation of Sexuality Since 1800.* New York: Longman.

DISCUSSION QUESTIONS: GILL

1. Many feminists interested in the media have characterized Buffy as a feminist icon, at least in the realm of the horror genre. Explain the basis of this characterization.
2. Describe the racialization processes Gill detects at work in the seven seasons of *Buffy the Vampire Slayer.*
3. Relate this critique to your favourite television series. How do you understand gender and race as social constructs organizing the plots and characterizations in that series?

DISCUSSION QUESTIONS: GAMSON

1. Explain how the visibility of gays, lesbians, bisexuals, and transgendered individuals in the media can be construed as positive social change.
2. What tactics do television show producers use when they invite these guests to participate in talk shows?
3. Discuss the conflict that has arisen between two particular subgroups of these talk show guests, paying attention to the questions of who gets to speak publicly for sexual minorities and what effect they have on larger societal relations of sexuality, class, and race.

FURTHER READINGS

1. Beck, Debra Baker. 1998. The "F" Word: How the Media Frame Feminism. *NWSA Journal,* 10(1), 139–153.
   Mainstream media tends to portray feminists and the women's movement in antagonistic ways. Beck explores how the media frames both feminism and feminists, and demonstrates the effects of that framing on people's acceptance of the movement and its goals.
2. Byerly, Carolyn, and Karen Ross. 2006. *Women and Media: A Critical Introduction.* Oxford: Blackwell Publishing.
   This monograph is a rigorously researched cross-cultural examination of the ways in which women have worked their way into, as well as outside, mainstream media organizations since the 1970s. Interviews with women media workers and activists highlight their experiences with the mainstream media, especially their efforts at organizing to improve media content and working conditions for women.

3. Lenskyj, H.J. 2003. *Out in the Field: Gender, Sport, and Sexualities.* Toronto: Women's Press.

Lenskyj draws together Canadian, American, and Australian case studies that explore the homophobia and sexual harassment enacted against women athletes by media and sports organizations.

4. Lind, Rebecca Ann (ed.). 2003. *Race/Gender/Media: Considering Diversity across Audience, Content, and Producers.* Upper Saddle River, NJ: Pearson Education.

The 44 essays collected in this book critically examine issues of race and gender in the media. Numerous topics are considered from several disciplines, including social science, cultural studies, and rhetorical studies, organized into the areas of media production, content, and reception.

5. Rose, Tricia. 1994. *Black Noise: Rap Music and Black Culture in Contemporary America.* Middleton, CT: Wesleyan University Press.

Using direct interviews with rappers, personal anecdotes, and the deconstruction of lyrics and music videos, Rose explores the sexual politics of rap. She addresses the sexism in rap lyrics and videos, as well as in the larger context of Black music production and distribution, including female rappers' critiques of this sexism.

RELEVANT FILMS

1. *And Still I Rose*, 1993, 30 minutes, Women Make Movies

The filmmaker, inspired by a poem by Maya Angelou, examines the images of Black women in the media, particularly images in popular culture. She shows how these representations are founded on myths about Black women's sexuality, which are a legacy of colonial-era scientific research on the Hottentot Venus.

2. *Carmen Miranda: Bananas Is My Business*, 1995, 92 minutes, Women Make Movies

Carmen Miranda was a Brazilian singer and Hollywood superstar in the 1940s. This film traces the story of her transformation from singer to American Latina star to independent artist, revealing the convergence of sexual politics and cultural imperialism in each stage of that transformation.

3. *Guerrillas in Our Midst*, 1992, 35 minutes, Women Make Movies

A 1980s group of feminist art terrorists called the Guerrilla Girls used unconventional tactics to bring sexism and racism to the attention of the larger art world. Their creative practices are understood as having radically changed the face of political and cultural activism.

4. *Dreamworlds 2: Desire, Sex, and Power in Music Video*, 1995, 57 minutes, Media Education Foundation

In this award-winning film that MTV attempted to ban, Sut Jhally provides a controversial look at the impact of images of sex and violence in music videos on men's and women's everyday lives. He includes scenes from almost 200 videos to demonstrate how the media portrays masculinity, femininity, and sexuality, as well as how these representations affect young people's self-images.

5. *Playing Unfair: The Media Image of the Female Athlete*, 2002, 30 minutes, Media Education Foundation

Despite 30-year-old legislation that grants equal journalistic time to the coverage of women's and men's sporting activities, the masculine world of sports journalism seems to exist in the far past. Women's sports are far less often covered than men's, and when they are the coverage tends to focus on women's femininity and sexuality rather than their athletic achievements.

RELEVANT WEB SITES

1. www.uiowa.edu/~commstud/resources/GenderMedia/index.html

The University of Iowa's "Online Communication Studies Resources" provides articles, content analyses and directories for the topic of gender, race, and ethnicity in the media. It also gives Web links in the areas of advertising, cyberspace, feminist media, print media, TV and film, and mixed media pertaining to groups such as African Americans, Asian Americans, Latin Americans, Native Americans, and the LesBiGay community.

2. http://pages.towson.edu/itrow/rgc.htm#Arts,%20Culture,%20Media,%20Sports

   This site constitutes a list of references to integrating race, gender, and class analyses in media and communication studies.

3. www.idst.vt.edu/ws/wsmodules/Gender_and_Media/MediaModule.html

   The "Gender and Media Module site" is rich with links to articles, journals, Web sites, documentaries, movies, and archives in the following areas: representations of women, film and television, print media, visual arts, music, pornography, and censorship. Sexuality, race, and class analyses are also included, as well as links to feminist art, literature, and music.

4. www.gendermediaandpolitics.org

   This Web site, called "Gender, Media, and Politics," is supported by the Social Sciences and Humanities Research Council of Canada, McGill University, and the University of New Brunswick. It is a great resource for people interested in the ways in which women in politics are represented in the media and the implications of this coverage for their electoral success. The site contains references to articles, book chapters, and conference papers on the media and women politicians in Canada.

5. www.thehoot.org/section.asp?section=S12&lang=L1&id=1

   "The Hoot" is a watchdog media organization in South Asia that reports on media activity in the subcontinent. On the "Media and Gender" portion of its site it provides up-to-date journalistic coverage of gender issues and gendered reporting in the South Asian media.

⊕ ⊕ ⊕

PART IX

THE GENDERED STATE

The state is usually defined either as a centralized set of social institutions—for instance that body which has the monopoly over legitimate coercion in a given territory to solidify its power—or in terms of its function in maintaining social cohesion. But neither of these accounts of the state, forwarded by Karl Marx and Max Weber respectively, considers the relationship between state institutions and actors and gender relations. The state is engaged with gendered political forces, its actions have gender-differentiated effects, and its structure is highly gendered. Consequently, feminists conceive the state as patriarchal, as well as capitalist, advancing the interests of both men and global capitalism.

Issues pertaining to gender and the state that have been identified by feminists include the role it plays in limiting women's access to paid work and welfare payments; criminalizing forms of fertility control (abortion and contraception); regulating the institution of marriage, in particular discriminatory income maintenance, parameters of divorce, and child custody policy; criminalizing homosexuality and denying custody of children to lesbian mothers; overlooking criminal violence against women; and implementing gender inequitable immigration and citizenship laws. In all of these ways, the state is patriarchal, meaning that it is structured in a way that its actions are more often in men's interests than in women's.

In my contribution to this reader, entitled "The Discursive Constitution of Pakistan Women: The Articulation of Gender, Nation, and Islam," I focus on the relationship between gender and the state in the context of Pakistan from its inception in 1947 to the present. I outline how the identities of Pakistani women have been historically forged through discourses of gender, nation, and Islam that are perpetuated by the Pakistani state for national purposes. More specifically, Pakistani women, who are constituted solely as wives and mothers, are used as national and religious tools in projects of nation-building and Muslim group identity construction. I detail exactly how women have been appropriated for state interests in ways that shift and change over time, as well as Pakistani women's organized resistance to gendered state appropriation.

Himani Bannerji, another Canadian feminist sociologist, expands my concerns about the gendered nature of the state in her analysis of the lives of immigrant women living in Canada. "Geography Lessons: On Being an Insider/Outsider to the Canadian Nation" constitutes a scathing critique, drawing on Bannerji's personal experience as a South Asian immigrant, of Canada as a sexist, racist, and classed entity that has been actively constructed through a White-patriarchal-capitalist national imaginary. Political constructions of Canadian citizens as White Euro-America men exclude racialized women (and men, as well as White women), dismissing them as merely "immigrants," "newcomers," "refugees," "aliens," "people of colour," and "multicultural communities." These categories place racialized Others in roles and niches of the nation that cannot project Canada. Therefore, they delimit state membership, constituting a racialized and gendered nation, as well as a citizenship crisis for those who are positioned outside the norm of "national subject."

CHAPTER 23

THE DISCURSIVE CONSTITUTION OF PAKISTANI WOMEN
The Articulation of Gender, Nation, and Islam

Nancy Cook

INTRODUCTION

Here, the women are always suffering. They give too many children birth. And they let men handle them like weak people. That's their lot. They can't be seen or heard. That's a big problem here for me, the plight of Pakistani women. (Nilofer Orange, 1999)[1]

The discourse of the passive, male-dominated Islamic "Woman" meanders through much of the interview material I gathered for my research on how western women living in Gilgit, Pakistan, negotiate their subjectivities in transcultural and postcolonial space.[2] Outside the interview transcripts, this discourse constitutes, in part, the practised subjectivities of both western and local women living and interacting in the small mountain town of Gilgit (Foucault 1978; Stoler 1995). My research participants are not alone. Many recent feminist analyses also "diagnose" the status of women in Islamic countries using such ethnocentric, homogenizing, and monocausal explanations (Brooks 1995; Ghoussoub 1987; Haddad and Smith 1996; Hasan 1995; Mohammad 1999). This occurs despite a large body of postcolonial and poststructural

feminist literature which recommends attempts to both understand how the category "Woman" is discursively constituted in specific and contingent contexts, and to identify how various discourses intersect to constitute gendered subjectivities and material practices (Frankenberg 1993; Mohanty 1984; Spivak 1985, 1988).

My aim here is to disrupt the givenness of this passive, oppressed, and unidimensional Islamic "Woman" by outlining the discursive constitution of gendered subjectivities and practices in Pakistan from 1947 to the late 1990s. Specifically, I trace the shifting intersection of discourses of gender, nationhood, and Islam during that time, demonstrating how they constitute, reproduce, and legitimate one another. Although individual Pakistani women practice these discourses in different ways depending on their situation in discourses of class, modernization, ethnicity, and location, one of the irregular regularities (Foucault 1980) of the discursive formation that results is the construction of an idealized "Pakistani Woman" who becomes available to state leaders and Islamic fundamentalists for ideological purposes. For example, when state and religious leaders restrict women to the confines of the private sphere through their politico-religious rhetoric, as well as in law, they fashion a "Pakistani Woman" almost exclusively as wife and mother. That wife and mother becomes useful in projects of nation-building and Muslim group identity construction.

Pakistani women's organized resistance to this disciplinary regime is a theme which runs unevenly throughout the paper. In the tradition of Hammani and Rieker (1988) and Sharoni (1994), I describe Pakistani women as active social participants engaged in negotiations of power as a way to undermine reified and Orientalist (Butz 1995) conceptions of homogeneous "Islamic" women as passive, helpless victims. Space limitations, however, prevent me from emphasizing Pakistani women's everyday resistance, the ways in which individual women disrupt disciplinary discourses and practices in and through their daily activities.

A brief outline of the rise of the Pakistani state will help contextualize my topic. In 1940, Mohammed Ali Jinnah, future founder of the state of Pakistan, presented the Lahore Resolution to the Muslim League, a political party founded in 1905 to advance the agendas of India's Muslim landowning class. This resolution inaugurated the Pakistan Movement, a nationalist crusade for an independent, non-theocratic Muslim state where Islam could be practised free from the constraints of the British government and Hindu-oriented Indian National Congress. The agenda of the Muslim League, similar to that of other colonized groups attempting to reassert a Muslim identity through nationhood, was grounded primarily in anti-colonialism (Shaheed 1986). The British Raj imposed on its colonial subjects laws and practices that left little room for Muslim colonial subjects to satisfactorily practice Islam in their daily lives (Hasan 1981). Jinnah incorporated a sense of beleaguered Muslim identity, along with growing dissent against British rule and the West more generally, into his fight for independence and an oppositional national identity. In his efforts to forge a common Muslim front, Jinnah consistently represented Muslim women as a vital nationalist resource.

Jinnah shared this practice of constructing and appropriating women for nation-building purposes with many other nationalist leaders in South Asia and elsewhere. Yuval-Davis and Anthias (1989), in their study of women's relation to national processes and state practices, provide a useful typology for understanding the historically contingent intersection of discourses of gender and nationhood. They identify five ways that women have been discursively constituted and utilized by nation-state leaders as (a) biological reproducers of state members, (b) propagators and defenders of the frontiers between nations, (c) transmitters of culture who socialize youth into the ideological framework of the nation, (d) signifiers of national difference, and (e) participants in national liberation struggles. An overview of the historical development of the Pakistani state reveals that various political leaders have drawn unevenly on these discursive complexes to support their nation- and identity-building agendas.

In the body of the paper, I augment this typology by outlining how discourses of Islam, including Islamic fundamentalism, have frequently mediated the coupling of discourses on gender and nationhood in Pakistan. This three-way intersection has strengthened the disciplinary regime and its effects on Pakistani women. However, since discursive formations are contingent and marked by series of ruptures and recuperations, this gender-nation-Islam trilogy has shifted with changing state mandates, with the effect that new discursive spaces, where tangential discourses can influence the discursive formation, are continually emerging and disappearing.

WOMAN-NATION-ISLAM

Women as Biological Reproducers of State Members

Several Pakistani political regimes have constructed Pakistani women as biological reproducers of the national collectivity. In the Pakistan Independence Movement of the 1940s, Jinnah represented Muslim women as "mothers of the nation" who embodied special, although politically limited, power. Willmer (1996) argues that this discursive use of women for the Muslim nationalist cause was constructed within a set of existing discourses of gender and modernization, which used the status of elite women to evaluate the modernizing potential of a polity. Thus, discourses of gender, nationhood, Islam, and modernization intersected in the Muslim League agenda. By incorporating these discourses into their program, the Muslim League's quest for emancipation from the Raj and the Indian National Congress gained ancillary social meaning. This alliance also meant that the concerns of elite Muslim women were coopted into the national checklist, thereby quelling the development of a modernizing feminist movement.

Jinnah encouraged all women to renounce their needs and interests, and those of their children, to support the development of a more glorious Islam. In a speech he gave on Radio Pakistan in 1948, he stressed that privileged women should take the lead, "not only in their homes, but by helping their less fortunate sisters outside in that great task" (as quoted in Hasan 1981, 71). This discourse constructs for women an identity as mothers and wives who nurture, support, socialize, and sacrifice for the good of the nation. Women were persuaded to confine themselves to the parameters of home and family in their support of nationalism, something the overwhelming majority of Muslim women assured Jinnah they were willing to do. As Hatem (1993, 45) notes in another context, "women's incorporation in the body politic as citizens is premised on their acceptance of nationalism as the only acceptable discourse."

Although Pakistani women were constituted as wives and mothers sacrificing for the Muslim nation, elite women within the Muslim League, including Mohtarma Fatima Jinnah (Jinnah's sister), had the discursive and spatial latitude during the parliamentary period of Pakistan's history (1947–57) to promote women's rights and public participation (Haq 1996). This latitude widened during successive governments, as the intersection of discourses of gender, nationhood, and modernization coalesced more confidently, shifting discourses of Islam to the sidelines. For example, Ayub Khan, who gained power through a military coup in 1958, and Zulifkar Ali Bhutto (1969–77) after

him, concentrated on modernizing Pakistan, identifying the status of women as an important gauge of their success. They both passed legislation, including the 1973 constitution, that gave women greater rights in marriage, divorce, educational opportunities, family planning, and employment.[3] In 1977, with General Zia-ul-Haq's (1977–1988) military coup, the formation of gender-nationhood-modernization shifted abruptly. Discourses of Islam were recuperated at the expense of modernization, although their nature altered radically.

In an effort to justify martial law, which lacked a social base of support (Gardezi 1985), Zia initiated a process of Islamization with the help of right-wing religious fundamentalist parties such as the *Jama'at-l-Islamii*. These fundamentalists claimed that anything "modern" was a tool of Western imperialism. In opposition to the "modern," they argued that the foundation of Islamic society lay in the sexual segregation of women and the reciprocal obligation of the sexes. This alternative socio-moral order could, simultaneously combat neo-colonialism and reassert a "true" Muslim identity (Haeri 1995). By promoting notions of a unified religion and national identity, as well as the moral honour of Islam, Islamic fundamentalism became the most influential discursive legitimation of Zia's military rule.

Zia exploited this reactionary form of Islam to justify destroying civil society and implementing oppressive laws. Legislative changes, including family planning restrictions and anti-abortion legislation, renewed and strengthened the discursive constitution of women as biological reproducers of the nation. Islamization policies reinforced the ideal of women's segregation in the home. For example, working women were constructed as liabilities due to their "lax" morality, which ostensibly disintegrated national, Muslim, and family values.

The *Hudood Ordinance* (1979), which narrowed the criteria for rape and included fornication and adultery in the criminal code, provided the legal context within which women were disciplined—by themselves, their families, and the state—to remain within the confines of their homes where they were less likely to be raped

(Mehdi 1990).[4] The law disciplines women's behaviour and spatial movement by constructing a vulnerable female identity in need of protection from strange men by male family members. Women are encouraged to remain safe at home, raising children in a segregated family setting.[5]

Zia's dictatorship roused Pakistani women to organized resistance. Despite the difficult climate for protest, urban middle-class women began to study the Quran for themselves, determined to reinterpret it as an empowering ideology rather than an oppressive one (Ayubi 1995). They also challenged Zia's junta by inaugurating an official Pakistan women's movement in 1981 with the formation of the Women's Action Forum (WAF). By uniting numerous women's groups under the WAF banner, feminists were able to organize a collective struggle and set the tone for debates over the status of women under martial and Islamic rule (Gardezi 1990). They were, however, ultimately unsuccessful in halting Zia's Islamization program. I will discuss his tenacious legacy in the 1990s later in the paper.

Women as Propagators and Defenders of the Frontiers between Nations

Pakistani women have also been constructed through state legislation as reproducers of national boundaries. The symbolic and material manifestations of nationhood are most strongly expressed through the allocation of citizenship, a process that is gendered throughout much of the world, including Pakistan (Joseph 1996). The state needs to specify who can claim legitimate citizenship, because potential citizens identify with multiple social groupings, many of which may pose a threat to the boundaries and identity of the nation. The state frequently draws on discourses of gender, as well as class, ethnicity, and religion, to differentiate between members of the polity and thus establish national boundaries.

Forging a Muslim, anti-Western national identity remained a state imperative during the first few years of Pakistan's independence. State leaders recognized that establishing strong national boundaries would buttress this objective.

The *Pakistan Citizenship Act* was passed in 1951. It was a law that consolidated intersecting discourses of gender, nationhood, and Islam to constitute Pakistani women as reproducers of the national frontier. The *Citizenship Act* prohibited Muslim women who married foreign or non-Muslim men from passing their Pakistani citizenship to their children, but it permitted the children of Muslim men married to non-Muslim women to become nationals. The legislation controlled the manner in which Pakistani women had children by stipulating that legitimate Pakistani nationals be born to a father of "authentic" Muslim identity. Since children gained citizenship and its attendant rights through their fathers and not their mothers, an explicit connection was forged between fathers and national citizenship (Joseph 1996). Pakistani women were denied the right to pass citizenship to children of non-Muslim fathers in order to enforce a national Muslim boundary and male citizenry. They became nationals only as appendages of their husbands and fathers. Through the process of conferring citizenship rights, the state constituted and utilized women as reproducers of the boundaries of the Islamic nation, while denying them citizenship as an autonomous right.

In April, 2000, General Pervez Musharraf's government amended Section 5 of the 1951 *Act* under the Pakistan Citizenship (Amendment) Ordinance 2000. The Ordinance provides that the children of Pakistani women married to non-Muslim men are also entitled to Pakistani citizenship. This releases women from their role as national frontier scouts and loosens slightly the gender-nation-Islam discursive trilogy.

Women as Transmitters of National Culture

By framing Pakistani women as "mothers of the nation," Jinnah implicitly represented them as "cultural transmitters of the nation." He drew on discourses of gender, nationhood, and Islam to constitute women as wives and mothers confined to the private sphere. As such, women were constructed as the main socializers of youth, those people responsible for perpetuating

Muslim cultural symbols and ways of life. Discourses of modernization that gained political purchase after Jinnah disrupted the discursive formation of gender-nationhood-Islam and produced discursive space within which some women could practice supplementary identities outside the home, loosening, however slightly, their exclusive tie to children. Zia's Islamization project, drawing on Islamic fundamentalism, coerced women back home to take up full-time duty as ideological reproducers.

Zia's 1984 *Law of Evidence*, for example, stipulates that the court requires evidence from two men or one man and two women for the conviction of a crime, reifying in legislation the notion that women's minds function at only half the capacity of men's (Doumato 1995). The law works from the premise that women's reproductive and socializing function renders them unsuitable for public responsibilities such as political and labour participation and, consequently, that their main value is as wives and mothers who socialize youth into Islamic culture.

Male household heads frequently utilize and legitimate these circulating discourses of gender and Islam to deny many non-elite women academic opportunities, or at least strongly dissuade them from pursuing their studies. They argue against women's education according to the logic that academic endeavours interfere with women's primary role as wives and mothers, that women's public and economic participation is culturally inappropriate, and that women ought to be obedient in most circumstances (Moghadam 1993). The discourse of women's obedience is premised on the notion that they surrender their rights to some realms of independent thought, action, and expression, including educational and employment opportunities. The low literacy level among Pakistani women (Malik 1995)—one effect of intersecting discourses of gender and Islam—traps women in the home where they remain economically and psychologically dependent.

Women's coerced entrapment in the home is somewhat paradoxical considering the profile of fundamentalists who exhorted it. Contrary to popular belief, fundamentalists in Pakistan tend not to be theological experts, but young, semi-worldly rural men who have migrated to the city in search of work, but whose lack of education and limited resources leave them disenfranchised in the urban social, economic, and political spheres (Ayubi 1995; Stowasser 1993). They are populist "scriptural activists" whose agenda is to transpose Islamic thought into holy practice with the view of establishing more egalitarian social relations; a fundamentally political, not religious, act (Stowasser, 1993). Fundamentalist notions of egalitarianism, however, do not extend to women, since they are constructed as the inviolate foundation of Islamic society.

The extremely discriminatory *Law of Evidence* incited Pakistani women to mass protest on a scale previously unprecedented in Pakistan. The WAF demonstrated their dissatisfaction with the draft bill through public lectures, discussion groups, resolutions, and artistic performances. The protest reached its climax in February, 1983, when women's organizations united in a demonstration march down Mall Road in Lahore. They planned to end their walk with a sit-in near the Court House, where the Chief Justice would hear their singing and poetry reading and be compelled to accept a formal memorandum against the draft legislation. Despite the peacefulness of the demonstration, the sheer number of women protesting unnerved the police. They surrounded the protesters, discharged tear gas, beat them until many were seriously injured, and arrested 50 women. Rather than vanquishing the protesters, this public "attention" impelled them to further action and greater solidarity.[6] Their continuing resistance to the *Law of Evidence* forced the government to delay implementing the bill for two years; it was eventually ratified in October, 1984.

Women as Signifiers of National Difference

Taking the previous intersection of discourses of gender, nationhood, and Islamic fundamentalism a step further, Zia cast Pakistani women as actual symbolic markers of the nation. These "women do not only teach and transfer cultural and ideological traditions of [the] national group, they constitute [its] actual symbolic figuration" (Yuval-Davis and Anthias 1989, 8). Through their constitution as wives and mothers, Pakistani women become both an alibi for, and an emblem of, cultural authenticity. By appropriating Islamist anti-imperialist discourses and advocating an "authentic" Muslim identity, Zia drew a cultural distinction on the actual bodies of Pakistani women, through their spatial movements and sexual behaviour. Women's "sexually appropriate" behaviour became legally and morally controlled since women were viewed as the touchstone of what it meant to be Muslim. This preoccupation with women's sexual and moral behaviour stems from the fact that "the woman question" constitutes one of the few Quranic legislative domains, and, moreover, from the fundamentalist conviction that "good" Muslims should be readily identifiable through appropriate clothing styles, polygamy practices, and adultery regulations (Keddie 1990). According to fundamentalists, women who reclaim for themselves the appropriate role of wife and mother re-establish an Islamic socio-moral order. Women's dress, domesticity, and behaviour thus constitute what Keddie calls an Islamic "badge of ideology" (101). In Stowasser's (1993, 22) words, "culture, religion, and morality stand and fall with [Muslim women]."

Purdah is one institutionalized form of restrictive behavioural codes for women. This social and spatial system of sexual segregation, where women are isolated from men who are not family members, was endorsed by Zia to ensure women's economic dependence on male family members and assure their "function" as wives and mothers. Moreover, *purdah* "protected" women from the dangers of the public sphere, while it safeguarded family honour by maintaining female modesty.

Rauf (1987) identifies four principles upon which *purdah* is founded: (a) women must not mingle with men who are not part of their immediate kinship network; (b) females should be physically sequestered from the time of puberty; (c) men bear the responsibility for being family breadwinners while women reproduce the extended household; and (d) women must dress, move, behave, think, and represent themselves

in culturally appropriate ways. Moral responsibility, therefore, rests mainly with women. These principles are instituted through the division of space (between the inside and outside of the home, and the male and female places within it) and the mandated use of a veil.

In Pakistan veiling takes diverse forms, from the scarf-like *dupatta* to the head-to-toe covering *burqa*. And, as a signifier, it has a range of meanings, depending on the social and political context in which it is used. While fundamentalists prefer women to veil completely in public as a sign of their Muslim identity, modesty, and sexual-spatial segregation, Pakistani women, like their Muslim counterparts elsewhere, veil to varying degrees and with varied meaning: to (a) be non-arousing, (b) promote an erotic culture, (c) protect themselves from sexual harassment in public, (d) express urbanism and their escape from the village (where veiling may be less common), (e) disguise their lower-class clothing, (f) support fundamentalist movements, reject western values, and assert nationalism, (g) garner sympathetic public reaction and comply with group norms, (h) pursue a career that they might not otherwise be permitted, and (i) signify their class status (Abu-Odeh 1992; Afshar 1994; Bulbeck 1998; Hammami and Rieker 1988; Mohammad 1999). Although many Pakistani women lead quite segregated lives according to the rules of *purdah*, most do not and cannot, follow strict clothing and boundary directives due to economic and labour materialities. Consequently, the *dupatta* and the *chaddor* are more common in Pakistan than is the *burqa*.

Despite its flexibility of meaning, Hammami and Rieker (1988, 93) argue that "the veil continues to signify its most historically constant meaning—class." Privileged women in Pakistan, who have access to often sizeable economic resources, are more rigorously regulated through *purdah* than most working- and middle-class women (Shaheed 1986). *Purdah* restrictions are frequently applied more strictly to women in feudal, landowning rural families to deny them access to their resources and the public sphere where they could mobilise them against both the men of their class and the dominant class monopoly of property ownership. However, some lower middle-class urban women also chose to follow stricter *purdah* regulations to distinguish themselves from working-class women (Shaheed 1986).

As part of his Muslim identity- and nation-building strategy, Zia drew a cultural distinction between Pakistan and the West on the actual bodies of Pakistani women. He reinforced and extrapolated the principles of *purdah*, a prevalent social/class system, as part of his agenda to re-establish an Islamic socio-moral order. By controlling women's spatial movements and sexual behaviour, Zia constituted them as the touchstone of what it meant to be a "good" Muslim. Whether most veiled Pakistan women actually constructed themselves as Islamic "badges of ideology," or merely covered themselves as a way to move unimpeded in public, get an education, or cover their shabby clothes, is open to question.

Women as Participants in National Liberation Struggles

During the Pakistan Movement and the early years of the new state, Jinnah consistently drew elite women into the struggle for a non-theocratic Muslim state. In so doing, he strengthened the intersection of discourses of gender, nationhood, and Islam. As part of his strategy of mobilizing Muslim women to the nationalist cause, he toured with his sister Fatima, advocating the organization of women's branches of the Muslim League in major urban centres, and foregrounding both his support of women's rights and his contempt for their subordinate position in society.

However, Jinnah and other Muslim League leaders deliberately constructed a Pakistan Movement narrative that mobilized women politically without ever promising them official political positions within the proposed nation (Willmer 1996). Once the state was formed, Pakistani women discovered that the Muslim League never intended to engage discourses of modernization as seriously as those of nationhood. The Pakistan Movement coopted elite women's concerns without forming any specific agenda for women. This

neglect marginalized women's concerns with the framework of the new state, and allowed Jinnah to constitute "modernization" for women within an Islamic national framework. For example, while he called on women to contribute to the national effort, they were asked to do so only in "appropriate" ways, as nurturers and supporters of the cause and its implicitly male citizenry. Women were posted in the Pakistan Women's National Guard and the Pakistan Women's Naval Reserve, but primarily to support and nurture men, by signalling, typing, and administering first aid (Mumtaz and Shaheed 1987). By drawing selectively on discourses of gender, modernization, nationhood, and Islam, Jinnah constituted Pakistani women as vital participants in the struggle for national liberation and resources for Muslim identity construction, without allowing that to outweigh the needs of nation or Islam.

ZIA'S LEGACY

As discourses of Islam mediate the coupling of discourses of gender and nationhood in Pakistan, disciplinary effects on Pakistani women are strengthened. However, ruptures to this discursive formation, realized through discourses of modernization during the middle period of Pakistan's history, left some women room to manoeuvre. Zia's program of Islamization, by rejecting discourses of modernization as Western imperialism, re-entrenched the gender-nationhood-Islam trilogy. And that discursive formation has been difficult to rupture in the years following Zia's rule.

Martial law was replaced by a pluralistic democracy after Zia's murder in 1988. Citizens angered by Zia's tyranny elected Benazir Bhutto (1988–90), who promised to continue her father's modernizing agenda. That a woman was elected prime minister indicated both a widespread dissatisfaction with Zia's Islamization program and elite women's discursive latitude within it. Not surprisingly, Bhutto was unable to repeal many of Zia's initiatives, despite her campaign promises to abolish the *Hudood Ordinance*. The fundamentalist *Jama'at-I-Islami* continued to exercise power due to its state ties. Bhutto maintained a defensive position vis-à-vis the fundamentalists who questioned her credibility as a female Muslim leader. The consolidation of discourses of gender, nationhood, and Islam in law and socio-cultural practice was also difficult to disrupt, as was the power of the military (backed by US military and economic aid) (Gardezi 1985). These factors frustrated Bhutto's efforts to steer a moderate course. She managed, however, to appoint women judges, open banks and police stations for women, restore freedom of the press, and draw women out of the home and back into public and political participation (Haq 1996).

In contrast to Bhutto, Main Nawaz Sharif (1990–93, 1997–99), leader first of the Islamic Democratic Alliance and later the Muslim League, made the *Jama'at-I-Islami* party an integral component of his coalition government to combat political instability and legitimate his rule. He resumed the process of Islamization begun by Zia and recuperated the trilogy once again. Specifically, he concentrated on making institutions and social arrangements conform to *Shari'a*, the traditional socio-religious law of Islam. Women's sexual and moral behaviour was state-monitored again as Sharif strengthened the Ordinances and censored female cultural representations (Pakistan News Service Nov. 2, 1997). In protest, Pakistani women formed Women Against Rape (1990) and challenged the Shariat Bill and a plan for separate women's universities.

Nawaz Sharif's government was overthrown through a military coup in October, 1999, and Pakistan is presently ruled by Chief Executive General Pervez Musharraf. Unlike the military leaders before him, Musharraf is sidelining repressive discourses of Islam in favour of those active during Bhutto's leadership. He has vowed to fight honour killings and violence against women, promote female literacy, encourage women's public participation, and, most importantly, modify the *Hudood Ordinance* (Pakistan News Service, Sept. 6, 2000; Pakistan News Service, Oct. 22, 2000). However, fundamentalists still exercise considerable power and influence throughout the country, especially through their support of the Taliban in Afghanistan (Pakistan News Service, Nov. 3, 2000).

Recently Musharraf inducted two religious scholars (*ulema*) into the National Commission for Women. Leaders of WAF criticize the appointments as a policy to appease "extremist and hardline parties" (Pakistan News Service, Sept. 7, 2000). Although Musharraf s government is not yet democratically run or elected, the discourses of Islam he is circulating may provide Pakistani women with fresh manoeuvring space.

CONCLUSION

I have attempted to follow the theoretical guidance of postcolonial and poststructural feminists in demonstrating the contingent and multifaceted discursive constitution of gendered subjectivities and practices in Pakistan through time. To understand more adequately the intersection of discourses of gender and nationhood in the process of subjectification, I augmented the typology outlined by Yuval-Davis and Anthias to demonstrate how discourses of Islam, appropriated and legitimated by non-theocratic and fundamentalist state leaders, have mediated this coupling. Tracing the shifting intersection of discourses of gender, nationhood, and Islam allowed me to avoid monocausal and homogenizing explanations of Pakistani women's situation in, constitution by, and resistance to discourses of power. It also demonstrated how the discursive formation of gender-nation-Islam fashions an ideological tool—the ideal Pakistani "Woman"—who is then utilized by state and religious leaders for nation- and Muslim identity-building practices.

This three-way intersection, which is characterized by various ruptures and recuperations over time, has had important but uneven disciplinary effects on Pakistani women. While political leaders like Zia-ul-Haq and Nawaz Sharif tightened the gender-nation-Islam trilogy through their appropriation of Islamic fundamentalism, others, such as Ayub Khan, Benazir Bhutto, and her father Zulifkar Ali Bhutto, loosened it through state mandates for modernization. What is most troubling about the uneven confluence of discourses of gender, nationhood, and Islamic fundamentalism is its tenacity in the context of continuing neo-colonialism and the persistent oppressive effects it has, with varying degrees, on Pakistani women.

But Pakistani women continue to resist this disciplinary regime. Recent debates in the literature (Gardezi 1990; Mumtaz and Shaheed 1987; Rouse 1988; Shaheed, 1995) illustrate the controversy between two prominent feminist agendas. Leaving explicit questions of nationalism aside, one feminist group argues that the struggle against gender oppression must engage discourses of Islam since they fundamentally constitute Pakistani culture, legitimate Pakistani feminism, and appeal to working- and lower middle-class women who have not participated widely in feminist struggles. Another group asserts that gender oppression is a secular issue of human rights. Shaheed's (1995) research identifies two factors that support a non-Islamic feminist agenda. First, many Pakistani women, despite viewing Islam as a participatory and communal spiritual experience, can be mobilized around a feminist critique of gender oppression independent of Islam. And second, the Islam practised by many Pakistani women does not resemble that preached by fundamentalists. This is well illustrated in fundamentalist parties' poor electoral showings in recent years. By nesting feminist demands in Islam justifications, feminists risk fundamentalist control of their movement by suggesting implicitly that all debates about women must be conducted in religious terms. This action undermines secular debates, which view women's emancipation as a worthy and valuable cause in itself, and constructs feminist activism as "alien" to Pakistani culture.

Despite these problematic elements of Islamic feminism, some feminist scholars (Kar 1996; Shaheed 1995) have argued recently that secular demands need not, and should not, be placed in a binary opposition to religious discourses. Rather than mobilizing one unified women's movement, a multifaceted approach to the struggle, realized through a network of independent groups and individual practice, may generate the momentum and altered subjectivities required to disrupt the gender-nation-Islam trilogy. This strategy, which involves deconstructing women's primary constitution as wives and mothers by state and religious leaders and establishing women as full legal and social beings, may be the most effective route to feminist advances in Pakistan.

ENDNOTES

1. My research participant's pseudonym is Nilofer Orange.

2. I conducted eight months of ethnographic fieldwork in Gilgit, northern Pakistan in 1999 and 2000. My research explores how disciplinary complexes that operate cross-culturally constitute the bodies and subjectivities of foreigners and locals in contemporary transcultural space. Specifically, I attempt to decipher how western women reproduce and legitimate imperialism as they negotiate their and "Others'" subjectivities in Gilgit. They do so, in part, by drawing on the Orientalist discourse of the passive, unidimensional Islamic "Woman." I write the paper to disrupt this discourse (in both practised and written form) and thereby undermine its imperialistic effects.

3. Khan eventually lost some of his credibility as the defender of women's rights during the 1965 election when he questioned the suitability of Fatima Jinnah's candidacy as the leader of the Combined Opposition Parties, arguing that a woman-headed Muslim state was un-Islamic.

4. Mehdi argues that most reported cases of rape in Pakistan, unlike those in the West, are perpetrated by men whom the victims do not know.

5. This less conspicuous intent of the *Ordinance* is echoed in other fundamentalist legislation based on the *Shari'a*, which identifies women's rights under Islam (and consequently their social contribution) as claims to male guardianship, full care in the home, children, house-task education, and the honour of preserving Muslim culture. See Doumato, E. 1995.

6. See Mumtaz, K. and F. Shaheed (1987) for a complete list of the dates and actions taken by women against the *Law of Evidence*.

REFERENCES

Abu-Odeh, L. "Post-colonial Feminism and the Veil: Considering the Differences," *New England Law Review*, 26.4 (1992): 1527–1537.

Afshar, H. "Muslim Women in West Yorkshire: Growing up with Real and Imaginary Values amidst Conflicting Views of Self and Society," *The Dynamics of "Race" and Gender—Some Feminist Interventions*. H. Afshar and M. Maynard, eds. London: Taylor and Francis, 1994.

Ayubi, N. "Rethinking the Public/Private Dichotomy: Radical Islamism and Civil Society in the Middle East," *Contention*, 28 (1995): 79–105.

Brooks, G. *Nine Parts of Desire: The Hidden World of Islamic Women*. New York: Anchor Books, 1995.

Bulbeck, C. *Re-orienting Western Feminisms: Women's Diversity in a Postcolonial World*. Cambridge: Cambridge University Press, 1998.

Butz, D. "Revisiting Edward Said's Orientalism." *Brock Review*, 4.1/2 (1995): 52–80.

Doumato, E. "The Ambiguity of Shari'a and the Politics of 'Rights' in Saudi Arabia," *Faith and Freedom: Women's Human Rights in the Muslim World*. M. Afkhami, ed. New York: Syracuse. 1995.

Foucault, M. *History of Sexuality*. New York: Vintage Books. 1978.

———. *Power / Knowledge: Selected Interviews and Other Writings, 1972–1977*. New York: Pantheon. 1980.

Frankenberg, R. *White Women, Race Matters: The Social Construction of Whiteness*. Minneapolis: University of Minnesota Press, 1993.

Gardezi, F. "Islam, Feminism, and the Women's Movement in Pakistan: 1981–1991." *South Asia Bulletin*, 102 (1990): 18–24.

Gardezi, H. "The Postcolonial State in South Asia: The Case of Pakistan." *South Asia Bulletin*, 5 2 (1985): 1–7.

Ghoussoub, M. "Feminism—or the Eternal Masculine—in the Arab World," *New Left Review*, 161 (1987).

Haddad, Y. and J. Smith. "Women in Islam: The Mother of All Battles," *Arab Women: Between Defiance and Restraint*. S. Subbagh, ed. New York: Olive Branch Press, 1996.

Haeri, S. "Of Feminism and Fundamentalism in Iran and Pakistan." *Contention*, 4.3 (1995): 129–49.

Hammani, R. and M. Rieker. "Feminist Orientalism and Orientalist Marxism," *New Left Review*, 170 (1988): 93–106.

Haq, F. "Women, Islam and the State of Pakistan," *The Muslim World*, 86.1 (1996): 158–75.

Hasan, R. "The Role of Women as Agents of Change and Development in Pakistan," *Human Rights Quarterly*, 3.3 (1981): 68–75.

———. "Rights of Women in Islamic Countries," *Canadian Women's Studies*, 15.2/3 (1995): 40–44.

Hatem, M. "Toward the Development of Post-Islamist and Post-Nationalist Feminist Discourses in the Middle East," *Arab Women: Old Boundaries, New Frontiers*. J. Tucker, ed. Indianapolis: Indiana University Press, 1993.

Joseph, S. "Gender and Citizenship in Middle Eastern States," *Middle East Report*, 198 (1996): 4–10.

Kar, M. "Women and Personal Status Law in Middle Eastern States," *Middle East Report*, Jan–Mar (1996): 36–9.

Keddie, N. "The Present and the Past of Women in the Muslim World," *Journal of World History*, 1.1 (1990): 77–108.

Malik, L. "Social and Cultural Determinants of the Gender Gap in Higher Education in the Islamic World," *Journal of Asian and African Studies*, 30.3/4 (1995): 81–193.

Medhi, R. "The Offense of Rape in the Islamic Law of Pakistan," *International Journal of Sociology of Law*, 18.1 (1990): 19–29.

Moghadam, V. "Patriarchy and the Politics of Gender in Modernizing Societies: Iran, Pakistan, and Afghanistan," *South Asian Bulletin* 13.1/2 (1993): 122–33.

Mohammad, R. "Marginalisation, Islamism and the Production of the 'Other's' 'Other'," *Gender, Place and Culture*, 6.3 (1999): 221–240.

Mohanty, C. "Under Western Eyes: Feminist Scholarship and Colonial Discourses," *Boundary* 2, 12.3/13.1 (1984): 333–353.

Mumtaz, K. and F. Shaheed. *Women of Pakistan: Two Steps Forward, One Back?* London: Zed Books, 1987.

Pakistan News Service. Http://www.paknews.com, 13(M31), November 2, 1997.

Http://www.paknews.com, 10(N246), September 6, 2000.

Http://www.paknews.com, 10(N247), September 7, 2000.

Http://www.paknews.com, 10(N292), October 22, 2000.

Http://www.paknews.com 10(N304), November 3, 2000.

Rauf, A. "Rural Women and the Family: A Study of a Punjabi Village in Pakistan," *Journal of Comparative Family Studies*, 18.3 (1987): 403–415.

Rouse, S. "Women, Religion, and the State," *South Asian Bulletin*, 8(1988): 54–8.

Shaheed, F. "The Cultural Articulation of Patriarchy: Legal Systems, Islam, and Women," *South Asia Bulletin*, 6.1 (1986): 38–44.

_____. "Networking for Change: The Role of Women's Groups in Initiating Dialogue on Women's Issues," *Faith and Freedom: Women's Human Rights in the Muslim World*. M. Afkhami, ed. New York: Syracuse University Press, 1995.

Sharoni, S. "Homefront as Battlefield: Gender, Military' Occupation, and Violence against Women," *Women and the Israeli Occupation: The Politics of Change*. T. Mayer, ed. London: Routledge, 1994.

Spivak, G. "Three Women's Texts and a Critique of Imperialism," *Critical Inquiry*, 12.1 (1985): 243–61.

_____. "Can the Subaltern Speak?" *Marxism and the Interpretation of Culture*. C. Nelson and L. Grossberg. London: Macmillan, 1988.

Stoler, A. *Race and the Education of Desire: Foucault's History of Sexuality and the Colonial Order of Things*. Durham: Duke University Press, 1995.

Stowasser, B. "Women's Issues in Modern Islamic Thought," *Arab Women: Old Boundaries, New Frontiers*. J. Tucker, ed. Indianapolis: Indiana University Press, 1993.

Willmer, D. "Women as Participants in the Pakistan Movement: Modernization and the Promise of a Moral State," *Modern Asian Studies*, 30.3 (1996): 573–590.

Yuval-Davis, N. and F. Anthias. *Woman-Nation-State*. New York: St. Martin's Press, 1989.

CHAPTER 24

GEOGRAPHY LESSONS
On Being an Insider/Outsider to the Canadian Nation

Himani Bannerji

My first encounter with Canada occurred during my geography lessons as a young girl. There, in an atlas of physical geography, coloured green, pink, and yellow, I came across Canada—a place of trees, lakes, wheat fields, ice caps, and an ancient rock formation cut through with glaciers. I don't remember reading anything of the history of this country in my geography book, but somehow there were faint echoes of people and nature blurring into each other—"red Indians," "eskimos," "igloos," "aurora borealis," and "reindeer." From where did these images come if not from my geography book? From literature and scattered visual images perhaps? There were, after all, the books of Fenimore Cooper or Jack London, which irrespective of national boundaries created mythologies of the "North," the "Indian," and wove tales of discovery of the Arctic—of Amundsen and others lost in blizzards on their dog sleds. Eventually, on my fourteenth birthday, I received a book called *The Scalpel and the Sword*, and I decided to be a doctor, like Norman Bethune.

What I am trying to recount is what Canada meant for me—all this jumbled-up information, this fusion of people and nature, my imagination moved by forests and the glow of Arctic ice. Certainly, "Canada" was a mental rather than a historical space. It was an idyllic construction of nature and adventure.

Many years later, the Canada I stepped into was vastly different from the Canada I had constructed in my childhood. When I immigrated to Montreal, I stepped out of my romantic construction of Canada and into a distinctly political-ideological one—one which impressed me as being both negative and aggressive. From the insistence and harshness with which I was asked whether I intended to apply for "landing"—a term I did not understand and that had to be explained—I knew that I was not welcome in this "Canada." I told the officer defiantly that this would never be my country; I had come as a foreign student and would leave upon receiving my degree. That is how it has remained to this day. Had I been received differently, had I been made to feel more "at home," would this be my home, my Canada?

This remains a hypothetical question, since upon "landing" six years later and being labelled an "immigrant," a "visible minority woman," I have remained in limbo. Even after years of being an "immigrant," and upon swearing allegiance to the same Queen of England from whom India had parted, I was not to be a "Canadian." Regardless of my official status as a Canadian citizen, I, like many others, remained an "immigrant." The category "Canadian" clearly applied to people who had two things in common: their white skin and their European North American (not Mexican) background. They did not all speak English. There were two colors in this political atlas—one a beige-brown shading off into black and the other white. These shades did not simply reflect skin colors—they reflected the ideological, political, and cultural assumptions and administrative practices of the Canadian State.

"Canada" then cannot be taken as a given. It is obviously a construction, a set of representations, embodying certain types of political and cultural communities and their operations. These communities were themselves constructed in agreement with certain ideas regarding skin color, history, language (English/French), and other cultural signifiers—all of which may be subsumed under the ideological category "white."[1] A "Canada" constructed on this basis contains certain notions of nation, state formation, and economy. Europeanness as "whiteness"[2] thus translates into "Canada" and provides it with its "imagined community." This is a process that Benedict Anderson (1991) speaks of, but he glosses over the divisiveness of class, "race," and ideology—the irreconcilable contradictions at the heart of this community-nation-state project. Furthermore, he does not ask about the type of imagination at work in this project. He does not ask either *whose* imagination is advanced as the national imaginary or what this has to do with organizing practical and ideological exclusions and inclusions within the national space. These questions become concrete if we look at how I was received in Canada. Why was I thus received? Was it just an accident? An isolated instance? What did it have to do with *who* I was—my so-called gender and race? Did this story of mine begin with my arrival, or was I just a tiny episode in a pre-existing historical narrative? Can I or similar "others" imagine a "Canada" and project it as the national imaginary?

So if we problematize the notion of "Canada" through the introjection of the idea of belonging, we are left with the paradox of both belonging and non-belonging simultaneously. As a population, we non-whites and women (in particular, non-white women) are living in a specific territory. We are part of its economy, subject to its laws, and members of its civil society. Yet we are not part of its self-definition as "Canada" because we are not "Canadians." We are pasted over with labels that give us identities that are extraneous to us. And these labels originate in the ideology of the nation, in the Canadian state apparatus, in the media, in the education system, and in the commonsense world of common parlance. We ourselves use them. They are familiar, naturalized names: visible minorities, immigrants, newcomers, refugees, aliens, illegals, people of color, multicultural communities, and so on. We are sexed into immigrant women, women of colour, visible minority women, black/South Asian/Chinese women, ESL (English as second language) speakers, and many more.[3] The names keep proliferating, as though there were a seething reality, unmanageable and uncontainable in any one name. Concomitant with this mania for the naming of "others" is one for the naming of that which is "Canadian." This "Canadian" core community is defined through the same process that others us. We, with our named and ascribed otherness, face an undifferentiated notion of the "Canadian" as the unwavering beacon of our assimilation.

And what is the function of the many names applied to us? They are categories for organizing the state apparatus, its regulations and policy functions, and for enabling the ideological organization of "relations of ruling."[4] These categories enable the state to extend its governing and administrative jurisdiction into civil society, while, at the same time, incorporating the everyday person into the national project. One might say, then, remembering Althusser, that they are appellations for interpellation.[5] These names are codes for political subjectivities and ideological/pedagogical possibilities, and they have embedded in them both immediate and long-term political effects. They help to construct "Canada" and to place us in certain roles and niches of the nation; and those who are not "Canadians" cannot directly project "Canada." This "Canada's" placement of "others," because it creates feelings of belonging and alienation, not only produces psychological and cultural problems regarding power, but is also integral to the structure of the Canadian polity itself. Its categories of otherness delimit the membership of this nation and this state (Ng, 1993). This situation reveals not only a raced or ethnicized state, but also—more importantly—a crisis in citizenship and a continual attempt to manage this crisis. It tells us that, in the polity of Canadian liberal democracy, there is always already a crisis of gender, race, and class. This becomes obvious if we look at the status of women, in particular the status of white women, in terms of their participation in the construction of "Canada." Their protracted struggle for enfranchisement, for inclusion in the nation, is marked by the fact that their gender was a barrier to them in spite of their status as mothers and daughters of the Canadian white male "race." Although Canadian suffragists such as Nellie McClung, following their white U.S. sisters, resented Chinese and non-white enfranchisement, they themselves were considered to be second-class citizens.[6] Privileged by class and race, but handicapped by gender, their situation exposes the fact that citizenship does not provide automatic membership in the nation's community. Living in a nation does not, by definition, provide one with a prerogative to "imagine" it. From the very inception of democracy, Athenian and after, the making of a national imaginary, the construction of its ideological political form and content, has been conditional. Such privilege, manifested as a belonging and conforming to regulatory norms and forms, has been restricted through criteria that are both constructed through and anchored in the social relations of the civil society. Being working class, being "raced," and being of a certain gender, all restrict access to citizenship in the here and now by modifying the conditions of freedom, property, and literacy.

Under circumstances in which wives and daughters of the white bourgeoisie do not qualify for citizenship, the issue of the enfranchisement of non-white women (usually working class) becomes ever more problematic. The latter are virtually erased from the political map. The non-white working-class male is at least referred to in the course of white bourgeois women's drives for social agency and citizenship, but their female counterparts are not even mentioned as potential members.[7] The othering or difference that is produced through the state's racist or ethnicizing policies with regard to importing and administrating labour[8] could only be further intensified through gendering. General disenfranchisement, deportation, head taxes, barrack lives, and so on (followed in more recent times by various types of immigration and refugee statuses, the reintroduction of a form of head tax through application fees, etc.) gave momentum to further oppression through patriarchy. Together, "sexing" and "racing" mark moments in a probation which qualifies one for a merely *formal equality*, a nominal citizenship.[9]

The making of Canada is thus accomplished through the exclusion and marginalization of women. Even formal equality has been hard for women to come by. Although not explicitly stated in the Constitution, this exclusive gendering is clearly present in the case of imported labour. At lower levels of labour, particularly, there was (and is) an active attempt to seek able-bodied young men in the industrial/manufacturing sector and young women in the service sector or for industrial piece-work.[10] This, too, was racialized and ethnicized as white and non-white, with the former being given permission to create families, to "settle" Canada and outnumber its indigenous peoples, and the latter, Chinese and Indian indentured workers, being restricted through head taxes, quotas, and miscegenation laws. A non-white labourer lived in a state of continual vulnerability, driven underground in search of jobs, company, and sex.[11] Even in the 1950s, when emigrating from the Third World with families first became possible, the emphasis was on masculinizing the labor force. "Independent immigration," therefore, has been a male preserve, with most women entering Canada "sponsored" by, or as "dependants" of, the "head of a family." This is the case even when women are as skilled (or unskilled) as their husbands. This patriarchal gesture of the state gave women's husbands (or male sponsors) complete control over them, while domestic workers (also, for the most part, women) were in the grip of their "Canadian" employers. Battering, rape, and general degradation could not and cannot be effectively resisted without risking the breakdown of these sponsorships, the withdrawal of work permits, and deportation. So, not only is there a mandate for importing able-bodied adult male labour and female reproducers (whose social production costs have been borne by another country), there is also a continual attempt to patriarchalize Canada's social organization. Thus, in Canada, gender and race have always mediated the overall social production and relations of class.

This patriarchalization has been at work since the era of the fur trade. It intensified when the white settler colonial state emerged, having race and gender deeply engraved in both its definition and its administration.[12] The socio-economic and cultural disenfranchisement of indigenous peoples has been both genocidal and patriarchal. Through the Indian Act, for example, racist and sexist constructions of "the Indian," "Indian culture," and "the Indian woman" became both possible and practicable.[13] This went together with ensuring that the white woman was out of bounds for non-white men, a process that did not exhaust itself with old-style settler colonialism. Canadian social organization was based on race, which was defined as being constituted by those of "pure blood" (either "Indians" or "Europeans") and those of "mixed blood" (the Métis).[14] The Indian Act created a zone of non-identity for indigenous women, and it ensured that they lost their economic bases. By marrying out of their prescribed locations and blood spaces as "Indians," they lost their "Indian" status in their own communities and did not gain white status in the non-Native communities.[15] This was a part of the overall process of excluding women from "Canada," and it came down most heavily on "raced" others.

In more recent times, the organized subordination of women comes out clearly in the context of the pro-choice movement, which is led by middle-class white women. Given that we live in a so-called liberal democracy (which supposedly enshrines individual rights and freedom of choice), and given that we live in what C.B. Macpherson has called a "market model of democracy" (Macpherson, 1977; 1973, 157–203), there should be no proscription against obtaining abortion on demand. But in spite of their formal equality with men as "citizens" and their being defined as possessive individuals, as owners of their own persons and other property, women's rights to abortion on demand is opposed by the Canadian state. And, their white, middle-class status notwithstanding, the leaders of the pro-choice movement were revealed to be, in political-ideological terms, of minority or non-age status. Unlike a man, who could consent to surgical procedures on any part of his body, a woman was against a legal wall. In fact, women turned out to be wards of the state, which, as their paternal guardian, got to decide what was good for them. With the help of protective/preventive laws and masculinized expert medical services, women were held in permanent tutelage. This role of reluctant breeders is forced, particularly, on white women, as they are of the majority culture and are thus held responsible for counterbalancing the "unassimilables" (i.e., non-whites) among us. Besides, as non-white women are considered to be overly fecund, there is a terror that they might change Canada's racial composition. Bloc Québecois leader Lucien Bouchard, while on his separatist campaign, has put the responsibility of the success of his national project squarely in the lap of Quebec's white women, since it is they who must breed in order to prop up the declining "white race."[16] In various euphemistic forms, this argument has underpinned Canadian immigration, refugee, and cultural policies. It is not hard to see that the Canadian state's overwhelming sense of guardianship over women's bodies amounts to a demand for white women to reproduce more and for non-white women to reproduce less. The overall mandate for women, here as in China (which has become a byword for repressive reproductive regimes), is to reproduce in keeping with the economic, cultural, and political ambitions of the state and within an overall population policy projected for the country. In the end, nationally appropriate reproduction becomes the white woman's burden, and it is not coincidental that this dovetails with the white supremacist desire to "Keep Canada White."

The fact that the state seeks to hold the white woman's womb hostage has profound repercussions for non-white women. Caught in the same legal labyrinth as are their white counter-parts, their motherhood is by implication also regulated. In the United States, a vast number of black women do not reach natural menopause (Sheehy, 1991); they are given complete hysterec-tomies or tubal ligations as early as during their thirties. It would be interesting to do a compara-tive study of the difficulties faced by black and white women, respectively, in their attempts to obtain abortions in Canada; it would also be interesting to look at this research in terms of class. At this point, however, I can only point to the general discouragement meted out to non-white people with regard to reproduction. Since there is already an attempt to criminalize "immigrants" or "visible minorities," any non-white woman's violation of the state's mandate against abortion on demand threatens to fur-ther criminalize her.

*****

The state constructs not only women in general, but also poor women, and impover-ished women of color in particular, as political/social subjects who are essentially dependent and weak (Fraser and Gordon, 1994; Alexander and Mohanty, 1997). As such they are seen as a burden on the state and the economy; that is, on the more competent, economically productive, masculinized "tax payer." The welfare recipient is often portrayed as a "she"—a "welfare moth-er" or a "single mother." Thanks to the com-bined effort of the state and the media, poverty is "feminized." It is seen as located in women's own social subjectivity, as their own creation. A whole world is conjured up—a world of mothers, strollers, babies, and recalcitrant, badly brought up children. This "female culture of poverty" is then condemned by the school system, child psychologists, the Ministry of Social Services, and the Ministry of Correctional Services. In fact, we are currently witnessing the revival of an eighteenth- and nineteenth-century cat-egory known as "the poor." "The poor" are now emerging as a character type, as (almost) a separate species. As with women, so with the poor in general: their character is their destiny. Not only does this category hide the production

of poverty by the state and the ruling mores of capital, it also results in a kind of political paralysis through the ontologization of poverty. The only action taken on behalf of the poor has to do with charity and the reinforcement of the nuclear family—action that assuages the consciences of the charitable rather than the hunger of those in need. It is worth consider-ing what a very different political and social persona would be projected if, rather than being categorized as "the poor," this same group of people was categorized as "the proletariat."

Racialization affects "the poor" just as it does others, such as unemployed workers. The category "immigrant/refugee welfare recipient," for example, includes both men and women who are thoroughly demonized as perennial welfare recipients and manipulators of unemployment insurance and workers' disability pension. The odour of dishonesty that haunts the world of "the poor" in general is most intense around those who are non-white. Whole communities live under suspicion and surveillance—Soma-lis, Tamils, Jamaicans, and so on. This raced poverty is both masculine and feminine, and even its feminine face does not fall within any code of chivalry or compassion and charity. Because of the alleged illegitimacy of their pres-ence in Canada, these people are not candidates for such treatment. This segment of "the poor" is thus quickly covered in a mantle of crime. The world of non-white poverty inspires media/state-produced images of desperate young men always ready to commit crime. What is aimed at them is "order"—either that of the police officer's gun or that of the deportation law. Both poor non-white men and non-white women are under perma-nent suspicion of "welfare fraud," a heightened version of what confronts poor whites.

That my assertions are not a matter of individual paranoia is evident in the fact that Ontario has established a "hotline" to prompt us to report anonymously on our neighbours and anyone else whom we think might be cheat-ing "the system." This "snitch line" violates human dignity/human rights, creates a state of legal surveillance, and organizes people into vigilante-style relationships with one another. It brings racism and sexism to a boiling point by stimulating an everyday culture of racist sexism, and it creates an atmosphere that can only be described as fascistic. Clearly, reporting "the jew" among us is not over yet!

Since these race-gendered class forms of criminalization, marginalization, and exclusion arise in present-day Canada—a supposedly liberal democratic state—the situation with which we have to deal becomes highly complex. [...] [B]y its very organization of social communities in "race" and ethnic terms, the state constantly creates "Canadians" and "others." This happens not only in the realm of state-constructed policy, but also in that of everyday life—within what Theo Goldberg (1993) calls a "racist culture." This "racist culture" is in a mutually constitutive relationship with the state.

*****

In the face of my assertion that "Canada," as a national imaginary, is a sexist-racist entity, some will advance a phenomenon known as "multiculturalism."[17] I will be told that, due to this phenomenon, which needs especial scrutiny with regard to citizenship of "others," the whole world looks up to Canada. Although, in practice, multiculturalism has never been effective, it can and does serve as an ideological slogan within a liberal democratic framework. It supplies an administrative device for managing social contradictions and conflicts. This is important since "Canada," as a nationalist project, is perceived to be a homogeneous, solid, and settled entity, though its history constantly belies this.

*****

Fractured by race, gender, class, and long-standing colonial rivalries, the construction of "Canada" entails two major forms of interconnected crises—that of citizenship and that of the legitimation of a "national" state formation. Differential status in citizenship is paired with a dual state formation, each aspect of which exerts pressures on the other. A white settler colonial state and a liberal democracy, while historically and contingently connected in many cases (such as in Australia, the former South Africa, the United States, the former Rhodesia [Zimbabwe], or Canada) are two separate political projects. They are not genealogically connected in terms of their political ideals and governing structures. This becomes clearer when we look at Britain, which had a vast colonial empire and ruled it autocratically, while developing a liberal democracy inside the country. In liberal democracy, even if it is only in the sphere of polity, the same state structures and legalities govern the entire subject population and show a reliance on the notion of enlightenment. The liberal democratic state, at least at the level of *formal equality*, is the antithesis of a colonial state. But in Canada, as in the case of Australia, for example, certain features of the colonial state coexist with those of a liberal democracy (Watkins, 1977). Different laws, with special departments such as the Department of Indian Affairs in Canada, govern the population differently. Indian reserves have laws governing them economically, politically, and socially which are different from the laws governing the rest of Canada. Viewed from the standpoint of indigenous peoples, the state of Canada is based on class, gender, and race, and it continues to administer these reserves as would a colonial state.

*****

These colonial relations and representations of "Canada," which run like rich veins throughout its state formation, were overlayered with liberal democratic aspirations in the course of the latter half of the twentieth century. The state faced many contradictions and complexities in this project due to the persistence of the colonial relations and also to the country's own inability to have a bourgeois revolution. Lacking a fully articulated bourgeois class in leadership, Canada has in effect a double dependency—on Britain for governmental and certain cultural forms, and on the U.S. for capital as well as for social and political culture. [...] Like all liberal democracies it is not only capitalist, but, as I said, colonial and dependent and autonomously imperialist at the same time. The problems of coherent state formation multiply as a result.

In fact, in the face of Canada's settler colonial origin and the weak development of its capital and capitalist class, the state in Canada has been a direct agent for capitalist development and has performed a substantial role in the accumulation of capital. It has also been the chief agent for procuring labour and creating a labour market, and has assisted in the regulation and exploitation of labour. Canada has depended on imported labour and has organized the labour market along lines of "race" and gender. This was not often an activity undertaken by the accumulating classes but primarily performed by the state, which took over a vast portion of the role of facilitation.[18] The current obedience of the state to NAFTA, or corporate transnational capital, is highly symptomatic of this. "Race" or ethnicity, translated into immigration policy quotas, has actually located different types of labour in different productional recesses.

By locking immigrant workers into zones of menial labour and low wages, the state has brought down the wage structure of the country as a whole. It has actively de-skilled and marginalized Third World immigrants by decertifying them and forcing them into the working class. Long before the present economic crisis, this device had created a reserve army of labour consisting of both males and females. As any study of homeworkers, piece-workers, cleaners of public spaces, or domestics will show, non-white or "immigrant" women occupy the worst position among these marginalized labour groups (Johnson and Johnson, 1982). These, then, are the people—straddling the line between surplus exploitation and unemployment—who stand permanently on the threshold of Canadian citizenship. Their paper-thin status is revealed when some family members are deported while others, such as children born in Canada, are allowed to stay. If these are not sufficient reminders of the crises of citizenship faced by non-white "others," one need only remember the Japanese internment.

*****

During the course of its tortuous formation, Canada has continued to exude irreconcilable contradictions. In following the imperatives of liberal democracy, in being motivated by the ideal of pluralism, and in responding to popular protests against inequality, Canada promulgated both multiculturalism and affirmative action, which both contained dissatisfaction and legitimated existing inequalities. At the same time, through various debates, the state called for sexist and racist responses to all its so-called multiculturalist and equity-oriented proposals. For example, at this moment, the fig leaf of equity and affirmative action has been altogether dropped in Ontario. By constantly calling on and constructing an entity called "Canadians" and pitting it against immigrants, the state has actually stimulated white supremacist attitudes and helped to establish their organizations, as was revealed by a government agent with regard to the Heritage Front.[19] By constantly signifying the white population as "Canadians" and immigrants of color as "others," by constantly stereotyping Third World immigrants as criminals, terrorists, and fundamentalists, the state manages to both manipulate and cancel its alleged dedication to multiculturalism.

*****

Due to its selective modes of ethnicization, multiculturalism is itself a vehicle for racialization. It establishes anglo-Canadian culture as the ethnic core culture while "tolerating" and hierarchically arranging others around it as "multiculture." The ethics and aesthetics of "whiteness," with its colonial imperialist/racist ranking criteria, define and construct the "multi" culture of Canada's others. This reified, mutated product, accomplished through a web of hierarchically arranged stereotypes, can then be both used against "ethnic" communities and commoditized with regard to fashion and current market tastes. Festivals of "ethnic" communities, from the Toronto Caravan to Caribana, provide excellent examples. Such "ethnic" constructs have serious consequences in the perpetuation of violence against women. Frequently, in the name of cultural sensitivity and respect, the state does not address violence against women when it occurs among the multiculturally defined "ethnic" communities. It is rumoured that the accused's behavior is a part of "their culture," and that "they" are traditional, fundamentalist, and uncivilized. In this way, an entire population is demonized even though particular men become exempt from indictment. Similarly, Canada's Islamic population has become permanently associated with terrorism and every Arab is seen as a potential terrorist.

One more issue that needs to be stressed with regard to multiculturalism is the fact that it arises at the convergence of a struggle between the state and otherized, especially non-white, subjects. Their demands for justice, for effective anti-racist policies and administration, for the right to a substantive social and cultural life, are overdetermined by the agenda of the state. As long as "multiculturalism" only skims the surface of society, expressing itself as traditional ethics, such as arranged marriages, and ethnic food, clothes, songs and dances (thus facilitating tourism), it is tolerated by the state and "Canadians" as non-threatening. But if the demands go a little deeper than that (e.g., teaching "other" religions or languages), they produce violent reaction, indicating a deep resentment toward funding "others'" arts and cultures. This can be seen in the Reform Party's stance on immigration and multiculturalism.

*****

This instance serves to show that "Canada," as a national imaginary, its multiculturalism and its lip service to Quebec's Canadianness notwithstanding, is actually an anglo-white male idea that blurs the class lines. There is little in the state's notion of multiculturalism that speaks to social justice. More than anything else, multiculturalism preserves the partisan nature of the state by helping to contain pressures exerted by "others" for social justice and equity.

We might, at this point, be asked what legitimized Canada, what provided the basis for its national project, before the arrival of the concept of multiculturalism. What was its justificatory, politically existential discourse? It seems that it was the notion of "survival." The white settler colonial entity devised for itself a threatened identity, whereby the colonizer

(erasing colonialism) was faced with the danger of extinction. In the works of Margaret Atwood (1972b), such a state of affairs is advanced as a truism, as a fact of "Canada." In Atwood's novel *Surfacing* (1972a), for example, a woman discovers her violated- and invaded-self in, or as, an equally violated and invaded wilderness. In spite of her gender and feminism, her race and class allow Atwood to project this particular vision of Canada. But this metaphor of the political psyche of Canada as a threatened femininity/nature obliterates indigenous people, swallowing them up in the myth of an empty wilderness that is to be invaded and populated by white people. In doing this, Atwood follows a literary and artistic tradition already in place, for example, in many of the works of the Group of Seven (Watson, 1994). The "Canadian," as the dreamer of the nation, must come to terms with the wilderness in order to find and found "Canada." S/he is white/European. The indigenous peoples are either not there or are one with the primal, non-human forces of nature. The threat to Canada, then, comes not only from south of its border but from within itself—from its denied, unincorporated, alienated nature and its human forms. In reaction to this can the settler, "the Canadian," take an option that Atwood's heroine in *Surfacing*, being a "woman" and pacifist, cannot? Can he, as he is a man, feel justified in killing or conquering that which he cannot comprehend or finally conquer? The "survival" ideological space holds that possibility in suspense. The other threat to Canada comes from without—from its fear of being overrun by, and incorporated into, the United States. This formulation, while anti-American and mildly anti-imperialist, erases Canada's own colonial and imperialist nature and aspirations. And this erasure certainly does not help to create politics or policies that challenge anglo-white nationalism, with its masculinist inflection, and that call for other ways of imagining and administering Canada.

The possibilities for constructing a radically different Canada emerge only from those who have been "othered" as the insider-outsiders of the nation. It is their standpoints which, oppositionally politicized, can take us beyond the confines of gender and race and enable us to challenge class through a critical and liberating vision. In their lives, politics, and work, the "others" hold the possibility of being able to expose the hollowness of the liberal state and to provide us with an understanding of both the refined and crude constructions of "white power" behind "Canada's" national imaginary. They serve to remind us of the Canada that *could* exist.

NOTES

1. On the construction of "whiteness" as an ideological, political, and socio-historical category, see Allen (1994), Frankenberg (1993), Roediger (1993), Roman (1993), and Ware (1991).
2. On Europeanness as "whiteness," see Stoler (1995).
3. See Carty and Brand (1993) and Carty (1994).
4. See D.E. Smith (1987), 3, 5–6, for a definition of this term.
5. For Althusser's concept of interpellation, see Althusser (1971, 162–70).
6. Much has been written on the suffrage struggle and second-class citizen status of white bourgeois women. For particular connections between these themes and the issue of race, see Stoler (1995) and Davis (1983).
7. See hooks (1981), chapters 4 and 5; Collins (1990), chapter 4; and B. Smith (1982).
8. On how the Canadian labour market and class system is organized through race and ethnicity, see Bolaria and Li (1988) and Avery (1995).
9. Much work still needs to be done with regard to considering class formation in terms of both race and gender, but Brand (1991) makes a beginning. See also Brand and Bhaggiyadatta (1985).
10. This is powerfully brought forth in the issue of the importation of domestic workers to Toronto from the Caribbean. See Silvera (1989).
11. See Bolaria and Li (1988), chapters 5, 7, and 8; and Arnopoulos (1979).
12. On Canada as a white settler colony and race/gender inscriptions in the formation and workings of the state, see Kulchyski (1994), and Monture-Angus (1995).
13. See Francis (1992). Also, Monture-Angus (1995) says: "The definition of Indian is a legal one based on the necessity of identifying the

population against which bureaucrats will administer the *Indian Act* regime. This definition is based on blood lines and residency on a reserve" (122, n. 5).

14. See Campbell (1983) and Emberley (1993).
15. See chapter 5 in Kulchyski (1994).
16. This was part of Lucien Bouchard's campaign speech prior to the Quebec referendum in October 1995.
17. On the history of multiculturalism, see Fleras and Elliot (1992).
18. See Law Union of Ontario (1981), as well as Canada (1974, 1986).
19. For details on the Heritage Front and other neo-nazi/white supremacist groups, see *Hearts of Hate*, a video produced by the National Film Board and aired on the Canadian Broadcasting Corporation in 1995. An exposé carried in the *Toronto Star* in 1994 uncovered evidence that one of the founders of the Heritage Front, Grant Bristow, was a paid agent of the Canadian Security and Information Service (CSIS).

REFERENCES

Alexander, M. Jacqui, and Chandra Talpade Mohanty. "Introduction: Genealogies, Legacies, Movements," in *Feminist Genealogies, Colonial Legacies, Democratic Futures*, edited by M. Jacqui Alexander and Chandra Talpade Mohanty. New York/London: Routledge, 1997.

Allen, T. *The Invention of the White Race: Racial Oppression and Social Control*. London: Verso, 1994.

Althusser, L. *Lenin and Philosophy*. London: New Left Books, 1971.

Anderson, B. *Imagined Communities*. London: Verso, 1991.

Arnopoulos, S. *Problems of Immigrant Women in the Canadian Labour Force*. Ottawa: Canadian Advisory Council on the Status of Women, 1979.

Atwood, M. *Surfacing*. Toronto: McClelland & Stewart, 1972.

———. *Survival: A Thematic Guide to Canadian Literature*. Toronto: Anansi, 1972.

Avery, D. *Reluctant Host: Canada's Response to Immigrant Workers, 1896–1994*. Toronto: McClelland & Stewart, 1995.

Bolaria, B.S., and P. Li, eds. *Racial Oppression in Canada*. Toronto: Garamond, 1988.

Brand, D. *No Burden to Carry: Narratives of Black Working Women in Ontario, 1920s to 1950s*. Toronto: Women's Press, 1991.

Brand, D., and K.S. Bhaggiyadatta, eds. *Rivers Have Sources, Trees Have Roots: Speaking of Racism*. Toronto: Cross Cultural Communications Centre, 1985.

Campbell, M. *Half Breed*. Toronto: Goodread Biographies, 1983.

Canada. *A Report of the Canadian Immigration and Population Study: Immigration Policy Perspective*. Ottawa: Manpower and Immigration, 1974.

_____. *Equality Now: Report of the Special Committee on Visible Minorities*. Ottawa: House of Commons, 1986.

Carty, L., ed. *And Still We Rise*. Toronto: Women's Press, 1994.

Carty, L., and D. Brand. "Visible Minority Women: A Creation of the Colonial State," in *Returning the Gaze: Essays on Racism, Feminism and Politics*, edited by H. Bannerji. Toronto: Sister Vision Press, 1993.

Collins, P.H. *Black Feminist Thought: Knowledge, Consciousness and the Politics of Empowerment*. London: Harper Collins Academic, 1990.

Davis, A. *Women, Race and Class*. New York: Vintage, 1983.

Emberley, J. *Thresholds of Difference: Feminist Critique, Native Women's Writings, Postcolonial Theory*. Toronto: University of Toronto Press, 1993.

Fleras, A., and J.L. Elliot, eds. *Multiculturalism in Canada: The Challenge of Diversity*. Scarborough, Ont: Nelson, 1992.

Francis, D. *The Imaginary Indian*. Vancouver: Arsenal Pulp Press, 1992.

Frankenberg, R. *White Women, Race Matters: The Social Construction of Whiteness*. Minneapolis: University of Minnesota Press, 1993.

Fraser, N., and L. Gordon. "A Genealogy of Dependency: A Keyword of the U.S. Welfare State." *Signs: A Journal of Women in Culture and Society* 19, no. 2 (1994): 309–36.

Goldberg, David T. *Racist Culture*. Oxford: Basil Blackwell, 1993.

hooks, b. *Ain't I a Woman: Black Women and Feminism*. Boston: South End Press, 1981.

Johnson, L., and R. Johnson. *Seam Allowance: Industrial Home Sewing in Canada*. Toronto: Women's Educational Press, 1982.

Kulchyski, P., ed. *Unjust Relations: Aboriginal Rights in Canadian Courts*. Toronto: Oxford University Press, 1994.

Law Union of Ontario. *The Immigrant's Handbook*. Montreal: Black Rose Books, 1981.

Macpherson, C.B. *Democratic Theory: Essays in Retrieval*. Oxford: Oxford University Press, 1973.

_____. *The Life and Times of Liberal Democracy*. Toronto: Oxford University Press, 1977.

Monture-Angus, P. *Thunder in My Soul: A Mohawk Woman Speaks*. Halifax: Fernwood, 1995.

Ng, R. "Sexism, Racism, Canadian Nationalism," in *Returning the Gaze: Essays on Racism, Feminism and Politics*, edited by H. Bannerji. Toronto: Sister Vision Press, 1993.

Roediger, D. *The Wages of Whiteness: Race and the Making of the American Working Class*. London: Verso, 1993.

Roman, Leslie G. "White Is a Color: White Defensiveness, Postmodernism and Antiracist Pedagogy," in *Race, Identity and Representation in Education*, edited by C. McCarthy and W. Chrichlow. New York/London: Routledge, 1993.

Sheehy, G. *The Silent Passage: Menopause*. New York: Pocket Books, 1991.

Silvera, M. *Silenced: Talks with Working-Class Caribbean Women about Their Lives and Struggles as Domestic Workers in Canada* (2nd ed.). Toronto: Sister Vision Press, 1989.

Smith, B. "Racism and Women's Studies," in *But Some of Us Are Brave*, edited by G. Hull, P.B. Scott, and B. Smith. New York: Feminist Press, 1982.

Smith, D.E. *The Everyday World as Problematic*. Toronto: University of Toronto Press, 1987.

Stoler, A.L. *Race and the Education of Desire: Foucault's History of Sexuality and the Colonial Order of Things*. Durham: Duke University Press, 1995.

Ware, V. *Beyond the Pale: White Women, Racism, and History*. London: Verso, 1991.

Watkins, M., ed. *Dene Nation: The Colony Within*. Toronto: University of Toronto Press, 1977.

Watson, S. "Race, Wilderness, Territory and the Origins of Modern Canadian Landscape Painting," *Semiotext[e]* 6, no. 17 (1994): 93–104.

DISCUSSION QUESTIONS: COOK

1. Discuss the five main ways in which the Pakistani state has constructed the identity of Pakistan women over time to enable nation-building projects and Muslim group identity construction. Include specific examples in your answer.
2. How have Pakistani women struggled against these constraints since the inception of the Pakistani state?
3. The Pakistani state is not the only state to exercise discourses of gender and religion in the name of national projects and priorities, including war. Consider Israel and the former Yugoslavia as two more examples.

DISCUSSION QUESTIONS: BANNERJI

1. Review Bannerji's argument that the Canadian state is a construction based on gender, race, and class relations.
2. Explain how non-White women are especially marginalized in the making of the Canadian state. Pay particular attention to labour and citizenship processes.
3. Bannerji argues that the state operates based on the organized subordination of women. What evidence does she give to support this claim, especially when considering state practices relating to welfare and women's reproductive activities?

FURTHER READINGS

1. Al-Ali, Nadje. 2000. *Secularism, Gender, and the State in the Middle East: The Egyptian Women's Movement.* Cambridge: Cambridge University Press.
   This book explores the political significance of women's secular activism against the Egyptian state as they fight for their political rights in the face of conservative forces. Al-Ali provides fascinating insights into the women's movement in Egypt and its struggle with the state and Islamic fundamentalists.
2. Amin, Cameron Michael. 2002. *The Making of the Modern Iranian Woman: Gender, State Policy, and Popular Culture, 1865–1946.* Gainsville: University Press of Florida.
   Amin examines the Women's Awakening Project undertaken in late 1930s Iran by Reza Shah Pahlavi. The book is a historical exploration of the rise of the modern concept of womanhood in Iran and Reza Shah's controversial attempt to forcibly Westernize Iranian women in order to "emancipate" and control them. It's a fascinating study of the relationship among Iranian women, state policy, and popular culture during this time period.
3. Ashwin, Sarah (ed.). 2001. *Gender, State, and Society in Soviet and Post-Soviet Russia.* Oxford: Taylor and Francis Group.
   This collection of noteworthy Russian contributors discusses the effects of the rise and fall of the Soviet state on gender relations. Important issues covered include women as breadwinners, men's loss of status at work, and changing gender roles in the press.
4. Dujon, Diane, and Ann Withorn (eds.). 1996. *For Crying Out Loud: Women's Poverty in the United States.* Boston: South End Press.
   Authors writing in this book outline the recent battle waged over welfare payments to unemployed women with children in the United States. In the 1980s and 1990s, the American political and media systems advocated cutbacks to so called "welfare queens." These scholars delve into pertinent statistics and myths to draw more humanizing portraits of these women who live on the economic margins of American society.
5. Meyer, Madonna Harrington (ed.). 2000. *Care Work: Gender, Labour, and the Welfare State.* New York: Routledge.

This collection of papers, written from a range of disciplines, examine the gendered nature of care work that is invisible and unpaid, yet constitutes the foundation upon which the modern welfare state is rooted.

RELEVANT FILMS

1. *Women of Niger: Between Fundamentalism and Democracy*, 1993, 26 minutes, Women Make Movies
    This film takes on the topic of the clash between democratic human rights and religious fundamentalism as it impacts women's lives in Niger. Muslim fundamentalists have called on the state to revoke women's civil rights as the country struggles for a more democratic system. In this clash, women become the most ardent defenders of democracy for all.
2. *Keep Her under Control: Law's Patriarchy in India*, 1998, 52 minutes, University of California Extension Centre for Media and Independent Learning
    In a Muslim village in Rajasthan, northern India, a single woman refuses to abide by the dominant patriarchal codes enshrined in local Islamic moral and legal laws. The film illustrates the practices she is resisting, including marriage customs, dowry issues, relationships with mothers-in-law, and women's rights to land ownership.
3. *To Walk Naked*, 1995, 12 minutes, Third World Newsreel
    A group of women from Dobsonville, South Africa reminisce about their 1990 struggle with the Afrikaaner National government, which destroyed their homes in makeshift squatter camps. In particular, they describe their tactic of stripping naked to protest, which further threatened their lives with social stigma.
4. *The Women Outside*, 1995, 60 minutes, Third World Newsreel
    This film explores the lives of some of the 27,000 South Korean women who "serviced" over 37,000 American soldiers in military brothels and clubs during the Korean War. The director compels us to think about the sexual politics of the US military, the South Korean government's complicity in these sexual transactions, and both governments' dependence on the sexual labour and exploitation of women.
5. *Something Like War*, 1991, 52 minutes, Women Make Movies
    India's family planning program is analyzed from the point of view of the women who have been targeted by it. The film traces the history of the state program, highlighting the brutality with which it was implemented. Women's explanations of their sexuality, fertility control, and health clearly contrast with those implied in this state program to control women's reproductive capacities.

RELEVANT WEB SITES

1. http://libarts.wsu.edu/polisci/rngs
    The Research Network on Gender Politics and the State is a group of 38 scholars from 16 North American and European countries whose purpose it is to study late 20th-century women's movements and the ways in which governments have responded to these movements. The site documents "state feminism," efforts made by institutions within states to open up policy-making processes to include women's interests. It also traces the impact of the women's movement on several policy areas in the 1970s: job training, abortion, political representation, and prostitution.
2. www.bridge.ids.ac.uk/reports/citizenship-report.pdf
    The Gender and Development Research Service, which is part of the Institute of Development Studies in the UK, provides an overview report on the relationship between gender and citizenship in a development context. The document explains why citizenship and gender are relevant to development practice,

and outlines critiques of citizenship through a gender lens, reframing citizenship from the perspective of gender equality in development. Seven case studies of women's efforts to challenge and reformulate citizenship and women's rights are documented in the Arab world, Namibia, India, Brazil, Mexico, South Africa, and Rwanda.

3. www.irp.wisc.edu/publications/dps/pdfs/dp108296.pdf

This Institute for Research on Poverty article on gender and the American welfare state summarizes current feminist understandings of the varying effects of welfare states on gender relations and vice versa. The article draws on data from Scandinavia, the United States, Canada, England, Australia, and France. Topics include the gendered division of labour, compulsory heterosexuality, discourses of citizenship, motherhood, and reproduction.

4. www-personal.umich.edu/~eandersn/biblio.htm

The "Gender, Race, and Affirmative Action" resource page provides an annotated bibliography of resources on race, gender, and affirmative action for those interested in the literature, including short articles, longer academic works, and other sources available only on the Web.

5. www.bridge.ids/ac.uk/reports/bbll.pdf

This Web site consists of a broad range of readings on gender and governance around the world, including gender and Third World politics, gender and participatory democracy, the masculinization of the neo-liberal state in Latin America, the state and sexual politics, and gender and international relations.

⊕ ⊕ ⊕

PART X

GENDER, RACE, AND RACISM

Various strands of classical feminist theory have been criticized for their tendency to essential-
ize gender, to depict women and men as uniform categories, which ignores the racial, class,
and sexual relations that differentiate groups of women. The modern feminist movement,
led mainly by White middle-class women, has also been criticized for its lack of attention to these
differences among women. Anti-racist feminists argue that the exclusion of "other" (non-White,
non-privileged) women has been a vital part of the privileged advancement of White women, marginalizing colonized, working-class, and immigrant women.

This critique has formed the foundation of new feminist understandings of gender relations as
overlapping with other axes of inequality, including class, race, ethnicity, sexuality, age, and ability.
It has also resulted in new accounts of the differentiated aspects of gendered lives, in relation to
education, employment, family life, and other major social institutions. In all of these analyses, race,
like gender, is construed as a social construct, one whose meaning has been social inscribed rather
than biologically given, and has differed over time and space. The arbitrarily constituted social classification system of race relations are socially constructed, as we see in the following articles, to serve
a range of social and political purposes such as colonialism, imperialism, and slavery.

Carolyn Egan and Linda Gardner, in their piece "Racism, Women's Health and Reproductive
Freedom," provide one of these accounts of the differentiated aspects of gendered lives through an
analysis of the racist nature of women's health care in Canada. They begin by reviewing research
that empirically details the experiences of racialized women in the Canadian health care system,
examining the intersection of race, class, and gender in those experiences. They demonstrate that
racism permeates medical services, which jeopardizes the health of these women. Research shows
that racialized women are often treated disrespectfully by medical professionals, in part because
of their lack of knowledge of the overall system. The authors end by analyzing how the Ontario
Coalition for Abortion Clinics has tried to improve the health care of women of colour primarily by
organizing for their reproductive rights.

To complete this section, French studies professor Denean Sharpley-Whiting focuses on the interplay between gender, race and sexual relations in the field of early 19th-century European science. At

this time French anatomist George Cuvier dissected the cadaver of Sarah Bartmann, a women who had been abducted from South Africa in 1810 by Europeans and exhibited naked throughout England and France. Known as the Hottentot Venus, Sarah Bartmann—her body more specifically—provided for the European scientific community the "crucial link" between Europeans and animals based on her "anomalous" anatomy and its sexual and racial connotations. Sharpley-Whiting's goal is to read this master scientific text of Black female sexuality and to relate Bartmann's influence on 19th-century Western racial-sexual science and the racial hierarchy that was constructed on it.

CHAPTER 25

RACISM, WOMEN'S HEALTH, AND REPRODUCTIVE FREEDOM

Carolyn Egan and Linda Gardner

Of all the forms of inequality, injustice in health is the most shocking and inhumane.

—Martin Luther King, Jr.

Unfortunately, there has been very little written on racism and women's health in Canada. We hope that this chapter will be a useful contribution to the body of knowledge available, and will lead to more work being done on the topic. In the article we intend to firstly review the findings of the research that is available that deals with the experiences of women of colour in the healthcare system, and examine the intersection of race, class, and gender. We will then analyze how one organization, the Ontario Coalition for Abortion Clinics, tried to relate to the health care needs of women of colour in its organizing for reproductive rights.

Racism has long been present in health care in this country. In Alberta between 1928 and 1972, 2844 people were forcibly sterilized through the province's sexual sterilization act. Under this legislation a eugenics board approved the operation, if reproduction involved the risk of "hereditary taint." Sixty-four percent of those sterilized were women, 20% were less than 16 years old. They were for the most part poor and working class. The racism of its application is obvious. First Nations and Metis people represented 2.5% of the population, but accounted for 25% of the sterilizations in the law's later years.[1] Both Alberta and British Columbia had such laws in effect, and it is believed that hundreds of such operations were carried out in Ontario as well.

We believe that racism still permeates every facet of Canadian society, and medical services are no exception. A recent study, "Immigrant, Refugee and Racial Minority Women and Health Care Needs," carried out by the Women's Bureau of the Ontario Ministry of Health, documents the health care experiences of minority women in Ontario. Researchers interviewed both individuals and groups of women in six regions: Ottawa, Thunder Bay, London, Windsor, Sudbury, and Toronto. These women outlined the situations they faced and the racism they experienced. The document concludes, "The most critical finding of this community consultation process was that immigrant, racial minority, and refugee women are discriminated against by the Ontario health care system."[2]

There are well over one million women who could be defined as immigrant, refugee, or racial minority in Ontario, at least one quarter of the female population of the province. There is, of course, an enormous range of difference in class, language abilities, racial, and ethnic backgrounds among these women, and therefore care has to be taken when making generalizations. The document does not differentiate between women of colour and other immigrant and refugee women, which is unfortunate for our purposes. We know that the majority of immigrants to Canada today are from non-European countries.

You will see from the comments of the women themselves that they perceive their health is being jeopardized because of the racism and discrimination they face. Racial barriers were clearly identified in the study. Many of the respondents observed that those who are racially different are seen as inferior by White, Canadian health-care providers. Women spoke of how they were treated disrespectfully and in a discriminatory manner. Structural barriers were outlined by the women, including the lack of access to language training and ghettoization in low-paying jobs, which restricts the time to access health services. Racism and limited language and literacy levels, combined with a lack of economic opportunities, inhibited the ability of respondents to use medical services, which has a huge impact on women's health.

Through no fault of their own, there is a lack of knowledge among immigrant and refugee women of health-care practices that are available, such as pap tests or breast screening. Very little effort is made in Ontario to make this information accessible in a racially sensitive manner, or in languages other than English or French. There is a lack of adequate translation and interpreter services, which creates real barriers and can greatly increase a sense of anxiety, alienation, and isolation. This can prevent women from using available services, and ensures that their needs remain unaddressed.

In Thunder Bay participants talked directly about their experience with racial discrimination and stereotyping by health care providers. Public health units were seen to be having a difficult time relating to them. Little effort had been made to develop programs and outreach initiatives, which were appropriate and responsive to minority women's needs. They spoke of how childbirth education programs were not reaching women. Concerns were also raised about the high number of Cesarean births and the over-medication of women involved in the study.

In Ottawa, women described a "softer but more pervasive" form of discrimination. Women spoke of a lack of understanding about their reality and the situations they were describing, as they spoke to health-care providers. They felt very reticent to express concerns or feelings about their health, which contributed to stress and mental health problems. Health professionals were often dismissive, treating women as though they were stupid. The women spoke of a lack of trust, and felt no confidentiality in their interactions with health-care providers. They felt that their experiences were devalued by the health care system.

In Sudbury women identified a particular need for information on gynecological care, and pre- and postnatal services. Women underutilized pap tests and breast exams, because of the lack of outreach to their communities. They were being denied basic health services because of who they are. Many physicians were not aware of conditions such as sickle cell anemia, which can have devastating effects on women of colour.

The authors of the study told us that women's reactions ranged from "polite disappointment to outright anger." The report documented that immigrant, refugee, and racial minority women have obvious health care needs, but they make use of health care services at a significantly lower rate than other women. This is clearly due to the barriers they encounter, which are not only the biases of individual providers, but systemic barriers integrated into the health care delivery system itself. As the study states, "This contradiction is due in large measure to ... racial, linguistic, gender and class barriers embedded within the system, their needs are not being met by existing programs and services ... many areas of the health care delivery system are simply inappropriate for or insensitive to the needs of minority women."[3] Unfortunately, we were not provided with a breakdown on the racial backgrounds of the women interviewed, how long they have been in Canada, or differences among the cities targeted. But the interviews make it clear that immigrant women and refugees, the majority of whom today are women of colour, experience the health care system differently than white women, because of the racism embedded within it.

An earlier study by the Immigrant Women's Health Centre (IWHC) in Toronto showed similar findings. The centre was established in 1975 and provides medical and educational services to women from a variety of communities. It also organizes around the health needs of immigrant women and women of colour. It is a multilingual, multiracial collective with a central focus on sexual health. The counsellors are members of the communities, which the centre serves. They deal with birth control, pregnancy, childbirth, abortion, sexually transmitted diseases, and other gynecological issues, as well as stress management, nutrition, and patients' rights. The centre was started because of the racism that women encounter in mainstream health services, and the need for health care geared to meet their needs. It established specific outreach services, such as the Black Youth Hotline, a mobile unit, and has responded to the needs of the Tamil community and other recent immigrants to Toronto.

The IWHC conducted a study with the women who were using its mobile health unit, which visited work sites between January 1984 and August 1985. The study focused on working women between the ages of 25 and 45 including women from the West Indian, Vietnamese, Chinese, and Spanish communities. Many of the women spoke very little English, did not have previous Canadian job experience, and were forced to work in low-paying jobs, often with unhealthy working conditions. They were often not able to find medical services that they could access and that were sensitive to their needs.

In the study, a health care worker at the IWHC said, "They ... are often taken advantage of without knowing what recourse to take. The implications for reproductive health, let alone reproductive rights, are limited. Unattended gynecological ailments, such as STDs, vaginal infections, information on breast examination, pap tests, and stress-related infections are seen at the Centre. The women are prey to poor qual-ity health services because of their economic, cultural, and political status in society."[4] Mainstream health care did not provide for these women, and this put their health at serious risk.

We don't have data on the numbers of women from each community that participated in the study; we do know that today the majority of the women who are seen at the IWHC clinics are women of colour. The study reached 1500 working women at 12 workplaces. Using information gathered in a 1983 community health survey, done by the city of Toronto health department, they compared the preventative health practices of women in the IWHC target group to those of other women in the city. They were asked questions about pap tests, breast examination by physician, and breast self-examination. The findings showed that only 43 percent of women in the IWHC target group had a pap test in the year prior to the interview, compared to 65 percent of other women. It was also found that women were even less likely to have had a pap test if they worked in semi-skilled or unskilled occupations. "The overall pattern suggests that women in the communities served by the IWHC, who worked in semi-skilled and unskilled jobs are at more risk of having undetected cervical dysplasia than women in any other groups."[5] In terms of breast examination by a physician, a similar pattern emerged in both number and percentage of women who had this performed in the year prior to the interviews. This was the case, not because the women had no concern about their health care needs, but because they had difficulty accessing services because of racism and systemic barriers.

The women seen by the IWHC tend to be concentrated in jobs where they work in assembly or product fabrication, as dishwashers, cleaners, cafeteria workers, waitresses, or domestic workers. The work makes women unable to take time off for routine health care. Treatable health problems, such as cervical or breast cancer, go undetected, jeopardizing chances of survival. Other health problems also go undiagnosed. For example, a woman with untreated high blood pressure is four times more likely to develop kidney disease. Women of colour face discrimination in employment, which makes it more likely that they will work in low-paying jobs, which do not allow easy access to medical services. They are denied health care that White, middle-class women take for granted.

In terms of reproductive issues, the study states, "women face a lack of options on family planning due to their economic condition and this has a direct relation to the measure of control they have or they don't have over their bodies. All of these must be taken into account; how the issue of birth control, pregnancy, abortion, etc., really affect women who work two jobs, who lack a facility in English, or who encounter racism in the society.... Women often seek abortions ... because their material conditions, i.e., housing, employment, lack of daycare, low salary jobs, have dictated to them how many children they may have at any given time in their reproductive life."[6] The intersection of race, class, and gender is very clear in the lives of the women interviewed in this study, and strongly impacts on how they experience health care in this country.

The racism that women of colour confront in the health care system is not confined to Ontario. In a study that specifically deals with the Chinese community in Vancouver, British Columbia the rate of cervical cancer was also found to be much higher.[7] A significant number of Chinese women in their late 40s through late 60s were being diagnosed with cervical cancer in a province that was said to be leading the world in pap test screening. This was significantly higher than the general population. We do not know the class background of the women, but it is likely that they are poor or working class. Again it was a question of systemic racism, and the lack of appropriate community programs. Many Chinese women also found it unacceptable to be examined by male doctors, and this was not being taken into account by health providers.

There were a number of structural barriers. Pap screening was a provincial responsibility, but there was a very real absence of creative thinking or support for changes in the program that would make it more accessible to specific communities. Also, the Ministry of Health lacked a funding mechanism to allow for more accessible programs.

Women from the Chinese community took up the issue themselves. A pap smear campaign was highlighted in the Chinese media, featured at community health fairs, and training was provided for volunteers and health professionals from the community. An evening program was launched providing women with information and services in their own language and women doctors from their own community. Chinese women developed their own solutions to a critical problem, which was being ignored by the medical community.

Interestingly Statistics Canada reported in 1996 that recent immigrants report fewer health problems of a chronic nature than people born in Canada, but the longer they are resident the greater the incidence of chronic health problems. "The difference is particularly marked for recent immigrants from non-European regions, who now account for most of the immigration flow.... The evidence suggests that health status of immigrants weakens the longer they stay in Canada," said Edward Ng, an analyst for Statistics Canada.[8] The health status of people of colour deteriorates at a greater rate than white immigrants the longer they are in the country.

It is clear that government cutbacks are having an impact on the health care of the most vulnerable in Canadian society. Insufficient nutrition, emotional stress, isolation, poverty, and job or family pressures are contributing factors to the situation. Women of colour, because of the systemic racism that exists in the delivery of health care and the class position that many of them occupy, are even more at risk.

We want to mention one last study that gives a national overview. At the fourth conference and biennial general meeting of the National Organization of Immigrant and Visible Minority Women, a document entitled "Political Participation for Change: Immigrant and Visible Minority Women in Action" was produced which examined a number of important issues confronting minority women. Health care was one of the concerns addressed. The document states, "The biological makeup of women and their role in society as child-bearers, mothers, nurturers, wives and sexual partners is an important component of life and calls for unique health care needs ... immigrant women with linguistic and cultural barriers are often denied and deprived of information and access to various options on reproductive health care services." This document identified sexually transmitted diseases, infertility, and unintended pregnancies as areas that had to be addressed. "With the advancement in reproductive technologies, women have options to control pregnancy with a variety of birth control measures or even to terminate their pregnancies. Even though these options are relatively accessible through mainstream health care services, immigrant and visible minority women's access to information on birth control options, information regarding their right to access these birth control options, and their awareness of making informed decisions in controlling pregnancy is severely limited because of language and cultural barriers. Other barriers also exist that prevent immigrant and visible minority women from accessing appropriate birth control options. These include cultural insensitivity, lack of cross-cultural awareness or even racism."[9] This indicates that the conclusions of the Ontario study cited earlier in this article, that women of colour face racial barriers in the health care system, appear to be applicable nationally.

In response to the fact that women of colour experience racism in the Canadian health system, they have tried to gain control over their health care. They have established centres that particularly meet their needs such as the Immigrant Women's Health Centre, and have developed community-based programs as did Chinese women in British Columbia. We believe that it is not only the role of women of colour to take up these concerns. Racism must be addressed by all organizations that work in health care.

The studies we reviewed deal with reproductive health. We are now going to examine the work of the Ontario Coalition for Abortion Clinics (OCAC), a reproductive rights organization, and how it attempted to meet the needs of women of colour in its organizing. We both worked for many years in the coalition, and are speaking from our own experience.

OCAC was formed in 1982. Women health care workers from the Immigrant Women's Heath Centre, Hassle Free Clinic, and the Birth Control and VD Information Centre in Toronto, felt they must challenge a system which was denying access to abortion to working-class women and women of colour. OCAC began as a grassroots, broad-based activist organization. Its immediate goals were to overturn the federal law, which restricted access to abortion, and to legalize freestanding clinics providing medically insured abortions. This campaign was one of the most hotly contested struggles between the Canadian women's movement and the state. OCAC worked with Dr. Henry Morgentaler and opened a clinic to challenge the criminal code restrictions on abortion. In 1983 the clinic was raided by the police, and the doctors were arrested. The clinic became a symbol of women's resistance to an unjust law, and a long campaign against two levels of government and an organized right wing movement began.

There was access to abortion in Canada at that time, but it was a very privileged access. In 1969 a federal law had been introduced which allowed an abortion to be performed, if it took place in an approved or accredited hospital with the approval of a therapeutic abortion committee. In practice, this resulted in access for middle-class women, primarily White, who could afford a private gynecologist or travel to the U.S. or Montreal. First Nation women, women of colour, and many working-class women did not have access to abortion services. In spite of claims that Canada had universal access to health care, in practice there was a two-tiered health system. The federal law was racist and class biased in its application.

Organizations such as the Immigrant Women's Health Centre and Women Working with Immigrant Women worked with OCAC and had a profound influence on its organizing. Women such as Linda Gardner, a Chinese-Canadian activist; Sherona Hall, a long-time organizer in the Black community; and Yuki Hayashi, leader of Students for Choice, were very active in the campaign. Today Rhonda Roffey, a First Nations woman, and Brenda Lee, from the Chinese community, are in the leadership. A broad reproductive rights perspective was fought for in the organization, and was won.

While OCAC organized a struggle with a very specific focus it did not mean that it was a single-issue group. The demand for abortion access was never seen in isolation, but as one of a number of interdependent struggles. OCAC found this reproductive rights perspective to be vital, not only because it reflects the reality of women's lives, but because it explicitly deals with class and race. In linking various struggles it was able to build a broad movement through demonstrations, marches, and rallies in which thousands of women could participate. Community leaders such as Judy Vashti Persad of the Cross-Cultural Communications Centre, Salome Lucas of Women Working with Immigrant Women, and Joan Grant-Cummings of the Women's Health and Women's Hands clinic spoke at many of OCAC's events about the needs of women of colour, the racism they encountered in seeking abortions, and the need for the movement to address these issues.

OCAC tried to make it clear in its organizing that it is a fundamental right for women to make the decision to terminate a pregnancy, but the pro-choice movement needed an analysis that went much further. It believed that it is equally important that women have the right to bear the children they choose to bear. It broadened the definition of "choice" beyond an individual right. For all women to truly have choices in our society regardless of race, class, sexuality, or ability, they require: safe and effective birth control with information and services in their own languages, and in their own communities, decent jobs, paid parental leave, free childcare, the right to live freely and openly as lesbians, an end to forced or coerced sterilization, employment equity, an end to sexual and racial harassment, and, of course, the right to full access to free abortion. All of these must be fought for in order for women to have reproductive freedom. It was argued that this must be more than simply a statement of principles. There had to be active involvement in and support for these interrelated struggles.

OCAC was very much aware of the limits of the notion of "choice." Full access to free abortion, as significant an advance as that would be, does not guarantee that all women have real choices over their lives or over having and raising children. It tried to show these limits concretely by stressing that the choice to have a child can never be free in a racist, sexist society in which women earn so much less than men, in which quality daycare and affordable housing are not available and where racism is systemic. OCAC actively supported these related struggles and believed that the alliance building, coalition work, and the concrete linking of these struggles strengthened each.

Its organizing included the fight against extra billing by doctors, supporting First Nations people at Oka, walking picket lines with striking workers, and marching against police violence in the Black community. OCAC always tried to engage in movement building. Its first outreach activities were to broaden and strengthen the involvement of working-class women in trade unions and immigrant women and women of colour organizations in the campaign. It worked to directly address the reproductive health issues and concerns of women of colour and working-class women. It fought for the provision of abortion services in clinics that served women of colour such as Women's Health and Women's Hands. It joined with First Nations women in demanding an end to abusive treatment and the lack of anesthetic during abortion procedures in a Yellowknife hospital.

To win demands from a racist and sexist government that was actively denying women reproductive freedom, a movement had to be built that included trade unions, people of colour organizations, lesbian and gay groups, and all of those who believe in the liberation of women. Without active involvement and broad support for its demands, no change would occur in the balance of forces in this country, and this was necessary to overturn the federal abortion law and increase access for every woman, regardless of race or class.

The lack of abortion rights impacts on women of colour in a different way than it would on a middle-class, White woman, and this had to be acknowledged. For example, OCAC challenged the coerced sterilization that women of colour were forced to undergo by therapeutic abortion committees. It fought the extra billing that gynecologists were imposing on their abortion patients which denied access to poor and working-class women. As the campaign continued, OCAC-sponsored forums brought together women with disabilities, lesbians, First Nations women, and women of colour to speak for themselves of their particular struggles for sexual and reproductive control and to support each other. The goal was to build a visible, mass movement, which spoke to a broad reproductive rights agenda. The full message was often lost in the media presentations of our campaign where more attention was given to the single issue and demand for abortion than to the broader context, and that was a problem.

Achieving the best balance between short- and long-term objectives, between the polemical value of the choice slogan and the constraints of such arguments, and between abortion and the broader struggle for reproductive freedom, was difficult. There were many debates. Such strategic complexities and dilemmas were made no easier in a movement that was constantly under direct attack from the state and the conservative right. Nonetheless, it was clear that these complex questions could not be left until after short-term objectives had been won. For example, do we put our limited energy or resources in an election campaign or do we fight anti-choice harassment at the clinics, when we know its targets are most frequently women of colour? Do we prioritize the lobbying of politicians or building mass actions with the active involvement of women of colour organizations putting forward their views and which give everyone an opportunity to be actively engaged in the struggle against a new law? Do we structure ourselves in a traditional manner with a board of directors or have general biweekly meetings open to anyone? We openly debated these questions and always tried to choose the activity that would involve the broadest and most representative number of people. At strategic junctures in the campaign, we advertised open public strategy meetings to involve the largest number possible in determining our direction. Many people who could not commit themselves to the organization in an ongoing way attended.

OCAC tried to be inclusive. For example, coerced sterilization could not be seen separately from the struggle for abortion rights. Prior to the overturning of the federal abortion law, the therapeutic abortion committees also functioned as a primary mechanism for coerced sterilization. Doctors denied women abortions unless they agreed to be sterilized. The Immigrant Women's Health Centre and the Birth Control and VD Information Centre had spoken to women who were subject to this coercion. It particularly affected women of colour, First Nations women, and women with disabilities. Strategically, OCAC believed that by fighting the federal abortion law, and winning free abortion, it would reduce the numbers of coerced sterilization in this country. This was made clear in our organizing.

OCAC also supported the Supreme Court case which stopped the practice of sterilization of women with disabilities without their consent. As Angus McLaren pointed out in his book, *Our Own Master Race*, the eugenic idea of "race betterment" legitimized state intervention to protect Canada from "degenerates."[10] As already stated, the governments of Alberta and British Columbia passed legislation, which allowed for sterilization of those deemed to be "unfit." Prior to the Second World War, this ideology impacted immigration laws, birth control, family allowance, and a range of social policies. Determining the extent of the abuse in northern communities was difficult. In the 1970s, 23 percent of women of the Inuit community Igloolek between the ages of 30 and 50 had been sterilized by government health services. Inuit women had been quoted as saying "if we had known exactly what the operation we were made to undergo meant, we would never have accepted it."[11] When the New Democratic Party raised a question in the House of Commons concerning a series of sterilization operations performed on Inuit women on Holman Island, regulations were changed clarifying the permanence of the procedure and translating the consent forms into Inuktitut. OCAC believed that it was important to outline the abuse that had taken place in this country. It initiated forums with First Nations women in Ottawa, Toronto, and Montreal to bring attention to and broaden awareness of the problem.

In 1991, during the Toronto mayoralty campaign, OCAC, along with the Ontario Coalition Against Poverty (OCAP), raised the fact that candidate June Rowlands, who later became mayor, had 20 years earlier called for the sterilization of low-income men on welfare. OCAC and OCAP called a press conference. Groups including the Black Action Defense Committee, the Coalition of Visible Minority Women, Women Working with Immigrant Women, and the Labour Council of Metropolitan Toronto and York region demanded that she retract her statement and clarify her current position. It was important to oppose this perspective whenever it appeared. AIDS activists often spoke at our rallies, outlining the pressures on HIV-positive women to have abortions and sterilizations, and why this must be opposed.

In 1992, the government of Saskatchewan was considering de-funding hospital abortions, giving in to anti-choice pressure through cutbacks to health care. In 1995, the Alberta Conservative government tried to do the same. In the U.S., the government denies poor women funding for abortions, but it still pays 90 percent of the cost of sterilizations. Angela Davis has said that when abortion is denied and sterilization is available, this constitutes coerced sterilization.[12] These government actions were fought by pro-choice groups in the provinces affected, as well as by organizations such as OCAC. If these changes had been successful, it would have forced poor and working-class women to make the decision to be sterilized, since they would no longer have access to abortion.

When the Supreme Court overturned the existing abortion law in January of 1988, it was through the strength of a broad-based movement with the active participation of working-class women and women of colour. It was a collective victory. Tens of thousands of supporters across the country played an active role. The fact that OCAC understood that the state was not neutral, that it was racist and class biased, and that it was actively working against our interests, was critical to our campaign. Only a mass movement could change the balance of forces in the interests of all women.

The Conservative government in Ottawa

began the process of introducing new legislation recriminalizing abortion. The campaign against a new law gained wide support from groups such as the National Organization of Immigrant and Visible Minority Women, the Canadian Labour Congress, the National Council of Jewish Women; the Federation des Femmes du Quebec, the Canadian Medical Association, the United Church of Canada, and a range of local labour and anti-racist groups. This broad support created the political pressure to defeat the legislation in the Senate in 1991, after it narrowly passed in the House of Commons.

At the same time, OCAC was also pressuring the provincial government to expand access in Ontario. It was quite difficult for the organization to do both, but we felt the struggle for the legal right could not be separated from the fight for full and free access, if we were to remain true to our principles. We were committed to eradicating race and class barriers for all women. In the end, the law was defeated and the Ontario NDP government announced that four freestanding clinics would be fully funded. It also established a Task Force on Abortion Access, which was to develop a strategic plan to expand access across the province.

As WWTW said in a statement released when the law was defeated: "Today, we applaud the death of Bill C43 acknowledging that collective visible actions by many different constituencies led to its defeat. We strongly support OCAC's position that the legal right to choose, as important as it is, is meaningless unless fully funded services exist to give every woman the opportunity to make that choice in her own language and her own community. WWIW will continue to work with OCAC to put pressure on the federal government to implement the Canada Heath Act to ensure that every province provides full access to free abortion and to insist that the provinces provide this critical service with all the other demands that will ensure real choices in our lives...."[13]

During the campaign against the new law and for increased access, anti-choice activists began another assault. "Operation Rescue," as they called it, started in Toronto, during the fall of 1988. Hundreds of anti-choice protesters blockaded the entrance of the Morgentaler Clinic. They physically and verbally assaulted women seeking abortion services. OCAC organized a defence of the clinics, rejecting the argument that it should be left to the police to protect the facilities. Many of the women using the clinics did not view the police as a friendly force. Women from working-class communities and communities of colour had seen the role of the police during strikes and in violent incidents with members of their communities. The police had previously raided the clinic, arrested the doctors, and followed and harassed patients. They also made it clear by their actions that they were in no hurry to remove the blockades, often viewing pro-choice activists as more problematic that the anti-choice vigilantes.

Supporters would link arms chanting, "Racist, sexist, anti-gay, born-again bigots go away," "Campaign Life, your name's a lie, you don't care if women die"—chants which reflected the politics of the campaign. It would not be unusual to see women and men from the United Steelworkers, the Black Women's Coalition, Canadian Auto Workers, AIDS Action Now!, Women Working with Immigrant Women, the Immigrant Women's Health Centre, and Eco-media standing shoulder to shoulder to defend the clinics. Because of the strong mobilization and community support, "Operation Rescue" was stopped. This speaks to the strength of the movement-building strategy, and the active alliance building. Those who defended women's access believed that the clinic was legal as a result of their collective struggle and were committed to defending it.

OCAC recognized that women's lives are such that not all women are able to actively participate in the day-to-day campaign. It is difficult to know how representative our organizing is, and we are sure more could have been done, but we try to be accountable to the groups with whom we work. Building strong alliances and working in coalition with organizations of women of colour and working-class women must always be key priorities in order to ensure their active involvement and a representative politic.

According to a recent poll, 77 percent of people in Canada believe that an abortion is a decision that should be made between a woman and her doctor. There is no federal law on abortion. Today, in Ontario, abortion is fully covered in hospitals, and in five free-standing clinics due to the struggle in this province. However, it is still a very fragile system of abortion services. Northern Ontario is very poorly served. In northwestern Ontario, First Nations women must make three trips off the reserve to obtain the procedure, which is a totally unnecessary burden and destroys any confidentiality. Anti-choice harassment has forced some doctors to stop providing these services. In 1992, the fire bombing of the Morgentaler Clinic in Toronto shows the extremes that anti-choice sympathizers take. In 1994, 1995, and 1997 doctors were shot in Vancouver, Ancaster, Ontario, and Winnipeg because they were providing abortions.

There are now 30 free-standing clinics offering abortions to women across the country, and access is much wider than in the early 1980s when the campaign began. In provinces other than Ontario, British Columbia, Alberta, Newfoundland, and Quebec (Quebec is not fully covered), governments are still refusing to pay the costs of clinic abortions. Abortion is entirely unavailable in Prince Edward Island and quite limited in the Atlantic provinces in general. In rural areas throughout the country access is still very difficult. The fight for the maintenance of universal health care, which is presently under attack through cutbacks, hospital closures, and reduction of services, particularly affecting working-class women and women of colour, must continue.

While the overall strategic situation has changed, and will always change, the lessons of this campaign will remain relevant. Issues of race and class must be prioritized in their organizing if movements are to speak to the realities of all women's lives. These are the principles and strategies that created a broad-based campaign to overturn the oppressive federal law, and create a network of abortion clinics in most provinces. Initial and partial victories certainly, but still major gains for women's reproductive freedom, and these are the principles that can continue to push the struggle forward.

It is only through the ongoing development of an anti-racist, class perspective, with the participation and leadership of women of colour and working-class women that the possibility exists to eradicate racism and class bias from the health care system, and win full reproductive freedom for all women.

NOTES

1. Janice Tibbets, *The Ottawa Citizen*, June 12, 1995.

2. *Immigrant, Refugee and Racial Minority Women and Health Care Needs: Report of Community Consultations*, Women's Health Bureau, Ontario Ministry of Health (August 1993), 17.

3. *Immigrant, Refugee and Racial Minority Women and Health Care Needs: Report of Community Consultations*, Women's Health Bureau, Ontario Ministry of Health (August 1993), iii.

4. *Immigrant Women's Health Centre, Annual Report* (1986), 8.

5. *Immigrant Women's Health Centre: Mobile Health Unit Project. Preventative Health Care for Immigrant Women* (September 1995), 6.

6. *Immigrant Women's Health Centre: Mobile Health Unit Project. Preventative Health Care for Immigrant Women* (September 1995), 7.

7. *What Women Prescribe: Report and Recommendations*, from the National Symposium, Women in Partnership: Working toward Inclusive, Gender-Sensitive Health Policies, Canadian Advisory Council on the Status of Women (May 1995), 68–9.

8. Edward Ng, "Immigrants Healthier Than People Born Here," *Toronto Star* (April 2, 1996).

9. *Political Participation for Change: Immigrant and Visible Minority Women in Action*, Fourth National Conference and Biennial General Meeting of the National Organization of Immigrant and Visible Minority Women of Canada (March 1995), 38.

10. Angus McLaren, *Our Own Master Race* (Toronto: McClelland & Stewart, 1990).

11. Robert Lechat, "Intensive Sterilization for the Inuit." *Eskimo* (Fall/Winter 1976): 57.

12. Angela Y. Davis, *Women, Race and Class* (New York: Random House, 1981).

13. Women Working with Immigrant Women. Statement issued on the defeat of Bill C 43 (1991).

CHAPTER 26

WRITING SEX, WRITING DIFFERENCE
Creating the Master Text on the Hottentot Venus

Denean Sharpley-Whiting

Cuvier

Science, science, science!
Everything is beautiful
Cranial measurements
crowd my notebook pages,
and I am moving closer,
close to how these numbers
signify aspects of
national character
Her genitalia
will float inside a labeled
pickling jar in the Musée
de l'Homme on a shelf
above Broca's brain:
"The Venus Hottentot."

The preceding excerpt from Elizabeth Alexander's poetic masterpiece *The Venus Hottentot* tersely recounts a definitive moment in the history of sexual science as it intersects with race, a moment when science and ideology merged and a Black woman's body mediated the tenuous relationship between the two—a moment when celebrated French anatomist and naturalist Georges Cuvier met the equally celebrated cadaver of Sarah Bartmann, the Hottentot Venus, a South African woman exhibited throughout England and France for some five years because of her "remarkable formation of person."

Notwithstanding Sander Gilman's seminal work *Difference and Pathology*,[1] little is known about either Bartmann's exhibition or about the public and popular responses to her exhibitions in France. And even less is known about Sarah Bartmann the person; mystery surrounds her date of birth, her date of death, her racial/ethnic origins—was she a Hottentot (Khoikhoi), a female Bushman (San), or a sang-mêlé? One can only speculate and approximate. But given the circumstances under which she was thrust into the limelight in the nineteenth century, these voids are not unusual. Most nineteenth-century French spectators did not view her as a person or even a human, but rather as a titillating curiosity, a collage of buttocks and genitalia.

For the scientific community she provided the missing link in "the great chain of being," the crucial step between humanity, that is, Europeans, and animals.[2] Indeed, among all the explorative undertakings of the French nineteenth-century medical community, this African woman figures as a treasured find, the key to the origin of an inferior species. As Georges Cuvier indicates, her body served in an equal degree as the master text on Black female sexuality for Europe's scientific community.[3] It

307

is the intention of this chapter not only to read excerpts from this phantasmal master text, but, more important, to relate Bartmann's immense influence on nineteenth-century Western racial-sexual science.

Born in Kaffraria in the interior of the Cape Colony of South Africa in approximately 1788, and renamed Saartjie Baartman when the region came under Dutch colonial rule, Baartman was one of six siblings. Her father was a drover of cattle who was killed by neighboring San, and her mother died when she was two years old. Her husband was a drummer, and she had had one child, who died shortly after birth.[4] She became a domestic of sorts to a Boer farmer, Peter Cezar, at the Cape of Good Hope.[5]

At the age of 21 or 22, on October 29, 1810, Saartjie entered into a contractual agreement with Alexander Dunlop of St. James, Middlesex, England, a surgeon of an African ship, and Hendrik Cezar, the brother of Peter Cezar. The contract stipulated that in addition to performing domestic duties, she was to be exhibited in England and Ireland. She would be paid a portion of the profits from her exhibition and repatriated in five years. However, upon Baartman's arrival in London, Dunlop attempted to sell his share in the "Hottentot," as well as the skin of a giraffe, to William Bullock, director of the Liverpool Museum in London. In offering Baartman, Dunlop described her as having "a very singular appearance" and predicted that "she would make a fortune for anyone who shewed [sic] her in London."[6] Bullock passed on both propositions.

In September 1810, Baartman was exhibited at 225 Piccadilly. The advertising bill read: "Parties of Twelve and upwards, may be accommodated with Private Exhibition of the Hottentot, at No. 225 Piccadilly, between Seven and Eight O'clock in the Evening, by giving notice to the Doorkeeper the Day previous."[7]

Standing a mere four feet six inches tall, Baartman's miniature frame was weighed down by her abundant buttocks. It was this riveting attribute, "large as a cauldron pot," as one bawdy English ballad attests,[8] that Europeans paid to see.

A sensation in England, leaving in her wake street ballads, caricatures, an appearance in the Chancery Court of England, and a name change to Sarah Bartmann [9] in December 1811, literally carrying her fortune behind her, Bartmann and her protuberant charms found themselves again in the limelight upon her arrival in Paris in September 1814. She and Cezar parted company in Paris; her new guardian was a showman of wild animals named Reaux. According to the widely read *Journal des dames et des modes*: "The doors of the salon open, and the Hottentot Venus could be seen entering. She is a 'Callipygian Venus.' Candies are given to her in order to entice her to leap about and sing; she is told that she is the prettiest woman in all society."[10]

The price to view this one-woman spectacle was three francs. At rue de Castiglione and for the same admission price, Reaux was also exhibiting a five-year-old male rhinoceros. Bartmann was exhibited from 11 a.m. to 10 p.m. at the ground level of 188, rue Saint-Honore.

Just as in England, Bartmann's persona filtered into satirical cartoons such as the ones titled *Les Curieux en extase ou les cordons de souliers* ("The curious in ecstasy or shoelaces") and *La Vénus hottentote*. In *Les Curieux en extase*, in which the French cartoonist pokes fun at the British fascination with the Venus, Bartmann is displayed on a pedestal engraved with *la belle hottentote*. She has arrested the gaze of three men, two British soldiers and one male civilian, and a female civilian. There is also a dog in the drawing, representing the base, animal-like nature of the human spectators, the proverbial "we are all animals" sentiment, and participating in its own sort of voyeurism as it looks under the kilt of one of the Englishmen. Each character comments on Bartmann's body. One soldier, behind Bartmann, extends his hand as if to touch her buttocks and proclaims, "Oh, godem, quel rosbif!" (Oh, goddamn, what roast beef!). The other soldier, looking directly into her genitalia, remarks: "Ah, que la nature est drôle!" (Ah, how amusing nature is!). The male civilian, peering through lorgnettes, declares: "Qu'elle étrange beauté!" (What strange beauty!), while the female civilian, bending down to tie her shoelaces—hence the cartoon's subtitle—looks through Bartmann's legs and utters: "A quelque chose malheureux est bon" (From some points of view misfortune can be good). The woman is, however, looking not at the "Hottentot," but through the opening between her legs and up the kilt of the soldier behind Bartmann. Thus, from her angle, she sees through Bartmann's "misfortune," her openness, or rather, the opening between her legs, something more pleasing. Bartmann's body is inscribed upon from the various perspectives. She becomes, all at once, roast beef, a strange beauty, an amusing freak of nature, and erased, invisible, as the female spectator privileges the penis. And while the points of view appear to reflect different positionalities, the ways of seeing the Other as exotic, amusing, invisible, and as something to be eaten or consumed like roast beef reflect sameness.

Bartmann was not only the subject of cartoons, but also of a popular vaudeville show at the Théâtre de Vaudeville entitled *La Vénus hottentote, ou haine aux Françaises*. A one-act vaudeville written by Théaulon, Dartois, and Brasier, the piece was first performed on November 19, 1814.[11] On and off stage, from cartoons to theater, Bartmann's body inspired a collective French obsession. And at the height of her career, the most profound evidence of her impact on the French imagination manifested itself among the medical community in the person of France's renowned naturalist Georges Cuvier.

For three days in March 1815 at the Jardin du Roi, at the request of Cuvier and with the permission of her guardian Reaux, a team of zoologists, anatomists, and physiologists examined Bartmann. The subsequent findings from this examination were published in 1824 in Frederic Cuvier's and Geoffroy St.-Hilaire's *Histoire naturelle des mammifères* and later in 1864 in *Discours sur les révolutions du globe* by Georges Cuvier et al. The prefatory note of *Histoire naturelle* explains the necessity for the text and its goals:

> The work that we have published has been requested and deemed necessary for many years by naturalists.... *The Natural History of Mammals* consequently proposes two problems: (1) the relationship that exists between these animals, and (2) the role that they play within the general economy of nature, that is, their relationship with other beings.[12]

The discipline of natural history is a combination of scientific writing, history, and ethnography that allows objects under the gaze to be ordered into a totalizing system of representation, that allows the seen body to become the known body. A significant problem within the constitutive framework of the discipline arises because of its dependency on the human eye. The human eye is faulty, often creating illusory images because of its "blind spot." Martin Jay notes in *Downcast Eyes: The Denigration of Vision in Twentieth-Century French Thought* that "the human eye has a blind spot where the optic nerve connects with the retina.... The blind spot's existence suggests a metaphoric 'hole' in vision."[13] Within this hole or empty space, alterity is invested.

Bartmann will be placed within this hole in the European system of representation as a highly developed animal, and then closely scrutinized in order to determine her relationship to other animals and human beings. She will be used as a yardstick by which to judge the stages of Western evolution, by which to discern identity, difference, and progress.

During the three-day examination, Cuvier asked Bartmann if she would allow herself to be painted nude. In that same prefatory note, the authors offer an explanation for the inclusion of etchings in the volume:

> Our drawings present each animal in a simple state and always in a profile because it is in this position that one can best seize the totality of the form and physiognomy; and we have taken care to provide a frontal drawing where necessary in order to better see and judge the animals.

The profile drawings permit the viewer to "best seize the totality of the form and physiognomy," "to better see and judge the animals." Seizing, seeing, judging, provided by the tool of the cameralike eye, are essential to the naturalist's project. The sketches, yielding up Bartmann's body, provide more visual clarity so that the gaze can fixate on the body in order to contemplate its anomalies. The sketches allow the viewer to observe, document, and compare her various physiognomic and physiological differences, differences that vastly differentiate the Other from the European self. Through this comparative/definitive exercise, Bartmann will be relegated to the terrain of the primitive—the lowest exemplum of the human species—while the European will always assume the pinnacle of human development. This process of mediating the self, of reflecting the self, through the body of the Black female Other begins and rebegins with every regard.

Of his initial observations, Georges Cuvier writes in *Discours sur les revolutions du globe*:

> When we met her for the first time, she believed herself to be about 26 years old.... Everyone who had been able to see her over the course of 18 months in our capital could verify the enormous protuberance of her buttocks and the brutal appearance of her face.... Her movements had something of a brusqueness and unexpectedness, reminiscent of those of a monkey. In particular, she had a way of pushing out her lips in the same manner we have observed in the Orangutan. Her personality was happy, her memory good, after several weeks she recognized a person that she had only seen one time ... she spoke tolerably good Dutch, which she learned at the Cape ... also knew a little English ... was beginning to say a few words of French; she danced in the fashion of her country and played with a fairly good ear upon a little instrument she called a Jew's Harp. Necklaces, belts, pieces of colored glass, and other savage trumperies seemed very much to please her; but that which flattered her taste above all else was brandy. (214)[14]

Cuvier's description abounds with associations of black femaleness with bestiality and primitivism. Further, by way of contemplating Bartmann as a learned, domesticated beast—comparing her to an orangutan—he reduces her facility with languages, her good memory, and musical inclinations to a sort of simianlike mimicry of the European race. By the nineteenth century, the ape, the monkey, and orangutan had become the interchangeable counterparts, the next of kin, to blacks in pseudoscientific and literary texts.[15]

Under the ever so watchful eyes and the pen of the naturalist, the master text on the Black female body is created; the light of White maleness illumines this dark continent:

> Her conformation was initially striking because of the enormous width of her hips, which surpassed forty-two inches, and because of the protrusion of her buttocks, which were more than half a foot. Of the remaining body parts, she had no other deformities: her shoulders, her back, the top of her chest were graceful. The bulging out of her stomach was not at all excessive. Her arms, a bit thin, were very well made, and her hand was charming. Her foot was also very alluring. (214)

Cuvier's gaze, it appears, is tempered with eroticism. The hand, foot, and other body parts, endowed with grace, charm, and allure, become a synecdoche for the palpably titillating Black female body. As he views Sarah Bartmann displayed before him nude, the scientist is as captivated by the Venus's charms as the male spectators at her rue St. Honoré exhibitions. Even Bartmann's belly bulge was not, for the equally short and paunchy Cuvier, disproportionate; rather, it was congruous with her beguiling arms, hands, and other extremities.

Wrenched from the seductive reverie induced by this African Delilah, the scientist violently readjusts his optic receiver and pen. Mistakenly identifying Bartmann as a San (Bushman), "people more backward than the Hottentots," instead of as a Khoikhoi (211), the now libidinally divested Cuvier observes:

> That which our female Bushman possessed that was the most repulsive was her physiognomy. Her face takes in part after the Negro by the jutting out of the jaw, the obliquity of the incisor teeth, the thickness of lips, the shortness ... of chin ... and in part after the Mongol by the enormity of the cheek bones, the flatness of the base of the nose....

Her hair was black and woolly like that of Negroes, the slits of her eyes were horizontal ... like that of Mongols ... her eyes were dark and lively; her lips, a bit blackish, and monstrously swelled; her complexion very swarthy.... Her ears were much like those found in many monkeys, small and weakly formed at the tragus. (214–15)

Cuvier reads Bartmann's face according to perceived racially specific characteristics. In this classificatory discourse based upon the all-knowing scientific gaze, he determines that Bartmann is a racial admixture: in part Negro because of her protruding jaw, short chin, pointy, cannibal-like incisor teeth, and woolly hair, and in part Mongol because of the slant of her eyes and large cheekbones. Her appearance insults his culturally biased aesthetic sensibilities. As he gazes back toward classical antiquity for icons of idyllic beauty and form,[16] Bartmann's starkly different—"swarthy"—complexion, monstrously swollen blackish lips, and anatomical and other physiognomic characteristics strike him as being so far removed from his ideals of beauty and goodness that he is moved again to find some relationship between her ears and those of a monkey. In negotiating Bartmann's tenuous place in the "great chain of being," he definitively concludes that the aforementioned characteristics are reminiscent of monkeys ("des singes") and forever destines blacks to a state of barbarity ("toujours restées barbares").[17]

In addition to the protuberant buttocks, which were not at all, according to the scientist, "muscular, but a mass of a shaking and elastic consistency, vibrating with the woman's every move" (215) and her "rebutante physionomie" (214), Cuvier describes at length Bartmann's massive hanging breasts:

Her breasts, usually lifted and held in place by her clothing, when left alone were a large hanging mass which terminated obliquely in a blackish aureole of more than four inches in diameter pitted with radiating wrinkles, near the center of which was a nipple so flattened and obliterated that

it was barely visible: the general color of her skin was a yellowish-brown, almost as dark as her face; and she had no body hair apart from a few short flecks of wool, similar to that on her head, scattered about her organs of regeneration. (214–15)

Breasts, the visible symbol of feminine seductive charm and of suckling, attracted particular interest in the medical literature of the eighteenth and nineteenth centuries.[18] According to eighteenth-century sexologist L.C.H. Macquart, "Nature destined the organ to nurture the newborn human being; she gave the breast a seductive charm by virtue of its form and bloom which powerfully attract men."[19] Bartmann's breasts, like her buttocks, represent for Cuvier an overdevelopment of female sexuality, a gross exaggeration of normalcy. She is excess (218).

However, at this juncture Cuvier's text on Black female sexuality and blackness remains superficial and incomplete. Or better yet, the text merely replicates earlier ethnographic works on Africans that had such words as *savage*, *primitive*, *monkey*, and *hideous* liberally sprinkled throughout them. As an anatomist, who at this moment of interpreting a Black female body was wading in the waters of theories in keeping with polygenesis, Cuvier endeavored to prove that Blacks were not only physiognomically and physiologically distinct, but that Black women were anatomically different. And what becomes crucial to his project lies in her organ of reproduction. Even in Bartmann's nakedness, Cuvier had yet to decipher her body, to undress the body. In the nineteenth century it is only through dissection that the hidden secrets of the body are fully revealed to the medical gaze,[20] and Bartmann still wore the veil of her skin.

The opportunity for dissection later presented itself, for on December 29, 1815, or January 1, 1816,[21] when she was mistakenly treated for a catarrh, a pleurisy, and dropsy of the breast, Sarah Bartmann died of smallpox aggravated by alcohol poisoning. Immediately following her death, Cuvier obtained permission from the prefect of police to examine Bartmann's body in greater detail. Again taking her to the Jardin du Roi, he began his groundbreaking anatomical study.

Cuvier made a plaster molding of her body. Realizing the importance of his study to the science of natural history, he immediately unveiled Bartmann. The protuberant charms of the Venus were still a curiosity. He discovered that underneath the buttocks, there was nothing but "une masse de graisse" (a mass of fat) (218). Attempting to solve concretely the riddle of the buttocks with respect to the cause of the excessive development, Cuvier writes that on the occasion of her first visit to the Jardin du Roi Bartmann "assured us that this undeniably bizarre conformation occurs during the first pregnancy." (218)

Bartmann's "monstrous" steatopygia was quickly superseded by the treasure Cuvier discovered between her thighs (218): "We did not at all perceive the more remarkable particularity of her organization; she held her apron ('*tablier*') carefully hidden, it was between her thighs, and it was not until after her death that we knew she had it" (215–16). The famous "Hottentot apron" is a hypertrophy, or overdevelopment, of the labia minora, or nymphae. The apron was one of the most widely discussed riddles of female sexuality in the nineteenth century. However, its existence, its intriguing origins, and its uses had been greatly debated in various travelogues of the eighteenth century. As Cuvier began his tract on the Venus, he noted: "There is nothing more famous in natural history than the apron of the Hottentots, and at the same time nothing has been the object of so many debates" (211). Some historiographers of the eighteenth century, such as French naturalist Francois Le Vaillant, thought that the apron—which he regarded as a monstrous example of a few African women's attempts at coquetry and fashion—was the prolongation of the outer vaginal lips, while others, like Englishman John Barrow, surmised that it was a natural development of the nymphae or "petites lèvres."[22] The writings of Le Vaillant and Barrow informed the work of their successor Cuvier, who while not the first naturalist to interest himself in the bodies of Black women, was the first to dissect a Black female cadaver of Bartmann's stature and to solve definitively at least one part of the apron's mysterious puzzle.

Performing a very thorough examination of Bartmann's genitalia, Cuvier notes:

The apron ... is a development of the nymphae.... The outer lips, scarcely pronounced, were intercepted by an oval of four inches; from the upper angle descended between them a quasi-cylindrical protuberance of around 18 lines long and over six lines thick, whose lower extremity enlarges, splits, and protrudes like two fleshy, rippled petals of two and a half inches in length and roughly one inch in width. Each one is rounded at the tip; their base enlarges and descends along the internal border of the outer lip of its side and changes into a fleshy crest.... If one assembles these two appendages, together they form a heart-shaped figure ... in which the middle would be occupied by the vulva.... As for the idea that these excrescences are a product of art, it appears well refuted today if it is true that all Bushwomen possess them from youth. The one that we have seen probably did not take pleasure in procuring such an ornament of which she was ashamed, thus hid so carefully. (216–18)

This very detailed examination of Bartmann's sex, proceeding by the nominating of the visible, consists of Cuvier's use of measurements, adjectives, and metaphors. His language is flowery and feminine: fleshy, rippled petals, crests, and heart-shaped figures. Bartmann's sex blooms, blossoms, before his very eyes; the body becomes legible. As he reads and simultaneously writes a text on Bartmann, the mystery of the dark continent unfolds. The *tablier* is nothing more than the overdevelopment of the nymphae caused by the hot climates in Africa: "We know that the development of the nymphae varies much in Europe, yet it becomes in general more considerable in hotter countries" (217). Moreover, because Bartmann refused to show Cuvier the *tablier*, which for Khoikhoi women was culturally a demonstration of disrespect, and because the *tablier* does not conform to European cultural standards of beauty and art, Cuvier racially naturalizes—in a few short paragraphs—its existence, suggesting primitivity, and consequently a difference in comparison to European women's sex.

Unlike his predecessor Le Vaillant and his undeniably Eurocentric ideals concerning the *tablier*, Cuvier is not interested in the apron's possible cultural significations; it is not a product of art because it is not beautiful; it is not even a "monstrous" signifier of coquetry because it is not alluring to his gaze; and it is certainly not fashionable because it is not *à la mode française*. The *tablier* had to be deemed a racially specific characteristic,[23] and thus representative of sexual pathology, in order to shore up claims of Africans' primitive origins.[24]

Nonetheless, for Cuvier, the *tablier* itself does not establish "a rapport between the women and monkeys," since monkeys' nymphae are barely visible (218). It is "ces enormes masses de graisse que les Boschimanes portent sur les fesses [qui] ... offrent une ressemblance frappante aux femelles des mandrills" (these enormous masses of fat that the Bushwomen carry on the buttocks which ... offer a striking resemblance to female mandrills) (218). Because of this "accroissement vraiment monstreux" (veritable monstrous growth) (218), Cuvier searches for a skeletal modification. Hence, the deciphering and dissecting does not stop at her genitalia. Examining the interior of her vulva and womb, and finding nothing particularly different, he moves on to her "compressed" and "depressed" skull and her pelvic bone ("les os du bassin"). Comparing her pelvic bone against "négresses" and "différentes femmes blanches," he concludes that Negro women share characteristics with female Bushmen and that these characteristics are similar to those of female monkeys ("des femelles singes") (218):

> I was curious to know if the pelvic bones had experienced some modification from this extraordinary overload that they carry. I have thus compared the pelvis of my Bushman female with those of negresses and of different White women; I have found it to be more similar to the first, that is to say, proportionally smaller, less flared.... All these characteristics link, but with a quantity nearly imperceptible, the negresses and the Bushmen females with female monkeys. (218–19)

Courtesy of the scientist's trained anatomical eye, Bartmann's body attests not only to Black women's nearly imperceptible evolutionary underdevelopment, but through Cuvier's use of phrenology—a pseudoscientific discourse that maintains that character and intellect can be read through the shape of the skull and "voluminousness" of the brain—wholly affirms Black inferiority (221). Neither the Bushmen "ni aucune race de nègres" (nor any race of Negroes) (221), according to Cuvier, could have been remotely responsible for the birth of Egyptian civilization (221). The naturalist "could easily assure" his reader that "they [Egyptians] belonged to the same race of men as us; that they had very voluminous skulls and brains; that in a word they were not the exception to that cruel law "which seems to have condemned to an eternal inferiority races with depressed and compressed skulls" (221–22). Stressing difference physiologically ("une ressemblance frappante avec celles qui surviennent aux femelles des mandrills, des papious, etc."), physiognomically ("rebutante physiognomie"), and phrenologically ("crane déprimé and comprimé"), this nineteenth-century master text on the Black female body reads as ultimate *difference* and *pathology*.

Besides molding Bartmann's entire body in plaster, Cuvier preserved her genitalia and skeleton. And in 1816, closing his chapter on the Black female body, he "had the honor of presenting the genital organs of this woman to the Academie, prepared in a manner so as not to leave any doubt about the nature of her apron" (216). Cuvier's work greatly influenced other nineteenth-century anatomical studies on Black women throughout Europe, the Antilles, and the United States.

Today Sarah Bartmann's remains are safely tucked away in Paris's Musée de l'Homme. According to the museum's director, Andre Langaney, the plaster body molding of Bartmann caused such excitement among museum visitors (one of the female tour guides was allegedly sexually accosted, and the molding itself had become the object of touching and many amorous masturbatory liaisons) that its exhibition was discontinued. It appears that Sarah

Bartmann, sadly and ironically commemorated in song, theater, and plaster, alive or dead remained a curious spectacle capable of inciting sexual frenzy and fervor well into the latter half of the twentieth century.

NOTES

1. Gilman, *Difference and Pathology*, pp. 76–108.

2. For more on "the great chain of being" and Bartmann in the nineteenth century, see John and Jean Comaroff, *Of Revelation and Revolution*, "Africa Observed."

3. Cuvier's influence was profound. After his dissection of Bartmann, autopsies were widely performed throughout Europe and the United States on Black American, Antillean, and African women. See Duchet, *Anthropologie et histoire*, for more on the opposing anthropological discourses of the eighteenth and nineteenth centuries: monogenesis and polygenesis.

4. Recounted by Bartmann at the Chancery Court in England and published in the "Law Report," *Times* (London), 29 November 1810.

5. Peter Cezar's original name was probably Pieter Kayser.

6. *Times* (London), 26 November 1810.

7. Reproduced in Edwards and Walvin, *Black Personalities*, p. 171.

8. Stott-Toole, *Circus and Allied Arts*, pp. 333–36.

9. The change in spelling from Baartman to Bartmann in the chapter follows literally and chronologically Bartmann's name change.

10. *Journal des dames et des modes*, 12 February 1815. See also Bernth Lindfors, "'The Hottentot Venus' and Other African Attractions in Nineteenth-Century England," *Australasian Drama Studies* 1 (1983): 88.

11. A copy of the manuscript is in the Bibliothèque Nationale in Paris.

12. Frédéric Cuvier and Etienne Geoffroy St.-Hilaire, *Histoire naturelle des mammifères* (Paris, 1824). All translations of excerpts are mine and from this edition of the text.

13. Jay, *Downcast Eyes*, p. 8.

14. The text on Bartmann by Georges Cuvier, besides appearing in *Histoire naturelle de mammifères*, can also be found under the title, "Extraits d'observation faites sur le cadavre d'une femme connue à Paris et à Londres sous le nom de Vénus Hottentote," in *Discours sur les révolutions du globe* (Paris: Passard, 1864), pp. 211–22. It is from this reprinted and more readily available version of the text in the United States that this and the following excerpts are taken. All translations are mine.

15. In addition to Cuvier's comparisons, see nineteenth-century naturalist Virey's *Histoire naturelle du genre humain* and his article in the *Dictionnaire des sciences médicales* 35 (1819): 398–403. Virey's discussion of Blacks is also included in Guenebault's *Natural History of the Negro Race*.

16. In his closing arguments on Bartmann and black inferiority, Cuvier reflects upon the greatness of the ancient race of Egyptians and concludes that they were definitely white in intellect (221).

17. See Cuvier, *Le Règne Animal*, p. 95.

18. See Jordonova, *Sexual Visions*, p. 29.

19. Cited in Jordonova, *Sexual Visions*, p. 29.

20. Jordonova, *Sexual Visions*, pp. 99–100.

21. There is some confusion as to her date of death. Records at the museum list the date as January 1, 1816, while Cuvier maintains it was December 29, 1815.

22. Both Le Vaillant and Barrow are cited in Avalon, "Sarah, La Venus hottentote." Le Vaillant says in his *Voyage dans l'intérieur de l'Afrique* (1790) that he had only seen four women and one young girl in this ridiculous state ("dans cet état ridicule").

23. "Labial hypertrophy" is not a racially specific characteristic. It has been found in Africans, African Americans, Asians, and European and Euro-American women. See the journal *Woman: An Historical Gynaecological and Anthropological Compendium* as well as a host of articles in contemporary medical literature, although most are shot through with racist-sexist discourse.

24. Gilman, *Difference and Pathology*, pp. 76–108.

WORKS CITED

Comaroff, John, and Jean Comaroff. *Of Revelation and Revolution: Christianity, Colonialism, and Consciousness in South Africa*. Chicago: University of Chicago Press, 1991.

Cuvier, Frédéric, and St. Hilaire, Geoffroy. *Histoire naturelle des mammifères*. Paris: A. Belin, 1824–27.

Cuvier, Georges. *Le Règne animal*. Paris: Chez Deterville, 1817.

Cuvier, Georges, et al. *Discours sur les révolutions du globe*. Paris: Passard, 1864.

Duchet, Michèle. *Anthropologie et histoire au siècle des lumièrs: Buffon, Voltaire, Rousseau, Helvétius, Diderot*. Paris: Librairie François Maspero, 1971.

Edwards, Paul, and James Walvin. *Black Personalities in the Era of the Slave Trade*. Baton Rouge: Louisiana State University Press, 1983.

Gilman, Sander. *Difference and Pathology: Stereotypes of Sexuality, Race and Madness*. Ithaca, N.Y.: Cornell University Press, 1985.

Jay, Martin. *Downcast Eyes: The Denigration of Vision in Twentieth-Century French Thought*. Berkeley: University of California Press, 1993.

Jordonova, Ludmilla. *Sexual Visions: Images of Gender in Science and Medicine between the Eighteenth and Twentieth Centuries*. Madison: University of Wisconsin Press, 1989.

Le Vaillant, Francois. *Voyage dans l' intérieur de l'Afrique*. Paris: De l'imprimerie de Crapelet, 1790.

Lindfors, Bernth. "'The Hottentot Venus' and other African Attractions in Nineteenth-Century England." *Australasian Drama Studies* 1 (1983): 83–104.

Stott-Toole, R. *Circus and Allied Arts: A World Bibliography 1500–1962*. Derby, U.K.: Harpur, 1962.

Virey, Julien-Joseph. *Histoire naturelle du genre humain*. 1st ed. Paris: Crochard, 1801.

DISCUSSION QUESTIONS: EGAN AND GARDNER

1. Enumerate the many ways in which racialized women in Canada, many of whom are immigrants and refugees, experience racism when they interact with the Canadian health care system.
2. Feminist organizations in Canada, especially the Ontario Coalition for Abortion Clinics, have responded to women's experiences of racism in the Canadian health system, attempting to help them gain control over their health care. Describe these efforts in detail.
3. What do the authors suggest the Canadian government can do to alleviate this problem? What further suggestions can you offer?

DISCUSSION QUESTIONS: SHARPLEY-WHITING

1. Sharpley-Whiting argues that the body of Sarah Bartmann was used by European scientists in the 19th century as a tool with which to devise a hierarchy of race and civilization based largely on constructs of sexuality. Explain.
2. How could this scientifically generated racial hierarchy justify particular European cultural, political, and economic practices in the 19th century?
3. The construct of the hypersexual Black woman, based on scientific "evidence" provided by the Hottentot Venus, continues to circulate in our 21st century. Examine cultural representations of Black women in magazines, music videos, television advertisements, and movies for this intersection of race, gender, and sexual relations.

FURTHER READINGS

1. Agnew, V. 1996. *Resisting Discrimination: Women from Asian, Africa, and the Caribbean and the Women's Movement in Canada.* Toronto: University of Toronto Press.

   The relationship among the Canadian women's movement, the Canadian state, and racialized women has been uneasy and conflicted. In this book Agnew analyzes the racist character of both the Canadian state and feminist theory and practice, while uncovering the long-invisible political activism of racialized women in this country.

2. Calliste, Agnes, and George Sefa Dei (eds.). 2000. *Anti-racist Feminism: Critical Race and Gender Studies.* Halifax: Fernwood Publishing.

   A collection of writings by a number of the leading feminist anti-racist scholars in Canada, this book introduces readers to the meanings and significance of "race" in social practice and to transnational feminist collaboration. Authors address many aspects of gendered racialization processes in the lives of Black, South Asian, African, and Muslim women.

3. Frankenberg, Ruth. 1993. *White Women, Race Matters: The Social Construction of Whiteness.* Minneapolis: University of Minnesota Press.

   This is a groundbreaking and award-winning book that is full of analytic insight. Frankenberg explores how whiteness as a racial category is socially constructed. Her argument is that race shapes White women's lives through racial privilege. In-depth interviews reveal the racism and challenges to it in White women's lives in the United States.

4. hooks, bell. 2004. *We Real Cool: Black Men and Masculinity.* New York: Routledge.

   hooks considers Black men and masculinity in this book. She argues they are taught violence and aggression as keys to survival, an ideology we see sometimes in hip-hop lyrics and culture, which dehumanizes them. In addition, Black men are put at emotional, social, and economic risk through unstable employment and alienation from their fathers and children. Through her analysis, hooks advises them to break with the macho demands and values of patriarchal culture in order to survive.

5. Lewis, Reina. 1996. *Gendering Orientalism: Race, Femininity, and Representation.* London: Routledge.

   Lewis takes up the question of how White European women contributed to imperial cultures in the late 19th century. She examines Henriette Brown's Orientalist paintings and George Eliot's writings, as well as their contemporary reception, to show how women contributed to the phenomenon of Orientalism.

RELEVANT FILMS

1. *Hollywood Harems*, 1999, 24 minutes, Women Make Movies

   In this documentary, Kamal-Eldin chronicles and analyzes Hollywood's enduring fascination with and fantasies about the Orient. Interweaving film clips from over 60 years of movie making, she demonstrates how relations of gender, sexuality, and race organize Hollywood's representations of harem keepers and dwellers, which (re)produce racist assumptions about people from the "East" while perpetuating the cultural, racial, and moral supremacy of the West.

2. *The Life and Times of Sara Baartman: The Hottentot Venus*, 1998, 53 minutes, First Run Icarus Films

   This film documents the life of Sarah Bartmann, a Khoi Khoi woman from South Africa who was abducted in 1810 and taken to Britain where she was exhibited countrywide as a sexual freak. In 1814, the Hottentot Venus was taken to France to become the object of scientific research into "primitive" sexuality. For centuries this research has been the source about discourses of Black women's sexuality.

3. *Coconut/Cane and Cutlass*, 1994, 30 minutes, Third Eye Productions

   An Indo-Caribbean lesbian who immigrated to Canada in the 1970s presents a poetic autobiographical narrative of that journey, including her experiences of and insights about exile, displacement, indenture, oppression, and shifting national identities.

4. *Brown Women, Blonde Babies*, 1992, 28 minutes, Productions Multi-Monde

Filipina domestic workers in Canada are the focus of this documentary. They have migrated to Canada in large numbers due to the unequal effects of economic globalization, which has caused increasing poverty in the Philippines. The film captures the nature and challenges of these women's working lives, including the pressure to send remittances back to the Philippines to support both their families and the state, which uses the foreign currency to pay back international loans.

5. *The Dreams of the Night Cleaners*, 1996, 47 minutes, National Film Board of Canada

This film constitutes an exploration of the working lives of Usha and Devika, two South Asian immigrants to Canada who are employed as night cleaners. It documents the racism, sexism, and employment anxieties these immigrants experience in an uncertain global marketplace.

RELEVANT WEB SITES

1. http://pages.towson.edu/itrow/rgc.htm

Yet again, this Web site contains an extensive bibliography of feminist literature that analyzes the intersection of gender, race, and class in many social sites, institutions, and academic disciplines.

2. http://academic.udayton.edu/race/05intersection/Gender/genderoo.htm

The University of Dayton School of Law's Web site on *Race, Racism, and the Law* lists many links to resources that explore the intersection of race and gender in the law, revolving around the experiences of India, African-American, Japanese, and Africa women. Topics include trafficking, female genital mutilation, single parenting, and the comfort women of World War II.

3. www.h-net.msu.edu/~women/bibs/venus.html

At this site you can find a discussion about and bibliography for the Hottentot Venus from a feminist perspective.

4. www.yorku.ca/gmcr/race_gender_class/garment.htm

The Gender, Migration, and Citizenship Project at York University in Toronto is doing research on the intersection of race, gender, and class in the lives of domestic, garment, and sex trade workers in Canada. On this Web site they provide a list of references on each of these topics.

5. www.awid.org/go.php?stid=1454

This Association for Women's Rights in Development Web site is an excellent resource that explains the status of Aboriginal women and Aboriginal feminism in Australia. It provides informative statistics outlining their unequal situation and social disadvantages, despite Australia's relatively strong global economic position.

PART XI

GENDER, IMPERIALISM, AND GLOBALIZATION

eminist scholars have recently addressed the dominant myths about globalization that pervade the social sciences. In particular, they criticize the conventional understanding that globalization is primarily a macro-economic process that is magically generated outside the context of everyday life and thus beyond our control. They are also concerned with the foundational gender myths that structure mainstream theories of globalization, especially the widespread assumption that globalization is a gender-neutral process. These authors contend that what is required in order to understand global processes more fully and precisely, without implicit gender baggage, is a style of analysis that shows how globalization operates through multiple modes and is effected through large-scale institutions, as well as by individuals who are engaged in a variety of locally situated activities that are embedded in, but at the same time actively transform, global processes, including imperialism in both its past and present incarnations.

The articles included in this last section of the reader provide such micro-level analyses that actually specify how global processes play out in particular locales for particular groups of people with particular consequences. Consequently, they render the links between gender and globalization more visible, which in turn contributes to a more measured overall understanding of the forms, impacts, experiences, and meanings of globalization. Gendering analyses of globalization improves our understanding of what globalization is, how it works, how it affects people's lives, how it is influenced by gender hierarchies and discourses, and how these gender hierarchies in turn shape global institutions and relationships.

Indira Ghose opens this section with the third chapter of her book *Women Travellers in Colonial India: The Power of the Female Gaze*. Her aim in this piece is to examine White European women's accounts of the Indian *zenana* (harem) during the colonial era, an early period of transnational migration and transcultural interaction for these women. During this time period in the West, White women suffered the male gaze, but as privileged travellers in a colonial setting, they were actively involved in the voyeuristic pleasure of gazing at "exotic" colonized women. Ghose argues that specific historical

319

and political circumstances informed this "female gaze," which was a vital part of the British imperial project in India. Consequently, European women did not enact one universal female gaze with which to judge and manage Indian women, but rather multiple and shifting modes of female spectatorship that were shaped by changing imperial priorities.

Robina Mohammad continues the theme of women's migration in a global context, but shifts directional flows and time periods by examining a contemporary community of South Asian immigrants in Britain. Expatriate Pakistanis suffer marginalization, exclusion, and racism within mainstream British society. As a coping mechanism they have taken efforts to create an autonomous and self-sustaining group identity as Muslims, which have positioned Pakistani women as conspicuous "markers" of the community. Women's bodies, sexuality, dress, and mobility are regulated and disciplined to enable the necessary sense of "separateness" that is required to construct and maintain the Islam/West binary. Mohammad stresses that women neither passively "receive" these disciplinary measures, nor passively participate in the construction of group identity. Rather, they simultaneously resist and comply.

In her recent yet influential article "Is Local:Global as Feminine:Masculine? Rethinking the Gender of Globalization," Carla Freeman examines the gendered nature of discourses of globalization, the ways in which they are infused with notions of masculinity, femininity, and gender roles. In her critique of mainstream treatments of globalization, she calls for feminist analyses that address the gendered nature of global processes, the local effects of globalization, and the impact of the local on the global. She then provides an example of such an analysis in her study of women higglers in Barbados who work at a transnational informatics firm, which highlights the gendered interplay between the global and the local.

The previous three readings all concern aspects of globalization that have been largely ignored by mainstream theorists of globalization because they do not deal with macro-economic processes. Lourdes Benería introduces a feminist economist's perspective on globalization in her piece "Globalization, Gender, and the Davos Man." Here she argues that globalization has precipitated the expansion of economic markets that transcend national boundaries. This expansion of markets has taken place within the context of a neo-liberal model of development, which has revived economic practices characteristic of 19th-century capitalism. This neo-liberal model has also created the Davos Man, an economic being characterized by the norms and behaviours associated with economic rationality such as individualism, competitive behaviour, and the acceptance of social inequalities and greed. Benería is concerned that the Davos Man, who controls our economic and military capabilities, and the market operate in gendered ways that disadvantage women economically, even though it is their paid and unpaid labour that sustains the economic system. She calls for more feminist economic analyses and visions that bypass models of free individual choice in a self-regulated market to instigate more equitable economic and social systems that do not take rational economic man's objectives as the desired norm.

In this final reading on gender and globalization, Michael Kimmel, a sociologist of masculinity, draws out the relationship between global processes and masculinity. He argues that globalization has transformed particular political, economic, and cultural arrangements at both the national and regional levels, and these transformations in turn have shifted domestic and public patriarchies. Lower middle-class men in North America, Europe, and some Islamic countries seem to have been affected most dramatically by these changes in ways that threaten their masculinity. These men resist the gendered threats that accompany globality by attempting to restore domestic and public patriarchies, which reveals that resistance to globalization does not always bring positive social change.

CHAPTER 27

THE FEMALE GAZE
Encounters in the Zenana

Indira Ghose

The first question that travellers to the East were confronted with on their return, according to Richard Burton, was: "What are the women like?"[1] Unfortunately, the gentlemen in question were unable to oblige in one important respect—it was virtually impossible for them to gain access to a harem or seraglio. Even Burton's disguises and contortions were of little use in this connection. This was no impediment to their fantasies, however. In 1598, Thomas Dallam claimed to have caught a glimpse of the Turkish Sultan's concubines playing ball in the royal gardens, and in the seventeenth century Sir George Courthope deftly conjured up a scene of royal sport with concubines in a pond in the same gardens (they were empty when he saw them). Alexander Pope fantasized about eunuchs and even cucumbers only being served cut in the harem; Burton's own account was both more drastic and more explicit.[2] And the painter Thomas Daniell's *A Zenana Scene* (1804), with its Oriental beauty draped in gauzy veils, was purely the product of his fantasy. It was only with the posthumous publication of Lady Montagu's *Letters* from Turkey in 1763 that an eyewitness account of life in the harem was made available to readerships in the West.

The issue of female spectatorship and the related questions of female desire and subjectivity as well as enmeshment in relations of power/knowledge are brought into particularly sharp focus in the case of eyewitness accounts of the harem by Western women. I wish to look specifically at accounts by Englishwomen and their encounters of the other kind in the Indian zenana.[3] Despite the fact that zenanas were only to be found in upper-class households in the North and East of India, they attracted an inordinately large portion of curiosity among women travellers.[4] Paradoxically, however, the travellers themselves—as women—were the focus of the male gaze in their own patriarchal home culture. The question to be probed is, what does it mean to look at the other woman from a woman's point of view? This issue is inextricably bound up with recent discussions on the female gaze.

Laura Mulvey's analysis of the position of female viewers of Hollywood films has emerged as a key text in discussions of the female gaze.[5] Originally Mulvey looks at the question of how spectators gain pleasure from mainstream films that are premised on the image of women as sexual commodities whose main *raison d'être* is to cater to male fantasies and desires. She concludes that in Hollywood films the location of the spectator is constructed as masculine, offering him the pleasures of voyeurism and/or the comforts of fetishism and identification with the (invariably male) hero. In other words: the gaze is male. In her later work Mulvey turns to the female spectator and identifies two possible viewing positions for her *vis-à-vis* Hollywood cinema's sexualized and fetishized female star—that of a vicarious identification with a male perspective or that of a narcissistic identification with the woman protagonist in the film, linked to the desire to be as sexually desirable as the film character. In fact, Mulvey posits the female spectator as continually oscillating between these two positions.[6] Thus, women have a choice only between objectifying the other woman in an adoption of the male perspective or identifying with the female character in her role as sex object of the male gaze.

These arguments have been further developed (and contradicted) by feminist critics in a variety of fields, who argue in favour of an autonomous female gaze. Thus Rosemary Betterton has examined the female nude in the oeuvre of the painter Suzanne Valadon and has come to the conclusion that the gender of the artist has left its trace in the images of women produced by her.[7] In these paintings, Betterton discerns a critical distance to the representation of the woman's body as an eroticized site. Reina Lewis has looked at women Orientalist painters' representations of the harem and detects a palpable difference to male Orientalist art and a latent threat to male Orientalist fantasies.[8] The harem is depicted as a social space rather than an eroticized space, with interactive relationships between the Oriental women focused on rather than the women being represented as merely awaiting the male gaze. Billie Melman, in her scrutiny of women travellers' accounts of their trips to Oriental (Middle Eastern) harems, observes a progressive domestication of the harem in Western women's writings.[9] Lady Montagu's famous claim of the greater (sexual) freedom of veiled women as contrasted to their Western sisters is gradually transmuted in later accounts to the depiction of the harem as a domesticated, bourgeois home, the women assiduously occupying themselves with needlework.

Many of the analyses of the female gaze draw on feminist psychoanalytic theory. However, in recent works on the female gaze the concept itself has come under fire. Feminist psychoana-

lytic theory is seen to unduly privilege gender.[10] An analysis drawing on discourse theory, on the other hand, would begin by dismantling the very notion of a female gaze: there is, of course, no "female gaze." A concept of identity as precarious and overdetermined by a plurality of factors makes it imperative to take coordinates other than gender into account. As Mary Eagleton points out,

> the notion of a "female imagination" can confirm the belief in a deep, basic, and inevitable difference between male and female ways of perceiving the world. Such "essentialist" or "biologistic" beliefs imply that there is something intrinsic in the experience of being female and thus render gender biological rather than cultural; they tend to privilege gender at the expense of class or race; and they can too easily become ahistorical and apolitical, presuming an unproblematic unity among women across culture, class and history.[11]

*****

In addition, determinants such as race and gender are themselves not characterized by an inherent essence, but are unstable and differential terms. Mulvey's spectator is predicated on a notion of gender as a fixed subject position of binary opposites. For a woman spectator to take up a masculinized viewing position involves, as it were, an act of transvestism. But recent feminist critics have shown gender to be a sophisticated political and social construction and gender identification to rather be a shifting and contradictory process. As Judith Butler explains, "Gender is the repeated stylization of the body, a set of repeated acts within a highly regulatory frame that congeal over time to produce the appearance of substance, of a natural sort of being."[12] "Woman," in other words, is only a myth.[13]

The question to be asked is: whose gaze is it anyway?[14] It is the power relations inscribed into the gaze that call for closer scrutiny, as discourse theory has shown. As various critics of Western feminism have pointed out, notions of universal womanhood re-enact the strategies of liberal humanism by setting up the yardstick by which to define the other and ultimately recolonize her.[15] These critics too have demolished the notion of "woman" and have pointed to the diversity of womanhood. In my analysis of Englishwomen's encounters with the Indian other, I wish to point to the historical dimensions of the gaze—instead of a universal "female gaze" I wish to look at specific political and historical configurations and how they have informed the gaze. Even within a circumscribed historical constellation, however, a plurality of gazes is discernible.

Finally, the notion of "the gaze" needs to be interrogated as well. The term "the gaze" assumes an autonomous viewing subject whose perception gives access to truth. In mimetic theories of art, texts are presumed to transparently reproduce this visual experience. In post-structuralist theory, however, experience is seen as culturally mediated and as historically produced and constructed within discourses. A reductive and homogeneous concept of the gaze needs to be replaced by a historicized notion of perception. As Betterton points out, "looking, and the psychic mechanisms which structure it, are themselves historically produced."[16] As regards the travel narratives of women travellers, for example, their encounters with the other woman were structured by the cultural norms and the ideological forces at work at the time. From their accounts we learn more about the fantasies of the viewers than about the material realities of the zenana.

THE EROTIC GAZE

Meyda Yegenoglu attacks the notion of a female gaze by deconstructing the harem account of Lady Montagu, one of the icons of feminist criticism.[17] She draws an analogy between women travellers' descriptions of the harem and Derrida's concept of the supplement: their accounts, while serving to complement male Orientalist accounts, were simultaneously disavowed as of minor significance. Nevertheless, for European women, barred admittance to scientific discourses, harem literature provided an opportunity to contribute to the discourses of Orientalism and thus gain in prestige. In Montagu's text she identifies a plea-

sure at being the first to penetrate the space of the other and thus add to the production of knowledge about the other. Yegenoglu attributes the Western subject's voyeuristic desire to "know" the Oriental woman to the fact that women were seen as the essence of the East, associated as it was with femininity, sensuality and irrationality in the discourses of Orientalism.[18] Yegenoglu sees Lady Montagu and her successors as implicated in Orientalism as they too constitute the other into an object of knowledge and contribute to the unequal power/knowledge nexus. [...]

We are thus faced with two irreconcilable readings of Western women travellers' accounts of the harem: critics such as Billie Melman see a sense of cross-cultural women's solidarity at work here, subverting patriarchal voyeuristic representations of the harem;[19] colonial discourse critics like Janaki Nair[20] and Yegenoglu see these accounts as an example of Western women's complicity in Orientalism and their assumption of a male gaze. There might, however, be another dimension to women's representations of the other hitherto insufficiently theorized. This is addressed in one of the most exciting essays on the female gaze to have appeared recently—"Desperately Seeking Difference" by Jackie Stacey.[21] Stacey looks at the phenomenon of fascination between women, which she considers hardly surprising "in a culture where the circulation of idealized and desirable images of femininity constantly surrounds us" (114). In particular, she takes a closer look at the pleasures produced for the female spectator by the film *Desperately Seeking Susan* (dir. Susan Seidelman, 1984), which virtually launched the Madonna cult. In this film the main protagonist, a bored and insecure American housewife, is drawn into a series of adventures through her fascination with the seductively anarchic Madonna, representing everything the housewife is not. This fascination, which the spectator is invited to share, "is neither purely identification with the other woman, nor desire for her in the strictly erotic sense of the word. It is a desire to see, to know and to become more like an idealized feminine other, in a context where the difference between the two women is repeatedly reestablished" (115).

Stacey's rejection of the rigid division between

objectification (as accomplice of the male voy-euristic look) and identification by pointing to an interplay of both elements offers one way of approaching the accounts of women travellers by focusing on issues of pleasure and fantasy. [...]

*****

"The perusal of Lady Mary Wortley Mon-tague's [*sic*] work has rendered me very anxious to visit a zenana, and to become acquainted with the ladies of the East," Parks announces (1:59). In her text Parks produces herself as Montagu's successor and is applauded by reviewers accord-ingly.[22] When she receives an invitation to pay a visit to a real zenana, she exults, "Was this not delightful? All my dreams ... were to be turned into reality. I was to have an opportunity of viewing life in the zenana, of seeing the native ladies of the East, women of high rank, in the seclusion of their own apartments, in private life" (1:37). A juxtaposing of Montagu's text with that of Parks is revealing for the insights it produces of an intertextual dialogue at work. Montagu's encounter with the fair Fatima is described in the following passage:

> I have seen all that has been called lovely either in England or Germany, and must own that I never saw anything so glori-ously beautiful.... I confess, though the Greek lady had before given me a great opinion of her beauty I was so struck with admiration that I could not for some time speak to her, being wholly taken up with gazing. That surprising harmony of fea-tures! that charming result of the whole! that exact proportion of body! that lovely bloom of complexion unsullied by art! the unutterable enchantment of her smile! But her eyes! large and black with all the soft languishment of the bleu! every turn of her face discovering some new charm![23]

In Parks' text Fatima has mutated to Mulka:

> How beautiful she looked! how very beautiful! Her animated countenance was constantly varying, and her dark eyes

struck fire when a joyous thought crossed her mind.... I felt no surprise when I re-membered the wondrous tales told by the men of the beauty of an Eastern woman....

*****

While the pleasure in gazing is presented in a similar way, Montagu's textualized gaze is far more self-reflexive, however. In one instance, the famous anecdote in the Turkish bath where she describes how the Oriental women marvel at the corset she is wearing, she produces herself as the object of the other's gaze and locates herself firmly in the viewing process. Here, for once, it is not only the corporeality of the Eastern woman that is under scrutiny by the disembodied viewer. The narrator is highly aware of the social and cultural implications of the voyeuristic gaze—at one point, her eye caught by some seductive slave girls, she notes, "I was sorry that decency did not permit me to stop and consider them nearer" (129). Her defense of the voyeuristic gaze attempts to de-eroticize the gaze, instead locating it within pseudo-religious and learned discourses as a legitimizing strategy and aestheticizing the object of the gaze.

*****

In both these travel accounts there is an undeniable sense of excitement, a frisson, in the descriptions of the Oriental other, which might, but not entirely, be attributable to homoerotic attraction. Stacey's development of the notion of the erotics of difference offers a useful analyti-cal tool here, especially in the light of a culture where eroticized images of Oriental women were continually circulated. An escapist ele-ment might well play a role here as well: in the projection of women's repressed sexual fantasies onto the other. Stacey does not seek to deny ho-moerotic desire—she sees purely erotic desire as only one element that informs a fascination with otherness between women. Above all, she points the way to a more active model of spectatorship for women, one that regains a space for women viewers to control the meaning of an image.[24]

Similarly, what I am arguing here is for a more ambivalent reading of female spectatorship in the harem—one that accounts for women's own voyeuristic pleasure in gazing at other women. Contrary to Mulvey's concept of fixed, pre-determined subjectivity, a notion of subjectivity as shifting and contradictory would take these women travellers' fractured gaze into account. To be sure, travellers like Montagu and Parks employ their privileged eyewitness status in the service of the voyeuristic male gaze. Women were, after all, both observer and observed—they themselves were particularly subject to the regulatory gazes of their own patriarchal society and their viewpoint is inflected accordingly. But not only do Parks and Montagu look vicariously from a male point of view, but they also derive their own pleasure from the sight—a pleasure that may well be inflected by homoerotic desire and that is, above all, attributable to the erotics of difference. This fascination with otherness is familiar to us from other travel narratives as well. Similarly, the reader constructed by their texts is not necessarily male—their texts cater to both male and female curiosity and voyeuristic fantasy.

The gaze is never innocent, however, but is located in specific relations of power. The voyeuristic gaze, whether male or female, is always linked to a sense of mastery over the image. The main difference between Madonna and Mulka/Fatima lies in the different political and historical formations they are located in. The texts of both travel writers put their own pleasure at the service of Orientalism in their production and dissemination of knowledge about the other. By the nineteenth century, moreover, the world equation of power had shifted significantly. Parks' gaze serves the colonial policy of "knowing" the other, a strategy to implement an improved surveillance of the colonized. [...]

THE COMPASSIONATE GAZE

The image produced of the zenana in most other women travellers' texts is quite different from that created by Parks. Many travellers to India never manage to visit a zenana and openly admit that their descriptions are based on second-hand knowledge. The globe-trotter Constance Gordon Cumming, for instance, spends a year travelling in India without catching more than a glimpse of a native woman (servants and peasant women excluded).[25] By the middle of the nineteenth century the policy of racial segregation had been well established, with the inter-dining and mutual visits of the previous century confined to a minimum. By analogy with the textual strategies which—as Billie Melman has shown—increasingly domesticize the harem in the texts of women travellers to the Middle East, the zenana, too, is produced less and less as a site of sensual pleasures and increasingly constructed as a bourgeois home. Any sense of fascination with otherness is repressed in these later texts. Instead, the image presented of the Indian woman is that of a Victim.[26]

This correlated with the increase of reforming zeal concerning Indian society fuelled by the Evangelical revival in England in the early part of the nineteenth century.[27] The position of women in a society was seen as an index of its level of civilization. For the Evangelicals as well as the Utilitarians who gained political control of Indian government policy in the 1830s, Indian civilization was degenerate and decadent. The "Indian women's question" became a political issue, with reformers clamouring for a radical transformation of Indian society. Large numbers of missionaries travelling to India filled in a crusading spirit to help uplift the downtrodden Indian woman. When Utilitarian influence on Indian politics ebbed, the banner for the reform of the condition of Indian women was taken up by the early feminists.[28] Women travellers' accounts of Indian women contributed to this image of Indian womanhood and thus served a further function—namely that of self-definition for the Western woman. By defining the other as backward, English women were able to define themselves as emancipated, civilized and rational creatures. The battles of feminism were also fought on the battlegrounds of the zenana. And here the Indian woman fulfilled the function of the "self-consolidating other."[29]

In Frances Duberly's account of her visit to a zenana in 1858, we see these discourses at work.[30]

First her account reveals a sense of fascination and bewilderment at the other, which is transmuted into a synecdochical obsession with ornamentation, perhaps not untinged with material envy:

> The ladies, who received us in the durbar room, were seated on chairs in a row.... The eldest lady conversed: the rest sat in silence. I never saw such a profusion of jewellery in my life. The forehead of each was hidden by a circular ornament of precious stones, and even their eyelids were fringed with diamonds; nose jewels, the size and weight of which distorted the nostril, completed the decorations of the face. Several necklaces, some apparently of solid gold, others of strings of pearls, covered the neck and bosom; while massive bracelets, blazing with rubies and emeralds, encircled their arms from elbow to wrist. One bracelet I particularly remember; it was a thick and heavy circlet of gold, studded with about thirty emeralds the size of peas. On their ankles they wore three or four chains and anklets of different patterns, and each toe was covered with an ornament resembling enamelled leaves. The Ranee who conversed appeared to be an unusually intelligent woman.... Her information was, I believe, acquired from a Persian newspaper, which she receives once a week (39).

It is perhaps not wholly misplaced to read a hint of class envy in the encounters between Englishwomen and Indian women, for most Englishwomen in India were from a middle-class background while the women they met were usually from the native aristocracy. Nevertheless, the narrator is convinced that the Indian woman envies her. After confirming, in answer to a query, that she had actually been present at a battle, the princess "fell back in her chair and sighed. A whole lifetime of suppressed emotion, of crushed ambition, of helplessness, and weariness, seemed to be comprehended in that short sigh" (41). No doubt personal motives predisposed the "heroine of the Crimea" (Duberly was the only woman to have accompanied the British troops during the Crimean War) to identify the Indian princess as unfortunate—including a portion of personal vanity. What is recurrent in Englishwomen's descriptions of Indian women, however, is the fact that they serve the project of self-presentation for the Western woman as more free than her Eastern counterpart.

Another celebrated traveller, Isabella Bird, is quoted on the same theme in the following way:

> I have lived in Zenanas, and have seen the daily life of the secluded women, and I can speak from bitter experience of what their lives are—the intellect dwarfed, so that a woman of twenty or thirty years of age is more like a child of eight, intellectually; while all the worst passions of human nature are stimulated and developed in a fearful degree: jealousy, envy, murderous hate, intrigue, running to such an extent that in some countries I have hardly ever been in a woman's house without being asked for drugs with which to disfigure the favourite wife, or to take away the life of the favourite wife's infant son. This request has been made of me nearly one hundred times. This is only an indication of the daily life of whose miseries we think so little, and which is a natural product of the systems we ought to have subverted long ago.[31]

In this horror scenario, rife with mutilation and murder, it is striking how Bird rhetorically aligns herself with the powers that be in the name of the higher cause—defined by Gayatri Spivak as that of "white men saving brown women from brown men." [32] The accounts of Englishwomen from the zenana served an ideological function, of course, namely that of supporting British colonial policy with regard to social reform. It was in the interests of the colonial power to define the Indian women as oppressed and Indian men as domestic oppressors to legitimize continued colonial rule over a people so obviously unfit to take up responsibility for itself.[33] Thus women travellers' accounts served both as an alibi for colonial policy and as a deflection of critique from their own oppression in Western society.

Despite the efforts to defuse the eroticism of Indian women, a sense of unease at the zenana as an uncolonized space remains: "This was the unreasonable, illogical space that resisted colonization and, thus, civilization."[34] Rumours about Indian women's obsession with sexuality remain in circulation. Paradoxically, the oppressed Indian women are constructed as immensely powerful in controlling their men and seen as a site of resistance to social reform instigated by the colonial power. As the social reformer Mary Carpenter remarks, "It is everywhere felt among the enlightened, that the stronghold of idolatry, and all its attendant evils, is in the home" (2:75).

The types of gazes looked at so far all reflect the two main modes of perceiving the other that dominate Western discourses. The other is presented as wholly other—the object of either fascination or repulsion (as in the voyeuristic harem accounts of Montagu and Parks). Conversely, the other is reduced to the same—but is presented as inferior to the self (as in the accounts of the backward Indian woman). In both cases the other serves as a foil for the fantasies and/or self-definition of the self.

THE CONSERVATIVE GAZE

With the emergence of the "New Woman" in England at the end of the nineteenth century, a further variation in the image of the Indian woman is to be observed. For conservative-minded travellers such as the journalist Mary Billington or the Anglo-Indian writers Maud Diver and Flora Annie Steel, the Indian woman now embodies all the feminine qualities that are under threat in England. Billington undertakes a lengthy journey to India for the *Daily Graphic* in order to investigate the hidden lives of Indian women. The conclusion she comes to is that "Indian women are not altogether in such pitiful plight as some of their so-called friends come and tell us."[35] Billington emphatically denies the reports of the immorality of Indian women and claims they are as moral as Englishwomen: "I am quite certain that if all present zenana restrictions were withdrawn, the Indian female population would stand woman for woman upon quite as high a platform as ourselves in this direction" (123). She

stresses her high respect for "the gentle fortitude that ... is one of the most admirable traits in the native female character" (4). In her account we gain a wealth of background information on what women's lives in the zenana are really like—among other facts she records "the wit of the zenana," the games girls play, as well as the regional variation in jewellery.[36]

Her benevolence towards Indian women is startling only if one overlooks the political agenda informing her text—written, after all, for the home market. Her text is haunted by the "noisy and assertive" feminists at home (20), either riding bicycles or wearing "uncompromising trousers" (25), who become increasingly threatening figures as the text progresses (on page 176 they are "in a frenzy" at the thought of their Eastern sisters' contentment with their more womanly lives). Similarly, she makes a visit to various communities of workers and denies reports of labour agitation, describing them instead as a "happy community" (152) kept busy with interesting and gainful employment. At one point she compares Indian women mine workers to English women workers: "Remembering, as one does, the terrible descriptions of the swearing, drunken, degraded disgraces to their sex that the north-countrywomen workers underground used to be, the most remarkable point about them was their perfect gentleness and modesty" (155). A variation on this theme is given in the following key passage, where the narrator cannot suppress a passing vitriolic dig at an insolent working-class at home getting above its place:

> According to modern "emancipated" lights, the answer of a poor Mohammedan woman in Calcutta to my question as to what she regarded as the chief happiness she would desire for herself might seem a contracted one. "To see my husband happy, and to know that what I have cooked and done for him has helped to make him so; to see my sons grow up as men, honest and strong, and to know that my daughters are well married"—is, in my view, a praiseworthy domestic ideal, enough even when set beside the possibilities of a bank holiday on Hampstead Heath. (173)

The gentle and docile Indian woman is conflated with the obedient worker. This conflation of race and class is a marker of colonial discourse, and finds its most absurd expression in the remark Lord Curzon is reported to having made on seeing British soldiers in India bathing—how strange it was that the poor should have such white skins.[37]

The conservative backlash against both the worker's movement and the women's movement in Britain represented by Billington and her ilk correlated to what historians have identified as the resurgence of Orientalism in colonial policy in India.[38] Francis Hutchins points out that with the waning of reformist fervour—in part due to the fact that a wholesale conversion of the teeming millions of India to Christianity was nowhere in sight—India became the preserve of conservative-minded officials who insisted it was in the best interests of Britain to conserve the traditional society of India—naturally with the British at the top of the hierarchy. They claimed to know the requirements of the Oriental mind and repulsed any attempt at reform that would destabilize the status quo.[39] A frequent lament is the decline of traditional Indian values under British reformist influence. Billington, for instance, lays the blame for the deterioration of traditional arts and crafts on missionaries: "drawn, as so large a percentage of their teachers are, from the lower middle classes, and imbued with the worst philistinism of their order" (189), they are unable to appreciate the true wonders of the East. As in (the equally conservative) politics of the picturesque, there is an implicit elitist element at work here. Maud Diver reproves missionaries for trying to break down social barriers by mingling with natives by reminding them that "the Oriental is a profound respector ... of all outward and visible signs of power,"[40] and Flora Annie Steel emphasizes "the absolute necessity for high-handed dignity in dealing with those who for thousands of years have been accustomed to it—they love it."[41]

Of course, the "thousands of years" of history that these imperial voices fall back on is a constructed history of India, just as the Oriental traditions of pomp and pageantry adopted by the rulers of India were, in the term employed by Eric Hobsbawm, an "invented tradition."[42] The late nineteenth-century imperialists in India were determined to freeze the country in a timeless Oriental tableau, which denied any possibility of social and political change. The image of the meek and docile Indian woman produced in Billington's text fits seamlessly into this frame. At the same time—in the wake of a long tradition of travelogues that idealize the other as a critique of their own culture—her text holds up an admonitory mirror to the society at home.

A DIFFERENT GAZE

Finally, I wish to look at the image of zenana women produced in the text of the Orientalist traveller, Marianne Postans. Her image transgresses the conventions generally employed in the description of Indian women and challenges reader expectations. While visiting a Muslim prince she is introduced to his four wives. Her descriptions of these beautiful and playful creatures draws heavily on discourses of Orientalism: in the royal gardens these birds of paradise disport themselves wreathing blossoms in their hair and adorning the narrator with their jewels, then inhale the smoke of "richly-adorned hookahs, whose delicately-scented goracco was tempered by the finest rose water" (2:107). Nevertheless, a more complex image of these women emerges in the course of her text. Her description of their chambers, though equally luxurious, sets a different note: "There was an air of privacy and quietness about this little Mohammedan boudoir, particularly inviting; and while its arrangement promised an unusual degree of comfort, a free circulation of air was insured by its height. Numerous windows of wrought stonework which surrounded it, afforded the fair inmate a charming view" (2:92).

Most descriptions of the zenana, on the contrary, stress the lack of elements like privacy, freedom, air, or a view. Postans discovers that the wives all have separate apartments, and learns to read the intricate jewelry (so often remarked upon) as a code for rank. She goes on to present an image of gender solidarity in the zenana—quite in contrast to the usual stereotype of female intrigue. When court intrigues are directed at the prince's concubine, who also inhabits the zenana, the four wives unite to support her cause. The most radical disruption of conventional constructions of the zenana is to be found in the following passage, when the narrator confesses herself to be "a little anxious on the matter of Mohammedan husbands' generosity, and the weighty affair of pin money." The Rahit Buckté (the principal wife) she is talking to sets her mind quite at ease by explaining that she has her own financial resources at her disposal: "The Rahit Buckté proved herself during our conversation, to be a good woman of business, quite *au fait* on the subject of grain, ploughs, mangoe trees, et cetera, from which her revenue is derived; large ledgers, written in the Guzzeratee character, were produced, and particular pages readily referred to, in explanation of the subject" (2: 94–5).

The downtrodden Indian woman as a hardheaded businesswoman, at a time when Englishwomen were still unable to own property in their own right after marriage—quite a morsel to swallow for her readers in England.

It is only appropriate to end this chapter based on eyewitness accounts from the zenana with a further eyewitness account—without, however, according it a greater degree of authenticity than the other accounts. In her *Indian Tales of the Raj* Zareer Masani quotes Tara Ali Baig, who grew up in a conservative Bengali family, on Indian women's reactions to visits by Englishwomen:

> The Indian women would say: "What sort of people are these? ... Look at those white arms; they look as if they haven't been cooked. And why do they wear those peculiar things on their heads?" And the British women would leave the place saying: "Really, isn't it shocking, these women are so backward...."[43]

This alternative account hints at more things going on in the zenana than are dreamt of in the travellers' tales. The traveller's transcendent gaze fails to penetrate the darkest recesses of the other's mind—the other eludes the epistemic grasp of the traveller.

NOTES

1. Richard Francis Burton, *Personal Narrative of a Pilgrimage to Al-Madinah and Meccah*, 2 vols. (London, 1856) 2: 85.

2. For early accounts of the harem, see Rana Kabbani, *Europe's Myths of Orient* 14–36.

3. Women's quarters, where the women lived in seclusion.

4. By contrast, the matriarchal society of the Nairs in South India is virtually ignored in these accounts.

5. Laura Mulvey, "Visual Pleasure and Narrative Cinema," *Screen* 16.3 (1975): 6–18.

6. Mulvey, "Afterthoughts on 'Visual Pleasure and Narrative Cinema' Inspired by *Duel in the Sun*," *Feminism and Film Theory*, ed. Constance Penley (New York Routedge, 1988) 69–79.

7. Rosemary Betterton, "How Do Women Look? The Female Nude in the Work of Suzanne Valadon," *Looking on: Images of Femininity in the Visual Arts and Media*, ed. Rosemary Betterton (London: Pandora, 1987) 217–34.

8. Reina Lewis, "Only Women Should Go to Turkey': Henriette Browne and Women's Orientalism," *Third Text* 22 (1993) 53–64.

9. Billie Melman, *Women's Orients: English Women and the Middle East, 1718–1918: Sexuality, Religion, and Work* (Basingstoke: Macmillan, 1992).

10. See Lorraine Gamman and Margaret Marshment, eds., *The Female Gaze: Women as Viewers of Popular Culture* (London: Women's Press, 1988) Introduction 1–7.

11. Mary Eagleton, ed., *Feminist Literary Theory: A Reader* (Oxford: Blackwell, 1986) Introduction 2.

12. Judith Butler, *Gender Trouble: Feminism and the Subversion of Identity* (New York: Routledge, 1990) 33.

13. A point Simone de Beauvior made more than 40 years ago in *The Second Sex* (Harmondsworth: Penguin, 1972). Also see Monique Wittig, "One Is Not Born a Woman," *Feminist Issues* 1.2 (1981): 47–54.

14. Also see Shelagh Young, "Feminism and the Politics of Power: Whose Gaze Is It Anyway?" Gamman and Marshment, 173–88.

15. See, for instance, Gayatri Spivak, "Three Women's Texts"; and Chandra Talpade Mohanty, "Under Western Eyes."

16. Betterton, "Introduction" 12.

17. Meyda Yegenoglu, "Supplementing the Orientalist Lack: European Ladies in the Harem," *Inscriptions* 6 (1992) 45–81.

18. See Said, *Orientalism.*

19. A similar argument is to be found in Lisa Lowe's *Critical Terrains: French and British Orientalisms* (Ithaca: Cornell University Press, 1991).

20. Janaki Nair, "Uncovering the Zenana: Visions of Indian Womanhood in Englishwomen's Writings, 1813–1940," *Journal of Women's History* 2.1 (1990): 8–34.

21. Gamman and Marshment, 112–29.

22. The reviewer of *The Court Journal:* "To the authoress of the 24 years' 'Wanderings' has been reserved the honour of superseding the vivacious correspondent of Alexander Pope, and of taking the first rank as the chronicler of the scenes of the Zenana." Quoted on the dust-jacket of Fanny Parks, *Asiatic Gallery, Baker Str. Bazar, Portman Square Grand Moving Diorama of Hindostan, displaying the Scenery of the Hoogly, the Bhagirathi, and the Ganges, etc.* (London, 1851).

23. Lady Mary Wortley Montagu, "Letter to Lady Mar, Adrianople, 18 April 1717," reprinted in Christopher Pick, ed., *Embassy to Constantinople: The Travels of Lady Mary Wortley Montagu* (London: Century, 1988) 129–30. Subsequent references in parentheses in the text.

24. Stacey develops her concept of active female spectatorship and the interplay of desire and identification in women's fascination with other women in her recent *Star Gazing: Hollywood Cinema and Female Spectatorship* (London: Routledge, 1994).

25. Constance Gordon Cumming, *In the Himalayas and on the Indian Plain* (Edinburgh, 1884) 14. All further references to be given in parentheses in the text.

26. See especially Janaki Nair, "Uncovering the Zenana."

27. For further historical background information, see Hutchins, *The Illusion of Permanence* 3–19.

28. See especially Antoinette M. Burton, "The White Woman's Burden: British Feminists and 'The Indian Woman', 1865–1915," *Western Women and Imperialism*, eds, Nupur Chaudhuri and Margaret Strobel (Bloomington: Indiana University Press, 1990) 137–57.

29. Gayatri Spivak, *In Other Worlds* 209.

30. Frances Isabella Duberly, *Campaigning Experiences in Rajpootana and Central-India, during the Suppression of the Mutiny, 1857–1858* (London, 1890). All further references to be given in parentheses in the text.

31. Quoted from an address at Exeter Hall on 1 Nov. 1893, in Irene H. Barnes, *Behind the Pardah. The Story of the Church of England Zenana Missionary Society Work in India* (London, 1897) 51.

32. Gayatri Chakravorty Spivak. "Can the Subaltern Speak?" *Marxism and the Interpretation of Culture*, eds. Cary Nelson and Lawrence Grossberg (Urbana: University of Illinois Press, 1988) 296.

33. See also Rosemary Hennessey and Rajeswari Mohan, "The Construction of Woman in Three Popular Texts of Empire: Towards a Critique of Materialist Feminism," *Textual Practice* 3.3 (1989) 323–59.

34. Nair 21.

35. Mary Frances Billington, *Woman in India* (1895; New Delhi: Amarko Book Agency, 1975) xiii. All further references to be given in parentheses in the text.

36. Indeed, as Leila Ahmed has pointed out, women living in seclusion have often developed an elaborate social world of their own. "Here, women share living time and living space, exchange experience and information, and critically analyze—often through jokes, stories, or plays—the world of men." Leila Ahmed, "Western Ethnocentrism and Perceptions of the Harem," *Feminist Studies* 8 (1982) 529.

37. Philip Mason, *Prospero's Magic: Some Thoughts on Class and Race* (London: OUP, 1962) 1.

38. See Hutchins 153–85; and Bearce 180–212.

39. In fact, a constant source of tension in colonial India was the friction between the government of India and its moderate attempts at reform and the official "man on the spot," who rejected these wholeheartedly—a motif that threads Kipling's fiction, for example.

40. Maud Diver, *The Englishwoman in India* (London: Blackwood, 1909) 133–4. All further references to be given in parentheses in the text.

41. Flora Annie Steel, *The Garden of Fidelity* (London: Macmillan, 1929) 133. All further references to be given in parentheses in the text.

42. Eric Hobsbawm and Terence Ranger, *The Invention of Tradition* (Cambridge: CUP, 1984).

43. Zareer Masani, *Indian Tales of the Raj* (London: BBC, 1987) 58.

CHAPTER 28

MARGINALISATION, ISLAMISM, AND THE PRODUCTION OF THE "OTHER'S" "OTHER"

Robina Mohammad

INTRODUCTION

Questions of identity and difference have become the subject of a renewed focus in recent years. [...] Colonized peoples, Black people, gays, women and the disabled now demand greater power to represent themselves, as well as seek to ensure that their representations are accepted as authentic and legitimate (Jay, 1994). [...]

In Britain such issues have been shaped by anxieties associated with the post-colonial period, and especially with the influx of Commonwealth immigrants arriving in the 1950s and 1960s who were seen to erode the putative authenticity of Britishness by hollowing it out from within (Gilroy, 1987). In the 1970s Margaret Thatcher infamously voiced her concern over this trend, remarking that "the country might be swamped by people with a different culture" (Brah, 1996, p. 37). Such concerns were also reflected in a spate of Raj nostalgia movies, and in the notion of a "return to" Victorian values, both part of a "neoconservative remythification of the imperial past" (Mercer, 1992, p. 425). And they were evident in the 1980s in the establishment of a "national" curriculum in schools, a key instrument for the transmission of national, hegemonic cultures and a shared national identity (Bourdieu & Passeron, 1990),

within which Prime Minister Thatcher insisted that British history should take precedence over world history (Judd, 1989). "Others," most notably Commonwealth immigrants, were to be included in British history as the excluded, as outsiders in the story of an "island race."

Brah (1996, p. 24) has noted how, for most white Britons, Asians "represent the epitome of ... outsider[s]," and have often been considered the antithesis of British culture, seen, for example, as "undesirable[s] who 'smelled of curry' ... wore 'funny clothes,' lived 'packed like sardines in a room' ... [and] practised 'strange religions'" (Brah, 1996, p. 23). First-generation Asian immigrants were often not concerned with acceptance or inclusion by *gore* or "the English" [...] (Anwar, 1979; Shaw, 1988; Hiro, 1992). As Valley & Brown (1995a, p. 2) point out, these groups "had scarcely any conflicts with the host society because they had scarcely any contact with it." This situation changed with the emergence of second-generation Asians. Born and bred in Britain, speaking in local dialects and holding British qualifications, many young Asians view themselves as British-Asians and hold similar socio-economic expectations to white people (Hiro, 1992; Valley & Brown, 1995b). But these expectations have not been realized. For example, Pakistanis, on whom I focus in this article, suffer very high rates of unemployment: the 1991 census gives unemployment rates of 20% for first-generation Pakistanis and 30% for second generation, rates exceeded only by Black Africans (Ballard, 1991). According to Modood (1992, p. 261), as a group, Pakistanis have the "worst housing and suffer from the highest levels of attacks on person and property" in Britain.

Persistence of these forms of disadvantage highlights the extent to which colour, "culture," and religion continue to act as markers of "Otherness" and bases for exclusion (Gilroy, 1987; Hiro, 1992, Al-Azmeh, 1993). One of the responses of "Others" to such exclusions has been to construct alternative or counter-identities as a way of recentring their experiences. In this article I examine the processes by which group identity is (re)constructed within one Pakistani Muslim group in a medium-sized urban locality in the south of England, in order to draw out the links between group marginality and processes of identity formation that create and reinforce internal gender hierarchies. I will show how narratives of group identity make women central to the processes through which group identity is constructed, but how, paradoxically, this centrality legitimates women's disempowerment. I will also show how, at one level, the pursuit of a distinctive identity disempowers women within the group in order to empower the group as a whole, while at another level, the conscious recognition and valorization of marks of marginality serve to encourage racist practices that lead to group exclusion. To develop my account I set the group studied here in the context of Asian immigration to Britain. Then [...] I focus on the significance of gender in a shift from Pakistani to Pakistani Muslim identity before exploring in more detail the gender dynamics of the latter.

ASIAN MIGRATION INTO THE "HEART OF DARKNESS"

The majority of Asian immigrants arrived in Britain during the 1950s and 1960s during a period of economic expansion. Immigration from the Asian subcontinent was encouraged in

order to ease job shortages in fields shunned by the existing British workforce. Most early Asian arrivals were men from rural areas throughout the Punjab (that is, including both Pakistani and Indian areas). Most had little formal education and entered the labour market in Britain at the lowest levels, enduring the worst working conditions. They tended to view their residence in Britain as a temporary sojourn undertaken purely for economic purposes. In conjunction with racist housing policies and practices, this encouraged Asian men to live together in large groups, sharing rental payments in order to maximize savings to send home (Brah, 1996). Within an alien and often overtly hostile environment, these early Asian immigrants shared in common aspects of their past lifestyles, their racialized immigrant status, and their aspiration for economic betterment across differences of nationality (Pakistani, Bangladeshi or Indian), religion (Muslim, Sikh or Hindu), and caste (Anwar, 1986; Hiro, 1992) as well as across more subtle cultural differences.

Automatic right of entry to Britain for Commonwealth immigrants was curbed by the Immigration Act of 1962, which limited entry to those filling jobs in specified sectors. Further limits imposed by the 1965 Immigration Act restricted entry to dependants only. These moves accelerated the rate of inward migration by precipitating "beat the ban" hysteria, and prompted a shift away from viewing residence in Britain as temporary. In this context, therefore, most first-generation Asian women arrived as dependants of men (Ballard, 1991).

*****

In the town investigated here, the Pakistani population is fairly homogeneous in terms of class and level of education. Most of the men are relatively fluent in English, but few first-generation women have adequate English language skills. Rates of male and female unemployment among the Pakistani population are close to national averages at just over 20% and 9% respectively. The majority of adult Pakistani women appear to be housewives: 58% are recorded as "economically inactive" for reasons other than full-time study, permanent ill health and retirement. Of Pakistani men and women in employment, the majority are in skilled manual jobs.

The most highly educated Pakistanis tend to occupy the upper levels of a group hierarchy, acting as "community leaders" who mediate between the group and the wider white community. They communicate the needs of the group and engage in the struggle for scarce resources, competing with other Asians (Indian, Hindu and Sikh), as well as White groups, on behalf of the community while also acting as gatekeepers for those resources.

*****

FROM PAKISTANI TO PAKISTANI MUSLIM IDENTITY: THE SIGNIFICANCE OF GENDER

The group on which this study focuses has, until recently, identified itself more closely with other Asian immigrant groups in the UK, that is they have emphasized their Asian affiliations rather than their identity as Muslims (Scantlebury, 1995). The Islamic revolution in Iran did little to change this, partly because the majority of British Asian Muslims belong to the Sunni sect (a sect which itself is divided) and did not identify closely with Khomeini, who, like the majority of Iranians, was from the Shia sect. In addition there was not much approval amongst British Asians of Iran's conflict with Iraq (Hiro, 1992).

The assertion of a Pakistani Muslim, or what some see as a British Muslim, identity was, however, facilitated by the Rushdie affair (Al-Azmeh, 1993; Hiro, 1992). Salman Rushdie's novel, *The Satanic Verses*, published in 1988, was charged by Muslims of all sects with blaspheming Islam. Muslims around the world argued that Rushdie's fictional character, Mahound (meaning false prophet), the protagonist of *The Satanic Verses*, who is depicted as unscrupulous and lecherous, was a not-so-hidden reference to Mohammed, the prophet of Islam. British Muslims joined with Muslims elsewhere to demonstrate against the publication of the book, with book-burning ceremonies in Bolton

(December 1988), Bradford (January 1989) and a march in London (January 1989) (Hiro, 1992). Reports in the media of the controversy in Britain and elsewhere in the world, along with the *fatwa* (death sentence) which Khomeini issued against Rushdie, served to emphasize the global nature of the links between Muslim groups.

The Rushdie affair also brought into sharper relief the differences between the Muslim diaspora in Britain and *gore log* (White people). It reminded Pakistanis of their religious and cultural difference from "English society" and facilitated a group identity based on such difference, which many felt that Rushdie had betrayed (Hiro, 1992; Al-Azmeh, 1993). Indeed, the strength of feeling about *The Satanic Verses* arose because the person of the prophet of Islam is a totem, a symbol of Islamic identity. The perception of such a highly visible attack on this totem, not just in far-off lands, but in Britain, fostered a collective cross-cultural Islamic consciousness, which was reinforced by acts of solidarity, such as the book-burning ceremonies in Britain. The moral panic generated by the Rushdie affair united globally dispersed and internally divided Muslims into a more cohesive imagined community in opposition to "the West" (Anderson, 1992; Alexander, 1998).

This collective identity served to empower British Muslims because it opened up the possibility that their minority status might be transformed into a counter-force on a global scale (Glavanis, 1998). It also provoked a re-evaluation of the fate of future generations who would grow up in a society that is non-Muslim and has in a variety of ways long been an adversary of Islam (Said, 1978). For Muslim leaders committed to maintaining Islamic values in a non-Islamic environment, the Rushdie affair provided a rallying cry to halt trends towards assimilation (especially among the second generation). It did so by ensuring that the Islam/West opposition persisted and remained dominant in the Muslim imaginary, fuelled especially by parental fears over their children's assimilation into a morally bankrupt, permissive society. Moreover, the first generation, who had largely rejected the idea of becoming part of a cultural melting pot, with a renewed consciousness of their difference, now focused their efforts on strengthening their selective socio-spatial and temporal apartheid in order to protect future generations from pressure to assimilate. In this way "religio-culture" became both the reason for, and the means of, constructing a strong group identity.

Group identity is always relational, and is publicly affirmed through rituals that construct shared experiences. Such affirmations mark the limits of the group by simultaneously defining what lies "inside" and what is "different," and therefore "outside" (Hall, 1991a, 1991b). Events such as the Rushdie affair do not create identities on the basis of new distinctions but facilitate the reworking or entrenchment of pre-existing, more or less latent, differences. Within Islamic societies membership in the collectivity is synonymous with adherence to religious doctrine ("religio-culture") so that those who do not comply exclude themselves by becoming viewed as non-Muslims (Kawar & Shaheed, 1988). In this way internal resistance and conflict is undermined and contained. Within diasporic communities, compliance with Islamic religio-culture both links local minorities with other Muslims across the globe, and provides a basis for resistance to the imperialisms and racisms that situate such communities as "Others."

Islamic discourses position women in a variety of ways, aspects of which can be traced to particular social and political contexts. These variations notwithstanding, a number of ideas appear across different Islamisms that place women at the heart of Muslim religio-culture identity (Afary, 1997). As mothers, women are seen as the biological producers of the group or nation, the transmitters of "religio-culture" to future generations, and the bearers of the markers of group identity. This centrality intensifies collective interest in the regulation of women's bodies and sexualities through measures which focus on both the body and the psyche, visually, spatially, and temporally (Kandiyoti, 1993; Yeganeh, 1993; Afshar, 1994; Yuval-Davies, 1997). It is also expressed in Islamic concepts of family life, which are construed as pivotal in the maintenance of social order and in the resolution of wider socio-economic problems (Yeganeh, 1993; Afary, 1997).

*****

As with the Taliban [in Afghanistan,] [in Iran] Khomeini [...] was concerned with women's appearance(s) outside of the home, denouncing women office workers "as painted dolls who 'displace and distract' men" (Afshar 1988, p. 232). Linked to this, the Iranian clergy understand the "power of female sexuality—[as a] satanic power [so strong, it] ... can annihilate the male species by its very presence" (Afshar, 1988, p. 237). Women's whole beings are understood to be involved in the operation of this power such that their bodies, their bodily movements, the style, shape and colour of their clothing, are all capable of unleashing male arousal. This has profound repercussions for the treatment of women, making them both the guardians of male honour and rendering them culpable if they are raped, as well as legitimating the need for male "protection" of women and the regulation of their bodies (Afshar, 1988).

The regulation of women's bodies provokes similar concern within Pakistani Muslim groups in Britain. Anwar's (1979) study of Pakistani immigrants in Rochdale emphasized the constraints on women in terms of visual marks and mobility, both of which are the focus of the practice of purdah. Legitimated in terms of Islamism and traditional culture, Anwar (1979, p. 165) notes that the practice of *purdah*:

> apart from veiling in the traditional sense, ... refers to the restrictions on the physical movement of Pakistani women ... They do not normally go out of the house without their husbands unless it is absolutely essential.

*****

Within the group on which my research focuses, these concerns are exemplified in two texts that interviewees referred to repeatedly to explain their understanding of Islamic doctrine (Sarwar, 1980; Khan, 1995). I was informed that these texts are used for teaching young people about Islam. Written in English, they target young people who would not necessarily be literate in a Pakistani language. Both rely on a binary opposition between Islam and the West, linking to this a series of binaries through which the superiority of Islam is argued. For example, in the foreword of his book, Sarwar (1980, p. 7) draws attention to the dangers of the non-Islamic environment, stating that the Islamic education of children is a "great challenge" in a non-Islamic society. He echoes Afghani and Iranian Islamist discourses about the power of female sexuality in his concern that women must refrain from arousing "man's base feelings" by concealing the contours of their bodies (Sarwar, 1980, p. 183). It becomes clear that this concern is central to his key argument about the maintenance of "the Muslim family" within which children grow and learn. This family both demands and is a means through which sexual regulation reproduces the collectivity both biologically and culturally. Female chastity ensures that children are conceived by "women [who] are not only biologically but also symbolically within the boundaries ... of the group" (Yuval-Davies, 1992, p. 285). Sarwar (1980, p. 168) suggests that the Western drive for gender equality is the main threat to this family because "total equality ... destroy[s] the social balance [leading to problems such as] broken marriages, illegitimate children, and the break up of family life ... problems [which] are already rife in ... Western society." These problems, Sarwar (1980, p. 170) argues, are the direct result of "a permissive outlook and [the] so-called freedom of women." The Western woman has been commodified, reduced to a male plaything for "enjoyment and fancy." Khan (1995) goes further in his condemnation of the West, which, he argues, has exposed the delicate female sex to the strong male world and so permanently lowered her status. This is the product of a hundred years of Western efforts to bring about an "unnatural" equality between men and women, influences that must be countered if Muslims are to maintain the Muslim family. Both Sarwar (1980, p. 169) and Khan (1995) argue that, unlike her Western counterpart, the Muslim woman's status is highly valued within the family: "[s]he is the queen of the family, ... her husband's help-mate ... a source of peace, happiness and contentment for [him]." Such constructions aim to eliminate

all shades of grey, and contain women within the binaries of black and white.

MODERN (RE)IMAGININGS: THE POLITICS OF NOSTALGIA

Separateness

The sense of separateness of the Pakistani Muslim group in this study, already facilitated by the Rushdie affair, is further strengthened by continuities across time and space, which support the notion of a primordial past in Pakistan, an "alwaysness." This imagining of Pakistan is both necessitated and made possible by modernity. The increased affordability of modern transport and communication systems has led to more transnational movements both to and from Pakistan. Even the poorest Pakistanis may return "home" as often as once a year. Improved communication facilities together with reduced telephone charges have made contact with relatives in Pakistan as easy and affordable as keeping in touch with relatives in Manchester or Bradford (Anderson, 1992).

This sense of "alwaysness" is reproduced by the group in question through shared rememberings, notably the telling of stories, an activity in which both women and men participate.[...] Social, cultural and religious mythologies are central themes in these narratives, and are given life by histories, landscapes, media, popular culture, and literature. Many of the stories narrated to me contrasted present lives in urban Britain with past lives in rural Pakistan. The former were often characterized as a "dull, drab, dreary" monotony, closeted and constrained in space and time by the fragmented individualism of urban modernity in Britain. [...]

*****

Periodic visits to Pakistan are mobilized to create a "life in a fantasy of rootedness" (Al-Azmeh, 1993, p. 3–4), and to make real in the imagination a Utopian "homeland."

*****

Trips to Pakistan certainly enable the maintenance of international kinship networks, which are consolidated through marriage [...] (Ballard, 1991), and Home Office statistics suggest that more Pakistani fiancés/husbands are accepted for settlement in the UK than for any other ethnic group (Berrington, 1991). For example, Sharon explained that her marriage to her double cousin (the son of her father's brother and her mother's sister) was arranged by her father as a way to conserve ties with her dead mother's family in Pakistan. [...] Thus, successive generations retain the past in the present and in so doing strengthen links that emphasize the separateness of the group to which they belong from others around them.

Separateness is also articulated through stories of moral dangers. Newly arrived Pakistani men, having moved beyond the gaze of their family and "community" in Pakistan, have long been perceived to be particularly at risk from several "Western" temptations, including the consumption of pork and alcohol, but above all sexual adventure(s), ranging from simply gazing at semi-naked girls on the beach to pre- or extra-marital sexual relationships, all of which are prohibited by Islam.

*****

Although today a "community" gaze in Britain operates as a constraining force for newly arrived women and men, it continues to be considered particularly important in relation to men, who are allowed greater spatial mobility and opportunities to stray than women both in Pakistan and in Britain. That Western spaces are still seen to offer considerably more freedom than the spaces of Pakistan is confirmed by Badruddin Khan's (1997) account of his experience as a gay Pakistani in both Pakistan and Canada. Turning to my respondents, Nina, a 15-year-old who attends a mixed-sex school and who spoke to me during a dressmaking class at the PCC, commented that Pakistani men "all want to come here. They believe that they will get a lot of freedom when they are here. They can do whatever they want. That is the only reason to come here." Sharon expressed her indignation about the unequal opportunities for men and women:

boys can go out and stay out late ... I know quite a few married men who go out night after night, have extra-marital affairs safe in the knowledge that their wives will never leave them.

Social exclusions generated by racism feed into and are used to maintain a sense of socio-spatial separateness. Modood (1992) has noted how the "Asian community" acknowledged and continue to invoke Enoch Powell's perceptiveness in his contention of the resistance to assimilation of Black populations. Publicans who banned Asians from their premises in the 1950s helped to prevent the consumption of alcohol, which was considered to be the devil's drink, capable of stripping away inhibitions and encouraging sexual adventure (Hiro, 1992).

[...] [S]ome of the women interviewed provided graphic accounts of racism. These accounts convey a sense of moral superiority that can be seen on the one hand as responses to racisms, while on the other hand as affirmations of "group" membership by women who have a greater stake in the notion of the "group" and as such contribute to the idea of a relatively "self-contained" and separate existence (compare Anwar, 1979; Hiro, 1992; Valley & Brown, 1995a). For example, Mrs Butt said:

when I first arrived 30 years ago I was treated as if I had just emerged from a jungle, was constantly asked questions like "have you ever seen a radio?" and "does your husband know how to make love to you?" One woman actually suggested that Pakistani men were so incompetent that their idea of making love was some kind of charging at the woman. These people are so ignorant.

*****

Such responses echo across the generations. For example, Shela, a 27-year-old who was born and brought up in Britain and now has five children, explained that "English people are different from us. They don't understand us. They think, because they are white they are better than us. They aren't." In this way exclusion becomes mutual.

*****

Gender and Socio-spatial Regulation

Fears that Western life would somehow seduce daughters and wives was a factor in the initial reluctance of male Pakistani migrants to permit their families to join them in Britain (Anwar, 1979; Shaw, 1988; Hiro, 1992). Young interviewees explained how such fears were again heightened in the late 1980s by two local incidents in which young Pakistani Muslim women left their parental homes against parental wishes. These incidents, together with a spate of media stories detailing young Pakistani women's resistances to cultural constraints, coincided with the Rushdie affair and rekindled anxieties about an erosion of morality (compare Al-Azmeh, 1993; Anwar, 1994; Alexander, 1998). This led to renewed efforts to protect "cultural authenticity" by redrawing the group's boundaries, for example, by imposing greater socio-spatial restrictions on young women.

*****

The representation of spaces as masculine or feminine is central to group identity. Feminine space is the space of home. It includes spaces for women and for their close male relatives, and is a domain into which the entry of other men is restricted. Spaces outside the home are largely masculine. These spaces are seen to conspire against group requirements both because they allow encounters between women and men in a culture seen to support sexual permissiveness, and because they are spaces that cannot be surveyed directly by parents. Female presence in these spaces is therefore contentious and problematic, especially for those past puberty.

The following comments illustrate how young women aged 17 or 18, all of whom were studying for A levels at all-girls schools, experience parental responses to this. Selina observed how her parents have aimed to control her movements throughout her life:

[W]e were not even allowed to visit the corner shop or friends. When I was seven my twin and I begged to visit my best friend but my mum refused because her father and brothers would be around. [When we were] at school we had to be back [home, at the end of the school day] by a minute past 4, if we were late we would be beaten. This ruled out any extra-curricular activities, as well as walking home in the summer, because we would inevitably be late.

*****

Leila drew attention to other girls who are "so restricted they can't even go off to college or stay on and do A levels or they have got to stay at home and look after so and so. They can't go off and fulfil their potential."

Finally, Polly contrasted the treatment of boys and girls, saying:

[W]e can't go to the cinema or even just shopping. It's different for the boys, though they are not allowed to go to the cinema either, but because they are allowed to wander around outside, at all hours, their visits to the cinema go unnoticed.

The main experiences outside the home for young Pakistani Muslim women take place in the spaces of the education system, and, for those who are permitted to enter it, the labour market. I explore the regulatory mechanisms mobilized in relation to each of these in turn.

(a) Separateness and education. The demand by Muslim groups for separate schools for Muslim girls accelerated considerably in the aftermath of the Rushdie affair (Hiro, 1992). Such schools would enable Muslim parents to ensure that girls remain in entirely feminine space. In the absence of Muslim schools, single-sex schools are preferred and schools in general are preferred to colleges and universities. Leila explained:

[W]hat they [parents] believe is at school you have the supervision of teachers. At our school that is definitely what it is. If they find some of the Asian girls doing things they shouldn't be doing then, because the teachers are so aware of Islamic culture and the Hindu culture and all the other multicultures, they do inform the parents and the parents are aware of that.

*****

[...] Polly found that her decision to attend university brought her into conflict with her parents, even though her father is more liberal than many. She explained that initially he had been keen for her to attend university, but as the time approached for her to take up her place, pressure from the group intervened:

> [F]riends of my father began to turn him against the idea. One [woman, the wife of a family] friend warned him, "they [young women] get up to all sorts of things [sexual activities]. I know because my son is at university and he tells me what girls get up to."

*****

Spaces of the education system are also threatening in terms of the possibilities they offer for exposure to radical thought (Hiro, 1992). This applies particularly to feminist thought, which challenges notions seen as fundamental to Islamic concepts of family. Selina reported that her parents disapproved of her decision to study sociology at A level and forbade her to spend time alone in her room, suggesting that they believed that this would encourage her to reflect on what she learnt on her course and might lead her to question the constraints on her life.

*****

One way of countering the effect of Western influences on second-generation Pakistanis is through marriages to spouses born and bred in Pakistan. Sometimes this magnifies differences between Pakistanis. For example, Tara, now a 30-year-old mother, was married at the age of 18 to a relative from Pakistan only two days after she was informed of his arrival and introduced

to him. She noted how newly arrived husbands from Pakistan "have a very different way of thinking to us. They expect women to be more subservient, but we have been brought up in Britain, we were taught at school to expect equality between men and women."

*****

For their parents, however, such remarks by young women often simply serve to justify marriages to spouses who have grown up distant from Western influences and have therefore been equipped to take over responsibility from fathers to counter such influences and regulate the next generation of daughters.

The need to monitor and sift influences on women was also evident in relation to adult education. The difficulties encountered by the WEA in assessing the need for, and in providing, adult education relevant to Pakistani women was in no small part attributable to the suspicions about courses that might be construed as carrying the potential to upset the status quo, and this included courses seen as more "academic." Single-sex adult education classes were established by the (predominantly male-run) PCC, partly as a form of rivalry with the WEA, but also so that Pakistanis could retain control of what subjects were taught to whom. Classes in subjects such as dressmaking and keep-fit were set up by the PCC and proved relatively successful in attracting women. Such classes could readily be classified as providing practical "feminine" knowledge useful for health and domestic work. [...] Women themselves were wary of courses which they thought would encourage changes in their ways of thinking, highlighting one way in which women resign themselves to their position within the internal structure of the group and are co-opted in the construction of oppressive forms of identity.

(b) The labour market. While education poses a threat to gender relations within the group through exposure to new ideas, the labour market is even more threatening because it can enable those ideas to become fully fledged resistances, and it can increase the capacity for women to undermine and destabilize the tradi-

tional family in which the head is always male. For example, speaking of her husband, Tara noted how "he feels that [a working woman] ... says something about his capacity to provide for his women as head of the family."

*****

While some members of the community assert "our women do not [do paid] work," and some women certainly are prevented from entering the labour market, all the young women interviewed indicated that they wanted to do paid work. Moreover, there are pressures from within the group itself for young women to enter the labour market. Changes to immigration laws enacted in the 1980s require women as well as men to provide evidence of their ability to offer financial support before overseas fiancés can be granted a British visa. This has led to an influx into the labour market of young Pakistani women who are awaiting the arrival of fiancés from Pakistan. [...]

*****

Thus, some young women are required to work in order to facilitate the entry of husbands and fiancés into the UK, sometimes at the expense of continuing their own education beyond age 16 or 18.

The types of work women are permitted to undertake are restricted by group requirements regarding spaces, times, dress and so on. Among interviewees, those in paid work and those expecting to enter the labour market said that they were limited to working in the daytime, in jobs that were close to home and that did not require any nights away from home. The scope for surveillance also limits job opportunities and is clearly illustrated by Sharon's experience. After arrangements were made for her marriage to her cousin in Pakistan, Sharon was expected to take up paid employment. However, her taking up of an office job with promotion prospects did not enthuse her father, despite the fact that she could wear Punjabi dress at work. Her father's concerns were prompted by the fact that the office space was hidden from his view so that he was not able to police her actions, and by the potential

for independence and therefore open resistance to parental control associated with employment with career prospects. By contrast, her move to a job in a town centre department store met with his approval despite the requirement that she wear Western dress (modified to ensure adequate bodily coverage). This was because the spaces of the shop were visible to him, enabling him to police her movements through periodic visits to the store. This prevented her from, for example, claiming to be at work in order to spend a day out of his (potential) sight. Fixing Sharon spatially in this way also fixes her economically: shop work is low paid with limited promotion prospects. Moreover, promotion would depend on participating in training courses away from home, which parental constraints will not permit her to undertake.

*****

Dress—the Visual Marker

Punjabi dress is regarded as a signifier not only of the morality of its women but also of the group as a whole. Through dress, therefore, "[women are made] ... the privileged signifiers of ... difference" (Kandiyoti, 1993, p. 376). Moreover, dress is an important means of countering fears associated with women's entry into public space. Although many young British Muslims do not approve of the conflation of Punjabi dress with Muslim dress, Pakistani Muslim groups from the Punjab remain committed to apna libaas (our dress), especially salwar-kameez. It is a form of dress that is understood to avert male sexual interest in women and so to assist the maintenance of sexual purity. In this context Anwar (1979) has noted that the central interest of the Bradford Muslim Society was in negotiating a "suitable" uniform for Pakistani Muslim schoolgirls.

While sons may dress "normally," daughters are constantly reminded of the need to dress modestly (Hiro, 1992, Afshar, 1994). Leila was indignant at the fact that "a Pakistani girl in jeans is ... automatically assume[d to be] bad [by the community] but none of the boys in [my locality] quite frankly, wear salwar-kameez outside [the home or the mosque]." Moreover, dress achieves much more than simply covering the body. Manna recalled how she heard one Asian man remark to another, as she walked past them on her way to work, that she was "an embarrassment to our culture despite the fact that I was modestly dressed in a pair of trousers and a blouse but because this was not *apna libaas* it was bad."

A visual contrast was maintained by all the women interviewed, although to varying degrees and for different reasons. They all indicated that they wore Punjabi dress in the home. Those wearing Western dress (most of whom were under 25 years of age) explained that they were doing so without parental knowledge or approval. Attitudes towards *salwar-kameez* vary. Shela, for example, declared that "I value our tradition, I am proud to wear our traditional costume." Sharon spoke of how she had resisted wearing *salwar-kameez*, but also how Punjabi dress now enhances her sense of her sexuality:

> at school when we had non-uniform days, all the other Pakistani girls would dress in Punjabi dress but I just wore my uniform because I felt it was more me. Today I dress in Asian clothes only at home and at weddings, when I feel pretty and sexy in them and the guys also like them.

[...] In addition to dress that is loose and long-sleeved so as to conceal all female curves, she was expected to wear the *hijab*, which has become a primary signifier of Islam both for Muslims themselves and for others. She told me how her forced adoption of the *hijab* isolated her from others, increasing her sense of being separate and different not only from Whites but also from other Pakistani Muslim girls. But, while the veil is often seen as an instrument of women's oppression, women also use the veil in other ways. For example, for Sara the desexualization offered by strict Muslim dress not only marks compliance with group regulations, but, in so doing, permitted her greater freedom to enter masculine spaces without parental or group conflict and to pursue a career that would not otherwise be permitted.

CONCLUSION

In this discussion I have constructed and narrated one story from the many stories that may be told about this Pakistani Muslim "group." I have examined links between the marginalization of the "group" within wider British society that has strengthened the need for a "group" identity, narratives of collective identity that make women central to the group, and regulatory practices that restrict women in a variety of ways. I have also illustrated that women are not passive recipients of these disciplinary measures, nor are they passive participants in the processes of identity construction. In conclusion, I draw out some of the dynamics at work within the "group" that are particularly significant in both the maintenance of, and resistance to, "group" identity.

Notions of group identity used by the Pakistani Muslim "group" construe cultural difference as immutable, absolute and incommensurable. [...]

*****

This naturalizes the borders within which the "group" is contained. But while the border implies that what lies within is singular, homogeneous and coherent, it is in fact dependent on internal divisions and hierarchies including those of gender and age.

The degree to which women accept or contest the construction of "group" identity varies both by age and between those born and brought up in Britain compared to those born and brought up in Pakistan. My evidence indicates that younger, second-generation women in full-time education or in the labour market are inevitably both more aware of and more influenced by opportunities that lie beyond the limits of the "group." They are therefore more likely than others to push against boundaries constructed to contain them. Women of the first generation, [...] together with older, married women born and brought up in Britain, tend to be more firmly ensconced "within" the "group," and are therefore more reluctant to voice any dissatisfaction. Thus, women born and brought up in Britain unite with those arriving from Pakistan in remembering, recovering, and celebrating the distinctiveness of the "group" and its "homeland," especially as they assume childrearing responsibilities. [...] Confirming "group" fears about the effects of "the West," they argue that these men expect greater subservience from wives than such women are accustomed to, or capable of, following a lifetime of exposure to Western ideas, especially the idea of "equality." In this they join with younger women born and brought up in Britain, many of whom are keen to speak out against multiple constraints that they feel prevent them from achieving their "potential." At times their anger was pronounced, for example, when Michelle used the term "sold" to describe the way marriage arrangements position young girls.

*****

Men, too, often experience difficulties in finding alternatives to this stark opposition. For example, those who wish to support their wives and daughters in pursuing their education or careers find themselves subject to moral disapproval from other members of the "group." By linking the honour of men to the chastity and morality of "their" women, the "group" exploits male fears in order to intensify the pressure to keep women, particularly those most at risk, within the boundaries of the "group."

This oppositional structure implies a high degree of "group" cohesion and homogeneity, but I have illustrated that this masks considerable internal diversity. In particular I have shown how women paradoxically both signify group identity and are positioned as the "Other's" "Other." Moreover, class and stage in the life-course further complicate this positioning. Race, gender, class, and age work as interlocking systems of domination, which not only uphold and sustain one another but also constitute the forms of oppression to which "Other" women are subjected in particular contexts (Maynard, 1994). Thus, Pakistani Muslim women in Britain may, for example, negotiate restrictions imposed over their movement in masculine spaces by adopting Islamic dress, and in so doing elicit different forms of oppression "outside" the "group." Islamic dress encourages Orientalist readings that constitute Muslim women as subservient, passive, and mute (Said, 1978), characteristics viewed in positive terms by the majority of "group" members, but reversed to signify oppression, barbarism, backwardness, and fundamentalism elsewhere, thereby intensifying exclusions in relation to the education system and the labour market.

Versions of identity politics constructed around a binary opposition between "Same" and "Other" can only offer a limited resistance to marginalization, because they do not challenge or address relations of exploitation. Instead, as I have shown, the tendency is to consolidate the power of the hegemonic "group" within the "group." Such conceptions of identity also work against the group in that they become complicit with newer, subtler, more covert, forms of racism: positing homogeneous ethnic or national communities, race is made synonymous with culture and is therefore legitimated as a basis of exclusion (Gilroy, 1992). This fosters versions of racism based on the idea of incommensurable difference that cannot be denied; as Al-Azmeh (1993, p. 6) puts it, "tandoori chicken [for example] is not roast chicken." [...]

In countering racism there is a risk that such constructions of group identity are merely revalorized while the oppositional structure is left intact. I hope that by examining the gender dynamics operating within one particular Pakistani Muslim "community" I have illuminated something of the complex internal hierarchies that co-exist with and problematize notions of group homogeneity.

REFERENCES

Afary, Janet (1997) The war against feminism in the name of the almighty: Making sense of gender and Muslim fundamentalism, *New Left Review*, 224, pp. 89–110.

Afshar, Haleh (1988) Behind the veil, in: Bina Agarwal (Ed.) *Structures of Patriarchy: The stale, the community and the household*, pp. 228–247 (London, Zed Books).

Afshar, Haleh (1994) Muslim women in West Yorkshire: Growing up with real and imaginary values amidst conflicting views of self and society, in: Haleh Afshar & Mary Maynard (Eds.) *The Dynamics of "Race" and Gender—Some Feminist Interventions*, pp. 127–147 (London, Taylor & Francis).

Al-Azmeh, Aziz (1993) *Islam and Modernities* (London, Verso).

Alexander, C. (1998) Re-imagining the Muslim community, *Innovation*, 11, pp. 439–451.

Anderson, Benedict (1992) New world disorder, *New Left Review*, 193, pp. 3–13.

Anwar, Muhammad (1979) *The Myth of Return: Pakistanis in Britain* (London, Heinemann).

Anwar, Muhammad (1986) *Race and Politics: Ethnic minorities and the British political system* (London, Tavistock).

Anwar, Muhammad (1994) *Young Muslims in Britain: Attitudes, educational needs and policy in implications* (Leicester, Islamic Foundation).

Ballard, Roger (1991) The Pakistanis: Stability and introspection, in: Ceri Peach (Ed.) *The Ethnic Minority Populations of Great Britain*, vol. 2, pp. 121–149 (London, HMSO).

Berrington, A. (1991) The Pakistanis: Stability and introspection, in: Ceri Peach (Ed.) *The Ethnic Minority in the 1991 Census*, pp. 178–212 (London, HMSO).

Bourdieu, Pierre & Passeron, Jean-Claude (1990) *Reproduction in Education, Culture and Society* (London, Sage).

Brah, Avtar (1996) *Cartographies of Diaspora: Contesting identities* (London, Routledge).

Gilroy, Paul (1987) *There Ain't No Black in the Union Jack: The cultural politics of race and nation* (London: Routledge).

Gilroy, Paul (1992) Cultural studies and ethnic absolutism, in: Lawrence Grossberg, Cary Nelson & Paula Treichler (Eds.) *Cultural Studies*, pp. 187–198 (New York, Routledge).

Glavanis, Pandeli M. (1998) Political Islam within Europe: A contribution to the analytical framework, *Innovation*, 11, pp. 391–410.

Hall, Stuart (1991a) The local and the global, in: Anthony D. King (Ed.) *Culture, Globalization and the World-System*, pp. 19–39 (Basingstoke, Macmillan).

Hall, Stuart (1991b) Old and new identities, in: Anthony D. King (Ed.) *Culture, Globalization and the World-System*, pp. 41–66 (Basingstoke, Macmillan).

Hiro, Dilip (1992) *Black British, White British: A history of race relations in Britain*, 2nd edn (London, Paladin).

Jay, G.S. (1994) Knowledge, power, and the struggle for representation, *College English*, 56, pp. 9–27.

Judd, J. (1989) Thatcher changes the course of history, *The Observer*, 20 August, p. 1.

Kandiyoti, Deniz (1993) Identity and its discontents: Women and the nation, in Patrick Williams & Laura Chrisman (Eds.) *Colonial Discourse and Post-colonial Theory: A Reader*, pp. 376–391 (New York, Harvester Wheatsheaf).

Kawar, Mumtaz & Shaheed, Farida (Eds.) (1988) *Women of Pakistan: Two steps forward and one step back* (London, Zed Books).

Khan, Badruddin (1997) *Sex Longing and Not Belonging: A gay Muslim's quest for love and meaning* (Oakland, CA, Floating Lotus).

Khan, M.W. (1995) *Woman between Islam and Western Society* (New Delhi, The Islamic Centre).

Maynard, Mary (1994) "Race," gender and the concept of "difference" in feminist thought, in: Haleh Afshar & Mary Maynard (Eds.) *The Dynamics of "Race" and Gender—Some Feminist Interventions*, pp. 9–25 (London, Taylor & Francis).

Mercer, Kobena (1992) "1968": Periodizing politics and identity, in: Lawrence Grossberg, Cary Nelson & Paula Treichler (Eds.) *Cultural Studies*, pp. 424–449 (New York, Routledge).

Modood, Tariq (1992) British Asian Muslims and the Rushdie affair, in James Donald & Ali Rattansi (Eds.) *Race, Culture and Difference*, pp. 260–277 (London, Sage in conjunction with Open University).

Said, Edward (1978) *Orientalism* (New York, Vintage).

Sarwar, G. (1980) *Islam, Beliefs and Teachings* (London, The Muslim Educational Trust).

Scantlebury, Elizabeth (1995) Muslims in Manchester: The depiction of a religious community, *New Community*, 18, pp. 425–435.

Shaw, Alison (1988) *A Pakistani Community in Britain* (Oxford, Basil Blackwell).

Valley, P. & Brown, A. (1995a) Pride and prejudice, *Independent*, 5 December, p. 2.

Valley, P. & Brown, A. (1995b) The best place to be a Muslim, *Independent*, 6 December, p. 4.

Yeganeh, Nahid (1993) Women, nationalism and Islam in contemporary political discourse in Iran, *Feminist Review* 44, pp. 3–18.

Yuval-Davies, Nira (1992) Fundamentalism, multiculturalism and women, in: James Donald & Ali Rattansi (Eds.) *Race, Culture and Difference*, pp. 278–291 (London, Sage in conjunction with Open University).

Yuval-Davies, Nira (1997) *Gender and Nation* (London, Sage).

CHAPTER 29

IS LOCAL:GLOBAL AS FEMININE:MASCULINE?
Rethinking the Gender of Globalization

Carla Freeman

Several years ago, Catherine Lutz posed what for me became a profound and troubling question, "Does theory have a gender?" (1995). At the time, I was designing a course called "Globalization and Culture" and was consistently struck by the two distinct categories into which the texts for the course fell: macroanalyses of the history, structure, and expansion of economic forms of globalization and microanalyses of women's insertion into the global economy as workers and members of third-world countries. Why have so many of the major treatises of globalization in the social sciences been systematically bereft of gender analysis when we have, by now, so many excellent accounts of the central role played by gender in the configuration of global production and global consumption when addressed at the "local" levels? In grappling with the implications of these patterns we might extend the critique made by Lutz about the more general "gender of theory" to argue that not only has globalization theory been gendered masculine but the very processes defining globalization itself—the spatial reorganization of production across national borders and a vast acceleration in the global circulation of capital, goods, labor, and ideas, all of which have generally been traced in their contemporary form to economic and

political shifts in the 1970s—are implicitly ascribed a masculine gender. Indeed, two interconnected patterns have emerged: the erasure of gender as integral to social and economic dimensions of globalization when framed at the macro, or "grand theory," level and an implicit masculinization of these macrostructural models. One outcome of these problems has been the implicit, but powerful, dichotomous model in which the gender of globalization is mapped in such a way that global:masculine as local:feminine.

This article asks what appears to be a simple question: What are the implications of a divide between masculinist grand theories of globalization that ignore gender as an analytical lens and local empirical studies of globalization in which gender takes center stage? How might alternative analytical approaches give rise to new understandings of globalization? As feminists have argued for some time, taking gender seriously not only adds to the analysis at hand but produces a different analysis (Enloe 1990; Massey 1994, 181). By taking up one empirical local case, the example of contemporary "higglers" (or marketers) in the Caribbean, I hope to illustrate that globalization works through many economic and cultural modes and is effected both through large powerful actors and institutions as well as by "small-scale" individuals engaged

343

in a complex of activities that are both embedded within and at the same time transforming practices of global capitalism. The particular case I will describe of contemporary transnational Caribbean higglers demonstrates quite literally that not only do global processes enact themselves on local ground but local processes and small-scale actors might be seen as the very fabric of globalization. By turning to the gendered qualities of globalization, this discussion aims to rethink the conceptual underpinnings that have implicitly construed global as masculine and local as feminine terrains and practices. As V. Spike Peterson has said,

> the binary logic of dichotomies frames our thinking in mutually exclusive categories so that masculinity, reason and objectivity are defined by the absence of femininity, affect and subjectivity. Once we reject the categorical separations presupposed in dichotomies, not only does the boundary between them change but so does the meaning of the polar terms: they are not mutually exclusive but in relation, which permits more than the two possibilities posited in either-or constructions. Moreover, changing the meaning of the terms and bringing them into relation (exposing their interdependence) changes the theoretical frameworks within which they are embedded. (1996, 18)

My goal here is to bring into relief several powerful dichotomies in need of dialectical engagement: global/local; masculine/feminine; production/consumption; and formal/informal sectors of the economy.

Perhaps like theory generally, as Lutz implied, sources that have become some of the leading expositions of "globalization theory" have been those hailed for their breadth and scope in grappling with the multitude of factors brought into play in today's era of late capitalism in its most general sense. Whether through evocative renderings of "scapes" within and across which people, capital, technology, media, and ideologies move (Appadurai 1990) or the broad exploration of political economic transformations in changing modes of accumulation as mapped through the "time-space compression" of postmodernity (Harvey 1989), some of the most prominent of globalization's macro theorists offer powerful models of circuits of movement and social and economic changes encompassing our world, but with little specificity about how these are configured in particular places, for particular groups of people, and to what particular ends. Certainly many fine studies have demonstrated the importance of an engagement between macrostructural analyses and the flesh and blood of people's lives as they are bound up within ever-changing localities and cultural and political configurations. By and large, however, many of the works that have become the defining sources of globalization within the social sciences have been macroanalyses that do not engage these linkages.

The point here is not merely to note the absence of gender in many grand treatments of globalization but to probe the ways in which this absence limits our overall understanding of globalization's forms and meanings. A gendered understanding of globalization is not one in which women's stories or feminist movements can be tacked onto or even "stirred into" the macropicture; rather, it challenges the very constitution of that macropicture such that producers, consumers, and bystanders of globalization are not generic bodies or invisible practitioners of labor and desire but are situated within social and economic processes and cultural meanings that are central to globalization itself. Some of the strongest examples of such an approach have been made within feminist critiques. However, achieving the weight of macrotheory that is embedded with local actors, culture, and a keen sense of the gendered, raced, and sexed qualities of these processes is a tall order.

REIMAGINING THE "LOCAL"

Discourses on globalization have emerged within roughly two categories—those that emphasize global economics and those concerned with culture. Each has proponents from both critical as well as conservative camps. In the first category, grand theorizing about globalization (works that attempt to trace both its roots and its current forms) has tended to equate contemporary globalization with advanced or fast capitalism whose ever-expanding reach expresses itself in the intensifying (and faceless) transnational flows of capital, labor, and the reconfiguration of global markets (Harvey 1989; Sklair 1991; McMichael 1997). Another set of accounts has focused on the spread of "global culture" through such media as television, the Internet, and the borderless, fast-paced dissemination and consumption of commodities and styles (Featherstone 1990; Waters 1995; Castells 1998). These two approaches have converged within specific accounts of local contexts of incorporation into the global arena. Scholars from a number of disciplines, including sociology, anthropology, and political science, have recently called for greater focus on "the local" contexts of globalization as a way of bringing home the lived realities of these mammoth forces.

In addition to humanizing (and thus providing means for both positive and negative readings of globalization "on the ground") these large-scale economic and social transformations, local studies promise to make clear that the historical and structural underpinnings and contemporary forms of globalization are themselves deeply imbued with specific notions about femininity and masculinity and expectations for the roles of women and men. In the recruitment of labor along the global assembly line, in modes of disciplining and controlling that labor, in the marketing of goods and the creation of consumers, and in the patterns of migration within and across national borders, there are embedded (and sometimes quite explicit) expectations that rely deeply upon ideologies and practices of gender. Close and detailed ethnography has been an integral part of such local analyses, for in order to register and interpret the dialectics of local/global processes and ideologies one needs (quite literally) to have a sense of how, for example, money is made, relationships are fostered, politics are transacted, and goods and services are circulated on the ground. Feminist critiques of globalization that

are steeped in ethnographic research have begun to yield important insights into the effects of globalization upon women, men, different ethnic and racial groups and classes, and different regional and national contexts, and they have made clear that macrostructural accounts are insufficient in describing the lived realities of globalization. However, localizing analyses of globalization helps to answer one set of problems while leaving another intact. This is particularly evident where gender is concerned, for the turn to gender on local terrain has inadvertently been the slippery slope on which the equation between local and feminine gets reinscribed. The assertion that we recast our view of contemporary processes we have labeled globalization through the study of the local cannot be a matter of subsuming one to the other, not a privileging of micro over macro, but rather a claim that understanding specific places, with their own particular and changing histories, economies, and cultures vis-à-vis the intensification of global movements (whether of trade, travel, commodities, styles, ideologies, capital, etc.), helps us to better grapple with the essence of these movements and their changing implications.

Where I begin is not to assert the primacy of the local against the generic or homogeneous global but rather, as Akhil Gupta and James Ferguson (1997) suggest, to highlight the "complex and sometimes ironic" processes through which "cultural forms are imposed, invented, reworked, and transformed" in a rapidly global arena (1997, 5). Further, I hope to suggest lines of development toward a framework in which these very cultural processes are themselves understood to be integrally local and global, mutually constitutive, and bound up in modes of gender at all levels. My aim, therefore, is twofold. First, I attempt to challenge the portrayal of the local as contained within, and thus defined fundamentally by, the global. My second goal involves a decoupling of the link that has fused gender with the local and left the macropicture of globalization bereft of gender as a constitutive force. In short, I will argue that seeing the specific dimensions of the Caribbean higgler's work as global processes (not as a result of them) prods us to think more flexibly about the relationship between gender and globalization at large. In particular, the higgler challenges any notion that global spaces are traversed by men and gendered masculine. She also disrupts familiar formulations in which the "third-world woman" is defined either outside globalization or as the presumed back upon which its production depends. Thus, she forces us to reckon with two related problems: the collapse of local specificity in macroanalyses of globalization and the slippery equation between local and women/gender that has effectively eclipsed the latter from the macromodels of globalization. If, as I suggested at the outset, the gendering of space as well as the social and economic processes associated with globalization imply that local and global become characterized in oppositional terms (feminine/masculine), then critiquing the effects of globalization on local ground can answer only one dimension of this conundrum. What is called for as well, then, is a feminist reconceptualization of globalization whereby local forms of globalization are understood not merely as effects but also as constitutive ingredients in the changing shape of these movements. A feminist reconceptualization of this sort requires a stance toward globalization in which the arrows of change are imagined in more than one direction, and where gender is interrogated not only in the practices of men and women in local sites but also in the ways in which both abstract as well as tangible global movements and processes are ascribed masculine or feminine value. Works by feminist social scientists across a number of disciplinary lines have begun to demonstrate the gains to be made by bringing together shifts in theorizing globalization with close empirical study of specific local contexts.

*****

GLOBALIZATION ACROSS FORMAL AND INFORMAL ECONOMIC FRONTIERS

The higgler in the Caribbean context is an age-old figure. Defined as a market intermediary, she is a buyer and seller, traditionally of produce and goods purchased from rural growers and sold in the town market. The country higgler has been a powerful figure in Afro-Caribbean history, a woman who symbolizes local economic ingenuity and female independence. Traditionally, she traveled from country to town and back again, buying and selling agricultural produce for manufactured and imported goods available in town, and, in turn, making these commodities available in rural areas. Her historical importance has been multifaceted. From the days of slavery, the higgler was integral to establishing the internal marketing systems that have come to define much of the Caribbean region (Mintz 1955; Katzin 1959; Le Franc 1989). Her role under slavery was profound, both symbolically and practically. By transporting and making available a wide array of produce, herbs, and root crops, grown by slaves on provision grounds during their "free" time, and by providing the dietary staples for slave and planter alike, she both subsidized and developed autonomy from the plantation system (Beckles 1989; Bush 1990). Traveling between peasant producers in the countryside and emergent urban areas, the higgler helped to establish a predictable national diet that has characterized West Indian life across class and racial boundaries. Over nearly two centuries, she also came to embody a figure of womanhood in which physical movement, travel, and business acumen were defining characteristics. In contrast to the plantation mistress, whose life was circumscribed by the limits of domestic duty and propriety and who was expected to inhabit the interior spaces of home and church, the higgler operated in the public space of markets and roads at home and in her travels to neighboring islands. She has been defined more by movement than by stasis, more by vivacity and grit than by a demure Victorian demeanor.

In the Caribbean, flux and movement have characterized models of livelihood and existence more than stasis and sedentarism. This is not surprising given the region's very invention as a global endeavor of colonialism. Perhaps out of the ashes of its bitter legacy of forced migrations of slavery and indenture emerged a cultural predisposition for flux and change (Mintz 1989, 1996; Trouillot 1992). The country higgler was the key bearer not only of produce and other consumer goods between country and town but of news, information, and gossip (Katzin 1959). Her style of banter and prowess over modes of negotiation are well-known and admired traits of West Indian womanhood. Indeed, this particular expression of femininity—of strength, size, and autonomy—has formed a powerful counterpoint to that of a more middle-class, European model denoted in the region's well-known concept of "respectability." This figure has been one of the most highly commodified images of West Indianness generally. The colorful country higgler, wearing a head tie and printed skirt, proudly balancing her bountiful tray of fruit atop her head or nestled beneath her generous bosom, has become a synecdoche for Caribbean womanhood and even nationhood. Her image is produced for touristic as well as local consumption, on postcards, key chains, tea towels, as well as finer artistic renderings. She signifies a femininity that is at once that of a mother and a worker, a provider and a consumer, at one and the same time the definition of locality and of movement.

Today, a new form of higglering has expanded in the region, in which women travel on commercial airlines, rather than on trucks, buses, or banana boats, buying clothing and other consumer goods, rather than mangoes or provision crops, and reselling these in an active (and illegal) informal market at home. Otherwise called "suitcase traders" or "informal commercial importers" (ICIs), Caribbean higglers are a well-known and much-discussed, but little-studied, group. The suitcase trade (named for the large bags carried abroad empty and returned full upon the higgler's return home) is an international phenomenon witnessed in many of today's major metropolitan areas as well as in third-world cities within Africa, Latin America, and the Caribbean. These informal commercial importers represent a growing dimension of an expanding informal sector in Barbados and the region at large. Today, the transnational higgler travels not only beyond the rural/urban loop of her agricultural counterpart but to cities in other parts of the region and, quite significantly, to places outside of the traditional interregional boundaries that colonialism established centuries ago.

*****

I turn attention here to those women employed within one of the region's newest and fastest-growing industries, offshore informatics, who find themselves propelled into the additional pursuit of weekend higglering and whose lives, as such, have become intimately bound up with a multitude of dimensions of globalization. I focus on this particular subcategory of higglers as a way of highlighting a number of hidden relationships within processes of globalization. In most cases for these women, higglering is not an explicit identity or form of work. Instead, it represents an economic strategy for supplementing their low formal wages or; as many women say, just a little extra way of "making do." Even more so than the traditional higgler dealing in produce and traveling across national and regional spaces, the informatics worker/higgler is multiply embedded in global processes, albeit in an unmistakably Caribbean form. The hyper-high-tech quality of the work they produce (transmitted in electronic form via satellite technology) and its inextricably global configuration, together with their transnational sojourns for profit and for pleasure, place this group of higglers in a category of their own. Though as global producers and as higglers their historical roots are deep, they demonstrate some of the convergences across structural spheres (culture/economy, production/consumption, and formal/informal sectors of the economy) that the globalization literature has narrowly (and separately) portrayed. Further, each of these realms and their dynamic intersections demonstrates the integral place of gender in the dialectics of local/global processes.

*****

Offshore informatics is a recent expansion of global industry and refers to the transnational movement of information-based service work for U.S., British, and other corporations outside metropolitan centers and into developing countries, where new, low-waged labor forces now perform it. As with other transnational production ventures that have shifted production operations "offshore" to the developing world, the draw of Barbados and some other Caribbean locales for offshore informatics is quite simple: comparatively lower wages; a well-educated, "disciplined," and English-speaking labor force (thanks to the legacy of British colonialism); and various tax and infrastructure inducements that the Barbadian government provides.

As in several other industries along the global assembly line (e.g., garments, textiles, electronics), informatics is a highly feminized arena. Nearly every computer cubicle of the dozen or so informatics "open offices" currently operating in Barbados is occupied by a woman between the ages of 18 and 35, who enters electronic data from airline ticket stubs, insurance claims forms, or legal briefs. Even a cursory glance at these women and their office-like production floors raises questions about their embeddedness in globalization. Operators commit to memory the place names and various associated data codes of North American cities to which they are electronically linked; they participate in American management practices such as "total quality management" (TQM) that British business consultants teach their Barbadian managers; they buy imported accessories displaying the logos of designers from Europe and the United States (jewelry, underwear, handbags, and the like); they rent pirated videos of movies taped from U.S. cable channels from mobile stalls parked outside their industrial zones during break times and between shifts; and many, on their vacation time or long holiday weekends, engage in transnational higglering trips to purchase the very goods (clothing, shoes, and accessories) that demarcate them visually from their sisters and neighbors working in a range of factories nearby.

Informatics employers directly foster these trips in a fascinating matrix involving corporate prescriptions for "professional" and disciplined workers, a reward structure in which airline tickets are exchanged for exceptional levels of productivity and commitment, and women workers' desire for new and reasonable fashions to further their workplace "professionalism" (and afterwork wardrobe) and for the opportunity to earn money through travel abroad. For example, Barbados's largest informatics employer (of over one thousand women workers) offers "thank-you cards," or productivity rewards, in the form of travel vouchers on American Airlines, which is owned by the same parent company as the informatics firm. These coupons enabled many of the women in this company to travel abroad for the first time in their lives. Again reflective of the youthful and feminine profile corporate managers held of their employees, these awards included companion tickets for a female family member chaperone. Networks of kin and friends living overseas influenced women's destinations, as did the limits of their coupons (e.g., two are required for a trip to San Juan, American Airlines' regional hub, and three are required for New York). In a more indirect way, a number of other factors have influenced employees' participation in the suitcase trade. I have argued elsewhere that the company's dress codes and emphasis on "professionalism" foster both discipline among the workers and a determination to distinguish themselves from other "ordinary" factory workers through particular modes of adornment and style. In order to do so, women go to great lengths to make, commission, and purchase new clothes and accessories that mark their nonfactory status. The suitcase trade represents one of the major sources of this distinctive attire. In this case, the demand for new styles and new consumer goods is integrally tied to the particular formation of a "pink-collar" worker within the informatics sector, a process configured by a complex set of factors including foreign and local modes of discipline and surveillance, gender ideologies, and aesthetics (Freeman 2000).

The fact that these high-tech working women juggle formal and informal sector work is not in itself remarkable in the history of Barbados nor the region more generally (Comitas 1964; Carnegie 1987; Senior 1990). However, the particular linkages, both structural and symbolic, between the formal transnational export sector and the emergent trade in consumer goods by suitcase traders remain unexplored as a dimension of (simultaneously) globalization, local culture and development, and identity.

*****

GENDERING GLOBALIZATION ACROSS PRODUCTION/ CONSUMPTION FRONTIERS

[...] [T]he pink-collar worker in the offshore informatics industry in Barbados takes her wage (and her corporate thank-you card) and invests it in the purchase of goods abroad, with the eventual goal of reselling them in informal networks back home. The challenge to a singular script of globalization, however, can be made not solely in the economic bases of production but by turning to the realm of consumption and, more generally, to cultural dimensions of these processes. Because the contemporary higgler's primary goal is the provision of consumer goods to such markets back home, she faces the task on her sojourns of translating tastes and desires between "home" and "host" cultures as well as managing her own relationships and movements on foreign territory, to a large extent through modes of consumption. In this sense, her consumption is both an individual personal practice carried out as she travels abroad and as an entrepreneur back home as well as a social practice that bears on the circulation of goods and, potentially, on their gendered enactments more broadly. For herself and her family, the transnational higgler is primarily involved in the pursuit of income and her own self-fashioning; but at the same time she is deeply engaged as an arbiter of styles and taste for the customers she supplies with goods. Her own embodiment of feminin- ity—the particular ways in which she occupies and traverses spaces, her adoption of new styles, modes of comportment, and articulation of "professionalism"—is conveyed through goods and her own expressions of self to her customer

networks of family, friends, workmates, as well as to the community at large. These practices, in turn, present possibilities for redefining gen- der and for redrawing conventional boundaries of class (Freeman 2000) and race (Ulysse 1999). How the higglering movements of contempo- rary Caribbean women help us think differently about the gendered relationships of production/ consumption, locality, and globalization may be read in part through Danielle's story.

Danielle was employed in one of the largest informatics firms in Barbados when I first met her in 1989. She was open then about her simul- taneous pride in and boredom with her job as "materials controller." She spent her day on slippered feet, handing out pages of text to sed- entary keyers who entered the text electronically for foreign publishers. Text pages were "double keyed" for higher accuracy, and Danielle's job involved keeping track of who had which pages and which pages needed to be double-keyed, all the while not keeping any of the typists waiting, as their pay depended upon fast and accurate data entry. Likewise, she was on-call to answer questions, interpret key-codes, and assist the supervisors and shift managers. While she complained about the boredom and frustration of being squeezed between keyers' demands and supervisors' mandates, she enjoyed the regular paycheck. "It helps me budget better and plan for things." Even in the early days of our meet- ing, she let on that her real ambition was to open her own business and "be my own boss." During those months, she perfected her sewing and made skirt-suits for herself and her fellow workmates on commission. Learning how to cut her own patterns by hand, she could soon turn out a simple suit in a matter of an hour or two. Soon, Danielle was supplementing her formal wage in informatics with fairly regular income earned informally as a needle-worker.

The relationship between her sewing pursuits and her formal job revolved closely around the conventions and expectations for professionalism—to dress and comport herself as an office worker in a transnational firm. In addition to seamstressing, transnational hig- glering trips had become a widespread practice among many of Danielle's workmates, and she and several friends arranged a trip together to San Juan over an Easter holiday weekend. As is typically the case, Danielle arranged a package ticket with a local travel agency, including ground transportation to a reasonable motel (costing roughly $55/night for a double room). On these trips, she travels with her friend and previous workmate, Marcelle, who has worked her way up in the informatics industry to a managerial position in a new firm. Their trips are planned so as to accommodate Marcelle's work schedule, and she arranges a day or two away from her formal job in order to extend the weekend over four days. Their husbands and other female relations take care of their children (two each), and these trips are eagerly anticipated with the simultaneous dimensions of profit-seeking work and pleasure-seeking escapade. They board a plane out of Grantly Adams International Airport, each woman having checked two large empty suitcases. Danielle carries with her ticket a wish list of orders to fill for herself, her family, and her customers.

On their last trip to St. Lucia, they were met by Danielle's cousin's husband, who has lived and worked in Castries for many years. Their four-day trip included a busy combination of shopping in reasonable retail stores for jeans, children's clothes, and casual leather shoes, an excursion to see the famous Pitons and dramatic waterfalls, and evenings out at popular nightclubs. They speak about being off on their own and out at night with an air of excitement, for these are activities they would be less likely to carry out at home. In the shops, Danielle straddles the roles of consumer and eventual broker and balances the requests on her list against prices, availability, and the new styles she ventures her customers will like. In her display of snapshots from this trip, which followed the familiar convention of posed portraits in front of national sites as well as inside the stores, one would be hard pressed to decipher this higglering journey as anything but a long weekend tourist excursion away from Barbados.

The particular meanings of Danielle's ventures are significant precisely in their multiplicity—they are opportunities for generating income but equally for seeing new sites, enjoy-

ing themselves, feeling fashionable and adept at finding "good deals," and in constructing forms of femininity that defy some traditional boundaries that are both gendered and formulated along the lines of class. Danielle and her friend Marcelle are both married women, mothers, and working women—one in a high-prestige industry in a position with responsibility, the other now having quit her job in informatics and running a bar/convenience store out of her home. They go to church with some regularity, and they could generally be described as straddling the upper-working/lower-middle classes. Their higglering pursuits when seen amid their wider relationships and responsibilities powerfully exemplify the false dichotomy of the persistently gendered paradigm of respectability and reputation. They are neither the "uptown ladies" nor the "downtown women" of Gina Ulysse's Jamaican paradigm (1999). They move easily between "proper," "respectable" etiquette of middle-class family life and work, facilitated by new modes of consumption they now enjoy, and the "reputation"-like practices of foreign travel, nightclubbing, bold bodily display, and self-fashioning formerly construed as masculine practices (Wilson 1969). The special combination of economic goals along with social desires (profit making and cost saving with pleasure seeking) gives these trips a dimension of both credibility as well as suspicion in the eyes of the women's husbands and boyfriends, and women are known to capitalize on the former to allay the latter. In short, they challenge the reputation/respectability dichotomy in many of the ways critics have asserted—by simultaneously enacting behaviors previously imagined to be the preserve of *either* men or women, middle or lower classes, white, brown, or black. Through modes of dress and travel that are tied both to their role as producer (higgler/informatics worker) and consumer, they are engaged in global processes that are locally distinct. They are incorporated into the international division of labor just as third-world women factory workers are in other countries; however, their incorporation is not generic nor is it in isolation from other modes of global activity and agency.

CONCLUSIONS

The case of the informatics worker/higglers helps to illustrate how through changing modes of production and consumption these social actors have become multiply "territorialized" across a global arena and, in the process, have become agents of globalization. They are local subjects living across and within a globalized terrain both within Barbados (as informatics workers as well as in numerous other forms of consumption and contact with global goods and culture) and on their higglering sojourns abroad (as consumers and marketers of goods and as "tourists" engaged in the consumption of other languages, people, and cultures). In a sense, they are rooted in Barbados, and their Barbadianness is increasingly defined and sharpened though new modes of production, consumption, and travel in ways that link Barbados with numerous other sites along the global terrain. Their notions of themselves as feminine, sexual subjects—as women, as members of the working/middle classes, and as Barbadian, West Indian, Caribbean, and Black—are, not surprisingly, increasingly defined in relation to others they encounter through their travel and their relationships forged as higglers. Higglering, then, as a form of labor and consumption and as such the nexus of social, economic, and cultural relationships, becomes a realm in which identities (national, regional, class, racial, gender, and sexual) are articulated and redefined.

*****

As a third-world female producer/consumer, the informatics worker/higgler represents an intriguing dimension of globalization in which participants within the informal sector and in global factories are themselves enacting new modes of globalization; they are not merely its effects. It is precisely their agency in doing so, as well as their mutually reinforcing engagements across formal and informal economies and across transnational spaces in which they produce and consume, that both the macro-models as well as many of the feminist ethnographic local accounts fail to illuminate. These engagements in production and consumption as they are configured across space and time have taken shape in ways that foundationally depend upon and redefine femininity and masculinity. As such, they make plain the gendering at work within modes of globalization and the limitations of interpreting such movements solely within the framework of masculinist models of capitalist expansion.

There is a dialectical process at work that begins with the informatics worker/higgler's first recruitment into her transnational firm. At this point, she is an instrument of multinational capitalism, and her incorporation is a gendered one. Her youthful and disciplined body and temperament are tapped and molded within this high-tech global production zone in a manner that fosters a form of professionalism such that she seeks other income sources and symbolic mechanisms for fostering her new feminine demeanor and appearance. The imperative for this new image quickly comes to be articulated both from above (management) and below (her fellow work-mates), and this image reflects not only corporate demands but also the creation of a new pink-collar identity she works hard to maintain. On buying trips to San Juan and Miami, the purchase of clothing and accessories is not only an act of consumption but of production—of new images, new modes of comportment, and new subjectivities in a transnational symbolic order. This production of self, while symbolic rather than material, has an economic value as well as a cultural one, as it is a vital dimension of the successful marketing of her goods back home. Through these complex practices, she is simultaneously imbricated in a dialectic of shopfloor production (albeit in an officelike setting), the consumption of clothing and style, and the production of new feminine selves. At each node of this imbrication, there is an exchange of economic as well as symbolic value. Significantly, in this process, she is transformed from being primarily *instrumental* in the forces of globalization (as an employee of a MNC) to becoming *agentive* when others pay for her privileged knowledge and attractive goods. In other words, disciplined and remade in the formal workplace of informatics, she further embellishes this new sense of self on her buying trips, through which she becomes a new agent of globalization. Her agency challenges us to rethink models of globalization more generally in which the local is construed as a space in which the heavy hand of the global makes its marks.

The informatics worker-cum-higgler is embedded within processes of globalization in multiple ways that are not unidirectional, just as Marchand and Runyan observe more generally (2000, 7). She demonstrates not only that local actors are resilient in *responding* to the demands of global capitalism (i.e., not only coping with low wages and a highly disciplined labor process but also redefining transnational prescriptions for "ideal" labor in light of local historical traditions of women's simultaneous expectations for wage work and motherhood) but also that they are involved in crafting multiple modes of global capitalism itself. Ironically, perhaps, she is involved not in "countering" global capitalism, as Gibson-Graham's (1996) model might be inclined to hope, but in intensifying its reach and, in a sense, democratizing its rewards. She gives a new shape to a long-standing female tradition of Caribbean marketing, and yet she continues its particular expression of femininity in which movement, sharp wits, and business acumen are vital ingredients. She capitalizes upon her formal wage-earning (and often exploited) status in the global informatics industry by turning productivity inducements (travel voucher rewards) into profit-making ventures and by utilizing her networks of workmates as a captive market for her imported wares.

In what way might we derive generalizable lessons from the story of a transnational higgler such as Danielle? She is distinct from Caribbean transnational higglers or suitcase traders who make their entire livelihood from this informal trade, as well as from agriculturally based higglers who continue to peddle their produce in the local marketplaces. In an effort to challenge tendencies within globalization literatures to make invisible local actors and their particular interventions in or initiations of global practices, one can run the risk of romanticizing as well as overplaying their

significance. While no one would claim that transnational higglers influence the direction or form of global production or consumption in the same ways or on the same scale as do more powerful global actors (e.g., finance capitalists or heads of multinational corporations), their roles as transnational informatics workers and marketers (travelers/tourists, consumers, producers, and arbiters of taste and styles between local and foreign sites) represent forms of global action on local stages whose significance affects directly the ways in which they and their customers live their lives and define themselves. They are significant in illustrating that globalization works in multiple and changing ways that are at once steeped in history, culture, and gender and that operate in and emerge out of local contexts in a relationship that is dialectical and in flux. They push us to challenge not only the dualisms of local/global and ethnography/theory but also the implicit gendered categories within them—local/ethnography as *feminine*: static, traditional, homebound, informal, and consumption oriented; and global/theory as *masculine*: mobile, modern, cosmopolitan, formal, and production oriented. The task before us, then, is not to disregard her as exceptional to the mainstream of global effects nor to ignore the ways in which globalization denies agency to many in its wake but to attune our critical gaze to the range of actors and practices on the global stage and thereby rethink the very concept of globalization itself—its roots, its forms, and its implications. In so doing, it will become more and more clear that broad theory and macrostructural models that do not attend to or account for such incursions and articulations are increasingly limited in their descriptive and explanatory power.

REFERENCES

Appadurai, Arjun. 1990. "Disjuncture and Difference in the Global Cultural Economy." *Public Culture* 2(3): 1–24.

Beckles, Hilary, 1989. *Natural Rebels: A Social History of Enslaved Black Women in Barbados.* London: Zed.

Bush, Barbara. 1990. *Slave Women in Caribbean Society, 1650–1838.* Bloomington: Indiana University Press.

Carnegie, Charles V. 1987. "A Social Psychology of Caribbean Migrations: Strategic Flexibility in the West Indies." In *The Caribbean Exodus,* ed. Barry B. Levine, 32–43. New York: Praeger.

Castells, Manuel. 1998. *End of Millennium: Volume III.* Oxford: Blackwell.

Comitas, Lambros. (1964) 1973. "Occupational Multiplicity in Rural Jamaica." In *Work and Family Life: West Indian Perspectives,* ed. Lambros Comitas and David Lowenthal, 157–73. New York: Anchor.

Enloe, Cynthia. 1990. *Bananas, Beaches, and Bases: Making Feminist Sense of International Politics.* Berkeley: University of California Press.

Featherstone, Mike, ed. 1990. *Global Culture: Nationalism, Globalization, and Modernity.* London: Sage.

Freeman, Carla. 2000. *High Tech and High Heels in the Global Economy: Women, Work and Pink-Collar Identities in the Caribbean.* Durham, N.C.: Duke University Press.

Gibson-Graham, J.K. 1996. *The End of Capitalism (as We Knew It): A Feminist Critique of Political Economy.* Oxford: Blackwell.

Gupta, Akhil, and James Ferguson, eds. 1997. *Culture, Power, Place: Explorations in Critical Anthropology.* Durham, N.C.: Duke University Press.

Harvey, David. 1989. *The Condition of Postmodernity: An Enquiry into the Origins of Cultural Change.* London: Blackwell.

Katzin, Margaret Fisher. 1959. "The Jamaican Country Higgler." *Theory and Practice.* London: Pinter.

Le Franc, Elsie. 1989. "Petty Trading and Labour Mobility: Higglers in the Kingston Metropolitan Area." In *Women and the Sexual Division of Labour in the Caribbean,* ed. Keith Hart, 99–123. Jamaica: Consortium Graduate School of Social Sciences.

Lutz, Catherine. 1995. "The Gender of Theory." In *Women Writing Culture,* ed. Ruth Behar and Deborah Gordon, 249–66. Berkeley: University of California Press.

Marchand, Marianne and Anne Sisson Runyan (eds.). 2000. *Gender and Global Restructuring: Sightings, Sites, Resistances.* London: Routledge.

Massey, Doreen. 1994. *Space, Place, and Gender.* Minneapolis: University of Minnesota Press.

McMichael, Philip. 1997. *Development and Social Change: A Global Perspective.* Thousand Oaks, Calif.: Pine Forge.

Mintz, Sydney W. 1955. "The Jamaican Internal Marketing Pattern: Some Notes and Hypotheses." *Social and Economic Studies* 4(1): 95–103.

_____. 1989. *Caribbean Transformations.* New York: Columbia University Press.

_____. 1996. "Goodbye Columbus: Second Thoughts on the Caribbean Region at Mid-Millennium." Walter Rodney Memorial Lecture, Centre for Caribbean Studies, University of Warwick.

Peterson, V. Spike. 1996. "Shifting Ground(s): Epistemological and Territorial Remapping in the Context of Globalization(s)." In *Globalization: Theory and Practice,* ed. Eleonore Kofman and Gillian Youngs, 11–28. London: Pinter.

Senior, Olive. 1990. *Working Miracles: Women's Lives in the English Speaking Caribbean.* Bloomington: Indiana University Press.

Sklair, Leslie. 1991. *Sociology of the Global System.* Baltimore: John Hopkins University Press.

Trouillot, Michel Rolph. 1992. "The Caribbean Region: An Open Frontier in Anthropological Theory." *Annual Review of Anthropology* 21:19–42.

Ulysse, Gina. 1999. "Uptown Ladies and Downtown Women: Informal Commercial Importing and the Social/Symbolic Politics of Identities in Jamaica." Ph.D. dissertation, Department of Anthropology, University of Michigan.

Waters, Malcolm. 1995. *Globalization.* London: Routledge.

Wilson, Peter J. 1969. "Reputation and Respectability: A Suggestion for Caribbean Ethnology." *Man* 4(1):70–84.

CHAPTER 30

GLOBALIZATION, GENDER, AND THE DAVOS MAN

Lourdes Benería

M uch has been said over the past 15 years about global markets. The process of accelerated globalization that we have witnessed during recent decades has been a powerful source of change driving national economies, deepening their international connections, and affecting many aspects of social, political, and cultural life. Despite the debate over the extent to which the degree of globalization is higher today than in other historical periods, few of us doubt that powerful forces are working toward the formation of "global villages." From an economic perspective, the basic features of globalization are the transformations linked to ever expanding markets and the rapid technological change in communications and transportation that transcend national boundaries and shrink space. The expansion of markets has taken place within the context of the neoliberal model of development, which has returned to a laissez-faire discourse and practice that characterized nineteenth-century capitalism. One argument presented in this chapter is that, despite its different framework, the current global expansion exhibits similarities to the earlier expansion of markets. This is the case for both high- and low-income countries, including those in transition to market economies from the centralized planning of the former Soviet Union....

THE SELF-REGULATED MARKET

The Great Transformation [by Karl Polanyi] was first published in 1944. It is an analysis of the construction and growth of the self-regulated market and of laissez-faire capitalism from the beginning of the industrial revolution up to the early twentieth century. Polanyi's "great transformation" was the "taming" of the market. It was represented by what he calls the "collectivist countermovement" that, beginning in the late nineteenth century and continuing through the twentieth, took refuge in "social and national protectionism" against "the weaknesses and perils inherent in a self-regulating market" (1957 [1944], p. 145).

Polanyi's analysis centers on the profound change in human behavior represented by market-oriented choices and by decisions in which gain replaced subsistence as the center of economic activity. Gain and profit, Polanyi argues, had never before played such important roles in human activity. Critical of Adam Smith's suggestion that the social division of labor depended upon the existence of markets and "upon man's propensity to barter, truck and exchange one thing for another" (p. 43), Polanyi argues instead that the division of labor in earlier societies had depended on "differences inherent in the facts of sex, geography, and individual endowment" (p. 44). For Polanyi, production and distribution in many earlier societies were ensured through reciprocity and redistribution, two principles not currently associated with economics. These principles were part of an economic system that was "a mere function of social organization," that is, at the service of social life. Capitalism, however, evolved in the opposite direction, leading to a situation in which the economic system determined social organization. Commenting on Smith, Polanyi argues that "no misreading of the past ever proved to be more prophetic of the future" (p. 43), in the sense that one hundred years after Adam Smith wrote about man's propensity to barter, truck, and exchange, this propensity became the norm—theoretically and practically—of industrial capitalist/market society. Although Polanyi may not always persuade us that the pursuit of economic gain is a result of market society, its fundamental role in a market economy—and in the theoretical models that sustain that economy—is unarguably central.

For Polanyi, a crucial step in this gradual transformation toward the predominance of "the economic" was the one "which makes isolated markets into a [self-regulated] market economy." Contrary to conventional wisdom, Polanyi argues, this change was not "the natural outcome of the spreading of markets" (p. 57). On the contrary, the market economy was socially constructed and accompanied by a profound change in the organization of society itself....

Polanyi mentions also the enormous increase in the administrative functions of a state newly endowed with a central bureaucracy, the strengthening of private property, and the enforcement of contracts in market exchange and other transactions.... He also ascribes the formation of a competitive national labor market in eighteenth- and nineteenth-century England to a series of policies that dislocated labor and forced the new laboring classes to work for low wages. In this sense, Polanyi's analysis suggests the seemingly contradictory notion of laissez-faire liberalism as "the product of deliberate state action," including "a conscious and often violent intervention on the part of

the government" (p. 250). As he points out, "all these strongholds of government interference were erected with a view to the organizing of some simple [market] freedom."

On the other hand, Polanyi points out that the "collectivist countermovement" or "great transformation"—the subsequent great variety of (re)actions taken against some of the negative consequences of the expanding market—started spontaneously as the critiques of capitalism led to political organizing and a variety of citizens' actions. Many of them constituted defensive actions on the part of different social groups. The left movements and social planning of the twentieth century were part of this transformation, although Polanyi sees its origins not in "any preference for socialism or nationalism" but in "the broader range of the vital social interests affected by the expanding market mechanism" (p. 145)....

The profound change represented by the gradual construction of a market society found a key expression in the changes in human behavior that led to the prevalence of rational economic man. As Polanyi puts it, "a market economy can only exist in a market society." That is, it can only exist when accompanied by changes in norms and behavior that enable the market to function. Economic rationality is based on the expectation that human beings behave in such ways as to achieve maximum gains. As any course in introductory economics emphasizes, while the entrepreneur seeks to maximize profit, the employee seeks to attain the highest earnings possible, and the consumer to maximize his or her utility. At the theoretical level, Adam Smith linked the selfish pursuit of individual gain to the maximization of the wealth of nations through the invisible hand of the market. He saw no contradiction between the two, and the orthodox tradition in economics continues to rely on this basic link.

In that tradition, and as feminist economists have often pointed out, the basic assumption of rational economic man has been embodied in neoclassical economic theory (Ferber and Nelson 1993; Folbre 1994). Economic rationality is assumed to be the norm in human behavior and the way to ensure the healthy functioning of the competitive market. This is expected to result in the most efficient allocation of resources and the maximization of production at the lowest possible costs. Feminist economists have also pointed out that most orthodox analysis excludes behavior based on other types of motivation, such as altruism, empathy, love, the pursuit of art and beauty for their own sake, reciprocity, and care. Selfless behavior is viewed as belonging to the nonmarket sector, such as the family....

THE CONSTRUCTION OF THE NATIONAL AND GLOBAL MARKET

> Capitalism without bankruptcy is like Christianity without hell.[1]

As the twentieth century nears its end, many parallels can be traced between the social construction of national market economies analyzed by Polanyi for nineteenth-century Europe and the expansion and deepening of both national and transnational markets across the globe. To be sure, a debate exists about the extent to which globalization represents a new historical trend; various authors, for example, have pointed out that some indicators of the degree of globalization are similar to those reached in earlier historical periods—such as before World War I. Yet the intensification of integrative processes during the past 30 years—for example, in terms of increasingly rapid movement of goods, communications, and exchange among countries and regions—has been unprecedented. The financial sector has led in the degree to which its markets have transcended national boundaries, while trade liberalization and the internationalization of production have accelerated the global integration of markets in goods and services.

At the national level, these processes have been facilitated by numerous efforts on the part of governments, which have played an active role in the globalization of domestic economies and of their social, political, and cultural life. This time, however, the construction of global markets has taken place in particular through the interventions of international forces beyond

national boundaries, such as the regional formation of free-trade areas and common markets, the growth of multinational corporations, the role of international organizations such as the World Bank and the International Monetary Fund, and the influence of foreign governments and other international actors, such as private banks, in determining policy in developing countries....

Although these policies have clearly increased the economic freedom of many actors involved in the market, they have also represented the use of a strong hand on the part of national governments and international institutions intent on building the neoliberal model of the late twentieth century, that is, achieving the great leap forward in the construction of national and global markets. To invoke Polanyi, these policies have been the product of deliberate state intervention—often carried out in the name of market freedoms—imposed from the top down and without a truly democratic process of discussion and decision making among all affected parties. As the *Wall Street Journal* put it for the case of Argentina, "[T]he reforms were largely accomplished by the political will of a presidential strongman who invoked executive decrees over 1,000 times" (O'Grady 1997)....

At the same time, the expansion of markets, associated also with the intensification of "modernization" across the globe, has been accompanied with triumphalist (re)statements and affirmations of discourses emphasizing the norms and behavior associated with economic rationality. These must be seen as part of the process of constructing markets à la Polanyi. We have witnessed this process in different forms, ranging from a strong emphasis on productivity, efficiency, and financial rewards, to shifts in values and attitudes—typified by the yuppies in the 1980s—such as a new emphasis on individualism and competitive behavior, together with an apparent tolerance and even acceptance of social inequalities and greed. The neoliberal weekly *The Economist* sees this set of factors as symbolized by the "Davos Man" who has replaced the "Chatham House Man" in his influence in the global marketplace.[2] The Davos Man, according to the weekly, includes businessmen, bankers, officials, and intellectuals who "hold university degrees, work with words and numbers, speak some English and share beliefs in individualism, market economics and democracy. They control many of the world's governments, and the bulk of its economic and military capabilities." The Davos Man does not "butter up the politicians; it is the other way around ... finding it boring to shake the hand of an obscure prime minister." Instead, he prefers to meet the Bill Gateses of the world. Written as a critique of Samuel Huntington's thesis in *The Clash of Civilizations and the Remaking of the World Order*, the praise of Davos Man by *The Economist* turns into an ode to the global and more contemporary version of economic man:

> Some people find Davos Man hard to take: there is something uncultured about all the money-grubbing and managerialism. But it is part of the beauty of Davos Man that, by and large, he does not give a fig for culture as the Huntingtons of the world define it. He will attend a piano recital, but does not mind whether an idea, a technique or a market is (in Mr. Huntington's complex scheme) Sinic, Hindu, Islamic or Orthodox. ("In Praise of the Davos Man" 1997, p. 18)

Thus, *The Economist* expects that Davos Man, through the magic powers of the market and its homogenizing tendencies, is more likely to bring people and cultures together than force them apart. In many ways, he is the rational economic man gone global.

What *The Economist* does not recognize is that the commercialization of everyday life and of all sectors of the economy generates dynamics and values that individuals and cultures might find repulsive. In many ways, we have witnessed, in Polanyi's terms, the tendency for society to become "an accessory to the economic system" rather than the other way around....

GENDER AND THE MARKET

This section argues that Polanyi's analysis of the social construction of markets has important

gender-related implications that he did not take into consideration. A central argument in this chapter is that the links to the market have been historically different for men and women, with consequences for their choices and behavior. Although Polanyi points out that all production in a market society is for sale, he fails to discuss the fact that, parallel to the deepening of market relations, a large proportion of the population engages in unpaid production, only indirectly linked to the market. Women are disproportionately concentrated in this type of work, which includes agricultural family labor, particularly but not solely in subsistence economies, domestic work, and volunteer work. In contemporary societies, women perform by far the largest proportion of unpaid activities. According to the United Nations Development Program's (UNDP's) "rough estimates" at the global level, if unpaid activities were valued at prevailing wages, they would amount to $16 trillion or about 70 percent of total world output ($23 trillion). Of this $16 trillion, $11 trillion, or almost 69 percent, represents women's work (UNDP 1995)....

Thus, to a large extent, men and women have been positioned differently with respect to both market transformations and the linkages between gender and nature (Merchant 1989). While the market has been associated with public life and "maleness," women have been viewed as closer to nature—often in essentialist ways instead of as a result of historical constructions. This perspective has in turn had an impact on the meaning of gender, a subject analyzed, for example, in the feminist literature dealing with the construction of femininity and masculinity (Gilligan 1982; Bern 1993; Butler 1993), and on our notions of the market itself (McCloskey 1993; Strassmann 1993). Clearly, Polanyi's 1944 analysis needs to be expanded to incorporate gender dimensions.

The norms and behavior associated with the market do not apply to the sphere of unpaid work that produces goods and services for use rather than for exchange. To the extent that unpaid work is not equally subject to the competitive pressures of the market, it can respond to motivations other than gain, such as nurturing, love, and altruism, or to other norms of behavior, such as duty and religious beliefs/practices. Without falling into essentialist arguments about men's and women's motivations, and keeping in mind the multiple differences across countries and cultures, we can conclude from the literature that there are gender-related variations in norms, values, and behavior (England 1993; Nelson 1993; Seguino, Stevens, and Lutz 1996). Likewise, the literature has discussed extensively women's concentration in caring/ nurturing work, either unpaid or paid (Folbre and Weisskopf 1996). Women have also concentrated in the service sector. To illustrate, the average proportion of women in this sector in the Organization for Economic Cooperation and Development (OECD) countries has been reported to be as high as 95 percent (Christopherson 1997).

Although the UNDP-type data show that the current predominance of women in unpaid work and that of men in paid activities is beyond dispute, engagement in nongainful activities is no more the exclusive domain of women than is market work the exclusive domain of men. In earlier societies, the principles of reciprocity and distribution described by Polanyi did not necessarily function according to the rules of market rationality. Instead, tradition, religion, kin, and community played an important role in setting up norms and affecting collective and individual values. But nonmaximizing behavior can also be found in contemporary societies. In subsistence economies, production is not geared to the market, and family labor is motivated primarily by needs rather than gain. Likewise, in market economies, behavior following norms of solidarity and choices between work and leisure, not necessarily pursuing gain or following the dictates of efficiency, competition, and productivity associated with economic rationality, has certainly not disappeared. This is symbolized by the large numbers of volunteer workers performing countless unpaid activities and by those engaged by choice in creative and/or in poorly remunerated work. In the case of volunteer work, such as that carried out at the community level, the motives might be associated with a sense of collective well-being,

empathy for others, or political commitment; in the case of artistic work, they might result from the pursuit of beauty and creativity, irrespective of their market value.

Feminist economists have written extensively about the way economic rationality, even in capitalist economies, may not be as prevalent as mainstream economics assumes. Their work has led them to recognize the need to develop alternative models based on assumptions of human cooperation, empathy, and collective well-being (Ferber and Nelson 1993; Strober 1994; Folbre 1994). In seeking alternative models, they join other scholars who have also questioned neoclassical assumptions on the grounds that they are predicated upon the Hobbesian view of self-interested individuals.

These authors argue that the numerous exceptions to this rule suggest that human behavior responds to a complex set of often contradictory tendencies (Marwell and Ames 1981; Frank, Golovich, and Regan 1993). Thus, neo-classical assumptions seem to contradict "real-life experiments in which collective action and empathetic connected economic decision-making are observed" (Seguino, Stevens, and Lutz 1996). Adopting a gender perspective, some authors have pointed out that this type of behavior is more frequently encountered among women than among men (Guyer 1980; Gilligan 1982; Benería and Roldan 1987)....

The claim on the part of feminist economists that models of free individual choice are inadequate for the analysis of issues of dependence/ interdependence, tradition, and power (Ferber and Nelson 1993) is particularly relevant for cultures in which individualistic, market-oriented behavior is more often the exception than the norm. Feminists have also pointed out that neoclassical analysis is based on a "separate self model" in which utility is viewed as subjective and unrelated to that of other people. As Paula England has argued, this model is linked to the assumption that individual behavior is selfish, since "emotional connection often creates empathy, altruism, and a subjective sense of social solidarity" (England 1993). Thus, to the extent that women are more emotionally connected than men, in large part because of their roles in child rearing and family care as well as because of the prevalent gender ideology, the separate self model has an androcentric bias. Moreover, to the extent that this model typifies Western individualism, it shares a Western bias and is foreign to societies with more collective forms of action and decision making. Neoclassical economic analysis has had little to say about these alternative modes of behavior and their significance for different forms of social organization and for policy and action.

We might ask if women's behaviors are changing as they enter the labor market in increasing numbers and as globalization intensifies the feminization of the labor force. Many studies have documented women's role in processes of industrialization in a variety of countries and their participation in production for global markets. During the past quarter century, we have witnessed the rapid formation of a female labor force in many countries. This labor force is often tied to the service sector and to production for export, even in countries where women's participation in paid work was traditionally low and socially unacceptable (Pyle 1982; Hein 1986; Ong 1987; Feldman 1992). In addition, the feminist movement, in its quest for gender equality, has contributed to this trend by emphasizing the need for women to increase their financial autonomy, bargaining power, and control over their lives....

The extension and deepening of markets across the globe raises many questions. What is the effect on individual behavior of being integrated in market activities? More specifically, what is the effect on women as the weight of their paid labor time increases relative to their domestic work? Does it imply that they are increasingly adopting the norms of economic rationality à la "economic man"? Are women becoming more individualistic, selfish, and less nurturing? Is market behavior undermining "women's ways of seeing and doing"? Are gender identities being reconstituted? The answers to these questions are not clear-cut. To begin with, a nonessentialist view of gender differences implies that social change influences gender (re)constructions; as women become continuous participants in the market, it is

likely their motives and aspirations will change, and they will adopt patterns of behavior traditionally observed more frequently among men. Casual observation and anecdotal evidence may persuade many of us that this is already happening. In addition, there remain areas of ambiguity, tension, and contradiction in the answers to these questions. These are rooted in different variables, some of which are historical and related to other factors.

The market can have positive effects, such as the breaking up of patriarchal traditions or the curtailment of arranged marriages that limit individual autonomy. On the cultural side, it can accelerate the diffusion of both "liberating" and "sexist" practices. It can also have negative consequences for those who suffer from discrimination and market exploitation. The literature on female labor in export-processing industries has provided examples of how an increase in women's autonomy and bargaining power can run parallel to discriminatory practices against them, at the workplace as well as at the community level (Pyle 1982; Hein 1986; Ong 1987; Cravey 1998)....

Several authors who have observed the changes in gender ideology in these countries have emphasized that the transition has exacerbated "latent and manifest patriarchal attitudes," increasing women's vulnerability both culturally and economically (Moghadan 1993). Bridger, Kay, and Pinnick note that "the initial rounds of democratic elections in Russia have virtually wiped women off the political map and their re-emergence is now painfully slow and fraught with difficulty" (1996, p. 2). In some Central Asian republics, new restrictions on women's lives have been imposed, such as barring them from appearing in public without a male or an elder woman, wearing pants, and driving cars (Tohidi 1996). A key question, however, will be the extent to which market forces will transform these norms and how the process of "modernization" spread through the market might shatter or erode patriarchal forms.

Ambiguity can also be found in feminist discourses themselves. For example, feminists have emphasized gender equality as a key goal, including the importance of women having the same access to the public sphere as men. In this sense, it is often assumed that women can behave as men do. Yet much feminist research has emphasized women's "difference." Gilligan, for example, documents the "different modes of thinking about relationships and the association of these modes with male and female voices." These different modes arise, she argues, "in a social context where factors of social status and power combine with reproductive biology to shape the experience of males and females and the relationship between the sexes" (1982, p. 2). Although Gilligan's work has been criticized for its essentialist overtones, it suggests that a key issue for feminism is how to combine an emphasis on difference with the pursuit of equality and how to preserve gender traits that contribute to individual, family, and human welfare without generating or perpetuating gender inequalities based on unequal power relations. One danger, for example, is to perceive difference in essentialist ways—a danger that is often encountered by those who view gender differences in oppositional ways, such as idealizing women's goodness and female superiority while viewing men as their opposite. This is different from understanding the extent to which it is important to maintain and even to foster, among men and women, what are identified as women's ways of knowing and doing, and the extent to which these can contribute to transforming knowledge and determining social change. The next section will deal with these questions.

BEYOND SELF-INTEREST?

I don't need money, I want the river's color back.
—Silas Natkime, son of the Waa Valley chief, Irian Jaya, Indonesia[3]

These words, a ringing affirmation of the value of a clean river over that of money, symbolizes one of the dilemmas of development, for it expresses an individual's desire to give priority to ecological over economic outcomes. It could also be interpreted as a reaction against the water-polluting outcome of "development." To return to Polanyi: his criticism of market society was that it is based on self-interest, leading to "disruptive strains" and "varied symptoms of disequilibrium," such as unemployment, class inequalities, "pressure on exchanges" and "imperialist rivalries" (1957 [1944]). We might now add environmental degradation to his list of disruptive strains....

For Polanyi, this tendency led to the need for planning or toward forms of market intervention that would counteract not only disruptive strains but also the domination of economic self-interest over all aspects of political and social life. This is not just history. As we observe the unfolding of global markets in the late twentieth century, we see these strains reappear. To be sure, the global market has displayed its dynamism and ability to supply unprecedented amounts of goods and services and to generate new forms of wealth. However, it has also generated new imbalances and economic and social crises, particularly in Africa and Latin America during the 1980s and in Eastern Europe and Asia during the 1990s. Evidence linking globalization with increasing inequalities and maldistribution of resources within and between countries has been growing (ECLAC 1995; Freeman 1996; Benería 1996; UNDP 1996, 1998, 1999).

Analogously, high unemployment or underemployment in many areas, including high-income countries such as in Europe, disrupts the social fabric of communities and countries. As Dani Rodrik (1997) has argued, globalization undermines social cohesiveness, requiring compensatory policies and the design of social insurance systems. In some Latin American circles, the tendencies of the past decade have been viewed as leading toward what some authors have called "socially unsustainable development" in the long run. In the same way, Asian, Russian, and Brazilian economic crises have raised new questions about the instability of financial markets, and they have begun to change course, initiating a new debate on global reforms and national controls over capital flows. Fifty years after *The Great Transformation*, Polanyi's call for subordinating the market to the priorities set by democratic societies resonates urgently, even though to achieve this goal we will have to accommodate new, late twentieth-century realities.

This prospect poses challenging questions for feminism, which could in fact be viewed as one of Polanyi's countermovements, representing an emphasis on gender equality but linked also to wider social issues. Can feminism make a contribution to the quest for new directions in human development? Can the alternative models discussed by feminists provide useful guidelines for constructing alternative societies? Can women offer different voices as they become more integrated in the market and public life? Can "difference" be maintained, and can it be a source of inspiration for those who work toward progressive social change? ...

Far from seeing this mode as "backward" or "irrational," we can perceive it as a source of inspiration leading to alternative ways of organizing society based on nonhegemonic conceptual/theoretical tools and models. This means, for example, not taking rational economic man's objectives as the desired norm, which does not necessarily imply a rejection of markets as a way to organize production and distribution of goods and services. As Polanyi stated, "the end of market society means in no way the absence of markets" (1957 [1944], p. 252). However, this view calls for subordinating markets to the objectives of truly democratic communities and countries. The goal is to place economic activity at the service of human or people-centered development and not the other way around; or to reach an era in which productivity and efficiency are achieved not for their own sake but as a way to increase collective well-being. Hence, in the same way that it is possible to think of Christianity without hell, it is also possible to design ways to reduce the social costs of bankruptcy. All of this implies placing issues of distribution, inequality, ethics, the environment, and the nature of individual happiness, collective well-being, and social change at the center of our agendas. It follows that an urgent task for economists and social scientists is to translate these general objectives into specific policies and action....

Feminism has played an important part in the struggle for solutions at the decentralized, local, and institutional level: it has fought discrimination and inequalities across countries; it has changed institutions and decision-making processes; it has incorporated new agendas in the politics of daily life; it has affected national policies; it has made an impact on international agendas; and it has been influential in bringing human welfare to the center of debates on economic and social policy. It now has to meet the further challenges posed by globalization.

Polanyi wrote that the endeavor of thinking of people first "cannot be successful unless it is disciplined by a total view of man and society very different from that which we inherited from market economy" (1957 [1944]). The principal message of this chapter is that this effort must be transformative and based on a "total view of wo/man and society." Rather than diminishing this view as "soft," "idealistic," and "female," we must dare to take up the challenge and continue to follow the concrete, bottom-up strategies that have made feminism such a powerful agent of social change.

NOTES

1. From a refrain attributed to Westerners in a *New York Times* article that argues that, during the Asian crisis, corporations in Asia failed in record numbers but without disappearing from the market (WuDunn 1998), that is, without "going to hell."

2. The reference is to the annual meeting in Davos, Switzerland, of "people who run the world." The Chatham House is the "elegant London home" of the Royal Institute of International Affairs, where "diplomats have mulled the strange ways of abroad" for "nearly 80 years" ("In Praise of the Davos Man" 1997).

3. See Shari and McWilliams (1995, p. 66).

REFERENCES

Bern, Sandra Lipsitz. 1993. *The Lenses of Gender: Transforming the Debate on Sexual Inequality.* New Haven, CT: Yale University Press.

Benería, Lourdes. 1996. "The Legacy of Structural Adjustment in Latin America." In *Economic Restructuring in the Americas*, ed. L. Benería and M.J. Dudley. Ithaca, NY: Cornell University, Latin American Studies Program.

Benería, Lourdes, and Martha Roldan. 1987. *The Crossroads of Class and Gender: Industrial Homework, Subcontracting and Household Dynamics in Mexico City*. Chicago: University of Chicago Press.

Bridger, Sue, Rebecca Kay, and Kathryn Pinnick. 1996. *No More Heroines? Russia, Women and the Market*. London: Routledge.

Butler, Judith. 1993. *Bodies That Matter: On the Discursive Limits of "Sex."* London: Routledge.

Christopherson, Susan. 1997. "The Caring Gap for Caring Workers: The Restructuring of Care and the Status of Women in OECD Countries." Paper presented at the Conference on Revisioning the Welfare State: Feminist Perspectives on the U.S., and Europe, Ithaca, NY: Cornell University, October 3–5.

Cravey, Althaj. 1998. *Women and Work in Mexico's Maquiladoras*. Totowa, NJ: Rowman & Allenheld.

ECLAC (Economic Commission for Latin America and the Caribbean). 1995. *Social Panorama of Latin America*. Santiago de Chile: ECLAC.

England, Paula. 1993. "The Separative Self: Androcentric Bias in Neoclassical Assumptions." In *Beyond Economic Man: Feminist Theory and Economics*, ed. Marianne A. Ferber and Julie A. Nelson, 37–53. Chicago: University of Chicago Press.

Feldman, Shelley. 1992. "Crisis, Islam and Gender in Bangladesh: The Social Construction of a Female Labor Force." In *Unequal Burden: Economic Crises, Persistent Poverty and Women's Work*, ed. Lourdes Benería and Shelley Feldman, 105–30. Boulder, CO: Westview Press.

Ferber, Marianne A., and Julie A. Nelson, eds. 1993. *Beyond Economic Man: Feminist Theory and Economics*. Chicago: University of Chicago Press.

Folbre, Nancy. 1994. *Who Pays for the Kids? Gender and the Structures of Constraint*. London: Routledge.

Folbre, Nancy, and Thomas Weisskopf. 1996. "Did Father Know Best? Families, Markets, and the Supply of Caring Labor." Paper presented at the Conference on Economics, Values and Organization, Yale University, New Haven, CT, April 19–21.

Frank, Robert, Thomas Golovich, and Dennis Regan. 1993. "Does Studying Economics Inhibit Cooperation?" *Journal of Economic Perspectives* 7 (2): 159–71.

Freeman, Richard. 1996. "The New Inequality." *Boston Review* (December–January): 1–5.

Gilligan, Carol. 1982. *In a Different Voice*. Cambridge: Harvard University Press.

Guyer, Jane. 1980. "Households, Budgets and Women's Incomes." Boston University, Africana Studies Center Working Paper No. 28.

Hein, Catherine. 1986. "The Feminization of Industrial Employment in Mauritius: A Case of Sex Segregation." In *Sex Inequalities in Urban Employment in the Third World*, ed. Richard Anker and Catherine Hein, 277–312. New York: St. Martin's Press.

"In Praise of the Davos Man." 1997. *The Economist*, vol. 342, February 1, p. 18.

Marwell, Gerald, and Ruth Ames. 1981. "Economists Free Ride, Does Anyone Else? (Experiments in the Provision of Public Goods)." *Journal of Public Economics* 15 (3): 295–310.

McCloskey, Donald N. 1993. "Some Consequences of a Conjective Economics." In *Beyond Economic Man: Feminist Theory and Economics*, ed. Marianne A. Ferber and Julie A. Nelson, 69–93. Chicago: University of Chicago Press.

Merchant, Carolyn. 1989. *The Death of Nature: Women, Ecology and the Scientific Revolution*. San Francisco: Harper & Row.

Moghadan, Valentine. 1993. *Democratic Reform and the Position of Women in Transitional Economies*. Oxford: Clarendon Press.

Nelson, Julie. 1993. "The Study of Choice or the Study of Provisioning? Gender and the Definition of Economics." In *Beyond Economic Man: Feminist Theory and Economics*, ed. Marianne A. Ferber and Julie A. Nelson, 23–36. Chicago: University of Chicago Press.

O'Grady, Mary Anastasia. 1997. "Don't Blame the Market for Argentina's Woes." *Wall Street Journal*, May 30.

Ong, Aiwa. 1987. *Spirits of Resistance and Capitalist Discipline: Women Factory Workers in Malaysia*. Albany, NY: SUNY Press.

Polanyi, Karl. 1957 [1944]. *The Great Transformation.* Boston: Beacon Press.

Pyle, Jean. 1982. "Export-Led Development and the Underemployment of Women: The Impact of Discriminatory Employment Policy in the Republic of Ireland." In *Women, Men and the New International Division of Labor,* ed. June Nash and Maria Patricia Fernandez-Kelly, 85–112. Albany, NY: SUNY Press.

Rodrik, Dani. 1997. *Has Globalization Gone Too Far?* Washington, DC: Institute for International Economics.

Seguino, Stephanie, Thomas Stevens, and Mark Lutz. 1996. "Gender and Cooperative Behavior: Economic Man Rides Alone." *Feminist Economics* 2 (1): 195–223.

Shari, Michael, and Gary McWillliams. 1995. "Gold Rush in New Guinea." *Business Week,* Issue 3451, November 20, pp. 66–67.

Strassmann, Diana. 1993. "Not a Free Market: The Rhetoric of Disciplinary Authority in Economics." In *Beyond Economic Man: Feminist Theory and Economics,* ed. Marianne A. Ferber and Julie A. Nelson, 54–68. Chicago: University of Chicago Press.

Strober, Myra. 1994. "Rethinking Economics through a Feminist Lens." *American Economic Review* 84 (2): 143–7.

Tohidi, Nayereh. 1996. "Guardians of the Nation: Women, Islam and Soviet Modernization in Azerbaijan." Paper presented at the conference on Women's Identities and Roles in the Course of Change, Ankara, Turkey, October 23–25.

UNDP (United Nations Development Program). 1995, 1996, 1998, 1999. *Human Development Report.* New York: Oxford University Press.

WuDunn, Sheryl. 1998. "Bankruptcy the Asian Way." *New York Times,* September 8.

CHAPTER 31

GLOBALIZATION AND ITS MAL(E)CONTENTS
The Gendered Moral and Political Economy of Terrorism

Michael S. Kimmel

Globalization changes masculinities—reshaping the arena in which national and local masculinities are articulated, and transforming the shape of men's lives. Globalization disrupts and reconfigures traditional, neocolonial or other national, regional or local economic, political and cultural arrangements, and thus transforms local articulations of both domestic and public patriarchy (see Connell, 1998). Globalization includes the gradual proletarianization of local peasantries, as market criteria replace subsistence and survival. Small local craft producers, small farmers and independent peasants traditionally stake their notions of masculinity in ownership of land and economic autonomy in their work; these are increasingly transferred upwards in the class hierarchy and outwards to transnational corporations. Proletarianization also leads to massive labor migrations—typically migrations of male workers—who leave their homes and populate migrant enclaves, squatter camps and labor camps.

In addition, the institutional arrangements of global society are equally gendered. The marketplace, multinational corporations and transnational geopolitical institutions (World Court, United Nations, European Union) and their attendant ideological principles (economic ratio-

nality, liberal individualism) express a gendered logic. As a result, the impact of global economic and political restructuring is greater on women. At the national and global level, the world gender order privileges men in a variety of ways, such as unequal wages, unequal labor force participation, unequal structures of ownership and control of property, unequal control over one's body, as well as cultural and sexual privileges.

The patterns of masculinity embedded within these gendered institutions also are rapidly becoming the dominant global hegemonic model of masculinity, against which all local, regional, and national masculinities are played out and increasingly refer. The processes of globalization and the emergence of a global hegemonic masculinity have the ironic effect of increasingly "gendering" local, regional, and national resistance to incorporation into the global arena as subordinated entities. Religious fundamentalism and ethnic nationalism use local cultural symbols to express regional resistance to incorporation (see especially, Jurgensmeyer, 2000; Barber, 1995). However, these religious and ethnic expressions are often manifest as gender revolts, and include a virulent resurgence of domestic patriarchy (as in the militant misogyny of Iran or Afghanistan); the problematization of global masculinities or neighboring masculinities (as in the former Yugoslavia); and the overt symbolic efforts to claim a distinct "manhood" along religious or ethnic lines to which others do not have access and which will restore manhood to the formerly privileged (White militias in the US and skinhead racists in Europe).

Thus gender becomes one of the chief organizing principles of local, regional, and national resistance to globalization, whether expressed in religious or secular, ethnic or national terms. These processes involve flattening or eliminating local or regional distinctions, cultural homogenization as citizens and social heterogenization as new ethnic groups move to new countries in labor migration efforts. Movements thus tap racialist and nativist sentiments at the same time as they can tap local and regional protectionism and isolationism. They become gendered as oppositional movements also tap into a vague masculine resentment of economic displacement, loss of autonomy and collapse of domestic patriarchy that accompany further integration into the global economy. Efforts to reclaim economic autonomy, to reassert political control and revive traditional domestic dominance thus take on the veneer of restoring manhood.

In this article, I examine the ways in which masculinities and globalization are embedded in the emergence of extremist groups on the far right and also in the Islamic world. Specifically, I discuss the ways in which global, political, and economic processes affect lower-middle-class men in both the economic North and the Islamic world, and describe several of their political reactions, especially their efforts to restore public and domestic patriarchy. It is the lower middle class—that stratum of independent farmers, small shopkeepers, craft and highly skilled workers and small-scale entrepreneurs—who have been hardest hit by the processes of globalization. This has resulted in massive male displacement—migration, downward mobility. And it has been felt the most not by the adult men who were the tradesmen, shopkeepers and skilled workers, but by their sons, by the young men whose inheritance has been seemingly stolen from them. They feel entitled and deprived—and furious. These angry young men

are the foot soldiers of the armies of rage that have sprung up around the world.

Here I discuss White supremacists and Aryan youth in both the US and Scandinavia, and compare them briefly with the terrorists of Al Qaeda who were responsible for the attack on the US on 11 September 2001. All these groups, I argue, use a variety of ideological and political resources to re-establish and reassert domestic and public patriarchies. All deploy "masculinity" as a form of symbolic capital, an ideological resource, (1) to understand and explicate their plight; (2) as a rhetorical device to problematize the identities of those against whom they believe themselves fighting; and (3) as a recruitment device to entice other, similarly situated young men to join them. These movements look backward, nostalgically, to a time when they—native-born White men and Muslim men in a pre-global era—were able to assume the places in society to which they believed themselves entitled. They seek to restore that unquestioned entitlement, both in the domestic sphere and in the public sphere. They are movements not of revolution, but of restoration.

By examining far right Aryan White supremacists in the US, and their counterparts in Scandinavia, we can see the ways in which masculinity politics may be mobilized among the some groups of men in the economic North; and while looking at the social origins of the Al Qaeda terrorists, we can see how they might work out in Islamic countries. Although such a comparison in no way effaces the many differences that exist among these movements, and especially between the movements in the economic South and North, a comparison of their similarities enables us to explore the political mobilization of masculinities, and map the ways in which masculinities are likely to be put into political play in the coming decades.

RIGHT-WING MILITIAS: RACISM, SEXISM, AND ANTI-SEMITISM AS MASCULINE REASSERTION

In an illustration in an 1987 edition of WAR, the magazine of the White Aryan Resistance, a working-class White man, in hard hat and flak jacket, stands proudly before a suspension bridge while a jet plane soars overhead. "White Men Built This Nation!!" reads the text, "White Men Are This Nation!!!" Here is a moment of fusion of racial and gendered discourses, when both race and gender are made visible. "This nation," we now understand, "is" neither White women, nor non-white.

The White Aryan Resistance that produced this illustration is situated on a continuum of the far right that runs from older organizations such as the John Birch Society, Ku Klux Klan and the American Nazi Party, to Holocaust deniers, neo-Nazi or racist skinheads, White Power groups like Posse Comitatus and White Aryan Resistance, and radical militias, like the Wisconsin Militia or the Militia of Montana. [...]

These groups are composed of young White men, the sons of independent farmers and small shopkeepers. Buffeted by the global political and economic forces that have produced global hegemonic masculinities, they have responded to the erosion of public patriarchy (displacement in the political arena) and domestic patriarchy (their wives now work away from the farm) with a renewal of their sense of masculine entitlement to restore patriarchy in both arenas. That patriarchal power has been both surrendered by White men—their fathers—and stolen from them by a federal government controlled and staffed by legions of the newly enfranchised minorities, women and immigrants, all in service to the omnipotent Jews who control international economic and political life. Downwardly mobile rural White men—those who lost the family farms and those who expected to take them over—are squeezed between the omnivorous jaws of capital concentration and a federal bureaucracy which is at best indifferent to their plight, and at worst, facilitates their further demise. What they want, says one, is to "take back what is rightfully ours" (cited in Dobratz and Shanks-Meile, 2001: 10).

In many respects, the militias' ideology reflects the ideologies of other fringe groups on the far right, from whom they typically recruit, especially racism, homophobia, nativism, sexism, and anti-Semitism. These discourses of hate provide an explanation for the feelings of entitlement thwarted, fixing the blame squarely on "others" whom the state must now serve at the expense of White men. The unifying theme of these discourses, which have traditionally formed the rhetorical package Richard Hoftsadter labeled "paranoid politics," is gender. Specifically, it is by framing state policies as emasculating and problematizing the masculinity of these various "others" that rural white militia members seek to restore their own masculinity. [...]

*****

White supremacists see themselves as squeezed between global capital and an emasculated state that supports voracious global profiteering. [...]

Of course, these are the same men whose ardent patriotism fueled their support of American involvement in Vietnam and the Gulf War. It is through a gendered rhetoric of masculinity that this contradiction between loving America and hating its government, loving capitalism and hating its corporate iterations is resolved. First, like others on the far right, militia members believe that the state has been captured by evil [...]. Environmental regulations, state policies dictated by urban and northern interests, the Internal Revenue Service, are the outcomes of a state now utterly controlled by feminists, environmentalists, Blacks and Jews.

In their foreboding futuristic vision, communalism, feminism, multiculturalism, homosexuality and Christian-bashing are all tied together, part and parcel of the New World Order. [...] Increased opportunities for women can only lead to the oppression of men. [T]he feminist now represents the confusion of gender boundaries and the demasculinization of men, symbolizing a future where men are not allowed to be real men.

The "Nanny State" no longer acts in the interests of "true" American men, but is, instead, an engine of gender inversion, feminizing men, while feminism masculinizes women. White men not involved in the movement are often referred to as "sheeple" while feminist women,

367

it turns out, are more masculine than men are. Not only does this call the masculinity of White men into question, but it uses gender as the rhetorical vehicle for criticizing "other" men. Typically, problematizing the masculinity of these others takes two forms simultaneously: other men are both "too masculine" and "not masculine enough," both hyper-masculine—violent rapacious beasts incapable of self-control—and hypo-masculine—weak, helpless, effete, incapable of supporting a family.

Thus in the logic of militias and other white supremacist organizations, gay men are both promiscuously carnal and sexually voracious and effete fops who do to men what men should only have done to them by women. Black men are both violent hyper-sexual beasts, possessed of an "irresponsible sexuality," seeking white women to rape (*WAR* 8(2), 1989:11) and less than fully manly, "weak, stupid, lazy" (*NS Mobilizer*, cited in Ferber, 1998: 81).

*****

In the militia cosmology, Jews are both hyper-masculine and hypo-masculine. Hyper-masculinity is expressed in the Jewish domination of the world's media and financial institutions, and especially Hollywood. They are sexually omnivorous, but calling them "rabid, sex-perverted" is not a compliment. *The Thunderbolt* claims that 90 percent of pornographers are Jewish. At the same time, Jewish men are seen as wimpish, small, nerdy and utterly unmasculine—likely, in fact, to be homosexual.

*****

Embedded in this slander is a critique of white American manhood as soft, feminized, weakened—indeed, emasculated. Article after article decries "the whimpering collapse of the blond male," as if white men have surrendered to the plot (cited in Ferber, 1998:127). According to *The Turner Diaries*, American men have lost the right to be free; slavery "is the just and proper state for a people who have grown soft" (Pierce, 1978: 33). Yet it is there that the militias simultaneously offer White men an analysis of

their present situation and a political strategy for retrieving their manhood. [...]

*****

If the state and capital emasculate them, and if the masculinity of the "others" is problematic, then only real White men can rescue this American Eden from a feminized, multicultural androgynous melting pot. The militias seek to reclaim their manhood gloriously, violently.

*****

WHITE SUPREMACISTS IN SCANDINAVIA

While significantly fewer in number than their American counterparts, White supremacists in the Nordic countries have also made a significant impact on those normally tolerant social democracies. [...] Norwegian groups number a few hundred, while Swedish groups may barely top 1000 adherents, and perhaps double that number in supporters and general sympathizers.

Their opposition seems to come precisely from the relative prosperity of their homelands, a prosperity that has made the Nordic countries attractive to ethnic immigrants from the economic South. Most come from lower middle-class families; their fathers are painters, carpenters, tilers, bricklayers, road maintenance workers. Some come from small family farms. Several fathers own one-person businesses, are small capitalists or self-employed tradesmen (Fangen, 1999b: 36). [...]

All the sons are downwardly mobile; they work sporadically, have little or no control over their own labor or workplace, and none owns his own business. Almost all members are between 16 and 20 (Fangen, 1999b: 84). Youth unemployment has peaked, especially in Sweden, just as the number of asylum seekers has peaked, and with it attacks on centers for asylum seekers. They struggle, Fangen (1999b: 2) notes, to recover a class identity "that no longer has a material basis."

Like the American white supremacists, Scandinavian Aryans understand their plight in terms of masculine entitlement, which is eroded by state immigration policies, international Zionist power and globalization. All desire a return to a racially and ethnically homogeneous society, seeing themselves, as one put it, as a "front against alienation, and the mixing of cultures" (Fangen, 1998a: 214).

Anti-gay sentiments also unite these White supremacists. [...] "With violence and terror as our weapons we must beat back the wave of homosexual terror and stinking perversion whose stench is washing over our country" (cited in Bjorgo, 1997: 127). And almost all have embraced anti-Semitism, casting the Jews as the culprits for immigration and homosexuality. [...]

*****

Another unifying set of symbols includes references to the Vikings, who are admired because they lived in a closed community, were fierce warriors, feared and hated by those they conquered (Fangen, 1999b: 36). Vikings also represent an untrammeled masculinity, an "armed brotherhood" of heroes and martyrs (Bjorgo, 1997: 136).

Masculinity figures heavily in their rhetoric and their recruitment. Young recruits are routinely savagely beaten in a "baptism of fire." One Norwegian racist recounted in court how his friends had dared him to blow up a store owned by a Pakistani in Brumunddal. He said he felt a lot of pressure, that they were making fun of him, and he wanted to prove to them that he was a man after all. After he blew up the shop, he said, the others slapped his back and cheered him. Finally, he felt accepted (Fangen, 1999b: 92). [...]

*****

Like their American counterparts, Scandinavian White supremacists also exhibit the other side of what Connell calls "protest masculinity"—a combination of stereotypical male norms with often untraditional attitudes respecting women. All these Nordic groups experience significant support from young women, since the males campaign against prostitution,

abortion and pornography—all of which are seen as degrading women (see Durham, 1997). On the other hand, many of these women soon become disaffected when they feel mistreated by their brethren, "unjustly subordinated," or just seen as "mattresses" (in Fangen, 1998a).

*****

One significant difference between the American and the Scandinavian Aryan movements concerns their view of the environment. While American Aryans support right-wing and conservative Republican efforts to discard environmental protection in the name of job creation in extractive industries, and are more than likely meat-eating survivalists, Nordic White supremacists are strong supporters of environmentalism. Many are vegetarians, some vegan. Each group might maintain that their policies flow directly from their political stance. The Nordic groups claim that the modern state is "impure," "perverted" and full of "decay and decadence" and that their environmentalism is a means to cleanse it.

THE RESTORATION OF ISLAMIC MASCULINITY AMONG THE TERRORISTS OF SEPTEMBER 11

Although it is still too soon, and too little is known to develop as full a portrait of the terrorists of Al Qaeda and the Taliban regime in Afghanistan, certain common features warrant brief comment. For one thing, the class origins of the Al Qaeda terrorists appear to be similar to these other groups. Virtually all the young men were under 25, well educated, lower middle class, downwardly mobile (see also Kristof, 2002a).

Other terrorist groups in the Middle East appear to have appealed to similar young men, although they were also organized by theology professors—whose professions were also threatened by continued secularization and westernization. The Taliban, itself formed in 1994 by disaffected religious students, seems to have drawn from a less fortunate class. Taliban soldiers were uneducated, and recruits were drawn often from refugee camps in Pakistan, where they had been exposed to the relative affluence of the West through aid organizations and television (see Marsden, 2002: 70).

*****

Most of these Islamic radical organizations developed similar political analyses. All were opposed to globalization and the spread of western values; all opposed what they perceived as corrupt regimes in several Arab states (notably Saudi Arabia and Egypt), which were mere puppets of US domination. Central to their political ideology is the recovery of manhood from the devastatingly emasculating politics of globalization. [...]

This fusion of anti-globalization politics, convoluted Islamic theology and virulent misogyny has been the subject of much speculation. Viewing these through a gender lens, though, enables us to understand the connections better. The collapse of public patriarchal entitlement led to a virulent and violent reassertion of domestic patriarchal power. "This is the class that is most hostile to women," said the scholar Fouad Ajami (cited in Crossette, 2001:1). But why? Journalist Barbara Ehrenreich (2001) explains that while "males have lost their traditional status as farmers and breadwinners, women have been entering the market economy and gaining the marginal independence conferred even by a paltry wage." As a result, "the man who can no longer make a living, who has to depend on his wife's earnings, can watch Hollywood sexpots on pirated videos and begin to think the world has been turned upside down."

Taliban policies were designed to both remasculinize men and to refeminize women. [...] Thus, not only were policies of the Afghani republic that made female education compulsory immediately abandoned, but women were prohibited from appearing in public unescorted by men, from revealing any part of their body, or from going to school or holding a job. Men were required to grow their beards, in accordance with religious images of Mohammed—but also, I believe, because wearing beards has always

been associated with men's response to women's increased equality in the public sphere. Beards especially symbolically reaffirm biological natural differences between women and men, even as they are collapsing in the public sphere. Such policies removed women as competitors and also shored up masculinity, since they enabled men to triumph over the humiliations of globalization, and as well to triumph over their own savage, predatory and violently sexual urges that would be unleashed in the presence of uncovered women.

MASCULINE ENTITLEMENT AND THE FUTURE OF TERRORISM

[...] But the terrors of emasculation experienced by the lower middle classes all over the world will no doubt continue to resound for these young men whose world seems to have been turned upside down, their entitlements snatched from them, their rightful position in their world suddenly up for grabs. And they may continue to articulate with a seething resentment against women, "outsiders," or any other "others" perceived as stealing their rightful place at the table.

The common origins and common complaints of the terrorists of September 11 and their American counterparts were not lost on American white supremacists (see also Kristof, 2002b). In their response to the events of September 11, American Aryans said they admired the terrorists' courage, and took the opportunity to chastise their own compatriots. Bill Roper of the National Alliance publicly wished his members had as much "testicular fortitude (*Intelligence Report*, Winter 2001). "It's a disgrace that in a population of at least 150 million White/Aryan Americans, we provide so few that are willing to do the same," bemoaned Rocky Suhayda, Nazi Party chairman from Eastpointe, Michigan. "A bunch of towel heads and niggers put our great White Movement to shame" (cited in Ridgeway, 2001: 41). It is from that gendered shame that mass murderers are made.

BIBLIOGRAPHY

Barber, B. (1995) *McDonalds and Jihad*. New York: Simon and Schuster.

Bjorgo, Tore (1997) *Racist and Right-Wing Violence in Scandinavia: Patterns, Perpetrators, and Responses*. Leiden: University of Leiden.

Connell, R.W. (1998) "Masculinities and Globalization," *Men and Masculinities* 1(1).

Crossette, B. (2001) "Living in a World without Women," *The New York Times* 4 October.

Dobratz, B. and Shanks-Meile, S. (2001) *The White Separatist Movement in the United States: White Power! White Pride!* Baltimore, MD: Johns Hopkins University Press.

Durham, Martin (1997) "Women and the Extreme Right: A Comment," *Terrorism and Political Violence* 9:165–8.

Ehrenreich, B. (2001) "Veiled Threat," *The Los Angeles Times* 4 November.

Fangen, Katrine (1999a) "Pride and Power: A Sociological Interpretation of the Norwegian Radical Nationalist Underground Movement," PhD dissertation, Department of Sociology and Human Geography, University of Oslo.

Fangen, Katrine (1999b) "Death Mask of Masculinity," in Soren Ervo (ed.) *Images of Masculinities: Moulding Masculinities*. London: Ashgate.

Ferber, A.L. (1998) *White Man Falling: Race, Gender and White Supremacy*. Lanham, MD: Rowman and Littlefield.

Jurgensmeyer, Mark (2000) *Terror in the Mind of God: The Global Rise of Religious Violence*. Berkeley: University of California Press.

Kristof, N. (2002a) "What Does and Doesn't Fuel Terrorism," *The International Herald Tribune* 8 May: 13.

Kristof, N. (2002b) "All-American Osamas," *The New York Times* 7 June: A-27.

Marsden, P. (2002) *The Taliban: War and Religion in Afghanistan*. London: Zed Books.

Pierce, W. (1978) *The Turner Diaries*. Hillsboro, VA: National Vanguard Books.

Ridgeway, J. (2001) "Osama's New Recruits," *The Village Voice* 6 November.

DISCUSSION QUESTIONS: GHOSE

1. Compare and contrast the three feminist theories of the "female gaze" as outlined by Ghose. Which of these theories does she use in this chapter and why?
2. Outline the dynamics of the three main "female gazes" Ghose discusses (erotic, compassionate, conservative), including their historical and political contexts.
3. How are these "female gazes" implicated in the process of imperialism?

DISCUSSION QUESTIONS: MOHAMMAD

1. Describe the responses of Pakistani immigrants to their social exclusion from British society. How do these responses feed into dominant racist constructs? What violence do these responses enact within the Pakistani community?
2. How does the Pakistani Muslim community in Britain construct its separation from "the West"?
3. Discuss the ways in which Muslim women are regulated to protect Pakistani cultural "authenticity" in the context of mainstream British morality. What are the consequences of these regulations for women's lives?

DISCUSSION QUESTIONS: FREEMAN

1. Detail Freeman's critique of mainstream treatments of globalization.
2. What kind of analyses does she feel are necessary to bypass these problems?
3. In the remainder of the article, Freeman produces one such analysis of the higgler in Barbados. Explain in detail how this particular analysis meets the parameters she has set out for a feminist reconceptualization of globalization.

DISCUSSION QUESTIONS: BENERÍA

1. Who is the Davos Man? What effects is "he" having on global economic organization?
2. According to feminist economists, what is women's relationship to the market under conditions of globalization and expanding markets?
3. How can women's different market experiences form the basis for a more just economic system that does not take the Davos Man's objectives as the desired norm?

DISCUSSION QUESTIONS: KIMMEL

1. Explain how lower middle-class men and their masculinity have been affected by globalization processes.
2. Explain what Kimmel means when he says that gender becomes a chief organizing principle of local, regional, and national resistance to globalization.
3. Compare the resistance strategies of Aryan youth in the United States, White supremacists in Scandinavia, and Al Qaeda and Taliban members.

FURTHER READINGS

1. Blunt, Alison, and Gillian Rose (eds.). 1994. *Writing Women and Space: Colonial and Postcolonial Geographies*. New York: Guilford Press.
   The essays collected here examine White women's "writing" during the colonial period, including their letters, travel writings, paintings, sculptures, maps, and political discourse. Each author explores how feminism and post-structuralism enable analyses of how these women, through their writings, have shaped Empire as they represent colonial landscapes and people.
2. Carty, Linda. 1999. The Discourse of Empire and the Social Construction of Gender. In Enaski Dua and Angela Robertson (eds.), *Scratching the Surface: Canadian Anti-racist Feminist Thought*. Toronto: Women's Press, pp. 35–45.
   Carty takes up the question of the role played by British women in shaping a White colonialist agenda and maintaining the exclusion of "other" women in the period of high imperialism. Her essay outlines the imperial context out of which Euro-American feminism emerged, and demonstrates Empire's legacy in academic feminist discourse in Canada today.
3. Folson, R.B. (ed). 2004. *Calculated Kindness: Global Restructuring, Immigration, and Settlement in Canada*. Halifax: Fernwood Publishing.
   Gender and migration are the two animating concepts of this book. Contributors write about Canadian immigrant women's education, training, and employment in different sectors, as well as migrant professionals and sex trade workers. Many papers develop sophisticated critiques of Canadian immigration policies.

4. Freeman, Carla. 2000. *High Tech and High Heels in the Global Economy: Women, Work, and Pink-Collar Identities in the Caribbean*. Durham: Duke University Press.

    This book is an ethnography of globalization as it is experienced by Afro-Caribbean women in Barbados, a new field for processes of transnational capitalism. These women work in the new high-tech computer industry called "informatics," where they are not only inculcated in the workings of globalization, but through their identity performances and everyday practices shape its very form.

5. Marchand, Marianne, and Anne Sisson Runyan (eds.). 2000. *Gender and Global Restructuring: Sightings, Sites, and Resistances*. London: Routledge.

    This collection of papers theorizes globalization as global restructuring, focusing on concrete sites or spaces of that restructuring and on the forms of resistance global restructuring has incited among women.

RELEVANT FILMS

1. *Earth*, 1998, 101 minutes, Deepa Mehta

    This feature film opens in Lahore, India, in 1947 at the end of British colonial rule in the subcontinent. As the British prepare to leave, a searing national process is underway that will split the Raj into two independent countries, India and Pakistan. Mehta depicts the horrors this process incites as millions of Muslims and Hindus are murdered as an outcome of Empire.

2. *Working Women of the World*, 2000, 53 minutes, First Run Icarus Films

    Economic globalzsation is the focus of this documentary. As Levi Strauss and Company garment factories are relocated from Europe to Indonesia, the Philippines, and Turkey where workers receive lower wages, affected women workers struggle against this transnational corporation and its working conditions and wage structures, as well as larger economic free trade policies. The film presents an intimate look at the working lives of these women, showing how they are interconnected around the globe.

3. *Women at Risk*, 1991, 56 minutes, Filmmakers Library

    This documentary portrays the lives of several women who attempt to survive as displaced refugees in Asia, Africa, and Latin America.

4. *Sisters and Daughters Betrayed: The Trafficking of Women and Girls and the Right to End It*, 1995, 28 minutes, University of California Extension Centre for Media and Independent Learning

    The trafficking of women is a global problem characterized by the illegal movement of millions of women and young girls across national boundaries for the purpose of prostitution. In this film we learn about the social and economic forces that shape this globe trade in women, as well as the exploitative effects it has on the personal lives of the women involved.

5. *Made in Thailand*, 1999, 33 minutes, Women Make Movies

    In the context of contemporary economic globalization, Thai women factory workers struggle to organize unions as a way to improve their working conditions. This film provides an intimate portrait of a group of workers whose cheap labour forms the foundation of the global economy.

RELEVANT WEB SITES

1. www.qub.ac.uk/schoos/SchoolofEnglish/imperial/imperial.ht,

    The Imperial Archive is a site devoted to the study of literature, imperialism, and post-colonialism. It provides resources for people interested in the influence of British imperialism on literature from the 19th, 20th, and 21st centuries using post-colonial theory, which is explained. Browsers can select from several colonized countries such as Australia, Canada, the Caribbean, India, Ireland, Nigeria and other African regions, and explore the key concepts in post-colonial studies. Click on "Feminism and Postcolonialism" to get an excellent introduction to this field of study and its theoretical concepts.

2. www.h-net.org/~women/bibs/mas.html

   Access this Web site for a list of references to masculinity and imperialism ... fascinating.

3. www.h-net.msu.edu/~women/bibs/bibl-imperialism.html

   A corollary to number 2: references to women's history and imperialism.

4. http://newmedia.colorado.edu/~socwomen/resources/globalization.html

   This Web site provides references to gender and globalization in the context of the Caribbean, Latin America, and Europe, as well as transnational feminist politics and global feminist movements.

5. www.crwh.org/programs/globalization.php

   The Centre for Research on Women's Health at the University of Toronto is studying the relationship among globalization, gender, and health. On this site it provides links to papers and other resources that explore the gendered impacts of globalization on health, including food security and nutritional well-being, occupational health and safety, mental health, gender violence, infectious diseases, HIV/AIDS, tobacco, reproductive health, women's access to water, and the health of indigenous women. The case studies of garment workers in Bangladesh, sex trade workers in Kenya, the privatization of waste in South Africa, women's access to anti-retrovirals in Malawi, and Youth against Global Tobacco are especially interesting.

COPYRIGHT ACKNOWLEDGMENTS

Chapter 8 by Judith Butler, "Introduction," from *Undoing Gender* (Oxford: Taylor and Francis Group Ltd., 2004): 1–16.

Chapter 9 by Andrea Doucet, "'It's almost like I have a job, but I don't get paid': Fathers at Home Reconfiguring Work, Care and Masculinity," from *Fathering* 2, no. 3 (2004): 277–303. Copyright © Men's Studies Press, LLC, 2004. Reprinted by permission of Men's Studies Press.

Chapter 10 by Enakshi Dua, "Beyond Diversity: Exploring the Ways in which the Discourse of Race has Shaped the Nuclear Family," from *Scratching the Surface: Canadian Anti-Racist Feminist Thought* (Toronto: Women's Press, 1999): 237–259. Copyright © Women's Press, 1999. Reprinted by permission of Women's Press.

Chapter 11 by Rose Weitz, "The History of Women's Bodies, " from *The Politics of Women's Bodies: Sexuality, Appearance and Behaviour* (Oxford: Oxford University Press, 2003): 3–11. Reprinted by permission of Oxford University Press.

Chapter 12 by Jacqueline Urla and Alan Swedlund, "Measuring up to Barbie: Ideals of the Feminine Body in Popular Culture," from *Gender in Cross-Cultural Perspective*, 4th ed., (Upper Saddle River, N.J.: Pearson Prentice Hall, 2005): 285-298. Copyright © Pearson Education Inc., 2005. Adapted from Jacqueline Urla and Alan Swedlund," The Anthropometry of Barbie: Unsettling Ideal of the Feminine Body in Popular Culture," in *Deviant Bodies: Critical Perspectives on Difference in Science and Popular Culture* (Bloomington: Indiana University Press, 1995): 277–213. Copyright © Jacqueline Urla and Alan Swedlund, 1995. Reprinted by permission of Pearson Education Inc. and Jacqueline Urla and Alan Swedlund, 1995.

Chapter 13 by Fatema Mernissi, "Size 6: The Western Women's Harem," from *Scheherazade Goes West: Different Cultures, Different Harems* (New York: Pocket Books, 2001): 208–220. Copyright © Fatema Mernissi, 2001. Reprinted by permission of Simon & Schuster, Inc and Edite Kroll Literary Agency Inc.

Chapter 14 by Fiona Sampson, "Globalisation and the Inequality of Women with Disabilities," from *Journal of Law and Equality* 2, no. 1 (2003): 17–28.

Chapter 15 by Susan Bordo, "Pills and Power Tools." In Michael Kimmel (ed.) from *Men and Masculinities* 1 (1998): 87–90. Reprinted by permission of Sage Publications, Inc.

Chapter 16 by Russell Dobash, "The Myth of Sexual Symmetry in Martial Violence," from *Social Problems* 39, no. 1 (1992): 71–91.

Chapter 17 by Helene Moussa, "Violence Against Refugee Women: Gender Oppression, Canadian Policy, and the International Struggle for Human Rights," from *Resources for Feminist Research* 26, no. 3/4 (1998): 79–111.

Chapter 18 by Jon Swain, "The Right Stuff: Fashioning an Identity through Clothing in a Junior School," from *Gender and Education* 14, no. 1 (2002): 53–69. Reprinted by permission of Routledge Taylor and Francis Group.

Chapter 19 by Diane Reay, "'Spice Girls', 'Nice Girls', and 'Tomboys': Gender Discourses, Girls' Cultures and Femininities in the Primary Classroom," from *Gender and Education* 13, no. 2 (2001): 153–166. Reprinted by permission of Routledge, Taylor and Francis Group.

Chapter 20 by Rhacel Salazar Parreñas, "The Care Crisis in the Philippines: Children and Transnational Families in the New Global Economy," from *Global Women: Nannies, Maids and Sex Workers in the New Economy* (New York: Metropolitan Books, 2003): 39–54. Reprinted by permission of Rhacel Salazar Parreñas.